D1083268

International Trade
and
Central Planning

International Trade and Central Planning "

AN ANALYSIS OF ECONOMIC INTERACTIONS

Edited, with an Introduction, by

Alan A. Brown

UNIVERSITY OF SOUTHERN CALIFORNIA

and

Egon Neuberger

STATE UNIVERSITY OF NEW YORK AT STONY BROOK

UNIVERSITY OF CALIFORNIA PRESS

BERKELEY AND LOS ANGELES

1968

University of California Press
Berkeley and Los Angeles, California

Cambridge University Press
London, England

Copyright © 1968, by
The Regents of the University of California
Library of Congress Catalog Card Number: 68–13821

Printed in the United States of America

TO
ABRAM BERGSON AND GOTTFRIED HABERLER
WHO HAVE TRAINED A GENERATION
OF ECONOMISTS, INCLUDING
THE EDITORS

Contributors

ROBERT E. BALDWIN	Professor of Economics, University of Wisconsin.
ABRAM BERGSON	Professor of Economics and Director of Russian Research Center, Harvard University.
JOSEPH S. BERLINER	Professor of Economics, Brandeis University.
MORRIS BORNSTEIN	Professor of Economics and Director of the Center for Russian and East European Studies, University of Michigan.
ALAN A. BROWN	Associate Professor of Economics, University of Southern California.
ROBERT W. CAMPBELL	Professor of Economics, Indiana University.
ROBERT F. DERNBERGER	Assistant Professor of Economics and Chairman, Committee on Far Eastern Studies, University of Chicago.
EVSEY D. DOMAR	Professor of Economics, Massachusetts Institute of Technology.
ALEXANDER ECKSTEIN	Professor of Economics and Director of the Center for Chinese Studies, University of Michigan.
GREGORY GROSSMAN	Professor of Economics, University of California at Berkeley.
GOTTFRIED HABERLER	Galen L. Stone Professor of International Trade, Harvard University.
OLEG HOEFFDING	Economist, The RAND Corporation.
FRANKLIN D. HOLZMAN	Professor of Economics, Tufts University and Fletcher School of Law and Diplomacy.

HARRY G. JOHNSON — Professor of Economics, University of Chicago and The London School of Economics and Political Science.

HERBERT S. LEVINE — Associate Professor of Economics, University of Pennsylvania.

TA-CHUNG LIU — Professor of Economics, Cornell University.

JOHN MICHAEL MONTIAS — Professor of Economics, Yale University.

AURELIUS MORGNER — Professor of Economics and Chairman, Department of Economics, University of Southern California.

EGON NEUBERGER — Professor of Economics, State University of New York at Stony Brook.

DWIGHT H. PERKINS — Associate Professor of Economics, Harvard University.

FREDERIC L. PRYOR — Associate Professor of Economics, Swarthmore College.

NICOLAS SPULBER — Professor of Economics, Indiana University.

BENJAMIN N. WARD — Professor of Economics, University of California at Berkeley.

PETER J. D. WILES — Professor of Russian Economics and Social Studies, the University of London.

RICHARD Y. C. YIN — Associate Professor of Economics, George Washington University (on leave from the University of Southern California).

Preface

This cooperative study of the interactions between international trade and the planning system in centrally planned (Communist) economies is based on papers and formal discussions originally presented at the Conference on International Trade and Central Planning and subsequently revised. The Conference, held at the University of Southern California in Los Angeles between December 30, 1966, and January 1, 1967, brought together economic specialists on central planning and on international trade. The program covered three major geographic areas: Eastern Europe, the Soviet Union, and Communist China. Among the fifty participants were representatives of research and government organizations, as well as members of the academic community from various universities and colleges in the United States and abroad.

As the first concerted study of the role of foreign trade in centrally planned economies, the Conference was organized under the sponsorship of the Research Institute of the School of International Relations and the Department of Economics at the University of Southern California, with generous financial support from the Joint Committee on Slavic Studies of the American Council of Learned Societies and the Social Science Research Council. Several universities and other institutions also made contributions by releasing time for their staff members and covering travel expenses. In the editing of this volume, we also received financial support from the Research and Publication Fund of the University of Southern California. It is a pleasure to express our appreciation to all these organizations.

The editors are deeply grateful to Professors Abram Bergson and Gottfried Haberler for their advice and encouragement from the inception of the idea of the Conference. Neither this symposium nor this volume would have been possible without their support. To them, with gratitude, this volume is dedicated.

Joseph S. Berliner, Evsey D. Domar, Alexander Eckstein, Gregory Grossman, Oleg Hoeffding, and Herbert S. Levine also served as members of the Advisory Board. Their counsel, which was repeatedly solicited, helped to make the Conference a success. Rodger Swearingen, as Director of the Research Institute and as specialist on Communist affairs, encouraged the idea of exploring the relationship between international trade and central planning. Both he and Aurelius Morgner, chairman of the Department of

Economics, gave their full support to the organization of the Conference. Richard Y. C. Yin devoted considerable time and effort to the Conference as co-chairman. Other staff members of the Research Institute and the Department of Economics at the University of Southern California were called upon from time to time for assistance. John L. Dominguez, who served as student coordinator of the Conference, deserves special acknowledgment.

Many individuals spent many hours to blend into a cohesive volume the twenty-five contributions presented at the Conference. To all of them we are twice grateful; in this joint endeavor they worked not only willingly but also with dispatch. *Bis dat qui cito dat.* Without such cooperation, we should have fallen far short of our ambitious time schedule, and the editing of the volume would have taken considerably longer. We wish, in particular, to thank our contributors, who were willing, in spite of competing demands on their attention, to make revisions and read proofs on time; if the pressure caused resentment, they were kind enough to conceal it.

We owe very much to the careful editing of Malcolm Palmatier; his skill greatly improved the volume and his remarkable forbearance never faltered, no matter how tight the deadlines. We are thankful to John C. Hogan, to whom we often turned for technical aid. We are indebted to Peter A. Berton, who gave expert advice on the preparation of the ten-language bibliography and made numerous creative suggestions for the design of the book. The preparation of the index — particularly in a cooperative volume — is an important task that challenges both competence and endurance; we are grateful to Heather Campbell, who compiled the index, and to Carol B. Pearson, who handled its editing. Philip E. Lilienthal and Maxwell Knight at the University of California Press were able to speed the work through its various stages of publication without compromising the exacting standards of the Press.

We should like to record an obligation to our research assistants — Clifford C. Burch, Kurt Charles, John Dominguez, Edward C. Erickson, Mahmoud Fouad, Janice L. Iles, Gary Stibel, and in particular, Douglas O. Walker — who checked the references, the proofs, and the index. Helen O'Connell commands our gratitude for her accurate typescript, always faithfully delivered, sometimes on very short notice.

The organization of the Conference and the preparation of this volume have made these past two years trying ones for our families. We would like to end this list of acknowledgments with an expression of warm appreciation to our wives, Barbara and Florence, for their patience, understanding, and encouragement.

Alan A. Brown
Egon Neuberger

December 1967

Contents

INTRODUCTION AND
THEORETICAL BACKGROUND

Foreign Trade of Centrally Planned Economies: An Introduction
  Alan A. Brown and Egon Neuberger 3
Theoretical Reflections on the Trade of Socialist Economies
  Gottfried Haberler 29
  Discussion: Robert E. Baldwin 46

FOREIGN TRADE
OF EASTERN EUROPE

Towards a Theory of Centrally Planned Foreign Trade
  Alan A. Brown 57
  Discussion: Robert W. Campbell 94
East-West Trade and the Paradoxes of the Strategic Embargo
  Nicolas Spulber 104
  Discussion: Morris Bornstein 126
*Socialist Industrialization and Trade in Machinery Products:
  An Analysis Based on the Experience of Bulgaria, Poland,
  and Rumania*
  John M. Montias 130
  Discussion: Frederic L. Pryor 159
Foreign Trade of Eastern Europe: A Summary Appraisal
  Peter J. D. Wiles 166

FOREIGN TRADE OF CHINA

The International Impact on Chinese Central Planning
  Dwight H. Perkins 177

Discussion: Ta-chung Liu 199

Prices, the Exchange Rate, and Economic Efficiency in the Foreign Trade of Communist China
Robert F. Dernberger 202

   Discussion: Richard Y. C. Yin 241

Foreign Trade of China: A Summary Appraisal
Alexander Eckstein 246

FOREIGN TRADE OF THE U.S.S.R.

The Effects of Foreign Trade on Soviet Planning Practices
Herbert S. Levine 255

   Discussion: Evsey D. Domar 277

Soviet Central Planning and Its Impact on Foreign Trade Behavior and Adjustment Mechanisms
Franklyn D. Holzman 280

   Discussion: Joseph S. Berliner 306

Recent Structural Changes and Balance-of-Payments Adjustments in Soviet Foreign Trade
Oleg Hoeffding 312

   Discussion: Aurelius Morgner 337

Foreign Trade of the U.S.S.R.: A Summary Appraisal
Gregory Grossman 340

CONCLUSION AND FUTURE PROSPECTS

Central Planning and Its Legacies: Implications for Foreign Trade
Egon Neuberger 349

   Discussion: Benjamin N. Ward 377

On Prospects for Communist Foreign Trade
Abram Bergson 384

Notes on Some Theoretical Problems Posed by the Foreign Trade of Centrally Planned Economies
Harry G. Johnson 393

APPENDIX

Basic Features of a Centrally Planned Economy
Alan A. Brown and Egon Neuberger...................... 405

Bibliography 417

Index of Names Cited................................ 433

Subject Index...................................... 437

TABLES

N. SPULBER

1. *World Trade by Areas and Trading Groups (Selected Years)*.. 111

2. *CEMA Trade, by Countries (Selected Years)*............. 112

3. *Eastern Europe's Pattern of Exports, by Regions and Areas (Selected Years)* 114

4. *Commodity Composition of East-West Trade (Selected Years)* 115

5. *Soviet Union's Share in the Foreign Trade of Individual East European Countries (Selected Years)*................. 116

6. *CEMA's Share in the Foreign Trade of Individual West European Countries (1953 and 1963)*................ 125

J. M. MONTIAS

1. *External Trade in Machinery of Bulgaria, Poland and Rumania*.................................... 132

2. *Investments in Domestically Produced Machinery in Bulgaria, Poland, and Rumania, 1949–1956* 133

3. *Surpluses and Deficits in "Hard Goods" (Raw Materials, Semifabricates, and Foodstuffs) and the Trade Balance of Bulgaria, Poland, and Rumania, 1949–1965*......... 138

4. *Changes in Poland's Imports, Exports, Consumption of Consumer Goods, and Gross Agricultural Output from 1950 to 1955*.................................... 141

5. *Simulated Expansion of a Soviet-Type Economy*.......... 149

6. *Number of Years of Positive Net Imports of Machinery and Equipment Under Various Assumptions About the Growth Rates of r, ρ, and σ* 151

  7. *Selected Factors Influencing Rumania's Trade in Machinery*
     Products 156

D. H. PERKINS

  1. *Chinese Exports* 180
  2. *Pre- and Post-1949 Export Levels* 181
  3. *Exports, Domestic Product, and Sales* 184
  4. *Major Commodities' Share in Exports* 195

R. F. DERNBERGER

  1. *Communist China's Annual Bilateral Trade and Payments*
     Agreements and Protocols with Communist Countries,
     1950–1965 208
  2. *Communist China's Trade and Payments Agreements with*
     Non-Communist Countries 212
  3. *Payments and Clearing Arrangements Created by Commu-*
     nist China's Bilateral Trade and Payments Agreements
     with Non-Communist Countries 214
  4. *Official Exchange Rate, Jen-min-pi per U.S. Dollar: April*
     1949 to Present 217
  5. *Changes in the Commodity Composition (Individual Com-*
     modities) of Communist China's Export Trade, 1955–
     1960 231
A-1. *The Volume and Balance of Communist China's Merchan-*
     dise Trade, 1949–1964 236
A-2. *The Commodity Composition of Communist China's For-*
     eign Trade, 1953–1964 238
A-3. *The Direction of Communist China's Foreign Trade, 1950–*
     1964 240

O. HOEFFDING

  1. *Soviet Trade in Crude and Processed Foodstuffs* 314
  3. *Soviet Hard-Currency Trade, 1959–1965* 316
  3. *Geographic Distribution of Soviet Trade with Hard-*
     Currency Area, 1959–1965 317
  4. *Soviet Trade in Food, 1959–1965* 319
  5. *Soviet Nonfood Hard-Currency Trade, 1959–1965* 322

6. *Changes in Total Nonfood Hard-Currency Balance, 1962–1965* 323

7. *Nonfood Exports to Hard-Currency Area by Commodity Group, 1962–1965* 324

8. *"Free World" Imports of Precious Metals and Stones, 1959–1965* 327

9. *Soviet Hard-Currency Nonfood Imports, 1962–1965* 329

10. *Commodity Composition of Hard-Currency Nonfood Imports* 330

11. *Soviet Hard-Currency Imports of Machinery and Equipment by Type* 331

12. *Soviet Imports and Exports of Rubber and Copper, 1962–1965* 334

E. NEUBERGER

1. *Balance of Trade of Yugoslavia, 1947–1966* 370

2. *Value of Output Subject to Price Control* 371

Introduction and
Theoretical Background

Foreign Trade of
Centrally Planned Economies:
An Introduction

ALAN A. BROWN
and
EGON NEUBERGER

Foreign trade of centrally planned economies (CPEs) has been, until recently, a relatively neglected field of study. Specialists have focused their efforts on market-type economies (MTEs), where government policies may be designed to influence the operation of the market, but do not try to supplant it. As a result, international trade experts have made no attempt to develop theoretical approaches that would explain the level, composition, and direction of foreign trade of CPEs, where direct government actions — subject to given planning mechanisms — play a determining role rather than the market, which performs only an ancillary function. Foreign trade has also been neglected by Marxist economists. Thus, as discussed below by Gottfried Haberler, neither the works of Marx nor the contributions of his followers pay much attention to the role of foreign trade in socialist economies. Similarly, the Western economic literature on CPEs has given almost exclusive attention to the domestic sectors. While these studies have produced many valuable theoretical and empirical insights, foreign trade has been treated over the years as an economic fifth wheel. Whatever effort has been devoted to foreign trade has failed to address directly one of the most important and complex issues, the interrelationships between the domestic economy and its foreign trade sector.

The relatively small dependence on foreign trade of the Soviet Union, the only CPE until the late 1940s, has undoubtedly been a major reason for this de-emphasis. During the past decade and a half, however, following the adoption of Soviet-type central planning in Eastern Europe and in the Far East, interest in centrally planned foreign trade has steadily increased. Because of the relatively important role of foreign trade in their countries' economic life, the economists of the smaller Eastern European CPEs were the first to turn their attention to foreign trade questions. During the 1950s, it became evident that most economic problems in these countries were closely connected with foreign trade. The naive confidence in the "socialist world market," which Stalin expressed early in that decade, has given way to soul-searching and doubt as to the compatibility of the traditional mechanisms of coordination and control and the requirements of foreign trade. It is now openly stated even in the orthodox Party newspapers that "the existing system of economic management has become outdated" [4, p. 5], and it is acknowledged that "one of the most serious shortcomings is the strict separation of production from foreign markets, due to lack of coordination between foreign and domestic markets" [4, p. 14].

In an attempt to attain a greater degree of economic rationality without abandoning the control exercised by the system's directors over crucial economic decisions, numerous economic reforms have been instituted; and, at least in Eastern Europe, foreign trade has played an explicit role in most of these reforms. As pointed out by Gregory Grossman, "to a significant extent *all* of the recent economic reforms or proposed reforms in Eastern Europe — though not in the Soviet Union — have as a main purpose to render the given socialist economy more effective as an earner of foreign exchange and as a gainer from the international division of labor." Despite these efforts, however, foreign trade problems have remained particularly acute in many of these countries.

Problems of foreign trade have not confined themselves to Eastern Europe. The steadily increasing demand for imports, coupled with difficulties over augmenting exports, has given rise to pressures in the balance of payments not only in the smaller CPEs but also in China, and finally even in the Soviet Union. In recent years, the recurrent balance-of-payments crises in the CPEs have received widespread public attention in the West, but serious study of the underlying causes of external disequilibria as well as of adjustment mechanisms has been hampered by the unavailability of data. As discussed by Oleg Hoeffding, the balance-of-payments accounts of CPEs have remained tightly kept state secrets, and no Communist country, except Yugoslavia, has published comprehensive balance-of-payments statements. This is not, however, an insurmountable barrier. Considerable foreign trade information is available, and specialists dealing with CPEs have proven over the years that valid conclusions may be drawn from available data.

In analyzing the foreign trade of CPEs, including the chronic balance-of-payments pressures, one may distinguish three aspects of the problem. First, as both Robert Baldwin and Harry Johnson point out forcibly in their contributions, the lessons of less-developed countries are applicable to the experience of CPEs, since in both cases a close relationship exists between the goal of rapid industrialization and chronic balance-of-payments difficulties. Their studies of less-developed countries lead them to the belief that the rapid industrialization goal, with the consequent neglect of traditional primary-product industries, is an even more significant factor in the explanation of foreign trade problems in CPEs than the institutional mechanisms of central planning. A large number of contributors to this volume, who have devoted themselves to the study of centrally planned economies, naturally view it as their primary task to stress the second aspect, attempting to examine the complex interactions — not yet fully explored in the literature — between the institutional mechanisms of central planning and the patterns of foreign trade. These functional relationships, which are of special interest to students of CPEs, are also of great importance to the international trade specialist, in view of the growing significance of centrally planned foreign trade in the world economy. The third aspect of the problem, stressed in Johnson's essay, is the existence of two general characteristics of all countries, regardless of their stage of economic development or their adherence to central planning or the market: (1) the adoption of protectionist policies, which to a greater or lesser extent restrict the volume of foreign trade; and (2) the fact that these restrictive trade policies are always devoted, in large part, to maintaining or expanding industrial production, a characteristic clearly associated with an ideology of nationalism. Thus, the study of centrally planned foreign trade has an even wider significance, for it sheds light on the interactions between domestic and foreign trade policies (and developments) even in market economies, where government policies do influence the conduct of foreign trade (although much less, of course, then in CPEs).

These considerations led to the organization of the Conference on International Trade and Central Planning, which was held at the University of Southern California, December 30, 1966, through January 1, 1967. The Conference was attended by leading Western experts on the economics of central planning and by international trade specialists, whose major contributions had heretofore fallen outside the field of centrally planned foreign trade. The aim of the Conference was to initiate the study of centrally planned foreign trade. This volume, a fruit of the Conference, contains a set of papers representing original contributions to this hitherto neglected area, as well as formal discussions. The papers and discussions were revised substantially after the Conference to incorporate the comments of the Conference participants, and to provide coherence to the volume. Thus, while this study is the end result of the Conference, it is not simply an official "proceedings" of the Conference. Instead, the volume might be characterized as a pioneering attempt to clarify and systematize the subject matter of centrally planned foreign trade, and, it is hoped, to stimulate further investigation in this new area of inquiry.

ORGANIZATION AND CENTRAL THEME

This volume contains five sections. The initial and final sections are designed to provide, respectively, a theoretical background and an overall perspective. In addition, there are three geographically oriented sections, arranged in order of the relative importance of foreign trade: Eastern Europe, China, and the U.S.S.R. While the geographical arrangement helps to emphasize the specific regional and national focus of the contributions, the lines of demarcation are not very sharp. The issues explored in each paper are essentially common to all CPEs. While certain differences are brought out between one geographical area and another (such as economic size and population density), in general the individual contributions do not dwell on them or on particularities of historical background, given stages of development, and the like. This general approach reflects the overall stress of the volume: the attempt to develop a common framework for the analysis of centrally planned foreign trade, which can then serve as a basis for further exploration of discovered diversities.

To broaden the perspective of individual contributions, an organizational innovation has been introduced. In addition to the customary, brief discussions of individual papers — emphasizing or criticizing certain specific points — each geographically oriented section concludes with a summary appraisal paper. These regional summaries not only attempt to assess some of the main arguments from a broader vantage point, but also offer further generalizations and insights. At the end of the volume are two major Conference discussion papers by Abram Bergson and Harry Johnson. These papers summarize, comment upon, and develop some of the key empirical and theoretical issues raised at the Conference, and thus provide a concluding synthesis for the volume. They also indicate important areas for further research, as does the contribution by Gottfried Haberler at the beginning of the volume.

The central theme of the book is the mutual relationships or interactions between central planning and foreign trade in given national economies. The purpose is to present an intensive treatment of certain issues directly connected with the theme, rather than a detailed analysis of trade patterns of particular countries or of economic relationships among various CPEs (as, for example, within the Council for Economic Mutual Assistance). The interrelationships between the planning system in a CPE (its goals and mechanisms) and its foreign trade sector include two major effects: the primary or direct effects of the domestic sector (or domestic planning system) on foreign trade, and the feedback effects of foreign trade on the domestic economy. Although this book attempts to investigate both sides of this two-way relationship, the greater emphasis is given to primary effects, which are generally stronger and easier to identify.

Several authors stress the first side of this relationship. The papers by John Michael Montias, Robert Dernberger, and Franklyn Holzman each deal with one of the three geographical areas, seeking to analyze the effects of planning on foreign trade. Three other papers, on the other hand, in the same respective areas — those by Nicolas Spulber, Dwight Perkins, and Herbert Levine — take a reverse direction, emphasizing certain influences of trade on the domestic economy. Thus, Levine's paper is devoted to the difficult question of the influence of foreign trade on central planning in the Soviet Union, where the literature on foreign trade planning is very sparse and much of the analysis has had to be conjectural. As an alternative, one may investigate jointly the primary and feedback effects, which form a set of dynamic interactions. The paper by Brown represents such an attempt, no doubt one of many possible approaches; it contains a conceptual framework designed to analyze the dynamics of centrally planned foreign trade. While this is a more comprehensive method, it also involves a higher degree of complexity, as Robert Campbell points out in his discussion.

The material presented in this volume is the result of original investigation in a new field of research. No attempt has been made, therefore, to reach a complete consensus on each specific issue. The basic purpose of the papers and discussions is to provide some new understanding and a measure of challenge for future study. Surely, the mutual interactions between trade and planning promise to provide a fruitful area for further economic analysis, both on the theoretical and on the empirical level.

KEY ISSUES

In examining the interrelationships between the domestic economy and foreign trade in CPEs, certain key issues are seen to emerge. These issues center around (1) the *level of trade* (i.e., the explanation of given trade levels by "autarky" or other theoretical approaches, effects of the Western embargo, determination of the level of trade by import needs or export

availabilities, and empirical problems of measuring trade-income ratios);
(2) the *structure of trade*, its commodity composition and geographical direction (role of machinery and of agricultural products; changes in the
structure of exports and imports; factors responsible for a given distribution and for changes over time); (3) the *institutional mechanisms* regulating the conduct of trade (state trading, bilateralism, inconvertibility);
(4) the *adjustment mechanisms* available for correcting balance-of-payments problems; and, finally, (5) some consideration of *future prospects*
(expected developments in the level and structure of trade, the role of
trade in the domestic economy, the problem of legacies, and the integration
of centrally planned foreign trade into international trade theory).

THE LEVEL OF TRADE

The level of aggregate trade and its relative significance present a set of
questions that are not only very important but, judging from the contributions to this volume and from the discussions at the Conference, also highly
controversial. Most of the Conference papers were to some extent concerned with theoretical explanations of given trade levels and their determination, and at least implicitly with empirical problems of assessing and
evaluating the relative importance of trade in CPEs.

Explanations of the relative importance of aggregate trade involve two
related issues: the size of the trading ratios at any given time, and dynamic
changes in the trading ratios. Since static and dynamic comparisons of the
trading ratios may yield different results, they should be examined separately.

According to all available evidence, the trade-income ratios in most CPEs
have generally been lower than those in comparable MTEs. Frederic Pryor
presents a summary of his statistical investigation which shows that in
1928 trade-income ratios of present-day CPEs did not differ significantly
from those of "comparable" countries in Western Europe. On the other
hand, he estimates that the volume of trade of CPEs in the 1950s — because of the decline of their trade during the 1930s and 1940s — was only
between 50 and 60 percent of that of "comparable" Western nations. A
similar point is stressed by Bergson, who shows that the current trade ratio
(combined export-income and import-income ratio) in the Soviet Union
is 5.3 percent, which is significantly lower than the United States ratio of
7.9 percent.

If, however, we compare the trading ratios over time, it appears that they
tend to increase much faster in CPEs than in MTEs. During the past decade
the gap between the trading ratios of CPEs and comparable MTEs has considerably narrowed. (See, for example, the documentation in Brown's paper, which contains intertemporal and cross-sectional comparisons of the
Hungarian trading ratios.) In China, according to the most recent esti-

mates, as presented by Perkins, the combined export-income and import-income ratio is 7 to 11 percent, which exceeds (taking the midpoint of the estimated range) the United States ratio of 7.9 percent.

In the past, the relatively low level of trade in CPEs was generally attributed to the planners' overt emphasis on self-sufficiency, or their "policy of autarky." The discussion at the Conference and the embarrassing variety of proposed definitions demonstrated, however, that there is little agreement as to the proper meaning of autarky. The problem, it further became evident, is not entirely semantic. On substantive grounds, autarky was attacked as a misleading oversimplification of the trade policy of CPEs, and most of the Conference members set aside the concept as an explanatory theory of centrally planned foreign trade.

As Peter Wiles emphasizes in his paper, "the attack on the orthodox Western notion that Soviet-type economies are autarkic" has been long overdue. Evsey Domar, in his discussion, calls attention to the difficulties that may arise from an unwary use of the term. He stresses, first, the importance of studying the commodity composition of trade, not simply the trading ratios. Then, he reminds us of the distinction between final equilibrium and the actual situation at a given time. He defines autarky as a desire to avoid dependence on imports of essential economic inputs. According to this definition, while ideal or equilibrium import structure would consist solely of "toys" (nonessential imports), a country's imports at a given time are likely to contain a large share of "machinery" (essential imports). Although a country may pursue a policy of autarky, technological progress in other countries may prevent the achievement of ideal, long-run equilibrium — the importation of "toys" only. We may add that even in equilibrium, the country may well continue importing "machines," since the goal of self-sufficiency is satisfied once the country is *able* to replace its "machines" at relatively low cost (in terms of real income) *if* the need for such replacement should arise.

But is the ambiguity or vagueness of the concept of autarky — the bewildering variety of definitions, or their overlapping and fuzziness, which is assailed in several contributions — the only difficulty? The problem goes beyond the absence of commonly accepted, clear definitions; it is the general inapplicability of specific definitions to centrally planned foreign trade. While this is hardly the place to attempt scrutiny of the great variety of definitions and their appropriateness, we may briefly consider as an illustration a distinction, which is rarely made, between *ex ante* and *ex post* autarky (intentional vs. actual trade developments).

One may say, for example, that a policy is motivated by *ex ante* autarky in a certain sense — i.e., *the desire to achieve the greatest possible self-sufficiency at some future time.* Perhaps one can argue that this was the case in the Soviet Union during the 1930s. In fact, Perkins finds that even more recently, in the 1950s, Communist Chinese policy was shaped by such a desire for autarky. He reasons that a government may continue to expand trade in order to take advantage of domestic-international cost differentials; but if it is bent on autarky, these differentials will be narrowed to the point where domestic products can be substituted for imports, if so desired, without great sacrifice. (Cf. Domar's preceding definition of autarky.) On the other hand, the stated objective of Soviet and East European planners after World War II implies a different notion of *ex ante* autarky — i.e., *the desire to reduce trade as much as possible, particularly essential imports, as soon as possible or at every point of time.*

Let us now turn to *ex post* autarky. How are we to determine to what extent the reduction of Soviet imports in the 1930s was a manifestation of autarky and to what extent it was the result of world-wide depression, which forced producers of primary exports in general (less by desire than by necessity) to curtail imports drastically? The low Soviet trading ratios during these years prove nothing. The period following the reconstruction after World War II, however, should be more revealing, since there was then no global collapse of trade relations as in the 1930s, while *ex ante* autarky (according to the second of the motivations in the preceding paragraph) was rampant. The rapid growth of trade — chiefly essential imports — seems to indicate that in spite of the planners' desire for self-sufficiency, the expansionary influences were permitted to prevail. In some instances, the most rapidly developing industries were heavily dependent, even in the long run, on imported supplies. This not only contradicts the hypothesis that the earliest possible attainment of economic self-sufficiency and independence from essential imports was indeed a significant operational goal of the trade policy — and not merely a frustrated wish, which is of little direct concern to the economist — but even renders questionable whether the planners tried to pursue future self-sufficiency as one of their primary objectives. Even vis-à-vis the West, CPEs did not become more self-sufficient than they had been, although their dependence on each others' trade increased much more. In absolute terms, imports from the West failed to decline, and what is more important, the relative significance of these imports (their strategic importance from the point of view of key supply procurement) in many cases increased.

In sum, simple notions of autarky tend to be discredited by anything but the most cursory examination, and as several contributions in this volume indicate, we must turn to alternative hypotheses if we want to explain how the level of trade in CPEs is established.

As for the actual development of foreign trade in CPEs, it is of course influenced by various (and often conflicting) policy considerations and specific institutional features (see the Appendix), in addition to given natural and *ad hoc* conditions. Traditionally, in formulating their foreign trade policy, CPEs have displayed a general aversion to trade. (Like most of these generalizations, this refers to CPEs in their orthodox form, which is currently in the process of considerable change.) Within this trade aversion, the desire to be economically self-sufficient is only one of several considerations. Since trade aversion leads primarily to a curtailment of nonessential rather than essential imports, its indirect consequence is less, not more, economic self-sufficiency. On the other hand, to be sure, there are also tendencies in CPEs to overtrade — i.e., to experience trade proclivity — which counteract to some extent the prevailing trade aversion.

Judging from the available evidence (i.e., policy announcements and generally lower trade ratios in CPEs than in MTEs), trade aversion in the past exceeded trade proclivity. This was particularly true where the planners did not feel compelled to use *ad hoc* imports, whenever unforeseen shortages occurred in key industrial branches, but could avail themselves of slackness in certain domestic low-priority sectors. No doubt, this is an important reason for the previously mentioned higher trade level in China, where the feeble shock-absorbing capacity of agriculture was quickly exhausted, than in the Soviet Union. (We may add, of course, that in both China and the U.S.S.R. the trade ratios tend to be relatively small, since they are inversely related to the size of the country.)

In any case, trade of CPEs tends to increase, in fact, more rapidly than in other economies (MTEs) where the traditional features of CPEs are absent. Trade increases relatively fast not only to support the industrialization effort and to provide *ad hoc* imports, but also indirectly to accommodate the dynamic interaction of certain variables. Let us take, for example, the average import-intensity of exports, which increases as commodities containing more imports are produced and exported. For various reasons, exports with very small import content are gradually replaced by exports that are highly import-intensive. Thus, the relative export share of neglected low-priority sectors requiring few imports (like agriculture) declines as their output stagnates. On the other hand, the export share of high-priority products (like machinery) rises, although they are most import-intensive, for both technological and institutional reasons — since the producers receive more favorable consideration when they request imported inputs. (It may be added, as Campbell rightly points out, that the notion of priority sectors and products is more complex than it appears and can be variously interpreted.)

As suggested by several contributors, this argument may help to illuminate — to a lesser extent, of course — the experience not only of CPEs but also of other developing countries that industrialize and become exporters of machinery rather than raw-material products. Their exports should also become more import-intensive. Because of their institutional features, however, average import-intensity tends to rise even faster in CPEs, where machinery exports tend to contain more imported materials, in part because the peculiarities of the incentive system place a premium on using more materials and making machines weigh more. The final result of the increasing import-intensity of exports is a cumulative expansion of trade. (See Brown's discussion of the "priority dilemma," and especially his "trade expansion multiplier.")

Several other influences also lead to unintended increases of centrally planned foreign trade over time. Thus, bilateral balancing of trade and payments causes a rapid growth of re-exports; furthermore, there is an increase also in re-imports, commodities that the country has originally exported.

In trying to explain how CPEs determine their trade levels, one may focus either on import demand or on export availabilities. The traditional view is that CPEs regard trade as a means of obtaining necessary imports, and that the level of trade is based primarily on the planners' evaluation of imports necessary to fulfill the plans, while exports are adjusted to finance these imports. This approach is supported in the papers on Soviet and Eastern European trade. Dernberger and Perkins, however, in their work on Chinese foreign trade, take a different position. They maintain that, at least after 1955, the level of Chinese foreign trade was determined by the availability of textiles and agricultural products for export.

It is, of course, not necessary to argue unequivocally that either import needs or export availabilities are the sole determinants of levels of trade. The significant question is whether the planners in CPEs are more likely to force a shift of goods from domestic consumption and investment toward exports to pay for a given level of imports (and assuming that they are willing, whether they are also able to do so), or to tailor the import plans to the readily available domestic surpluses of exportable commodities. It is noteworthy that in Eastern Europe and in the Soviet Union primary emphasis has been placed on satisfying a given import demand (using a sequential process in which "an import plan is worked out on the basis of the production plan, and an export plan on the basis of the import and production plan" [3, p. 78]), while in China analyses of the trade level begin with the limitation of export supply. Although export supply does play a role in either case, it only becomes a primary restraint when domestic "surpluses" can no longer be readily mobilized — a problem that China had to face, at least after 1955.

Empirical verification of hypotheses regarding the relative significance of trade in different countries requires international comparisons of CPE trading ratios. For this, one needs, first of all, reliable and comparable statistics for both trade and income in each country. External trade statistics present the lesser problem. Official data, which most CPEs have been publishing since the 1950s (in some cases even earlier), are given in special accounting units that can easily be translated into actual dollar amounts paid for imports and received for exports. Additional information can be obtained, if necessary, from the trading partners' trade statistics. National income data, on the other hand, have to be recalculated laboriously, or the official figures adjusted to eliminate methodological shortcomings (e.g., inclusion of turnover tax and exclusion of interest and rent) and incomparabilities (e.g., exclusion of services).

Second, aside from questions of the reliability of the statistics, one must face the crucial problem presented by the virtually complete separation of domestic prices in CPEs from foreign trade prices. Gross national product or national income statistics are given in inconvertible domestic currencies, based on domestic prices, while foreign trade is reported in terms of foreign exchange rubles or forints, which are accounting units based on external (world market) prices. Therefore, the numerator of trade-income ratios is in dollars converted to rubles at the official exchange rate, while the denominator is in rubles at internal Soviet prices. Since the official exchange rates are arbitrary, one would need, if imports and exports are to be expressed as given percentages of income, an independent set of disaggregated ruble-dollar conversion ratios. (Without such ratios, one could only compare changes in the trade-income ratios over time, in one country, by using constant price data to measure both trade and income.)

THE STRUCTURE OF TRADE

The thorough explorations by Montias, Perkins, and Hoeffding of the commodity composition of trade in Eastern Europe, China, and the Soviet Union, respectively, represent significant contributions to our knowledge of centrally planned foreign trade. Specific implications of this issue are further examined in the appraisal papers of Wiles and Alexander Eckstein. The novelty of these contributions is their analysis of trade composition in relation to domestic economic development. To a large extent, this is a question of the relative priority of machinery versus that of agriculture in the domestic plans, and the resulting effect on foreign trade. Spulber examines a converse aspect of the same issue, i.e., the effect of Western export controls on the relative priority of various products in the domestic plans of CPEs.

The paper by Montias presents a simulation model, buttressed by substantial empirical analysis, which attempts to isolate major factors influencing the rate of transition from a net import to a net export balance of machinery trade in less-developed CPEs. The key variables governing the demand for imported machinery are the total volume of investment and the capacity of the domestic machine-building industry. The government's policies with respect to relative priorities given to consumption and investment determine the total investment demand. Priority allocation of investments to the metallurgical and metal-fabricating complex promotes the rapid growth of machinery output. Since the planners are intent on maintaining full employment in the machine-building industry, imports of machinery must fall when investment demand declines.

The ability to pay for imported manufactured products, of which the most important part is machinery, depends on the net availability of foreign loans, the volume of exportable raw materials, semi-fabricates and foodstuffs, and the economy's requirements for imported materials. The simulation model of Montias' focuses on variables that determine the availability of export surpluses of primary products; it attempts to trace their long-run effects on foreign exchange earnings for given rates of agricultural and raw-material production. Within his experimental range of values of the exogenous variables and of the parameters, the growth rates of industrial labor and capital productivity and the growth rate of real wages exert a paramount influence on the long-run substitution pattern of domestic for imported capital goods. In particular, the larger the differences between the rate of growth of labor productivity and of real wages in industry (which together determine the change in wages per unit of output, and hence the domestic absorption of exportable foodstuffs and light industrial products), and the smaller the rate of growth of capital productivity in industry (which determines the output of industry and the raw-material requirements associated with this level of output), the longer will be the period during which the industrializing economy will remain a net importer of machinery products. In reality, as Montias observes, discontinuous, short-term changes in the balance of payments and in the ratio of agricultural procurement to output may postpone the decline in net imports, or even reverse it temporarily, as occurred in Bulgaria and Rumania between 1958 and 1963.

Pryor, in his discussion, presents a simplified two-sector model which, he argues, will approximate the major propositions provided by the more complex model of Montias'. The greatest contribution of Montias' study, to which Pryor pays tribute, is the exploration of interrelations between investment and trade cycles. In this connection, Pryor presents an interesting argument that the still relatively low trading ratios in CPEs make them more "dependent" on marginal units of trade, and that this should logically lead them to try to dampen the natural cyclical activity and make their trade volume more stable than that of MTEs. He then quotes the results of a study by George Staller which shows that the volume of foreign trade was, in fact, less stable in Eastern than in Western Europe.

Getting back to the question of the CPEs' trade balance in machinery, we find that the achievement of an export balance leads to a paradox. Instead of improving the position of CPEs in international markets, it actually forces them into a very weak bargaining position because of the relatively low quality and backward technology of most of their equipment, as well as the difficulties they face in providing the necessary long-term credits needed to finance machinery exports. CPEs in this position, such as Czechoslovakia and East Germany, are supinely dependent for their prosperity on their partners' demand for machinery. Their difficulties may serve as a caveat for less-developed countries, where import-substitution, particularly in producer goods, is strongly promoted.

Wiles, who further considers the significant role of machinery in the trade of CPEs, argues that "imperialism used to depend on the export of manu-factures, including light manufactures, but now to be successfully imperialist one must export technology (especially military) and agricultural prod-ucts." He finds several reasons for the CPEs' emphasis on machinery pro-duction and trade: the influence of Marx, Stalin, and the Western embargo — adding, however, that "technology rides the backs of machines, not raw materials; it is *educative* to make machines."

The interrelationship between growth strategy and the volume and com-modity composition of foreign trade is strikingly illustrated by Perkins in his case study of China. He chiefly emphasizes the effects of foreign trade on the pattern of domestic development. This approach is reasonable if one takes the initial decision of the Chinese government as given. Specifically, China, following in the footsteps of other CPEs, stressed from the outset a capital-intensive development of industry at the expense of agriculture; more particularly, she concentrated on steel-producing and steel-consuming in-dustries at the expense of chemicals that could have served as agricultural inputs. As Perkins maintains, "once [the Chinese planners] rejected mod-ern investment in agriculture, they had little real choice unless they were willing to accept a significantly lower rate of growth." Thus, foreign trade possibilities determined, in effect, what industries China had to develop domestically. Given the initial commitment to steel and machinery, foreign exchange earnings could not expand sufficiently, and as a result, "Peking had to develop a whole range of industries more or less simultaneously." Perkins argues that before the direction of its domestic development was set, China did have an option. If the original decision, for instance, had been to develop the output of fertilizers and insecticides (by importing chemical machinery or complete chemical plants), China could have generated an agricultural export surplus, instead of having to import grain. This surplus could then have been used either to import more chemicals and chemical plants, or, if desired, to support the long-run development of steel-oriented industries.

Ta-chung Liu is basically in agreement with this analysis of Perkins', although he feels that Perkins underestimates the cost to Chinese policies with respect to both agriculture and foreign trade. He argues that China could have increased with relative ease the value added in agriculture by 10 percent during the First Five-Year Plan period, and, by exporting this increased output in payment for additional imports, the trade-income ratio could have been virtually doubled. Similarly, Liu argues, on the basis of Taiwan's experience, that China could have gained considerably in terms of economic growth by shifting investment to light manufacturing industries. This would have permitted a rise in exports and thus a rise in capital goods imports.

Eckstein stresses the extreme importance of agriculture in the Chinese case. He argues that domestic goals, the stability of the economy, and the developments in the international sector all depend on the trends and annual fluctuations in agricultural output. "Given China's economic backwardness and the weight of agriculture in the national product, and even more so in the labor force, agriculture acts as a most effective constraint on growth in all sectors of the economy, including the international sector."

THE INSTITUTIONAL MECHANISMS

The institutional framework within which centrally planned foreign trade is conducted is analyzed in the literature, and the contributors to this volume have, to some extent at least, assumed an acquaintance with it on the part of the reader. For the benefit of those who are less familiar with the internal and external institutions of CPEs, an Appendix has been added to the volume. It presents a summary description of domestic planning in a CPE, its objectives and mechanisms.

The Appendix is designed to consolidate and elaborate somewhat on the background descriptions contained in some of the papers. An analytical description of foreign trade organization and planning is included in Levine's paper, serving as background for his investigation of the problems of co-ordination. The most important foreign trade institutions and *modi oper-andi* — the state monopoly of foreign trade, bilateralism, and inconverti-bility — are reviewed by Holzman and Dernberger. The latter attempts to fill an important gap in the literature on centrally planned foreign trade by dealing with the institutional framework as developed in China.

In order to understand the foreign trade institutions and mechanisms in CPEs, it is essential to focus first on two key features of a CPE: physical planning and the methods of domestic price formation. These features, together with the arbitrary exchange rates, tend to isolate these countries' prices from their foreign trade price structure. Several contributors deal with the relationship between differentiated price structure and efficiency in the conduct of foreign trade. Dernberger, in fact, makes this important issue one of the central points of his paper; and Richard Yin, commenting upon Dernberger's paper, says that the relationship between artificial price structure and exchange rates, on the one hand, and efficient resource allocation, on the other, "in a nutshell, appears to be the plot of the whole story." While Yin agrees with Dernberger that a price structure that does not reflect relative scarcities will hinder the efficient conduct of trade, he adds that since we do not know enough about the degree of distortion in the Chinese price structure or the actual determination of prices, we therefore cannot determine to what extent this lessens the Chinese gains from trade.

The foreign trade monopoly is considered to be "the keystone of the foreign trade system in the U.S.S.R." [1, p. 11]. This is also true in the other CPEs; the principle is even embodied in the national constitutions of these countries. The state monopoly of foreign trade means that all external economic activities must be channeled through state enterprises; and until the foreign trade reforms in the late 1950s, which led to the establishment of some direct trading abroad by the producing enterprises in Eastern Europe, it was also generally accepted that only enterprises specifically established for this purpose (the foreign trade enterprises) should be permitted to have any direct economic contact outside the country. This latter provision, which served to separate domestic production and distribution from foreign trade, was designed to safeguard the supremacy of the domestic plan. Dernberger suggests a different interpretation of the motives behind the institution of the foreign trade monopoly in China from that for the U.S.S.R. He argues that while Lenin's goal was to protect the weak Soviet economy from the undermining influence of capitalist trade, the monopoly of foreign trade in the Chinese case was an integral part of the attack on domestic inflation. Although he recognizes the theoretical possibility of divorcing the domestic price structure from the influence of foreign prices, as part of the anti-inflationary campaign, without the imposition of state trading, he argues that it would be administratively most difficult. Eckstein, who questions this interpretation, suggests that many countries have used exchange controls, import quotas, export licensing, and similar methods to maintain artificial exchange rates and fight inflation, while trade was carried on by private business enterprises.

Inconvertibility and its relationship to bilateralism are discussed by both Holzman and Dernberger. Bilateralism, Holzman argues, is a logical consequence of inconvertibility. This economic interpretation is essentially corroborated by Dernberger, who considers bilateralism to be a necessary result of trade among CPEs with foreign trade monopolies and inconvertible currencies, although not a necessary condition for central planning in any single country. In addition, Dernberger stresses the influence of a political factor that has been partially responsible for bilateralism in the Communist world — namely, the desire of the U.S.S.R. to assure control over the foreign trade of other CPEs.

Holzman in his analysis distinguishes between foreign exchange and commodity inconvertibilities. Thus, CPEs have maintained not only a strictly inconvertible system of exchange (making the transfer, for instance, of accumulated rubles from one trading partner to another impossible without special agreements) but also a commodity inconvertibility, which is defined as "[a prohibition on] foreigners who hold your currency to spend it on imports (from you)." While MTEs frequently resort to foreign exchange inconvertibility if faced with persistent external deficits, commodity inconvertibility, which restricts unplanned exports, is a "direct antithesis of the attitude of Western nations in balance-of-payments difficulties."

An important aspect of bilateralism, which has been neglected so far in the literature, is the use of re-exports as a means of mitigating the worst effects of bilateralism. This issue is raised in the paper by Brown, who shows that a significant part of the increase in Hungarian trade in the 1950s was due to the rapid rise of re-exports (goods which the Hungarians accepted from their trading partners under bilateral agreements but for which they had no use domestically). The ability of countries to overcome the disadvantages of bilateralism by such means, as well as the economic cost of re-exports, deserves further study. Johnson points out that, given the possibility of re-exports, "bilateral trading appears as a means of avoiding the explicit use of money, but not as a partitioning of the market into segregated sectors with widely different exchange ratios; and the economic waste involved may be only a rather trivial cost of shipping goods to their final users by more indirect routes and through the hands of more transactors than would be the case in a market employing money." Haberler suggests, in the appendix to his paper, that future investigation comparing trade levels and the degree of bilateralism should make allowance for re-exports, although he notes that lack of information may prove to be an obstacle.

The establishment of a separate organizational structure in foreign trade, whatever its merits for central planning, adds to the existing difficulties in achieving effective coordination. The paper by Levine contains a detailed analysis of this problem. The economic literature of Communist countries is replete with sharp attacks on the separation of the producing firm in a CPE from its potential buyers and suppliers abroad. Paradoxically, the very efforts to maintain maximum central control leads to a *de facto* erosion of this control. The administrative rigidities tend to create periodic interruptions in the flow of essential supplies, and these lead to greater permissiveness in the effort to cope with the crises (as discussed in the paper by Brown under "the flexibility dilemma"). Campbell further stresses the importance of studying the interactions between lower and upper levels in the planning hierarchy for a more complete understanding of the dynamics of centrally planned foreign trade.

The formulation of the plan becomes much more complicated when foreign trade is taken into account. As emphasized by Eckstein, information on this relationship between foreign trade and domestic planning — which Levine analyzes in the Soviet case — has been one of the most important gaps in our knowledge of Chinese planning. Levine shows that Soviet planning practices, until recently, have not been very significantly affected by the pressures for rationality arising in the foreign trade sector, because of the relatively small size of this sector. Grossman generally agrees with Levine, but adds an interesting qualification. He suggests that while trade had relatively little effect *after* the domestic system had been established, it could have played a major role in shaping the economic system during its formative years. Thus, Grossman questions whether Stalin would have ordered a collectivization drive of the same extent and severity had he not been concerned with the availability of grain exports to pay for machinery imports.

A major contribution of Levine's paper is his explicit comparison of material balancing in the closed economy with material balancing in the open economy. The basic difference, on which he concurs with Brown, is the substitution of relatively unstable coefficients, based on changes in world prices (when trade is with the West), for the more stable technological coefficients of the domestic production plan. Domar, in commenting on Levine's paper, expresses reservations about the validity of applying input-output analysis to Soviet import and export planning. He argues that the whole essence of the input-output method lies in the rigid interrelationships between the outputs and the required inputs, and that once this rigidity is absent, the input-output approach fails to clarify the foreign trade problems.

The implications of a basic, and probably integral, problem of central planning is scrutinized in the paper by Haberler. He emphasizes that the inability of centrally planned systems to provide aggressive, innovative entrepreneurs, willing to take risks, is one of the fundamental weaknesses of centrally planned foreign trade. This type of entrepreneurship, Haberler argues, while vital in the domestic economy, is even more crucial in the field of international trade, where the range of possible gains and losses (i.e., the variance of their probability distribution) is much greater. Haberler's stress on the entrepreneurial factor is seconded by several other participants, including Baldwin, Domar, and Egon Neuberger.

THE ADJUSTMENT MECHANISMS

Hoeffding discusses the effect upon the Soviet balance of payments of the inability of Soviet agriculture to meet domestic needs — which has led to substantial imports of grain. In addition to complementing Perkins' discussion of the crucial role of agriculture, Hoeffding provides — what is, in view of the unavailability of regular balance-of-payments accounts, a rarity — an empirical analysis of the balance-of-payments adjustment process in a CPE. On the basis of his study of Soviet foreign trade data, Hoeffding finds that Soviet responses to the balance-of-payments problem induced by grain imports were speedy, vigorous, and comprehensive. Surprisingly, export expansion accounted for more than half of the improvement in the nonfood trade (although these exports included some uncommon export commodities, such as platinum, silver, and diamonds); and less than half of the improvement was achieved by import restrictions (rubber and copper being the major victims). Hoeffding raises an interesting question as to the extent to which the Soviet Union may have used conscious management of commodity reserves, as a supplement to the management of gold and foreign exchange reserves, in balancing external accounts.

We may note that the apparent success of the U.S.S.R. in handling its balance-of-payments adjustment problem does not mean that this lesson can be applied to other CPEs without qualification. The size and diversification of the Soviet economy, its relatively small trade-income ratio, available gold reserves, and strong bargaining power vis-à-vis Eastern European countries, which enabled the U.S.S.R. to reduce its food exports and increase its food imports from these countries, are generally absent from the experience of CPEs, with the partial exception of China.

Aurelius Morgner adds two interesting points to Hoeffding's analysis. First, he calls attention to a major difference between the adjustment mechanism in the Soviet Union and that in a MTE. In the Soviet case, response to the need for increased wheat imports consisted of significant changes in exports, and imports of a limited number of commodities only. In a MTE, on the other hand, the changes in individual exports and imports would probably have been very small, but spread over a large number of commodities. Further, Morgner reminds us of how significantly the Soviet leaders' preference functions have changed and of the implications of this change. While "in past periods, it has been charged that even in the face of famines, the Soviet Union maintained food exports in order to pay for equipment imports," this has now given way not only to "a remarkable solicitude for the consumer" but also to a noteworthy rigidity in trying to maintain the "planned wheat consumption." Thus, instead of adjusting the food consumption pattern, the Soviet leaders display a curious willingness to reduce reserves (not only of gold but also of basic raw materials, such as rubber and copper) and to alter significantly the commodity and geographical structure of trade, so that Soviet consumers "should not be inconvenienced" by a slight reduction in the consumption of bread.

Hoeffding's contribution may be studied jointly with that of Holzman, who presents a theoretical treatment of the balance-of-payments adjustment under central planning. Deficits in the balance of payments are restored in CPEs (whether through restriction of imports or increase of exports) by means of direct government action and not by automatic income or price effects. The income mechanism and the foreign trade multiplier are absent, not only because the government does not allow foreign trade to interfere with internal goals, but also, as Joseph Berliner points out, because "since the Soviet planners have the power to reduce imports directly it hardly makes sense for them first to let incomes fall so as to motivate themselves to reduce imports." In any case, as long as trade is transacted by means of bilateral agreements, income effects, even if present, could not go far in correcting the deficit with any given trading partner, since the results would be diffused and imports from all partner countries would be reduced.

Neither can the traditional price effects operate in CPEs, since domestic price policy is divorced from foreign trade developments, and the fulfillment of domestic plans is of such high priority that the short-run elasticity of demand for imports approaches zero and the export supply curve may even be backward-bending. Of course, one can argue, as in the case of income effects, that the planners have no use for superfluous, indirect signals if they can adjust imports and exports directly. Holzman not only shows — using Berliner's vivid metaphor — that certain "keys made to fit the locks of a market economy [cannot] pick the locks of the Soviet economy," but, by taking pains to demonstrate why this is the case, also helps to illuminate an important aspect of the interactions between the planning system and foreign trade.

Although one cannot consider the exchange rates in CPEs to be an adjustment mechanism either, an interesting parallel is drawn in Holzman's paper between the "real" exchange rate in a CPE and the freely floating exchange rate in a MTE. Since the official exchange rate has little economic significance, he considers instead the ratio of domestic to world prices — i.e., the purchasing power parity. This "shadow exchange rate" acts in a CPE somewhat as a freely floating exchange rate acts in a MTE: both create a buffer between external and internal price level changes. Thus, an increase or decrease of domestic prices will have an inverse effect on the "real" exchange rates, but will not disturb the pattern of trade. Conversely, movements in the terms of trade will have no influence on domestic prices, only on the "real" exchange rates. Nonetheless, the functions of these exchange rates are rather different. While world market price changes have an immediate effect on the flow of trade in MTEs — where the freely floating exchange rate does serve as an adjustment mechanism — a shift in the purchasing power parity, owing to external price changes, has no such result in CPEs. In any case, the analogy with the freely floating system would only apply to the trade of CPEs with MTEs. In trade among CPEs, foreign trade prices are kept relatively stable for several years; therefore, the exchange rate is like an adjustable-peg system. Analysis of these differing types of exchange rates — flexible with MTEs and rigid with CPEs — leads to an important conclusion regarding the methods of adjustment. CPEs, in trading with MTEs, can rely chiefly on price adjustments, at least in the short run, to maintain a perfectly inelastic import demand. In trade with other CPEs, on the other hand, price adjustments are excluded; therefore, external imbalances tend to be corrected by more painful quantity adjustments. Brown's discussion of the "trade reorientation dilemma" leads to a similar conclusion.

The paper by Spulber, which provides a concise analytical survey of the Western strategic embargo, shows the impact of foreign trade on the domestic planning strategy of CPEs. Perhaps the most interesting of the paradoxes emerging from this paper is that the strategic embargo created the greatest difficulties in CPEs, not when it was applied with full force, but when it was gradually removed. This effect is to a large extent, although of course not wholly, the result of the institutional setting of centrally planned foreign trade. The rigidities of the planning system, the stress on quantity rather than quality and output rather than cost, and the traditional sellers' markets make it difficult to respond readily to certain types of changes, particularly if the changes involve qualitative adaptation to new demand conditions. The inability to obtain certain key items of equipment and essential raw materials from the West has fostered a hothouse development — on the basis of an assured market within the Soviet bloc — of certain industries in the more advanced Eastern European CPEs.

The relaxation of Western export controls, beginning in the middle 1950s, made Western equipment available that was of higher quality and technologically more advanced than that of the CPEs. This, in turn, led to a reduction of the demand, above all, for heavy industrial machinery from other CPEs; although this decline of demand was long and gradual, the planning systems were unable to provide effective mechanisms of readjustment. Morris Bornstein, while in general agreement both with Spulber's analysis and with his interpretation of actual events, finds that the consequences of the strategic embargo, strictly defined, were not "paradoxical." Thus, for example, Bornstein says that "the strategic embargo was imposed to retard the build-up of military and economic power of what was then generally regarded as a unified 'bloc' of hostile nations, rather than with the aim of splitting this 'bloc.' " It becomes chiefly a matter of semantic interpretation whether the resulting reorientation of the domestic industrialization program in the CPEs, which was a logical by-product of the exogenous restriction of trading opportunities, should be considered a paradoxical development or not. In discussing the effects of the strategic embargo, Bornstein also makes the noteworthy suggestion that the strategic control system itself may be conceptualized as "an interesting attempt at central planning of international trade," which, as he points out, deserves much more thorough investigation than it has yet received.

In passing, it may be mentioned that, despite the emphasis placed on the economic aspects of central planning and foreign trade, one should not overlook the impact of *ad hoc*, noneconomic events, a point stressed by Wiles. Nonetheless, as Spulber demonstrates, even when such exogenous political influences as the strategic embargo are dominant, the economist can still properly investigate the economic response of the system. Two approaches are possible, and probably both are necessary. The first is a theoretical analysis of the available alternatives — e.g., an attempt to explain the events and make predictions by means of a conceptual model, which is derived from the given assumptions of the system. Alternatively, one may examine how the system reacts to certain exogenous shocks — in reality — as is done by Spulber. Even though the approach in the latter case is empirical, interpretation of events still presumes at least an implicit formulation of certain assumptions, which one may generalize. In any case, in spite of strong political overtones, as Spulber concludes, "changes in Eastern Europe's foreign trade practices . . . are largely, though not exclusively of course, conditioned by economic necessities."

FUTURE PROSPECTS

Both Bergson and Neuberger deal with the prospects of centrally planned foreign trade. As discussed earlier, foreign trade has been, in some CPEs, an important force behind economic reforms, culminating in recent years in an overall quest for economic rationality. Bergson, in his role as a discussant of the entire Conference, elaborates on the findings of the other contributors and offers some further thoughts on the relationship between foreign trade and economic rationality. Since he looks into the future, his interest centers mainly on the question whether the current trend to economic rationality will continue to have an impact on foreign trade (its level, structure, and direction). Neuberger's paper, on the other hand, is chiefly concerned with the inherent restraints on the dynamic adjustment process, which is a question of transition. He examines various features of a CPE that tend to affect both the path towards economic rationality and the speed of readjustment.

Before turning to the future, Bergson presents a concise summary of the CPEs' past foreign trade performance, with liberal references to the other contributions in this volume. He analyzes how the conduct of centrally planned foreign trade has diverged from economic rationality, and comments on the degree of this divergence. At first he defines economic rationality in foreign trade as conformity with the norms of comparative advantage, but later he turns to the possibility of rational departures from free trade (e.g., if a CPE enjoys some monopoly power). In considering future prospects, Bergson faces the difficult question of short-run versus long-run comparative advantage. Using Soviet agriculture as an example, he argues that short-run comparative advantage would probably require the Soviet Union to increase its imports of agricultural products, paying for them by raising machinery exports. In the long run, however, he questions whether the apparent comparative disadvantage of Soviet agriculture would persist if the past neglect of agricultural investment were corrected — and, we may add, if the organizational and incentive problems were solved more satisfactorily.

On balance, Bergson believes that CPEs are not likely to move rapidly toward full implementation of measures needed to introduce economic rationality, either in the domestic sectors or in foreign trade. He cites with approval the conclusions reached by Neuberger, who deals with the obstacles standing in the way of achieving economic rationality and reaping the full gains from trade. Neuberger begins by asking what legacies a Soviet-type CPE is likely to bequeath to its successor system. These legacies include the absence of entrepreneurs able and willing to take full advantage of the possibilities of foreign trade (a point stressed in Haberler's contribution), vestigial influences of an interventionist psychology, investment in "infants" that refuse to grow up, a high investment rate that exerts a continuous inflationary pressure, difficulties of correcting a price system divorced from both domestic and foreign scarcity relationships, and the absence of specialized and technologically advanced export sectors.

Legacies are presented by Neuberger not only as a tool of theoretical analysis, but also as elements of an empirical study, using the Yugoslav experience for illustration. Benjamin Ward, in his discussion, refers to the distinction between the theoretical concept of legacies, which he accepts as a potentially "very useful tool of comparative economic analysis," and "the empirical isolation of legacies, [which] is a very difficult matter." There are possible pitfalls, as Ward observes, when one moves from theoretical treatment to empirical observation (his comparison of Yugoslavia and Greece is particularly illuminating). Therefore, in considering the legacies in Yugoslavia that affect the move towards efficiency in foreign trade, one ought to listen to the Yugoslav economists' own evaluation. Perhaps the most eloquent testimonies to the difficulties of attaining a new, more rational equilibrium are the statements of Yugoslav economists who still complained in 1965 that ". . . our whole economic system is unfinished, so that one should regard it more as a transitional category which contains in itself elements of the old and the new (we suppose future). Under the new form there often hides the old content, so that, objectively regarded, *that which is old in the present system is more than dominant"* ([2, p. 40] with emphasis added). This is a sobering assessment after 13 years of reforms.

Johnson, as the second discussant of the entire Conference, concentrates on the question of the integration of centrally planned foreign trade into the general field of international trade. Both his critical comments on the papers of other participants and his own theoretical contributions are focused on this particular point.

Johnson stresses those aspects of centrally planned foreign trade which bring it into the mainstream of international trade theory and policy, rather than those aspects which differentiate it from foreign trade under other systems. As mentioned earlier, he believes that foreign trade policy in CPEs can be best understood if compared with the policy of other countries that also stress rapid economic growth as a primary objective. There are, of course, similar attempts to promote the industrial sector — which is considered crucial to national power and economic growth — in less-developed countries with other types of economic systems, whose restrictive foreign trade policies are overtly associated with the ideology of growing nationalism.

In conceptualizing government behavior, Johnson expands the idea of "public goods" to include preference for industrial production as an item of collective consumption. He argues that the public may be "prepared to sacrifice private consumption via the inefficiency entailed by protection; and that a rational government will push protection to the point where the marginal cost of protecting industrial production is equal to the marginal social utility derived from the collective consumption of it." Wiles, who objects to this approach, suggests that rather than appropriate the term "public goods," it may be better to call them "ideological goods." He adds whimsically that economists should not engage in intellectual imperialism; they should restrict their contributions to the exploration of the cost side, openly admitting that they have little to say professionally about the demand side for such goods. Conversely, he stresses that such "goods" as protectionism, national airlines, and parks have an important element of income redistribution and that economists have been deficient in assessing this aspect of public goods. Johnson refuses to accept the notion that the public-goods approach is any closer to intellectual imperialism than is the consumer-preferences approach in traditional economic theory, since neither tries to explain why some goods are preferred over others. Our function here is not to enter into this interesting discussion, no matter how great the temptation, but merely to call it to the reader's attention.

Johnson's theoretical discussion also leads to interesting empirical questions. In his view, a prime question is how much, in terms of real resources, the types of policies pursued by CPEs have cost them, as compared with free trade, and how much of this cost was necessary to the kind of development policies pursued and how much of it was due to inconsistencies and inefficiencies of the central control system. He argues that the probable real income cost of protection is likely to be much lower than is usually thought to be the case. A major exception would be an economy where, under free trade, production would be highly specialized for the world market, and where attempts to reduce dependence on trade would encounter rapidly rising costs of import-substitution.

CONCLUSIONS

Having considered in detail the key issues developed in the Conference papers, let us briefly restate the most significant conclusions of this cooperative study on centrally planned foreign trade.

Trade Aversion and Trade Proclivity vs. Autarky. The planners in CPEs have traditionally mistrusted and feared foreign trade; they have considered it a *pis aller*, trying to restrict it as much as possible. While to some extent this "trade aversion" has been counteracted by "trade proclivity" (i.e., an inclination to overtrade), on the basis of theoretical considerations one could expect trade aversion to prevail in all CPEs (i.e., a relatively low and decreasing level of trade). Trade has been growing in CPEs, however, at a strikingly rapid rate relative to total output, even during the early 1950s, when trade policy was highly restrictive, and according to the available evidence even faster than in comparable MTEs. In sum, as Johnson remarks, "it is hopelessly naive and futile to attempt to appraise the foreign trade policies of these economies in terms of 'autarky' as an objective."

Gains from Trade. The planning mechanisms of CPEs are unable to create a favorable environment for efficiency in foreign trade; therefore, the CPEs in their traditional form have been unable to reap the maximum possible gains from trade. Various aspects of the system share the responsibility for this, particularly its lack of flexibility and its inability to develop entrepreneurial initiative.

Instability. In spite of the planners' desire for stability, centrally planned foreign trade has been very unstable, not only in level of aggregate trade but also in commodity composition and geographical distribution. These acute short-term fluctuations have been transmitted also to the domestic sectors and have adversely affected their performance.

Machinery vs. Agricultural Exports. The preference of the planners for industry, particularly for machinery production and for industries that serve machine-building, has led to an anomaly in foreign trade. As CPEs have become industrially more advanced, they have encountered increasing difficulties in selling their exports; this in turn has tended to weaken, rather than strengthen, their position in world trade. This erosion of bargaining position, paradoxical for industrially better developed countries, is not simply a problem of adjustment to new markets. More lasting difficulties are presented by the fluctuations in foreign demand for capital goods and by the traditional association of machinery exports with long-term credits (a particularly burdensome requirement for CPEs in view of their relative scarcity of capital and their balance-of-payments pressures). A further handicap has been the long-standing neglect of agriculture in CPEs, which has caused losses of potential exports as well as direct and indirect increases in imports.

Balance-of-Payments Adjustment. The mechanisms of central planning are not designed to guard against the development of balance-of-payments pressures; neither do they provide for a painless adjustment if imbalances do occur. The planners, to be sure, can correct external disequilibria without having to face certain undesirable indirect effects induced elsewhere in the economy, such as those caused by the multiplier and accelerator. Thus, theoretically, the planners could avoid stop-go policies triggered by balance-of-payments deficits. Certain other secondary consequences, however, tend to be particularly troublesome. Since "nonessential" (low-priority) imports constitute a small proportion of total imports, and since foreign trade reserves are inadequate, balance-of-payments pressures periodically force the planners to cut imports of raw materials and capital equipment, giving rise to recurrent supply bottlenecks.

Legacies. Once principles of Soviet-type central planning become firmly established in a country, it is exceedingly difficult to abandon their specific features and remove their direct — and indirect — deleterious effects on foreign trade. Thus, an evaluation of trade and planning interrelationships must take into account the legacies that a Soviet-type CPE is likely to bequeath to its successor system.

Further Research. Various contributions to this study, from the opening paper by Gottfried Haberler to the concluding ones by Abram Bergson and Harry Johnson, repeatedly imply that this study is but a necessary first step in the analysis of interactions between international trade and central planning. In fact, Johnson stated at the conclusion of the Conference "that it would probably have been difficult, in advance of this Conference, to lay out what problems could be fruitfully discussed."

While this study is chiefly concerned with the interactions between central planning and foreign trade, in addition, quoting Johnson once again, other "important contributions, either of new understanding or of fruitful new lines of investigation, have emerged." Future research efforts might be directed to examine similarities and differences in the interactions between foreign trade and the domestic economy under various types of economic systems and in countries at various stages of economic development. This type of analysis would also serve to bring the study of centrally planned foreign trade more closely into the broader framework of international trade theory. Between the covers of this volume, surely more questions have been raised than answered. This is as it should be in a pioneering venture which attempts to probe into uncharted territory.

REFERENCES

1. Baykov, Alexander. *Soviet Foreign Trade* (Princeton: Princeton University Press, 1946).
2. Gorupic, Drago, and Ivo Perisin. "Prosirena reprodukcija i njeno financiranje," *Ekonomski Pregled*, Nos. 2–3 (1965); as quoted by Egon Neuberger, *Central Planning and Its Legacies*, P-3492 (Santa Monica: The RAND Corporation, December 1966).
3. Liska, Tibor, and Antal Máriás. "A gazdaságosság és a nemzetközi munkamegosztás" ("Economic Efficiency and International Division of Labor"), *Közgazdasági Szemle*, I:1 (October 1954), pp. 75–94.
4. *Rude Pravo*. October 17, 1964; translated by JPRS, November 2, 1964.

Theoretical Reflections on the Trade of Socialist Economies

GOTTFRIED HABERLER

At the outset it should be made quite clear that what I have to say is not more than "theoretical reflections" or "speculations of a theorist." I have no first-hand knowledge of Soviet-type economies and their trading problems. Nor have I made a really thorough study of the Western literature on those problems. I have read books and articles on the subject and am familiar with the broadest facts — that is all. I am somewhat better versed in the theoretical literature on the subject, but am far from having made an exhaustive study.

Statements will be made that should be supported by facts and figures. In my opinion, they can be verified, although I have not fully done so myself.[1] Experts on Soviet economies have a clear comparative advantage in this area. To them I leave the task of verifying — or proving false — what I have to say. For brevity, I shall state my propositions somewhat more dogmatically and unqualifiedly than I should.

EARLY SOCIALIST VIEWS

It is not surprising that Marx and Engels had nothing to say on the trade problems of socialist countries. Marx' was a theory of capitalism, and he refused to theorize or give advice on how to manage socialist economies. Marx and Engels did write, though not much, on trade between capitalist countries. They took issue with the problems of free trade and protection of their time. Later, when Marxist parties entered parliaments in Central Europe, Marxist theorists had to come to grips with the actual

[1] Some of them are listed in the Appendix to this paper.

trade problems and policies of the capitalist countries. Rudolf Hilferding and Otto Bauer on the theoretical level, and many others on a more practical level, tried to develop normative principles for trade policy and economic-sociological explanations of the actual policies pursued by capitalist countries — but there is nothing, so far as I know, in their writings, on the trade problems of the future socialist economies.[2]

Only a few Marxists were attracted by the free trade doctrine based on comparative cost grounds. Let me mention a personal experience. In Austria in the late 1920s and early 1930s, I had to deal with practical trade problems in the Vienna Chamber of Commerce (which was the official representative of private business), and I attempted to oppose protectionist proposals and policies. In these endeavors I was supported by Benedict Kautsky, the son of Karl Kautsky and a scholarly Marxist in his own right, who was the representative of the Chamber of Workers on these matters. He fully shared the free trade position and opposed protectionist tendencies in the trade union wing of the Social Democratic Party.

Marx himself favored free trade for the capitalist world, not on static comparative cost grounds but rather as a means of spreading capitalism to the four corners of the world and thus speeding it toward its eventual downfall. From the narrower technical standpoint, Marx' views on trade and protection were closer to those of Friedrich List than to those of the English classical economists and the Manchester School. The same is true of many later Marxists. What Marx and List had in common was their historical approach to economic problems, which led them to believe that different policies were indicated for the same problem — such as foreign trade and commercial policy — at different stages of economic development: protection in the early stages, free trade in the late stages of economic development.

MODERN THEORISTS OF SOCIALIST PLANNING

Modern non-Marxist theorists of socialist planning have a little more to say than the Marxists on the trade problems of centrally planned economies, but very little on trade between the socialist countries. Oskar Lange, in his famous *Economic Theory of Socialism* [13], does not discuss international trade. H. D. Dickinson, in his well-known *Economics of Socialism*, discusses briefly how socialist communities should trade with "other communities" — that is, with non-socialist countries [4, pp. 172–188]. Relegated to a footnote is an explanation of why he does not deal with the trading problems arising between socialist countries. The footnote is worth quoting because it is revealing in itself and probably also explains Lange's silence on the problem of intra-socialist trade:

[2] The literature is well reviewed in [9] and [10].

These other communities are assumed to be non-socialist. It is improbable that a number of independent socialist commonwealths would isolate themselves, each in its own distinct economic system, when self-interest and socialist principle alike would impel them to adopt an integrated system of economic planning and costing [4, p. 173n].

This passage seems to say that there is no need to worry about intra-socialist trade, because there will be no nationalistic bias under socialism. There will be either central planning by a supranational authority, which almost by definition excludes thinking in terms of national economies, or there will be competitive pricing. In the latter case, all that would be necessary is to instruct the managers of plants and industries in each country to disregard national boundaries and to refrain from "discrimination."[3] The rules of marginal pricing and costing would apply universally without regard to national boundaries. The state may not wither away; the modern socialist (and non-socialist) planners do not share that nebulous and mysterious article of faith of the Marxists' creed. But nationalism would disappear or be banished by the stroke of the pen — that is, by the promulgation and universal application, without regard to national boundaries, of Lerner's *Rule* [15, pp. 128 ff].

GREATER DEGREE OF ECONOMIC INTEGRATION IN THE WEST THAN IN THE EAST

It should have been clear from the beginning that this was wholly unfounded and naïve idealism. There is no question that bureaucratic planners and managers of public enterprises, both in the mixed economies in the West and in fully socialized, centralized or decentralized economies in the East, are much more averse to engage in international economic transactions, more conscious of national interests and constrained by national boundaries, than private, profit-seeking businessmen. "Private enterprise, as such, is normally non-patriotic, while government is automatically patriotic," as Viner puts it.[4]

There can hardly be a doubt that despite real or alleged monopolies, oligopolies, and other deviations from perfect competition, and despite the disregard of real or imagined externalities, the "invisible hand" of often imperfect competition, impeded though it is by tariffs and other government restrictions of trade, has managed to integrate the Western economies to a much greater extent than the centrally planned economies of the East have been integrated by their planners. Or to express it differently, market

---

[3] Both Dickinson [4, pp. 172–188] and Lerner [14, Chap. VII] use this expression. Lerner characteristically does not distinguish between true economic liberalism and socialism. The economies of the two systems are the same for him.

[4] Viner [22] discusses several real and apparent exceptions to this rule.

forces, although impeded and falling short of the ideal of perfect competition, have brought the Western economies much closer to the ideal international division of labor along the lines of comparative cost, as pictured both by the free trade classical and neoclassical theorists and by the theorists of competitive socialism, than the centrally planned or decentralized socialist economies of the East have been brought by their methods of central or "competitive" planning.

There are three reasons. The first is political and sociological in nature. Nationalism has proved to be an extremely hardy plant. The state has not withered away, and planners in the Soviet countries are probably more nationalistic than their counterparts in the West — those planners responsible for public policies and public enterprises in most Western countries. At any rate, national bias is largely absent from private business, which still is responsible for most of Western trade.

Second, Eastern planners have been severely handicapped by their upbringing in Marxian dogmas. Marxist economic theory is not only useless, it is a positive impediment to the efficient management of socialist economies. It inculcates a complete disdain for and disregard of market forces, price mechanisms, and competition. This attitude is all-pervasive, but it has been especially damaging for the efficient allocation of resources in the area of investment and international trade. The refusal to use interest rates systematically and explicitly prevents the efficient use of resources in the area of investment and international trade. True, time preference and capital cost cannot possibly be disregarded completely without courting famine and catastrophe. But failure to allow for it systematically and explicitly must cause serious inefficiencies and losses [2]. Similarly, in the field of international relations ignorance of the theory of international division of labor is a handicap. The Eastern planners have been taught that the doctrine of comparative cost in its old or modern form is bourgeois economics — that it is irrelevant or worse.[5] True, as in the case of resource allocation over time, even the most doctrinaire Marxist planner cannot do without some international division of labor. Literal autarky would be suicidal for the smaller socialist countries and extremely costly even for large Russia her-

---

[5] Wilczynski quotes the following description of the theory of comparative cost by some Soviet economists: "a pseudoscientific, reactionary foreign trade theory disseminated by bourgeois economists . . . to serve as a theoretical basis for the Western discriminatory foreign trade policies towards Socialist countries." This quotation is probably especially harsh in tone, but it is typical in substance. See [23, p. 66].

The fact that the theory of comparative cost was originally based on the labor theory of value has not endeared it to the Marxists. It is true, however, that in actual, practical planning, literal interpretation in terms of labor cost (neglecting capital cost, land, and other resource cost) would lead to very costly misallocations of resources. Western attempts at verifying the theory have been vitiated by exclusive regard to comparative labor cost. See, e.g., MacDougall's well-known papers on the subject [16].

self. What is lacking is systematic allowance for trading opportunities; this defect is implicit in the rejection of comparative cost theory.

Ignorance of modern theory of efficient resource allocation over space and time is, however, a handicap that can be alleviated or removed. There is plenty of evidence, with which other participants in this Conference are more familiar than I am, that it is in the process, in fact, of being gradually removed — that Eastern economists are learning Western economics and are engaged in substituting modern economic theory for sterile Marxian clichés.

The third reason for the comparatively low degree of international economic integration and suboptimal division of labor among the Socialist countries in the East is more subtle and requires careful elaboration.

THE DUAL APPLICATION
OF MODERN ECONOMIC THEORY

I shall argue that the benefits flowing from a better grasp of modern economic theory are limited. I do not deny that the substitution of modern economics for Marxian dogmas, systematic attention to the time profile of production (acknowledgment of time preference and interest cost), and recognition of the possibility of increasing national income by procuring many commodities indirectly via international trade — that all this can improve planning, eliminate numerous crude inefficiencies of present procedures, and, thus, lead to a considerable increase in output. But it is no more than a very imperfect substitute for real competition and is subject to serious limitations.

Let me develop what I have in mind at greater length.

Neoclassical and modern microscopic price theory — whether and whereever one wishes to draw a line between the two — has become much more operational than it was fifty years ago as a tool of policymaking and advising policymakers. It was always operational in the logical sense, but now it is highly operational and useful from the practical policy standpoint, too — primarily *public* policy, but also to some extent *private* business policy. This is due to the improvement of the theory itself, to advances of econometric and statistical procedures, and to the greater availability of statistical data.[6]

It is a remarkable fact that neoclassical microscopic price theory, which describes the working of an idealized, smoothly functioning, competitive, capitalistic economy, has turned out also to provide the answer to the problem of how an ideally efficient, socialist economy, either centralized or

[6] This statement does not exclude the possibility, some would say the probability, that improved and more highly operational theory brings with it the danger of luring governments into premature or ill-judged, and possibly very costly, policy interferences in the free-market mechanism. But I need not go into this problem for the purpose of my paper.

decentralized, should allocate scarce resources. In a sense this has been known, or more or less vaguely felt, by neoclassical theorists.[7] But it has been precisely formulated in the modern theory of linear and nonlinear programming. In many respects, the theory of the idealized, perfectly competitive, capitalist economy is the same as the theory of shadow and efficiency prices in the planned economy.[8] This identity or duality explains why modern theorists of socialist planning could learn so much from the neoclassical masters, and why good treatises on socialist planning, such as the books by Dickinson and Lange, can be and are being effectively used as texts in courses dealing with the competitive functioning of capitalist economies.

THE LIMITATIONS OF ECONOMIC THEORY: DEPRESSIONS, IMPERFECT COMPETITION, AND EXTERNALITIES

I turn to the alleged limited applicability of microscopic competitive price theory and its complement or dual, the theory of efficient resource allocation, to the capitalist economies of the West.

Modern proponents of central planning forcibly express the opinion that the application of neoclassical economic theory to the explanation of the functioning of capitalist economies is severely restricted, or made altogether impossible, by three factors: the proneness of the capitalist economies to develop more or less severe and prolonged periods of depression or stagnation, the absence of perfect competition, and the disregard of numerous existing externalities. Because of these alleged defects, modern socialists — including Dickinson, Lange, and Lerner — assert that modern economic theory is, in fact, more useful for socialist planning than for explaining what actually happens in the Western economies of today.

[7] Some older theorists made the mistake of giving an ethical interpretation to the attainment of Paretian efficiency under competition. J. B. Clark was one of the sinners. Many socialists and reformers, on the other hand, rejected marginal analysis on the ground of their mistaken belief that its acceptance would imply ethical approval of the capitalist system. However, many neoclassical writers correctly distinguished the "efficiency" function and the distributional function of the price mechanism, and pointed out that the two are not only theoretically distinct but also separable, to some extent at least, by policy.

[8] The former is sometimes called "descriptive" or "positive," and the latter "normative" or "technocratic." See [21, p. 15].

Since either version presents but an idealized picture of the actual operation of any capitalist or planned economy, either can be interpreted alternatively as descriptive or as normative. But Solow [21] may be right to call the competitive version "descriptive" and the planned version "normative" in the sense that the capitalist economies would seem to approach the efficient ideal much closer than the planned economies, at least the existing specimens of centrally planned economies. (I am not sure, however, whether Solow actually wished to convey that judgment.)

Concerning the first factor, I confine myself to saying that prolonged, deep depressions constitute, of course, a serious deviation from equilibrium as described in micro-theory. In a sense it can be said that such conditions suspend, or at any rate seriously distort, the working of the micro price mechanism on the national, and especially on the international, level.[9] Naturally, the views of Lange, Dickinson, and others were strongly influenced by the traumatic experience of the great depression of the 1930s and by the fact that the Soviet economy was, not surprisingly, spared the ordeal of the great depression.[10] But there is fairly general agreement among economists — which is beginning to be shared, though grudgingly, by Western and Eastern Marxists — that the time of deep and prolonged depressions is past. Mild recessions are a different matter altogether. I would argue that mild fluctuations of economic activity, implying occasional lapses from full employment, far from impede long-run growth; on the contrary, they are a condition for long-term growth. The corollary of this statement is that a high-pressure system that tries, with more or less success, to prevent even mild deviations from full employment leads to overfull employment, inflation, rigidity, numerous bottlenecks, and wasteful attempts at government interference with the economy to suppress the symptoms of inflation — and thus results in the end in slowing down rather than accelerating long-run growth.

The analogue in the socialist economy to the condition of overfull employment in the capitalist economy is what experts of Soviet economics call "taut planning."[11]

Closely connected analytically and empirically with the problem of cyclical fluctuation is that of inflation. Inflation, too, disturbs and distorts micro-equilibrium, although probably to a much smaller extent — except in very severe cases — than deep depressions. But socialist countries have by no means been spared the evils of inflation, even in peaceful periods — notwithstanding the fact that the authors of blueprints of centrally planned or decen-

---

[9] Micro general equilibrium theories, both of the "marginal productivity" and of the "linear" type, assume competition, hence price and wage flexibility. This assumption implicitly excludes wage and price rigidity, unemployment, depressions, and the like.

[10] Some Western countries managed to extricate themselves more quickly than the United States, the United Kingdom, and France from the deflationary spiral: e.g., Australia, Sweden, and Nazi Germany.

Interestingly, although again not surprisingly, it was only during the worst depression years in the 1930s that Soviet trade amounted to a substantial factor for some Western countries and industries. For example, in 1932 the U.S.S.R. took 11 percent of German exports. In 1931 Russia accounted for 55 percent of all machine tools exported from the United States. In no other year, before or after, were such high percentages reached. (The figures are taken from [5, p. 20]. See also [8].)

[11] Compare the trenchant analysis of that condition in Professor Brown's paper in this volume.

tralized socialist economies take it for granted that inflation as well as deflation could never become a problem under socialism.

As far as the second factor, the absence of perfect competition, is concerned, I am convinced that many theorists *in all camps* take much too seriously the existence of literally perfect competition, in the sense of horizontal demand curves, "the parametric function of prices" (Lange) as a condition for efficient functioning of the free-enterprise economy. Perfect competition in that sense is indeed a rarity. But the requirements of workable and efficient competition are much less exacting. I return to this point below.

The trouble with the third factor, the disregard of externalities (external economies and diseconomies in the broad sense), is that many of them, especially the important ones, are not readily recognizable and are almost incapable of quantitative evaluation. The theorists of central planning have an easy solution for that problem: they simply endow their "Supreme Economic Council" (Dickinson) with perfect knowledge and instruct it to allow, in their cost calculations, for all externalities.[12] This, I am afraid, is much too simple. If it were really so easy to ascertain the sign and magnitude of the externalities, it would not be difficult to correct the price mechanism in capitalist countries through taxes and subsidies so as to eliminate this source of inefficiency. This, in fact, is often done or attempted. Actually, however, it is extremely difficult in most cases to determine the existence and magnitude of external economies. One should never forget that they can be negative as well as positive. The fact that important branches of economic policy (for example, infant industry or development protection) are based on the explicit or implicit assumption that external economies are always positive (and located in the import-competing, rather than in the export, industries) illustrates the difficulties of correctly diagnosing and efficiently allowing for external economies. Every day, great economic crimes are committed in the name of giving due weight to external economies.[13]

There is no reason to assume that the detection and quantitative ascertainment of external economies are easier in a centrally planned economy.

---

[12] See, e.g., [4, p. 174].

[13] Let me make one qualification. There are certain types of externalities that are easier to recognize, to evaluate, and to correct — at least in principle. I mean such things as pollution of water and air, smoke damage to crops, and (on a larger scale) overforesting and overgrazing. In the Western countries, such conditions, which usually are *dis*economies (rather than economies), are dealt with by *ad hoc* legislative or administrative action. They may also have international implications, if the industries concerned (that emit the smoke or get damaged) are engaged in or affected by international trade.

There is no evidence that the socialist countries have been better aware of, or more effective in dealing with, these problems than the Western countries.

Controversial and difficult to diagnose and measure are the broad, all-pervasive externalities alluded to in the infant-industry theory of protection and in modern development theory.

The notion that there are no "vested interests" in the centrally planned economies, as there are in the free-enterprise economies, seems to me a myth. Vested interests firmly lodged in the rigid structure of bureaucracy constitute a formidable obstacle to change and reform. The assertion that centrally planned economies are free of these impediments to efficiencies suggests a type of reasoning that was perhaps natural and understandable, though not justifiable, fifty years ago when we had no experience with centrally planned economies — namely, the habit of comparing the *ideal* type of a centrally planned economy with the *real* type of a predominantly free market economy with all its imperfections, deviations from competition, and externalities, including those introduced by bad government policy. (The latter may well be a large fraction of all imperfections in existence. Think of the innumerable monopoly positions created and sustained by import restrictions.) Today, there is no longer any excuse for that procedure. We have to compare either the *ideal* types of both systems (in which case there is not much difference) or the *actual* pictures of both — but not the ideal type of the one with the actual picture of the other.

ECONOMIC THEORY AND THE ROLE OF THE ENTREPRENEUR

I now come to a point that in my opinion is of crucial importance. I have argued that modern micro-theory has become operational in the sense of being of considerable use to public and even private policymakers. But we must not exaggerate. It is not operational in the sense of being capable of telling the businessman how to conduct his business, and the entrepreneur where to look for new profitable ventures and how to carry them out. It is not a substitute for entrepreneurial qualities — vision, judgment, drive, persuasiveness. Entrepreneurial, innovational activity is still of vital importance for economic growth. It may be possible today, thanks to advances in managerial economics, to routinize certain activities that formerly belonged to the domain of decisions where the vision and hunches of the entrepreneur ruled supreme. But Schumpeter himself has probably greatly exaggerated the extent to which it is possible to routinize the entrepreneurial functions [20].

The uncertainties and risks that the innovating entrepreneur faces cannot be completely eliminated by any device. Existing price and cost structures provide a framework for entrepreneurial activity; market research based on micro-theory and elaborate statistics and econometric procedures (input-output analysis, etc.) may help to gauge the future response of the market to a reduction in price, to product differentiation, to improved quality of an existing product, or to an entirely new product. But the innovating entrepreneur cannot be guided mechanically by existing prices. This is quite clear if he contemplates production of an entirely new product, because no price exists for products not yet on the market. If the innovator undertakes to produce a better or a differentiated product, he must guess the price differential that will make it sufficiently attractive; if he intends to market a cheaper product, he must undercut the prevailing price and must have some idea of how his competitors and potential rivals will react.[14]

CRITICISM OF THE THEORY
OF PERFECT COMPETITION

Too literal an interpretation of perfect competition has obscured the functioning of the dynamic free-enterprise economy. First, it is perhaps not superfluous to remind ourselves that perfect competition, in the sense that producers and buyers take the price as given (horizontal demand curve), does *not* imply that the future price will be the same as the present; even the most perfect competition does not remove the risks and uncertainties connected with future price changes.

Second, it is in the nature of entrepreneurial activity that the innovating entrepreneur can usually count on a temporary monopoly position resulting from his innovations; in many cases the great risks of innovations would deter the entrepreneur from going ahead if there was no reasonable expectation of reward through a temporary monopoly position. Schumpeter saw that clearly, and it made him (rightly, I believe) critical of the extreme antimonopoly attitude of many modern theorists and antitrust lawyers. Rigid enforcement of perfect competition, if it were possible, would in many cases not conduce to rapid growth, because it would unduly restrain entrepreneurial activity. E. H. Chamberlin's static theory of monopolistic competition points up the necessity of relaxing the strict definition of perfect competition as a horizontal demand curve. F. A. Hayek has repeatedly criticized the rigid interpretation of perfect competition, and J. K. Galbraith has expressed similar reservations concerning the wisdom of a doctrinaire antimonopoly position and policy.

[14] I find it necessary to spell out these matters in some detail, because they are so often misunderstood. I think here especially of the modern theory of the so-called "dynamic external economies," which has become very influential among theorists *and practitioners* of economic development. This theory states that the individualistic price and market mechanism as described by modern general equilibrium theory, which includes the theory of comparative cost, works only so far as *current* production is concerned; for investment problems, where the future is involved, the price mechanism breaks down, because there are no future prices to guide the investor. This theory was developed by P. N. Rosenstein-Rodan and Tibor Scitovsky, and has strongly — and perniciously, in my opinion — influenced development planning. See my criticism in [7].

ENTREPRENEURSHIP IN
CENTRALLY PLANNED ECONOMIES

The reader may now ask — true or not, what has all that to do with the trade problems of Soviet-type countries? Briefly this: There is no room in centralized socialist economies for the innovating entrepreneur, and entrepreneurial activity is vitally important for international trade — in fact, perhaps, more than for internal growth and development.

That there is no room for private entrepreneurs in the Eastern economies will hardly be denied. It is true, of course, that some plant and industry managers develop exceptional drive and initiative. (So do some managers of public enterprises in the West.) But it can hardly be open to doubt that they have much less scope and opportunity for daring innovation than the private entrepreneur in the capitalist countries. The existence of enterprising plant or industry managers is no substitute for the multitude of large, medium, and small entrepreneurs and innovators in a free-enterprise economy. This judgment is not invalidated by the recognition that in certain areas investments are so big and their future value and usefulness so uncertain that private initiative cannot be relied upon to undertake them. Space exploration (if it has, in fact, economic value or significant economically valuable by-products) and atomic energy in the early stages of its development are examples that come readily to mind. But Western societies have not been precluded from exploiting these opportunities for public development. That public enterprise can fall back on private contractors and subcontractors for all those jobs where the private entrepreneur has a clear advantage, has made public investment much easier and more efficient than it would otherwise be. I need not dwell on what I regard as obvious, that the choice which Western countries have made of the areas they reserve for public management has not always been wise — to put it mildly.[15] This is not the point. The point here is that the possibility of choosing between public and private enterprise gives the West a great advantage over the East, which denies itself this option, even though the Western countries rarely make the best use of their opportunity.

One more remark on this matter. The proposition that centrally planned economies are severely handicapped, compared with capitalist economies, by the absence of innovating private entrepreneurs, and that this deficiency reduces their growth below the potential, does not imply that centrally planned

---

[15] I personally have no doubt that practically all Western countries have gone much too far, from the standpoint of economic efficiency, in reserving more and more areas for public management. This is especially true of less-developed countries, because they are in a much poorer position than the mature countries to manage public enterprises with a tolerable degree of efficiency. Grossly inefficient and overstaffed public enterprises are one of the major sources of inflation and impediments of growth in many less-developed countries.

economies cannot give a high priority to the stimulation of technological progress and cultivate in their people by a variety of measures (education, propaganda, etc.) attitudes and qualities favorable to technological advance and to the dissemination of technological knowledge. On the contrary, creation, acquisition from abroad, and dissemination of technological knowledge are, in fact, accorded high priority and are lavishly provided with material resources both in Russia and other Communist countries. But high priority and lavish financing do not guarantee tolerably efficient use of resources. Productive resources can be wasted by overinvestment and misdirected investment in technological knowledge, just as much as in the manufacture of tangible goods. There is a good deal of evidence that this has actually happened and is happening on a large scale in Communist countries.[16]

THE ROLE OF ENTREPRENEURS IN INTERNATIONAL TRADE

International trade, especially overseas trade with backward areas, has always been an arena for adventurers, explorers, conquerors, and traders. This was so both in the precapitalist and in the capitalist eras — early, high, and late capitalism. Methods have, of course, changed greatly. Gone are the days of the East India Company and colonies, gunboat diplomacy, and protection of investors in backward countries by military and political intervention. True, Marxists like to dwell with nostalgic attachment on the grisly tales of exploitation in those "golden ages" — golden not only for the conquerers and exploiters, but also for the critics of exploitative capitalism, who make heroic efforts to demonstrate that only appearances have changed while the basic facts of "monopolistic exploitation" of backward areas have remained the same through the centuries.[17] In reality, things have changed profoundly. As far as the exploitation of backward countries is concerned, in the era of the U.N., the United Nations Conference on Trade and Development (UNCTAD), the International Bank for Reconstruction and Devel-

[16] See the American Economic Association panel discussion [6] [12] [19]. The theory of "optimum investment" in that area has been developed by F. Machlup in several places, especially in [17, pp. 187–199] and [18].

[17] In non-Marxist circles the exploitation theory nowadays takes the form of the proposition that the terms of trade have a secular tendency to change to the disadvantage of the less-developed countries, largely or partly because labor and business monopolies in the industrial countries, by keeping the prices of their products high, manage to appropriate the fruits of technological progress to themselves instead of passing them on to the consumer. This theory is very popular, especially in less-developed countries. Despite the fact that the theory of secular deterioration of the terms of trade for less-developed countries has been disproved a hundred times, every meeting of the United Nations Conference on Trade and Development and other specialized U.N. subsidiaries abounds with talks of the "victimization" of the less-developed countries by the terms of trade.

opment (I.B.R.D.), the International Development Association (I.D.A.), and innumerable other international and interregional agencies dealing with development problems and distributing development funds to less-developed countries,[18] the shoe is clearly on the other foot — *pace* Myrdal, Prebisch, Singer. But what has remained true to this day is that greater risks and uncertainties are usually attached to international trade than to internal trade. While physical risks of delays, losses, and damage in transit have diminished and transport costs and shipping time have been slashed, other risks have increased — not everywhere, of course, but in many areas. Thus the legal protection of foreign investors and traders is less certain than it was, and the risk of foreign government interference in numerous ways has sharply increased. Greater risks, fiercer competition, greater uncertainties, and lack of firm knowledge give a special comparative advantage in the field of international trade to the freewheeling private entrepreneur over the bureaucratic managers of public enterprises, in the West as well as in the Communist countries.

It stands to reason that thousands of small, medium, and large private entrepreneurs — producers, merchants, traders, investors — will uncover and create more opportunities for fruitful division of labor than managers of public enterprises, of state-owned industries, or of government trade monopolies.[19] Heavy investments, not only in productive equipment but also in sales and service facilities, are necessary to carry trade beyond the "vent of surplus" stage (Adam Smith). In the West, an army of international traders, specialized according to product and geographic area, stand ready to act as intermediaries, to sell their specialized knowledge to the producers, and to spread the risks and take them off the shoulders of the manufacturers. The risk of failure and loss can be reduced by specialization and transferred from the timid to the adventurous, from those who specialize on production to the knowledgeable "speculators." But the risks cannot be wholly

[18] The less-developed countries have organized an effective representation that has managed, through political pressures — by skillfully playing off rivalries between Western powers and the rift between East and West — to extract from the rich countries huge annual contributions to the poor through numerous channels and international, interregional, and national agencies, development banks, and the like. That much of the money is wasted in costly bureaucratic structures, monster conferences, and international travelling in tremendous amounts; that much of the advice given by the various agencies is bad or diverts attention from necessary internal reforms; that the net effect of the enormous effort to speed up the economic development of the poor countries is comparatively small and may even be negative — all of this does not alter the fact that it is today the rich who are squeezed by the poor and not the other way around.

[19] Chinese merchants in Hong Kong are infinitely more successful in selling Chinese products all over the world than the bureaucrats of the mainland. The latter know it; therefore, they have tolerated, and have funneled hundreds of millions of dollars' worth of exports through, Hong Kong.

eliminated. There must be some who are willing and able to assume the
irreducible hazards. Can there be any doubt that the supply of the highly
productive function of "risk-bearing" is much more plentiful among private
"capitalists" than among bureaucratic managers, especially on the plant and
intermediate industry level? The top managers of the socialist economy,
especially those in totalitarian countries who are not responsible to democratic parliaments, may have more leeway to invest in very large and very
uncertain ventures than the private managers of even the largest Western
corporations.[20] But further down the line, managers on the plant and intermediate industrial level in socialist countries are certainly much more
constrained and less adaptable and flexible in their investment and production decisions than their colleagues in the capitalist world. Investment
in predominantly export industries must appear to them to be a highly
hazardous venture.

In the West, with many independent firms of different size and management with a variety of outlook and policies, it is much more likely that
there are some who are willing and able to venture into uncertain fields
than in the East with their standardized setup.[21] Inside the area covered
by the same plan, plant and industry managers naturally feel safer and more
at home than outside the country's boundaries where the economy is either
unplanned, which to those who have grown up in a planned economy looks
like utter chaos and confusion,[22] or subject to the rules and regulations of
a foreign planning authority. It is one of the facts of life that plans of different countries do not easily mix or mesh, and that the difficulties of mutual
adjustment of different national plans are formidable and increase rapidly
as the plans become more comprehensive and detailed.[23] The result is
"trade aversion," to use Professor Alan Brown's felicitous expression, leading to "undertrading" — that is, a volume of trade falling far short of
the optimum as determined by the comparative cost situation.[24]

[20] But as was pointed out above, Western societies have not been debarred by the
predominantly individualist organization of their economy from having recourse to
public investment and management when that has seemed advisable.

[21] In the West, the existence of numerous "pure traders" — modern department stores,
for example — who have no interest in production and buy where products are cheapest
and most attractive without regard to national boundaries, assures maximum utilization
of international trading opportunities.

[22] Imagine an Eastern manager being confronted with *to-hu-bo-hu* of an American stock or commodity exchange.

[23] Experience in the Western countries fully supports these conclusions. The more
planning, the more difficult the international division of labor, the smaller the volume
of international trade. See [1] for comprehensive documentation and numerous empirical illustrations.

[24] It is true that there are also cases of "trade proclivity" (see Professor Brown's paper)
on the record. These would tend to lead to "overtrading." Trade proclivity, however,
would seem to be the exception. It is probably best regarded as occasional overreaction
to extreme trade aversion. A tendency seems to exist for a vicious cycle: excesses of

SUMMING UP

The absence of independent entrepreneurs who, lured by profits and prepared to assume the risks of losses, seek out trading opportunities irrespective of national boundaries tends to foster a "vent of surplus" mentality in the export field. Investments in production and sales facilities for the prime purpose of selling in foreign markets, which are subject either to the unpredictable vagaries of the unregulated forces of demand and supply or to the whims of foreign planning authorities, are much too risky for the bureaucratic managers on the plant and industry level of a socialist economy.

Similarly on the import side, the tendency is to import what is absolutely necessary, but not to become dependent on deliveries from abroad for anything that can be produced, though at much higher cost, at home. Of course, import requirements are often very large and pressing when important raw materials are not available domestically or modern equipment cannot yet be produced. Import needs are also subject to wide fluctuations, especially in the agricultural area, or when something goes wrong (as often happens) in the coordination of different activities. All of this provides a stimulus to push exports and even occasionally to undertake special investments for export purposes — e.g., in the tourist trade (hotels, etc.) to provide the means for unavoidable imports. Naturally, in the small Communist countries international trade plays a much greater role than in Russia. This makes these countries more receptive to proposals of reform of their trading system, and provides a strong inducement for decentralization. The exigencies of foreign trade may yet become the wedge for far-reaching changes in the economic regime.

The overall result of the attitudes and policies of socialist countries concerning international trade is that in the socialist economies international trade plays a much smaller role than in Western countries of comparable size and economic structure. Trade aversion and undertrading are the rule, notwithstanding occasional cases of trade proclivity and overtrading. International division of labor between the socialist countries themselves, and between the socialist countries and the non-socialist world, falls far short of the optimum. The deviation from the optimum is probably much greater than in the most protectionist countries of the Western world.

In all socialist countries there have been great stirrings in recent years to loosen rigid centralized planning, to decentralize, and to allow the price mechanism and market prices to play a greater role. Some Eastern countries

trade aversion leading to a reaction which overshoots the optimum into trade proclivity, which in turn gives way, after glaring inefficiencies have been discovered, to trade aversion, and so on. It is similar to the oscillation between overcentralization and overdecentralization, which can be observed in Soviet-type countries.

have moved farther and faster in this direction than others. It is not surprising that the movement toward a greater reliance on market forces has
made less progress in the international area than in the domestic field. In the
international trade sphere, the substitution of market or competitive socialism for rigid central planning could bring about substantial improvements;
although, for the reasons given earlier in this paper — especially because
of the absence of independent entrepreneurs — no close approach to the
optimum can be expected.

In actual practice, the most centralized of the Communist countries tend
to set the pace of reform of international trading methods.[25] Trade still
seems to be almost completely centralized. The result is that things are much
worse than they could be if there was an approach at uniform speed to
competitive socialism. The descriptions of trading methods and arrangements given us by knowledgeable Eastern economists convey a picture of
utter confusion. One gets the same impression from Western studies, such
as Professor Brown's as yet unpublished dissertation on Hungarian international trade [3]. Strictly bilateral trading and outright barter seems to
dominate trade between the socialist countries.[26] The tales one hears remind one vividly of the worst periods of disorganization of Western trade at
the depth of the great depression in the 1930s, and again for a short period in
Europe immediately after World War II.

Rigid exchange rates will probably always be a serious impediment to
more efficient and freer trade of the socialist countries. That this hurdle is
not easy to surmount, even under market socialism, is suggested by the
fact that in the European Economic Community (Common Market), which
is, of course, much less given to controls than the Eastern countries. The
amount of planning — especially in the agricultural sector, where they have
gone farthest in the direction of central planning (although even here not

---

[25] Western countries have had much the same experience. When dealing with socialist
countries, or for that matter with other Western countries that have adopted highly
protectionist and non-market-type methods of trade controls (quotas, exchange control,
and state trading monopolies vs. mere tariffs), liberal Western countries themselves
have been forced, in self-defense, to resort to illiberal trading methods. In this area,
Gresham's law seems to operate: Bad trading methods drive out good, or bad examples
corrupt good manners.

[26] The consequences of strict bilateralism are somewhat reduced by "re-exports"
which seem to loom large in Communist trade. Communist countries often cannot avoid
accepting unwanted things in bilateral deals. These are then re-exported. This procedure
obviously is but a very imperfect and expensive substitute for true multilateralism.
Another device that Eastern countries use to reduce the crudities of bilateralism is the
so-called "switch-deals." There they employ Western specialized traders to dispose of
unwanted commodities in third markets — at a discount — for the delivery of which
they have contracted in bilateral deals. This method is probably more efficient than
re-exports, but it is still a very imperfect substitute for multilateral trade. (See [11,
p. 143].)

nearly so far as the East) — seems to make changes in exchange rates virtually impossible, short of situations of extreme, strangling disequilibrium.

Through the substitution of modern principles of resource allocation, especially over time and space, for sterile, nonoperational Marxian dogmas; through decentralization and a gradual approach to "competitive socialism"; through these measures, the crudest inefficiencies of the present trading methods of the socialist countries can be eliminated or alleviated. But, for reasons given earlier, no close approach to the optimum can be expected. "Synthetic competition" among managers of government enterprises and shadow pricing are no more than a very imperfect substitute for "real competition." Real competition must not be interpreted in the narrow sense of perfect competition of pure theory (horizontal demand curve). The existence of numerous private entrepreneurs, freedom of entry (i.e., free enterprise in most branches of the economy), absence of comprehensive government price-fixing and regulation of entry into numerous areas of economic activity — these are sufficient conditions for efficient and workable competition. Private property and the pursuit of profit are necessary ingredients, because that system, in Alfred Marshall's words, "harnesses man's strongest though not necessarily highest motives."

Appendix

Empirical Propositions That Are Assumed To Be True, Could Be Verified, and Should Be Made the Object of Systematic Factual-Statistical Studies

1. The trade of the Soviet countries, both among themselves and with the rest of the world, constitutes a substantially smaller fraction of gross national product than the trade of "comparable" Western countries. I have consulted several Soviet experts; no one doubts that the proposition is true, but I could not find a systematic investigation.

The main difficulties of such a study are probably to find appropriate deflators and to define "comparable" Western countries. Geographic size or even "economic size" (gross national product, or gross national product per capita) is probably not a sufficient criterion of comparability. If possible, consideration should be given to internal structural diversity with respect to climate, resource endowment, and transportation facilities (e.g., land-locked countries vs. seafaring nations). "Re-exports" ought to be eliminated; in other words, "specific" not "general" trade ought to be compared. Statistically, it may not be easy in many cases to eliminate re-exports.

2. The degree of multilateralism and bilateralism and the proportion of outright barter in the total trade of Communist countries, including intra-Communist trade, could be measured — again making allowance for re-exports. It is generally assumed that bilateralism and barter play a much greater role in Communist trade than in Western trade; but, again, I could not find a Western study of that question.

3. My statement concerning nationalistic bias, bureaucratic rigidity, and aversion to international economic transactions and entanglements on the part of Eastern managers, negotiators, and policymakers could be supported by reference to the Eastern literature.

4. It can probably be shown that the trade of Eastern countries is, to a much higher degree than in the West, concentrated on commodities that are wholly or almost completely unavailable in the importing countries: on raw materials and equipment rather than finished consumer goods; on "necessities" rather than "luxuries."

DISCUSSION

Robert E. Baldwin

I should stress at the outset that Professor Haberler's opening remark concerning his lack of detailed knowledge about CPEs applies with even greater force to me. My comments on the issues raised in his paper will be based not upon any special knowledge concerning the trading problems of CPEs but upon general trade analysis plus some special knowledge concerning the nature of trade problems in non-centrally-planned (market-type) less-developed countries (LDCs). The final verification or falsification of the propositions he lists in the appendix to his paper will, for example, have to await more of a specialist on these matters than myself.

One issue raised by Professor Haberler and several others, where an analogy between the trade experience of market-oriented LDCs and CPEs is evident, concerns the level of export and import trade in CPEs compared with the level of their gross domestic products. It has been brought out in the Conference that apparently there is no simple, safe generalization about how these export and import ratios compare with those in market-oriented economies, or indeed about how the ratios behave over time in CPEs. The resource structure of these economies — their size, their per capita income levels, and the like — is simply too diverse to permit a sweeping generalization, at least until more careful statistical analysis is feasible. However, one can speak quite properly, as Professor Brown has done, about the various forces tending either to increase or to decrease these trade ratios in CPEs.

One set of factors that Professors Haberler, Holzman, and others have mentioned as tending to decrease these ratios is associated with what have been termed the mechanisms of planning in CPEs (see the Appendix). The particular techniques traditionally followed by CPEs tend, Professor Brown suggests, to produce the result that both the benefits of trade are — or seem to be — lower and the costs of trade are higher than they are in market-oriented economies. For example, such factors as the high degree of nationalism in Soviet-type economies, the reluctance of planners to accept responsibility for the performance of a sector outside their direct control, and the inability to determine lines of comparative advantage because of the chaotic character of internal prices and foreign exchange rates — all tend to reduce the volume of international trade.

Another factor held by some of the authors to decrease the export ratio— in contrast to the import ratio, where it has the opposite effect — is the implementation, in CPEs that are traditionally primary-product-oriented, of the goal of rapid growth with particular emphasis on producer goods. It seems to me that experience in non-centrally-planned LDCs supports this point and indeed suggests that this development goal may be considerably more important in explaining trade behavior in CPEs than the particular planning mechanisms adopted by these countries to carry out this goal. One finds, for example, in the non-centrally-planned LDCs of Southeast Asia, where the goal of industrialization ranks high but where planning is under-taken on a much less detailed and less doctrinaire basis than in Soviet-type economies, that the share of exports to gross domestic product generally fell between the early 'fifties, when vigorous growth efforts were just getting underway, and the early 'sixties. Basically, it was due to an absorption of resources from the export sector into domestically oriented industries. The governments of market-oriented LDCs in Southeast Asia and elsewhere made little provision in their early development planning for increasing their traditional exports of primary products. The typical view was that world demand conditions made such export expansion undesirable. Coupled with this notion was a belief that these traditional exports would be able to maintain their relative importance in gross domestic product without any special development efforts in the export sector. Furthermore, it was thought that the balance-of-payments pressures associated with the need for imported capital goods to initiate industrial expansion could be successfully met on a short-term basis by foreign aid and investment, and on a longer-run basis by the import substitution benefits resulting from the industrialization program.

The sequence of events that in fact took place in the non-Soviet-type LDCs is similar in many ways to what apparently tended to take place in some of the CPEs as they carried out their development efforts. Relatively neglected sectors such as traditional exports and domestic agriculture did not turn out to be independent of the industrial sector. Instead, resources were withdrawn from these sectors into industry, with the result that exports tended to fall in relative terms. But perhaps the most disappointing outcome for many LDCs has been their lack of success in easing balance-of-payments pressures through import substitution. Instead of decreasing the need for industrial and raw material imports, the new industries have been much more import-intensive than it was initially thought they would be. To help provide the large quantities of capital goods and raw materials needed to carry out their industrialization goals, the typical LDC drastically curtailed imports of consumption goods. But, of course, in the absence of appropriate restraining fiscal and monetary policies directed at the private sector, import restrictions of this type merely make the domestic production of these items highly profitable, and *domestic* resources instead of *internationally traded* resources tend to be bid away from the heavy industries that the government wishes to promote.

Fortunately, many LDCs have been able to meet part of their need for capital goods through foreign loans and grants. Thus, we find that while exports have tended to decline as a fraction of gross domestic product in the non-centrally-planned economies of Southeast Asia, imports have tended to increase. The combined total of exports plus imports in relation to gross domestic product has remained roughly constant in these countries. Perhaps it is in connection with foreign investment that the ideology and mechanisms of CPEs play an important role. Soviet-type economies seem to give considerable weight to their desire not to become indebted to other countries, because of the risks of being subjected to economic warfare at a later date. Furthermore, the chaotic nature of internal prices and the existence of unrealistic exchange rates must seriously discourage possible lenders from making long-term lending commitments on strictly economic grounds. However, it would seem that even with respect to foreign borrowing it is likely that the rapid industrialization goal, rather than the mechanisms of planning, would play the more important part in determining the extent of foreign trade.

When a government is able to undertake central planning of the Soviet-type, it has the political power to carry out a much more massive industrialization program than the typical market-oriented LDC. The market orientation of the latter is in part a manifestation of its unwillingness to go as far as a CPE in the direction of rapid, massive industrialization. The faster and the more extensively resources are forced into the industrial sector with little regard for comparative costs, the more severe becomes the type of trade problems so familiar in the market-oriented LDCs. Exports of primary products fall more rapidly and the demand for imported capital goods tends to rise at a faster pace. In addition, as the economy moves more and more resources into productive lines that are highly inefficient in terms of existing international prices, the less profitable and the more risky it becomes to invest in such an economy. Thus, setting aside politically motivated foreign aid, CPEs that have traditionally relied on primary-product exports are likely to be forced to carry out their industrialization programs with internal resources to a greater extent than similarly structured market-oriented LDCs with the same general goals, both because their foreign exchange earning from exports tend to fall faster and because they are poorer risks for foreign lenders. Even so, it seems likely that the ratio of exports plus imports to gross domestic product would have declined in the market-oriented LDCs of Southeast Asia as it did in some Soviet-type economies had it not been for governmental loans and grants made to these Southeast Asian countries, not on narrow economic grounds but for political reasons.

As experience with industrialization programs is gained, however, both market-oriented and a number of the centrally planned economies tend to conclude that greater attention must be paid to increasing exports as a means of increasing imports of capital goods. The notion of comparative advantage is initially rejected in favoring the industrial sector and in neglecting domestic agriculture as well as exports of primary products, but eventually planners come to recognize that comparative costs are relevant even to the establishment of a productive pattern that itself may be inefficient in terms of world resource allocation. Given the same set of across-the-board industrialization goals in primary-product-exporting market-type and centrally planned economies that are inconsistent with comparative-costs relationships (both statically and dynamically), and ruling out massive external aid based on noneconomic considerations, it follows that the level of trade is likely to be lower than for countries that follow comparative-advantage lines to a greater degree in their industrialization efforts. However, it also appears for market-oriented and centrally planned countries that, given a particular pattern of desired industrialization goals, there is still some minimum level of trade activity below which its industrialization goals are made considerably more difficult to achieve. Indeed, some CPEs have apparently been able to raise their relative export levels and to increase their rates of industrialization at the same time. One would think that, unless countries defined their industrialization goals in rather selective terms, this would occur mainly in countries that rely on industrial rather than primary-product exports. Actually the market-oriented LDCs think they have discovered the potentialities of this approach and are now pressing for tariff preferences so they can increase their exports of manufactured goods.

The main point of Professor Haberler's paper does not, however, deal with factors that determine the level of trade in CPEs or with their ambivalent trade behavior over time(to use Professor Brown's language), but instead with the limitations of central planning in a dynamic world economy. On these matters I am in substantial agreement with him, and will only try to elaborate on some of his points.

As Professor Haberler notes, one of the favorite arguments of those who support planning in Soviet-type economies and wish for a greater use of planning in market-oriented LDCs is that socially significant investment interdependencies and technological spillover effects tend to be neglected in free-market economies. The price system, it is claimed, is a poor signaling mechanism for directing investment allocations among industries. To use a frequently cited example, it may be that investment in each of two complementary industries would be profitable if undertaken in both together but not if undertaken alone. However, because investors in either industry are unaware — or at last uncertain — of investment plans in the other, neither set of firms will increase its capacities, and socially productive investment opportunities will be lost. Actually, as Scitovsky points out, this argument has its greatest force when there are significant economies of scale in both industries. In industries with large numbers of firms and with no significant capital indivisibilities, relative prices are more likely to change in a smooth, continuous manner and to act in turn as reasonably reliable indicators for capital accumulation on a relatively smooth, continuous basis. However, in industries where capital must be accumulated in sizable lumps, prices tend to change in such a discrete fashion that existing prices or recent price trends are not reliable indicators of what prices will be after the lumpy investments have been undertaken.

It seems to me that the argument of Scitovsky and Rosenstein-Rodan does have validity as far as it goes. But, as Professor Haberler points out, in jumping from this argument to the conclusion that central planning is needed, these writers neglect some of the key elements in the actual operations of a dynamic free-enterprise economy. They are using as their model of a free-market economy an idealized, static version.

Industries in which economies of scale are important and where Scitovsky's argument supposedly has its greatest force are precisely those industries where — because of these economies — the number of firms engaged in production is relatively small. As Chamberlin and Mrs. Robinson taught us long ago, these are the industries in which "mutual dependence is recognized." Not only do producers within an oligopolistic industry not rely on the current price and output policies of their rivals within the industry in making their own current and future output decisions, but they recognize their interdependence with producers in other closely related oligopolistic industries. And, because they are aware of these interdependencies, they do not rely solely on current prices in complementary industries in determining their investment behavior. Their relatively small number makes it comparatively easy to exchange information through more direct channels than the price system, and thereby to cooperate in mutually profitable investment opportunities. Where the interdependencies are particularly important, a common ownership arrangement among closely related industries tends to emerge. To argue that firms in industries characterized by economies of scale act in the same way as firms in large numbers (the competitive model) is to ignore the whole behavioral side of the theory of imperfect competition.

We tend too often to overlook this particular benefit from oligopolistic industries. Schumpeter stresses the advantages of monopoly profits in stimulating innovation, and Galbraith points out the countervailing power benefits that can emerge from the market structures. But, in a complex industrial economy, perhaps more important than these is the tendency of oligopolistic industries to exploit socially profitable investment interrelationships among themselves to a greater extent than in a purely competitive market structure.

Of course, the argument that a dynamic free-market economy operates in a reasonable socially efficient manner can be overemphasized. In some cases the restrictive aspects of monopolistic behavior may outweigh any dynamic benefits. This is one of the arguments used by planners against the free-enterprise economy. But, as Professor Haberler also stresses, if we are talking about the actual and not the idealized model of free enterprise, where government ownership of some sectors and antimonopoly regulations are part of the model, it would seem that cases where restriction is clearly a real danger can be satisfactorily handled within a predominantly free-enterprise environment.

I think we also must agree with Professor Haberler that the argument that CPEs are superior to market economies because of their ability to prevent costly depressions is no longer very convincing. Market economies seem to have learned how to prevent deep depressions by general fiscal and monetary policies without the need to engage in detailed planning.

What then is left to the advantage of central planning if the alleged disadvantages of ignored externalities, imperfect competition, and prolonged depressions — supposedly associated with free-market economies — are not accepted as valid? It seems to me that — as Professors Brown and Neuberger emphasize in their list of desirable consequences of the Soviet-type system (see the Appendix) — if a nation desires to undertake a massive industrialization program favoring heavy industry, central planning does have advantages over a free-market economy. Conceivably it would be possible, by an elaborate set of tax and subsidy policies, to accomplish the same goal through the market mechanism; but, in practice, this kind of program so departs from the preferences of consumers that a nonquantitative system of incentives and penalties is not likely to work effectively. The thousands of profit-oriented entrepreneurs will tend to find loophole after loophole in the programs used by the government to direct investment into the special channels it desires, and thereby will prevent achievement of the government goals. Consequently, it is likely to be less costly to undertake a massive industrialization effort by central planning. The free-market-oriented entrepreneur may be an impediment to achievement of a government's growth goals if these goals depart radically from the economic preferences of the people. In short, perhaps much of the

planning system itself in CPEs is influenced by the goal of rapid industrialization rather than by static doctrines about planning.

The same point may also apply to the use of a decentralized market
system within an overall planning framework. There is no doubt about the
great inefficiencies of the planning mechanisms followed at present in the
typical Soviet-type economy. Decentralized socialism of the Lange-Lerner
variety can undoubtedly improve resource allocation in a Pareto-optimality
sense. But, in so doing, the preferences of consumers may operate in such
a way as to draw resources from the industrial activities desired by the
government. Again, taxes and subsidies can conceivably be used in such
a way that the economy picks up these efficiency benefits without sacrificing
its massive industrialization efforts; but in practice this seems questionable.
Central planning of the Soviet type easily results in costly misallocation
errors, but it would seem that many of these tend to be borne by the consumer sector rather than by the industrial investment sector. A decentralized
market system, on the other hand, is likely to permit the open expression
of competing goals that may cut more seriously into industrialization activities.

Once a planned economy reaches the development stage where it is
prepared to shift production toward consumer goods and to ease off on its
level of forced saving, the advantages of decentralized planning — and, even
more, the benefits from encouraging entrepreneurial activity — become evident. An economy at this stage is presumably interested mainly in stimulating rapid overall growth as indicated by consumer preferences rather than
in directing a massive dose of resources into a particular sector. Professor
Haberler makes a very important point when he emphasizes the advantages,
under these conditions, of a dynamic free-market economy — in which entrepreneurs can flourish — over a socialistic economy, whether it be centrally
or decentrally controlled. His point about the significant but still limited
benefits that flow from substituting market socialism for rigid central planning
is especially worth stressing. It is a matter of static efficiency gains compared
with dynamic growth benefits. A decentralized market system in which firms
still are not permitted to exercise entrepreneurial functions tends to bring
only static gains. Perhaps, as Professor Neuberger suggests, socialist economies will eventually hit upon a compromise system where some room is
left for private entrepreneurial action yet where "the commanding heights"
are socialized. But as we move in this direction, there would seem to be even
less reason for seeing these economies as a separate and unique group of
countries whose problems cannot be understood without reference to their
particular planning mechanisms.

REFERENCES

1. Balassa, Bela. "Planning in an Open Economy," *Kyklos*, XIX:3 1966), pp. 385–403.
2. Bergson, Abram. *The Economics of Soviet Planning* (New Haven: Yale University Press, 1964).
3. Brown, Alan A. "The Economics of Centrally Planned Foreign Trade: The Hungarian Experience" (Unpublished doctoral dissertation, Harvard University, 1966).
4. Dickinson, H. D. *Economics of Socialism* (London: 1937).
5. Gerschenkron, Alexander. *Economic Relations with the USSR* (The Committee on International Economic Policy in Cooperation with the Carnegie Endowment for International Peace, 1945).
6. Grossman, Gregory. "Innovation and Information in the Soviet Economy," *American Economic Review*, LVI:2 (May 1966), pp. 118–158.
7. Haberler, Gottfried. "An Assessment of the Current Relevance of the Theory of Comparative Advantage to Agricultural Production and Trade," *International Journal of Agrarian Affairs*, IV:3 (May 1964), pp. 130–149.
8. ———. "Economic Consequences of a Divided World," *The Review of Politics*, XVIII:1 (January 1956), pp. 3–22.
9. Hoselitz, Bert F. "Socialism, Communism and International Trade," *Journal of Political Economy*, LVII:3 (June 1949), pp. 227–241.
10. ———. "Socialist Planning and International Economic Relations," *American Economic Review*, XXXIII:4 (December 1943), pp. 839–851.
11. "How Switch Trading Works," *The Economist*, January 14, 1966.
12. Johnson, D. Gale. "The Environment for Technological Change in Soviet Agriculture," *American Economic Review*, LVI:2 (May 1966), pp. 145–153.
13. Lange, Oscar. "On The Economic Theory of Socialism," in Benjamin E. Lippincott (ed.), *On the Economic Theory of Socialism* (Minneapolis: University of Minnesota Press, 1938).
14. Lerner, Abba P. "Economic Liberalism in the Postwar World," in Seymour Harris (ed.), *Postwar Economic Problems* (New York: McGraw-Hill, 1943), pp. 127–139.
15. ———. *The Economics of Control* (New York: Macmillan, 1944).
16. MacDougall, G. D. A. "British and American Exports: A Study Suggested by the Theory of Comparative Costs, Part I," *Economic Journal*, LXI (December 1951), pp. 697–724; Part II, *Economic Journal*, LXII (September 1952), pp. 487–521.
17. Machlup, Fritz. *The Production and Distribution of Knowledge in the United States* (Princeton: Princeton University Press, 1962).
18. ———. "The Supply of Inventors and Inventions," *Weltwirtschaftliches Archiv*, LXXXV:2 (1960) pp. 210–254.
19. Neuberger, Egon. "Libermanism, Computopia, and Visible Hand: The Question of Informational Efficiency," *American Economic Review*, LVI:2 (May 1966), pp. 131–144.
20. Schumpeter, Joseph A. *Socialism, Capitalism and Democracy* (New York: Harper, 1947).
21. Solow, Robert. *Capital Theory and the Rate of Return* (Amsterdam: North-Holland Publication, 1963).

22. Viner, Jacob. "International Relations between State-controlled National Economies," *American Economic Review*, XXXIV, Supplement (March 1944); reprinted in *Readings in the Theory of International Trade* (Philadelphia: Blakiston, 1949), pp. 437–456.
23. Wilczynski, J. "The Theory of Comparative Costs and Centrally Planned Economies," *Economic Journal*, LXXV:297 (March 1965), pp. 63–80.

Foreign Trade of
Eastern Europe

Towards a Theory of Centrally Planned Foreign Trade*

ALAN A. BROWN

INTRODUCTION

Students of Soviet-type centrally planned economies (CPEs)[1] will probably concur with the recent observation of Professor Robert Campbell that "most of our fraternity experience a typical sense of frustration" as they approach the study of CPEs after years of graduate training in economics. Because of the basic fact of scarcity, "much of the logic of our model of

* To Professors Abram Bergson and Gottfried Haberler I am very grateful for encouragement and advice. I am indebted to Professor Egon Neuberger for his patience and insight in commenting on numerous drafts of this paper. For enlightenment on specific issues of centrally planned foreign trade, I am thankful to Dr. Rudolf Nötel. Along with several Hungarian economists, he also helped by calling to my attention valuable and not easily accessible statistical data. Professors Evsey Domar and Harry Johnson read early drafts of this paper. Finally, I wish to acknowledge my indebtedness to the Ford Foundation, the Harvard University Russian Research Center, and the Research Institute and Economics Department of the University of Southern California for financial assistance.

[1] This term includes the U.S.S.R., the smaller East European countries, and the non-European Communist countries. A sketch of the key features of CPEs, prepared by the editors, appears in the Appendix to this volume. My own conceptualization of a closed CPE was strongly influenced by Professor Granick's well-known organizational model of Soviet planning [22]. Since the mid-1950s, an increasing number of Western and a few East European economists have constructed models dealing with certain domestic aspects of CPEs, and the following list is not meant to be complete. Professor Bergson presented in one of his recent books an analytical framework of the Soviet economy, within which he interpreted the Soviet behavior pattern and assessed its economic efficiency [8]. Professor Montias appraised the Polish experience and provided a thorough introduction to the theory of central planning [49]. Both Balassa and Kornai used theoretical models of central planning to analyze economic planning in Hungary [4] [41]. A very comprehensive treatment of the different models of CPEs and of some alternative Communist economic systems appeared in a book by Professor Wiles [73]. The rich fruits of a collective undertaking on various aspects of planning in the Soviet

allocation and rationality ought to apply even in the Soviet economy. But despite the logical relevance of this body of thought, the institutional peculiarities of the Soviet economy make it not very operational" [15, p. 186]. This frustration is even more strongly felt in the study of centrally planned foreign trade. Over the past century and a half, Western economists have erected an impressive edifice of foreign trade theory, but some of the key assumptions of this theory have only limited applicability to CPEs. The theory of comparative costs, for example — in spite of the increasing intellectual appreciation of the doctrine in East Europe since the early 1950s [2] — has remained inconsistent with the CPEs' administrative and planning mechanisms, the lack of competition, and the irrationality of domestic prices and disequilibrium exchange rates. (See the Appendix, "Basic Features of a Centrally Planned Economy.") [3]

As for a theory of autarky, while many students of centrally planned foreign trade have correctly stressed the undeniable desire of the planners for economic self-sufficiency, the very concept of autarky has remained vague and ambiguous. [4] If we are willing to set aside the conceptual complexities and accept a simple, conventional definition — *autarky*: a policy designed to achieve the greatest possible economic self-sufficiency, or a policy to reduce trade as much as possible — we find that the hypothesis of autarky is contradicted by the dynamic trade pattern that can be expected to emerge, and does in fact emerge, in a CPE. On both theoretical and empirical grounds we will have to reject the hypothesis that the foreign trade behavior of CPEs, in general, has effectively been governed by their manifest desire to

Union and in East Europe were published in a volume edited by Professor Grossman; the editor's Introduction contains not only a summary of the other contributions but also a succinct model of CPEs [24]. A later article by Professor Grossman serves as an excellent theoretical frame of reference for Soviet-type systems [23]. In the *Festschrift* honoring Professor Gerschenkron there were several models of Soviet planning [57]. As we proceed, reference will be made to other contributions that relate to specific features of CPEs.

[2] During the mid-1950s the East European economists rediscovered, and since then have sought to rehabilitate, the theory of comparative costs. This intellectual effort was spearheaded by the Hungarians. See [47]. A brief analysis of the subsequent debate is contained in my article [12, pp. 11–28]. The increasing intellectual acceptance notwithstanding, the effective operation of the theory of comparative costs has been impeded by a continued adherence to the traditional system.

[3] A recent Western analysis appeared in *The Economic Journal* [71], showing "the irrelevancy of the theory of comparative costs in the centrally planned economies" [71, p. 63].

[4] Autarky seems to be a very simple term, but behind the apparent simplicity lurks a variety of meanings; and on closer examination it becomes evident that the term has little operational significance. I have tried to analyze the difficulties of defining autarky precisely (its vagueness) and to examine differing definitions (its ambiguity), attempting to apply several concepts of autarky to centrally planned foreign trade, in a paper given in 1963 at The RAND Corporation. (This paper is being revised for publication under the title, "The Theory and Practice of Autarky.")

achieve economic self-sufficiency.[5] To avoid any misunderstanding, let me add that I do not claim that the hypothesis cannot be supported in certain specific cases.[6] My point is simply that we shall need a balanced conceptual framework, *based on the key features of CPEs,* which will explicitly take into account the *passage of time and interaction among the variables,* if we want to analyze the relationships between central planning and foreign trade.

The purpose of economic theory is to clarify fundamental economic relationships and to help us understand and forecast economic events. Thus, theories of foreign trade attempt to explain what a country will trade and where (the level, the composition, and the direction of trade), how the gains from trade are divided (the terms of trade), and how an external disequilibrium is corrected (the balance-of-payments adjustments). Let us begin by considering some concrete examples of the foreign trade of Hungary,

[5] The two definitions of autarky — self-sufficiency and utmost trade restriction — do not necessarily imply each other, although this implication is often assumed. Liska and Máriás, for example, the two Hungarian economists who were the first in East Europe to attack in print the inefficiencies of centrally planned foreign trade, spoke of "the theory of autarky, which holds essentially — without expressing it openly — that participation in the international division of labor is not possible or not advisable, and therefore, we should adjust ourselves as completely as possible to self-sufficiency" [47, p. 78]. On the other hand, Professor Thomas Schelling, who has provided (without using the term "autarky") the most thorough theoretical discussion of the policy of economic self-sufficiency that I could find, argues that a country wanting to be self-sufficient should try to move to the importation of nonessentials and pay with exports of essentials [59, pp. 512–532]. "Why learn to do without bananas before we have to?" asks Professor Schelling rhetorically [59, p. 514]. We can easily dispose of the possible objection that the elimination of nonessential imports would help the balance of payments. If the planners have already decided the level of real consumption, then it can be shown that the balance of payments could be even improved by giving domestic consumers a wider variety of choice through the increased importation of nonessential consumer goods. (For a proof see my discussion of the "orange-apple paradox" in [12, pp. 15–16].) As Professor Haberler observes, "If . . . [a country's objective is] to induce different habits of consumption, and to lead people to spend less on luxuries, then, logically, there is no ground for discriminating between imported and home-produced luxuries; both should be taxed equally" [26, p. 249]. In CPEs, as discussed later, the emerging pattern of trade restriction is the opposite of the one suggested by Professor Schelling, not only in the short run — one could still argue that this implies some kind of autarky — but also in the long run.

[6] For example, in the Soviet Union during the early 1930s, as argued by Professor Holzman in his detailed analysis of Soviet foreign trade. (See [31, pp. 283–332].) We may briefly note, however, that after World War II, when the Soviet Union became richer and more able to afford the luxury of greater self-sufficiency, its dependence on imports did not diminish. We may also refer to Professor Pryor, who calculated in a pioneering study of the centrally planned foreign trade system [56] that the actual trade in East Europe was below the "trade potential." This observation is certainly not without interest, but it does not prove the existence of "autarky." Consideration of a single year does not tell us about the dynamic pattern of trade. During the supposedly most autarkic period, trade in fact increased more rapidly than income, not only in Hungary, as will be discussed, but also in the other CPEs.

along with some empirical observations.[7] The statistical findings may be summarized under the headings of aggregate trade, commodity composition, regional direction, and price developments. In each instance the observer is confronted with a set of paradoxes, or contradictions, between the planners' explicitly stated policies and the actual developments.

The most striking phenomenon is the growth of Hungarian trade volume, which increased faster than national income during the entire planning era. Paradoxically, the most rapid increase of trade occurred during the early 1950s, when the planners' opposition to the country's involvement in international division of labor was strongest. Although in this period foreign trade was considered a necessary evil to be reduced as much as possible,[8] the relative importance of trade increased faster than it did subsequently when opposition to trade became less. In fact, overt restrictionary sentiments notwithstanding, the trade-income ratio increased much faster in Hungary than the corresponding propensity-to-trade [9] did in similar market-type economies.[10] Foreign trade was also much more unstable in Hungary than, for example, in Austria during the same period. This instability was evident both in the absolute level of trade and in the trade-income ratios. (Thus, in the Hungarian trade-income ratios there was a recurrent annual cycle, which is further examined in the concluding section of this paper.)

Neither did developments in commodity composition reflect official policy goals. First, in spite of strenuous efforts to expand machinery imports, for

[7] The choice of the Hungarian case for study suggests itself for two reasons. First, the Hungarian foreign trade statistics are the most comprehensive among the CPEs; second, the remarkably candid and incisive self-appraisal by Hungarian economists covers the longest time period. The statistical results cited in this paper were derived from my analysis of Hungarian foreign trade. (For further details and a discussion of the statistical methodology, see [13].)

[8] The following was called a "classical formulation" of this view: "The primary task of foreign trade is the assurance of imports that cannot be produced within the country, by means of the exports" [35, p. 98].

[9] The terms "import-income ratio" and "export-income ratio" (or briefly, "trade-income ratio") will be used as measures of the relative importance of trade instead of the customary "propensity-to-trade," since propensities (as well as elasticities) imply unidirectional cause-and-effect relationships, while in CPEs there is a more complex functional relation between trade and income. (See the analysis of the Hungarian trade-income cycle in the Conclusion, below. The methodological issue is discussed more fully in [13, Chap. IV, pp. 154 ff.].)

[10] My time-series comparison of Hungarian and Austrian trade experiences showed that between 1950 and 1955, when the Hungarian import-income ratio increased by 7.6 percent per annum, the average growth of the Austrian import propensities was only 2.7 percent. During the entire decade of the 1950s, on the average Hungarian import-income ratio increased by 5.7 percent; the corresponding increase of the Austrian import propensity was 2.3 percent. Compared with the pre-war period, the average Hungarian import-income ratios in the 1950s were 44 to 70 percent above the 1924–1938 average, in contrast to the experience of 12 Western countries whose average post-war propensities exceeded the inter-war averages by only 7 percent (the range was minus 32 to plus 47 percent) [13, Chap. IV].

example, their share was less in 1955 (12.3 percent) than in 1949 (18.2 percent) [13, Table V-1]. Second, there was also a steady decline in the proportion of industrial raw material imports, notwithstanding continued complaints about their scarcity (76.8 percent in 1949, 67.6 percent in 1955, and 59.7 percent in 1960) [13, Table V-1]. Third, the unprecedented increases of agricultural imports conflicted with the unrelenting stress on imports for industrial growth, which were continuously emphasized. Finally, short-term fluctuations overshadowed long-term trends in every category, although planning incessantly stressed stability.

There were similar short-term gyrations in the geographic distribution of trade, which also conflicted with official planning policy. While Hungarian trade with both major trading areas increased in absolute terms, the relative share of Western trade at first very substantially declined, then increased, and then again declined. Given the political pressures of the period, the initial decline is not surprising. By 1955, however, the 1950 distribution was re-established (43.4 percent of the imports came from the West in 1949, and 45.4 percent in 1955) [13, Table V-5]. But this change, too. proved to be temporary, in spite of the political thaw and the strenuous policy efforts during the second half of the 1950s to increase trade with the West.

The relative regional price changes, although most pronounced during the rapid geographic shifts, provide no explanation for this trade diversion. In fact, the causal relationship seems to be reversed, the price changes being the dependent and the regional redistribution of trade the independent variable. The relative changes in regional terms of trade (while the overall terms of trade steadily deteriorated) were inversely related to the shifts of regional trade; that is, the terms of trade deteriorated with region A relative to region B when the share of trade with region A increased, and vice versa.

In the concluding section of this paper, an attempt will be made to explain these contradictions or paradoxes by means of a theoretical model of foreign trade. This theoretical or conceptual framework, while it was conceived in an effort to illuminate the Hungarian experience, should be relevant to other CPEs as well, since the basic assumptions of the model are the goals and mechanisms of CPEs in general. The conclusions of the model should therefore be applicable to other economies with similar objectives and planning systems. We may add, at the risk of emphasizing the obvious, that the theoretical conclusions tend to emerge less forcibly in large CPEs, like the Soviet Union, than in small countries where participation in international specialization is of relatively greater importance from the standpoints of both demand and supply.

THE THEORETICAL MODEL

This section examines how some of the key features of a CPE affect the conduct of foreign trade. The conceptual model is presented in two parts, statics and dynamics. In the first part, attention is focused on factors that would either tend to lower the equilibrium level of trade in a CPE as compared with a similar market-type economy (MTE), or tend to raise it. The method of analysis is, therefore, comparative statics. Two opposite sets of shift variables are examined. The effects of the first set, which have a restrictionary influence, are discussed under *trade aversion*,[11] while the effects of the second set, whose influence is expansionary, are examined under *trade proclivity*. Trade aversion may be thought of as the thesis of a dialectical process, and trade proclivity as the antithesis. The synthesis emerges in the second part of the model, dynamics; it is termed *trade ambivalence*, alluding to the difficulty of attaining a stable equilibrium in the level, composition, and direction of trade.

STATICS: TRADE AVERSION AND TRADE PROCLIVITY

TRADE AVERSION

The shift variables with a restrictionary effect on trade — those that would result in a lower level of trade in a CPE, *ceteris paribus*, than in a MTE — may be further divided into two subsets. The first of these includes those shift variables that tend to increase the implicit costs of trade (*cost sensitivity*),[12] while the second subset includes those shift variables that tend to reduce the explicit benefits from trade (*benefit denial*).[13]

[11] The point deserves some emphasis, in view of the frequently "hasty identification of self-sufficiency with a policy of discouraging trade" [59, p. 512], that trade aversion and autarky are very different concepts. Neither the motives nor the results are necessarily the same (although some aspects of trade aversion may also play a role in autarky). Autarky is a policy of self-sufficiency, which in accomplishing this purpose may or may not lead to trade restriction. Trade aversion, as we shall see it, implies to some extent an opposition to trade in general; in fact, some restriction of trade which would not be an illogical result of trade aversion, such as a restriction of nonessential imports, may well lead to a reduction of a country's self-sufficiency.

[12] These do not include the explicit costs of trade (i.e., exports and freight charges) but only the implicit cost or the consequences of foreign trade which have adverse effects outside the trade sector. To illuminate the concept, we may refer to Kalecki's principle of increasing risk. Just as "the fear of the worst" increases the subjective risk aversion of private firms, the planners are also more hesitant to engage in activities that might irreparably undermine their position [37].

[13] An analogy based on the theoretical model of the firm may help to clarify these concepts. If we consider the foreign trade sector as a multiproduct firm, which can produce a variety of outputs (i.e., imports) by utilizing certain inputs (i.e., exports), then trade aversion can be represented by a lower position of the profit schedule (i.e., of the total gains from trade) and trade proclivity by a higher position. To analyze

Cost Sensitivity

Cost sensitivity is based on factors that create greater implicit costs in a CPE than in a MTE. These factors are both noneconomic and economic.

Noneconomic Factors

We may distinguish between two noneconomic factors of cost sensitivity: the danger of foreign trade to national independence or security, and the conflict with (Marxian) ideology. These need not detain us long. Centralization, one of the basic objectives of a CPE, could be considered to be a means within a broader, noneconomic means-ends chain, the more ultimate end being the desire to safeguard the country's national sovereignty and its given ideological orientation. While all countries are concerned in a general way with the effects of foreign trade on national security, these effects tend to play a more decisive role in the trade relations of CPEs. To cite Professor Jacob Viner's classic observation, "private enterprise, as such, is normally nonpatriotic, while government is automatically patriotic" [70, p. 439]. In addition, foreign trade represents a greater implicit cost on ideological grounds for the planners who are steeped in Marxist-Leninist ideology. There is, first of all, the deep-seated suspicion that foreign trade is nothing but a notorious tool of imperialism, which enables the capitalist system to rid itself of its three surpluses — capital, commodities, and population. A further ideological impediment is fear of the "anarchy of the market," as revealed in the concern voiced by Stalin that foreign trade may make it impossible to limit indefinitely the operation of the "law of value" (i.e., the market) if a CPE is heavily dependent on foreign trade.[14]

Problems of Planning and Control

The economic causes of cost sensitivity are connected with the problems of planning and control. Two chief problems will be considered: the transmission of external fluctuations and the increased complexity of planning and control.

Transmission of External Fluctuations. The fear of the central planners that participation in foreign trade will expose their economies to the influence of the "law of value," or the market mechanism, is not entirely a question of ideological orthodoxy. International market fluctuations — being,

---

trade aversion further, we can separate that part of trade aversion which is directly related to the operation of foreign trade (benefit denial) from the indirect effects of trade (cost sensitivity). These can be represented, respectively, by a downward shift of the revenue curve and by an upward shift of the cost curve. (For a more elaborate discussion of this analogy, see [13, Chap. VII].)

[14] Stalin mentioned Great Britain specifically, where "the law of value," he said, "would continue to operate because of the importance of foreign trade to Britain and the vast part it plays in her national economy" [62, p. 13].

of course, beyond the control of the central planners — may also endanger the stability of the overall economic plan.

The destabilizing influence of external fluctuations on domestic planning depends on the degree of taut planning. In the domestic sectors, taut planning means that the planners attempt to set both input coefficients and reserves lower, and output norms higher, than the most likely estimates. (See the Appendix.) Taut planning in foreign trade is manifested in overestimation of export prices and underestimation of both import prices and foreign exchange reserves needed to smooth out short-run fluctuations. Therefore, with taut planning, foreign trade plans are established on the basis of more optimistic forecasts than are objectively warranted. In fact, the foreign trade plans are likely to be even more unrealistically taut than domestic plans, for two reasons: first, because the possible range of estimates in foreign trade is much wider than in domestic production; and second, because the planners — who consider foreign trade a particularly sensitive sector, where central control is very difficult to enforce — are not likely to relax the tautness coefficients used in formulating the foreign trade plans.[15]

Increased Complexity of Planning and Control. Apart from the difficulties caused by world market price fluctuation, foreign trade tends to make the implementation of central planning more cumbersome. In domestic planning, argues Maurice Dobb, "the actual complexity of the situation with which any group of central planners is likely to be confronted, is substantially reduced because the coefficients of production are often fixed by a given technology" [17, p. 81]. A similar proposition is presented by Paul Baran, who writes that the task of the planners is facilitated because, instead of "slow adjustments to small changes, . . . [there is] a choice between few technological alternatives involving large indivisibilities and 'fixed coefficients'" [6, p. 385]. But these arguments lose their validity in an open economy. Foreign trade reduces the existing discontinuities and indivisibilities of the production functions, since there are numerous ways to "produce" any given commodity by means of foreign trade. The high degree of substitutability, which is usually considered to be a major advantage of trade, also means a potential increase in the number of plan variants, and this is an added burden — an increase in the implicit cost of foreign trade — for the CPE.

[15] In Hungarian foreign trade it was estimated that within a given year there was a 25 percent fluctuation in world prices [see 44, pp. 410–442], which is certainly a much greater variability than one would expect to find in the domestic production coefficients. As for the optimum tautness coefficients — since in taut planning the "intention is to set the targets somewhat beyond the full capacity so as to force the enterprise to seek out reserves" [46, p. 27] — I am assuming that these coefficients will be higher (the plans being more taut) in those sectors where the planners feel more uncertain, if they are particularly distrustful of the enterprises or have but scant advance knowledge of what the objective conditions will be. (See also Professor Hunter's article on "Optimum Tautness" [34].)

Foreign trade also tends, as noted, to make the implementation of central plans more difficult and to reduce the effectiveness of central control. While foreign trade is considered to be one of the most sensitive areas of the economy (one of the "commanding heights"), the supervision of foreign trade activity is particularly hampered by a lack of competent and reliable experts.[16] Given the planners' preference for centralization, the *de facto* reduction of effective central control becomes another source of higher implicit cost.

Benefit Denial

Benefit denial is based on factors that tend to make the explicit gains from foreign trade less in a CPE than in a MTE. This may be partly an objective phenomenon and partly a subjective one, given the planners' assessment of gains. Benefit denial is a function of the unreliability of valuation standards, of overcentralization in administration and planning, and of dysfunctional material incentives. Let us briefly consider these.

Unreliable Valuation Standards

The standards of valuation are generally unreliable in a CPE; that is, the domestic price system is irrational, and the disequilibrium exchange rates fail to reflect accurately the real cost of obtaining a unit of foreign currency. This unreliability precludes the use of accounting profits as a reliable measure either to compare planning alternatives or to assess fulfillment of the plan.

Although accounting losses suffered in foreign trade are not allowed to play a decisive role in the formulation of foreign trade plans, price equalization deficits seem to have a negative effect on the planners' subjective assessment of the benefits from trade. There has been evidence of such a subjective benefit denial in the East European economic literature, where arguments are presented against foreign trade, based on the large and increasing price equalization deficits.[17]

[16] Because of the scarcity of competent and reliable foreign trade staff, the Hungarian planners, for example, did not even attempt to institute an independent control system in foreign trade. The foreign trade plan was based "primarily on the recommendation of the FTEs" [65, p. 8]. (The problem of the scarcity of foreign trade cadres is discussed further below.)

[17] [1, p. 292]. The so-called "price equalization deficits" are the accounting losses in terms of domestic currency. (For a good description of the system of price equalization in East Germany, see [56, pp. 101–105].) In a compilation of official documents by the Hungarian Central Statistical Office, it was stated, in effect: As a result of the price policy, it is almost impossible to determine which foreign trade transaction is advantageous for us, and which is not [1, p. 292]. While the size of the price equalization deficits is no reliable measure of the real gains from trade, these deficits are not without economic significance: (a) The subsidies lead to financial expansionary pressures, which require special countermeasures to avoid inflation. (This is what Professor Holzman called "the financial effect" of trade. See his discussion in [33, especially pp. 436–440].) (b) If the subsidies increase over time, they give a downward bias to

In any case, actual benefits from trade are likely to be less in a CPE than in a MTE if there are no reliable criteria by which to evaluate alternatives. Inefficiency will be fostered not only in macro-planning but also on the micro-level; neither have the enterprises accurate yardsticks for comparing real costs with derived benefits, nor can their activities be controlled effectively.[18]

Overcentralization in Administration and Planning

Macroeconomic inefficiencies (administrative and planning maladjustments) caused by certain traditional features of CPEs tend to be intensified by foreign trade, which results in benefit denial. Let us consider four of the principal features — vertical coordination and control, the method of material balances, taut planning, and discontinuous planning — along with a phenomenon that is more or less transitory, the relative shortage of foreign trade cadres. (The analysis at this point is still restricted to static consequences; dynamic interactions are to be taken up in the succeeding section.)

Vertical Coordination and Control. A chief cause of benefit denial is stress on vertical channels of coordination and control, with a corresponding threefold weakening of the horizontal connections: (a) between the foreign trade and domestic sectors (i.e., between, on the one hand, the foreign trade enterprises — FTEs — and, on the other hand, the industrial firms), (b) among the individual organizational units within the foreign trade sector (i.e., among FTEs), and (c) within given organizational units (i.e., among departments of given FTEs, or within the Ministry of Foreign Trade). As a result of the compartmentalization among sectors, enterprises, and departments, the normal operational lags increase, efficiency becomes more difficult to evaluate, and the response to changing conditions becomes less elastic.[19] The

the rate of growth of national income (since the subsidies appear as negative entries in the national income accounts).

[18] According to an official release, "our methods of planning, control, and incentives, as well as the wage and bonus system led to a tendency in general for the individual interests of the workers in foreign trade to oppose the interest of the people's economy" [1, p. 292]. One of the chief criteria used to measure the performance of FTEs in various CPEs is the so-called "price equalization index" (PEP-index), which compares the domestic with the foreign cost by means of the exchange rate. In spite of some improvements, the index is universally condemned as an efficiency standard, since it is affected by aberrations of domestic prices and the exchange rates. (For further discussion see [12, pp. 17–18].) The other major yardstick is the "net foreign exchange earning index" (NFE-index), which measures the net foreign exchange derived by exporting a given good [12, p. 17]. In describing this index, a Hungarian textbook of economic statistics conceded that it was "no efficiency index at all" [75, p. 349].

[19] The intersectoral separation has frequently been attacked. In Poland, for example, Fiszel complained that the producing firms did not know foreign market conditions and the FTEs were ignorant of domestic production; but even if they had been aware, neither set of enterprises would have been interested in making the socially desirable adjustments [20, pp. 27–30]. The interfirm separation (among the FTEs) presents difficulties in case of tied agreements, since one FTE, for example, may be unable to

consequent reduction of benefits presents a more serious problem in foreign trade than in the domestic economy, since the opportunities to take advantage of rapid changes in world market conditions, which may be lost, are one of the most important sources of gains from trade.

Method of Material Balances. The traditional method of formulating and revising plans also tends to reduce potential gains from trade in a CPE. The method of material balances denotes that the various economic plans are sequentially established (as discussed in the Appendix). In the planning of foreign trade, the import commodity plan (analogous to the physical output plan in domestic planning) is formulated first, and the other foreign trade plans (the export plan, financial plans, geographical plans) are set up in sequence. The initial guidelines for the import plan are based on anticipated domestic deficits, while the export plan tends to utilize available surpluses. This could still lead to an optimal foreign trade plan if the plans for domestic production were to be adjusted in subsequent rounds, taking into account opportunities in foreign trade. While this is possible in theory, in practice the planners find it cumbersome to consider the numerous primary and secondary feedback effects between foreign trade and the domestic sectors, and they likewise tend to neglect atypical conditions and unusual circumstances. The use of material balances causes benefit denial not only when plans are formulated but also when plan revisions are considered, since the planners generally try to avoid readjustments of the balances that require extensive coordination. As a result, the options for their taking advantage of available substitutabilities in trade are limited.[20]

conclude an export deal if the interest of the appropriate importing FTE is not harmonized. Finally, because of the interdepartmental separation (e.g., one ministerial department being in charge of *ad hoc* exports, and another of issuing import licenses), as documented by a Hungarian economist, it was only years later discovered "that exports . . . [in given cases] . . . required more foreign exchange than the total earnings derived from the exportation . . ." [5, p. 319]. Similar cases were reported in Poland and in Hungary, even in the 1960s [e.g., 12, p. 7].

[20] While there have been many complaints about the use of material balances in foreign trade and its corollary, trading in surpluses and deficits, there have been few detailed descriptions of the process. We find an explicit account in the article by Liska and Máriás: ". . . an import plan is worked out on the basis of the production plan, and an export plan on the basis of the import and production plans" [47, p. 78]. Also, "the financial plan was set up subsequent to, and simply on the basis of, the already approved foreign trade commodity plan" [2, p. 1]. For a lucid description of the use of material balances in East German foreign trade, with ample documentation, see [56, especially pp. 55–63]. The consequences of this practice were condemned by numerous economists in various CPEs. In Hungary, it was said that foreign trade "was only a passive observer in economic planning" [67, p. 3]. A plea was entered in East Germany, too, that foreign trade should be actively considered when the national plan is prepared [76]. In Poland several economists spoke out against the practice of exporting left-over domestic surpluses and only buying imports to cover deficits in the material balances [55]. By the end of the 1950s, even the Hungarian First Deputy Minister agreed that "importing to cover commodity deficits . . . and selling surpluses . . . was an oversimplified view of the tasks of foreign trade" [39, p. 1143].

Taut Planning. Taut planning affects benefit denial as well as cost sensitivity. Since the plans are not drawn up on the basis of what is most likely, but according to forecasts that are more optimistic than facts would warrant, and because of attempts to keep reserves and inventories at unrealistically low levels, there is less opportunity to exchange the most desirable assortment of commodities under the most advantageous conditions. Both the inadequacy of foreign exchange reserves and the low level of salable inventories interfere with the flexibility of foreign trade policy, providing less opportunity to take advantage of world market fluctuations. Taut planning in foreign trade not only tends to reduce potential gains from trade directly but also contributes to benefit denial indirectly, making it more difficult to correct problems that arise from other causes. If, for example, the planners are faced with unexpected domestic shortages in the supply of key commodities, they may find it more difficult to alleviate this problem by means of foreign trade because — as a result of taut planning — additional foreign exchange can only be secured by an immediate increase of exports. Since importing and exporting thus occur under emergency conditions, the terms of trade are adversely affected. Also, because of efforts to expedite deliveries, transportation costs are increased.[21]

Discontinuous Planning. This feature of the planning system also contributes to benefit denial. In centrally planned foreign trade, the operational plans are the yearly ones. But conditions in world markets are highly volatile; thus, predictions made in any given year on the basis of information available from the preceding year tend to be even more unreliable in foreign trade than in domestic production. To guard against uncertainties, final approval of the plans may be delayed; this, however, motivates FTEs to postpone as many of their activities as possible until late in the year, with consequent losses in gains from trade. The result is benefit denial in either case: if the foreign trade plans are approved late, operation of foreign trade is impeded; but even if the plans are approved earlier, there is a reluctance to take changing conditions into account and to sanction thoroughgoing plan revisions.[22]

[21] This was frequently attacked [e.g., 42, p. 20; 43, p. 19]. In general, the FTEs "did not consider what extra expenses were created in those transactions which were concluded for the sake of plan fulfillment" [1, p. 292].

[22] "Only when a good part of the year elapsed were the details of the foreign trade plan ready" [68, p. 3]. For example, the Hungarian 1955 foreign trade plan was approved as late as June 1955 [1, p. 297]. As Hicks said, "an inefficient firm will make major plans as rarely as possible, and do all its planning by small adjustment of detail, which takes only a few elements of the situation into account . . ." [30, p. 124]. According to the testimony of the Hungarian economists, major revisions of the foreign trade plan were only undertaken under emergency conditions [2]. Uncertainty is, however, so great in foreign trade that in 1955, when the foreign trade plan was revised in Hungary as late as in October, the revised plan deviated from the actual fulfillment no less than the original plan did [1, p. 297].

Relative Shortage of Foreign Trade Cadres. The relative shortage of foreign trade cadres is a joint result of demand pressures and supply limitations. An economic advantage frequently claimed for centralization is that it enables a system to concentrate the most competent personnel in the center, thus conserving technical and administrative skills. But skilled personnel are needed not only for decisionmaking and operational activities but also for supervision and control. Therefore, there are pressures on the demand side because effective centralization requires the maintenance of independent checks. This problem tends to be particularly serious in foreign trade because the sources of information there are more diverse than in domestic production, and world market conditions are more changeable. In foreign trade, consequently, the amount of data which needs to be collected is larger, and the difficulty of gathering and processing the data is greater. On the other hand, the supply of foreign trade personnel tends to be more limited in a CPE than in a MTE, because, in the former, personnel — particularly those who are sent abroad — are expected to be not only technically competent but also ideologically reliable. While this may be a short-run problem that tends to correct itself over time, even in the long run the foreign trade cadres should find it difficult to adjust to the very different environment of foreign trade, having received their training and experience in a CPE. Specifically, they have to unlearn the pattern of behavior appropriate only within the persistent sellers' markets that prevail domestically.[23]

Dysfunctional Incentives

The system of incentives is dysfunctional in a closed economy — i.e., social and private interests are improperly synchronized. This is partly due to the unreliability of performance evaluation standards and partly to the discontinuity of incentives. (See the Appendix.) Let us consider how the dysfunctional incentives affect the operation of foreign trade.

On the import side, discontinuous incentives, which specify success as 100 percent fulfillment of the quota, lead to a more absolute dichotomy than in exports. An unauthorized overfulfillment of the import quota is as unacceptable as an underfulfillment is reprehensible. Unlike a domestic producer of shoes, for instance, the enterprise that imports shoes is not permitted to overfulfill its "output" quota; therefore, its success indicator registers only dichotomous results, either success or failure. In an effort to overcome this problem, the planners give more weight on the import side to other success indicators, particularly to the price equalization percentage index (PEP-index), which rewards a FTE if the accounting profit exceeds the planned profit. But be-

---

[23] Reasons for the shortage of foreign trade cadres and the consequences of this shortage are discussed, *inter alia*, in [38]. According to a more recent account, lack of knowledgeable and reliable supervisory staff was responsible for simply allowing credit for foreign claims, without even checking them [19, p. 4].

cause of the irrationality of domestic prices and the disequilibrium exchange rates, the importing firms can show more favorable results by "informally" substituting domestically overpriced import goods.[24]

On the export side, the dichotomy of incentives is not absolute but the benefit denial is no less serious. The exporting firms are urged to fulfill their "output" quotas, which are measured in terms of (net) foreign exchange earnings (NFE-index). Consequently, exporters are motivated to lower the foreign selling prices, since they thereby increase their aggregate foreign exchange earnings as long as foreign demand is elastic (not a very restricting assumption).[25]

The benefit denial tends to be particularly strong, since the traditional incentive system is even more dysfunctional when applied to foreign trade than in the closed economy. In foreign trade, on the one hand, there is a greater danger of simulation: first, the "assortment problem" tends to be more serious, because the products in international trade are more variable and conditions are more volatile (and, in general, controls are less reliable); and second, "storming" in exporting is also greater than in domestic production, because it is a combined result of the activities of the domestic producers of exports and of the FTEs.[26] On the other hand, the danger of a tendency towards lethargy is much greater in foreign trade, since the level of incentives is at the mercy of unpredictable world market fluctuations, and individual responsibilities are especially difficult to assess. Since success or failure is often mainly determined by fortuitous price variation, the FTEs may well decide that their most rational alternative is to opt for a quiet life.[27]

[24] "Profitability can be improved by a shift of the product assortment towards items which contain larger profits. The determination of product assortment entirely from the standpoint of profitability must be condemned as harmful also in foreign trade" [3, p. 12]. (For an explanation of the PEP-index, see note 18 above.)

[25] There have been many complaints that the FTEs often do not mind selling at less than "world market prices" [66, p. 16], thereby creating "hidden reserves" in foreign trade. According to a rough estimate of a Hungarian economist, these "hidden reserves" amounted to $4–6 million annually in Western trade alone (about 2 to 3 percent of Western exports) [38, p. 10]. (For an explanation of the NFE-index, see note 18, above.)

[26] This point is made, for example, in an official Hungarian document [Forg. 19/1951. jul.; as cited in 1]. "The activities of the FTEs are often planless and generally campaign-like. They try to make up for their underfulfillments at the end of the planning periods; therefore, the activities are pushed to the end of the planning cycles. This, however, is the fault of the FTEs only on the import side" [1, p. 306]. The report also shows comparative statistics and mentions some specific consequences — e.g., breakdown of the transportation system, loss of sales, etc. [1, pp. 301–302].

[27] This conclusion is implicit in many bitter complaints. For example: "Try to find a manager or trade union representative who can decide in this case 'the quantity and quality of the performed work'! I am giving away no secrets when I say that *it takes weeks after each premium disbursement until the dissatisfaction subsides*" [27, pp. 19–20; my italics].

TRADE PROCLIVITY

This section analyzes the methodological features of the CPE that would result in a higher level of trade in a CPE, *ceteris paribus*, than in a MTE. Two main causes of trade proclivity will be examined: the emphasis on rapid industrial growth, and the use of foreign trade as an external safety valve.

Rapid Growth and Industrialization

Rapid economic growth, along with a disproportionately fast development of the industrial sector (particularly certain high-priority heavy industrial branches), is one of the chief objectives of CPEs. Foreign trade can be used as a vehicle to accomplish this objective. Access to the goal of rapid growth and industrialization can be generally facilitated in the short run by exploiting foreign technology (e.g., by importing capital goods). But trade proclivity may also occur in the long run, since the stress on heavy industrial development is independent of the individual CPE's resource endowment; and some CPEs, as they pursue their typical pattern of growth, may become more dependent on imported industrial raw materials. In addition, neglect of agriculture, the other side of stress on heavy industrial growth, may result in a higher agricultural import demand, and therefore in trade proclivity. These long-run effects depend, of course, on the relationship between required and actual resource endowments.[28]

Safety-Value Role of Foreign Trade

The second major cause of trade proclivity is the use of foreign trade as a safety valve in an attempt either to prevent short-run disequilibria in the domestic supply system or to mitigate their consequences. Temporary supply imbalances may be the result of errors in planning or of *ad hoc* changes during implementation of the plans. Specifically:

(a) There is always a certain degree of uncertainty in forecasting because of random disturbances.

(b) The method of taut planning creates systematic shortages in the supply system, since both output targets and input coefficients tend to be overoptimistic, and reserves are kept too low to serve as efficient shock absorbers.

(c) There are uncoordinated departures from the plan, since the degree of plan fulfillment varies among different industries.

(d) Within the broader commodity categories, the actually produced assortment of commodities can, and frequently does, deviate from the required assortment.

---

[28] The emphasis on steel production, for example, caused a very considerable trade proclivity in a country like Hungary, which has to depend almost exclusively on imported iron ore and coking coal.

(e) There may be problems of timing, since the suppliers of commodities tend to regulate the rhythm of deliveries with little regard for the needs of the buyers. (The suppliers in persistent sellers' markets can easily disregard demand considerations.)

The planners might, of course, consider other methods than *ad hoc* imports to alleviate supply bottlenecks. They could maintain emergency reserves, undertake large-scale replanning, or sanction the transfer of resources from low-priority industries. It is, however, frequently more expedient — faster and less costly — to utilize additional imports than to employ alternative methods. In general, the more rigidly centralized a CPE and the more reliance it places on taut planning, the more it will resort to the flexibility provided by foreign trade.

In addition, foreign trade is used as a safety valve, not only because the planners consider imports to be a convenient adjustment device, but also because industrial enterprises are motivated to press for inflated import plans. Thus, enterprises whose fulfillment of production targets depends on the availability of supplies (their adequate and timely flow, and their proper assortment) try to diversify their supply sources and reduce their dependence on less reliable domestic suppliers. While this practice is officially condemned, it tends to persist as an informal, surreptitious mechanism. It is tolerated because it reduces the inherent rigidities of the supply system; but, in any case, it would be difficult to eliminate it in the absence of reliable evaluation standards. This aspect of trade proclivity is further enhanced by the stress on vertical coordination and control levers, which makes it difficult to evaluate given foreign trade transactions efficiently.[29]

DYNAMICS: TRADE AMBIVALENCE

We have seen that two opposing sets of forces affect centrally planned foreign trade: one of these tends to reduce the level of trade in a CPE as compared with a MTE (trade aversion), while the other tends to increase it (trade proclivity). But the final outcome is not simply a net total of these two forces, since addition of the partial derivatives would neglect interactions among the variables. These interactions, occurring over time, lead to a synthesis of the model of trade dialectics (trade ambivalence).

The following main conclusions emerge. While on the basis of the static analysis one may initially expect more trade aversion than trade proclivity

[29] For example, as a Hungarian economist complained, the producing enterprises were motivated "to buy and use the best quality [of imports], regardless whether these were the most efficient" [40, p. 13]. It was difficult to evaluate the efficiency of given import requests, since administrative control was divided among several ministries (e.g., foreign trade, heavy industry, and finance), and among several departments within the same ministry. Thus the exportation was even encouraged when it subsequently required more imports than the value of exports. (See note 19, above.)

(i.e., a positive net trade aversion), changes over time in the dynamic analysis lead to gradual increase of trade, worsening of the commodity and the single factoral terms of trade, deterioration of the balance of payments, and development of increasingly acute domestic supply bottlenecks. Also, the Marshallian offer curve becomes increasingly inelastic as a result of the growing inelasticity of both import demand and export supply.[30] Although these results are interdependent, forming a set of vicious circles, for expositional convenience the dynamic processes will be separated into three dilemmas of centrally planned foreign trade: the *priority dilemma*, the *flexibility dilemma*, and the *trade reorientation dilemma*.[31]

THE PRIORITY DILEMMA

The priority dilemma involves certain dynamic adjustments of the commodity composition and level of trade. The choice is between two alternatives: whether to increase the trade-income ratios of a CPE relatively slower, or faster, than trading propensities tend to increase in a comparable MTE.[32] These two alternatives mean, respectively, that foreign trade will be either a comparatively low-priority or a comparatively high-priority sector of the economy.[33] According to the preceding static analysis, trade could only become a high-priority sector if trade proclivity were to increase relative to trade aversion. Because of dynamic changes, however — as will be demonstrated — this is not a necessary requirement. Even though the planners may prefer the second alternative and try to reduce the trading ratios, over time the unintended growth of trade will exceed the intended rate. Foreign trade, therefore, may be a low-priority sector *ex ante*, but it will tend to be a high-priority sector *ex post*.

[30] For a mathematical derivation of the relationship between import demand and export supply, on the one hand, and the Marshallian reciprocal demand, on the other, see [74, pp. 52–56]. (If E = elasticity of Marshall's reciprocal demand, η = elasticity of import demand, and ϵ = elasticity of export supply, then $E = (\eta + \eta\epsilon) / (\epsilon - \eta)$.)

[31] It may be added that the choices offered within the dilemmas need not be considered to be strictly dichotomous; the disjunctive premises of the dilemmas will be modified accordingly in the subsequent discussion.

[32] The purpose at this point is to examine only those factors in centrally planned foreign trade which would make its pattern diverge from that in the trade of MTEs (the method of analysis being comparative dynamics), without implying that the propensity to trade in MTEs would actually increase. It may be noted in passing that in the long run, according to statistical evidence, total volume of international trade in general has not increased as fast as world real income [21, pp. 23 ff]. This phenomenon has been discussed in the past by several economists: for example, Werner Sombart at the end of the nineteenth century even developed a "law of the falling export quota." See [36, p. 183].

[33] Assuming that an economic sector in a CPE is of comparatively high priority if its output increases faster than national output as a whole, compared with the performance of a similar MTE, and of low priority if the increase is comparatively slower.

Changes on the Import Side

The structural changes on the import side are the starting point in the process of the priority dilemma. These structural changes may be separated into two phases: an increase of high-priority and a decrease of low-priority imports.

Increase of High-Priority Imports

As discussed under trade proclivity, there is a tendency for import demand to increase both in the long run (because of the emphasis on rapid growth and industrialization) and in the short run (because of *ad hoc* imports). In either case, the additional imports will be high-priority goods, or they will achieve high priority temporarily to alleviate acute domestic shortage or bottlenecks in domestic high-priority sectors.[34]

Decrease of Low-Priority Imports

As high-priority imports increase, there will be a concomitant gradual decrease of low-priority imports in response to balance-of-payments pressures. While external financial pressures are certainly not absent in MTEs stressing rapid growth, the balance-of-payments problem tends to be more chronic in CPEs, for reasons directly or indirectly attributable to the goals and mechanisms of the CPE. Several direct causes of persistent external disequilibria have already been identified: the steady demand for imported capital goods, the continual *ad hoc* imports needed to avoid input-output disproportions, and the tendency to use import and export price forecasts that are — according to the method of taut planning — more optimistic than the most likely estimates. Since taut planning in foreign trade also implies that foreign trade reserves are to be kept at a low level, a CPE must either reduce its imports or be forced to increase its exports when balance-of-payments deficits develop, unless it can resort to foreign loans. As long as there are imports that are considered, in the domestic economy, to be of relatively low priority, their emergency curtailment offers the planners the simplest short-run solution. But, *ceteris paribus*, temporary reduction of nonessential imports tends to be carried over into the succeeding plan periods because of the general reluctance of the planners to restore imports that could be eliminated without causing obvious damage to growth.[35]

---

[34] Thus there is an important difference between the domestic shock absorbers and the foreign trade safety valve. Although both mechanisms serve to relieve bottlenecks due to planning errors and unexpected circumstances, in foreign trade this function is fulfilled by increasing the "outputs" (i.e., the imports) — which tends to increase the priority level of foreign trade — while domestically the role of shock absorber is performed not by increasing the output of low-priority sectors but by diverting their inputs to high-priority industries.

[35] In Hungary, for example, manufactured consumer imports declined steadily during the first planning years: 132 million DF (*deviza forint,* or "foreign exchange

The end result is an increase of the average priority level of imports, which in turn implies that the offer curve becomes inelastic. On the one hand, the elasticity of import demand approaches zero, import prices having little or no effect on the quantities imported (within a range, of course); on the other hand, the elasticity of export supply declines to minus unity (i.e., becomes backward-sloping), as the planners try to keep the total value of exports constant, regardless of price changes.[36]

Exports and Import-Export Interactions

As the average priority level of imports rises, further curtailments of imports to alleviate external disequilibria become increasingly difficult. But when imports can no longer be easily reduced, the burden of equilibrating the balance shifts to the export side. This then leads to a pressure to augment exports, which *pari passu* increases their order of priority.

Dichotomous Priority System

The planners, when faced with the need to mobilize more exports, are initially likely to turn to domestic low-priority goods — i.e., to "nondeficit commodities" — which are thought to be least difficult to withdraw from domestic markets.[37] But this is only a short-run solution — as will be shown below — since the emphasis on exportation of low-priority products (e.g., agricultural, light industrial, and consumer goods) creates a dichotomy in the priority system (i.e., low priority for domestic use but high priority for exports), causing subsequent repercussions. Let us consider these consequences.

Dual Pressures on Priority Planning. The low-priority industries, having

forint") in 1950, 88 million in 1951, 81 million in 1952, and 74 million in 1953. (The *deviza forint* is not a medium of exchange but only a unit of account; 11.48 DF is equivalent to U.S. $1.) Nonessential imports such as oranges virtually disappeared [63, pp. 264–270]. During the same years, however, the current value index of total imports increased by more than 50 percent. We can observe a similar movement in the commodity series of Soviet imports during the First Five-Year Plan. (See Holzman in [31, pp. 296–297].)

[36] In a MTE, according to Professor Haberler, "it is most unlikely that the elasticity of demand of a country, as shown on a Marshallian curve [the reciprocal demand], will in practice be less than unity" [26, p. 157]. (Marshall analyzed the consequences of inelasticity, "some of them quite remarkable," in [48, Appendix J].) The usual proposition of elastic reciprocal demand rests, however, on the very assumptions that are violated in centrally planned foreign trade: (a) in a CPE the demand for the majority of import goods is not inelastic; (b) the range of export goods becomes more limited (there is less responsiveness to external price changes); and (c) changes in the terms of trade will not lead to a quick expansion or contraction of domestic production. (For a discussion of these considerations in MTEs, see [26, pp. 157–158].)

[37] Professor Levine, for example, uses the term "nondeficit materials," but he says that in Soviet planning "they are always described as 'fully substitutable substitutes'" [46, p. 164]. See also the previous discussion of trading in deficits and surpluses, note 20.

for a long time suffered neglect in supply allocation, will have to accommodate themselves to the increasing export demand. This intensifies existing tensions in low-priority industries and leads to a more rapid exhaustion of their shock-absorbing capacity, thereby weakening one of the traditional adjustment mechanisms, priority planning.[38]

Deterioration of the Terms of Trade. Since the instructions are usually violated with impunity so long as output quotas are successfully met, the quality of exports is likely to suffer. Producers of low-priority products (e.g., consumer goods) are particularly unaccustomed to stringent demand specifications, and quality control in these industries is said to be especially lax.[39] They are lacking, as a rule, both in motivation and in ability to accommodate buyers of their products. Therefore, efforts to increase foreign sales of domestic low-priority products lead to a decline of export prices and a deterioration of the terms of trade.

Single Factoral Terms of Trade. The traditional neglect of low-priority industries — lack of investments, obsolete equipment and technical skills — retards their technical progress and reduces their rate of productivity improvement, if not absolutely at least relative to other sectors. Stressing the exportation of these products will cause — in addition to deterioration of the commodity terms of trade — a comparative decline in the single factoral terms of trade, forcing the CPE to surrender for any given quantity of imports the products of more factors. Because of the adverse movement of the single factoral terms of trade, the total value of exports will rise in terms of domestic scarcity prices: (a) relative to the foreign exchange value, and also (b) in absolute terms (since the offer curve is likely to be inelastic).[40]

[38] In fact, it may be argued that, over time, the traditional low-priority industries cease to be of low priority, a development that causes further problems, since a rigidly centralized economic planning depends on the existence of low-priority sectors. Partly, the recent reform movements were initiated because the shock absorbers had worn thin. For a discussion of this point, see [14].

[39] An official Hungarian document [Forg. 40/1955. marc.; cited in 1] took note of greater unreliability in light than in heavy industrial production. Over time, the gap even widened. In the last quarter of 1953, for example, the light-industrial vs. heavy-industrial rejection rates were 20.0 and 14.6 percent, respectively; while during the final quarter of 1954, the corresponding figures were 16.9 percent and 7.4 percent. (The rejection ratio was reportedly much higher in some branches of light industry, and it reached 49 percent in one of the shoe factories [1, pp. 304–305].

[40] This is again in terms of comparative dynamics. Assuming that (a) the marginal productivity of the low-priority good relative to the high-priority good increases abroad in comparison with the productivity changes in a CPE, and that (b) the relative export share of the low-priority commodities increases, then it follows that (c) the single factoral terms of trade will be comparatively worse in a CPE than in a MTE, even without adverse movement in the commodity terms of trade. (For a concise discussion of the relationship between the commodity and factoral terms of trade, see [25, pp. 24–25].)

The Trade Expansion Multiplier

While the dichotomous priority system becomes increasingly untenable because of shortages that develop in low-priority industries and adverse movement of the terms of trade, the growth of high-priority industries facilitates the exportation of the domestically produced high-priority commodities. But as high-priority export goods are substituted for low-priority ones and the average priority level of exports increases, an induced demand for imports results, since high-priority goods tend to be more import-intensive (as demonstrated below). The feedback effect for induced imports, caused by the initial increase of import-intensive exports, culminates in a gradual expansion of both imports and exports: more imports will be necessary to produce the import-intensive exports, requiring more exports to restore equilibrium in the balance of payments, causing a further increase in the import demand to produce the additional exports, and so forth. Trade will rise through a convergent series of increments, achieving a new equilibrium when the new level reaches the old level times the coefficient of the *trade expansion multiplier*, which is determined by the difference between the old and new import intensities.[41] (A mathematical derivation of this coefficient is given in the Appendix to this paper.)

Let us now consider the reasons for the greater import-intensity of high-priority goods. (At this point, only the logical arguments are presented; statistical evidence can be found in the concluding section of this paper.) First, heavy industry is generally much more import-intensive than agriculture, which employs domestic inputs predominantly. Second, the coefficient of the trade expansion multiplier is especially large in countries where the import-intensity of high-priority branches of industry, for special technological reasons, greatly exceeds that of the low-priority branches (e.g., in Hungary).[42] Third, in all CPEs, regardless of relative factor endowments, some trade expansion occurs because of the previously discussed features of CPEs, which tend to increase import-intensity. Thus, importation of machinery, equipment, and raw materials is sanctioned, as a rule, to facilitate the growth of high-priority industries. Induced import demand tends to be strong, leading to further increases of trade, because (a) the industrial

[41] The coefficient of the trade expansion multiplier (due to a structural change of exports) — μ — depends on the initial import-intensity of exports (λ_o) and on the final import-intensity (λ_n). The formula is: $\mu = (1 - \lambda_o) / (1 - \lambda_n)$.

[42] At the end of the decade in Hungary the median direct and indirect import-intensity of light industries was 13.5 percent vs. 17.4 percent in heavy industries; the average import-intensity in agricultural production (crop raising and animal husbandry) was only 5.6 percent. These figures are based on the 1959 import-output table, and in the early 1950s the disparity was probably considerably more [13, Appendix]. (For the overall average import-intensity of exports, see the mathematical Appendix to this paper.)

incentive system favors production of bulkier, heavier commodities and substitution of imported inputs for domestic inputs, and (b) high-priority producers are in a more favorable position to have their requests implemented.[43]

THE FLEXIBILITY DILEMMA

By the flexibility dilemma is meant a choice between a flexible and a rigid trade policy. Let us first suppose that the planners only consider two extreme alternatives: whether to formulate the foreign trade plans (i.e., the prices and quantities of imports and exports) in terms of point estimates, requiring special approvals for any modification; or to use interval estimates (i.e., contingency plans), giving discretionary power to the operational units for making changes within certain limits.[44] The disadvantages of both of these alternatives were discussed above in the static analysis; flexibility, as we have seen, is a source of cost sensitivity, while a rigid trade policy results in benefit denial.

The planners, one may object, should attempt to escape between the two horns of the dilemma by reducing flexibility to a point where there is an equal trade-off between cost sensitivity and benefit denial. But this optimal static solution is very difficult to attain, as shown below. The traditional features of CPEs activate certain feedback mechanisms, which lead to fluctuations in trade policy, official inflexibility periodically giving way to excessive, *de facto* flexibility, unlikely to yield a stable equilibrium. The planners, anxious to avoid the consequences of further fluctuations, may logically try to grasp one of the horns of the dilemma. As long as incentives are dysfunctional, a high degree of flexibility cannot provide a satisfactory solution. The other alternative is to increase the use of trade agreements, which implies maximum rigidity in foreign trade, but only at the expense of domestic centralization. Thus, while reliance on trade agreements helps to maintain centralization in foreign trade (at the expense of further benefit denial), it also tends to paralyze one of the chief adjustment mechanisms of

[43] When there is a dispute with a high-priority industry, "foreign trade cannot go against the opinion of the interested industrial experts. In the case of a conflict of opinion, it is the industry which — rightly or wrongly — puts its demand through" [60, p. 24]. (In Hungarian aluminum production, for example, an economist estimated that excessive import demand by industrial firms was 50 percent [58, p. 8].) Low-priority industries are not in such a favorable position. For example, local and small-scale industries, "on a lower priority scale than large-scale industry even when they produce exports," experienced great difficulties in getting imported raw materials [45, p. 8].

[44] Of course, *ex post* changes will be required if external prices are incorrectly estimated. As discussed below, whether planning is flexible or not, given an inelastic import demand, the parameters will be the quantities of imports, and the prices and the required foreign exchange will be dependent variables. (Cf. Professor Baumol's "equilibrium method" of adjustment [7, pp. 126–130].) The important difference is that, in case of inflexible planning, price changes require special *ad hoc* authorization from the planners, while flexible planning permits decentralized price changes.

the system, the use of foreign trade as a safety valve, which in turn seriously handicaps domestic centralization. Let us analyze this in somewhat greater detail.

Crisisphilia

There is a tendency towards excessive crisis-creation in CPEs, not, to be sure, by the planners themselves but by the FTEs. Given various aspects of trade aversion discussed earlier, particularly the desire to insulate the planning system from unpredictable effects of world market fluctuations, planners in CPEs attempt to formulate and execute their foreign trade plans with a high degree of inflexibility, even more so than in domestic planning. But the effectiveness of official policy is periodically undermined; in the face of acute bottlenecks in domestic high-priority sectors, deviations from the plan are readily approved. The agents of FTEs not only learn to take advantage of supply crises but are even motivated to intensify them, since their own interests are best served by inducing *de facto* flexibility.[45]

How is this accomplished? According to traditional foreign trade planning principles, FTEs are instructed to import and export certain bundles of commodities; within the short-term operational plans, the composition of the trade bill and the prices are rigidly specified.[46] In case of favorable price movements (i.e., a fall in import prices or a rise in export prices) the amounts of imports and exports are not stipulated to change — this implies perfectly inelastic short-run import demand and export supply. While import demand may be perfectly inelastic also when price changes are unfavorable (i.e., if high-priority imports are involved), this will require additional foreign exchange allocation, to be secured from the central authorities by means of specific approval. Unless, however, the original quotas are formally revised, unfavorable price movements tend to jeopardize the bonuses of FTEs. Such formal quota revisions are much easier to secure when the need for imports has become acute within the country, giving FTEs an in-

---

[45] In the Hungarian economic literature we find frequent references that describe with amazing candor how the staffs of FTEs acted to induce the desired response, especially during the highly centralized era until the mid-'fifties. (Among the previously cited sources, see, e.g., [3, 65, and 66].) The motivation was very strong to create a more favorable environment, since the major part of the FTEs' remuneration used to be based on plan-fulfillment bonuses and premium payments. Even after 1959, when the incentive system was modified and the bonus plus premium payments were to be officially frozen at 25 percent of the base salary, the actual ratio in many cases was reported to be much higher (e.g., 44.5 percent for Importtex; see [29, p. 14]). One of the chief purposes of the Hungarian foreign trade incentive system at the end of the 1950s was to increase "the foreign bargaining propensity of the FTEs" [18, p. 10]; it is doubtful, however, that this purpose was achieved, since the new system became so complex that "most of the employees cannot comprehend them" [27, p. 19].

[46] The traditional planning system described here is currently being modified in several East European CPEs. The Hungarian foreign trade reforms, which largely still remain to be implemented, are discussed in [50].

centive to delay their negotiations abroad until domestic shortages have created a proper atmosphere.[47]

Although such delays further reduce foreign exchange earnings on the export side and increase exchange requirements for imports, they make it easier for the FTEs to secure additional foreign exchange allocations, and to have their quotas revised — which then improves their prospects of obtaining plan fulfillment bonuses. This leads to systematic procrastination in foreign trade, and, as an immediate consequence, to periodic crises in domestic supply procurement. Further, the terms of trade are likely to deteriorate, especially when the trading partners become aware of the pattern.[48]

As a result of willful, periodic delays and excessive crisis creation — *crisisphilia*, if you will — short-term fluctuations develop in foreign trade deliveries and in domestic supplies. These fluctuations (accentuated perhaps by the prevailing seasonal *storming* at the end of each planning period) may give rise to self-sustaining cycles. Namely, the initial rigid trade policy causes supply bottlenecks, which lead to *de facto* flexibility; since this helps to alleviate bottlenecks, the rigid policy can be reinstated and a new phase of the cycle is ready to start. Over time, as the trading agents become more sophisticated and the planners more concerned over bottlenecks, the cycle is likely to intensify, and may become explosive.

Trade Agreements

Increasing reliance on trade agreements — a characteristic feature of centrally planned foreign trade — is partly an attempt to deal with the consequences of *crisisphilia*, such as the uneven flow of imports and recurrent supply bottlenecks. But trade agreements, while they may reduce somewhat the uncertainties of supply procurement, create new problems, in turn, by imposing a fixed, prearranged pattern of trade. The structure of trade will be more inflexible (a) the greater the proportion of trade covered under specific commodity and payment agreements, and (b) the earlier the negotiation of agreements. As for the extent of coverage, although original agreements usually contain provisions for supplementary agreements to guard against total inflexibility, the more the planners rely on such provisions, the more

[47] See, *inter alia*, [3, 65, and 66]. Economists in other CPEs have been, in general, somewhat more reticent in their analyses of the clandestine activities of the FTEs than their Hungarian colleagues; although it was reported in East Germany, too, that in the foreign trade plans "discrepancies were not corrected until some crisis occurred during the plan year," and the activities of the FTEs tended to present the planners with a *fait accompli* [56, p. 62].

[48] They similarly learn to take advantage of the cyclical ("storming") pattern in foreign trade. As stated in an official document, "The capitalist buyers and sellers have come to expect the increases in the level of trade [which occur] for the sake of plan fulfillment, and they set the prices accordingly . . ." [Alt. 6/1965. aug.; as cited in 1, p. 300].

the specter of *crisisphilia* is likely to reappear. In general, trade agreements tend to reduce both the gains from trade and the elasticity of substitution.

Let us look at some of the specific problems. First, certain problems are implicit both in short-term and long-term agreements. Short-term agreements increase the negotiation lag, since trade in any given commodity category becomes contingent upon approval of the entire agreement, and they tend to impede the flow of trade at the beginning of the year because of delays in ratification of the trade protocol.[49] Long-term agreements, on the other hand, which are negotiated sufficiently in advance, must use very outdated information. Second, the agreements are based on information that is not only outdated but also frequently unreliable because of the conscious manipulation of the agents of FTEs, who realize that the data submitted to the central authorities will affect their own compensation in the next planning period. Third, trade agreements make it difficult either to take advantage of new opportunities in foreign markets or to adjust the commodity composition of trade if domestic conditions change. Finally, reliance on trade agreements encourages bilateralism, which further reduces the opportunity to select the best sources of supply or the most favorable export markets.

We may pause momentarily to consider whether bilateralism also necessarily reduces, along with the gains from trade, the level of trade, as is usually assumed. One should not forget, however, that re-exports — which are a means of disposing of unwanted imports — are likely to increase under bilateral trade agreements. Therefore, general trade (i.e., trade including re-exports) may well rise.

In sum, whether general trade increases or not, the gains from trade will be reduced. Also, the effectiveness of trade as a safety valve will be curtailed. This, from the standpoint of a CPE, is probably the most serious consequence of trade agreements. In fact, as the planners resort to trade agreements to make centralization more effective in foreign trade, they deprive themselves of a principal adjustment mechanism on which centralization in the domestic sectors depends. If, on the other hand, domestic centralization is maintained, the economy will require *ad hoc* imports; but this, in turn, limits the use of trade agreements and thereby interferes with centralized foreign trade. Ultimately, therefore, the flexibility dilemma resolves itself into a conflict between centralization in domestic production and in foreign trade.

THE TRADE REORIENTATION DILEMMA

The trade reorientation dilemma involves a choice between two alternatives: continued dependence on imports from MTEs, or a gradual diversion

[49] See note 22, above.

of trade to other CPEs. While both have disadvantages, those of the second alternative are less immediately obvious. We may, therefore, expect that at first a CPE will try to shift its trade to other CPEs. Although switching to ideologically more reliable sources of supply tends to reduce noneconomic cost sensitivity, the results over time are increased problems of planning and control (i.e., greater *economic* cost sensitivity) and reduced gains from trade (i.e., more benefit denial).

A static solution to the problem of regional distribution is relatively simple: the planners could aim at a new regional equilibrium, which would be reached at a point where the total gains from trade (i.e., explicit benefit minus implicit cost) are maximum. It is more difficult, however, to reach such an equilibrium dynamically. There is a tendency at first to overshoot the mark, since the consequences of the original trade diversion only become evident over time. Whether subsequent trade reorientation can lead to a desirable equilibrium depends on the frequency of the exogenous shocks and on the readiness of the planners to make regional readjustments. There is a danger, one may add, that even the long-term trade distribution will not be optimal, since reorientation of trade in a CPE requires more effort (greater real cost), which the planners try to avoid. Let us consider the dynamic effects, step by step.

Initial Effects

It may be expected that a CPE will initially try to reduce its dependence on imports from MTEs. The planners would probably like primarily to shift high-priority imports, but they can more easily reorient the importation of nonessentials. In fact, high-priority imports from MTEs may even increase: (a) *ad hoc* imports needed to smooth out temporary supply disturbances can be more readily secured from MTEs (in view of the similarities in their priorities, it is unlikely that the shortages and surpluses in different CPEs will be complementary); and (b) rapid industrialization creates a greater import demand for high-priority materials and equipment, some of which are likely to be sought in MTEs for reasons of technological advantages, better quality, and smoother timing of deliveries. Consequently, *the relative importance of trade with MTEs tends to increase, although the proportion of this trade may decline.*

We have already seen, in connection with the priority dilemma, that import demand as well as export supply (therefore, also, the offer curve) become inelastic. If imports and exports constitute a smaller share of the totals, demand for imports from MTEs will be even more inelastic than total import demand and will become so even more rapidly (because of the growing concentration of high-priority imports). Export supply to MTEs will be also very inelastic (i.e., changes in selling prices will have little effect on the quantities offered, because of the planners' unwillingness to readjust the overall economic plan in response to external price changes). Moreover, if trade with MTEs becomes a decreasing share of total trade, there will be a lack of responsiveness to price changes not only in the short-run planning period (during which the established plans are kept as little changed as possible) but in the long run as well, since the elasticity of expectations will also be reduced.[50]

Problems of Increasing Trade with CPEs

Trade with other CPEs constitutes a *dual risk* for a CPE that becomes greater, *pari passu*, as the proportion of this trade increases. Thus, imports may be abruptly curtailed not only because of domestic plan failures (which prevent fulfillment of export commitments) but also because of plan failures in other CPEs.

In an effort to reduce these risks, CPEs seek to formalize their relations by means of bilateral commodity and payments agreements. These agreements among CPEs are usually based on compulsory quotas that can be easily integrated into the overall economic plans of the trading partners. (Trade agreements with MTEs, on the other hand, are only permissive; they merely contain maximum quota limitations.) Agreements with compulsory quota provisions not only specify quantities and prices for both imports and exports but they also stipulate exact payments conditions and delivery terms. To some extent — as long as they help to alleviate problems of uncertainty — these provisions are attractive to CPEs.[51]

But, to be sure, there are also disadvantages. Although a clause is usually included allowing for supplementary agreements, subsequent changes after compulsory agreements are ratified tend to be limited.[52] Compulsory agreements, having a tendency to predetermine the trade pattern and its conditions with a very high degree of inflexibility, not only reduce the gains from trade but, perversely, may even give rise to periodic threats against stability in domestic planning. Thus, compulsory agreements — with hardly any provision for swing credits — promote the customary insistence of CPEs on immediate settlement of bilateral balances.[53] The strict discipline that this implies becomes from time to time very burdensome for CPEs continually

[50] Cf. Hicks' definition of the elasticity of expectations in his discussion of prices and production plans. (See [30, p. 205].)

[51] During the initial planning years, the complaint was that the country "could not be sure for years in advance that it would definitely get everything it needed from other countries with planned economies, or that it would definitely supply them with certain goods" [Gay, as quoted in 61, p. 429]. To correct this, compulsory long-term agreements were introduced on an increasingly wide scale.

[52] Thus, for example, compulsory long-term agreements covered more than 80 percent of Hungary's trade with other CPEs by the end of the 1950s [68, p. 1].

[53] As Professor Holzman argues, out of the desire for an overall payments balance arises the less justifiable tendency for bilateral balancing "by limiting imports [*in every direction*] to the level of exports" [32, p. 249].

beset by balance-of-payments pressures. *Ad hoc* credit, if granted at all, is made available only after a long time-lag, since it requires cooperation at various administrative levels.[54] (In real emergencies central approval can be swift — although it is likely to come after crises when the planners are anxious to avoid further repercussions.)

Repercussions and the Quest for Equilibrium

Eventually, as the disadvantages of trade with other CPEs become more and more apparent, and as, in any case, the dependence on MTEs for essential imports continues (its significance may even grow), it becomes evident that the initial trade diversion was excessive. Nonetheless, the process of reorientation to MTEs tends to be delayed because of certain irreversibilities. It is hindered not only by the atavism and inertia of the planners but also by the self-interest of the domestic producing firms, since these have no incentive to adjust to the more exacting requirements of Western trade. There is, therefore, a ratchet effect in the regional trade diversion which affects exports directly and imports indirectly, since under bilateral trade and payments the regional direction of imports and exports is jointly determined.

Of course, as pressures increase in intensity and shortages become critical in essential commodity supplies, there is likely to be a hasty retreat to the previous regional distribution of trade. But unless this reorientation of trade is carefully prepared, the result is a deterioration in the terms of trade with MTEs, followed by a new balance-of-payments crisis. At this point the pendulum tends to swing once again in the direction of CPEs.

If the exogenous shocks are relatively frequent, or if the reaction is delayed by an unwillingness to change, the broad back-and-forth swings in regional distribution of trade may well continue indefinitely without approaching a stable, long-term equilibrium. Generally, since external disturbances can be expected to recur, attainment of equilibrium will depend on whether the planners are willing to formulate contingency plans. Of course, the planners can learn from past mistakes; but the more centralized the system, the more cumbersome the job of making advance preparations for the transitions — instead of waiting for crises to develop and then responding abruptly. (In Hungary, as we shall see below, there was no such advance preparation and no attempt to institute an effective mechanism within the framework of the CPE to meet contingencies.)

CONCLUSION

The preceding theoretical analysis showed that a CPE tends, over time, to become increasingly dependent on foreign trade. This dynamic process

[54] Difficulties at various administrative levels in approving credit requests are cited, for example, in [16, p. 21].

leads, on the one hand, to an intensification of the familiar economic problems of the closed system,[55] and, on the other, to a gradual erosion of the effectiveness of traditional domestic adjustment mechanisms.

Instead of recapitulating the abstract model at this point, we may apply its conclusions to a concrete case. We shall use the conceptual framework in an attempt to illuminate contradictions or paradoxes in the foreign trade of Hungary, to which we referred briefly in the introduction to this paper.

Hungary has always depended heavily on imports. Under central planning, foreign trade became an important means of supporting the goal of rapid industrialization and alleviating unforeseen disturbances in the domestic sectors. Nonetheless, in view of the planners' violent opposition to trade, one would reasonably have expected a gradual reduction in the country's dependence on external trade. Surely, official policy announcements, as well as frequent diatribes against trade in the Hungarian economic literature, indicated that trade aversion far exceeded trade proclivity during the early 1950s. In spite of this strong net trade aversion, however, there was no observable trend towards greater self-sufficiency. On the contrary, the country's dependence on foreign trade steadily increased. What evolved was not a policy of autarky, as is often claimed, but an undesired growth of trade within an unstable pattern. Instead of a gradual movement toward a new equilibrium, there were constant fluctuations in the commodity composition and regional distribution of trade; these were largely responsible for the steady deterioration of the terms of trade, and contributed to worsening crises in the balance of payments and the domestic supply system. As demonstrated above in the dynamic part of our theoretical analysis, such consequences tend to follow logically in centrally planned foreign trade.

What was the reaction of the Hungarian planners? Briefly, they did not — and within the framework of the orthodox system of central planning, they probably could not — institute a set of effective foreign trade adjustment mechanisms. Instead, they tried to introduce various experimental, *ad hoc* measures, chiefly on an emergency basis. These measures failed to check certain unwanted developments: (1) unintended increases in the aggregate trade level; (2) instability in the regional distribution of trade; and (3) vicious circles of increasing balance-of-payments pressures, worsening terms of trade, and acute supply bottlenecks.

These problems are addressed separately in the following discussion.

THE LEVEL OF TRADE

The theoretical analysis showed (see particularly the priority dilemma) that, for several reasons, there would be a more rapid increase of trade in a

---

[55] See the discussion of the undesired consequences in the Appendix, "Basic Features of a Centrally Planned Economy."

CPE than in a MTE; such an increase was in fact experienced in Hungary during the initial years of the planning era, contrary to the planners' explicit desire.

As shown theoretically, trade tends to increase, first of all because of changes in the structure of exports (see the analysis of the trade expansion multiplier). Second, there is an undesired growth of trade as the terms of trade deteriorate and the offer curve becomes increasingly inelastic. (If, for example, the plan rigidly specifies the import volume, a deterioration of the terms of trade will require a proportionate expansion of exports, which tends to increase both imports and exports in subsequent rounds, depending on the import content of the additional exports.) Third, bilateralism leads to an expansion of re-exports (see the flexibility dilemma); because exports are usually included in aggregate trade statistics, this expansion becomes another factor in the growth of trade. In addition, re-imports also tend to rise, further inflating the aggregate level of trade. (Since taut planning results in a systematic underestimation of domestic supply requirements, the country is forced, on occasion, to re-import some previously exported commodities in order to avoid critical shortages.) Finally, disproportionate increases in transportation costs also contribute to the expansion of total trade (Foreign trade enterprises not only lack incentives to minimize transportation costs but are frequently motivated to choose the most expensive means.)

The Hungarian data lend empirical support to these theoretical propositions. Structural changes of exports led to a growth of trade as the planners substituted import-intensive exports (e.g., machine tools) for traditional exports with low import requirements (e.g., agricultural products). As estimated in an official report, "[Hungarian] machinery exports (machine tools, trucks, etc.) weigh one-and-a-half to two-times as much as competitive machinery, although in our case the raw material requirements are largely imported" [1, p. 317]. According to my calculations, structural changes in Hungarian exports between 1950 and 1953 were responsible for 20 to 30 percent of the increase in real imports (and for 46 to 70 percent of the increase in import-income ratio).[56]

The deterioration of Hungarian terms of trade directly increased exports and led to subsequent, indirect increases of both imports and exports. I have calculated that between 1950 and 1956 the average annual increment in exports attributable to deterioration of the terms of trade amounted to 40 to 50 percent, and that during the same period this caused an increase of imports by 22 to 33 percent.[57]

[56] As shown in the mathematical Appendix at the end of this paper. (For further details, see [13, Appendix].)

[57] According to my calculations, the commodity terms of trade deteriorated between 1950 and 1956 from 100 to 80.1 [13, Table V-10]. Assuming an inelastic import

The drastic growth of Hungarian re-exports also contributed to the rapid increase of aggregate trade. (Hungarian trade statistics are in terms of general trade — i.e., special trade plus re-exports.) In an effort to equilibrate the flow of trade bilaterally, re-exports increased by 114 percent between 1951 and 1955 (the period for which data were available), while the growth of special exports (i.e., domestically produced exports) was only 44 percent during the same period. The increase of re-imports (i.e., imported commodities that had been exported earlier in the same year) was even faster; they rose by 194 percent, while the increment in special imports was only 30 percent. The effect of this disproportionate rise of re-exports and re-imports on the expansion of aggregate trade was substantial. The ratio of re-exports to special exports increased from 8 percent in 1951 to 14 percent in 1955, and the ratio of re-imports to special imports grew from 7 to 16 percent. As a result, 20 percent of the total increase in general exports during these years was due to the growth of re-exports, and 33 percent of the increase of general imports was due to the expansion of re-imports [13, Appendix.]

In sum, at least two-thirds of the increase of trade between 1950–1951 and 1955–1956 was the joint result of the factors mentioned. Although the importance of these indirect effects declined after 1956, and the expansion of trade became mainly tied to the upward shift of demand for direct imports, some of the increase of trade was still unintended even during the second half of the decade. Thus, transportation costs, which rose much more rapidly than trade (excluding transport), affected the c.i.f. value of imports. Relative freight charges increased as more expensive means of transport were used to speed up the delivery of shipments in an effort to alleviate domestic supply bottlenecks. As a proportion of the import value, transportation costs increased by more than 50 percent between 1956 and 1959, which means that over 5 percent of the average annual increase of imports was the result of higher transportation costs.[58]

THE REGIONAL DISTRIBUTION OF TRADE

One could expect a gradual reorientation of Hungarian trade to other CPEs after the establishment of central planning in 1949. Although there

demand, the direct result of this deterioration is a 24.8 percent increase of exports. Given the estimated range of the trade-expansion-multiplier coefficient (1.096 to 1.147), the 24.8 percent direct increase of exports leads to a further 12.0 to 18.3 percent indirect increase of imports, which was 22 to 33 percent of the total increase in real imports during these years. The total effect on the export side is the sum of the direct and indirect increases (34.8 to 43.1 percent), which was 40 to 50 percent of the real export growth.

[58] Official Hungarian sources referred to some "unnecessarily expensive means of transportation," which were used in desperate attempts to hasten deliveries: e.g., "passenger automobiles to border points, etc." [1, p. 306].

was movement at first in this direction, the initial shift did not lead to a stable equilibrium in the regional distribution of trade. The back-and-forth trade diversion during the 1950s was a direct consequence of the recurrent balance-of-payments crises.

The pressure on the Hungarian balance of payments began in 1952, although on the commodity account there was no substantial deficit until 1957. But in spite of the balance-of-payments difficulties, imports did not have to be cut in 1952, 1953, or 1954, since the country was able to obtain last-minute credits. Then suddenly — according to official testimony, without any advance warning — the Hungarian trade negotiators were notified in January 1955 that their imports from other CPEs would be reduced to 50 percent of the previous year's level, which was only 36 percent of the imports they had expected to obtain when annual trade negotiations began [51, p. 189]. These Draconian measures were imposed in spite of the Hungarians' promise to reduce their indebtedness by 1 billion DF (*deviza forint*, or foreign exchange forint). In fact, Hungary's actual 1955 export surplus to CPEs was even more, 1.2 billion DF — exports having exceeded imports by more than 33 percent [13, Table IV-1].

The unexpected reorientation of imports led to a forced and totally-unprepared-for reorientation of Hungarian trade to MTEs. This was candidly acknowledged in an official Hungarian report: "The plan tried to divert to capitalist countries products, which had been originally made for socialist countries, in spite of the much higher quality requirements in capitalist markets" [1, p. 295].

The immediate result of this hasty reorientation of trade was a drastic decline of the Hungarian terms of trade with MTEs; consequently, the short-term indebtedness to the West "very significantly increased" [1, p. 290]. This led to a return of the pendulum, and once again the other CPEs became the chief suppliers of Hungarian imports. Unlike before, however, this was an undesired move, judging by official announcements and by the belated revision of the foreign trade incentive system in 1955–1956. Thus, in an effort to encourage trade with MTEs, the bonus for above-plan exports to MTEs became three times as high as for those to CPEs.[59]

It would seem, from a casual inspection of the statistics, that during the second half of the 1950s a relatively stable balance was achieved in the regional distribution of trade. But this apparent stability had a weak base. It was only maintained by repeated injections of large *ad hoc* credits extended to Hungary by the other CPEs, first in the wake of the 1956 revolt and again at the end of the decade.[60]

[59] See [28, p. 9]. These "correction coefficients" were again tripled in 1960.

[60] See, *inter alia*, [69, p. 255 ff.]. For example, Professor Vajda says: "We obtained

THE VICIOUS CIRCLES: INFLEXIBILITY AND FLUCTUATIONS

Earlier, in connection with the flexibility dilemma, we discussed in theoretical terms the genesis of certain vicious circles: balance-of-payments pressures, deterioration in terms of trade, and domestic supply bottlenecks. At this point, we shall analyze empirically the development of these interactions, which culminated in a series of crises during the 1950s, eventually disrupting both foreign trade and domestic production in Hungary.

Let us first examine the recurrent annual cycles that affected Hungarian import-income and export-income ratios, as mentioned in the introduction to this paper. These fluctuations can be related to the phenomenon of *crisisphilia* — the predilection of the FTEs for crisis-creation — which emerges from the mutual interaction between excessive (and periodically frustrated) inflexibility in foreign trade planning and critical domestic shortages. The concept of *crisisphilia* was developed from various comments of Hungarian economists regarding the behavior of their own foreign trade agents. Lacking appropriate microeconomic data to verify the consequences of this mechanism, we may substitute a test on the macro-level by observing the interrelationship between aggregate imports and aggregate production.

We state the following two hypotheses:

(1) Changes in the growth rate of domestic production result in inverse changes of the growth rate of imports during the following year. (The relationship is inverse, since a rapid expansion of domestic production permits the maintenance of a more rigidly restrictionary trade policy, and vice versa.)

(2) Changes in the growth rate of imports result in direct changes of the growth rate of domestic production during the same year.

Let us use the following definitions:

$$M_t = \text{aggregate imports in period } t$$
$$Y_t = \text{aggregate domestic production in period } t$$
$$m_t = \log M_t$$
$$y_t = \log Y_t$$
$$\triangle m_t = m_t - m_{t-1}$$
$$\triangle y_t = y_t - y_{t-1}$$
$$\triangle^2 m_t = \triangle m_t - \triangle m_{t-1}$$
$$\triangle^2 y_t = \triangle y_t - \triangle y_{t-1}$$

Then the hypotheses can be expressed symbolically as follows:

a significant portion of the deliveries by means of credits from the Soviet Union. During the years of 1957–1958, two-fifths of our imports from the Soviet Union were covered from these credits" [69, p. 258].

(1) $\triangle^2 m_{t+1} = f[\triangle^2(y_t)]$,   where $f' < 0$

(2) $\triangle^2 y_t = g[\triangle^2(m_t)]$,   where $g' > 0$

During the 1950s, especially until the revolt of 1956, the Hungarian data confirmed both hypotheses.[61] If we combine Eqs. (1) and (2) into ordinary difference equations, we can show that the growth rate of both imports and domestic output will alternately increase and decrease. From Eqs. (1) and (2), we have:

(3) $\triangle^2 m_{t+1} = u[\triangle^2(m_t)]$,   where $u' < 0$

(4) $\triangle^2 y_{t+1} = v[\triangle^2(y_t)]$,   where $v' < 0$

This, then, provides an explanation for the annual cyclical fluctuations in the Hungarian trading ratios.[62]

Let us now see how balance-of-payments pressures, deterioration of the terms of trade, and domestic supply bottlenecks affected the Hungarian economy. In their initial efforts to safeguard central control of the economy, the Hungarian planners refused to let considerations of foreign trade play an active role in the overall planning process. This implied a cavalier disregard of external market conditions. Thus, for example, "when it was decided to build the great industrial establishments, a complete lack of information prevailed as to the cost or the amount of imported materials that would be required to establish and maintain them" [51, p. 186].

Acceleration of the industrialization program was only the initial cause of the upward shift of import demand. Indirectly, the structural changes in production led to subsequent increases in the demand for imports: [63] "The demand for heavy industry, which was producing export goods largely from imported materials, grew disproportionately, and this demand could be and was met solely through still further imports" [51, p. 186]. This increase was further intensified by periodic, sharp spurts in *ad hoc* imports, particularly after 1951. It was then that Hungarians began to use foreign trade as an external safety valve, not only to alleviate unforeseen shortages in the traditional high-priority sectors but also to relieve tensions developed in the previously low-priority sectors (see the theoretical analysis of the dichotomous priority system).

According to a release of the Hungarian Central Statistical Office, the country's first short-term debts were incurred in 1952, when agricultural imports greatly increased. These debts progressively increased in size during

---

[61] The hypothesis of independence was rejected for both equations (using linear least-square regression) at the 5 percent level of significance. (See [13, Appendix].)

[62] For further details, see [13, Appendix].

[63] Cf. the above discussion of the growth of trade level because of the structural changes of exports. See also the theoretical analysis of the trade expansion multiplier.

the following years. In 1953, in spite of a trade surplus of 150 million DF, it was reported that in the overall balance of payments there was a deficit of 270 million DF. The deficit doubled by 1954 — to 540 million DF — amounting to about 10 percent of total imports.[64]

The steady increase in the balance-of-payments deficit was accompanied after 1952 by a drastic deterioration of the terms of trade.[65] Although no systematic official analysis has been released, the Hungarian planners, judging by scattered evidence, were aware of the interconnections between the increased import demand, the balance-of-payments crisis, and the deterioration in the terms of trade. We have, for example, the account of Imre Nagy, Hungary's ill-fated premier: "Industrial development required more and more imported basic and raw materials, which we acquired on less and less favorable terms" [47, p. 184]. To this he later added: "Payments . . . on expensive short-term foreign credits constantly used up our foreign exchange, making it impossible to purchase essential imports" [51, p. 191].

Thus came the vicious circle to a full revolution. First, balance-of-payments pressure developed, because of the need to supplement domestic with foreign supplies and as a result of the indirect increase in import demand. This led to an adverse movement of the terms of trade. Then came a drastic curtailment of imports, culminating in critical domestic supply bottlenecks. The seriousness of these bottlenecks was later officially documented, with citation of specific cases, in a report of the Hungarian Central Statistical Office. For example: "Reserves of imported materials were so significantly reduced that in many instances the flow of production was endangered. . . . Because of uneven and reduced imports . . . the wool reserves were even insufficient for a single day's operation. . . . Due to the shortage of coking coal, for instance . . . foundry operations had to be curtailed." Therefore, even heavy industrial plants had to suspend production because of the shortage of imported materials [1, p. 301].

During the second half of the 1950s the Hungarians instituted various pioneering reforms in an effort to improve their foreign trade system.[66] These reforms, however, were neither sufficiently thoroughgoing nor suf-

[64] See [1, pp. 308–315]. Aside from such fragmentary information, Hungary, like other CPEs, did not publish any balance-of-payments statistics. (No wonder that Professor Campbell wistfully remarked, in a paper on Yugoslav foreign trade, that happiness is having a balance-of-payments account.)

[65] The Hungarians only began to publish terms-of-trade statistics at the end of the 1950s. For the earlier years, only sporadic references appeared in the literature. The terms-of-trade figures to which I have been referring are based on my own calculations, derived from official statistical sources. (They were computed from the average unit values of 350 to 400 import and export goods over a period of 12 years.) See [13, Chapter V].

[66] These reforms are discussed in detail in [13, Chaps. II and III]. For price and exchange rate reforms in various CPEs, see [12].

ficiently integrated. Consequently, pressure on the balance of payments continued [67] and the terms of trade deteriorated further, although this time to a much lesser extent. Only with the help of sizable long-term loans from other CPEs has the recurrence of the earlier interruptions in domestic production been prevented. Currently, a new set of reforms is being promulgated in Hungary, and foreign trade is prominently mentioned among the motivating forces. This is also true in the other CPEs.[68] As before, the reforms are directed against the three major problem areas: pricing, incentives, and hypercentralization.[69]

In spite of considerable improvements during the past decade, however, the reforms have remained a patchwork of insular measures, lacking overall coordination.[70] In view of the complex economic interactions, one may justly wonder how much relief further suboptimization schemes can offer. The legacies of central planning, as Professor Neuberger convincingly argues in his paper in this volume, have a tendency to haunt the present.

APPENDIX

THE TRADE EXPANSION MULTIPLIER

DERIVATION OF THE COEFFICIENT

(1.1) $M_o = M_a + M_{io}$ [by definition]

(1.2) $M_{io} = \lambda_o X_o$ [by definition]

(1.3) $X_o = M_o$ [initial equilibrium]

(1.4) $X_o = \dfrac{1}{1 - \lambda_o} M_a$ [from Eqs. (1.1), (1.2), and (1.3)]

(2.1) $M_n = M_a + M_{in}$ [by definition]

(2.2) $M_{in} = \lambda_n X_n$ [by definition]

(2.3) $X_n = M_n$ [final equilibrium]

[67] In 1957, in the aftermath of the revolt, Hungary had a negative trade balance of 2.3 billion DF. Then, after a brief respite in 1958 (when there was a surplus of 600 million DF), the deficits reappeared in spite of officially announced efforts to repay the earlier loans. Thus, during the ensuing seven years a deficit of 5 billion DF was accumulated on the commodity account alone — nearly 1.5 billion between 1959 and 1960, and more than 3.5 billion between 1961 and 1965, under the Second Five-Year Plan. (See [64, p. 215].)

[68] As analyzed in [14]. For example, the Czechoslovakian Party newspaper, *Rude Pravo*, stated: "One of the most serious shortcomings is the strict separation of production from foreign markets . . . in our export trade, increasing difficulties force us to sell goods for which there is little demand" (As quoted in [14, p. 7].)

[69] Or, employing Professor Neuberger's felicitous phrase, "the reforms may be interpreted as a partial move toward the introduction of a visible hand" [53, p. 139].

[70] The foreign trade and investment efficiency indices have not been harmonized, nor have the efficiency calculations been incorporated into the foreign trade incentive system. (As discussed, e.g., in [12].)

(2.4) $X_n = \dfrac{1}{1-\lambda_n} M_a$ [from Eqs. (2.1), (2.2), and (2.3)]

(3.1) $M_a = (1-\lambda_o)\, X_o = (1-\lambda_n)\, X_n$ [from Eqs. (1.4) and (2.4)]

(3.2) $\dfrac{X_n}{X_o}\; \dfrac{1-\lambda_o}{1-\lambda_n}$ [from Eq. (3.1)]

(3.3) $\mu = \dfrac{X_n}{X_o} = \dfrac{M_n}{M_o}$ [by definition]

(3.4) $\mu = \dfrac{1-\lambda_o}{1-\lambda_n}$ [from Eqs. (3.2) and (3.3)]

NOTATION

$\mu =$ Coefficient of the trade expansion multiplier

$M_o; M_n =$ Aggregate imports in the initial period; in the nth (final) period

$M_a =$ Autonomous imports (i.e., determined by the requirements of domestic production)

$M_i =$ Induced imports (i.e., used to produce export goods)

$M_{io}; M_{in} =$ Induced imports in the initial period; in the nth (final) period

$X_o; X_n =$ Aggregate exports in the initial period; in the nth (final) period

$\lambda_o; \lambda_n =$ Total (i.e., direct and indirect) import content of exports (ratio to value) in the initial period; in the nth (final) period

ESTIMATION OF μ IN HUNGARIAN FOREIGN TRADE

According to my calculations, most of the expansionary effect due to the structural changes of exports occurred between 1950 and 1953. (The structural changes after 1953 had no appreciable effect on the size of the coefficient.) Let us define:

$\lambda_o =$ Average import intensity of the exports in 1950

$\lambda_n =$ Average import intensity of the exports in 1953

The estimates of the average import intensities were based on the Hungarian input-output tables, which were inverted in 1959 and in 1961. The following two estimates (λ and λ,* based on the inverted tables of 1959 and 1961) were derived for 1950 and 1953:

$\lambda_o = 7.9$ percent $\lambda_o^* = 6.6$ percent

$\lambda_n = 16.0$ percent $\lambda_n^* = 18.4$ percent

Therefore, from Eq. (3.4), we have:

(4.1) $\mu = \dfrac{100 - 7.9}{100 - 16.0} = 1.096$ (9.6 percent increase)

(4.2) $\mu^* = \dfrac{100 - 6.6}{100 - 18.4} = 1.147$ (14.7 percent increase)

Since imports (in constant prices) increased by 48.6 percent between 1950 and 1953, the increase due to the trade expansion multiplier (based on the structural change of exports) was 20 to 30 percent of the total increase. In the same period, the import-income ratio increased by 20.9 percent; therefore, of this increase, 46 to 70 percent was caused by the trade expansion multiplier.

DISCUSSION
Robert W. Campbell

Professor Brown has given us an intricate model, full of special concepts and novel terminology. My first reaction to the paper was one of exhaustion from the effort of swinging from branch to branch of the taxonomic tree the author has constructed, and trying to understand, say, how a deterioration in the terms of trade was caused when some twigs of the trade-proclivity branch brushed against the benefit-denial branch. It is a tightly constructed argument, in which each effect and each conclusion depends on the interaction of numerous mechanisms and ideas developed elsewhere in the argument. But it is an interesting and indeed an exhilarating paper. It has an ambitious goal and it well repays the care taken to assimilate the argument.

The thesis of the paper is developed in two steps. The first is an explanation of how the general systemic characteristics of the centrally planned economy affect foreign trade behavior in static terms — how the distinctive incentive system and special pressures influence decisionmakers to conduct greater or lesser amounts of trade, and different kinds of trade, than would occur in a comparable economy organized along market lines. The second then describes the dynamic interaction of those effects in an effort to explain the paradoxical results that Professor Brown has observed in his study of Hungarian foreign trade: namely, that despite an expressed desire for self-sufficiency the volume of trade has grown more rapidly than gross national product, that its composition seems to belie the priorities the leaders said they had in mind, and so on. This is an intriguing line of argument, and one is eager to see the magic done. Anyone who can explain away paradoxes is bound to command our attention.

The individual elements, such as peculiarly constructed incentive systems, inaccurate pricing, and bargaining behavior between upper and lower levels of management, are well enough established, and are well documented in Professor Brown's Hungarian sources. (The supporting citations are a valuable part of the study.) I am not certain, however, that the author has succeeded in integrating into a unified model all his knowledge of how foreign trade decisions get made in a centrally planned economy like that of Hungary. Nor has the elaborate terminology really justified itself. Indeed, I think the terminology often gets in the way of the argument.

To begin with the argument of the statics section, some of the distinctions seem to me to be forced. The significance of the distinction between benefit denial and cost sensitivity, for example, is not very clear. The idea of benefit denial is that the centrally planned economy is less able than a market-organized economy to capture the benefits of trade, and that there will be a corresponding reluctance to engage in trade. Cost sensitivity is related by the author to "implicit costs," a concept taken from the theory of the firm. The idea is that the existence of the foreign trade sector makes it more difficult to administer the rest of the economy, and the planners will try to limit foreign trade. It seems to me that this distinction is irrelevant to the point that the author wants to establish — namely, that the people in charge of designing and controlling this system will try to limit the amount of trade by direct commands or by biased rules. More important, there is a failure to complete the argument here — it is not demonstrated at all unambiguously that benefit denial means that there will be less trade in a centrally planned economy than in a market-organized economy. Indeed some of the features noted as aspects of benefit denial, such as inability to evaluate the rationality of a given trade act, could work as effectively to increase trade as to inhibit it.

Benefit denial is also said to result from the use of net foreign earnings as a success indicator, since that will induce the exporters to cut the price and so worsen the terms of trade. But note that in the process of making trade less advantageous and so causing the controllers of the system to try to keep down the volume of imports, the volume of exports necessary to pay for imports is increased. Thus, the effect on the quantum of total trade is ambiguous, with a tendency for imports to be lower than in a comparable market-organized economy, and for exports to be higher.

There is an unremarked distinction in the decisionmaking for foreign trade that would really be much more relevant than some of those that are made: namely, a distinction between the different levels of the administrative system. That is what really lies behind the differentiation of cost sensitivity and the implicit costs of trade from the explicit costs of benefit denial. The former refers to behavior at higher levels, the latter to behavior at lower levels of the system. When we get to the dynamics section, it turns out, I think, that many of the stepwise interactions that occur in the system and lead to the dynamic effects are interactions between the lower and upper levels of the system; and so the dynamics would be more easily understood if this distinction were made more explicit in the description of the statics.

It is also said that there is a "relative" shortage of foreign trade personnel, and that the personnel charged with responsibility for foreign trade activity are less well prepared to cope with their responsibilities than those in charge of domestic production. This is supposed to follow from the fact that people recruited into foreign trade operations will be inefficient because the habits they learned in dealing with the domestic sellers' market do not fit the conditions of the world market. Let us analyze this in detail. Working in a sellers' market in the domestic economy means that one must hustle in order to buy, but need not worry about selling. Let us grant that experience in the domestic economy will develop people with this skill as the modal type. If we assume that the world market is a buyers' market, then it is true that the personnel of the foreign trade sector find themselves in an atypical situation. The exporter has to hustle to buy domestically and must also hustle to sell externally — that is indeed a change. But for each of these exporters there is an importer who, as a buyer in a buyers' market and a seller in a sellers' market, need hustle in neither. Therefore, the benefit denial would only apply on the export side.

The real deficiency of the section on trade aversion is that the connection is never developed between these various mechanisms and the level, composition, and direction of foreign trade. The argument is that since there is benefit denial the level of trade will be less than in a market economy. But who decides this, and how is an equilibrium reached? Even if the argument is accepted that the centrally planned economy cannot get the benefits from trade that a market economy could, does this mean that trade is simply to be abandoned altogether? Obviously not, but the question of what criteria will guide the curtailment of trade is not explained. It is true that this question is taken up a bit in the dynamics section; but, as I expect to show below, the answer is not very clear there either.

The heart of the paper is its explanation of the dynamic effects, the way one thing leads to another. The case is built around three dilemmas: the priority dilemma, the flexibility dilemma, and the trade reorientation dilemma. I do not find discussions couched in terms of dilemmas very satisfying — it seems to me that dilemmas and vicious circles are more a rhetorical device than a feature of the real world. Let us analyze one of these — the priority dilemma — in some detail. This is the most important one, and the one that is most intricately developed. The central concept in the dynamics of the priority dilemma is a continuing change in the relative importance of high-priority and low-priority goods in the import mix and the export mix, which has further consequences for the elasticity of demand and supply, changes the elasticity of the offer curve and the terms of trade, leads to balance-of-payments problems, and affects the level of trade.

The problem with this line of argument is that the distinction between high- and low-priority goods has at least four different meanings. Thus, even though Professor Brown defines what he means by priority, other common meanings attach to this term. His argument starts with an explicit definition "that an economic sector in a CPE is of comparatively high priority if its output increases faster than national output as a whole, compared with the performance of a similar MTE, and of low priority if the increase is comparatively slower" (footnote 33). This definition, however, leads to an ambiguity when we try to apply it to commodities rather than to sectors. Some good may be a high-priority good in the sense that its output is growing faster than gross national product. But it may be a good formerly imported (after all, import replacement is one of the main reasons in the planners' view for stimulating the growth of some sector), and this may mean that, considered as an import, the good is a low-priority one by definition — imports of the good are growing less rapidly than gross national product, and less rapidly than all imports.

A second implicit interpretation of the distinction between high and low priority, used in numerous places in the development of the argument, is whether a good is in excess supply or in excess demand. There is much talk of deficit goods, surpluses, bottlenecks, etc. Third, in still other places the concept clearly refers to elasticity of demand; those goods with inelastic demands are in some sense goods of higher priority than those with low elasticities. Under conditions of taut planning, actual performance will involve retrenchments vis-à-vis *ex ante* expectations, and in this situation goods with highly inelastic demands are those that the planners will be most reluctant to cut back. There are several references to substitution, to willingness to sacrifice consumption rather than something else, and all these ideas are related to the elasticity of demand. Finally, in discussing the factoral terms of trade, there is an implication that a low-priority industry is one where the input mix is irrational — an industry where the marginal productivity of capital is above and the productivity of other factors below that elsewhere in the economy. (These examples all underscore the fact that priority is a disequilibrium concept — we can make it meaningful only in a disequilibrium situation.)

All of these are perfectly legitimate interpretations of the priority concept, sanctioned by common usage. But the difficulty is that these different meanings can be contradictory — a given good might be a high-priority good by one of these definitions but a low-priority one by another. For example, it is easy to imagine that some good will have an inelastic demand for all the standard textbook reasons, such as relative unimportance as a jointly demanded input, limited possibilities for substitution, and so on. But such a good could still be in excess supply, or could be experiencing a lower rate of output growth than the average, and so be a low-priority good by the other definition. Similarly, since the whole concept assumes disequilibrium in the first place, there is no reason to suppose that a good whose output is growing at a faster-than-average rate is therefore in deficit supply — it may be that the planners have raised the rate of its output growth sufficiently above the average that it is in surplus supply. After working through this section repeatedly, it occurs to me that the priority dilemma is rather a result of these contradictions in the meaning of the central concept than of any inability of the central planners to regulate the growth of foreign trade. Or possibly it may be that their efforts to control the growth of trade are confounded by the fact that they themselves are thinking in terms of these contradictory notions of what their priorities are.

The other two mechanisms are rather simpler and more readily understood. The flexibility dilemma is built on the idea that there is a cyclical
tightening and loosening of the controls over foreign trade organs, and that
the latter manipulate this cycle. This centralization-decentralization cycle is
a frequently noted feature of centrally planned economies in other contexts,
and this is another interesting elaboration of it. But it is not very clear what
the consequences are for trade levels, for composition of trade, or for geographic direction. The process worsens the terms of trade but it is not clear
what its implications are for the rest.

The trade reorientation dilemma is explained essentially by the failure of
the planners to see far enough ahead what they are getting into. In turning
away from the market economies to escape certain disadvantages in that kind
of trade, and in shifting their trade more to centrally planned economies,
the foreign trade planners fail to foresee certain disadvantages involved in
dealing with the latter. When they have learned through experience what
these disadvantages are, they turn once again to the market economies; but
the process does not come to a neat dynamic equilibrium, since there are
irreversibilities, threshold effects, and the like.

The trade reorientation dilemma suggests a conclusion that, though somewhat prosaic, probably deserves a more important role in this discussion
than Professor Brown has given it. Surely much of the paradoxical development of the foreign trade of these countries — the dynamic behavior of trade
levels, the rapid growth in imports of raw materials, the heavy emphasis
on agricultural imports, and so on — is due to the fact that the planners
failed to foresee the foreign trade implications of their development policies. They had a short planning horizon and a limited acquaintance with
indirect effects. They could build factories without thoroughly thinking
through what this meant in terms of raw materials requirements. They could
slight agricultural development, either not believing or not wanting to see
what this would imply with respect to foreign trade and the balance of payments. When they started their planning operations, they were simply not
sophisticated enough about planning or about economics to understand such
subtle but powerful effects as the trade expansion multiplier.

If this is true, it also suggests a final point about the kind of model Professor Brown has developed. The model as presented attempts to explain
foreign trade behavior in terms of inherent behavioral characteristics of the
centrally planned economic system. Apart from his success in bringing this
off, I am not sure that this is necessarily the best tactic to follow. Surely a
great deal of the history of foreign trade behavior in the centrally planned
economies thus far is the result of non-repeating influences. If the planners
were not sophisticated enough in the early years to see ahead more than a
step or two at a time, they now have experience and improved theory to

guide them. The mechanisms lean heavily on transitory phenomena — the surpluses, deficits, and priority rankings that come about because of a determination to change the structure of output. For example, the priority dilemma is due in part to the effort to change the structure of the economy — to build a heavy industrial base. Once that is accomplished, or is given up as an inappropriate goal, then the very notion of priority items becomes less meaningful.

In concluding, I want to emphasize that these comments are offered in a constructive spirit. I am much impressed with the boldness of the conception Professor Brown has started from. The integration of static and dynamic equilibrium analysis of a whole economy on a detailed enough level to explain fluctuations in balance-of-payments pressures and changes in the commodity composition of trade is a task that few would dare attempt for any economy. My real conclusion, in fact, is that it is *too* ambitious an approach, especially in a short paper. I, for one, would have been more instructed, if perhaps less challenged, by a fuller and more rigorous explanation of a few of the basic dynamic mechanisms, especially those involved in the priority dilemma.

REFERENCES

1. *Adatok és adalékok* (Budapest: Központi Statisztikai Hivatal, 1957).
2. Akar, László. "A külkereskedelmi tervezés fejlesztéséröl" ("On the Development of Foreign Trade Planning"), *Külkereskedelem*, II:6 (June 1958), pp. 1–2.
3. Bakos, György. "A termelés anyagi ösztönzése a külkereskedelmi célkitüzések elérésére ("Material Incentives in Production To Achieve Foreign Trade Programmes"), *Külkereskedelem*, V:5 (May 1961), pp. 10–13.
4. Balassa, Bela A. *The Hungarian Experience in Economic Planning* (New Haven: Yale University Press, 1959).
5. Balàzsy, Sándor. "A külkereskedelem gazdaságosságához" ("On the Economic Efficiency of Foreign Trade"), *Közgazdasági Szemle*, IV:3 (March 1957), pp. 303–320.
6. Baran, Paul. "National Economic Planning," in Bernard F. Haley (ed.), *A Survey of Contemporary Economics*, II (Homewood, Ill.: Irwin, 1952), pp. 355–403.
7. Baumol, William J. *Economic Dynamics* (New York: Macmillan, 1951).
8. Bergson, Abram. *The Economics of Soviet Planning* (New Haven: Yale University Press, 1964).
9. Berliner, Joseph S. *Factory and Manager in the USSR* (Cambridge: Harvard University Press, 1957).
10. Bornstein, Morris. "A Comparison of Soviet and United States National Product," U.S. Congress, Joint Economic Committee, *Comparisons of the United States and Soviet Economies* (Washington, D.C.: 1959), Part II, pp. 377–395.

11. ———. "The Soviet Price System," *American Economic Review*, LII:1 (March 1962), pp. 64–103.
12. Brown, Alan A. "Centrally-Planned Foreign Trade and Economic Efficiency," *American Economist*, V:2 (November 1961), pp. 11–28.
13. ———. "The Economics of Centrally-Planned Foreign Trade: The Hungarian Experience" (Unpublished doctoral dissertation, Harvard University, 1966).
14. ———, and Richard Yin. "Communist Economics: Reforms vs. Orthodoxy," *Communist Affairs*, III:1 (January–February, 1965), pp. 3–9.
15. Campbell, Robert. "On the Theory of Economic Administration," in Henry Rosovsky (ed.), *Industrialization in Two Systems: Essays in Honor of Alexander Gerschenkron* (New York: Wiley, 1966), pp. 186–203.
16. Déri, Gusztáv. "Utazói tapasztalatok Közép-Amerikában" ("Experiences of Commercial Travelers in Central America"), *Külkereskedelem*, III:7 (July 1959), pp. 20–21.
17. Dobb, Maurice. *Economic Theory and Socialism* (New York: International Publishers, 1955).
18. Facsády, Kálmán, and László Várkonyi. "Prémiumrendszer a külkereskedelemben" ("Premium System in Foreign Trade"), *Külkereskedelem*, II:6 (June 1958), pp. 9–12.
19. *Figyelö*, July 3, 1963, p. 4.
20. Fiszel, H. *Gospodarka Planowa*, Nos. 7–8 (1957), pp. 27–30; cited in *Közgazdasági Szemle*, V:6 (June 1958), pp. 614–625.
21. Gordon, Wendell C. *International Trade: Goods, People, and Ideas* (New York: Alfred Knopf, 1962).
22. Granick, David. "An Organizational Model of Soviet Industrial Planning," *Journal of Political Economy*, LXVII:2 (April 1959), pp. 109–130.
23. Grossman, Gregory. "Notes for a Theory of the Command Economy," *Soviet Studies*, XV:2 (October 1963), pp. 101–123.
24. ——— (ed.). *Value and Plan: Economic Calculation and Organization in Eastern Europe* (Berkeley: University of California Press, 1960).
25. Haberler, Gottfried. *A Survey of International Trade Theory*. Revised and enlarged edition, Special Papers in International Economics, No. 1, July 1961 (Princeton, N.J.: International Finance Section, Princeton University, 1961).
26. ———. *The Theory of International Trade*, English translation (London: William Hodge, 1936).
27. Hamburger, László. "Az exportforgalmi jutalék és az árkiegyenlitési prémiumrendszer néhány hiányossága" ("Some Shortcomings of the Export Turnover Bonus and of the Price-Equalization Premium System"), *Külkereskedelem*, III:1 (January 1959), pp. 19–20.
28. Hantos, Miklós. "A külkereskedelem vállalati prémiumrendszeréröl" ("On the Premium System of the FTEs"), *Külkereskedelem*, IV:3 (March 1960), pp. 7–9.
29. ———, and László Várkonyi. "A külkereskedelmi prémiumrendszer módositásáról" ("On the Modification of the Foreign Trade Premium System"), *Külkereskedelem*, III:5 (May 1959), pp. 12–15.
30. Hicks, John R. *Value and Capital*, Second Edition (Oxford: Clarendon Press, 1946).
31. Holzman, Franklyn. "Foreign Trade," in Abram Bergson and Simon Kuznets

(eds.), *Economic Trends in the Soviet Union* (Cambridge: Harvard University Press, 1957), pp. 283–332.
32. ———. "Foreign Trade Behavior of Centrally-Planned Economies," in Henry Rosovsky (ed.), *Industrialization in Two Systems: Essays in Honor of Alexander Gerschenkron* (New York: Wiley, 1966), pp. 237–265.
33. ———. "Some Financial Aspects of Soviet Foreign Trade," U.S. Congress, Joint Economic Committee, *Comparisons of the United States and Soviet Economies* (Washington, D.C.: 1959), Part II, pp. 427–443.
34. Hunter, Holland. "Optimal Tautness in Developmental Planning," *Economic Development and Cultural Change*, IX:4 (July 1961), pp. 561–572.
35. Illyés, Éva. "A külkereskedelem szerepe és tervézésének jelenlegi feladatai" ("The Role of Foreign Trade and the Current Tasks of Its Planning"), *Társadalmi Szemle*, IX:5 (May 1954).
36. Iversen, Carl. *Aspects of the Theory of International Capital Movements* (Copenhagen: Levin and Munksgaard, 1936).
37. Kalecki, M. "The Principle of Increasing Risk," *Economica*, N.S., IV:4 (November 1937), pp. 440–447.
38. Kálmán, Dezsö. "Az importmunka felelössége" ("Responsibility of the Import Work"), *Külkereskedelem*, III:8 (August 1959), pp. 10–11.
39. Karádi, Gyula. "Új vonások külkereskedelmünkben" ("New Trends in Our Foreign Trade"), *Közgadasági Szemle*, VI:11 (November 1959), pp. 1141–1158.
40. Katus, László. "Termelöi árrendezés, import ármegállapitás" ("Producer Price Reform, Import Price Determination"), *Külkereskedelem*, II:3 (March 1958), pp. 13–14.
41. Kornai, János. *Overcentralization in Economic Administration: A Critical Analysis Based on Experience in Hungarian Light Industry*, translated by John Knapp (London: Oxford University Press, 1959).
42. *Külkereskedelem*. III:3 (March 1959).
43. *Külkereskedelem*. III:4 (April 1959).
44. *Külkereskedelmi Kislexikon* (Budapest: Közgazdasági és Jogi Könyvkiadó, 1960).
45. Lakos, Gyula. "A helyi és kisipari export néhány problémájáról" ("On Some Problems of Local and Small-Scale Industrial Exports"), *Külkereskedelem*, I:2 (November 1957), pp. 7–8.
46. Levine, Herbert S. "The Centralized Planning of Supply in Soviet Industry," U.S. Congress, Joint Economic Committee, *Comparisons of the United States and Soviet Economies* (Washington, D.C.: 1959), Part I, pp. 151–176.
47. Liska, Tibor, and Antal Máriás. "A gazdaságosság és a nemzetközi munkamegosztás" ("Economic Efficiency and International Division of Labor"), *Közgazdasági Szemle*, I:1 (October 1954), pp. 75–94.
48. Marshall, Alfred. *Money, Credit and Commerce* (London: Macmillan, 1923).
49. Montias, John Michael. *Central Planning in Poland* (New Haven: Yale University Press, 1962).
50. ———. "Planning with Material Balances," *American Economic Review*, XLIV:5 (December 1959), pp. 963–985.
51. Nagy, Imre. *On Communism* (New York: Praeger, 1957).
52. "Napirenden: A külkereskedelem harmadik ötéves terve" ("Agenda: The

Third Five Year Plan of Foreign Trade"), *Külkereskedelem*, X:7 (July 1966), pp. 193–194.

53. Neuberger, Egon. "Libermanism, Computopia, and Visible Hand: The Question of Informational Efficiency," *American Economic Review*, LVI:2 (May 1966), pp. 131–144.

54. Nove, Alec. *The Soviet Economy: An Introduction*, Revised Edition (New York: Praeger, 1965).

55. Pajestka, J. *Ekonomista*, No. 5 (1957), pp. 42–62; cited in *Közgazdasági Szemle*, V:6 (1958), p. 625.

56. Pryor, Frederic L. *The Communist Foreign Trade System* (Cambridge: Massachusetts Institute of Technology Press, 1963).

57. Rosovsky, Henry (ed.). *Industrialization in Two Systems: Essays in Honor of Alexander Gerschenkron* (New York: Wiley, 1966).

58. Sattler, Tamás. "Gazdaságos aluminiumkohászati segédanyag import" ("Economical Importation of Auxiliary Materials for Aluminum Metallurgy"), *Külkereskedelem*, III:12 (December 1959), pp. 8–11.

59. Schelling, Thomas C. *International Economics* (Boston: Allyn and Bacon, 1958).

60. Sebestyén, Tibor. "A Chemolimpex és az ipar együttmüködése az importban" ("Cooperation of Chemolimpex and Industry in Importing"), *Külkereskedelem*, III:2 (February 1959), pp. 24–25.

61. Spulber, Nicolas. *The Economics of Communist Eastern Europe* (New York: The Technology Press of Massachusetts Institute of Technology and Wiley, 1957).

62. Stalin, Joseph. *Economic Problems of Socialism in the USSR* (New York: International Publishers, 1952).

63. *Statisztikai Évkönyv, 1949–1955* (Budapest: Központi Statiszikai Hivatal, 1956).

64. *Statisztikai Évkönyv, 1965* (Budapest: Központi Statisztikai Hivatal, 1966).

65. Szabó, Tibor, and Tamás Sugár. "A külkereskedelem ipari kapcsolatai és ösztönzési rendszerek a szocialista országokban" ("Relations between Foreign Trade and Industry and the Incentive Systems in Socialist Countries"), *Külkereskedelem*, IV:2 (February 1960), pp. 4–9.

66. Szányi, Jenö. "Moszkvai tapasztalatok . . ." ("Experiences from Moscow . . ."), *Külkereskedelem*, I:3 (December 1957), pp. 15–16.

67. Tallós, György. "Az 1958 évi külkereskedelmi tervröl" ("On the 1958 Foreign Trade Plan"), *Külkereskedelem*, II:3 (March 1958), pp. 1–3.

68. ————. "Az 1959 évi külkereskedelmi tervröl" ("On the 1959 Foreign Trade Plan"), *Külkereskedelem*, III:1 (January 1959), pp. 1–3.

69. Vajda, Imre. *Szocialista Külkereskedelem* (Budapest: Közgazdasági és Jogi Könyvkiadó, 1963).

70. Viner, Jacob. "International Relations between State-Controlled National Economies," *American Economic Review*, XXXIV, Supplement (March 1944), pp. 315–329; in Howard S. Ellis and Lloyd A. Metzler (eds.), *Readings in the Theory of International Trade* (Philadelphia: The Blakiston Company, 1950), pp. 437–456.

71. Wilczynski, J. "The Theory of Comparative Costs and Centrally Planned Economies," *Economic Journal*, LXXV:297 (March 1965), pp. 63–80.

72. Wiles, P. J. D. "Are Adjusted Rubles Rational?", *Soviet Studies*, VII:2 (October 1955), pp. 143–160.

73. ———. *The Political Economy of Communism* (Cambridge: Harvard University Press, 1962).
74. Yntema, Theodore O. *A Mathematical Reformulation of the General Theory of International Trade* (Chicago: University of Chicago Press, 1932).
75. Zala, J. (ed.). *Gazdaságstatisztika* (Budapest: Közgazdasági és Jogi Könyvkiadó, 1959).
76. "Zur Aussenhandelskonferenz," *Aussenhandel*, No. 3 (1958).

East-West Trade and the Paradoxes
of the Strategic Embargo

NICOLAS SPULBER

Two sets of problems affect East-West trade. The first — affecting imports from the U.S.S.R. and Eastern Europe into the United States and Western Europe — concerns the possible reduction to a common denominator of trade policies and practices in market-directed and in centrally planned economies. The second — affecting imports bound in the opposite direction — concerns the need for systematic restrictions on exports which may directly or indirectly strengthen the military potential of any Communist country.

The first set of problems is unobtrusive, deep-rooted, and only slowly changing; the second is conspicuous, always in the public eye, and often changing. The lasting and ramifying impact of the first complex of problems has been dealt with painstakingly, particularly by experts of international organizations, who have tended to dismiss the second set of problems as "overly politically motivated" and hence outside their particular expertise.[1] On the other hand, the shifting consequences of the second complex of problems have been dealt with extensively, notably by the press and by various congressional committees who have precisely stressed the political implications of export inducements or denials. Actually, trading policies and practices, and so-called "political" trade inducements or denials, affect each other continuously; they cannot be analyzed fruitfully if this interaction is ignored.

[1] See "Trade Problems between Countries Having Different Economic and Social Systems" and "Implications for Trade between the Centrally Planned Economies and Developing Countries" (both by the Secretariat of the United Nations Economic Commission for Europe) in [14, pp. 113–169, 121, 238–403].

I

United Nations forums, reports, and studies have gone a long way toward explaining the difficulties of adjusting the divergent views of, and approaches to, international trade that have been adopted in the market-directed and the centrally planned economies [14, pp. 117ff., 122ff., and 238ff.]. The basic approach to international trade of the Western economies, embodied in the provisions of the General Agreement on Tariffs and Trade (GATT) and in some related documents, is that in "normal times" virtually no direct governmental controls will be exercised over trade. In addition, tariffs will be applied without discrimination by area and origin of imports except for certain temporary or permanent cases concerning arrangements pre-dating GATT, or custom unions and free trade areas. Only by exception will quantitative trade restrictions be resorted to; non-discrimination *among members*, embodied in the *most favored nation* clause (MFN), may be suspended only in case of a custom union's preferential tariffs, temporary needs of import controls and payment restriction for current transactions, or restrictions for income price supports, for instance. Furthermore, the obligations under GATT have been interrelated with mutual obligations extending virtually "to the full range of governmental action which may affect competition and imports."

These principles underlie trade practices among *developed* market economies. In the centrally planned economies (defined for the purposes of this paper as encompassing all the Communist or "socialist" economies except Yugoslavia), quantitative regulation of international trade has been, up into the 1960s, not the exception but the rule. The import plan, directly linked to the scope, structure, and targets of the national plan, has been the key element of foreign trade planning. Tariffs have had hardly any bearing upon level or area trade patterns. The Soviet Union, Czechoslovakia, Hungary, and Poland, followed by East Germany, have adopted a two-column tariff; but no country has been subjected to the higher duty rates. Choices among suppliers have been largely guided by the planners' need of guaranteeing definite deliveries at predetermined prices for specified planning periods. The arrangements within the Council for Economic Mutual Assistance (CEMA) [2] have reflected efforts to coordinate import requirements according to the national plans, and, on a higher plane, to coordinate the production plans themselves as they bear upon import requirements without resort to formal tariff or other policy measures used in the West for influencing the decisions of exporters and importers.

The Western governments have repeatedly stressed that under these con-

[2] The CEMA, CMEA, or COMECON countries are now the U.S.S.R., Bulgaria, Czechoslovakia, East Germany, Hungary, Poland, Rumania and Outer Mongolia (since 1962). The trade of the last-named country is not covered in this paper.

ditions they could not meaningfully compare their "principles and practices" with those of the centrally planned economies, and that hence they could not insure in all cases "effective reciprocity" and verification of the application of MFN treatment in the planned economies. Given these differences, the governments of the market-directed economies have declined to apply GATT principles to centrally planned economies, even when one of the latter was a full member of GATT.[3] Clearly, they wished to insure their "satisfactory access to the markets of the centrally planned economies, in total or for individual products," as well as to protect themselves against certain dangers arising from centralized state trading — namely, market disruption due to abrupt shifts in big trading orders. "Completely non-discriminatory treatment of imports from centrally planned economies is rare (or possibly even non-existent)," notes a United Nations source. The range of imports subjected to control, the degree of effectiveness of the restriction, and the extent to which transferability of earnings is granted to the centrally planned economies vary, however, from country to country.[4]

The governments of the centrally planned economies have stressed, for their part, that their own differential tariff was but a "defensive response to the application of such tariffs by certain market economies," that consideration of relative costs actually plays an increasingly significant role among their various planning criteria, and that "unconditional MFN" in respect to both tariffs and quantitative trade controls must prevail in any and all transactions if international trade is to develop on a healthy course. Increasingly, the higher ranking economists of certain planned economies have drawn attention to the fact that planning concepts are changing in Eastern Europe, and that the overall planning of foreign trade, the connection of imports to the national plan, the quantitative regulation of trade flows, and the whole

[3] Czechoslovakia is the only centrally planned economy whose membership in GATT was established before it came under Communist rule. Poland established relations with GATT by a declaration in November 1959, but only certain members extend to it the MFN. Its situation is thus similar to that of Czechoslovakia. Yugoslavia associated itself with GATT by a declaration in May 1959, and acceded to full membership in November 1962, after important changes in its foreign trade and foreign exchange systems. Rumania is authorized to follow the work of GATT as observer. Hungary applied for a similar authorization in November 1966.

[4] [14, p. 121]. The United States has denied by law, since January 1952, the application of MFN to the U.S.S.R. and the East European countries, excluding Yugoslavia. Accordingly, imports from these countries have been subjected to the 1930 Tariff Acts, not the rates as reduced by trade agreements entered into since the 1934 Trade Agreement Act. In 1960, the Administration granted MFN to Poland and warded off a number of congressional efforts to deny this treatment to Poland and Yugoslavia. The so-called Miller Report [10], released by the White House on April 29, 1965, anticipated, as a key tool in "building bridges" to the East, the vesting of "discretionary authority in the President to grant as well as withdraw MFN treatment [to selected Communist countries]." See, notably, [5, p. 39], [6, pp. 1005 and 1010], and [10, p. 10 and *passim*].

organizational setup of sales and purchases abroad are bound to change appreciably. Such changes would most likely help reduce substantially the differences in principles and trading practices prevailing in the developed market-directed economies and in the East European planned economies.

II

Besides these underlying differences, a number of special trading restrictions have been enacted by the Western countries since 1948–1949 with respect to exports directed toward the Communist countries. Changes in the scope and nature of these restrictions have been numerous and have at times sharply affected the overall volume, value, and structure of East-West trade.

Special export controls toward the "Soviet bloc" — consisting, in the early post-war years, of most of the Eastern European countries, including Yugoslavia and the Soviet Union — were initiated first by the United States and then by the Western European countries at a time when international tensions seemed to push the world inexorably toward political bipolarization and toward the compartmentalization of international trade into Soviet bloc and non-bloc areas. From 1948 until the end of 1953, export controls interlocked to form a tight and complicated mesh covering virtually all Western exports. First, the United States devised unilateral controls and established a number of procedures meant to ensure that any country receiving U.S. aid would not ship to the bloc. Second, the Western European countries developed their own export restrictions on trade with the bloc. Finally, multilateral export controls were locked together by all the developed world powers, including Canada and Japan.

U.S. controls over exports to Communist countries started in 1948 and operated through the general system of controls over shipments to foreign countries in existence since 1940 [3, pp. 38ff.]. Two basic documents — the *Exports Control Act* of 1949 and the *Battle Act* of 1951 — embodied the effort to systemize U.S. trade controls and to relate this effort to countries then receiving U.S. aid.

The Exports Control Act, administered by the Department of Commerce, aimed to exercise the necessary vigilance over exports from the standpoint of their significance to the national security of the United States. The Department of Commerce was empowered to control all exports to Communist countries via two types of licenses: "validated license" for specific key goods in specific quantities, and "general license" for commodities of secondary importance. All exports to the Communist countries — including China after 1949 — were thereafter deemed to require a validated license.

The Battle Act, administered by the Department of State, required on the other hand that no U.S. assistance "be supplied to any nation unless it applies an embargo" on specified goods that might be directed toward the bloc. The administrator of the act grouped into two categories the items to be embargoed under the provision of Title I: Title IA, covering arms, ammunitions, and atomic energy materials, contained 21 listings of numerous items; Title IB, specifically covering petroleum, transportation materials, and items of strategic importance used in the production of war materials, had 264 listings, each with many hundreds of items. Shipment of category "A" materials required mandatory cessation of U.S. aid to the exporting country; shipment of category "B" items, cessation of aid unless such a measure would be "clearly detrimental to the security of the United States." Title III of the act enjoined the continuous review of existing restrictions and of the items that might need more effective controls. Finally, after the beginning of the Korean conflict, the *Trading with the Enemy Act* was invoked against China and North Korea; and, as mentioned, special import restrictions from all Communist countries were put into force at the same time.

Following the U.S. lead, the United Kingdom and France formulated in 1949 an Anglo-French list of export items placed under similar control. That same year a series of bilateral discussions was conducted in Paris by the United States and its allies. There, the United States, Canada, and the Western powers established an informal committee — the so-called Consultative Group (CG) — aimed at carrying out cooperative action in the field of security trade controls on a world scale. The CG approved three international lists: an *embargo* list, a *quantitative controls* list, and a *surveillance* list, conforming to classifications of the "strategic" importance of the goods considered. These lists, representing areas of international agreement, did not, however, replace the individual lists of each of the participating countries, which in certain cases continued to be far more extensive. Immediately prior to the adoption of the Battle act, a special control system was applied by all the cooperating countries to prevent transshipment of embargoed goods through either allied or neutral ports toward the bloc. This system, known as *Import Certificate Delivery Verification* (ICDV) empowered the authority of the exporting country to require the importer to obtain a certificate and have it recorded by his government before issuing an export license for goods subject to control. Finally, in 1949, the United Nations General Assembly followed the U.S. lead and recommended the establishment of world-wide controls over exports to China.

Thus, from 1948 on, export restrictions and delivery controls over export to the Sino-Soviet bloc expanded systematically in both range of items and tightness of application. By the close of 1953, however, the multilateral embargo reached its zenith. Shifts within both Eastern and Western Europe brought about an increasing differentiation in the type of restrictions applied to each of the former by each of the latter, and thus opened a second period in the history of the embargo.

Already, in 1954, the CG had decided to revise sharply the Soviet bloc lists while maintaining unchanged the controls concerning China. The organization had established two working committees composed of representatives of the fifteen NATO powers (including Japan, but excluding Iceland): the Coordinating Committee (COCOM) to examine controls with respect to the Soviet bloc, and the China Committee (CHINCOM) to examine controls with respect to China. The international lists concerning the U.S.S.R. and Eastern Europe were revised as follows: List I (embargo list), reduced from 260 to 170 items; List II (the quantitative controls list), from 90 to 20 items; List III (the surveillance list), from 100 to 60 items. A special atomic energy embargo list was added to List I. Two years after these measures were taken, pressures started to build against keeping the so-called "China differential," the difference in embargo policies with respect to China. In 1956, a resounding British deal broke the embargo concerning rubber, and the following year CHINCOM failed to achieve unanimity over the extent of control revisions concerning China. The United Kingdom, deciding to take the initiative, completely dropped the differential, an act soon repeated by the other participating powers in the CG — except the United States. A year later, the CG decided to narrow its embargo lists still further. List I was substantially revised, and Lists II and III were replaced by a new "watch" list consisting mainly of items formerly on List I and still considered to be of some strategic importance. Finally, the CG adopted a procedure for frequent revision of the international lists. Indeed, a new review began immediately afterward, reducing the embargo list to some 100 items and the watch list to 20.

After 1953, the United States, once the pace-setter for all its allies in this sphere, had to pursue an unilateral course in many respects, according to its own evaluations of the changes taking place in the Sino-Soviet bloc as a whole. As differentiation increased in the bloc and produced various degrees of centrifugal forces, the United States relaxed or tightened its export regulations affecting some countries. Yugoslavia received, in respect to exports, the same treatment as non-Communist countries. Certain exports to Poland and Rumania no longer required a validated license. On the other hand, the term "strategic" was extended in 1962 to encompass goods of economic as well as military importance — an extension that led to the denial of certain non-military goods to the U.S.S.R.[5] Finally the *Trading*

---

[5] The United States has applied a full embargo on the export and import trade with Communist China and North Korea, has blocked their assets in the United States, and has denied all financial transactions with them since December 1950. On the other

with the Enemy Act was extended to Cuba and North Vietnam. By the mid-1960s, the embargo as defined by the COCOM became quite limited and covered, apart from implements of war and atomic energy items, a "selective range of the most advanced industrial materials and equipment." In contrast, the range of goods covered by the U.S. export controls was far more comprehensive. This is illustrated by the positive list which is used to identify strategic goods as defined by the Department of Commerce. As of the end of the first quarter of 1964, 1,303 separate entries were on the positive list [3, p. 42].

A third period of the embargo was finally opened in the second half of the 1960s. As the conflict deepened between the Soviet Union and most of Eastern Europe, on the one hand, and China, on the other hand, the United States moved to bring its own standards concerning the strategic and economic embargo of the former into closer agreement with those of the Western countries. In the fall of 1966, Washington announced its decision to remove hundreds of items from its embargo lists (including textiles, metals, machinery, and a variety of other products) [7, October 8, 1966]. Thus a *de facto* Western consensus was re-established on a limited but highly flexible range of embargoed goods, except in the case of China and of the other Communist countries against which the United States invokes the *Trading with the Enemy Act* and against which it alone applies a total embargo.

III

The political and economic shifts within the former Sino-Soviet bloc itself and the shifts in the nature and range of the embargo interacted in different ways during the three broad periods into which the post-war years may be conveniently divided: (1) the period from 1949 to 1953, the period of clear-cut world bipolarization; (2) the decade 1954–1963, or the transitional period during which the Sino-Soviet bloc started to split in various ways; and, finally, (3) the period immediately following, characterized by increasing heterogeneity in planning and management under "socialism."

During the first period, the Sino-Soviet bloc appeared as a menacing political monolith, though at the time it was already being shaken by deep centrifugal economic undercurrents. After the expulsion of Yugoslavia in 1948, the Soviet Union dominated unchallenged the intra-bloc economic relations. Each East European country was tied to the U.S.S.R. by innu-

hand, the United States has denied only those goods that could make "a significant contribution," first to the military and later (after the building of the Berlin Wall) to the "economic potential" of the U.S.S.R., CEMA, and Albania. U.S. controls, however, have never been used to deny *all* types of commodities to these countries. Hence the term "strategic" (selective) embargo has been applied to these restrictions from the inception of this policy. Cf. [6, p. 1003].

TABLE 1

WORLD TRADE BY AREAS AND TRADING GROUPS (SELECTED YEARS)

Areas and Trading Groups	Exports f.o.b. ($ million)						Imports c.i.f. ($ million)					
	1938	1948	1953	1958	1963	1964	1938	1948	1953	1958	1963	1964
World[a]	23,500	57,400	82,600	108,000	153,700	172,200	25,400	63,600	84,300	113,700	161,500	180,600
Developed areas[b]	15,200	36,700	53,700	71,100	103,500	117,500	17,900	41,200	55,000	73,500	110,200	124,900
Common Market	4,360	6,680	14,680	23,440	37,550	42,560	5,130	10,650	15,510	23,620	40,410	44,890
Free trade area	4,150	9,560	12,000	15,760	21,770	24,050	6,290	12,880	14,570	18,400	25,970	30,290
United States	3,064	12,545	15,661	17,738	23,102	26,229	2,180	7,183	10,915	13,340	17,076	18,666
Underdeveloped areas[c]	5,900	17,100	21,000	24,700	31,500	34,400	5,800	18,600	21,400	27,700	32,400	34,900
Communist world[d]	2,380	3,690	7,910	12,100	18,660	20,290	1,700	3,800	7,800	12,500	18,800	20,800
CEMA[e]	1,151	3,118	6,451	10,100	16,934	18,436	1,075	3,017	6,521	9,925	16,571	18,338

Areas and Trading Groups	Exports f.o.b. (%)						Imports c.i.f. (%)					
	1938	1948	1953	1958	1963	1964	1938	1948	1953	1958	1963	1964
World[a]	100.0	100.0	100.0	100.0	100.0	100.0	100.0	100.0	100.0	100.0	100.0	100.0
Developed areas[b]	64.8	63.8	65.0	65.9	67.4	68.2	70.5	64.8	65.2	64.6	68.3	69.2
Common Market	18.6	11.6	17.8	21.7	24.4	24.7	20.2	16.7	18.4	20.8	25.0	24.9
Free trade area	17.7	16.7	14.5	14.6	14.2	14.0	24.8	20.3	17.3	16.2	16.1	16.8
United States	13.0	21.9	19.0	16.4	15.0	15.2	8.6	11.3	12.9	11.7	10.6	10.3
Underdeveloped areas[c]	25.1	29.8	25.4	22.9	20.5	20.0	22.8	29.2	25.4	24.4	20.1	20.0
Communist world[d]	10.1	6.4	9.6	11.2	12.1	11.8	6.7	6.0	9.3	11.0	11.6	11.5
CEMA[e]	4.9	5.4	7.8	9.3	11.0	10.6	4.2	4.7	7.7	8.7	10.2	10.1

[a] Excluding intra-trade of Asian planned economies.
[b] United States, Canada, Western Europe, Japan, Australia, New Zealand, and South Africa.
[c] Total of regions other than developed areas, Eastern Europe, the U.S.S.R., and Asian centrally planned economies.
[d] Eastern Europe, the U.S.S.R., and Asian centrally planned economies.
[e] Bulgaria, Czechoslovakia, East Germany, Hungary, Poland, Rumania, and the U.S.S.R.
SOURCE: United Nations Statistical Yearbook 1965 (New York: United Nations, 1966), pp. 390–393.

TABLE 2

CEMA TRADE, BY COUNTRIES (SELECTED YEARS)

CEMA Countries	Exports f.o.b. ($ million)						Imports c.i.f. ($ million)					
	1938	1948	1953	1958	1963	1964	1938	1948	1953	1958	1963	1964
U.S.S.R.	251	1,250	2,875	4,298	7,272	7,681	268	1,250	2,875	4,350	7,059	7,737
Bulgaria	68	128	206	373	838	969	60	123	200	367	915	1,057
Czechoslovakia	295	753	994	1,513	2,462	2,668	239	681	879	1,357	2,160	2,429
East Germany	(a)	142	706	1,704	2,471	2,670	(a)	154	920	1,511	2,130	2,380
Hungary	155	166	498	684	1,206	1,352	123	167	488	631	1,306	1,495
Poland	225	533	831	1,060	1,770	2,096	248	516	774	1,227	1,979	2,072
Rumania	157	146	341	468	915	1,000	137	126	385	482	1,022	1,168
Total East Europe	900(b)	1,868	3,576	5,802	9,662	10,755	807(b)	1,767	3,646	5,575	9,512	10,601

CEMA Countries	Exports f.o.b. (% of world trade)						Imports c.i.f. (% of world trade)					
	1938	1948	1953	1958	1963	1964	1938	1948	1953	1958	1963	1964
U.S.S.R.	1.07	2.18	3.48	3.97	4.73	4.46	1.06	1.97	3.41	3.83	4.37	4.28
Bulgaria	.29	.22	.25	.35	.55	.56	.24	.19	.23	.32	.56	.58
Czechoslovakia	1.26	1.31	1.20	1.40	1.60	1.55	.94	1.07	1.04	1.19	1.33	1.34
East Germany	(a)	.25	.85	1.58	1.61	1.55	(a)	.24	1.09	1.33	1.32	1.32
Hungary	.66	.29	.60	.63	.78	.78	.48	.26	.58	.55	.80	.83
Poland	.96	.93	1.01	.98	1.15	1.22	.98	.81	.92	1.08	1.22	1.15
Rumania	.67	.25	.41	.43	.60	.58	.54	.20	.46	.42	.63	.65
Total East Europe	3.84(b)	3.25	4.32	5.37	6.29	6.24	3.18(b)	2.77	4.32	4.89	5.86	5.87

a Data not available.
b Not including East Germany.
SOURCES: As in Table 1; completed with *United Nations Economic Survey of Europe* for 1954 and 1957 (New York: United Nations, 1955 and 1958 resp.), p. 113 and Chap. VI, p. 23.

merable economic threads: the former enemy countries, East Germany, Hungary, Rumania, and Bulgaria, were tied to it through reparations, restitutions, or joint companies; the former allied countries, Poland and Czechoslovakia, by a number of direct and indirect obligations. In these conditions, the East European countries lost significantly in their *relative* importance in world trade. While the total exports of the East European countries reached $1,868 million in 1948, their share in world exports fell from 3.8 percent in 1938 (excluding East Germany) to 3.2 percent (including, this time, East Germany's exports). (See Tables 1 and 2.)

At the time, each of these countries was attempting to reproduce in miniature the Soviet economy and was proceeding on parallel lines of development. Within each country, investment was allocated according to the Soviet pattern with its well-known stresses on heavy industry. A feverish atmosphere of industrialization prevailed in the area, an atmosphere further surcharged by the exigencies of the Korean war. The rapid expansion within each country of the metallurgical industries and of military output produced, in turn, growth (regardless of cost) in domestic outputs of coal, iron, and ores; an intensive demand for iron, fuel, and grains (notably from the Soviet Union); and a brisk intra-bloc trade in steel profiles, machinery, and equipment. The embargo, which was closing its tight grip around the bloc, consolidated this new pattern of trade. In 1938, Western Europe and the United States absorbed some 72 percent of East Europe's exports (including the U.S.S.R. but excluding East Germany); but in 1948 this share fell to 40 percent and in 1953 to only 15 percent. On the other hand, intra-CEMA trade rose from 10 percent of area exports in 1938 to 44 percent in 1948 and 64 percent in 1953 (Table 3).

Patterns of supply and demand of the East European goods entering foreign trade were rapidly changing under the multiple impact of industrialization, of the deliberate inclination of the centrally planned economies to trade among themselves, of the key position acquired by the U.S.S.R. in the area, and of the import-export restrictions established by the Western countries; at the same time, the East-West trade of the East European countries proper underwent sharp contraction while Soviet-West trade actually expanded. Between 1950 and 1953, Eastern Europe's imports f.o.b. from countries of the Organization for Economic Cooperation and Development (OECD) (excluding Spain), Finland, and Yugoslavia fell from $498 million to $473 million; those of the U.S.S.R. rose from an estimated $140 million to $311 million. During the same period, Eastern Europe's imports of machinery and equipment from the same sources fell from $151 million to $100 million, while those of the U.S.S.R. rose from $87 million to $107 million. While all the East European countries were losing in various degrees their former markets in the West — where their exports fell between 1950

TABLE 3

EASTERN EUROPE'S PATTERN OF EXPORTS, BY REGIONS AND AREAS (SELECTED YEARS)

Year	Total[a] ($ million)	North America				Western Europe			Eastern Europe			Areas		
		Total	U.S.	Canada	Latin America	Total[b]	EEC	Free Trade Area	Total	U.S.S.R.	Other[c]	All Other	Developed	Under-developed
1938	1,960	86	80	6	100	1,340	670	535	198	23	175	236	1,470	215
1948	3,170	120	115	5	36	1,180	330	600	1,405	475	930	429	1,320	195
1953	6,780	41	37	4	31	980	275	460	4,340	1,530	2,810	1,388	1,040	170
1958	10,100	82	70	12	120	1,810	695	620	6,060	2,220	3,840	2,028	1,930	710
1963	16,980	111	90	21	630	2,960	1,240	1,010	11,050	4,140	6,910	2,229	3,240	1,810
1964	18,480	131	103	28	600	3,300	1,330	1,140	11,960	4,500	7,460	2,489	3,650	1,900

Year	Total[a] (%)	North America				Western Europe			Eastern Europe			Areas		
		Total	U.S.	Canada	Latin America	Total[b]	EEC	Free Trade Area	Total	U.S.S.R.	Other[c]	All Other	Developed	Under-developed
1938	100.0	4.4	4.1	0.3	5.1	68.4	34.2	27.3	10.1	1.2	8.9	12.0	75.0	11.0
1948	100.0	3.8	3.6	0.2	1.1	37.2	10.4	19.0	44.3	15.0	29.3	13.6	41.6	6.2
1953	100.0	0.6	0.5	0.1	0.5	14.4	4.1	6.8	64.0	22.6	41.4	20.5	15.3	2.5
1958	100.0	0.8	0.7	0.1	1.2	17.9	6.9	6.1	60.0	22.0	38.0	20.1	19.1	7.0
1963	100.0	0.6	0.5	0.1	3.7	17.4	7.3	6.0	65.0	24.3	40.7	13.3	19.1	10.7
1964	100.0	0.6	0.5	0.1	3.2	17.8	7.2	6.2	64.4	24.4	40.0	14.0	19.7	10.3

[a] Including East Germany and Albania throughout. Excluding certain exports whose destination could not be determined.

[b] Total Europe, excluding East Europe and transactions between East and West Germany valued as follows:

	1953	1958	1963	1964
West to East Germany	60	191	215	288
East to West Germany	70	211	242	264

[c] Albania, Bulgaria, Czechoslovakia, East Germany, Hungary, Poland, and Rumania.

SOURCE: United Nations Statistical Yearbook 1965 (New York: United Nations, 1966), pp. 398, 402-403.

TABLE 4

COMMODITY COMPOSITION OF EAST-WEST TRADE
(SELECTED YEARS)

Commodity	West Europe[a] Exports f.o.b. ($ million)				West Europe[a] Imports c.i.f. ($ million)				West Europe[a] Exports f.o.b. (%)				West Europe[a] Imports c.i.f. (%)			
	1950	1953	1956	1962	1950	1953	1956	1962	1950	1953	1956	1962	1950	1953	1956	1962
Machinery and equipment																
East Europe	151	100	88	441	31	42	95	150	30.3	21.1	11.3	30.7	5.0	7.3	3.8	10.1
Soviet Union	87	107	220	502	1	4	18	39	62.1	34.4	41.0	46.8	.6	1.2	2.7	3.2
Manufactured and semi-manufactured goods, including chemicals and metals																
East Europe	196	179	338	605	[b]	170	394	596	39.4	37.8	43.2	42.2	[c]	29.5	40.8	39.9
Soviet Union	27	92	221	443	[b]	88	213	423	19.3	29.6	37.4	41.3	[c]	26.3	31.9	35.1
Crude materials and fuels																
East Europe	84	99	151	175	[b]	222	348	424	16.9	20.9	19.3	12.2	[c]	38.5	36.0	28.4
Soviet Union	18	42	50	67	[b]	145	388	748	12.9	13.5	9.3	6.2	[c]	43.4	58.1	62.1
Food, beverages, and tobacco																
East Europe	42	90	204	203	156	172	240	479	8.4	19.0	26.1	14.1	25.0	29.9	24.8	32.1
Soviet Union	7	70	65	59	83	133	135	169	5.0	22.5	12.1	5.4	47.4	39.8	20.2	14.0
Total (incl. unspecified)																
East Europe	498	473	782	1,435	625	576	966	1,492								
Soviet Union	140[c]	311	537	1,073	175	334	668	1,205								

[a] OECD countries (excluding Spain), Finland, and Yugoslavia.
[b] Data not available.
[c] Estimated.
SOURCE: Based on *Economic Bulletin for Europe*, XVI:2, pp. 78–79.

Nicolas Spulber

and 1953 from $625 million to $576 million — Soviet exports to the same countries were rising from $175 million to $334 million (Table 4). The Soviet Union was in fact able at the time not only to maintain an expanding volume of trade with the West, notwithstanding the embargo, but also to expand significantly its intra-bloc trade. In fact, during 1952–1953, the relative shares of the Soviet Union in the exports and imports of the East European countries reached their higher levels of the 1950s (Table 5).

TABLE 5

SOVIET UNION'S SHARE IN THE FOREIGN TRADE
OF INDIVIDUAL EAST EUROPEAN COUNTRIES
(SELECTED YEARS)
(Percentages)

	Exports				Imports			
Country	1948	Peak year in early 1950s[a]	1956	1964	1948	Peak year in early 1950s[a]	1956	1964
Bulgaria	51	57	50	54	59	63	42	53
Czecho-slovakia	16	36	31	37	16	39	33	38
East Germany	34	46	40	47	42	47	42	46
Hungary	17	37	25	36	15	30	23	33
Poland	21	38	27	34	29	37	34	31
Rumania	33	58[b]	50[c]	42	34	58[b]	50[c]	42

[a] Peak years for exports: 1952 for Bulgaria, 1953 for Hungary. and 1954 for other countries.
Peak years for imports: 1951 for Bulgaria, 1954 for Poland, and 1953 for other countries.
[b] Estimated.
[c] 1958.
SOURCES: *Economic Survey of Europe* for 1957 (New York: United Nations, 1958), Chap. VI, p. 6; and *Economic Bulletin for Europe*, XVII:1 (November 1965), pp. 32–33.

After a short period of readjustment in planning targets and in investment allocation, the East European countries again engaged, essentially on autarchic lines, in a second round of long-term plans. This time, however, various trading opportunities opened in the West for at least certain East European countries; consequently, the share of intra–East European trade in their total trade started to contract, hitting its lowest level in 1956. Simultaneously, the Soviet Union's share in the foreign trade of some East European countries declined, while its role in certain key imports and exports of other CEMA countries (notably East Germany, Czechoslovakia, and Poland) remained decisive. Attempts at integrating either the foreign trade plans or the underlying output plans became increasingly ineffective, however; opening trade opportunities in the West strengthened the centrifugal tendencies of the least developed countries (Rumania, for instance) to avoid any supranational integration schemes. After 1956, the intra-CEMA trade expanded again in every case except that of Rumania, involving anew up to 65 percent of CEMA's trade; but this time the expansion took place because of a corresponding sharp contraction in the trade with China (Table 3).

During the decade 1954–1963, the main Western exporters and importers to and from the East were West Germany (excluding its trade with East Germany), Italy, and the United Kingdom; in the preceding period, the main exporters had been the United Kingdom, Sweden, and Switzerland [8, pp. 69ff.]. In turn, during this decade the main CEMA exporters and importers to and from the West were the U.S.S.R. and, increasingly, the least developed countries of the area, in contrast with the early post-war period, when Czechoslovakia and Poland were the main traders with the West. During the 1950s, the combined share of these two countries in total East-West trade declined from close to 60 to roughly 30 percent.

The foreign trade linkage between East and West took again the pre-war form of interchanges of food, fuels, and crude materials from the East, against steel, machinery, and industrial equipment from the West. A shift occurred within this broad group, however, during the 1950s; East European exports changed from cereals and coal to primarily oil, pig iron, and timber. The East European exports of cereals to the West contracted sharply during the 1950s, and tended to rise again only briefly in the late 1950s and early 1960s, thanks to Soviet and Rumanian exports. Poland's coal exports were squeezed out of Western markets, first by expanding American coal exports in the 1950s and then by expanding Russian coal exports after the beginning of the 1960s. Finally, since 1954, Soviet petroleum exports have risen sharply, primarily toward Italy, Germany, and Finland. In turn, the imports of machinery and equipment, of processed steel, and of metal from the West have risen significantly during these years in the Soviet Union and in the least developed East European countries (notably Rumania). Soviet imports of fully equipped plants and ships and of manufactured and semi-manufactured goods from the West made up to 88 percent of the total Western exports to the Soviet Union, as against 73 percent of the Western exports to the other CEMA countries in the early 1960s. The total value of Western exports of machinery and equipment to the Soviet Union — prompted by the latter's modernization effort in the chemical industry, light industries, and fishing — reached over half a billion dollars in the early 'sixties, as against $440 million for the rest of the CEMA countries combined (Table 4).

Since the mid-1960s, further centrifugal tendencies have developed within

CEMA. The upper tier of Eastern European countries — East Germany and Czechoslovakia, the most industrialized of the area — have been attempting to break away from their dependence on certain Soviet and CEMA import requirements. This has posited a significant reorganization in the output patterns of some of their industries, changes in their management and planning practices, and bold realignment of their domestic price structures with the patterns prevailing in Western markets. The East Germans, followed up to a point by the Czechs, have been trying to lessen the steel-intensiveness of their industrial economy and to shift toward outputs with a lower specific steel content. They have shifted partially from heavy products, like large generators and turbines, toward machine construction, equipment for the chemical industry, precision instruments, and electric equipment. Their dependence on Soviet food, fuel, and raw materials rendered such changes possible only insofar as they were mapped with Soviet acquiescence. Czechoslovakia and East Germany have indeed accepted to pay prices higher than those of the world market for their imports of Soviet fuel and raw materials; furthermore, they have agreed to invest heavily in Soviet fuel and raw-material-producing industries.[6] Acquiescence has been granted also because of the Soviet Union's own access to alternative sources of supply of industrial products.

The middle tier of CEMA countries — Poland and Hungary — while attempting also to expand their trading opportunities in the West, seem in certain respects to be in far less favorable positions. Both have been squeezed out of the Western markets for a variety of products (particularly farm products) and must rely increasingly on the Soviet market for their exports of machinery and industrial articles in the years to come.[7]

Finally, the lower tier of Eastern Europe — particularly Rumania and up to a point Bulgaria — put their hopes on expanding trade with Western

[6] The discussion on the prices of Soviet fuel and raw materials has been opened in *Voprosy ekonomiki* by an important article of I. Dudinski, "Toplivno syr'evaia problema stran SEV i puti ee resheniia" ("The Fuel Raw Materials Problem of the CEMA Countries and the Road of Its Solution"), stressing the expanding role of the U.S.S.R. as CEMA's supplier of fuels and raw materials, and the "burden" that this expansion puts "on the entire national economy" of the U.S.S.R. Dudinski stresses that world prices do not reflect Soviet opportunity costs. To establish new ore centers in Siberia, notes Dudinski, enormous infrastructural investments along with large investment in mining and a long gestation period are required. Cf. [14, No. 4 (1966), pp. 84–94]. See also [7, September 11, 1966] concerning Soviet–East German trade up to 1970, and [7, November 27, 1966] concerning Soviet-Czechoslovakian trade relations.

[7] Poland has had to cope with the uncomfortable problem of import surpluses from the West payable in hard currency, and export surpluses to the East payable in nonconvertible currency. The prospects have brightened since the U.S.S.R. has become able, in the fall of 1966, both to sell a large amount of grain to Poland and to step up its imports of consumer goods from Poland. The Poles acknowledge that their manufactured goods cannot compete effectively on the developed capitalist markets. See [7, November 12, 1966].

Europe, notably Germany and France, with the other Balkan countries, and with underdeveloped areas, particularly the countries of the Middle East. CEMA trade is thus pulled in various directions by a variety of factors which will deepen the centrifugal tendencies further, as trading opportunities diversify in the West and as awareness and need of taking advantage of these opportunities increase in the East.

IV

Some of the entries in the overall balance sheet of the strategic embargo seem quite straightforward and obvious after close to two decades since its inception; others appear more doubtful and more difficult to pinpoint. It seems certain that, "below the nuclear ceiling," the embargo played an effective role during heightened East-West political tensions in denying various decisive exports to the bloc. This denial sharpened intra-bloc conflicts between the richer and the less well-endowed countries, and prepared in a way the launching of "New Course" policies that at times de-emphasized heavy industry investment. For a number of years, the U.S. economic defense policy prevented a more decisive shift in the structure of bloc imports from the West toward highly manufactured goods (notably fully equipped plants and various other strategic goods), imposed a real cost on these countries by denying them the benefits of foreign trade, discouraged the extension of long-term Western credits to bloc countries, and, at critical times, kept in check pressures from both West and East toward indiscriminate trade expansion. This contributed indirectly to the keeping of East-West trade at low levels, though the key aim of this policy was to deal with the composition rather than with the overall volume of this trade.

On the other side of the balance sheet, one may note, to start with, that the main, ambitious objective of the embargo — the reduction of the rate at which the Soviet Union and the bloc would be able to build their capacity "to wage war" — could be attained only in a highly uncertain measure via trade controls.[8] In the atomic age, this ability may depend on the existence within the given country of certain scientific skills or on the ability to import them, and on the capacity and the will to develop and integrate a set of domestic industries and supporting facilities. These are factors on which an embargo may have only a limited impact. As we now know, not only the

[8] In a statement on "U.S. Policy on East-West Trade" made in 1964, Professor Robert Loring Allen suggests that during the early 1950s "there were some rather far-out notions concerning economic war and the nature and effectiveness of the strategic embargo." According to him, this thinking was at the time: "Stop the Soviet Union from importing these items, and stop the economy. This seemed to be an easy solution, and as in the case of most easy solutions, quite incorrect." See [2, p. 214].

U.S.S.R. and China, but even Israel and Egypt can develop atomic capabilities.

Furthermore, as could have been foreseen at the very inception of the embargo, such a policy applied indiscriminately to a whole set of countries could only accentuate the dependence of some of the less endowed of these countries on the better endowed in the area. Indeed, the middle and lower East European tiers grew more dependent on the U.S.S.R. and on the more advanced East European countries. The embargo hit the former harder than the latter.[9] For a while — until the opening of new trading opportunities with the West — the embargo helped consolidate the monopoly positions within the bloc of the U.S.S.R. and the industrially advanced East European countries, strengthened the newly emergent trading patterns, reduced the less-developed countries of the area to captive markets of the more-developed countries of the bloc, and completed the loss of these markets for certain Western products. In turn, this policy provoked harassing strains among the Western countries themselves, which, as one report to Congress once put it, "marched always together though not always in perfect step." Last, the vast and costly machinery of the embargo could not prevent the U.S.S.R. and advanced countries of the area either from finding substitutes for the denied imports or from purchasing illegally on the Western markets various amounts of highly strategic goods; the penalty incurred in this case was higher prices rather than denial of goods.[10]

Thus, paradoxically, the policy in its initial phase, when the embargo was at its strongest, consolidated rather than weakened the Soviet Union's position in the bloc, facilitated rather than hampered its capacity to "displace" the output plans of the weaker countries of the CEMA group, and accelerated rather than retarded national drives toward heavy domestic industry building in each of these countries. On balance, these factors may ultimately have increased the capacity of the bloc to wage war. Even though the U.S.S.R. started in 1953 to liquidate its reparation claims and its joint-companies in Eastern Europe, it found itself in an enhanced economic position as the main supplier of raw materials for the expanding industries of the area and as the main importer of its machinery and equipment. Being also in the

---

[9] See my article [12, p. 126 and *passim*].

[10] By denying the benefits of international trade to the bloc, the United States imposed via the strategic embargo a cost on these countries. "That cost," Professor Allen correctly notes in the paper quoted previously, "can be measured precisely by the difference between what it costs the importing country to develop import substitutes for the previously imported products and the value of exports previously exported to pay for the imports, taking into account the delays and disturbances caused by the disruption of trade" [2, p. 213]. It is a large part of this cost that the U.S.S.R. was able to push on the shoulders of various East European countries, particularly in the early phase of the embargo; it was the East European countries who had to develop in particularly difficult conditions some of the import substitutes needed by the U.S.S.R.

position of supplying the West with grains, timber, and other commodities, the U.S.S.R. managed to cut through the nets of the embargo as none of the other East European countries could do.

Paradoxically again, during the second phase of the embargo, from 1954 on, the foreign trade of the area increased sharply, in no mean measure because the U.S.S.R. itself and some East European countries became able both to intensify further their own interchanges and at the same time to turn the tables and export to the West some of the strategic goods that had previously been banned from export to the East. In 1955, for instance, the U.S.S.R. exported to the West some 116,000 barrels of oil daily; in 1960, its exports rose to some 486,000 barrels a day and in 1965 to an estimated 1,020,000 barrels per day. By mid-1960, the Soviet Union was exporting to the West some $250–300 million worth of oil and oil products, and some $350–400 million worth of raw materials other than fuels. Rumania also became able to export fuels in significant quantities. In exchange, the U.S.S.R. obtained from the West not only some of the steel pipe needed for carrying its oil and oil products to the heart of Europe [11] but also new tankers for carrying these products all over the world.

The usual fallacy at the inception of the embargo seems to have been to assume that Soviet exports had no alternative markets or that the resources released because of the Western purchase restrictions could in no way help import substitution and the reorientation of these economies [2, p. 216]. After a very difficult initial period of readjustment and high cost of import substitution, foreign trade turnover, at current prices, grew over the transitional decade 1954–1963 at the yearly rate of over 8 percent for Poland; 9.5–10 percent for Czechoslovakia, East Germany, Hungary, and the U.S.S.R.; and over 10 and 15 percent for Rumania and Bulgaria, respectively. CEMA countries became exporters of armaments, oil, and machinery, notably to the underdeveloped areas; it is evident that great advances were made with respect to commodities previously considered in scarce supply in Eastern Europe.

Paradoxically, finally, the increasing relaxation of embargo controls in

[11] The so-called "Friendship Pipeline" connecting the Soviet oil fields to Poland, Czechoslovakia, and East Germany, and scheduled to branch out eventually toward Italy and France, was completed in late 1964 instead of early 1963 as originally planned. The embargo on 40-inch pipe, imposed by COCOM in 1962, cut the Soviet imports of large-gauge pipe from more than 300,000 tons in 1962 to 50,000 tons (supplied by Sweden). But, on the other hand, the Soviet Union stepped up its own production of 40-inch pipeline from zero in 1961 to 600,000 tons in 1965. From 1959 to 1962, Soviet purchases of pipe from Western Europe — notably Western Germany, Japan, and Sweden — totaled $150 million. The embargo on sales of large-gauge pipeline was lifted by COCOM in the fall of 1966 at the insistence of West Germany; the Soviet demand for pipe remains strong, *inter alia*, for the expansion of gas transmissions. See [7, September 17, 1966].

Western Europe did not bring about truly significant shifts in the respective overall relative shares of intra-CEMA and East-West trade in the total East European trade. A broader revision of the embargo in the early years of this second phase would perhaps have brought about a shift in the structure of the East European imports toward more strategic goods from the West rather than toward a spectacular increase in intra-CEMA trade. But for this purpose special credits were needed, and the West was neither ready nor willing to furnish them at the time. The United States has officially relaxed export controls toward all the CEMA countries since October 1966, waiving the previous requirements of industrial licensing for each transaction. But the East European countries may not necessarily be interested in the goods excepted henceforth from special licensing; moreover, the foreign trade planners may remain reluctant to spend their hard currency earnings in a country which, because of tariff bars, offers only a restricted market to their products.

While East-West trade may not necessarily expand much more rapidly in volume and value than it did in the early 1960s, the methodic relaxation of West European controls and of U.S. licensing procedures is already exercising some interesting effects on CEMA intra-trading. Up till the 1960s, Czechoslovakia and East Germany's industries, "sheltered" by the embargo restrictions, could and did maintain monopoly positions in the East European markets. They could supply high-priced, low-quality products, and find eager takers. The opening of alternative sources of supply for higher quality goods at lower prices "exposed" the inefficiency of certain CEMA industries, and forced policymakers, planners, and managers to drastic reorganizations to make them more competitive both within and outside CEMA. Thus, in its heyday the embargo cemented an apparently monolithic socialist bloc; at its ebb, paradoxically, it has helped to strengthen a variety of centrifugal tendencies within what appears to be an increasingly divided socialist camp.

V

Slowly but unmistakably, a new setting of East-West trade relations is emerging. A variety of changes is taking place in the foreign trade principles and practices of the U.S.S.R. and the other East European planned economies (excluding Albania). For more than a decade — from the mid-1950s to the mid-1960s — intensive discussions have centered on the question of prices in foreign trade, on the underlying problems of how an optimal export structure could be achieved for each state, and on how intra-CEMA prices could be determined. These discussions on the so-called effectiveness of foreign trade, which started usually from the assumption of a rigidly determined import level and structure, tried to establish criteria for rationally determining which goods to export — given the existing international price constellation — in order to obtain the foreign currency needed to cover the given imports.[12] After branching off into discussions on how to correct domestic prices to make them valid for foreign trade comparisons, the debate on prices has finally involved the problem of planning and managing the national economy as a whole as well as the problem of its underlying principles.

Along with these changes, an increasing readiness can be observed on the part of all these countries to search aggressively in and out of CEMA for markets for their industrial products and for fuels and raw materials in scarce supply in the area. Clearly, the efforts to turn CEMA into a supranational, all-around coordinating-planning body of either output or foreign trade have failed. As a Czech deputy premier once put it, bilateral and multilateral paths of action are easily combined in the *preparation* of plan coordination in the area; in the *actual realization* of the cooperation required, the application of one path or the other depends "on the nature of the matter" on hand. Multilateralism has been applied to clearing in convertible rubles within certain limits, to power systems linking, and to associations among three or four countries for given outputs, lending or marketing. Bilateral agreements have continued, however, to dominate all the rest, including basic aspects of foreign trade.[13]

The ongoing changes in planning principles and methods, and the overhauling of foreign trade practices, do not, of course, mean that price considerations alone will shape the foreign trade of even the most developed countries of the area or those most vitally interested in foreign trade, such as East Germany and Czechoslovakia. As the central planners attempt to free their foreign trade companies from dependence on an inflexible domestic output-import plan and let them be guided by the market and by price considerations, and as the planners increase the flexibility in output to cope with the requirements of Western markets, they in turn may have to resort to wide use of the traditional array of tariffs, export taxes, subsidies, and exchange rate manipulations to control, up to a point, the level and composition of their trade, as the market-directed economies do.

On the other hand, the end of supranational coordination in CEMA does not mean that the U.S.S.R. does not retain important levers for influencing the foreign trade flows into each of the countries. In the early 1950s, given the key position it secured in the area after the war, the U.S.S.R. was instrumental in developing there high-cost production and overdiversification in keeping with its own requirements for a variety of machines, equipment, and other products. After industrialization of these countries along parallel

[12] For an illuminating discussion on the early price debates in foreign trade, see [13, pp. 41 ff.]; see also [9, Chap. V, pp. 131 ff.].

[13] See interview with Deputy Premier D. Simunek [11].

lines had led area trade into numerous snags, the U.S.S.R. tried to bring about a more rational allocation of resources via intra-CEMA coordination. This ran afoul of the national goals of a country like Rumania and the diverging orientations of the other countries of the area. A third phase of Soviet-CEMA relations was then started. As the U.S.S.R. remains the key supplier of crucial raw materials for all these countries (including Rumania), it started to exercise a serious impact not only on intra-bloc prices, but on trade flows as well. The U.S.S.R. might, in fact, be increasingly inclined in the future to encourage the development of a wide variety of temporary or more permanent triangular arrangements involving itself, a CEMA country, and another CEMA or non-CEMA partner. In such an arrangement, the recipient of imports of Soviet fuel and raw materials would compensate with exports of machinery or raw materials to third countries in whose exports the Soviet Union itself would be interested.[14]

While these changes are taking place in the East, significant changes are also occurring in the West. Attempts to unify Western European trading policies with respect to Eastern Europe as a whole have not been successful except in some cases, the most conspicuous of which have been agricultural products.[15] Broader U.S.–West European unification attempts, with respect to credit policies toward the East, have also apparently not met with success.[16] Trade with the East continues to be dominated by agreements between pairs of Western and Eastern countries specifying goods and trade conditions, including tariffs and credits. But within this framework, each of the Western partners feels free to make its own assessment of the changes occurring in the East and to act accordingly. The United States is reducing its export restrictions and orienting itself toward a flexible employment of MFN in its relations with each East European country. The major West European countries are attempting to increase significantly their shares in the opening markets for consumers' durables and for the re-equipment of light industries in the CEMA countries. The latter, which already play a significant role in the foreign trade of some West European countries, are in all likelihood going to increase significantly this share, particularly in the foreign trade of such countries as Italy (Table 6).

Paradoxically, while changes in Eastern Europe's foreign trade practices, as related to the West, are largely (though not exclusively, of course) con-

[14] Such arrangements have been made in the past but on a limited scale. See [9, pp. 193 ff.].

[15] The EEC common regulations concerning agrarian policy which became effective in 1962 have severely affected Polish and Hungarian exports to the Common Market. Thus, for instance, charges on Polish eggs rose from $50 per ton in 1961 to $340 per ton in 1964.

[16] Cf. the U.S. suggestions at the Paris OECD meetings in November 1966 [7, November 25, 1966].

TABLE 6

CEMA'S SHARE IN THE FOREIGN TRADE OF INDIVIDUAL
WEST EUROPEAN COUNTRIES (1953 AND 1963)
(Percentages)

Country	Exports f.o.b.		Imports c.i.f.	
	1953	1963	1953	1963
EEC,[a]	2.0	2.9	1.6	3.4
of which				
Italy	3.9	5.3	1.9	5.6
Western Germany[a]	1.2	3.0	1.7	3.5
France	1.4	2.8	1.0	2.9
Belgium-Luxembourg	2.9	1.5	1.7	2.2
Netherlands	2.6	1.5	2.2	2.0
EFTA[b] and Finland,	3.5	4.8	4.0	4.7
of which				
Finland	30.4	20.5	34.1	20.8
Austria	10.9	14.9	10.8	12.0
Sweden	4.5	4.2	3.8	4.6
Denmark	4.9	4.3	3.9	4.0
Norway	6.3	4.3	4.4	2.8
United Kingdom[b]	0.6	3.0	2.2	3.6
Rest of Western Europe,	5.7	12.4	2.3	8.0
of which				
Yugoslavia	....	26.7	....	22.8
Iceland	20.0	17.3	9.1	17.7
Greece	6.4	19.9	1.3	8.5
Turkey	7.4	9.6	5.5	7.3
Total, Western Europe[a, b]	2.8	4.0	2.8	4.3

[a] Excluding trade between Eastern and Western Germany.
[b] Excluding re-exports from the United Kingdom.
SOURCE: *Economic Bulletin for Europe*, XVII:1 (November 1965), p. 46.

ditioned by economic necessities, the Western changes in relation to the East are in principle advocated primarily for the sake of political necessities. Referring to the Soviet Union's foreign trade policy, a U.S. document contrasts the Soviet intra-CEMA trade with her trade with the West, as follows:

In terms of this general direction of trade policy, therefore, it is fair to assert that, by contrast, the trade of the U.S.S.R. with the countries of the industrial West has been marked by a motivation that has been more economic than political [4, p. 939].

The already quoted *Special Committee on U.S. Trade Relations with East European Countries and the Soviet Union* (the Miller Report) states for its part:

In sum, trade with European Communist countries is politics in the broadest sense — holding open the possibility of careful negotiations, firm bargaining, and constructive competition. . . . Trade should be brought into the policy arena. It should be offered or withheld, purposefully and systematically, as opportunities and circumstances warrant [10, pp. 3 and 10].

In the view of the special Committee, the entrusting of MFN permission or denial to executive decision corresponds indeed to the need for rapid, discretionary, and selective decisionmaking in relation to the East. Economics and politics thus intermingle in a way that renders questionable the fine distinction drawn by some United Nations experts between "politically motivated" export restrictions and "economically motivated" import restrictions. As a result of this intermingling, some East European countries might fare better because of the easing of restrictions on the U.S. market for *political* reasons, while at the same time faring worse in the Common Market for *economic* reasons, such as discrimination through the common external tariff (for instance, Poland for its farm products).

Whatever each specific case may be, increased flexibility in output patterns and trade practices in the East and increased flexibility in trade inducement and trade denial in the West should combine henceforth in a wide variety of ways to shape new settings for East-West trade in the 1970s.

DISCUSSION

Morris Bornstein

Professor Spulber's paper provides a concise review and appraisal of the evolution of the NATO countries' strategic trade controls and of concurrent changes in the levels and patterns of East-West trade and intra-CEMA trade.[17] Because I am in general agreement with his analysis and his conclusions, my comments will focus on some differences in interpretation and on some suggestions for further work on the subject.

The paper distinguishes three phases in the evolution of the strategic trade control system. (1) From 1948 to 1953, in a period of increasing world tension and bipolarization into Eastern and Western blocs, a comprehensive scheme of export controls was developed by the NATO countries at the initiative of the United States. (2) From 1954 to 1965, as East-West relations gradually improved and as increasing differentiation among Communist countries became evident, the lists of embargoed goods were steadily reduced. During this period, however, the United States followed a more

[17] For convenience, I refer to the members of the COCOM strategic trade control system as "the NATO countries," although this is not strictly correct, because COCOM is not formally a part of NATO and because it excludes one member of NATO (Iceland) and includes Japan. Similarly, I refer to the grouping of the U.S.S.R. and the East European Communist countries as "CEMA."

restrictive policy than its allies, by embargoing various goods not covered in the NATO embargo, by restricting the extension of credits to the CEMA countries while other NATO countries permitted them, and by applying a complete embargo against the Far Eastern Communist countries. (3) In 1966, in an effort to improve Soviet-American relations and to encourage the East European Communist countries to act more independently of the U.S.S.R., the United States relaxed its restrictions on exports to the CEMA countries, bringing them much closer to those of its allies.[18]

In examining these developments, Professor Spulber finds a number of "paradoxes": (1) In its first phase, the embargo consolidated the U.S.S.R.'s position vis-à-vis the East European Communist countries and accelerated efforts to develop heavy industry in each CEMA country, thereby indirectly contributing in some measure to building up an industrial base for military strength. (2) In the second phase of the embargo, the CEMA countries even began to export to the West some goods previously embargoed by NATO as "strategic," notably oil. (3) During this period, the relaxation of the embargo did not lead to "truly significant" shifts in the trade of CEMA countries from intra-CEMA trade to East-West trade. (4) In summary, "in its heyday the embargo cemented an apparently monolithic socialist bloc; at its ebb, paradoxically, it has helped to strengthen a variety of centrifugal tendencies within what appears to be an increasingly divided socialist camp."

While our differences of interpretation may be only semantic, I do not consider these developments in the strategic embargo to be as "paradoxical" as Professor Spulber does.[19] (1) The strategic embargo was imposed to retard the build-up of military and economic power in what was then generally regarded as a unified "bloc" of hostile nations, rather than to split this "bloc." It was to be assumed, however, that the CEMA countries would attempt, as part of their industrialization programs, to reorient their economies as best they could to meet the impact of the embargo. (2) Soviet and Rumanian oil exports do not appear to me to be surprising in the light of these countries' natural resource endowments, their export patterns in the 1930s, and the greater ease of breaking into world markets for fuels and raw materials than into markets for more sophisticated manufactured goods. (3) It would have been somewhat optimistic to expect a major reversal in trade patterns when embargo restrictions were relaxed in the middle of the 1950s. On the one hand, the reorientation of production and trade which the Communist countries had undertaken could not be easily reversed; and in any case the CEMA countries were still engaged in an effort, under Soviet aegis, to develop

---

[18] However, the United States still has a more restrictive policy on credits to the European Communist countries, and it continues its complete embargo against the Far Eastern Communist countries and its virtually complete embargo against Cuba.

[19] *Webster's New Collegiate Dictionary* defines a paradox as "A tenet contrary to received opinion; also, an assertion or sentiment seemingly contradictory, or opposed to common sense, but that yet may be true in fact."

their "socialist world market" through closer coordination of trade and production. On the other hand, the NATO countries did not accompany the reduction of export restrictions with offers of credit — which to the present remains a key requisite for the expansion of East-West trade. (4) It does not appear to me to be coincidental or paradoxical that Western export restrictions should be relaxed at a time when Communist East Europe is characterized by increasing diversity in economic organization, international politics, and foreign economic policy. Rather, one purpose of the relaxation is precisely to encourage such diversity and to try to influence it along certain lines.

In short, while I concur on the whole with Professor Spulber's account of what has happened and why, I find these developments more consistent and less paradoxical than he does.

In any case, although it is not possible to measure precisely the impact of the strategic embargo on the evolution of East-West trade and on the economic development of the CEMA countries, its importance should not be overestimated. Western analysts generally hold that the embargo had its greatest impact in the early 1950s, and that by, say, 1956 it was no longer a dominant factor in East-West trade [9, pp. 164–170]. Even during the "first phase" from 1948 to 1953, the embargo was only one of a number of factors altering East-West trade. Other factors, as Professor Spulber points out, were the key position that the U.S.S.R. acquired in East European trade, the consequences of national industrialization programs, and, last but not least, the deliberate decision of the CEMA countries to trade among themselves.

Since the relaxation of Western export restrictions in the middle 1950s, the chief obstacles to the expansion of East-West trade have included the Communist countries' continued though unsuccessful efforts to integrate production and trade in CEMA, the lack of Eastern export products that could compete in Western markets, the inexperience of the CEMA countries' foreign trade organizations in selling to the West, the limited amount of Western credits, problems in extending most-favored-nation (MFN) treatment to state-trading nations, the CEMA preference for bilateralism, and the like. Because NATO export restrictions are now so relatively insignificant, their further relaxation cannot have much impact on East-West trade, although further elimination of restrictions may have a symbolic value as a gesture of good will. The subjects for real negotiations concerning East-West trade are, instead, credits, multilateralism, and Eastern reciprocity for Western MFN treatment.

In conclusion, I should like to point out that the strategic trade control system itself is an interesting attempt at central planning of international trade, which, so far as I know, has not been thoroughly analyzed and appraised by independent scholars. Among the questions that seem worthy of investigation are the following: How sound have been the criteria for defining strategic goods? How sensibly and consistently have they been applied to the thousands of items covered at different times by the embargo? How effectively has the embargo been enforced? How important has the more restrictive U.S. embargo been in denying the Communist countries goods that they could not buy in Western Europe? These questions involve various aspects of "plan construction," "plan implementation," "the effectiveness of foreign trade," and the like. It is interesting to speculate whether a careful study of this case of central planning of Western foreign trade would yield a more favorable evaluation than that usually accorded central planning of Eastern foreign trade.

REFERENCES

1. Dudinskii, I. *Voprosy ekonomiki*, No. 4 (1966); translation in *American Review of Soviet and Eastern European Foreign Trade*, II:5 (September–October 1966), pp. 84–94.
2. *East-West Trade: A Compilation of Views of Businessmen, Bankers and Academic Experts*, U.S. Congress, Senate Committee on Foreign Relations (Washington D.C.: 1964).
3. Herman, Leon M. *A Background Study on East-West Trade*, U.S. Congress, Senate Committee on Foreign Relations (Washington D.C.: 1965).
4. ————. "Soviet Foreign Trade and the United States Market," U.S. Congress, Joint Economic Committee, *New Directions In The Soviet Economy* (Washington D.C.: 1966), Part IV, pp. 935–946.
5. McKitterick, Nathaniel. *East-West Trade: The Background of U.S. Policy* (New York: The Twentieth Century Fund, 1966).
6. Metzger, Stanley D. "Federal Regulation and Prohibition of Trade with Iron Curtain Countries," *Law and Contemporary Problems*, XXIX:4 (Autumn 1964), pp. 1000–1018.
7. *The New York Times*.
8. "Note on Post-war Developments in East European Trade," United Nations, *Economic Bulletin for Europe*, XVI:2 (Geneva: 1964).
9. Pryor, Frederic L. *The Communist Foreign Trade System* (Cambridge: Massachusetts Institute of Technology Press, 1963).
10. *The Report to the President of the Special Committee on U.S. Trade Relations with East European Countries and the Soviet Union* (April 29, 1965).
11. *Rude Pravo*, February 12, 1964.
12. Spulber, Nicolas. "Effects of the Embargo on Soviet Trade," *Harvard Business Review*, XXX:6 (November–December 1952), pp. 122–128.
13. Svendsen, Knud Erik. "Notes on the Economic Relations between the East European Countries," *Economy and Economics of the East European Countries, Development and Applicability*, Ost Okonomi, Special Number (Oslo: Norwegian Institute of International Affairs, 1961).
14. "Trade Expansion and Regional Groupings," in *Proceedings of the United Nations Conference on Trade and Development, Geneva, 23 March–16 June 1964*, VI, Part I (New York: United Nations, 1964).

Socialist Industrialization and Trade in Machinery Products:

An Analysis Based on the Experience of Bulgaria, Poland, and Rumania*

JOHN M. MONTIAS

Perhaps the most powerful single force determining the level of trade among the members of the Council for Economic Mutual Assistance (CEMA) is the net import demand for manufactured goods on the part of the U.S.S.R. and the less-developed members of the organization. Whenever the demand for machinery and industrial consumer goods is buoyant, as in 1949–1953 and again in 1958–1963, total trade expands at a rapid pace; whenever it flags, as in 1953–1957 and in 1964–1965, the expansion of trade slows down.[1] The more advanced industrial countries of CEMA, Czechoslovakia and East Germany, are largely dependent for their prosperity on the strength of their partners' demand for manufactured products. It is of some importance, therefore, to gain insight into the determinants of this demand, especially for machinery products, which at one time made up the near-totality of exchanges in manufactures within CEMA and still represent the majority of these exchanges today.

The capacity of the machine-building industries in the less-developed countries of Eastern Europe, particularly in Rumania and Bulgaria, was still quite small when the first long-term plans were launched after World War II; hence, the inflated demand for equipment resulting from high rates of investment in the national economy had to be met, in the initial years,

* I am grateful to Mr. Jozef van Brabant for verifying my calculations and for his assistance at various points in this paper.

[1] I will not attempt here to support this conjecture, which is based on my previous analysis of trade trends in CEMA. For some evidence, see [6].

largely from imports. During the first period of intensive industrialization, starting with 1949–1950, as a result mainly of lavish investments incorporating recent technical progress and of generous allocations of skilled and semi-skilled manpower, the machine-building industry in all Soviet-type economies grew at a very rapid pace — typically, 15 to 25 percent per year.[2] The principal question I wish to study in this paper is what happens to imports of equipment as industrialization proceeds and the capacity of the domestic machine-building industry expands.

The present study is a crude first attempt to explore the problem. The organization of the paper reflects its tentative, experimental nature: I first examine *prima facie* evidence to identify the proximate causes of fluctuations in the machinery trade of Bulgaria, Poland, and Rumania. Subsequently, I construct a simple model of import substitution to gain insight into the more deeply embedded forces acting on trade. Finally, I single out Rumanian development from 1950 to 1965 for the purpose of comparing the model with "reality," insofar as I have been able to ascertain it.

I must at once acknowledge that I could find no satisfactory way of determining the demand for imported machinery or the supply of raw materials and foodstuffs for export due to international specialization *within* these branches. Deepening specialization among CEMA members causes each country's imports and exports of machinery and primary products to be higher than they would otherwise be. But it has only a minor effect on the net surplus or deficit in these trading categories. To get around this problem, I shall attempt, wherever possible, to analyze trends in net machinery imports and in net exports of primary products (i.e., in imports minus exports in each group).[3]

TRADE PATTERNS

Rumania, Poland, and Bulgaria — the least developed members of CEMA, now that Albania has been excluded from the organization — all had a net deficit in imports of machinery during the 1950s and early 1960s. (In 1964, for the first time, Poland became a net exporter of capital goods.)

From the data in Table 1 it appears that in Poland and Rumania both net and gross machinery imports increased rapidly in the first years of industrialization and then fell off. In Poland imports reached their peak in 1951, in Rumania in 1953. The subsequent declines were steep and prolonged in

[2] For data on Rumania, see Table 7 below.
[3] Specialization will affect the net demand for imported machinery and equipment to the extent that more efficient, specialized production will make it possible to release labor and materials that can be used to expand exports. For the purposes of my model, it is immaterial whether a reduction in input coefficients is brought about by technical progress or by specialization.

the two countries. In Bulgaria, by contrast, the cycle was of much smaller amplitude: imports rose slowly until 1953, then remained more or less at the same level until 1955, after which they resumed their upward climb. In all three countries a sharp acceleration in the expansion of gross imports occurred after 1958–1959. The level of these imports peaked out in Poland

TABLE 1

EXTERNAL TRADE IN MACHINERY OF BULGARIA, POLAND, AND RUMANIA

(Millions of U.S. dollars at foreign exchange prices)

	Bulgaria (1955 prices until 1960, current prices thereafter)		Poland (1955 prices until 1955, current prices thereafter)		Rumania (Current prices)	
				Surplus (+)		
Year	Machinery and Equipment Imports	Deficit (−) in Machinery Trade	Machinery and Equipment Imports	or Deficit (−) in Machinery Trade	Machinery and Equipment Imports	Deficit (−) in Machinery Trade
1949	51	− 51	154	−139	n.a.[a]	n.a.
1950	52	− 52	216	−167	90	− 81
1951	60	− 60	313	−261	81	n.a.
1952	62	− 58	310	−240	131	−118
1953	76	− 72	319	−218	162	−133
1954	78	− 73	294	−198	108	− 78
1955	77	− 71	288	−167	97	− 71
1956	97	− 82	339	−185	72	− 32
1957	101	− 73	300	−102	68	− 29
1958	131	−100	328	− 43	125	− 69
1959	226	−170	390	− 89	113	− 85
1960	273	−195	405	− 34	211	− 92
1961	311	−208	491	− 70	330	−203
1962	355	−205	627	−133	408	−261
1963	428	−248	675	− 89	427	−276
1964	443	−209	635	+ 67	458	−276
1965	515	−224	767	+ 1	420	−216

[a] Not available.

NOTE: As a result of changes in the method of recording trade, the data for Poland for the years 1949–1955, for Rumania for 1950–1957, and for Bulgaria for 1949–1957 are not fully comparable with those for later years.

SOURCES AND METHODS: *Bulgaria*: 1949–1957: G. Popisakov, *Vŭnshna tŭrgovia na N.R. Bŭlgaria* (Sofia: 1959), pp. 95, 122; 1958–1962: *Vŭnshna tŭrgovia na N.R. Bulgaria: Statisticheski sbornik* (Sofia: 1963); 1963–1964: United Nations, Economic Commission for Europe, *Economic Survey of Europe in 1964* (Geneva: 1965), Chapter I, p. 46. *Poland*: 1949–1955: based on total imports and exports at 1955 prices in *Polska w liczbach 1944–1958* (Warsaw: 1959), p. 40, and on the percentage breakdown of trade at 1955 prices in *Rocznik statystyczny 1956* (Warsaw: 1956), p. 248; 1956–1960: *Rocznik statystyczny 1961* (Warsaw: 1961), p. 268; 1961–1965: *Rocznik statystyczny 1966* (Warsaw: 1966), pp. 356–357. *Rumania*: sources and notes to Tables 2 and 9, Chapter 3, J. M. Montias, *Economic Development in Communist Rumania* (Cambridge, Mass.: Massachusetts Institute of Technology Press, 1967).

TABLE 2

INVESTMENTS IN DOMESTICALLY PRODUCED MACHINERY
IN BULGARIA, POLAND, AND RUMANIA, 1949–1956
(Millions of national currency units at constant domestic prices)

Year	Investments in Domestically Produced Machinery			Same Investments as a Percentage of Total Investment in Machinery and Equipment		
	Bulgaria[a]	*Poland*	*Rumania*	*Bulgaria*	*Poland*	*Rumania*
1949	36	n.a.[b]	n.a.	6	n.a.	n.a.
1950	105	10,130	1,032	16	80	50.8
1951	311	8,430	1,663	27	70	58.2
1952	437	11,860	2,111	38	77	59.4
1953	394	14,660	2,804	31	80	63.5
1954	404	18,560	2,782	37	84	73.2
1955	587	20,240	3,210	42	86	74.5
1956	572	20,440	3,279	41	84	76.8

[a] "Limited" investments only. (Limited investments in equipment and structures came to 82 percent of all investments in 1950.) All data are expressed in post-1952, pre-1963 levas.
[b] Not available.
SOURCES AND METHODS: *Bulgaria*: all investment data for 1949 to 1956 and investments in domestically produced equipment from 1953 to 1956 are from *Razvitie narodnogo khoziaistva Narodnoi Respubliki Bolgarii (Statisticheskie pokazateli)* (Moscow: 1958), p. 95; 1949 to 1953: total machinery imports from 1949 to 1953, in 1955 foreign exchange prices, are given in G. Popisakov, *Vŭnshna tŭrgovia na N.R. Bŭlgaria* (Sofia: 1959), p. 99. It was assumed that the 1953 ratio of machinery imports in foreign trade prices to "limited" investments in domestically produced equipment also held in earlier years. On this assumption, imports in foreign-exchange levas were converted into domestic levas and subtracted from total investments to arrive at the value of investments in domestically produced equipment for the years 1949 to 1952. *Poland*: the value of imported equipment at domestic prices was available only for 1956 from a percentage in V. Wacker and B. Malý (eds.), *Mezinárodni socialistická dĕlba prace* (Prague: 1964), p. 200. The same method was used as for Bulgaria to estimate these data for other years, starting from the series of investments in machinery and equipment in 1961 prices in *Rocznik statystyczny 1961* (Warsaw: 1961), p. 71, and the import statistics in Table 1 above. *Rumania*: 1950 to 1956. *Anuarul statistic al Republicii Socialiste România, 1965* (Bucharest: 1965), pp. 344–345.

and in Rumania after 1962, but continued to expand in Bulgaria until at least 1964.[4]

Exports of machinery followed a steady upward course throughout the entire period under consideration (1949 to 1965). Since exports were much larger in the second spurt of accelerated growth than in the first, the deficits in the machinery group became smaller relative to imports in all three countries (in Poland, absolutely smaller in the second than in the first).

[4] After 1962 the expansion of trade in machinery products slowed down in the entire CEMA area. The volume of exchanges of machinery products within CEMA rose by 22.2 percent from 1961 to 1962, by 13.5 percent from 1962 to 1963, by 9.4 percent from 1963 to 1964, and by 6.4 percent from 1964 to 1965 [12, p. 14].

Why did imports of machinery in Poland begin to flag as early as 1951, while they continued to grow in Rumania and in Bulgaria until 1953? Why was the recession in these imports so deep and long-lasting in Rumania and so mild in Poland and Bulgaria? The answers to these questions hinge in part on the total volume of investments and on the capacity of the machine-building industry in each of these countries.

One measure of a country's capacity to produce the type of equipment called for in the investment program is the ratio of domestically produced investment goods to total investments in machinery. In Table 2 I have esti-mated these ratios for the initial round of post-war industrialization, along with the trends in the domestic production of investment goods in the period 1949–1956.

While the statistics for Bulgaria and Poland for earlier years are subject to some degree of error,[5] I believe that the shares in total investments in machinery and equipment of home-produced capital goods are sufficiently disparate in the three countries to help explain why the turning points in their imports occurred in the order they did. Poland, which was already producing some four-fifths of all the equipment invested in her economy in 1950, was obviously more capable of reducing her dependency on machinery imports in a short time by the further expansion of her industry than Ru-mania, which started off by importing approximately half of her investment needs, and *a fortiori* more capable than Bulgaria, which imported nearly all the equipment she needed for her investments in 1949. In the case of Poland, unfortunately, these differences are obfuscated by the effects of the Korean War, which was probably responsible for reducing the absolute level of total investments in machinery and equipment in 1951, as domestic productive capacities were shifted to defense production.[6]

Imports of machinery were also conditioned by the policy in force in each country to protect the domestic machine-building industry from fluctuations in the total level of investments. Rumanian statistics available on a com-

[5] The assumption that the ratio of total machinery imports to investment in imported equipment was the same in 1949 to 1952 as in 1953 (in the case of Bulgaria) and in 1950 to 1955 as in 1956 (in the case of Poland) is not strictly accurate. For one thing, imports of machinery in the Korean War years may have included armored cars, planes, and other products of the armaments industry, which did not enter into invest-ments. For another, a higher proportion of machinery imports is believed to have been stockpiled in 1954–1955 than in 1950–1951 in Poland as well as in Bulgaria. The absolute drop in investments in domestically produced equipment in Poland in 1951 is particularly suspicious. It may be that imports of machinery in that year contained a large proportion of items not destined for investment purposes, which when subtracted from total investments in machinery and equipment artificially reduced the estimates of the domestically produced component of this total. Such an underestimation, how-ever, would reinforce rather than weaken the comparison with Rumania in the text below.

[6] This shift toward the production of armaments was undoubtedly more pronounced in Poland than in the "ex-enemy" countries, Rumania and Bulgaria.

parable basis for an extended period throw light on the planners' strategy of using machinery imports as a complementary source of supply, which could be compressed or expanded at will, depending on the state of the balance of payments or of the total level of investments contemplated.

In Fig. 1 I have plotted data for fifteen years on the volume of Rumanian investments in machinery and equipment, both imported and of domestic origin.[7] The data were also fitted to semi-logarithmic trend lines, the simplest functional relation capable of approximating the plotted points. The three equations corresponding to these regressions are the following:

$$\log I = 3.29 + 0.059X$$
$$(0.008)$$
$$\log P = 3.08 + 0.066X$$
$$(0.007)$$
$$\log M = 2.83 + 0.049X$$
$$(0.012)$$

where X is any year between 1950 and 1965, I is the volume of investments in machinery and equipment, P is the domestic component of these investments, and M is the imported component. (The standard deviations of the regression coefficients are shown in parentheses.)

The percentage deviations of data from the trend lines were then calculated for all three variables. The deviations from trend for the imported machinery and for the domestically produced components of investments were separately regressed on the deviations from trend of total investments in machinery and equipment. The results are shown below:

$$\hat{P} = 0.53 + 0.55 \, \hat{I}$$
$$(0.13)$$
$$\hat{M} = 10.13 + 2.14 \, \hat{I}$$
$$(0.28)$$

where a "hat" over the symbols denotes a percentage deviation from trend.

The regression coefficients in the last two equations indicate that fluctuations in investments in machinery and equipment have had a moderate influence on domestically produced investments but a very powerful impact on imports. Thus imports bore the brunt of fluctuations in investments, both in the downward (1953–1958) and in the upward (1961–1963) direction.[8]

[7] I am grateful to Professor Pong S. Lee for running these regressions and those that follow.

[8] The immediate consequences of the New Course in Bulgaria and Poland were similar to those just observed in Rumania. From 1953 to 1954, investments in imported equipment fell (by 24 percent in Bulgaria, by 8 percent in Poland, and by over 30 percent in Rumania), while investments in domestically produced equipment stayed approximately constant in the two Balkan countries and rose by 26 percent in Poland. The upswing in investments after 1958 caused the proportion of imported machinery

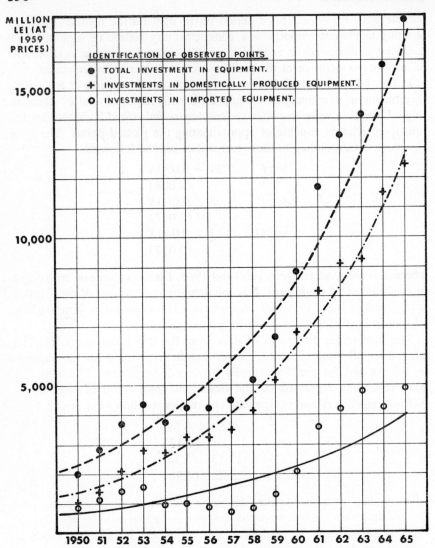

FIG.1–VOLUME OF RUMANIAN INVESTMENTS IN MACHINERY AND EQUIPMENT, IMPORTED AND DOMESTIC, 1950–1965

The effective demand for imported machinery on the part of the under-developed Communist countries was also influenced by the credits they received from the Soviet Union and from Czechoslovakia, and by their ability to pay for machinery with surpluses in other commodity groups, especially in raw materials, semifabricates, and foodstuffs. The data in Table 3 on surpluses in non-manufactured goods and on the overall balance of merchandise trade — whose year-to-year changes presumably reflect variations in the capital account of the balance of payments and in the balance of receipts and outlays on tourism and shipping — throw light on the fluctuations in machinery imports of the three industrializing countries.

The "improvement" in the balance of trade of all three countries during the years of the New Course, starting with 1953–1954, corresponded to a reduction in their exogenous sources of foreign exchange. Thus, from 1954 to 1956, Bulgaria and Rumania had to use their surpluses in the raw materials and foodstuffs groups to cover a positive trade balance, in addition to financing their net imports of manufactured goods. Except for 1953, Poland continued to run an overall deficit, although a much smaller one than in the early 1950s. These changes in the balance of trade were apparently related to the repayment of debts incurred by these nations in the first years of their post-war industrialization program.[9]

The New Course seems to have had a more powerful impact on Rumania's trade than on Bulgaria's or Poland's. Machinery imports, as we have seen, plummeted after 1953 in Rumania, while they rather stagnated than declined in the other two countries. Almost the entire drop in the Rumanian deficit in

in total investments to rise again in Bulgaria and in Rumania; however, the long-run trend in the substitution of domestic for imported equipment kept the ratios from reaching the peaks attained in the early 1950s. In Poland, the long-run trend was strong enough to prevent the ratio from rising at all, even though the absolute level of machinery imports still went up in the early 1960s. In 1961, a year from which we have apparently reliable data for all three countries, the import ratio stood at 67 percent for Bulgaria (compared with an average of 78 percent from 1949 to 1951), at 11.9 percent in Poland (24 percent from 1950 to 1952), and at 30.9 percent in Rumania (44 percent from 1950 to 1952). For Poland the ratio for 1961 is given in [20, p. 260].

[9] The possibility cannot be ruled out that the curtailment of machinery imports, some of which were normally bought on credit, was a cause as well as an effect of the apparent decline in net borrowing. However, the fact that Bulgaria's balance radically "improved" in 1954, 1955, and 1956, whereas her imports of machinery remained approximately constant, suggests that the apparent change in the capital account was exogenous rather than related endogenously to the level of imports.

The above speculations are based on the reasonable assumption that the balance of trade in "invisible items" (tourism, shipping, insurance, etc.) did not shift in such a way as to render them invalid. There is also some arbitrariness in computing a balance of trade from imports and exports measured at constant prices, as I have done for Bulgaria and Poland for the period 1949–1955. However, price changes in foreign trade affected only the magnitude, not the general direction, of the changes in the overall trade balance discussed in the text. (In Poland, the positive shift in the balance of trade from 1952 to 1953 was even stronger in current than in constant prices.)

TABLE 3

SURPLUSES AND DEFICITS IN "HARD GOODS" (RAW MATERIALS,
SEMIFABRICATES, AND FOODSTUFFS) AND THE TRADE BALANCE
OF BULGARIA, POLAND, AND RUMANIA, 1949–1965
(Millions of U.S. dollars at foreign exchange prices)

Year	Bulgaria (1955 prices until 1960, current prices thereafter)		Poland (1955 prices until 1955, current prices thereafter)		Rumania (Current prices)	
	Surplus (+) or Deficit (−) in Hard Goods	Total Surplus (+) or Deficit (−) in Merchandise Trade	Surplus (+) or Deficit (−) in Hard Goods	Total Surplus (+) or Deficit (−) in Merchandise Trade	Surplus (+) or Deficit (−) in Hard Goods	Total Surplus (+) or Deficit (−) in Merchandise Trade
1949	− 27.8	− 81.2	+140.8	+ 29.3	n.a.[a]	+ 2.2
1950	+ 40.7	− 17.0	+165.0	+ 30.2	+ 64.0	− 31.0
1951	+ 58.0	− 3.1	+146.1	−110.1	+ 43.5	− 9.3
1952	+ 72.7	+ 13.1	+128.6	− 82.3	+ 90.0[b]	− 28.2
1953	+ 72.6	− 1.8	+170.1	+ 13.7	+ 89.0	− 42.8
1954	+ 93.1	+ 26.2	+133.3	− 19.0	+ 98.3[b]	+ 13.0
1955	+ 77.4	+ 34.7	+130.2	− 12.1	+ 89.6	+ 9.0
1956	+134.1	+109.9	+122.1	− 37.1	+ 82.6	+ 5.0
1957	+ 52.0	+ 56.9	−164.9	−276.5	n.a.	− 6.2
1958	+ 81.6	+ 6.7	− 79.6	−167.5	+ 58.8	− 13.3
1959	+ 90.0	− 32.3	−160.3	−274.5	+ 86.0	+ 22.2
1960	+ 80.1	− 61.1	−188.5	−169.5	+152.3	+ 69.1
1961	+134.8	− 3.4	−186.2	−183.1	+176.9	− 22.2
1962	+113.6	− 10.3	−175.0	−239.3	+133.4	−123.1
1963	+123.1	− 76.1	−223.7	−209.0	+166.3	−107.0
1964	+ 87.0	− 82.0	−189.3	+ 24.2	+ 90.0	−168.0
1965	+128.0	+ 1.0	−229.6	−112.5	+190.0	+ 24.3

[a] Not available.
[b] Estimates.

SOURCES: *Bulgaria*: 1949–1957: G. Popisakov, *Vŭnshna tŭrgovia na N.R. Bŭlgaria* (Sofia: 1959), pp. 95, 122; 1958–1962: Tsentral'no statistichesko upravlenie, *Vŭnshna tŭrgovia na N.R. Bŭlgaria: statisticheski sbornik* (Sofia: 1963); 1963: *Ikonomichesko i sotsialno razvitie na NRB* (Bŭlgarska akademiya na naukite) (Sofia: 1964), p. 264; 1964–1965: *Zahraniční obchod*, No. 9 (1966), pp. 8–9. *Poland*: total imports and exports from 1949 to 1955, in 1955 prices, are from *Polska w liczbach 1944–1958* (Warsaw: 1959), p. 40; the commodity breakdown of trade, in 1955 prices, for 1949 to 1955 is from *Rocznik statystyczny 1956*, p. 248. All other data are from *Rocznik statystyczny 1966*, pp. 356–357. *Rumania*: sources to Tables 3.18 and 3.19 in J. M. Montias, *Economic Development in Communist Rumania* (Cambridge, Mass.: Massachusetts Institute of Technology Press, 1967).

the machinery group — roughly $60 million from 1953 to 1954–1955 — may be explained by the change in the balance of trade, from a deficit of nearly $43 million in 1953 to an average surplus of $11 million in 1954–1955.[10] The surplus in trade in raw materials and foodstuffs remained at approximately the same level from 1952 to 1956. If the New Course policy favoring an improvement in consumers' living standards had an effect on the composition of trade, it was rather on the relative importance of producer and consumer goods in exports and in imports than on the surplus in "hard goods," as the following figures,[11] expressed in millions of U.S. dollars, indicate. Rumania's surplus (+) and deficit (−) in producer and consumer goods were as follows:

Year	*Producer Goods*			*Consumer Goods*		
	Machines	Raw Mate- rials	Total	Food stuffs	Industrial Consumer Goods	Total
1953	−133	+41	−92	+48	+ 2	+50
1955	− 71	+51	−20	+39	−10	+29

The drop in the export surplus in foodstuffs in 1955, in an agricultural year when gross output was said to have exceeded the level of 1953 by 20 percent, reflects the government's decision to alleviate the burden that the export sector imposed on the consumers' market. The net increase in the surplus in the raw materials' group, despite the rise in industrial production which must have absorbed increasing supplies of imported materials, was made possible by the reallocation of building materials, including lumber and cement, from the stagnant construction industry to exports.

Thanks to the structural changes carried out in foreign trade in 1954 and 1955, the New Course in Rumania was implemented with minimum adverse consequences for industrial output and employment. The construction sector was the only one forced to contract and dismiss a part of its working force,

---

[10] The repayment of debts contracted in 1947–1948 and the settlement of obligations to the Soviet Union arising from the liquidation of the joint Soviet-Rumanian companies are believed to be the main causes of sudden changes in the balance of trade. Note that Rumanian exports for reparations are not included in available statistics, which represent "commercial trade" exclusively. However, these reparations were declining in the early 1950s, and by 1953 were probably more than offset by the capital inflow reflected in the deficit in the balance of commercial trade, which equaled 42.8 million U.S. dollars in that year. (On the decline in reparations payments, see the budget data in [14, p. 192].) There is no reason to believe that the sudden elimination of the deficit in merchandise trade and the accrual of a 13-million-dollar surplus in 1954 were compensated by a simultaneous reduction in reparations payments of the same magnitude.

[11] Based on Table 3.9 of [5].

which, as it happens, was less skilled and more easily relocated than that of other sectors.

In Poland, peak imports of machinery occurred in 1951, two years before the launching of the New Course. At that time the country was running an overall deficit in merchandise trade of $110 million at 1955 prices ($162 million at current prices). By 1953 the deficit had turned into a surplus of $13.5 million ($56.7 million at current prices). In terms of 1955 prices, Poland's net imports of machinery declined by only $43 million between 1951 and 1953, compared with a $123.7 million reduction in the availability of foreign exchange owing to the "improvement" in her trade balance. The difference between these two sums was entirely covered by increases in net food exports — from a $55 million surplus in this commodity group in 1951 to a $95 million surplus in 1953 — and in net exports of manufactured consumer goods — from $5.5 million to $43.5 million. These adjustments at the expense of domestic consumption were characteristic of the austere economic policy in effect before Stalin's death.

During the New Course period, from 1953 to 1955, Poland's balance of trade turned again to a small deficit. This change in the balance of trade added about $26 million (at 1955 prices) to endogenously generated sources of foreign exchange ($69 million at current prices). The deficit in machinery trade kept on declining, however, as the surplus in foodstuffs fell to less than a quarter of its 1953 level and the surplus in consumer goods dropped to $27 million (Table 4).

From the differential trends in the four years 1951 to 1955 we may tentatively conclude that the availability of foreign exchange to import machinery was depressed, at first, by the elimination of the capital inflow that had stimulated these imports in the past and, later on, by the deflection of consumer goods from the external to the domestic market. The New Course not only reversed previous trends in exports of consumer goods but also exerted its influence on the composition of exchanges in raw materials and semifabricates through the substitution in the imports program of "light" for "heavy" raw materials. These changes and their effects on individual consumption are illustrated by the statistics of Table 4.

The statistics on consumption and gross agricultural output adduced in Table 4 reinforce the conclusions already drawn from the analysis of foreign trade. Poland's net exports of food were stepped up between 1950 and 1953, when agricultural output was constant or declining, and then were scaled down during the years of the New Course, when output was again on the rise. If we did not know about the political changes that occurred in 1953, we might infer from these statistics that trade was used to intensify rather than to mitigate the effects on home consumption of fluctuations in farm output.

In Bulgaria, as we have seen, there was little or no decline in machinery imports during the years of the New Course, even though the overall balance of trade shifted from a small deficit position in 1953 to a surplus of $35 million in 1955 and to the comparatively large sum of $110 million in 1956, or 31 percent of total exports in that year (all trade statistics expressed in 1955 prices).[12]

TABLE 4

CHANGES IN POLAND'S IMPORTS, EXPORTS, CONSUMPTION OF
CONSUMER GOODS, AND GROSS AGRICULTURAL OUTPUT
FROM 1950 TO 1955
(Trade in millions of U.S. dollars at 1955 prices)

Item	1950	1951	1952	1953	1954	1955
Imports:						
Raw materials for light industry	219	211	170	173	204	221
Foodstuffs	65	61	82	48	117	121
Manufactured consumer goods	36	43	31	20	30	40
Exports:						
Foodstuffs	120	116	110	142	151	141
Manufactured consumer goods	68	48	52	63	74	67
Consumption per capita:						
Grain (kilograms)	166	160	161	163	166	171
Meat and animal fats (kilograms)	38	38	33	36	37	39
Cotton textiles (meters)	15	16	16	15	16	17
Woolen textiles (meters)	2.1	2.2	2.3	2.3	2.2	2.5
Gross agricultural output (index, 1950 = 100)						
Crops	100	90	93	93	101	101
Animal products	100	97	96	103	105	111

SOURCES: All data except for those cited below are from J. Pajestka, "An Interpretation of the First Stage of Poland's Economic Development," in *Studies on the Theory of Reproduction and Prices* (Warsaw: 1964), pp. 219–220. Consumption per capita and the index numbers of gross agricultural output are from *Polska w liczbach* (Warsaw: 1959), pp. 26 and 38.

How were the Bulgarian planners able to maintain the level of machinery imports under these adverse conditions? We may, in any case, rule out the possibility that the agricultural sector supplied the additional goods for export that made this balancing act feasible. Agricultural output, in fact, receded by 4 or 5 percent from 1951–1953 to 1954–1956, and net exports of foodstuffs did not, on the average, surpass the level of 1953. The two commodity groups responsible for the sudden increase in the positive balance

[12] In current prices, a small surplus of $5 million was already earned in 1953; it grew into a $90 million surplus by 1956.

of trade were raw materials and manufactured consumer goods. The increased surplus in the first group was linked to a rapid expansion in the production and export of nonferrous minerals, including zinc-lead and copper ores,[13] and to a dramatic improvement in the balance of trade in heavy chemicals, "as a result of the full satisfaction of domestic requirements" [7, p. 130]. From less than $8 million in 1953, Bulgarian exports of manufactured consumer goods, excluding processed foods, rose to $58 million in 1956; there was no increment in imports to offset this deflection of consumer goods from the domestic market.

The evidence from trends in domestic output and foreign trade suggests that in Bulgaria the New Course had relatively little effect on the allocation of resources at home, and that foreign trade made only a token contribution to the improvement of household consumption, in contrast to the situation in Poland and Rumania. To establish this contention, however, a much more detailed analysis of the internal economic situation in Bulgaria would have to be undertaken.

The chief variables governing the level of machinery imports have been brought out in this brief study of trends in the first half of the 1950s. The marked acceleration in imports of machinery and equipment — associated with higher investment rates — starting with 1958, can be explained in terms of the same variables as in the first period of rapid industrialization. In Rumania, as we shall see in the analysis of the concluding section, an extraordinary increase in agricultural procurements made it possible to more than triple food exports from 1958 to 1963, while imports of these goods remained virtually constant.

In Poland, the curtailment in the deficit in machinery imports was made necessary by a precipitous rise in the deficit in raw materials, which could be financed neither by net food exports nor by the surplus earned in trade in consumer goods. In 1964, the situation was aggravated by the necessity of financing a surplus in total trade; the deficit in machinery trade, for the first time since 1953, turned into a surplus. In Bulgaria, the boom in machinery imports starting in 1958 was accompanied by a growing trade deficit — the counterpart of an increase in earnings from tourism and of Soviet loans, extended in the late 1950s, for the construction of the Kremikovtsy steel mill and for other projects — but also by a more than twofold increase in net exports of foodstuffs and manufactured consumer goods from 1958 to 1962 (in current foreign-exchange prices). As in Rumania, the rise in exports of foodstuffs was made possible by a combination of growing farm output and higher ratios of procurements to output.[14] In more recent years the net

[13] Output of nonferrous ores in Bulgaria grew by nearly 30 percent from 1953 to 1956. This favorable evolution in the output of a key export staple contrasts with the slow growth of coal extraction in Poland and oil output in Rumania during this period.
[14] On state procurements and their ratios to output, see [17, p. 226].

deficit in machinery trade has been more or less stabilized, owing partly to a major effort to expand exports of standardized heavy equipment, including electric motors, pumps, railroad cars, and metal-cutting machines.

In all three of the less-developed countries of CEMA, the forces that boosted machinery imports after 1958 seem to have been spent by 1963. The long-run trends depressing machinery imports — rapid expansion of domestic machinery output, the pressure on the balance of payments of fast-growing imports of raw materials, the rise in the domestic consumption of foodstuffs and industrial consumer goods, the relatively slow rates of increase of food production after the temporary spurt of 1958–1962 — finally overcame the factors of strength that propelled equipment imports in the period 1958 to 1963. To offset these adverse trends, credits would have to be extended on a larger scale by the more- to the less-developed countries of CEMA — at a time when the former are much less able to afford to expand their loans than in 1958–1959 (owing in part to their own balance-of-payments problems). Sufficiently rapid gains in labor productivity in the industrializing countries, if they were not "taken out" in increased consumption, could also release resources for export that would enable them to finance a larger gap between their imports and their exports of machinery. By quantitative analysis, we may form some notion of how strong these counteracting forces would have to be to overcome the long-run tendency toward smaller deficits in machinery trade. The analysis is based on the following model of trade determination in a developing Soviet-type economy.

SIMULATION

The purpose of the exercise about to be described is to determine the level of machinery and equipment imports of a country pursuing an industrialization strategy resembling that of a typical Soviet-type economy at an early stage of development. To keep the problem within manageable dimensions, only the most basic variables and the principal links relating them have been considered. Despite this aggregation, the model should be able to capture the essential features of the phenomenon under study.

The economies whose development will be simulated adhere to two strategic principles: (1) total investments are maximized, subject to the constraint that real wages in non-agricultural sectors must not fall, or must rise at a given rate, and (2) investments in each period are distributed among sectors according to a fixed pattern, with heavy industry (represented in the model by the machine-building sector) receiving a relatively large proportion and light industry a relatively small proportion of the total (as compared, for example, with their respective capital stocks in the initial period).

In addition, certain behavioral characteristics are posited on the part of the centralized decisionmakers governing this system. (These characteristics were suggested by the analysis of actual developments in the preceding section.)

1. All domestic industries are operated at full capacity. Imports of raw materials are determined by the capacities of the raw-material-consuming industries; net imports of machinery and equipment equal total investments in capital goods minus their domestic output.

2. Employment in the non-agricultural sectors is strictly determined by the demand originating in these sectors, under the assumption that there is a sufficient supply of farm laborers seeking off-farm employment to satisfy this demand at the wages set by the government.

3. Investments in industry are made in new plants, whose labor, material, and capital coefficients are determined independently of the relative scarcities of these inputs (i.e., on the basis of technologies borrowed from abroad).

4. Agricultural output and the production of raw materials are exogenously determined, even though both sectors receive some inputs from the industrial sector and both employ labor. (The relation between inputs and outputs in these two sectors is, in reality, so sensitive to the influences of institutional factors beyond the scope of the model that there was little point in trying to tie the two together by rigid coefficients.)

5. All variables are expressed in physical quantities weighted by fixed prices with the exception of labor, whose wages rise at a constant rate. Development has no influence either on domestic or on foreign trade prices. (In particular, all exportables may be sold abroad in any desired quantity at constant prices.) [15]

6. Raw materials are produced by the extractive industry using only labor and capital. Manufacturing industry is composed of two sectors: the first producing machinery and equipment, and the second producing industrial consumer goods excluding foodstuffs (the output of the latter, whether processed or not, is assigned to the agricultural sector). Semifabricates, such as steel and chemicals, are not represented explicitly in the models, and it is assumed that their net effect on the balance of trade is zero. However, the two industries producing for final demand are taken to consume labor, raw materials, and capital goods not only directly but also via the semifabricating industries. To take this into account, the direct labor and raw-material input coefficients have been raised substantially, and investments have been allotted to the two final-demand industries as if they accounted for the entire industrial sector.

[15] This assumption is more realistic for raw materials and foodstuffs than for industrial consumer goods. However, exports of the latter by the less-developed countries of CEMA can be "tied" to exports of "hard goods" in such a way that their outlets at "world prices" can be fairly well protected.

The model that follows is essentially mechanical, in the sense that there is no choice or explicit maximization to be made at any point, and all its relations are expressed in terms of equalities. The "maximization" of investments referred to above simply follows from the postulate that all foreign exchange not used for meeting the endogenously determined requirements of the productive system are devoted to the purchase of machinery and equipment.

The production relations of the model, within any one period or "year," are linear both in the inputs and in the outputs. However, the introduction into the model of gestation periods of three years, between the time when investment outlays are made in light and in heavy industry and the time the resulting capital stocks are put into operation, generates a third-order system of difference equations which cannot be solved by ordinary methods. This was the principal reason for resorting to simulation in this attempt to explore the typical behavior of the system.[16]

I have chosen initial conditions and input coefficients that were meant to represent very approximately the levels of these variables and coefficients in Rumania around 1950.

The funds of foreign exchange from which imports of machines and equipment are financed are derived from the net exports of raw materials, agricultural products, and industrial consumer goods as well as from the foreign credits already referred to.[17] All three of the net exports are residuals obtained after meeting domestic requirements for production and consumption purposes, according to the following equations.

Net exports of raw materials (S_R) equal raw material output minus the total consumption of raw materials:

(1) $$S_R = R - 0.2\,I_p - 0.1\,I_b - 0.35\,L_p$$

where R is the exogenously determined output of raw materials, L_p is the production of industrial consumer goods excluding foodstuffs, I_p is the production of machinery and equipment, and I_b is the production of the construction sector. In this and in all other equations where the variables are not dated, the form of the functional relation is assumed to hold in any year. However, the input coefficients, which may vary over time in ways to be described, refer to an initial year.

Net exports of agricultural products (S_A) equal total procurements or

[16] This simulation was carried out for me on an IBM 7094 by Mr. Marcus Miller, with whom I also had fruitful discussions on the nature and operation of the model. Mrs. Melanie Weaver programmed further variants of the model. I am most grateful for their help.

[17] Imports of raw materials and foodstuffs may be conceived as exogenous additions to the output of the extractive and farm sectors, which are financed by a corresponding subtraction from the exports of these sections. Although imports do not appear explicitly in the equations, their effect was taken into account in estimating the input coefficients.

marketings minus their consumption by industry minus household consumption by the non-agricultural population:

(2) $$S_A = 0.6\,A - 0.2\,L_p - C_{AI}$$

where A is agricultural output, net of consumption for productive purposes, and C_{AI} is the consumption of agricultural products by the non-agricultural population. (Procurements and marketings are set at 60 percent of net agricultural output.)

Net exports of industrial consumer goods (S_L) equal the output of these goods minus their consumption by the agricultural and non-agricultural populations:

(3) $$S_L = L_p - 0.42\,A - C_{LI}$$

where C_{LI} stands for the consumption of industrial consumer goods by the non-agricultural population; $0.42A$ is estimated on the assumption that for every unit of agricultural produce sold to the state or otherwise marketed, farmers obtain 0.7 unit of industrial commodities in return.

The input coefficients in Eqs. (2) and (3), as well as in the labor equation below, are meant to represent the total (direct and indirect) demand for inputs per unit of final demand in the two industrial sectors.[18]

The balance of payments matches net imports of machinery and equipment (I_N) against the (algebraic) sum of net exports in the three groups plus the deficit in merchandise trade (D):

(4) $$I_N = S_R + S_A + S_L + D$$

where I_N represents the difference between total investments in machinery (I_c) and the (fully utilized) capacity of the domestic machine-building industry (I_p).

(5) $$I_N = I_M - I_X = I_c - I_p$$

where I_M and I_X stand, respectively, for machinery imports and exports.

[18] The simplified Leontief matrix of the aggregated economy, in which all other interdependencies have been assumed away, may be represented as follows:

	1	2	3	4	5	6
1. Agriculture and foodstuffs industry	1	0	0	0	0	0
2. Construction	0	1	0	0	0	0
3. Machine-building	0	0	1	0	0	0
4. Consumers' manufactures	0	0	0	1	0	0
5. Industries producing semifabricates	0	$-a_{52}$	$-a_{53}$	$-a_{54}$	1	0
6. Raw materials	0	$-a_{62}$	$-a_{63}$	$-a_{64}$	$-a_{65}$	1

It is assumed that sector 5 generates no net output. The raw-material input coefficients in Eq. (1) of the text correspond to the second, third, and fourth elements in the last row of the inverse of the above matrix. All input coefficients include imported as well as domestic demand.

The deficit in the balance of trade was set at 1 billion units for the first five years of the simulated industrialization program, minus 1 billion for the next five years, plus 1 billion for the next five, and so forth. These changes are meant to reflect the periodic pattern of capital movements, starting with inflows from loans contracted, followed by outflows due to the reimbursement of these obligations (as disclosed earlier in this paper).

Let us now consider wage costs and consumption in this hypothetical economy. We have first an equation to compute total wage costs, W, of non-agricultural production:

$$(6) \qquad W = \frac{w_o r}{\rho} \, (0.5 \, L_p + 0.4 \, I_p + 0.6 \, I_b + 0.35 \, R)$$

where w_o represents the (uniform) wages in the non-agricultural sector in the initial period, r and ρ are respectively an index of wage rates and an index of labor productivity, both rising at constant rates from unity in the first period. The other symbols refer to the outputs of sectors already identified. The labor coefficients for L_p, I_p, I_b and R comprise both direct and indirect expenditures of labor, including those incurred in the production of intermediate goods.

If, as I shall assume, households spend their entire incomes, consumption in the non-agricultural sectors (C_I) will equal the wage bill W:

$$(7) \qquad C_I = C_{AI} + C_{LI} = W$$

where C_{AI} and C_{LI} are, respectively, the consumption of agricultural products and industrial consumer goods by non-farm employees. It is easily verified from the above equation that imports of capital goods are invariant to changes in the proportions in which the non-agricultural population consumes agricultural and industrial products. (As the share of foodstuffs in workers' budgets falls and that of industrial goods rises, more of the former goods are released for export at the expense of the latter.)

We now consider investments, which consist of outlays on machinery and equipment — domestically produced and imported — and on structures. The latter (I_b) are assumed to be exactly equal to investments in machinery and equipment.

$$(8) \qquad I_b = I_c$$

Total investments in any year are distributed among the economy's sectors in fixed proportions:

$$(9) \qquad I_T = I_b + I_c = I_{I_T} + L_{I_T} + N_{I_T},$$
$$I_{I_T} = 0.25 \, I_T; \; L_{I_T} = 0.07 \, I_T; \; N_{I_T} = 0.68 \, I_T$$

where I_T represents total investments, I_{I_T} investments in the machine-building and ancillary industries, L_{I_T} investments in light industry, and N_{I_T}

investments in all remaining sectors, including construction, housing, transportation, raw materials, and agriculture.

We finally introduce elementary production functions for the two industrial sectors:

$$(10) \qquad\qquad I_p = 0.3\,K_I$$
$$L_p = 0.8\,K_L$$

where K_I and K_L are the capital stocks of the machine-building and light-industrial sectors.[19] While, as we have seen, both industrial sectors employ labor, the supply of labor to industry is considered sufficiently elastic to make it possible for industry to develop as if labor were not a constraint on output. It should be noted that, even though at any point of time the labor and capital coefficients are fixed, *ex post* factor proportions are variable, owing to the different rates of decline of the two coefficients.

At any time t the capital stocks of the industrial sectors are made up of the depreciated value of last year's capital stock plus investments in the sector expended three years ago. Thus:

$$(11) \qquad\qquad K_I^t = 0.92\,K_I^{t-1} + I_{I_T}^{t-3}$$
$$K_L^t = 0.95\,K_L^{t-1} + L_{I_T}^{t-3}$$

The capital stocks are depreciated on a straight-line basis at 8 and 5 percent per year, respectively.

Gross national product in this model is defined in terms of the preceding equations,

$$(12) \qquad\qquad \text{GNP} = I_T + A - AP + C_I + C_{LA} - D$$

where AP stands for agricultural procurements.

The initial levels of the exogenous variables A and R and of the capital stocks in the two manufacturing industries were roughly estimated from Rumanian data for 1950. The input coefficients were derived from Soviet input-output data, with some rule-of-thumb adjustments to approximate Rumanian conditions more closely [11, Vol. I, pp. 97–99].

The initial labor and capital input coefficients in Eqs. (1) and (10) were reduced at alternative rates (ρ and σ) of 1, 3, and 5 percent. Material consumption coefficients, which actually tend to decline much more slowly than labor and capital coefficients, were held fixed. The real wage index r was also increased at rates varying between 1 and 7 percent.

Table 5 shows the results of two of the simulated expansions. In both cases, net agricultural output and raw-material production grow at 3 and 5 percent per year, respectively; real wages rise at 3 percent per year; and labor productivity ρ rises at 5 percent. In Case I capital productivity σ rises

---

[19] Note that the output-to-capital ratios presumably take into account the indirect demand for capital via intermediate-goods industries.

SIMULATED EXPANSION OF A SOVIET-TYPE ECONOMY
(Billions of units)

Year No.	Net Agri-cultural Out-put	Raw Mate-rial Out-put	Deficit (−) or Surplus (+) in Merchan-dise Trade	I_p I	I_p II	L_p I	L_p II	I_T I	I_T II	GNP I	GNP II	Net Imports (−) or Exports (+) of Machinery and Equipment I	Net Imports (−) or Exports (+) of Machinery and Equipment II
1	15.0	3.0	−1.0	1.3	1.3	6.2	6.2	7.6	7.6	25.8	25.8	−2.5	−2.5
2	15.5	3.2	−1.0	1.6	1.6	6.3	6.4	8.2	8.2	27.0	27.1	−2.5	−2.5
3	15.9	3.3	−1.0	1.9	2.0	6.5	6.8	8.7	8.8	28.3	28.5	−2.4	−2.4
4	16.4	3.5	−1.0	2.5	2.6	6.8	7.2	9.5	9.6	29.9	30.3	−2.3	−2.2
5	16.9	3.7	−1.0	3.0	3.3	7.2	7.8	10.2	10.4	31.6	32.2	−2.1	−1.9
6	17.4	3.9	+1.0	3.6	4.0	7.6	8.4	8.6	9.0	32.3	33.2	−0.7	−0.5
7	18.0	4.0	+1.0	4.3	4.9	8.1	9.1	9.6	10.0	34.2	35.4	−0.5	−0.1
8	18.5	4.3	+1.0	5.0	5.8	8.6	9.9	10.6	11.2	36.3	37.9	−0.3	+0.2
9	19.1	4.5	+1.0	5.6	6.6	9.1	10.7	11.5	12.3	38.2	40.3	−0.2	+0.5
10	19.6	4.7	+1.0	6.2	7.6	9.6	11.5	12.5	13.6	40.2	42.9	−0.0	+0.8
11	20.2	4.9	−1.0	7.0	8.7	10.2	12.6	16.2	17.7	43.7	47.0	−1.1	+0.1
12	20.9	5.2	−1.0	7.8	10.0	10.8	13.7	17.5	19.4	46.2	50.4	−0.9	+0.3
13	21.5	5.5	−1.0	8.8	11.6	11.6	15.1	19.0	21.4	48.9	54.2	−0.7	+0.9
14	22.2	5.7	−1.0	10.1	13.7	12.7	17.0	20.8	24.0	52.3	59.0	−0.3	+1.7
15	22.8	6.0	−1.0	11.6	16.2	13.9	19.2	21.8	26.9	56.1	64.5	+0.2	+2.7
16	23.5	6.4	+1.0	13.2	19.1	15.3	21.7	22.4	27.8	59.0	69.5	+2.0	+5.2
17	24.2	6.7	+1.0	15.0	22.4	16.9	24.6	24.0	31.8	63.4	76.7	+2.6	+6.6
18	25.0	7.0	+1.0	17.1	26.4	18.6	28.1	29.8	36.5	68.4	85.0	+3.2	+8.2
19	25.7	7.4	+1.0	19.1	30.7	20.4	31.9	30.6	41.6	73.4	94.0	+3.8	+9.9
20	26.5	7.8	+1.0	21.4	35.8	22.4	36.5	33.9	47.8	79.0	104.5	+4.5	+11.9

NOTE: σ rises at 3 percent per year in subcolumns I and at 5 percent per year in subcolumns II.

Initial conditions: $I_T^{-3} = 4.1$, $\quad K_I^{-1} = 3.6$,

$\qquad\qquad\qquad I_T^{-2} = 4.7$, $\quad K_L^{-1} = 7.8$

$\qquad\qquad\qquad I_T^{-1} = 5.5$,

where I_T^t is total investment in year t ($t = -1, -2, -3$) and K_I^{-1} and K_L^{-1} are the capital stocks of the machine-building and light industries, respectively, in the year preceding the onset of the simulation period.

at 3 percent, in Case II at 5 percent. The same levels of agricultural and raw-material production apply in both cases (shown in the columns at the left).

The expansion in both cases sets off with a very high ratio of gross investments to gross national product (29 percent) and a domestic saving rate equal to 25 percent of gross national product. The investment ratio stays below 30 percent for 9 years in Case I, and for 10 years in Case II. From then on it rises perceptibly, eventually reaching unrealistically high levels.

Net imports of machinery and equipment start at a level equal to nearly twice the domestic production of these goods (I_p). After the third year they taper off at a rapid rate. When capital productivity rises at 3 percent per year, it takes 15 years for the country to become a net exporter of capital goods. With capital productivity in industry going up at 5 percent per year, the turning point occurs after only 7 years. An essential feature of the model is that imports of machinery and equipment are gradually curtailed by reason of the diminishing availability of foreign exchange to pay for them (as raw materials and foodstuffs are deflected from exports to domestic consumption). The curtailment of machinery imports is not due to protectionist measures of any sort. An upper limit placed on the investment rate, coupled with a policy of maintaining full utilization of capacity in the machine-building industry, would make for a still faster decline of machinery imports.[20]

A general downward trend in net imports of machinery, followed eventually by the transformation of the economy into a net exporter of these goods, was a feature of most of the variants explored. As it turns out, for net imports of machinery to remain positive throughout the simulation period, *the rate of growth of labor productivity minus the rate of increase of real wages* has to be larger than the rate of growth of capital productivity. This point can be verified from the summary in Table 6 of all the simulations run, on the basis of the initial parameters of the basic set of equations.[21] This critical relation among the three parameters ρ, r, and σ may be explained as follows. If ρ exceeds r then wage costs per unit are falling, and the expansion of industrial output entails a less-than-proportional domestic absorption of exportables. The rate of industrial expansion, total employment, and total consumption of raw materials are determined, in turn, largely by the rate of growth of the productivity of capital, the bottleneck factors in this

---

[20] A ceiling on the investment rate could be incorporated in the model by letting real wages rise at an accelerating rate.

[21] It can be deduced from the equations or observed in Table 6 that the pattern of expansion of the economy depends only on the difference between the growth rates of labor productivity and real wages, not on their actual levels. Thus, whether ρ and r equal 5 and 1, or 7 and 3, respectively, the economy remains a net importer of capital goods for 27, 16, or 14 years depending on whether capital production rises at 1, 3, or 5 percent per year.

TABLE 6

NUMBER OF YEARS OF POSITIVE NET IMPORTS
OF MACHINERY AND EQUIPMENT
UNDER VARIOUS ASSUMPTIONS
ABOUT THE GROWTH RATES OF r, ρ, AND σ

r	ρ	σ	T_1	T_2
1	1	1	8	13
1	1	3	6	6
1	1	5	5	5
1	3	1	17	21
1	3	3	14	14
1	3	5	7	8
1	5	1	27+	27+
1	5	3	16	16
1	5	5	14	14
1	7	1	27+	27+
1	7	3	27+	27+
1	7	5	15	15
3	1	1	5	5
3	1	3	5	5
3	1	5	5	5
3	3	1	8	13
3	3	3	6	6
3	3	5	5	5
3	5	1	17	21
3	5	3	14	14
3	5	5	7	8
3	7	1	27+	27+
3	7	3	16	16
3	7	5	14	14
5	1	1	5	5
5	1	3	5	5
5	1	5	5	5
5	3	3	5	5
5	3	5	5	5
5	5	1	8	13
5	5	3	6	6
5	5	5	5	5
5	7	1	17	21

$T_1 =$ Number of consecutive years, starting from year 1, during which net imports of machinery and equipment are positive.
$T_2 =$ Total number of years of positive net imports of machinery and equipment during the entire thirty-year simulation period.
NOTE: The rates of growth of agricultural production and of raw materials output were set at 3 and 5 percent, respectively, in all the above variants.

model. Hence, the larger the ratio $(\rho - r)/\sigma$, the smaller the total domestic absorption of exportable raw materials, light industrial products, and foodstuffs. Given a sufficiently rapid expansion of agricultural procurements and raw-material output, enough of these exportables will be left after meeting domestic requirements to generate an increasing export surplus in these commodity groups, making it possible to finance imports of capital goods for an indefinite period.

As one might expect, the span of years during which the economy continued to be a net importer of capital goods varied positively with the rate of growth of farm output. This growth parameter, however, appeared to exert less influence on the pattern of import substitution than the rate of decline of input coefficients in industry. There was only one constellation of growth parameters where the speed of import substitution was critically affected by the rate of expansion of the agricultural sector. Here, labor productivity grew faster than capital productivity, but the rate of growth of real wages was in excess of the rate of growth of agricultural production. In this case an alignment of the agricultural growth rate on r made it possible to run a deficit in capital goods for a much longer time. Raising the agricultural growth rate above r, however, had only a minimal effect on the critical period.[22]

A number of experiments were conducted to gauge the sensitivity of the model to changes in the structural relations of the hypothetical economy. The principal variants explored consisted of (1) a differentiation of the growth rates of labor productivity in the three industrial sectors, (2) the introduction of a growth factor in the ratio of agricultural procurements to output, and (3) shifts in the terms of trade between the agricultural sector and light industry.

For the first experiment, the rates of growth of labor productivity in the production of machinery, light industrial goods, and raw materials were taken to be in the proportion of 3 to 2 to 1.[23] In one variant, for example, the rate of growth of labor productivity in the extraction of raw materials, ρ_r, was set at 3 percent; the corresponding rate for light industry, ρ_l, was set at 6 percent; and the rate for the machine-building industry, ρ_I, was set at 9 percent. Again the crucial determinant of the speed of substitution of domestic for imported capital goods was found to reside in the relation

[22] With $r = 3$ percent, $\rho = 5$ percent, and $\sigma = 3$ percent and the net output of agriculture rising at 1 percent per year, net imports of machinery were wiped out in 6 years. Raising the agricultural growth rate to 3 percent delayed this turning point to 14 years. Raising it to 5 percent only delayed it by another year.

[23] The faster growth of productivity in the machine-building industry than in raw-material extraction, postulated here, is less realistic if productivitly is measured in terms of both direct and indirect labor inputs, since (direct) labor productivity in industries producing intermediate goods tends to grow somewhat more slowly than in those producing final investment goods.

of ρ_r, ρ_l, and ρ_I to the rate of growth of capital productivity in light industry and machine building, and to the trend in real wages. For the rates of labor productivity given in the example above, with real wages rising at 3 percent, the economy remains a net importer of capital goods for the entire 30-year period of simulation so long as σ, the rate of growth of the productivity of capital, is kept as low as 1 percent per year. But the economy becomes a net exporter in the nineteenth year, when σ rises to 3 percent. The turning point comes in the eleventh year, when σ is as high as 5 percent. The pattern of expansion does not differ markedly from the pattern that would obtain in the basic model if labor productivity were made to rise at a uniform rate equal to a weighted average of the rates of increase of labor productivity in the three sectors in the present variant.

To investigate the effect on trade in machinery products of increasing the marketed share of agricultural production, the ratio of procurements to agricultural output was raised at alternative rates of 1, 2, and 2.5 percent per year from an initial ratio of 40 percent (lower than the constant ratio in the basic model, to allow for subsequent increases). The initial impact of raising the marketed share was to expand exports of agricultural goods, which made it possible to import more capital goods. But these added imports raised total investments; hence, after a lag of three years, the capital stock and the output of the domestic machine-building industry were larger than they would have been if the marketed share had remained constant. This caused more exportables to be absorbed domestically, thereby offsetting the initial gain in foreign-exchange availability. Eventually the second effect dominated the first, and higher net *exports* of capital goods were generated than if the share had been constant. When agricultural output grew at 5 percent, r was set at 1 percent, ρ at 5 percent, and σ at 3 percent, the economy turned into a net exporter of machinery (a) in 21 years when the procurement ratio grew at 1 percent per year, (b) in 23 years when it grew at 2 percent per year, and (c) in 22 years when it grew at 2.5 percent per year. Net exports of machinery in year 30 were 5.9 units in the first case, 6.9 in the second, and 7.4 in the third.

In the model, the state pays for agricultural procurements by supplying the agricultural population with light industrial products. Initially, it was assumed that for every unit of agricultural output, measured at market prices, the state delivered 0.7 unit of industrial products. How does the structure of the economy evolve when more disadvantageous terms of trade are imposed on the agricultural population — when the state supplies substantially less than 0.7 unit of light industrial products for each unit of farm product procured? Simulations were run for trade ratios of 0.6, 0.5, and 0.3 in addition to the ratio of 0.7 in the initial model.[24] The short-run effect,

---

[24] The procurement ratios were increased at the rate of 2 percent per year in all the variants examined.

as usual, differed from the long-run effect: a lower exchange ratio enabled the state to spare light industrial products for urban consumption; this released agricultural products for export or diminished import requirements for these goods; so that, in either case, more foreign exchange machinery became available for importing machinery. On the other hand, higher machinery imports made for a larger volume of investments and a more rapid accumulation of capital in the machinery sector receiving the lion's share of industrial investments. This made possible a more rapid substitution of domestic for imported machinery than if the state had offered more advantageous terms of trade to the farm sector. In general, however, it was not until the last few periods that the long-run effect began to predominate. Lowering the trade ratio from 0.6 to 0.5, for instance, helped to sustain higher net imports of machinery for 26 years (in the eighth year, imports were 27 percent larger for the lower ratio).[25]

As in all other variants, the relation between σ and $(\rho - r)$ remained a crucial determinant of the scale of machinery imports and of the incidence of the turning point.

THE MODEL AND REALITY

When we move from the mythical world of simulation to historical reality — at least, as nearly as it can be recorded — we are forced to deal with a whole complex of interacting factors, dominated by abrupt changes in economic policy, which have the effect of obscuring (if not of totally effacing) the long-term trends that emerged so clearly in the simulations. In Table 7 I have assembled statistical data from Rumania on the factors that would appear, on the basis of the simulations carried out, to be most pertinent to the determination of net machinery imports.

If the model of the preceding section is relevant at all, the yearly growth rates in the lower part of Table 7 should help to explain the volume of net trade in each commodity group in the upper half of the table. In some (but by no means all) instances, the signals point in the right direction. In most cases we must look to combinations of growth rates to find anything like a satisfactory explanation. The forces acting on net material exports (raw-material output and the pace of industrial expansion, which determine the requirements for domestic and imported materials) should first of all be distinguished from those acting on net food exports (agricultural procurements, labor productivity, real wages, and household consumption).

The main Rumanian exports of raw materials throughout the period under consideration were petroleum products and lumber (raw and processed). It is instructive to compare the growth of petroleum and lumber output in each

[25] In this example, r was 0.01, ρ 0.07, and σ 0.03; the procurement ratio rose at 2 percent per year, starting from 0.4.

period with the rate of growth of industrial output, which governed imports of raw materials and semifabricates. Until 1960, the two trends, fluctuating in more or less parallel fashion, approximately offset each other.[26] From 1961 on, import requirements began to outrun the supply of raw-material exportables, and a deficit opened up in this commodity group.

Net exports of foodstuffs were determined as the resultant of several interacting forces. Agricultural procurements fixed the potential supply of these exportables. Domestic non-agricultural demand was shaped by trends in employment and in unit labor costs (the rate of growth of labor productivity minus that of real wages). Moreover, thanks to the growth of light industry, whose products displaced foodstuffs in household consumption, a large volume of agricultural produce could be released for the export market, even in years of rapidly mounting total consumption. In general, the data in Table 7 suggest that periods of rapid increases in employment were associated with relatively slow gains in labor productivity and in real wages, and vice versa. From 1950 to 1953, when non-agricultural employment rose at a faster rate than in any subsequent period, labor productivity in industry increased at 5 percent per year and the real wages of all non-agricultural employees at 2.8 percent per years — the lowest rate of increase officially recorded for any period.[27] The rapid rise in employment resulted in an increased total domestic consumption of foodstuffs, in spite of falling unit labor costs. This differential trend, coupled with relative increases in agricultural procurements amounting to about 5–6 percent per year, left only a modest surplus of foodstuffs available for export.

From 1954 to 1958 employment grew much more slowly; however, because real wages were rapidly raised to higher levels, unit labor costs in industry failed to resume their downward trend. Even though agricultural procurements were stepped up, the net increase in the availability of foodstuffs on urban markets was relatively small, as the peasant market, which used to provide a substantial share of urban consumption, dwindled in importance. Moreover, the pent-up demand for food during the period of rationing had to be satisfied before households could be induced to substitute consumer manufactures for victuals. During the entire period 1954–

[26] The years 1959–1960 were exceptional in that the surplus in the raw-material group increased in spite of a marked acceleration in industrial output and relatively small increases in the output of the petroleum and lumber industries. The explanation may lie in the more intensive utilization of inventories of imported raw materials. It is known, at least, that total industrial inventories failed to rise with output in these two years (see [8, p. 178]). We may infer from the steep rise in imports of raw materials in 1958 and from their constant level in 1959 that some stockpiling of imported materials took place in the former year.

[27] Because of the rationing of consumers' goods that prevailed in this first period as well as the errors in deflating current incomes by a price index under conditions of repressed inflation, the official index is likely to be more upward-biased than in later periods, when consumers' choice prevailed.

John M. Montias

TABLE 7

SELECTED FACTORS INFLUENCING RUMANIA'S TRADE
IN MACHINERY PRODUCTS
(1950 TO 1965)

Factor	1951–1953	1954–1955	1956–1958	1959–1960	1961–1963	1964–1965
Percentage of imported machinery in total machinery investments	39.2	26.1	19.6	21.4	32.5	28.1
Average yearly values (millions of U.S. dollars):						
Net machinery imports	90	75	43	89	247	246
Net imports (−) or exports (+) of:						
Foodstuffs	+50[a]	+39[b]	+47[c]	+77	+158	+178
Raw materials and semifabricates	+17[a]	+51[b]	+22[c]	+48	+ 1	− 38
Manufactured consumer goods	+ 2[a]	−10[b]	−13[c]	+ 9	+ 3	+ 33
Surplus (+) or deficit (−) in total merchandise trade	−27	+14	+ 1	+46	− 84	− 72
Yearly growth rates:[d]						
Industrial output	13.7	5.8	9.5	15.4	12.2	n.a.[e]
Machine-building and metal-processing industry output	24.4	9.1	26.0	22.0	10.1	n.a.
Light industry[f]	7.1	9.2	2.2	14.4	7.4	n.a.
Labor productivity in industry (ρ)	5.0	8.1	7.2	10.8	5.0	n.a.
Capital productivity in industry (σ)	3.6[g]	1.4[g]	1.5	7.4	2.7	n.a.
Non-agricultural employment	9.3	3.6	0.6	4.0	6.5	4.5
Real wages of all non-agricultural employees (official index) (r)	2.8	6.8	8.0	7.9	4.3	3.8
$\rho - r$	2.2	1.3	− 0.8	2.9	0.7	n.a.
$\dfrac{\rho - r}{\sigma}$	0.6	0.9	− 0.5	0.4	0.3	1.2

[a] 1951 and 1953 only.
[b] 1955 only.
[c] 1956 and 1958 only.
[d] The indices from which growth rates are computed are based on the year preceding the period indicated at the head of the column.
[e] Not available.
[f] Textiles, leather and hides, glass and ceramics, and soap and cosmetics only. The food-processing industry has been purposefully excluded from the index to avoid overlapping the farm-procurements index.
[g] Based on the capital stock in state and cooperative industry only.

TABLE 7 (Continued)

Factor	1951–1953	1954–1955	1956–1958	1959–1960	1961–1963	1964–1965
Agricultural procurements	5.6	11.4	7.3	11.8	6.7	10.4[h]
Petroleum industry output	19.3	7.7	5.4	7.3	9.8	4.3
Lumber industry output	16.5	7.3	8.9	6.8	13.1	13.0
Terms of trade of farm sector (improvement +, deterioration −)	n.a.	n.a.	8.5	− 3.5	n.a.	n.a.

[h] 1964 only.

NOTE: The industrial output index, on which all growth rates and labor and capital productivity data are based, was calculated independently, from a sample of 187 physical series. The indices of machine-building and metal-processing output, and of light industry output, used for 1950 to 1963 are component parts of the independently constructed index cited above.

SOURCES: Indices of output and trade data: J. M. Montias, *Economic Development in Communist Rumania* (Cambridge, Mass.: Massachusetts Institute of Technology Press, 1967), Table 3.9 and Appendix A. Capital stock 1951–1955: *Anuarul statistic al R.P.R. 1959*, p. 83. Agricultural procurements 1950–1955: M. Levente, E. Barat, and M. Bulgaru, *Analiza statistico-economica a agriculturii* (Bucharest: 1961), p. 20, and *Dezvoltarea agriculturii R.P.R.* (Bucharest: 1961), p. 368; 1955–1965: *Dezvoltarea agriculturii R.P.R. Culegere de date statistice* (Bucharest: 1965), pp. 576–577. Terms of trade: M. Levente, E. Barat, and M. Bulgaru, *op. cit.*, p. 48. Trade data: Tables 1 and 2 above. All other data were computed from *Anuarul statistic al Republicii Socialiste România 1966*, 105–106, 116–117, 152–153.

1958, exports of foodstuffs fluctuated at a level slightly below that attained in the period 1950–1953.

From 1959 on, net exports of foodstuffs begin to climb at an unprecedented pace. For the rise in exports of 1959–1960, the aggregated statistics in the table appear to give a satisfactory explanation: procurements were expanding at a record rate; the rise in employment, which was limited to a modest 4 percent per year, was in large part offset by declining labor costs in industry (because of unusually large labor productivity increases); food consumption was also held down as the products of light industry became available in vastly greater volume and quality and were substituted for foodstuffs in household budgets.[28] But the doubling of food exports in the next period (1961–1963) cannot be accounted for at all in these highly aggregated terms. Agricultural procurements rose more slowly than in the preceding period; but it so happens that procurements of corn, the chief item accounting for the upsurge of exports, increased at the record rate of 18 percent per year

[28] The reversal of the improvement in the terms of trade of the agricultural sector of 1955–1958 — a reversal that coincided with the campaign for total collectivization — had the effect of reducing, relatively, the volume of light industrial products that the government had to supply to the peasantry to buy foodstuffs, and made it possible to accelerate the substitution of these products for foodstuffs in urban consumption.

from 1960 to 1963 [3, p. 578]. Exports of corn hardly affected domestic urban consumption directly; however, by cutting deeply into available fodder supplies, they jeopardized future increases in the consumption of meat and milk products.[29] Although total procurements rose at a somewhat slower rate than in 1959–1960, they were sufficient to accommodate the demand for foodstuffs generated by large (and partly unplanned) additions to non-farm employment.

The impact of trends in capital productivity in industry on export performance cannot be detected in the data presented in Table 7. Capital inputs were highly correlated with industrial output during every period except 1959–1960, when a sudden upward shift occurred in capital productivity. This shift, if it was not caused by an overstatement of output in the independently constructed index for these two years, was due to the fuller utilization of the existing capital stock made possible by a perceptible improvement in the supply of materials (especially of foreign origin).[30] This particular explanation, on the face of it, conflicts with the assumption of the model that provided for the maintenance of full utilization of capacity at all times.

The critical relation of the model between $\rho - r$ on the one hand and σ on the other was apparently swamped, in the actual development of the Rumanian economy, by short-run changes in the exogenous variables (in procurements, in the overall balance of merchandise trade, and so forth). From the available data, it would seem that the ratio of $\rho - r$ to σ was smaller than unity in all periods. If there had been no oscillations in the exogenous variables, we should have expected net imports of capital goods to decline "in the long run." We know that they actually tripled from 1956–1958 to 1961–1963, thanks mainly to capital imports, tourist earnings, and a discontinuous increase in procurements of exportable farm products. They dropped slightly in 1964–1965; it is fairly safe to predict that they will continue to drop in the next few years, as the growth rates of agricultural procurements and raw-material output regress toward their long-run values. It remains to be seen whether the relative rates of growth of labor and capital productivity and of real wages — if they continue their present course — will reinforce this downward trend.

To recapitulate, the classical development strategy of a Soviet-type economy consisting in the concentration of investments in heavy industry, and particularly in the metallurgical and machine-building complex, leads us to expect a steady, systematic decline in net machinery imports owing to the contraction of exportable surpluses of raw materials and foodstuffs, required in increasing amounts to feed the expansion of industry. Several offsetting factors, however, may postpone or even temporarily reverse this decline. Capital borrowing and invisible earnings from more-developed countries,

[29] For a detailed analysis, see [5, Chap. 2].
[30] See note 26 above.

especially if they occur after a protracted period of debt reimbursement —
as in Rumania in the period 1954–1957, when all allotments of foreign exchange had to be cut to the bone — may be a powerful stimulant to capital
goods imports. Despite the low-priority status of agriculture in the industrializing state's investment program, a sudden upsurge in the availability of
exportable foodstuffs may come about as a result of a discontinuous increase
in the ratio of procurements to agricultural output (associated, for example,
with the collectivization of agriculture). Finally, we should keep in mind the
possibility that the expansion of industrial branches other than those linked
to the machine-building and metalworking complex may promote rather
than retard imports of capital goods: light industry and chemicals may, on
balance, earn foreign exchange at a later stage of industrialization, rather
than drain these earnings as they did at an earlier stage.[31]

The weaknesses inherent in the confrontation of the crude model of the
previous section with the realities of Rumanian development are painfully
obvious: (1) The model is too mechanical and operates at an excessively
high level of aggregation; (2) the input and output indices are not sufficiently
reliable to compute precise differences in yearly rates; (3) the export surpluses are the resultant of numerous, mutually offsetting forces, and are
highly sensitive to errors in the measurement of any of the factors involved;
and finally (4) the data have not been subjected to systematic statistical
treatment (no attempt was made, for example, to run a multiple regression
of the surpluses and deficits in each commodity group on their putative causa-
tive factors). I have only drawn such conclusions as the data appeared capable of supporting without further testing. Manifestly, a great deal of work
is left to do in model-building, data-gathering, and statistical testing before
the pattern of domestic substitution for foreign capital goods in a period of
socialist industrialization can be definitively established. If this paper has
shed light on the critical variables and coefficients that condition this process
of import substitution, it will have served its purpose.

DISCUSSION

Frederic L. Pryor

Professor Montias' provocative and ambitious essay focuses on both
empirical and theoretical aspects of the commodity composition and volume
of trade, the balance-of-payments situation, and the cycles and growth of
the domestic economies of three East European nations: Bulgaria, Poland,
and Rumania.

[31] In 1965, for the first time, Rumania exported more chemical products than she
imported. A decade earlier the value of imports of chemicals had been more than four
times as great as the value of exports in this group [1, pp. 472–473].

In attacking such a problem nexus, finding a suitable base from which to unravel the various causal interrelations is the first difficult task. After distinguishing between machine goods (which are difficult to sell in the West for hard currency) and raw materials and agriculture (which are more easily marketed in the West), Montias presents a series of propositions and observations based on the assumption that it is the demand for machine goods in the three nations which determines their trade in raw materials and agriculture, rather than some reciprocal or reverse determination. This basic assumption assigns to the Soviet Union, which is the largest trading partner of all three nations under consideration, a curiously passive role. Certainly changes in Soviet trade policies have greatly affected the trade pattern of these three nations, especially in the middle 1950s.[32] However, the real effect of omitting such considerations can only be judged by Montias' success in explaining the problems he is examining.

In the descriptive half of the paper, where some extremely useful data are presented, Montias quantitatively dissects some of the important factors linking trade in machinery to domestic production capacities and investment cycles. While not complete, this analysis reveals a number of elements in the intra-bloc trade situation which have not received their proper due, especially in the examination of the balance-of-payments adjustment process.

The heart of the paper is the author's 26-variable, six-sector simulation model, which is based on a number of crucial assumptions: growth in the agricultural and raw material sectors is exogenously determined; in the other sectors the major restraint on production is capital, these sectors can draw on an unlimited supply of labor, and their production functions are simple fixed capital/output types; there is complete substitution between domestic and foreign production; the consumption of agricultural workers rises at a constant rate (the procurement policy and the terms of trade between agriculture and industry are fixed) while the consumption of industrial workers depends on a preset policy variable concerning the rise in real wages;[33] and the distribution of investments is held constant. This is a complex and intriguing model; unfortunately, its purpose is not entirely clear.

---

[32] The Soviet Union's initiation of the New Course in 1953 and its refusal to increase export quotas for certain key products to Eastern Europe in 1956 played a major role in the commodity composition of East Bloc trade in the middle 1950s. (The effects of these two measures on East German trade are graphically described in [13].) Other examples of Soviet influences on the commodity composition of trade of the CEMA nations in later years can also be given.

[33] It seems unduly complicated to separate the growth coefficient of the output/labor ratio and also the growth coefficient of the wage rate when, in reality, together both determine the rate of growth of consumption, which is easier to understand. Thus in Table 6, it appears that the really important determinant of the T_1 and T_2 data is the ratio of r to ρ and to the capital coefficient σ. When the former ratio is unity (e.g., r and $\rho = 1$, r and $\rho = 3$, etc.), the resultant T_1 and T_2 for different values of σ are exactly the same.

If the aim in constructing the model is to generate a number of solutions from which a set of propositions about the relative short-run effect of different growth rates can be induced, then a much simpler model can be used. For instance, from a simple two-sector model the static equivalent of every one of the dynamic propositions derived from the complex model, which are presented in various parts of the paper, can be easily deduced.[34] Although it is good to know that these propositions are valid in both simple and complex cases, such a result could be expected; most of the propositions, upon reflection, are intuitively clear after we have mastered the simple two-sector model presented in the footnote. Of course this does not make the propositions any less useful in analysis. Certainly, Montias' dissection of the em-

[34] Assume that national income (Y) is produced in two sectors, an "autonomous sector" (A) making consumer goods whose growth is independent of investment, and a capital-goods sector (B), whose production depends on the capital stock in the sector (K) and the output/capital ratio (b). Assume further that the national income is used either for consumption (C) or investment, that there is no lag between investment and its use, and that capital only lasts one period. (This assumption can be easily changed without changing the derived propositions.) Thus, $B = bK = b(Y - C)$. Because the economy initially imports capital goods and exports consumer goods, it can be shown that b is greater than zero and less than unity. Finally, assume that consumption is some fraction of the wage bill in the capital-goods sector, which depends in turn on the labor/output ratio (m) and the wage rate (w): $C = mBw$. Since consumption is less than the value of output in sector B, mw is greater than zero but less than unity. Through elementary algebra it can be shown that $B = bA/(1 - b + bmw)$.

Now, net imports of capital goods (T) are equal to total investment minus home production of capital goods: $T = Y - C - B$, which can be transformed into the following: $T = A \left\{ 1 - [bmw/(1 - b + bmw)] \right\}$. The following relationships, which are the static equivalents of the most important propositions derived by Montias from his model, can be easily deduced from the more simple model:

1. If the capital/output ratio declines (as b rises), net imports of capital goods (T) decline if A remains constant. (This is equivalent to the following proposition: If capital productivity increases, net imports of capital goods decline.)
2. If the labor/output ratio declines (as m declines), net imports of capital goods (T) increase if A remains constant. (This is equivalent to the following proposition: If labor productivity increases, net imports of capital goods increase.)
3. If the labor/output ratio declines more rapidly than the capital/output ratio (if mb declines), net imports of capital goods increase if A remains constant. (This is equivalent to the proposition: If labor productivity rises more rapidly than capital productivity, net imports of capital goods increase.)
4. If consumption rises, net imports of capital good decline if Y remains constant. Similarly, an increase in wages (w) has the same effect.
5. If the labor/output ratio declines more rapidly than the wage rate increases (if mw declines), net imports of capital goods increase if A remains constant. (This is equivalent to the proposition: If labor productivity rises more rapidly than wages, net imports of capital goods increase.)
6. If production in the autonomous sector (A) increases, net imports of capital goods rise if B and Y remain constant.
7. If the autonomous sector grows at a faster rate than the increase in capital productivity (decrease in the capital/output ratio), imports of capital goods rise.

pirical data of the three countries in the first section of the paper (which is based on a number of intuitively clear propositions from a less restrictive model) is extremely provocative, illuminates many facets of the phenomena under examination, and provides important and new insights into the process of Eastern European foreign trade.

If the purpose of the model is to show long-run changes in the composition of trade (abstracting from the trade cycles caused by investment cycles, or from the effects brought about by short-run policy changes), then two types of objections can be raised:

First, several of the basic assumptions seem quite unreal for the long run, especially the lack of labor restraints and the existence of autonomous sectors whose growth is independent of investment.

Second, the long-run results of the simulation experiments do not correspond with the actual long-run events. Using the parameters of Rumania, the change-over from importation to exportation of machine goods should occur in a relatively short period of time. But, as Montias shows in Table 1, Rumania had a considerable net deficit in machinery and equipment 15 years after 1950. Further, unless properly constrained, certain variables in any simulation model tend to explode; certainly the rise in the ratio of investment to gross national product in the experiment recorded in Table 5 is disquieting.

In addition to using the model for deriving propositions about the differential growth of the variables and for long-run simulations, a third and much more important use can be envisioned — exploring the interrelationships between investment and trade cycles which Montias empirically analyzes for Rumania. Since changes in the autonomous loans generate some cyclical behavior (Table 5), changes in investment should even accentuate such cycles. Applying the model to such problems provides not only a rigorous explanation of the results of Fig. 1 but also an interesting insight into one neglected aspect of "autarky," a topic touched upon in many of these Conference papers. The major difference between the Montias and autarky models of trade in East Europe lies in expectations about instabilities of trade.

If the East European nations are more autarkic than nations in West Europe, then they should be more "dependent" on the marginal unit of trade. We might therefore argue that the foreign trade of these nations would be conducted in such a manner as to dampen "natural" cyclical activity, so that the volume of foreign trade would show *more* stability than in West Europe. However, we know that fluctuations in construction (and presumably investment as well) are greater in East than in West Europe [15]. From the Montias model we might therefore conclude that the volume of trade in East Europe would show *less* stability than in West Europe.

To resolve this matter in an empirical way, we must determine whether the East European nations are the more autarkic and, if this is so, determine their differential degree of foreign trade stability.

The relative degree of autarky of a nation depends very much on world trade conditions (average level of tariffs and other trade barriers, transportation costs, and the like). Therefore, autarky can only be measured through cross-sectional comparisons. Of course, measuring empirically the degree of autarky raises a number of knotty statistical problems. For instance, comparisons between domestic and world market prices would not be very useful except in some special cases.[35] Furthermore, computation of meaningful trade/GNP ratios in domestic prices is extremely difficult for the East European nations because of problems arising from the evaluation of exports, imports, and GNPs in comparable "adjusted" prices. One easier way of doing this is to use calculated estimates of the GNPs of these nations in dollars, and the dollar values of their trade, which are also published.

For seven East European and twenty-one developed West European and North American nations, comparisons of trade, GNP, and population were made for 1956 and 1962 — and, to check for any structural bias in the trade of the East European nations, for 1928 as well.[36] Trade was assumed to be a multiplicative function of GNP, population, and a dummy variable designating whether the nation is in Eastern Europe.[37] The resulting regression model yielded (cross-sectional) correlation coefficients over 0.90 for all three years. Other calculations were made with a smaller sample that excluded very large nations such as the United States and the U.S.S.R., and very small nations such as Iceland.

The results with respect to the dummy variable designating "East Europe" (or, in 1956 and 1962, the fact that the nation was centrally planned) can be easily summarized. In 1928 there was no statistically significant difference in the volume of trade of "comparable" (i.e., having about the same GNP and population) East and West European nations. In 1956 and 1962, how-

[35] One such special case is for imported tropical products. For such a price comparison, see [9].

[36] For 1928 a sample of 22 nations was used; for 1956 and 1962, a sample of 28 nations. Data for 1928 come from [2], [4], [5], [18], and [19]. The GNP estimates are based on calculations which are described in my joint article with George Staller [10].

[37] A multiplicative model (i.e., one in which the regression was calculated in logarithms) was chosen, for two reasons. First, it can easily be shown that with various forms of the model (e.g., trade as the dependent variable, GNP and GNP/capita as the independent variables; trade as the dependent variable, GNP and population as the independent variables; trade/GNP as the dependent variable, GNP/capita and population as the independent variables) the numerical value and the significance of the dummy variable representing "Eastern Europe" is not affected. Second, such a regression model accounts for over 80 percent of the variance of trade for the nations in the sample.

ever, the calculated coefficient was significant, and showed that the volume of trade among the East European nations was between 50 and 60 percent of the trade volume of comparable West European nations.[38] Although the trade/GNP ratio, as several Conference participants have pointed out, is only one facet of the vague phenomenon that we call autarky, we unfortunately have no other convenient statistical handle with which to analyze the problem. From the regression results, therefore, we must conclude that the East European nations have experienced a relatively autarkic development pattern in comparison with West Europe.

A clear test of the hypotheses about the instability of foreign trade, which derive from the Montias or the autarky models, can now be made. According to the autarky hypothesis, trade in East Europe should be more stable than in West Europe; and according to the Montias model, such trade should be less stable.

From the results of an extensive econometric study by George Staller of trade fluctuations in European nations [16], the volume of East European foreign trade shows a much more unstable pattern than West European foreign trade.

Thus, the ideas and analytical tools presented by Professor Montias in his paper lead to a tentative prediction about the nature of East European trade which cannot be deduced from autarky considerations and which has not been foreseen by other Western observers. It is in the analysis of cyclical activity that I believe Montias' simulation approach will prove, in the future, to yield many more insights.

REFERENCES

1. *Anuarul statistic al Republicii Socialiste România* (1966).
2. Clark, Colin. *The Conditions of Economic Progress*, Third Edition (London: Macmillan, 1957).
3. *Dezvoltarea agriculturii R.P.R.: Culegere de date statistice* (Bucharest: 1965).
4. League of Nations. *Statistical Yearbook, 1933/4* (Geneva: 1934).
5. Montias, John M. *Economic Development in Communist Rumania* (Cambridge: Massachusetts Institute of Technology Press, 1967).
6. ———. "Economic Nationalism in Eastern Europe: Forty Years of Continuity and Change," *Journal of International Affairs*, XX:1(1966), pp. 51–61.
7. Popisakov, G. *Vŭnshna tŭrgovia na N.R. Bŭlgaria* (Sofia: 1959).

[38] These results do not imply that the trade/GNP ratios have risen less (or fallen more) in all East European countries vis-à-vis the various West European nations. Indeed, the standard error of the dummy variable was so large in the 1928 calculations a faster relative rise of the trade/GNP ratio than most West European nations (the problem is complicated, of course, by the fact that many East European nations lost population between 1928 and 1945).

8. *Probleme economice*, No. 12 (1962).

9. Pryor, Frederic L. "Trade Barriers of Capitalist and Communist Nations against Foodstuffs Exported by Tropical Underdeveloped Nations," *Review of Economics and Statistics*, XLIII:4 (November 1966), pp. 406–412.

10. ————, and George Staller, "The Dollar Values of the Gross National Products in Eastern Europe 1955," *Economics of Planning*, VI:1(1966), pp. 1–26.

11. Research Analysis Corporation, *The 1959 Soviet Intersectoral Flow Table* (Washington, D.C.: November 1964), Vols. I and II.

12. Savov, M., and N. Velichkov. "Spetsializatsiata na proizvodstvoto i tsenite v tŭrgoviita mezhdu sotsialisticheskite strani," *Planovo stopanstvo i statistika*, No. 7 (1966).

13. Schenk, Fritz. *Die Magie der Planwirtschaft* (Cologne: Kiepenheuer and Witsch, 1960).

14. Spulber, Nicolas. "National Income and Product," in Stephen Fischer-Galati (ed.), *Romania* (New York: Praeger, 1957).

15. Staller, George J. "Fluctuations in Economic Activity: Planned and Free Market Economies, 1950–1960," *American Economic Review*, LIV:4 (June 1964), Part I, pp. 385–395.

16. ————. "Patterns of Stability in Foreign Trade, OECD and COMECON," *American Economic Review*, LVII:4 (September 1967), pp. 879–888.

17. *Statisticheski godishniak na N.R. Bulgaria 1963* (Sofia: 1963).

18. United Nations. *Demographic Yearbook* (New York: various years).

19. ————. *Yearbook of International Trade Statistics* (New York: various issues).

20. Wacker, V., and B. Malý (eds.), *Mezinárodní socialistická dělba práce* (Prague: 1964).

Foreign Trade of Eastern Europe: A Summary Appraisal

PETER J. D. WILES

To discuss in a unified manner three such disparate papers as those of Professors Brown, Spulber, and Montias would be the merest pretense. I am forced to pick three points of general interest (one from Professor Johnson) and expatiate upon them.

I

First and most generally, the title of Professor Brown's paper. The operative words are the first two: "towards" and "a." I am deeply convinced that we shall never be able to say "at" or "the." For international trade takes place between states — so it is in all cases highly political. Indeed, when one considers the Polish obsession with exporting machinery, or the Mexican obsession with oil ownership, one must say psychological. Such matters will never be brought into the compass of any one theory, still less by a pure economist. But now add to this the fact that in these particular states the government and the economy coincide, and all general theories must be essentially ones that predict government behavior. Therefore, there are and will be no valid *general* theories.

It suffices to name a very few of the more important obstacles to such a theory. First, it must take Marxism fully into account — while not itself being wholly Marxist, for then it would be wrong. My most serious objection specifically to Brown's theory is that Marxism is not given enough emphasis. And, second, it is for this reason that he does not elaborate upon the role of trade in machinery, which, as we shall see, is all-important. Third, the interpretation put upon Marxist orthodoxy differs by country. Most orthodox, according to my interpretation of holy writ, are the parties of the CEMA bloc. The Yugoslavs have misread Marx as blessing decentralization and a market economy; the Chinese have dropped his preference for capital-intensity down the memory-hole. Fourth, the rate of decay of these varying orthodoxies itself varies. Poland, Hungary, and Czechoslovakia have an easy lead in this respect. Then, too, national traditions and the whims of particular leaders differ greatly.

Thus, it results — in my opinion — from this book that what we have previously called "Communist" autarky was really only Stalinist; and great credit accrues to Brown for being perhaps the first person to put this in print. The U.S.S.R. itself is moving away from autarky; but other countries — notably China, Hungary and Poland — have abandoned it very much more rapidly, if ever they had it. In this respect, both Czechoslovakia and Rumania have been lagging. Differing national traditions also make for differences in the geographical distribution of trade. Obviously nothing but politics can explain the behavior of non-CEMA members, but how do we explain that loyal Poland and disloyal Rumania alike do only 60 percent of their trade with the rest of CEMA? What makes this proportion fidelity in the one case and betrayal in the other (see below for the answer!)? Or in Brown's own Hungarian case (cf. Conclusion of his paper), is it possible to explain the shifts in the trade pattern in 1954–1956 without giving the specific political background? From July 1953 to April 1955 Imre Nagy was premier, and he sought in a number of ways to break the Soviet stranglehold. Nagy fell because Khrushchev had ousted Malenkov, and one of the specific policies of the Kremlin's new master was a tightening of CEMA bonds.

It is clear that no general theory will encompass this historically based diversity. The Soviet-type economies are not, where foreign trade is concerned, closely bunched around some norm or *Idealtypus*. Despite undoubted domestic similarity, their foreign economic policies differ substantially. This should perhaps distress, but surely not surprise, the pure economist. For his anxiety to seek economic explanations for economic phenomena is after all without the slightest theoretical or empirical justification. It is the straight, unblushing admission of this truth that I miss in Brown's paper.

II

Nor do I find Johnson's proposal very illuminating, that some of these policy aims be re-christened "public goods." This idea originates in the insight of Mr. Albert Breton into Quebec nationalism.[1] If the Quebec provincial government buys up a power station in order to replace

[1] [1, 1964]; cf. H. G. Johnson, in [2, 1965]. One might, to keep a just balance, mention that innumerable anti-United States measures taken by the English-speaking Dominion government are susceptible to the same analysis, and doubtless inspired the Quebec imitation.

X English-speaking with *Y* French-speaking engineers, such a change in staffing may be regarded by the population at large as a public good, purchased at a definable cost. This cost might be, for instance, the yield to the provincial government of the power station minus debt redemption, assuming no change in the government's policy on debt management and the price of electricity.

Now the public good has also its *Idealtypus*: the park. The park is enjoyed in a definable way by specifiable people, who are (*ex hypothesi*) not asked to pay. But when we move away from goods and services into government policies, the analogy becomes very dubious; and less sophisticated minds might be tempted to push it deeper than the very shallow level at which it floats. Thus a heavily subsidized national airline indeed renders definable services, but it is the *contemplation* thereof that constitutes the "public good." The actual passengers simply pay. The contemplators are a select group from among the watchers at the airport, the passengers, the readers of newspapers, and the governing elite. Steel was this kind of a good to Stalin. This kind of enjoyment is not economic, and *ideological good* would be a far better phrase. For unlike the park, the ideological good may be of negative economic marginal utility; and even if this is known it may still be bought, or produced, quite consciously.

The Quebec case is different again, since on top of the ideological benefit, as Mr. Breton points out, there is the pure redistribution of income — from mostly French-speaking taxpayers to only French-speaking managers. Similar redistribution from taxpayers to royal families is indeed an ideological good, but I find the Quebec case difficult to classify in that way: surely it is simply the result of group pressure, and is a straightforward source of private economic good for the members of the group.

Institutional systems, again, are ideological goods for some, while for others they have redistributive effects and thus yield private economic gains and losses. Yet others undergo both influences. Moreover, policies, such as free trade or the use of the labor theory of value, are similarly ideological goods or the (redistributive) means to private economic goods, or both. And both policies and institutions may in all cases be rationally or irrationally valued. Also they have perfectly straightforward effects on the volume of production and Pareto optimality.

There are, too, many private ideological goods, such as faith and chastity, seen as personal ideals alone and not enforced on others. But all this analysis takes us very far from the park, the genuine public good.

These various categories have only this in common: they are wanted by human beings, they cost something, and payment is not collected by the price mechanism — so they must be produced by planning. To be wanted is, in the very vaguest sense, to have "utility," even if it is not "economic." But if all human wants are to be the province of economics, then psychology, politics, and sociology are branches of economics. The "public good" line is therefore intellectual imperialism. We give a piece of politics an economic name, and hope we can become professors of economics by talking about it. So indeed we may, but human knowledge will advance only if we are cleverer — at politics — than the professors of politics; or if our economic training gives us a better vantage point and enables us to propound a unified social science of humanity. Such a time is not yet, and premature attempts will waste much energy. In particular we economists are deficient in assessing the importance of income redistribution, which is so common in these problems and so near to our science, even when narrowly defined.

It is on the cost side only that we can as yet contribute. Parks, national airlines, useless steel, protectionism, free trade, war, and incorrect theories of value all have an opportunity cost in real income. These costs are indeed for economists to calculate, but the benefits of many of them escape us. There is no cost-benefit analysis for the decision to use the labor theory of value: only a cost analysis.

To return to Professor Brown, it would do him very much less than justice if I simply pointed to his excessive faith in Western economics. Our discipline must be admitted to have *some* explanatory force in competent hands, never mind what excessive claims are made for it. And his are highly competent; he says very many of the things that needed, in the present state of the art, to be said. Virtually everything he says is true, and much of it is new — especially his attack on the orthodox Western notion that Soviet-type economics are autarkic. I would only complain here that he does not go far enough. He does not show the utter incompatibility of autarky inside the bloc with Marxism, and he does not fully bring out the point that "unreliable valuation standards" may at all times lead to *too much* trade. Thus the "price equalization" may well cause the monetary authorities to resist imports, since it means that they must subsidize exports; but *eo ipso* it encourages consuming enterprises to press for imports — who wins?

A word here on the assumed structural similarity of Hungary to other Soviet-type economies. There have always been sizable differences, and these are now growing very rapidly. Thus the Hungarian "price equalization" has usually shown a tremendous deficit, without parallel in any other Soviet-type economy known to me. In Hungary, import subsidy exceeds export levy. In East Germany, where the official rate was nearly right, prices were so irrational that both imports and exports used to be subsidized! The Chinese for the most part, and the Russians fitfully, have chosen such rates of exchange as will eliminate a price equalization. China, again, is so decentralized that she permits her regions to trade abroad to some extent independently; and the same may shortly hold for Czechoslovak enterprises, and the Soviet Far East. Finally, machinery exporters are very different from machinery importers. And to this point we must now turn.

III

From Professors Spulber and Montias alike — but also from reading Communist works on foreign trade — I have learned of the absolutely crucial role of trade in machinery. For a few very underdeveloped countries — say Guinea in its Communist period — consumer good imports may be of major concern, and all small countries are naturally exercised about raw material imports. For the rest the only import, or indeed export, that permanently occupies Communist attention is machinery. There could, for instance, as Professor Franklyn Holzman has proposed [3], be free trade in consumer goods on a very large scale at virtually no sacrifice to the Soviet-type system. But the possibility has been entirely neglected.

In earlier work [6, Chap. 15] I have poured scorn on the Communist countries' obsession with producing their own machinery. I stand by everything there written, but must now correct a very serious omission: technology rides the backs of machines, not raw materials — it is *educative* to make machines. It follows that mild autarky or protectionism in machine-building is a good thing. In any case, so long as growth is favored, machinery must be acquired somehow. A "growth product," as I point out in [6, Chap. 15], can be any product temporarily in very short supply: e.g., imported cotton yarn if looms are standing idle, or even bread if there is a famine and people are physically run-down. But I should have added that, since investment and skill are always necessary for growth, machines are a "growth product" nearly all the time.

The principal effect of the embargo, then, was to substitute Czechoslovakia and East Germany for the West as suppliers of growth products. One machine is exceedingly unlike another, so in the absence of comparable price information we cannot say what this did for their intra-bloc terms of trade. But it is a fair guess that, at least vis-à-vis the other satellites, they did not do badly in the prevalent machine famine while Stalin lived. Granted the growth policies of their Eastern neighbors, they would have specialized in machinery anyway. But once this had happened they were stuck with it, and their allies had to buy the machines even under changed circumstances, because they were, after all, allies. So in a sense the embargo, in flat opposition to Marxist prejudice and doctrine, marked many countries as raw material exporters, notably Rumania and U.S.S.R.; and by turning trade inward, it marked the central country, Poland, as a purveyor of transit services. It is to be deplored, *en passant*, that so little has been said of invisibles in all these contributions, as if they were not trade. Data on tourism and shipping are not all that scarce: they are not state secrets to the same extent as total balance-of-payments data.

But after the death of Stalin the cold war, and consequently the embargo, began to relax in Europe, and his promotion of machine-building in the more eastward-lying countries began at length to pay off. Moreover — a point which is in a way accidental, but of crucial importance to the argument — Communist machinery, even if made in the more advanced Western fringe, was and remains for various reasons unquestionably inferior to capitalist machinery. It is therefore extremely difficult to sell outside the bloc, even in the *tiers monde*, except on credit. Thus there must have begun a severe deterioration in the Czechoslovak and East German terms of trade, which I suggest elsewhere is the true lesson of the Holzman-Mendershausen controversy.[2] Mendershausen, the non-specialist should be told, was the first to present statistical evidence for the orthodox point of view that the Soviet terms of trade are exploitative. Holzman sought to prove that they are not. I believe that the true reconciliation of seemingly conflicting data is that all other CEMA members "exploit" East Germany and Czechoslovakia, the worst "offenders" being Hungary and Bulgaria, not the U.S.S.R.; and that this may constitute a Prebisch-type "aid through trade" to these two poor and small countries.

It is not clear to me how East Germany has reacted, except that its principal planner, Erich Apel, killed himself in December 1965 on the conclusion of a Soviet-East German trade agreement. Striking evidence, this, of the presence of "exploitation," but either my ignorance or a deeper mystery obscures the practical steps that East Germany has taken. Czechoslovakia, on the other hand, has become by far the greatest Communist aid-giver per capita; i.e., she has "called the underdeveloped world into existence to redress the balance of the CEMA." But these are all soft loans and have no real effect on the terms of trade. The great balance-of-payments crisis of 1962 was the result.[3] But both countries remain the prisoners of their previous specialization, and are thus living refutations of the anti-raw-material, pro-manufacture bias of Prebisch, Stalin, Myrdal, and Marx. We cannot doubt that their subservient foreign policies find here a partial explanation.

By contrast, Rumania and little loyal Bulgaria have been liberated by the same turn of events. If the one has been polite where the other has been brusque, that is a political difference. Note above all that Rumania succeeded in giving such great offense without much shift in the geographical distribution of her *overall* trade; it was the decision to import Western machinery that brought her into disfavor.

[2] See [5, Chap. 9] and the references therein.
[3] For proof that this *was* an externally induced crisis, and for a discussion of its unique severity among Communist balance-of-payments crises, cf. [5, Chap. 5].

But by far the most interesting case of a raw material exporter is the U.S.S.R. herself. Marxism and imperialism sit ill together, and it should surprise no one, in retrospect, that this country was truly imperialist only for a brief eleven years. Annex in haste, subsidize at leisure. In 1956 the post-imperial or paying-out phase set in, and one can see no end to it. For if the U.S.S.R. were to "do a Rumania" on the CEMA, it would fall apart; and she is responsible before history for keeping world Communism together. She must therefore refrain from rerouting her raw materials westward, and must continue to buy East German and Czechoslovak machines. But where Rumania simply cut out, the U.S.S.R. exacts a price for staying in. And this is the significance of "terms-of-trade Bogomolov," as he should be known by now in professional circles. For Mr. Bogomolov can always be relied upon at the right psychological moment for an article on the monstrous cost of Soviet raw materials.[4] That he uses a strange theory of value, stressing marginal capital-output ratios and forgetting labor costs (!), is less important. Doubtless he is right for the wrong reasons; after all, returns diminish even under the dictatorship of the proletariat.

Thus international trade in machinery is a key that unlocks almost too many doors. Its general explanatory power is so great as to render it suspect — for consider yet other applications. Both the Yugoslav (1948) and the Rumanian (1962) splits were on this issue; in both cases the CEMA members refused to supply machinery for long-term plans of which they disapproved. In the Yugoslav case there were many more important questions, but at least this was the chief economic one. In the Rumanian case it was far and away the principal bone of contention. Poland, on the other hand, is in approximate machinery balance; and so since 1956 we have never heard of any serious trouble between her and the U.S.S.R. or CEMA. Sitting athwart the trade routes, her problems are "invisible."[5]

China too is a sort of Rumania, or at least a Bulgaria. For if tung oil is more dispensable than petroleum, it is surely as necessary to human kind as attar of roses. If in this case politics was altogether dominant, we must at least allow that there was an economic prerequisite for a split. Could China get her machines elsewhere? The answer was yes, and better and cheaper too: better, since as we have seen, capitalist machines *are* better; cheaper, because transport costs are far lower. Moreover, the Far East and the West had far more use for China's traditional exports of raw materials and light manufactures than had Eastern Europe or the U.S.S.R., which had been absorbing these frivolous and unMarxist objects as a concession only.

We may go further. Imperialism used to depend on the export of manu-

4 E.g., O. O. Bogomolov in [4].

5 In particular, as she is able to hold her own in merchandise trade, the invisibles tend to pile up in currency surpluses; hence her demand for a convertible ruble.

factures, including light manufactures; but now to be successfully imperialist one must export technology (especially military) and agricultural products. The new importance of agriculture is due to the new unwillingness of governments, especially the successor governments in ex-colonies, to let their citizens starve. Of course, to sell technology is to sell the newest and most expensive machines, since of all other kinds there is no dearth in the world. If Cuba wants buses, the Czechs and the British will rush to oblige. There is no monopoly of buses, and imperialism cannot base itself on the simple technology of wheeled vehicles. The great imperialist power is the one that provides, so to speak, both guns and butter, while leaving simpler products to others.

Thus the logic of factor endowment, including education, suits the United States very well for an imperial role. It condemns China and India to export light manufactures and import food — strategically the least enviable situation. The U.S.S.R. will clearly never be a major food exporter, and is really in much the same situation as East Germany, Czechoslovakia, and Northwest Europe: a serious competitor with the United States in high technology, and a natural exporter of the more obvious kinds of machine.

REFERENCES

1. Breton, Albert. "The Economics of Nationalism," *Journal of Political Economy*, LXXII:4 (August 1964), pp. 376–386.
2. Johnson, Harry G. "A Theoretical Model of Nationalism in New and Developing States," *Political Science Quarterly*, LXXX:2 (June 1965), pp. 169–185.
3. Rosovsky, Henry (ed.). *Industrialization in Two Systems: Essays in Honor of Alexander Gerschenkron* (New York: Wiley, 1966).
4. *Voprosy ekonomiki*, No. 1 (1966).
5. Wiles, P. J. D. *Communist International Economics* (forthcoming).
6. ———. *The Political Economy of Communism* (Cambridge: Harvard University Press, 1962).

Foreign Trade of China

The International Impact on Chinese Central Planning*

DWIGHT H. PERKINS

Economists in underdeveloped economies frequently complain that their countries' dependence on foreign trade is unprofitable and hazardous. It is unprofitable, they argue, because long-run price movements go against raw material exporters, wiping out short-run gains based on static comparative advantage. It is hazardous because wide fluctuations in export earnings make meaningful long-term planning impossible. Under such circumstances, the obvious solution is to minimize one's dependence on foreign trade by developing industry as fast as possible.

Although these arguments have been placed in modern analytic dress, in origin they probably owe much to the premodern belief that if one competing party gets a bigger slice of the economic pie, someone else has to receive a smaller share. This view was reinforced by a century and more of imperialist domination and damaged pride. For China, as for many other underdeveloped countries, therefore, the development of an "independent" industrial economy is assumed to be the most effective if not the only route to a higher standard of living or to greater military power. This assumption has become a part of the ideology and is seldom questioned.

If a failure to fully comprehend Adam Smith's principal message accounts in part for China's dogged faith in economic autarky, it still does not follow that this goal is irrational. The decision of the Chinese Communist leadership to maintain a less than pacific posture toward all the world's major powers would in itself dictate a high degree of autarky, for military reasons if no other.

* I am indebted to Professors Franklyn Holzman and Gottfried Haberler for carefully reading and criticizing a draft of this paper. I have also received a number of helpful comments from the discussants of my paper, Professors Ta-chung Liu and Alexander Eckstein, and the editors of this volume. Finally, I would like to thank Professor Robert Dernberger for permission to use data from his doctoral dissertation.

In this paper, I do not plan to deal at length with these military and ideological considerations. They are stated at the outset because they are crucial to any understanding of the intent behind Chinese foreign trade policies.

In the analysis that follows, I shall concentrate less on intentions and more on the nature of the alternatives available to Peking. In particular, did the maximum attainable level of Chinese trade dictate an investment program directed at import substitution, or was such a direction the result of autarkic trade policies? Put somewhat differently, did Peking by investing heavily in such industries as steel and machinery in the 1950s sacrifice large potential gains from trade, or did she in fact reap whatever benefit there was to be had? [1]

Perhaps the principal conclusion in this paper is that Peking's investment allocation and planning techniques were severely constrained by limits on the extent to which mainland China's trade with the rest of the world could be expanded. It is, therefore, desirable to start with an analysis of whether the size of China's trade ratio $[(X + M)/\text{GNP} = 7 \text{ to } 11 \text{ percent}]$ [2] was primarily a result of deliberate policy (including mistaken policy) or of the Chinese economy's comparative advantage (i.e., relative cost structure) vis-à-vis actual and potential trading partners.

In the second section of this paper, the question asked is, given the level of trade and a policy oriented toward rapid economic growth, could Peking have avoided major investments in steel, machinery, and related industries? The answer will be seen to depend on the required level of modern investment in agriculture. In the final section, I shall turn to the narrower and more technical issues of the impact of the international sector on methods of planning, particularly the achievement of balance between industrial inputs and outputs.

CHINA'S EXPORT POTENTIAL

In many Communist countries, it is generally believed that central planners first decide how much they will have to import in any given year, and only

[1] For a somewhat similar attempt to discuss some of these same issues for the Soviet Union, see [8].

[2] I am indebted to Professors Eckstein and Haberler for pointing out a number of difficulties in connection with the calculation of this trade ratio. The upper end of this range, 11 percent, is the figure one obtains by converting the Chinese export and import data for 1953–1957 from dollars into yuan using Eckstein and Chao's exchange rates for consumers' goods and producers' goods respectively [6, pp. 120–121]. If one converts using the official exchange rate, one gets a figure of 8 percent. If instead of converting trade, one converts GNP into dollars using the producers' and consumers' goods exchange rates where applicable, one gets a figure of 7 percent. One can get an even higher trade ratio than 11 percent by converting exports into yuan using the producers' goods rate, but this makes little sense given that very few producers' goods are exported.

after making such a determination do they set the level of exports. For China the reverse procedure is closer to the truth.[3] That is, the principal constraints on China's ability to expand trade have been limits on her ability to expand exports whose foreign exchange earnings could be used to increase desired imports.

The size of China's trade has also been reduced by her inability to obtain large amounts of foreign aid or credit. The small share of foreign aid in total foreign exchange earnings and as a proportion of investment of national product has resulted partly from China's size and partly from deliberate policy. Because aid-giving nations have generally been more concerned with strategic military-political considerations in the distribution of economic support funds than with questions of equity, the aid share of large nations such as China relative to their national product has tended to be less than that of many smaller nations.

For China, however, a more important limitation on funds received has been her posture in international politics. The decision of Mao Tse-tung upon attaining power to "lean to one side" and subsequently to enter the Korean War effectively eliminated any possible support from the world's principal aid-giving nations, the United States and countries of Western Europe. The effect of this step was reinforced when in late 1957 Peking began to put pressure on the Soviet Union in ways that culminated in the Soviet decision in 1960 to break off all economic relations other than trade. Thus in a fundamental sense China's low level of foreign economic assistance, which probably resulted in a reduction of the size of her trade, has been a consequence of a deliberate desire to go it alone in international politics.[4]

The level of Chinese commodity exports has also been brought about both by China's size and by steps initiated by the government. China is a large country, in population, in geographic extent, and in terms of gross national product. Because large countries possess within their own borders sufficient demand to operate modern industrial plants at an efficient level, because distances to alternative sources of supply outside their borders are often great, and for a variety of other reasons, the share of trade in the product of large countries tends to be less than that in small countries. Thus whatever the policies pursued by the government, a small trade ratio (relative to, say, that of the Netherlands or Malaya) will undoubtedly continue to be a characteristic of the Chinese economy.[5]

[3] The causality in China and other Communist economies is, of course, more complex than this statement implies. A "desired" level of imports certainly has some influence on the level of exports in China, and the reverse is the case for the Soviet Union and East Europe.

[4] A lower level of foreign aid or credit does not necessarily imply a reduced trade ratio. The receiving country may simply raise its exports to make up the difference caused by the loss of credit.

[5] For a fuller discussion of these issues, see [14].

Dwight H. Perkins

The area where government policy has had its greatest impact on trade is agriculture. Like most underdeveloped countries, China must rely particularly heavily on agricultural exports. About three-quarters of Chinese export earnings come from farm products or what Peking refers to as processed agricultural products — principally processed food and cotton, i.e., textiles. The issue that concerns us here is whether Chinese export earnings have grown as rapidly as rising international demand for these products would allow; or, alternatively, whether there were policies in-

TABLE 1

CHINESE EXPORTS
(1950–1965)

Year	Total Exports[a] (Million yuan)	(Million U.S. dollars)	(Million U.S. dollars)[b]	Textile Exports (Million U.S. dollars)[c]	(Million yuan)[d]	Exports of Oilseeds and Oils (Million U.S. dollars)	(Million yuan)[d]
1929–1931[e]	[2,900]	[950]	.....	.....	.....	.....	.....
1950	2,030	630	.....	.....	.....	.....	.....
1951	2,440	760	.....	.....	.....	.....	.....
1952	2,710	830	.....	.....	.....	.....	.....
1953	3,480	970	.....	.....	130	.....	.....
1954	4,070	1,160	.....	.....	250	.....	.....
1955	4,940	1,367	.....	104	440	196	990
1956	5,570	1,628	.....	187	640	196	930
1957	5,450	1,609	1,600	247	860	145	710
1958	6,700	1,890	.....	354	1,290	128	800
1959	7,650	2,147	2,230	524	2,110	159	630
1960	6,570	1,869	.....	554	2,140	123	.....
1961	4,332	1,270	.....	479	.....	34	.....
1962	4,182	1,249	1,512	481	.....	37	.....
1963	.....	.....	1,554	449	.....	38	.....
1964	.....	.....	1,780	.....	.....	.....	.....
1965	.....	.....	2,085	530	.....	.....	.....

  [a] [5, pp. 389, 439, 446, 452–454]. Essentially comparable (but generally somewhat higher) figures appear in [6, p. 95].
  [b] These are estimates made by the U.S. Consulate in Hong Kong and appearing in [4, p. 10] and [3, p. 2].
  [c] [5, pp. 114–115]. The 1965 figure is from [2, p. 11]. The 1955–1963 figures exclude raw fiber exports. Whether this is the case with 1965 is not clear. Such exports were about U.S. $50 million in 1961–1963.
  [d] [5, pp. 497, 499, and 501]. The coverage of these figures is not quite the same as the Eckstein data.
  [e] These figures have been converted to 1952 prices. Chinese exports in the years 1929–1931 averaged 1,464 million yuan in current prices [26, p. 64]. Agricultural and handicraft prices about doubled in China between the early 1930s and 1952 [16, p. 24]. The 1952 yuan figure in the table was obtained by multiplying the current price total by two. The dollar figure was obtained by converting the 1929–1931 yuan figure into dollars at the then current exchange rate and multiplying by the U.S. wholesale price index, 1930 to 1952. Needless to say, these estimates are very crude.

hibiting the ability of China to sell abroad all that overseas markets were willing to take.

Chinese exports grew rapidly between 1952 and 1959 (Table 1), but they dropped sharply thereafter and had not quite recovered their 1959 level by 1965. Nevertheless, taking the period as a whole, 1952–1965, the rate of increase of Chinese exports about matched the performance of the world as a whole and surpassed that of the underdeveloped world. Superficially this is an impressive record, but it is less so when one takes into account the artificially low level of exports in 1952.

TABLE 2

PRE- AND POST-1949 EXPORT LEVELS

| | Metric Tons Exported | |
Commodity	1929–1931[a] (avg.)	1957[b]
Tea	47,274	43,500
Soybeans	2,431,959	972,000
Peanuts	51,593	250,000
Tung oil	62,531	46,100
Silk	9,628	3,400

  [a] [26, pp. 74–75].
  [b] [5, pp. 499–500].

Basically by 1952 or 1953 Chinese exports had only recovered their previous peak (1929–1931) level (Table 1). By way of contrast, exports of the rest of the underdeveloped nations in 1952–1953, in real terms, were 50 percent or more above their pre-war peaks.[6] China, of course, was struggling with the effects of the Korean War embargo and 13 years of wartime destruction. By the late 1950s neither of these factors was operative and China caught up with the other developing countries.

Conclusions drawn from aggregate data of this kind, however, are only of limited use. An analysis of individual commodities suggests that certain Chinese policies did in fact significantly inhibit the expansion of Chinese exports.

First of all, a number of China's major exports, particularly soybeans, have not come close to their 1929-1931 levels (Table 2). Although there are specific exceptions, many of the commodities whose export level has dropped are ones for which world demand has grown rapidly, not declined. Soybeans are an important case in point. China and the United States account for about 90 percent of the world's production, but where U.S. production and

  [6] See [23, p. 444]. This percentage is not changed much if one picks a year not affected by the Korean War boom in raw material prices, instead of 1952.

exports of soybeans have expanded rapidly in the post-war period, China's production and exports have remained stagnant [6, p. 118]. Tea is another example. China lost her dominant position in the tea trade around the turn of the century. The point here is that Peking has done nothing to recoup China's lost position or even to maintain her 1950 share of world tea exports. Although a definitive explanation of this performance cannot be made here, it is difficult to believe that China is incapable for economic reasons of competing with Ceylon and India, the two other major tea producers.[7] India, in particular, has not been noted in the post-war period for a dynamic export promotion policy.

This discussion could easily be extended to a number of other major Chinese exports. Such an effort, however, is best left to someone who is willing to study world marketing and cost conditions for each commodity in much greater detail than is possible in a short paper.

One further point regarding the potential market for Chinese exports is worth making. The event of the past decade of perhaps most significance for China's export potential has been the rapid growth of Japan's national income and trade. A comparison of U.S. and Chinese exports to Japan in 1965 will illustrate the main point. Overall, U.S. exports to Japan were almost ten times those of China.[8] Nearly $800 million (of a total of U.S. $2 billion) was agricultural products, even after excluding cotton.[9] Another $76 million was coal, and $100 million iron ore and iron and steel scrap. In contrast, Chinese exports of these same items amounted to only about U.S. $200 million in 1965, and the figure is much smaller in earlier years. Although again a definitive judgment must await further study, it would appear that China has not even begun to exploit the full potential of the Japanese market.

Why has China not attempted to take greater advantage of this potential?[10] In part, of course, politics has played a role. The Korean War embargo and

[7] By economic reasons I mean that China's long-run comparative advantage in tea would not seem to be markedly different from India or Ceylon's, at least not to the degree indicated by China's small contribution to world tea exports. China lost her virtual monopoly position in tea around the turn of the century because of such things as her inability to maintain quality. Such shortcomings, however, can be readily overcome by government quality controls.

[8] All U.S.-Japan trade figures for 1965 are taken from [24]. Sino-Japanese figures are from [3, pp. 7–8].

[9] Cotton is excluded because the U.S. probably has a substantial comparative advantage vis-à-vis China in the production of cotton (particularly if U.S. subsidies are taken into account). China will probably not be able to export much cotton until she raises the quality of her product. In any case, it is more advantageous for China to use the cotton to produce cloth and export the cloth.

[10] This is a relative statement since China is rapidly expanding her trade with Japan. In the first half of 1966, Japan exported U.S. $30 million more to China than in all of 1964. For a somewhat more conservative estimate of the future of Sino-Japanese trade, see [6, pp. 209–212].

its aftermath made it impossible to develop trade relations with Japan in the early 1950s. The break in Sino-Soviet relations in 1960 probably also reduced the willingness of the Soviet Union to buy certain kinds of Chinese goods. But it was the Chinese who broke off growing economic relations with Japan in 1958, and the Soviet Union in 1960 was apparently willing to buy more than the Chinese were able to sell.[11]

The principal reason China was unable to expand exports more rapidly was her failure to raise production of key items at home (Table 3). The products involved were mostly from the farm. The inability to raise exports was in a basic sense part of a more general failure of policymakers to recognize the key role of agriculture in the Chinese economy.

The problem was more than an inadequate overall rate of growth of farm output. Chinese agricultural difficulties were particularly severe in certain key areas. Output of crops with the greatest potential export markets, such as oilseeds (Table 3), did not rise at all, even before the bad harvests of 1959–1961. If one ignores the inflated figure for 1959, cotton textile output was never able to significantly surpass the level reached in 1954. As already mentioned, soybean output was stagnant, and tea, silk, and tobacco production never got close to pre-1937 levels. Together, the commodities in Table 3 plus soybeans made up 35 to 40 percent of Chinese exports.

Maintenance of exports would not have been so difficult if it had not been for the fact that the share of exports in the total output of a number of these commodities was quite large. Total agricultural exports (including processed farm products) accounted for about 8 percent of the value added of agriculture plus consumers' goods industry and handicrafts.[12] For a number of individual products, however, this percentage was much higher. Between 15 and 19 percent of edible oils output was exported in the 1950s in one form or another (Table 3). Given the key role of these oils in the Chinese diet, it is difficult to see how their export could have been greatly expanded without causing severe hardship. After 1960, in fact, it appears that the government felt it was impossible to export these items at all.

The case of cotton textiles is somewhat different. There Peking was able to postpone consumption during the 1959–1961 crisis and thus maintain roughly the 1959 peak level of textile exports. The postponement, however, could not have been prolonged indefinitely. Presumably it was carried to the lengths it was because of the need to keep export earnings from disappearing altogether.

The one commodity whose trade was comparable in importance to textiles in determining the availability of foreign exchange for the purchase of

---

[11] The principal evidence in support of this is the fact that the Soviet Union had to extend China unanticipated credits in 1960 because of China's inability to ship what had been agreed to for the year.

[12] The value-added data are from [16, pp. 140–141].

TABLE 3
EXPORTS, DOMESTIC PRODUCT, AND SALES

Commodity	1952	1953	1954	1955	1956	1957	1958	1959	1960	1961–1962
Textiles (million meters)										
Production[a]	3,830	4,680	5,230	4,360	5,770	5,050	5,700	7,500	....	(3,500)[b]
Retail sales[c]	2,813	3,899	3,791	3,849	5,101	4,150	4,860	5,200	....	(1,500)[d]
Exports[e]	....	....	....	162	281	696	913	2,658	2,188	(2,000)[f]
X/Prod. (%)	....	....	....	4	5	14	16	35	....	57
Oilseeds (1000 metric tons)										
Production[g]	3,800	3,600	4,200	4,500	4,750	3,750	4,000+	....	....	....
Exports[e]	....	....	....	386	404	268	113	101	63	5
X/Prod. (%)	....	....	....	9	8	7	3	....	....	....
Edible oils (1000 metric tons)										
Production[a]	983	1,009	1,060	1,165	1,076	1,100	1,250	1,140	....	....
Retail sales[c]	778	....	....	1,060	1,230	1,050	1,065	....	....	....
Exports[e]	....	....	....	113	119	103	155	146	87	9
X/Prod. (%)	....	....	....	10	11	9	12	10	....	(2)
Hogs (1000 head)										
Used[h]	71,800	76,900	81,400	70,300	67,200	69,000	....	....	....	....
Exports[e]	....	....	....	626	549	502	773	692	861	354
X/Used (%)	....	....	....	1	1	1	....	....	....	....
Pork (1000 metric tons)										
Retail sales[c]	2,396	....	....	2,420	2,350	1,454	1,764	....	....	....
Exports[e]	....	....	....	145	128	74	176	134	62	37
X/Sales + X (%)	....	....	....	6	5	5	10	....	....	....
Tea (1000 metric tons)										
Production[a]	83	85	92	108	121	112	....	....	....	....
Exports[e]	....	....	....	35	38	44	46	44	37	36
X/Prod. (%)	....	....	....	32	31	39	33	27	....	....

[a] Except where otherwise noted, production figures are those published by [22, pp. 99–100, 125] and [15, p. 4].
[b] Derived by adding sales to exports.
[c] These figures are official figures or ones derived from published official percentages. For the original sources, see [19, pp. 250–251].
[d] Refugee sources indicate that rations in 1961–1962 tended to be about 2 meters per person, although these figures were not uniform throughout the country.
[e] All export data are taken from [5, pp. 493–501].
[f] This is a rough estimate based on Dernberger's estimates of the value of textile exports.
[g] ...... there is [16, p. 125] except for the 1958 figure, which is an estimate based on official peanut and rapeseed figures. The

industrial imports was grain. Traditionally, China has been a net importer of grain, but in the 1950s the Communists were able to eliminate most imports and actually exported a million tons a year, two million tons in 1959 [5, p. 494]. Depending on the year, grain exports provided Peking with between 5 and 10 percent of her export earnings. In 1961, however, this policy was sharply reversed, and China began to import about 6 million tons a year at a cost of U.S. $300–$400 million a year, or the equivalent of 15 to 20 percent of peak export earnings.

This turnaround in grain trade policy was not the result of the large share of imports or exports in total Chinese grain output. In fact, even at the bottom of the agricultural crisis in 1960–1961, grain imports accounted for at most 4 percent of total grain consumption.[13]

The per capita level of grain consumption in 1960–1961 was, as is now well-known, very low; but a 4 percent increase in consumption was not sufficient to significantly alleviate the shortage. It was distribution problems, in part resulting from the drop in farm output but really more a cause than a result of the fall in production, that led Peking to resort to importing grain. If distribution were not the principal problem, it would be difficult to explain why grain imports have continued unabated in the face of a nationwide 10 to 20 percent increase in per capita grain consumption, and why Peking has apparently decided to import large quantities for several more years at least. It is true that in 1965 China's grain trade was partly simply a substitution of wheat for rice and corn, but net imports still amounted to U.S. $250 million [3, II, p. 11].

The nature of the distribution problem was and is twofold.[14] First, by taking more grain from key marketing areas than the peasant in those areas was willing to market voluntarily, a damper was placed on his incentive to raise production (the 1962–1965 increase was essentially only a recovery to 1957 per capita levels). Between the 1955–1956 grain year and that of 1958–1959, the compulsory portion of purchases (excluding the agricultural tax) rose from about 10 million to 20 million tons.[15] The reason this portion rose so rapidly was principally the rapid rise of large urban centers, particularly in Manchuria and North China. Six million tons went a long way toward relieving the burden that urbanization placed on the peasant, and hence toward raising his incentive to increase output. In a fundamental sense, therefore, grain imports were similar in nature to investment in agriculture.

[13] There were no grain imports in 1960, but in 1961 they reached a level of 6 million tons. Estimates of total grain output in China in 1961 are generally around 160 million tons.

[14] This discussion is based on my forthcoming article, "Urbanization and the China Grain Market, 1700–1966."

[15] These figures are derived from official data. For the original sources, see [19, pp. 248–249].

The second problem was the strain placed on China's badly overburdened railroads by these increased marketings. The difficulty was that the cities to be supplied were 1000 and more miles from the principal surplus area of the upper Yangtze river, particularly Szechwan. Grain imports were a means of substituting foreign ships for Chinese railroads.

Thus China's limited ability to expand export earnings was primarily a result of her failure to raise agricultural production. Even the grain marketing problem could have been alleviated if grain output had risen fast enough to provide a voluntary surplus. China's political difficulties with the United States and the Soviet Union were by comparison less significant. Whatever the influence of such factors as secularly declining export prices and world income inelasticity of demand for agricultural products on the trade of other underdeveloped countries, they were of minor importance in curtailing Chinese export earnings.

Even if Chinese policies had succeeded in raising farm output on a sustained basis and had taken full advantage of potential export markets, however, the share of trade in China's national product would have remained small relative to all but the largest nations. Perhaps the trade ratio $[(X + M)/\text{GNP}]$ could have been raised from 10 to 15 percent (or from 7 to 11 percent), but it is difficult to see how a much greater increase could have been achieved.[16]

IMPORTS AND CHINESE GROWTH STRATEGY

Given this level of export earnings and the lack of foreign aid, it follows that there were also rigid limits on the degree to which imports could be expanded. What then are the implications of this limited amount of imports for China's investment strategy? The principal question of relevance here is whether Chinese Communist import and investment policies were derived from a deliberate policy of emphasis on autarky or were simply a necessary result of limited foreign exchange earnings.

To anticipate, the principal conclusion of the analysis in this section is

---

[16] I am indebted to Professor Liu for pointing out the need to elaborate on my reasons for picking the 15 percent figure. Total trade could undoubtedly, over time, be raised by more than 50 percent, but in the meantime GNP would presumably also be rising. If GNP were not rising by at least 4 percent per year, it is difficult to see how exports and hence imports could be expanded at all. If GNP were rising at 4 percent a year, total trade would have to rise at a rate of 10 percent a year to reach 15 percent of GNP in 10 years. By way of comparison, between 1948 and 1961 the trade of the developed world grew at about 6.5 percent per year, while that of the underdeveloped world grew at under 4 percent per year. Since 1955, the latter rate has declined slightly. A 10 percent rate is not unprecedented, but it is extraordinarily high. Hence 15 percent seems to be a reasonable upper limit on the Chinese trade ratio for the next decade or two. A really definitive upper limit could be determined, however, only by an elaborate analysis of China's potential export markets.

that, whatever their desires, the Chinese Communists were compelled by economic considerations to follow a policy that led to an increasing ability to do without imports. Put differently, China's restricted import capacity together with limits on the variability of input-output coefficients within heavy industry meant that Peking had to pursue a policy of more or less balanced growth, at least within the producers' goods industrial sector. By balanced growth, I simply mean that China could not have built one type of industry (such as machinery) and then relied on imports to supply the necessary inputs (e.g., steel). The bulk of these inputs had to be produced domestically.

It is not meant to suggest that the Chinese had no alternatives. The principal choice, it will be demonstrated, was between investment in industrial output that could be used to make more industrial products and in industrial products that were inputs to agricultural production. It is thus useful to begin the analysis by dividing the argument into two parts. The first part of the argument proceeds under the assumption that no investment is made in agriculture except for internal investment by the agricultural sector itself. In the second part of the discussion this assumption is removed. This approach has the added advantage of being the way in which the Chinese Communists approached the problem — that is, by first assuming as they did in the 1950s that agriculture could take care of itself.

The first question in essence is, could the Chinese Communists have allocated investment in the 1950s differently, given that all of the investment was to go into industry (or supporting sectors)? Certainly large-scale investment in light industry would not have made much sense. A high proportion of these industries depended on agricultural raw materials, and these raw materials would not be increasing rapidly enough to require a major rise in plant capacity. In a few cases (e.g., cotton and wool), raw materials could be profitably imported provided that most of the finished product were then exported. This was, to some extent, done, but one should not exaggerate the gains from such a procedure or the extent to which maximum use of this procedure would have required a shift in investment priorities. Greater investment in light industries that did not depend on farm inputs might also have been possible. Increased allocation of funds for bicycles, thermos bottles, and particularly artificial fibers would have made possible more exports as well as greater consumption at home. But again one should not overemphasize the degree to which exports of these items could be expanded. When this limit was reached, further expansion of capacity and output would be entirely at the expense of investment and the rate of growth.[17]

[17] This statement makes the implicit assumption that the key operational constraint limiting the rate of investment is the ability of the Chinese to pay for imports of investment goods. If, instead, the operational constraint on investment is the low level of per

If one eliminates from consideration modern investments in agriculture, then the range of choice available in the producers' goods industrial sector is not much wider than for consumers' goods. Within any particular sector there will be many alternatives. Any industrial program will require the development of sources of energy, but there is considerable variation in the kinds of energy used. Buildings can be constructed from different kinds of materials, but machines must be housed and mine shafts shored up in some way. Thus between sectors, broadly defined, the degree of flexibility is not great.

If all construction materials including steel could be imported, or if the same were possible for energy resources or machinery, Peking's possible investment strategies would be many and varied. Such, however, is not the case, because of China's inability to find enough foreign exchange for more than a fraction of her machinery and industrial input requirements. If, for example, one looks at the situation prevailing in, say, 1957 and assumes that all steel and machinery had to be imported, the Chinese Communists would have had to more than double exports.

In a sense, China's options as of 1966 are less limited in this regard than in 1957. They are less limited because from 1953 through 1960 China imported "machines to make machines" and devoted considerable domestic resources to the same end. Thus Chinese steel output as of 1965 was about 10 to 12 millions tons annually, up from 1.3 million tons in 1952.[18] If China had had to import 10 million tons of steel in 1965 instead of producing it at home, the foreign exchange cost would have come to at least U.S. $2 billion in that year.[19] A comparable figure for machinery imports cannot be estimated so readily, but it must be about the same as that for steel.[20] Because of this development of machinery and steel, China could pursue a considerably wider range of economic programs, without resort to excessive imports, than would have been possible in the 1950s.

One should not exaggerate, however, the degree to which the growth of these industries has widened Chinese options. Ten to twelve million tons

capita consumption of cloth, this statement would have to be modified — but this is improbable.

[18] The 1965 figure is that reported in *Nikkan Kogyo* (Japan Industrial News), which was in turn based on a report of a visit to China by a director of the Yawata Iron and Steel Co. (reported in [1]).

[19] The unit value of steel imports from the Soviet Union in the years 1955–1959 was U.S. $124 to $226 per metric ton for rolled iron and steel and up to U.S. $561 for cold-drawn strips [18, p. 112].

[20] The gross value output of the machine-building industry was about the same as that of steel in 1957 [22, p. 92]. If these same commodities had all been imported, however, it may be that the relative international prices of machinery and steel would have been significantly different from relative domestic prices. There is also a problem of double counting, arising principally from the fact that the gross value figure for machinery presumably includes steel inputs used in making the machinery.

of steel is not large in relation to the needs of a developing economy of China's size. In 1957, Japan produced 12 million tons with a gross national product that was somewhat less than half that of China in 1965, and an industrial sector that was no larger than China's 1965 level.[21] From 1957 to 1965 Japan's national product about doubled, but her steel output increased even more rapidly, to 42 million tons.[22] China may not require such a large increase, but a growth rate of, say, 5 percent a year will certainly require an at least comparable rate of increase in steel.[23] Present indications, principally the apparent lack of expansion of steel capacity beyond the 1959 or 1960 level and the desire to buy a steel plant from West Europe, imply that this rise in steel output will have to be supplied by imports either of steel or of steel mills. China is not yet able to build the needed mills completely from domestic resources, or so it seems.[24]

Given that imports must be limited, and that domestic requirements for such commodities as steel and machinery will be large, the only reasonable policy is to purchase specialized items where the country's comparative disadvantage is particularly great. Thus China in the 1950s imported special alloy steels and advanced varieties of machinery and equipment.[25] Certain raw materials that were not produced within her borders also had to be imported. This was the case with rubber, and throughout the 1950s it was also the case with petroleum.

As Chinese economic development proceeded in the 1950s imports were made up of progressively more advanced items. Although total imports increased rapidly until 1959, the share of imports in the consumption of most general categories of products declined with roughly equal speed [6, Table 4–10, p. 126]. In a sense, this shifting import pattern could be thought of as simply reflecting China's determined drive toward autarky. But if the above line of argument is correct, these shifts can also be thought of as reflecting the course taken by any large country undergoing rapid industrial-

[21] International comparisons of industrial product are always difficult for both theoretical and statistical reasons, and this statement is only meant to indicate that the two countries' productions were roughly comparable in size.

[22] Same source as footnote 18.

[23] A precise figure can only be obtained by postulating a set of output targets (or final demand targets) and then working out the results with the aid of an input-output table for some country whose coefficients roughly approximate those for China (perhaps the Japanese table for the early 1950s would be appropriate). The principal users of steel in the Japanese economy, besides shipbuilding, were transport equipment, machinery, iron and steel itself, non-metallic minerals, metal mining, coal mining, and petroleum — i.e., most of heavy industry but not chemicals [2, pp. 216–217].

[24] The issue is not whether China can build at reasonable cost any steel mills at all, but whether she can build mills that produce the needed quality and varieties of steel. The statement in the text is not meant to be definitive and could be proved wrong by further analysis.

[25] For an attempt to determine commodities in which China has a comparative advantage, see [13].

ization. In this context it is interesting to note that heavy industry in Japan, whose trade ratio was more than double that of China, rose from 19.1 percent of industrial output in 1895 to 38.0 percent in 1920, and producers' durable equipment production rose 40 to 50 times [21, pp. 95, 99, and 321].

Perhaps the greatest difference between Chinese Communist investment policies and those that would have been undertaken by any Chinese government with a program for rapid industrialization (and ignoring agriculture) was in the treatment of transport. By the end of the 1950s, Chinese railroads were being utilized at a rate far exceeding that of any other large country,[26] and the strain had a detrimental effect throughout the economy. Greater investment in railroads, however, would have meant a shift in demand toward, not away from, steel and machinery. Except for such difficult-to-produce items as locomotives, this demand would still have to be supplied from domestic sources.

If Chinese industrial investment followed a pattern dictated largely by her size and her desire for rapid industrial growth, what then is the meaning of Chinese statements about the vigor of their pursuit of autarky? A belief in autarky has been an article of faith with Chinese economic planners and there is no reason to doubt the sincerity of the belief. One of the principal reasons this belief has never been questioned, however, is because it never had to be. In a real sense, the Chinese economy has been increasing its degree of independence of foreign trade.

The term autarky as used here does not imply that the share of foreign trade in China's national product has declined. The Chinese Communists have never really defined the term, but what they seem to mean is the progress of the Chinese economy to a point where economic growth and military production could be continued unabated even if all or most trade were cut off. Thus the government may continue to expand trade to take advantage of domestic-international cost differentials, but these differentials will be narrowed to the point where domestic production could be substituted without greatly increasing cost. Autarky in this sense is as much (or more) a function of a country's scientific and technical capacity, particularly its ability to develop inexpensive substitutes, as it is of its industrial plant in being. The primary significance of the concept is as a measure of a nation's capacity to counteract an embargo imposed for military or political reasons.

If China has increased her potential ability to do without imports, she is still a long way from the level achieved by such countries as the United States or the Soviet Union. There are many key commodities that China either cannot produce at all or can produce only at a very high cost. Still,

---

[26] Even in 1957, the number of ton-kilometers carried in China per kilometer of road exceeded that of the Soviet peak level of the 1930s. The Soviet Union is normally thought of as a country with an excessively high rate of utilization, and yet Chinese utilization in 1958 and 1959 was well above the high level of 1957 [11, p. 79].

the effect of the withdrawal of Soviet technicians in 1960 was far less severe than it would have been if it had occurred in, say, 1956. Increased potential autarky, therefore, is the result of China's industrialization and scientific manpower development programs.

The above arguments have been made on the assumption that the only investment in agriculture is that by the rural sector in itself, using only traditional inputs. How is the argument changed when this assumption of no modern investment in agriculture is removed? The principal change is in the relative priority given to the chemical industry. Depending on the priority given to agriculture, it is conceivable that a very high proportion of imports for and investment in the heavy industrial sector could be shifted to chemicals. Chemicals are among the few products of heavy industry that do not make great use of ferrous metals and machinery. In fact, the chemical industry depends primarily on inputs of other chemicals, rubber products, and various agricultural products.[27] Thus it would be conceivable for China to expand development of the chemical industry, which would in turn increase agricultural output and exports, which could then be used to import more chemicals or chemical plants — all without any great expansion in steel and machinery output.

If one assumes that grain output must be raised by 3 to 4 percent per year [28] and further that China's production function for grain is not radically different from that of other countries, it is likely that such an increase could be attained with an annual increase in fertilizer application of 300–400 thousand metric tons (in terms of plant nutrient). If the entire amount were to be imported, the annual net increase in imports would amount to U.S. $60–70 million, or about 3 percent of China's past peak export levels (in 1959 and 1965). Within 15 years, total imports of chemical fertilizer would reach U.S. $1 billion. If one takes into account disincentives and poor managment resulting from the introduction of cooperatives in agriculture, then the cost of any given increase in output would have to be raised.

Over the long run, importing fertilizer is undoubtedly much less expensive than importing grain (about one-fifth as expensive),[29] but the burden on China's foreign exchange earnings would still be heavy, although not prohibitive. In contrast, essentially the same increase in chemical fertilizer consumption could be achieved by the annual importation of under U.S. $300

[27] This statement is based on input-output tables appearing in my "Industrial Planning and Management" (forthcoming in a conference volume of the Committee on the Economy of China) and those in [2].

[28] Population in China is growing by 2 percent or more per year. Grain output would have to grow at least that fast and enough more to make possible a rising standard of living and a rising surplus that could be shipped to the cities on a voluntary basis, or at least on some basis that did not badly damage rural incentives.

[29] This does not mean it is irrational to import grain under all circumstances.

million in complete plants.[30] Thus it is clearly in China's long-run interests to develop her own chemical fertilizer industry. Whether it is in her interest to import complete plants or to build industries capable of supplying the equipment needs of such plants from domestic sources is less clear. Available evidence suggests that Peking has opted for the latter course but that she still imports a few complete fertilizer plants.[31]

It is not so easy to make comparable calculations for other agricultural inputs, but I expect that the results would be similar for such items as insecticides, power pumps, steel plows, and the like. Any reasonable estimate of the real value of foreign exchange to Peking and of the opportunity cost of producing these basically simple items with domestic resources would, I believe, favor domestic production over imports.

To argue that China could invest in chemicals without a commensurate development of steel and machinery, and further that Chinese export earnings are more than sufficient to pay for the imports required for such a program, is not to argue that such a one-sided development strategy is necessarily desirable. The choice between steel and machinery, on the one hand, and chemicals, on the other, need not be a mutually exclusive one. In fact, if the above cost estimates are roughly accurate, China could still afford to devote the bulk of her foreign exchange earnings to the development of heavy industries other than chemicals. This assumes, of course, that the annual import of several hundred million dollars of chemical plants would in fact raise agricultural output by the desired amount, thus allowing for the elimination of farm imports and an expansion of exports. Such an assumption is tenable only so long as Peking avoids any further radical reorganizations of rural society, such as those in 1958–1959.

The point of this discussion is that once one abandons the assumption of no modern investment in agriculture, it is no longer inevitable that a large share of investment funds must go into steel and machinery. This is true, in part, because of the different inputs required by the chemical industry and, in part, because increased exports of agricultural products would make possible a greater, although still limited, dependence on imports. Thus international trade placed the greatest constraints on the range of investment choices open to China when Peking excluded large investments in agriculture. As long as the government mistakenly believed it was possible to raise farm output by mass labor mobilization, planners had to concentrate heavily on the development of steel, machinery, and inputs of coal, power, and the like required by these industries.

[30] Individual fertilizer plants of under 50,000 tons capacity (probably in terms of gross weight) cost China $7–10 million in 1964 [17].

[31] In the past several years China has imported several chemical fertilizer plants from Japan and West Europe, but most of her increase in fertilizer output, which has been substantial, appears to have come from domestically produced plants.

These constraints on Chinese investment behavior became particularly severe from 1960 on, with the effects of the agricultural crisis and Soviet withdrawal. Inability to pay meant a sharp cutback in imports, and the Soviet posture perhaps also made it impossible to purchase certain key items, although this is not clear.[32] But the cutback in trade alone would have accounted only for a cutback in the rate of industrial development and perhaps a gradual shift in funds to chemical fertilizers. What actually happened in 1961 was a virtual cessation of new investment in industry, including chemicals. The primary cause of this drastic step was the disruption of industrial production resulting from the "great leap forward." From 1958 through 1960, factories had been built without much consideration for what varieties of products they would produce or whether a particular commodity was needed at all. From 1961 on, what was needed was not more investment and more factories, but a redirection of the activities of existing plants toward the production of useful items.

Agriculture from 1960 on also played a major role in slowing down industry, completely aside from its effect on export earnings. Feeding the increased population in the cities became a major marketing and transport problem, particularly during the "great leap forward." Even if exports had somehow been maintained, therefore, it is likely that events during the years 1961–1962 would not have been greatly altered.

Foreign trade constraints thus had the greatest impact on development strategy and the direction of investment when industrial growth was proceeding at a rapid pace. How severe these constraints were depended in turn on the rate of increase of exports. Any reasonable level of exports, however, would have been too low to allow China to pursue a policy of unbalanced heavy industrialization. China's determination in the 1950s to build a basic industrial system that would make possible further heavy industrial growth largely from domestic resources, together with small foreign exchange earnings, meant that Peking had to develop a whole range of industries more or less simultaneously. Otherwise import requirements for such items as steel or machinery would rapidly outstrip the ability of exports to pay for them.

The principal option open to the Chinese was to give greater emphasis to the development of a chemical industry. Such an emphasis had the advantage that it tended to raise export earnings, because it would raise agricultural productivity, and also that it reduced the need to develop a broad range of industries, because the inputs to the chemical industry were somewhat more limited in scope. After the agricultural failures of 1959–1961, a shift toward chemicals became not so much an option as a necessity.

[32] The Soviets apparently stopped selling China complete industrial plants, but they may have been willing to deliver those previously ordered and they have continued deliveries of other products to the present.

FOREIGN TRADE AND
TECHNIQUES OF PLANNING

Once a basic strategy of growth is decided upon, one of the principal remaining problems for central planners is to draw up the material balances. Specific output and input targets must be decided upon for each enterprise, and these targets must be consistent with each other and the general goals of the government. Foreign trade enters into these calculations as a potential source of inputs and as a market for output. The latter function, however, does not present much of a problem for those responsible for drawing up the material balances. Because exports are mainly consumers' goods, mistakes in setting export levels for specific commodities generally lead simply to an adjustment in consumption and do not reverberate throughout the industrial sector, as would, say, a mistake in steel allocation.

The overall level of exports is, of course, important to planners, since it determines to what degree they can depend on imports of commodities not produced in sufficient quantity domestically. As stated at the beginning of this paper, it is a common argument among economists in many underdeveloped economies that the prices of raw material exports, and hence foreign exchange earnings, fluctuate wildly. Under such circumstances meaningful planning is almost impossible unless a stabilization plan of some sort is instituted.

Fluctuating raw material prices are not a serious problem for China, however. Unlike many other underdeveloped countries, China, is not dependent for foreign exchange on the export of one or two agricultural products such as rubber or coffee. This situation is partly another reflection of China's size. A large country is apt to have a comparative advantage in a larger number of major commodities than a small country. But China is better off than several other large countries as well. China is not dependent on any single commodity, as India is on tea and jute, for example (Table 4).

The rising share of cotton textiles in Chinese exports in the 1960s did increase the vulnerability of Chinese foreign exchange earnings to a degree, not because of fluctuating prices but because of the potential loss of markets to competitor nations. But loss of export markets for textiles is more of a long-run problem than a factor complicating short-run planning. The principal source of export instability is, as indicated previously, domestic not foreign in origin — namely, the instability of agricultural output.[33]

Harvest fluctuations, however, are not so destabilizing for planners as one might suppose. As stated in the first five-year plan, once a plan (presumably an annual plan) is drawn up, fulfillment of the export portion of

[33] Professor Haberler has pointed out to me that various studies have shown that export instability in many if not most developing nations, not just China, is domestic rather than foreign in origin.

the plan has priority over competing domestic requirements [7, p. 163]. Fluctuations within any particular year can usually be offset by short-term credits. Thus, in principle, a bad harvest will not affect the annual plan once it has been adopted, but only future annual plans that have yet to be drawn up. With the exception of the extreme conditions of 1960, it would appear that China has held to this set of priorities, although I have no concrete evidence regarding foreign trade plans of 1961–1965. In at least

TABLE 4

MAJOR COMMODITIES' SHARE IN EXPORTS
(Percentages)

Commodity	India (1956)[a]	Commodity	China (1956)[b]
Tea	23.6	Oilseeds	12.2
Jute manufactures	20.2	Textile manufactures	11.4
Cotton manufactures	10.3	Cereals	9.6
Hides and skins	4.8	Metals	6.9
Raw cotton	4.1	Meat and fish	8.8
Manganese ore	3.7	Raw textile fibers	7.4
...		Ores	6.6
Other	33.3	Other	37.1
Total	100.0	Total	100.0

[a] [12, p. 343].
[b] [5, pp. 459–462]. These percentages are based on Chinese exports to reporting countries only (i.e., about 80 percent of all Chinese exports).

1954, 1957, 1958, and probably 1956, foreign trade plans were slightly overfulfilled [9] [10] [20, p. 167] [25].

For periods extending beyond an annual plan, exports did not enjoy a comparable priority. According to Yeh Chi-chuang, the Minister of Foreign Trade [25], exports of commodities that are crucial to the people's livelihood and that are in tight domestic supply must be strictly limited. He also describes an intermediate category, and then a third category of "commodities which don't have much influence on the people's needs or the domestic market." For this third category only, goods are first to be exported, and then, if there are any surpluses left over after foreign demand has been fulfilled, they can be sold on the domestic market.

Generally, Peking seems to have roughly followed these priorities in actual practice, although one might change the first category's definition to include only goods whose domestic supply is "extremely tight." Although Yeh Chi-chuang's statement was made in 1957, he specifically mentions grain and edible oils as being in this category. In the 1960s under the impact of the poor harvests, it was these commodities whose share in exports dropped most dramatically. The fact that exports of cotton textiles were maintained at such a high level in the 1960s, however, indicates that commodities "crucial to the people's livelihood" were rather narrowly defined. There is also a question of how these priorities would have been applied in the 1960s if the economic difficulties had been entirely agricultural in origin. If greater imports for industry could have been used efficiently — that is, if the disruption of the "great leap forward" had not occurred — there might have been a greater willingness to cut back further on consumption. In general, however, Peking had not given anything approaching an absolute priority to exports; hence planners had to take into account fluctuations in imports that could not be completely anticipated more than a year in advance.

Another source of instability in Chinese imports has been China's political relations with key trading partners. Heavy dependence for imports or export markets on any single country can be a problem for any nation, but usually the threat is a long-term one and not a major difficulty for those drawing up short-term plans. Not so for China, largely for political reasons. China's decision to "lean to one side" and the embargo imposed by most non-Communist nations after Chinese entry into the Korean War required China to completely reorient her trading pattern within a very short time. Similarly, in 1960 the break with the Soviet Union forced Peking to obtain imports of many key items in the West. In the latter case, individual machines and even entire enterprises had to halt production temporarily, and in some cases permanently. Under such circumstances, the annual balancing of inputs and outputs was obviously greatly complicated. Still the major cause of the lack of balance in the industrial economy of the early 1960s was domestic, not foreign, in origin. The virtual abandonment of planning in the "great leap forward" of 1958 through 1960 and the resulting anarchic production policies would have thrown the industrial sector out of balance even if international trade relations with the Soviet Union had remained normal.

Thus with the exception of the political problems connected with the Korean War and the Soviet break, instability in the overall level of total Chinese trade has been largely domestic in origin. Generally when trade has fluctuated, particularly when it has dropped, the difficulties thus created for central planners have been dwarfed by errors and instability wholly unrelated to foreign economic relations.

If total trade fluctuations were of secondary importance in complicating planners' calculations, there remains the question of to what degree planners retained a choice over the commodity composition of a particular trade volume. In the preceding discussion of the effect of foreign trade on growth strategy, it was argued that the range of choices among the industries China had to develop domestically and those where she could depend on imports was limited. Hence the basic kinds of commodities to be purchased from abroad were fairly obvious once an overall development strategy was decided upon.

There remains, as well, the question of whether the particular technology used in constructing an individual enterprise was an equally clear choice. If, for example, China had a wide range of alternative kinds of steel mills or machinery plants to import, the task of central planners could be a complicated one. For the task to be really difficult, however, the different technologies would have to involve significantly different combinations of material inputs and outputs. The experience of other countries suggests that this is not the case. As Chenery and Clark have shown, the input-output coefficients of several industrial countries at varying stages of development and possessing different factor endowments are similar [2, pp. 205–213]. Although there is not sufficient evidence to firmly establish that similar coefficients prevail in China, such is probably the case. Among other reasons, China's plant designs have generally been copies of Western or Soviet and Japanese models. Given similar input-output coefficients, the principal decision to be made by central planners is not how much of a commodity to produce, but whether to buy the equipment from, say, Japan or France or perhaps to decide between several alternative Japanese plants. To a substantial degree such decisions can be made individually without having to alter the material balances every time a change is made.

It is an open question whether this state of affairs would be greatly changed if Peking finally succeeded in developing small-scale labor-intensive enterprises in a number of industries. The efforts of 1958–1959 were not rewarded with success because of the haphazard way in which they were carried out, but this may not always be the case. Even if China did develop efficient small-scale plants, one suspects that the savings would be rather in terms of shorter gestation periods (capital savings) than major reductions of material inputs into the production process itself. Smaller-scale plants might also require less complicated machinery, which would allow planners a somewhat wider choice in selecting what to import. Whatever the case, these changes would take time and would not greatly complicate the year-to-year balancing process.

Thus problems of taking into account the international trade sector do not greatly complicate the task of Chinese central planners in drawing up the annual material balances. Again it is the limited size of the trade sector relative to national product that accounts for this situation. If trade were, say, 30 or 40 percent of gross national product, fluctuations of the size of those in Chinese trade in the 1950s and 1960s would have had a traumatic effect on Chinese central planners. As it was, the effect was only one of several in determining the rate of investment in heavy industry. If trade had been a larger share of national output, planners would also have had to face up to such issues as whether to concentrate on light industry and agriculture and import capital equipment, whether to import steel and produce machinery or vice versa, and so on.

These latter issues, however, are rather ones of long-term strategy than of short-term material balances. Furthermore, although a small trade ratio places limits on the scope of short-term decisions as well, it also increases the cost of planning errors. A country with a large trade ratio can usually fall back on imports to make up deficits in particular items caused by faulty planning. Often these imports can be made at the expense of consumers' goods or relatively low-priority investment items. Shortages in China of items normally produced domestically, in contrast, would most likely be made up at the expense of high-priority investment goods. Not surprisingly, China has generally not used foreign trade as a buffer against short-term planning errors.

CONCLUSION

The principal determinant of the international impact on Chinese central planning, therefore, is the limited share of trade (potential as well as actual) in national product. Most important is the effect of this limited size on Peking's choice of development strategies. It is doubtful that the Chinese Communists in the 1950s seriously considered alternative strategies; but if they had, they would have seen that, once they rejected modern investment in agriculture, they had little real choice unless they were willing to accept a significantly lower rate of growth. Increased awareness of the needs of agriculture after 1959 broadened these alternatives, but still within a narrow scope.

In the more limited sense of drawing up the material balances, the impact of the international sector was also shaped by its small size relative to that of most small countries. Errors in planning had to be covered by adjustments in domestic output and distribution. Fortunately for the central planners, trade fluctuations were not themselves a major source of short-run commodity imbalances. The annual foreign trade plan, once made, was generally fulfilled. In the short run, exports could always be maintained by reducing domestic consumption. If trade had been a larger share of gross national product, this too would not have been possible.

As China's economic and technical capacity grows, barring an extraordinary growth of exports, these limitations will not change radically. The principal difference will be that the cost differential between foreign and domestic production of complex machinery and the like will narrow. This in turn will give Chinese planners greater scope in deciding what to import, but basically most key items will still have to be produced at home.

DISCUSSION
Ta-chung Liu

Professor Perkins has contributed a useful paper on the impact of international trade on central planning in Communist China. My comments are limited to certain technical details in his analysis.

Perkins says that "even if Chinese policies had succeeded in raising farm output on a sustained basis and had taken full advantage of potential export markets . . . the share of trade in China's national product would have remained small relative to all but the largest nations. Perhaps the trade ratio $[(X + M)/\text{GNP}]$ could have been raised from 10 to 15 percent (or from 7 to 11 percent), but it is difficult to see how a much greater increase could have been achieved." Perkins may have underestimated the importance of agriculture in this connection. If agricultural policies had been sounder than they were, it would not have been difficult to increase value added by agriculture by 10 percent during the First Five-Year Plan period. Take 1957 as an example. A 10 percent increase in agricultural net value added would have increased agriculture output by about 4.32 billion yuan, equivalent to 4.5 percent of the domestic product. If the entire increment were then exported and the proceeds used to finance imports of the same amount, the ratio $[(X + M)/\text{GNP}]$ would increase from 10 to 19 percent. In fact, the increment in agricultural output could have been significantly greater than 10 percent if proper policies had been pursued. Moreover, if the additional imports mentioned above (amounting to 4.5 percent of the total product) consisted entirely of capital equipment, it would represent a 25 percent increase in Communist China's investment in 1957. The favorable effect on growth would have been very great.

Similarly, Perkins may also have underestimated the possibility and advantages of shifting investment toward light manufacturing industries. Taiwan does not produce much cotton, yet exports of textile products are now the most important single export category. There is no reason why the same shift could not have been attempted on a much larger scale on the mainland than it actually was. The same is true of light manufactured products that do not use agricultural products as raw materials. As Perkins says, there was of course a limit beyond which attempts of this kind could not go. But the limit was far from approached in the case of Communist China. Expanded exports of agricultural and light manufactured products would have enabled Communist China to import a great deal more capital equipment that she was unable to produce or could only produce at higher costs. The emphasis on autarky has cost Communist China more in terms of growth and development than is indicated by Perkins.

In the last section of his paper, Perkins may also have underestimated the complications in drawing up the annual material balances with respect to export products. Much of Communist China's exports consisted of agricultural and handicraft products, which had to be collected from small producing units scattered over the country. It is now common knowledge that the Communists had rather limited knowledge about these small producing units.

REFERENCES

1. *The Boston Globe*, August 1, 1966, p. 21.
2. Chenery, Hollis B., and P. G. Clark. *Interindustry Economics* (New York: Wiley, 1959).
3. "China in World Trade," *Current Scene*, IV:3 (February 1, 1966), pp. 1–8, Part I; and IV:4 (February 15, 1966), pp. 1–11, Part II.
4. "Decision for an Upsurge," *Current Scene*, III:17 (April 15, 1965), pp. 1–10.
5. Dernberger, Robert F. "Foreign Trade and Capital Movements of Communist China, 1949–1962" (Unpublished doctoral dissertation, Harvard University, 1965).
6. Eckstein, Alexander. *Communist China's Economic Growth and Foreign Trade* (New York: McGraw-Hill, 1966).
7. *First Five-Year Plan for Development of the National Economy of the People's Republic of China in 1953–1957* (Peking: Foreign Languages Press, 1956).
8. Holzman, Franklyn D. "Foreign Trade," in Abram Bergson and Simon Kuznets, *Economic Trends in the Soviet Union* (Cambridge: Harvard University Press, 1963), pp. 283–332.
9. *Hsin-hua Pan-yueh-k'an*, March 10, 1958, p. 20.
10. *Hsin-hua Yueh-pao*, October 28, 1955, p. 169.
11. Hunter, Holland. "Transport in Soviet and Chinese Development." *Economic Development and Cultural Change*, XIV:1 (October 1965), pp. 71–84.
12. *India, 1960* (Delhi: Government of India, 1960).
13. Ishikawa, S. "Strategy of Foreign Trade under Planned Economic Development — with Special Reference to China's Experience," *Hitotsubashi Journal of Economics* (January 1965).
14. Kuznets, Simon. *Six Lectures on Economic Growth* (Glencoe: Free Press, 1959), Lecture V.
15. Li Fu-chún. "Report on the Draft 1960 National Economic Plan" (March 30, 1960), *Second Session of the Second National People's Congress of the People's Republic of China (Documents)* (Peking: Foreign Languages Press, 1960), pp. 1–48.
16. Liu, T. C., and K. C. Yeh. *The Economy of the Chinese Mainland: National Income and Economic Development, 1933–1959* (Princeton: Princeton University Press, 1965).
17. MacDougall, Colina. "Eight Plants for Peking," *Far Eastern Economic Review*, XLIII:4 (January 23, 1964), pp. 156–158.
18. Mah Feng-Hwa. *Communist China's Foreign Trade: Price Structure and Behavior, 1955–1959* (Santa Monica: The RAND Corporation, October 1963), RAND Memorandum RM-3825-RC.

19. Perkins, Dwight H. *Market Control and Planning in Communist China* (Cambridge: Harvard University Press, 1966).
20. Po I-po. "Report on the Results of the 1956 Plan and the Draft 1957 Plan," *Chung-hua Jen-min Kung-ho-kuo Fa-kuei Hui-pien*, No. 6, pp. 145–178.
21. Rosovsky, Henry. *Capital Formation in Japan* (Glencoe: Free Press, 1961).
22. State Statistical Bureau. *Ten Great Years* (Peking: Foreign Languages Press, 1960).
23. United Nations. *Statistical Yearbook, 1962* (New York: 1963).
24. United States–Japan Trade Council. "United States Exports to Japan by Customs District of Shipment, 1965."
25. Yeh Chi-chuang. "A Discussion of Foreign Trade," *Jen-min Shou-ts'e, 1958*, pp. 557–559.
26. Yen Chung-p'ing. *Chung-kuo chin-tai ching-chi shih t'ung-chi tzu-liao hsuan-chi* (Peking: Science Press, 1955).

Prices, the Exchange Rate, and Economic Efficiency in the Foreign Trade of Communist China[*]

ROBERT F. DERNBERGER

In January 1966, Fidel Castro publicly denounced Communist China for canceling a sugar-rice barter agreement after it had been implemented for only one year. In proposing the agreement, Cuba had argued that the price of sugar in China was four or five times the price of rice, while the price of rice in Cuba was two or three times the price of sugar. Thus, it was mutually convenient to trade Cuban sugar for Chinese rice. Cuba offered two tons of sugar for one ton of rice, but the Chinese surprisingly agreed to exchange one ton of rice for one ton of sugar. This agreement, however, was canceled at the end of one year. Why?

According to China's Ministry of Foreign Trade, China agreed to trade rice for sugar in the first place only to help Cuba out and because China had rice to trade. However, the two countries are no longer "able to meet the needs of the other." According to the Editor of the *People's Daily*, Cuba has a single-crop economy — the legacy of imperialism — and has reinforced this situation by putting into practice what the "Khrushchev revisionists call 'the principle of international division of labor'," creating "grave difficulties for Cuba." The Editor of the *People's Daily* asks, "Is this the result of advice given by the Chinese?"

Have the Chinese Communists ignored the gains from trade based on the international division of labor? In what way has the institutional reorganization of their international trade weakened or hindered rational decision-

* I wish to express my appreciation to the editors and discussants of my paper, not only for the many helpful suggestions they have made, but also for their willingness to allow me to reorganize and substantially revise the paper for publication.

making on the basis of the international division of labor? Upon what basis do the Chinese Communists make decisions concerning the commodity composition or level of exports and imports? The answer to each of these questions is important in determining the impact of planning upon Communist China's foreign trade. This paper represents a preliminary investigation into the possible answers; complete and definitive answers must await further work.

INTRODUCTION

Central planning and state foreign trade are like unwanted stepchildren in discussions of foreign trade theory. The specific institutional organization or mechanics of central planning of foreign trade and of state foreign trade companies have, of course, been studied by students of the Communist economies. The results of these institutions and their effect on the foreign trade and domestic economy of particular countries have also been investigated in some detail.[1] The aforementioned studies often include suggestions as to how central planning and state foreign trade negate the assumptions and conclusions of the traditional theory of international trade; but the traditional theory remains unchallenged as both the analytical apparatus for interpreting developments in foreign trade — why Canada exports wheat — and the basis for normative judgments of developments in foreign trade — why Canada should export wheat.

It would be possible, if sufficient data were available, to analyze Communist China's foreign trade on the basis of deviations from these normative judgments of the traditional theories, but the purpose of this paper is to examine various impacts of planning upon trade. In view of current trends in world trade, deviations from the optimum allocation of resources — optimum according to the traditional theory — are widespread; our purpose is to discover those distortions particularly due to planning and the relationship between planning and the resulting foreign trade.[2] In a specific analysis of the relationship between planning and foreign trade in Com-

[1] For examples of studies that describe the specific institutional organization or the mechanics of central planning of foreign trade and of state trading, see [3], [4], and [5]. For examples of studies that analyze the impact of these institutions on the foreign trade and domestic economy of a particular country, see [28], [29], [30], [34], and [35]. For an example of a study that incorporates both approaches, see [41].

[2] Professor H. G. Johnson has pointed out that, insofar as domestic prices and the exchange rate are concerned, a system of tariffs and exchange controls can achieve the same results that are obtained by means of state foreign trading and central planning. In this sense, one could argue that some of the literature on tariffs and exchange controls serves as a proxy for a theoretical investigation of the impact of state foreign trading and central planning. While I agree with Johnson's argument, I have been unable to find in the literature any attempt to show how tariffs can be used to maintain a specific exchange rate and domestic price level and structure. See [24] for Johnson's development of a model that could be used in such an attempt.

munist China, it also would be possible to accept the conclusions of investi-gations of the relationship between planning and foreign trade in other Communist countries with similar institutions. For example, Professor Franklyn Holzman's paper in this volume investigates many of the same problems discussed in this paper. Yet, to accept without verification the hypothesis that similar institutions in each of the Communist countries will produce the same results may lead to serious errors in interpreting those results.

Thus I have divided the argument of my paper into two distinct parts. First, I attempt to describe the particular institutional reorganization of Communist China's foreign trade and to investigate why this reorganization was made by the Chinese Communists. I examine how it has isolated the level and structure of domestic prices from the effects of foreign prices, making it difficult for the planners to use these prices as a guide to the allocation of resources for securing the gains from trade based on the international division of labor. Much of the discussion will repeat the anal-yses and conclusions of similar studies of the institutional reorganization of the foreign trade sector in other Communist countries. Nonetheless, I believe it to be worthwhile to show explicitly that the analyses and conclusions of these other studies also apply to Communist China.

Second, I turn to an analysis of the impact of planning on Communist China's foreign trade by investigating the rationale of changes in the level, direction, and commodity composition of the trade itself. The preliminary findings in this second part of the paper suggest that foreign trade has been used by the Chinese Communist planners to secure gains from trade by ex-changing exports of commodities not required for plan fulfillment or mini-mum levels of domestic per capita consumption for imports of commodities needed for plan fulfillment, especially those essential to the realization of planned investment.

I

BILATERAL TRADE AGREEMENTS AS A
PRECONDITION FOR INTRA–COMMUNIST BLOC TRADE

Empirically, bilateral trade and payments agreements would appear to be a fundamental aspect of the interrelationship of central planning and foreign trade. All trade between Communist countries is carried out under the provisions of bilateral trade and payments agreements, and, in 1955, Com-munist country trade with non-Communist bilateral-trade-agreement part-ners accounted for 70.5 percent of the Communist bloc's total trade with the non-Communist world [36, p. 13]. Central planning in the Communist coun-tries relies upon a system of material balances for planning the production and allocation of goods and materials, and imports are included in the available supply while exports are included in the allocation of output [26, pp. 162–167]. Bilateral trade agreements, therefore, could be considered to be the means of assuring the delivery of planned imports and the sale of planned exports. An examination of both the history and the actual purpose of these bilateral trade and payments agreements, however, reveals that they are not a necessary condition for central planning. Bilateral trade and payments agreements between Communist countries result from the internal organization of the domestic economy in those countries, and in trade with non-Communist countries they have been utilized to avoid the use of hard currency in paying for Communist country imports.

The argument that bilateral trade and payments agreements are neither necessary nor even beneficial to a planned economy with state foreign trading is supported by the experience of the Soviet Union from 1918 to 1940. Prior to World War II, the Soviet Union carried out foreign trade without resort to bilateral trade agreements. Soviet foreign trade was made a state monopoly in 1918, and with the introduction of planning in 1928 the state foreign trading companies operated within the framework of a foreign trade plan. Nonetheless, subject to the condition that total imports were balanced by total exports plus available foreign exchange and loans, export commodities could be sold and import commodities could be purchased in their best world market. The multilateral character of Soviet foreign trade was possible as long as there existed a general multilateral transferability of foreign currencies, especially the pound sterling and the U.S. dollar.[3] During the 1930s, the European countries that did not have planned economies, especially the Eastern European countries, sought refuge in bilateral trade and payments agreements from the foreign exchange and international payments problem caused by the world depression; while the Soviet Union, with central planning and state trading, did not adopt these agreements to any significant extent [19].[4]

The creation of the Soviet bloc following World War II led to the imposition of closer Soviet-satellite economic ties upon the countries of Eastern Europe. The large reparations assessed by the Soviet Union committed much of the satellite export capacity to trade with the Soviet Union.[5] Postwar Soviet-satellite trade did not appear to be a long-run phenomenon,

[3] "Russia's interwar trade was largely multilateral in character and she made relatively little effort to use her trade as a bargaining weapon for creating economic or political advantage" [36, p. 3].

[4] The difference between the European countries and the Soviet Union during the 1930s was not entirely due to differences in government policy concerning bilateral trade and payments agreements. The Soviet Union had already adopted measures to isolate the Soviet economy from the influence of world markets, while the smaller countries of Eastern Europe were still integrated in the world economy and were subject to the inter-war currency and payments difficulties in Europe to a much greater extent.

[5] Harry Schwartz estimates that East European reparations shipments to the Soviet Union were four to five billion U.S. dollars by the end of 1950 [46, p. 600]. Closer

however, and the Soviet Union's trade with several of the satellite countries actually declined in 1947. Moreover, the European satellites were invited to participate in such international organizations as the World Bank, the International Monetary Fund, the United Nations Food and Agriculture Organization, and the Marshall Plan. Faced with the threatened loosening of its control over the resources of the satellite countries that were needed in its own rehabilitation and development, the Soviet Union sought to en⁻ force maximum dependence of the satellites upon the Soviet economy. The satellites were not allowed to join the aforementioned international organizations, and an attempt was made to create an intra-bloc market by means of bilateral trade and payments agreements. By 1949, all of the Soviet-satellite and inter-satellite trade was being carried out under the provisions of these agreements.

The desire to assure Soviet control over the foreign trade of satellite countries may have been a major political factor responsible for the creation of bilateral trade and payments agreements in intra–Communist bloc trade. Yet economic factors were also responsible for the adoption of these agreements, for, with the attempt to create a separate "world market" and with the introduction of foreign trade monopolies in all of the satellite countries by 1949, these agreements became the natural result of annual negotiations between bilateral foreign trade monopolies. The Soviet Union did hold a superior bargaining position in these negotiations, but it was still necessary to determine the types of commodities, their quantities, their prices, and the whole framework of commercial law that was to govern the trade. Furthermore, inasmuch as the trade ruble could not be transferred multilaterally, it was necessary to create a system of bilateral payments and clearing mechanisms, not only for Soviet-satellite bilateral trade, but for inter-satellite bilateral trade as well. Thus, bilateral trade and payments agreements, while not a necessary condition for central planning, became a necessity in intra-bloc trade. Upon joining the Communist bloc at the end of 1949, China also adopted bilateral trade and payments agreements as a precondition for trade with other Communist countries.

Communist China began signing these bilateral agreements with other Communist countries immediately after coming to power in 1949, and the increase in the number of Communist countries with which China signed such agreements closely follows the development of Sino-Communist bloc trade relations. In the European bloc, bilateral trade agreements were signed with the Soviet Union, Czechoslovakia, and Poland in 1950; East Germany and Hungary were added in 1951; Rumania and Bulgaria in 1952; and finally Albania in 1955. Formal trade agreements were not signed with North

Soviet-satellite economic ties were reinforced by the creation of Soviet-satellite joint-stock companies, partly in the nature of seized German property.

Korea and North Vietnam until 1954, undoubtedly due to the military nature of China's relations with those two countries in earlier years. It was not until 1953 that China was able to break the Soviet Union's almost complete monopoly of Outer Mongolia's foreign trade, with the signing of a Sino–Outer Mongolian bilateral trade and payments agreements. Thus, from 1949 on, all of China's foreign trade with the countries of the Communist bloc involved the signing of an annual bilateral trade agreement or annual protocol under an already existing bilateral trade agreement (Table 1).[6]

BILATERAL TRADE AGREEMENTS AND THE PLANNING PROCESS

While bilateral trade and payments agreements are neither necessary nor beneficial to a planned economy, the need for bilateral agreements for trade between planned economies with state monopolies of foreign trade has made the annual negotiations of these agreements an integral part of the planning process. When I refer to planning or plans, I mean the process of drawing up a consistent set of national balances, with imports included as one of the input categories and exports as a category of output distribution. With multilateral free trade and in the absence of bilateral trade agreements, "planned" import requirements can be purchased from their cheapest source and "planned" exports can be sold in their best market by the state trading companies. Communist China's bilateral trade agreements with the countries of the Communist bloc specify the types and amounts of commodities that can be considered "planned" exports and imports, and the countries with which they can be traded. Thus the annual negotiations of bilateral trade agreements to determine what and how much is to be traded with whom becomes an integral part of the planning process.

Although Communist China did not introduce comprehensive planning until 1953, the increase in the role of the state trading companies, the growing share of China's trade with the Communist bloc, and the rapid increase in the domestic socialist sector before 1953 were interrelated aspects of the

[6] The annual bilateral trade and payments agreements and protocol signed by Communist China with Finland and effective since 1953, with Yugoslavia since 1956, and with Cuba since 1960 have not been included in Table 1. All of the agreements and protocols listed there are completely standardized. The methods of payments in trade with Finland, Yugoslavia, and Cuba are identical with those in trade with the Communist countries — bookkeeping entries in clearing accounts held at both countries' central banks — and the account currency is in both international currency and in rubles. On the other hand, the agreements with Finland, Yugoslavia, and Cuba — unlike those with the Communist countries — contain no provision for the determination of prices, and the final settlement of the clearing account balances at the end of the trading period is to be made in international currency. Therefore, Communist China's annual bilateral trade and payments agreements and protocols with these countries are similar in some respects to China's agreements and protocols with the Communist countries and similar in other respects to China's agreements and protocols with non-Communist countries.

TABLE 1

COMMUNIST CHINA'S ANNUAL BILATERAL TRADE AND PAYMENTS AGREEMENTS AND PROTOCOLS WITH COMMUNIST COUNTRIES, 1950–1965
(Date signed)

Year	U.S.S.R.	Czech.	E. Ger.	Hungary	Poland	Bulgaria	Rumania	Outer Mong.	N. Korea	Albania	N. Viet.
1950	4/19/50	6/14/50	10/10/50								
1951	6/15/51	6/21/51		1/22/51	1/29/51						
1952	4/12/52	7/15/52	5/28/52	7/21/52	7/11/52	7/21/52	7/30/52				
1953	3/21/53	3/ 7/53	4/30/53	3/20/53	5/25/53	12/ 3/52	1/19/53	8/20/53			
1954	1/23/54	4/27/54	3/30/54	4/30/54	2/19/54	3/25/54	4/19/54	4/ 7/54	9/ 4/54	12/ 3/54	
1955	2/11/55	4/ 6/55	4/24/55	4/26/55	3/21/55	1/27/55	1/20/55	12/16/54	12/31/54		
1956	12/27/55	11/11/55	11/20/55	1/27/56	12/21/55	1/21/56	1/ 3/56	2/ 7/56	1/12/56	3/13/56	7/26/56
1957	5/11/57	3/ 6/57	4/ 5/57	6/ 8/57	4/ 1/57	1/28/57	4/19/57	12/22/56	1/24/57	3/ 8/57	7/31/57
1958	4/23/58	4/16/58	4/23/58	3/21/58	4/ 7/58	3/13/58	3/31/58	1/28/58	1/21/58	3/12/58	3/31/58
1959	2/26/59	3/12/59	2/ 5/59	3/17/59	3/ 6/59	12/18/58	3/22/59	1/30/59	11/19/58	1/16/59	2/18/59
1960	3/29/60	2/ 2/60	3/23/60	2/28/60	2/22/60	3/15/60	3/15/60	2/23/60	2/29/60	3/15/60	3/ 7/60
1961	4/ 8/61	10/20/61	5/15/61	7/15/61	7/13/61	3/ 8/61	7/ 7/61	4/26/61	3/18/61	2/ 2/61	1/31/61
1962	4/20/62	7/17/62	8/ 4/62	3/30/62	3/28/62	3/30/62	5/29/62	2/25/62	3/29/62	1/13/62	1/22/62
1963	4/20/63	4/19/63	6/22/63	4/10/63	4/30/63	3/ 5/63	4/ 8/63	3/18/63	11/ 5/62	1/17/63	12/ 5/62
1964	5/13/64	4/24/64	8/ 1/64	3/28/64	2/ 5/64	4/14/64	12/27/63	1/20/64	10/14/63	12/ 6/63	10/24/63
1965	4/29/65	4/ 8/65	2/19/65	3/26/65	3/16/65	12/21/64	12/ 9/64	3/24/65	9/24/64	10/10/64	9/30/64

Number of bilateral trade and payments agreements and protocols signed each year and median month agreements signed:
1950 — 2, May; 1951 — 5, Feb.; 1952 — 7, June; 1953 — 8, April; 1954 — 9, April; 1955 — 10, Feb.; 1956 — 11, Jan.; 1957 — 11, March.
1958 — 11, March; 1959 — 11, Feb.; 1961 — 11, May; 1962 — 11, April; 1963 — 11, April; 1964 — 11, March; 1965 — 11, Jan.
Long-term bilateral trade agreements with Communist countries:

Country	Years covered by agreement	Date signed	Years covered by agreement	Date signed
1. Poland	1959–1962	4/7/58	....	....
2. Rumania	1959–1962	7/21/58	....	....
3. North Korea	1959–1962	9/27/58	1963–1967	11/5/62
4. Czechoslovakia	1959–1962	4/11/59	1966–1970	6/8/65
5. Albania	1961–1965	1/16/59		

increasing direct government control over the economy. Therefore, Communist China's pre-1953 trade agreement negotiations with the countries of the Communist bloc involved the bargaining of "planned" available exports for "planned" import requirements.[7] On the basis of the resulting trade agreements, the Chinese economic planners could revise the tentative production plan to fit the assured foreign supply of machinery, equipment, and raw materials.[8] With the formal introduction of planning in 1953, the change was more in the nature of enlarging the scope of the economy under the control of the state plan than of changing the principle involved.

The late date at which many of these annual bilateral trade agreements were signed is but another facet of the extreme difficulty the Communist countries have had in coordinating the many decisions among the various production and trading organizations and in adapting to the time required to formulate a consistent and meaningful plan. In the area of foreign trade, the difficulty encountered in attempting to arrange the bilateral exchange of available exports for required imports on an annual basis led to the introduction of long-term bilateral trade agreements. After 1950, most of the European bloc countries followed the recommendation of the Council for Economic Mutual Assistance in signing these long-term bilateral trade agreements, but the evidence suggests that the agreements have served only as minimum guidelines and have not been integrated into the planning process [41, pp. 65–69]. Despite the existence of these long-term agreements, intra–Communist bloc trade is still integrated with domestic economic planning by means of the annual bilateral trade agreements and protocols.[9]

THE RELATIVE UNIMPORTANCE OF
COMMUNIST CHINA'S BILATERAL TRADE AND PAYMENTS AGREEMENTS WITH
THE NON-COMMUNIST COUNTRIES — AN ASIDE

While bilateral trade and payments agreements were a precondition for intra–Communist bloc trade, the Chinese Communists, immediately after coming to power, were content to trade in the non-Communist world without adopting inter-government trade agreements. With the exception of

[7] According to Yeh Chi-chuang, Minister of Foreign Trade, the planning of exports and imports was carried out "since the founding of the Chinese People's Republic" [52]. According to a Soviet study of Chinese planning, the Chinese Communists adopted the Russian practice of drawing up material balances in kind. Exports and imports are included in these material balances, which show available resources and their distribution [31].

[8] In actual practice, the appearance of both domestic and foreign unplanned shortages led to constant revisions in both the domestic and foreign trade plans, caused by changes either in the domestic sector or in the foreign trade sector.

[9] Communist China never became a member of CEMA and has signed long-term trade agreements with only five other Communist countries. Four of these agreements were for the five-year period, 1959–1962. Only the long-term agreements with North Korea and Albania have been renewed (Table 1).

three Sino-Indian contracts concerning the sale of Chinese rice to India in 1951, trade between China and the non-Communist countries did not involve inter-government negotiations or the signing of trade agreements before 1952. Before 1952, China was building up a sterling balance in trade with the non-Communist countries, and thus did not encounter a payments problem — the major cause of the adoption of trade agreements in the Far East. While building up a favorable balance in trade with the European industrial countries, however, China was in desperate need of imports of machinery, metals, and chemicals for the rehabilitation and development of the Chinese economy. Following the implementation of restrictive trade controls on trade with China, adopted in the non-Communist countries in 1951, imports of these needed equipment and materials were not possible. Therefore, China first negotiated both inter-government and private trade agreements in trade with the non-Communist countries in an attempt to secure required imports when faced with the non-Communist embargo.

Communist China signed trade agreements with private delegations from eleven non-Communist countries immediately following the Moscow International Economic Conference in 1952; but, inasmuch as she was unable to obtain the desired imports by means of these agreements, they were not renewed. After 1953, with the exception of agreements signed with West Germany and Japan, Communist China negotiated no further private trade agreements with non-Communist countries.[10] Unlike the agreements with private delegations, China's first trade agreement with a non-Communist government, one signed with Ceylon in October 1952, was successful in obtaining needed imports of rubber. Ceylon, neither a member of the United Nations nor a recipient of U.S. aid in 1952, was hard hit by the rapid decline in the price of rubber at the end of the Korean War boom and received

[10] See Table 2, Section A. The agreement signed by Communist China with West German businessmen in 1957 represents the latter's success in having arbitration transferred from the Chinese Inspection and Testing Bureau to Zurich. The Chinese did not reply to West German invitations to negotiate a renewal of the agreement in 1958. The agreements signed by Communist China and private and semi-official Japanese delegations in 1952, 1953, 1955, 1958, and 1962 were much more involved with political relations between these two countries than was true of China's private trade agreements with other non-Communist countries. Communist China continually put pressure on the Japanese government to sign a payments agreement between the Bank of China and the Bank of Japan to eliminate the necessity of financing Sino-Japanese trade in pound sterling through letters of credit opened in London. The signing of such an agreement would have involved *de jure* recognition of Communist China by Japan, and when the Japanese government refused to take any action on the Sino-Japanese Trade Agreement of 1958, China unilaterally suspended direct trade relations with Japan. Sino-Japanese trade slowly revived in 1959–1961. A fifth Sino-Japanese private trade agreement involving the principle of barter trade with private Japanese concerns was signed in 1962, and Sino-Japanese trade rose to a level of 260 million U.S. dollars each way in 1965.

favorable price concessions from Communist China for signing this first of a continuing series of Sino-Ceylonese Rubber-Rice Trade Agreements. With the exception of these Sino-Ceylonese trade agreements, Communist China's trade and payments agreements with non-Communist governments were an integral part of what has come to be called the Communist "economic offensive." As such, they are but one aspect in the development of political and economic relations with the underdeveloped countries of Southeast Asia, the Near East, and Africa (Table 2, Section C).

Two important aspects of Communist China's bilateral trade agreements with the non-Communist countries differ significantly from her bilateral trade agreements with the Communist countries. First, those with the non-Communist countries involve a relatively small portion of China's total trade with that area. In 1950–1964, China's trade with non-Communist trade agreement partners was never more than 22 percent of Sino–non-Communist country trade (Table 2, Section C). Second, with the exception of the Sino-Ceylonese agreements, China's bilateral trade agreements with the countries of the non-Communist world do not include any discussion of prices. As is indicated by the relatively small portion of China's total trade with the non-Communist countries carried out under the provisions of these agreements, it is not necessary to determine prices by means of inter-government negotiations before trade can take place between China and the non-Communist countries.

The motivations of the non-Communist governments in entering into these bilateral trade agreements with Communist China can be summarized under four categories: (1) the spirit of Bandung and the desire to reduce dependence upon the Western industrialized nations and to assert policies of neutralism; (2) the desire to dispose of accumulated stocks of export commodities and improve the terms of trade; (3) the desire to continue negotiations for the extension of Chinese economic aid; and (4) the desire to create a payments mechanism that would eliminate the need for using international currencies.[11]

The payments and clearing mechanism created by China's bilateral trade and payments agreements with the non-Communist countries is shown in Table 3. With the exception of trade with India, Pakistan, and Sudan, the bilateral trade between China and the non-Communist trade-and-payments-agreement partner is financed through bilateral clearing accounts in the People's Bank of China and in the central bank, or the designated bank, in the partner country. In this manner, it is not necessary for either country to use international currencies to finance the trade, even in those cases

[11] Later developments showed that these agreements created as many problems as they solved. For a detailed discussion of the non-Communist countries' experience with bilateral trade agreement with the Communist countries, see [2] and [36].

TABLE 2

COMMUNIST CHINA'S TRADE AND PAYMENTS AGREEMENTS WITH NON-COMMUNIST COUNTRIES

A. Trade agreements signed with private representatives and delegations from non-Communist governments:
   1. Signed in 1952: Belgium, Ceylon, Chile, Finland, France, West Germany, Indonesia, Japan, the Netherlands, Pakistan, Switzerland, and United Kingdom.
   2. Signed in 1953: France, Japan, and United Kingdom.
   3. Signed in 1955: Japan.
   4. Signed in 1957: West Germany.
   5. Signed in 1958: Japan.
   6. Signed in 1962: Japan.

B. Commercial agreements signed with non-Communist governments: [a]
   1. Signed in 1955: Lebanon.
   2. Signed in 1956: Sudan.
   3. Signed in 1957: Denmark and Sweden.
   4. Signed in 1958: Norway, Pakistan, and Yemen.

C. Trade and payments agreements with non-Communist governments: [b]

	Country	Date First Agreement Signed	1953	'54	'55	'56	'57	'58	'59	'60	'61	'62	'63	'64	'65
1.	Ceylon	10/ 4/52	X	X	X	X	X	X	X	X	X	X	X	X	X
2.	Indonesia	11/30/53		X	X	X	X	X	X	X	X	X	X	X	X
3.	Burma	4/22/54		X	X	X	X	X	X	X	X	X	X	X	X
4.	India	10/14/54			X	X	X	X	X	X	X	X	X	X	X
5.	Egypt (U.A.R.)	9/25/58				X	X	X	X	X	X	X	X	X	X
6.	Syria	8/22/55				X	X	X	X	X	X	X	X	X	X
7.	Cambodia	11/30/55					X	X	X	X	X	X	X	X	X
8.	Afghanistan	4/24/56						X	X	X	X	X	X	X	X
9.	Tunisia	7/28/57						X	X	X	X	X	X	X	X
10.	Morocco	5/23/62							X	X	X	X	X	X	X
11.	Iraq	10/27/58							X	X	X	X	X	X	X
12.	Guinea	1/ 3/59								X	X	X	X	X	X
13.	Mali	9/13/60									X	X	X	X	X
14.	Ghana	2/28/61									X	X	X	X	X
15.	Sudan	8/18/61										X	X	X	X
16.	Pakistan	1/ 5/63										X	X	X	X
17.	Somali	5/15/63											X	X	X
18.	Congo (Brazvle.)	7/23/64												X	X
19.	Algeria	9/19/64												X	X
20.	Central African Republic	9/29/64													X
21.	Burundi	10/22/64													X
22.	Kenya	12/18/64													X

where international currencies are used as the unit of account. Exports and imports are financed by credits and debits in the bilateral trade accounts in the central banks, and no problem arises so long as exports and imports are bilaterally balanced. In the interim between periodic settlements or within the limits of the stipulated swing credits, however, there is nothing to prevent China, or the partner country for that matter, from acquiring an import surplus at the temporary expense of the other country's central bank. One of Communist China's principal aims in negotiating these agreements was to remove the need for using international currency to finance trade, and thus to increase the bilateral trade ties by increasing the partner country's imports from China. This aim is in accordance with the whole history of bilateralism. The history of bilateral trade and payments agreements shows that these agreements have also been utilized by a country to gain a debtor's position at the expense of the partner country's banking system. Judging by the four cases of significant imbalance in China's bilateral trade with non-Communist trade-and-payments-agreements partners — Ceylon, Burma, Egypt, and Indonesia — there is little evidence to suggest that China utilized these agreements to gain a debtor's position in trade with these countries.[12]

·Inasmuch as China's bilateral trade and payments with the non-Communist countries did not involve more than one-fifth of China's trade with that area, the goods traded under these agreements were to be those normally traded and were to be valued at world prices, and they were utilized in an attempt to increase China's trade relations with the underdeveloped countries; the existence of these agreements is not a major consideration in the relationship of China's foreign trade and domestic economic planning.

[12] In their analysis of 240 trade agreements between the Communist bloc and the Free World, Raymond Mikesell and Jack Behrman conclude, "The results do not indicate a greater tendency on the part of either bloc countries or Free World countries to run surpluses under these agreements" [36, p. 86].

NOTES TO TABLE 2:

Percent of Sino–non-Communist country trade with non-Communist trade-and-payments-agreements partners: 1952, 0%; 1953, 13.3%; 1954, 13.3%; 1955, 12.2%; 1956, 19.4%; 1957, 19.2%; 1958, 16.0%; 1959, 21.4%; 1960, 20.5%; 1961, 18.4%; 1962, 20.4%; 1963, 19.7%; 1964, 16.1%; and 1965, not available.

[a] The commercial agreements are principally statements of intent to stimulate trade between Communist China and the non-Communist partner country. They include the reciprocal granting of most-favored-nation treatment, lists of commodities for which no quotas are assigned and which are traditional exports of both countries, and provisions that payments are to be made in the domestic currency of the non-Communist trading partner or a currency acceptable to both parties. Inasmuch as these commercial agreements are found in the normal trade relations among all nations and do not affect the methods of trade, they are not discussed in this paper. For a discussion of the significance of most-favored-nation privileges in trade with a Communist country with state trading, see [15].

[b] An X entered in a particular row and column means that a bilateral trade and/or payments agreement covered Communist China's trade with that particular country in that year.

TABLE 3

PAYMENTS AND CLEARING ARRANGEMENTS CREATED BY
COMMUNIST CHINA'S BILATERAL TRADE AND PAYMENTS
AGREEMENTS WITH NON-COMMUNIST COUNTRIES

Country	Clearing Accounts in Both Central Banks?	Payments and Accounts Currency	Settlement in:	Swing Credit*
1. Afghanistan	Yes	Sterling	Currency or goods[a]	0.085
2. Algeria	Yes	Algerian dinars	Goods[b]	7.0[c]
3. Burundi	Yes	Burundi francs	Currency or goods[d]	30[e]
4. Cambodia	Yes	Sterling	Currency[f]	2.8[g]
5. Central African Rep.	Yes	CFA francs	Goods[h]	250[i]
6. Ceylon	Yes	Ceylon rupees	Currency or goods[j]	
7. Congo (Brazzaville)	Yes	French new francs	Goods[k]	2.5[l]
8. Egypt	Yes	Sterling or agreed currency	Goods[m]	5.6
9. Guinea	Yes	Guinean francs	Currency or goods[n]	
10. India	No[o]	Indian rupees or sterling	Sterling	
11. Indonesia	Yes	Sterling	Currency[p]	1.68
12. Iraq	Yes	Iraq dinars	Currency or goods[q]	
13. Pakistan	No[r]	Sterling or agreed currency		
14. Somali	Yes	Sterling	Currency or goods[s]	0.28
15. Sudan	No[t]	Sterling or agreed currency		
16. Syria	Yes	Sterling	Currency or goods[u]	
17. Tunisia	Yes	Swiss francs	Currency or goods[w]	1.5[v]

* In million U.S. dollars unless otherwise specified.
[a] After balance surpasses amount of permitted swing credit, or at end of every six months, balance to be paid in goods, sterling, or accepted currency. Balance may be transferred to next trading period, but 3 percent interest charged on all balances carried over. [b] After balance surpasses amount of permitted swing credit, excess balance to be paid in goods within six months. If not paid within six months, method of payment to be decided by agreement of both parties. [c] Million Algerian dinars. [d] Balance at end of one year, if balance surpasses amount of permitted swing credit; excess balance to be paid in goods or accepted currency within three months. [e] Million Burundi francs. [f] Settlement every six months. [g] After balance surpasses amount of permitted swing credit, either country may suspend imports from or exports to the other country. [h] After balance surpasses amount of permitted swing credit, excess balance to be paid in goods within six months. If not paid within six months, method of payment to be decided by agreement of both parties. [i] Million CFA francs. [j] Settlement by conversion into agreed currency or balance carried forward. [k] After balance surpasses amount of permitted swing credit, excess balance to be paid in goods within six months. If not paid within six months, method of payment to be decided by agreement of both parties. [l] Million French new francs. [m] Balance every three months. Balance to be settled: i, through trade by delivery by the debtor country to the creditor country of exports of

STATE TRADING AND THE MAINTENANCE OF
INDEPENDENT DOMESTIC PRICE LEVELS
AND STRUCTURES — THE EMPIRICAL EVIDENCE

State trading in the U.S.S.R. had been introduced as a policy of self-defense during a period of instability in the 1920s. Lenin was fearful that Western capitalists would submerge the domestic Soviet economy with goods, weakening its economic and political position. Bukharin felt that domestic producers could be adequately protected by a system of high tariffs, but Lenin argued that "no policy of tariffs can be effective in the imperialist epoch when there is a monstrous difference between the poor countries and those of unbelievable wealth" [20, p. 245]. At the end of World War II, Communist governments were established in the countries of Eastern Europe, and each of these new satellites adopted state trading in both domestic and foreign trade. While Communist China also followed the Soviet institutional model in the early 1950s, several important economic factors figured in the evolution of state trading in Communist China after 1949.

State trading creates the necessary conditions for isolating the domestic economy from the influence of foreign prices, and therefore enables the Chinese Communists to replace consumer preferences with those of the state planners in the domestic price structure. In March 1950, however, when the principle of state foreign trading was introduced in China, the principal problems faced by the Chinese Communists were not the creation and implementation of planning but stemming the rampant inflation, reviving pro-

the debtor country or exports of a third country; ii, through the transfer of a credit balance held by the debtor country with a third country, subject to the approval of all parties concerned; or iii, through delivery of exports from the debtor country to the other country for resale to a third country. [n] Balance at the end of one year, balance to be settled within six months in goods or in accepted currency. [o] Trade to be financed through accounts established by Chinese deposits of sterling in the Reserve Bank of India and in Indian commercial banks. [p] Settlement at end of one year. Any balance in excess of permitted swing credit to be paid in pound sterling or other accepted currency upon demand. [q] Balance at the end of one year, balance to be settled in goods or in accepted currency. [r] China and Pakistan have not signed a payments agreement; all Sino-Pakistan agreements have been barter agreements. [s] After balance surpasses amount of permitted swing credit, payment of excess balance in accepted currency within thirty days. Balance at the end of one year to be settled within six months in goods or accepted currency. [t] Payments and clearance according to "general international practice," procedures and currency to be agreed upon by both parties. [u] Balance to be settled within six months in goods, balance remaining after that period to be settled in sterling. [v] Million Swiss francs. [w] Balance at end of one year to be settled in goods within six months, balance remaining after that period to be settled in Swiss francs or accepted currency.

SOURCE: *Chung-hua Jen-min Kung-ho-kuo T'iao-yueh-chi* (Treaties of The People's Republic of China). The 1961 volume is not available in the United States, and the payments and clearing agreements with Burma, Ghana, Mali, and Morocco, signed in 1961, are not included in this table. Kenya and Tanzania have not been included, because the 1965 volume has not yet been published. There is no reason to believe, however, that the payments and clearing arrangements excluded from the table would differ significantly from those included.

duction, and reducing (or financing) the large import surpluses. Throughout 1949, various measures were adopted to alleviate the inflationary pressures and to hold them in check. Because of continued military operations in the civil war and the low level of revenues, however, the sources of inflationary pressure remained and prices rose rapidly in the last half of 1949.[13]

At the beginning of 1950, the Chinese launched an all-out assault on the inflation. Expenditures and revenues were to be centralized and the budget deficit was to be reduced that year — to be partially offset by the sale of government bonds. A National Monetary Conference in February adopted a cash control program, and the People's Bank was given control over all short-term loans, with long-term investments to be regulated by the Ministry of Finance [12]. A National Urban Supply Conference, also held in February, recommended the creation of twelve national trading companies, six for domestic trade and six for foreign trade, to regulate the supply and wholesale prices of the commodities under the control of these companies [13]. Therefore, the Chinese Communists adopted state trading in foreign trade in March 1950 as an integral part of their overall attack on inflation.[14]

It is true, of course, that state trading itself was not essential in an attack on inflation. Yet, with continued large-scale military operations and the task of rehabilitating the economy, the best the Chinese Communists could hope for was to limit, or possibly stop, the increase in the domestic price level. A deflationary policy was not desirable under the given circumstances. As long as private trade remained the principal means of foreign trade, a realistic or meaningful exchange rate was required to enable both exporters and importers to realize profits and to balance imports and exports. Experience had shown that, with increases in domestic prices, the maintenance of meaningful exchange rates meant a continuous depreciation of the *Jen-min-pi* (People's currency). Table 4 shows this relationship most clearly. That these rates tended to follow developments in the domestic price level is supported by comparing the estimated thirty-fold increase in domestic prices between April and December 1949 (Tientsin, [23, p. 298]) with the thirty-fold increase in the exchange rate from April 17 to December 10, 1949.

Depreciation of the Chinese currency was unfavorable from the Chinese

---

[13] According to Ti Chao-pi, Director of the Statistical Department of the Committee on Financial and Economic Affairs, the budget deficit in 1949 accounted for 40 percent of total expenditures [17]. An article in the *New China Monthly* discusses the rapid price rise during this period, but does not provide statistics to indicate its magnitude. The article claims that the price rise was due to the imbalance between the fiscal expenditures and revenue and the resulting "excessive issue of paper money" [40].

[14] State foreign trading companies without monopoly or monopsony power over specific export and import commodities were engaged in foreign trade before March of 1950; the granting of monopoly and monopsony power in the sales and purchase of specific commodities in both domestic and foreign trade was the result of the National Urban Supply Conference in February 1950. For the regulations applying to the state trading companies, see [13].

TABLE 4

OFFICIAL EXCHANGE RATE, *JEN-MIN-PI* PER U.S. DOLLAR:
APRIL 1949 TO PRESENT

Date	Rate[a]	Place	Source
April 17, 1949	613	North China	1
May 30–June 4, 1949	1,100	Tientsin	2
July–November, 1949	2,000	Shanghai	3
July–November, 1949	3,600	Tientsin	4
	4,500	Tientsin	5
	7,000	Tientsin	6
November 21, 1949	10,000	Tientsin	7
December 10, 1949	18,000	Bank of China	8
January 1, 1950	21,000	Bank of China	9
January 6, 1950	23,000	Bank of China	9
January 21, 1950	25,000	Bank of China	9
February 1, 1950	27,000	Bank of China	9
February 8, 1950	29,000	Bank of China	9
February 23, 1950	31,000	Bank of China	9
February 24, 1950	34,000	Bank of China	9
March 2, 1950	39,000	Bank of China	9
March 11, 1950	42,000	Bank of China	9
April 2, 1950	41,000	Bank of China	9
April 10, 1950	40,000	Bank of China	9
April 19, 1950	39,000	Bank of China	9
April 24, 1950	37,500	Bank of China	9
July 3, 1950	35,500	Bank of China	9
July 8, 1950	35,000	Bank of China	9
August 7, 1950	32,200	Bank of China	9
September 5, 1950	31,000	Bank of China	9
December 25, 1950	31,000	Bank of China	9
January 4, 1951	24,900	Bank of China	9
January 20, 1951	22,890	Bank of China	9
May 22, 1951	22,270	Bank of China	10
December 6, 1952	23,430	Bank of China	10
Present rate	2.343[b]		

[a] Rates before January 1, 1950 have been selected from the various rates that existed throughout China in 1949. While these rates differed with the locality, they closely followed both the level and rate of increase depicted above. The rates after January 1, 1950, are the buying rates of the Bank of China, the rates in different cities becoming more uniform. The rates for May 30 through November 21, 1949, are for telegraphic transfers in New York. All other rates are for U.S. dollar notes.

[b] All of the rates, with the exception of the present rate, are in "old" *Jen-min-pi* (People's Currency). On March 1, 1955, a currency conversion was introduced that called in all "old" *Jen-min-pi* in exchange for new notes at the rate of 10,000 "old" to one "new."

SOURCES:
1. [18], May 11, 1949.
2. [18], July 7, 1949.
3. [18], July 28, 1949.
4. [18], September 29, 1949.
5. [18], October 20, 1949.
6. [18], November 24, 1949.
7. [18], January 12, 1950.
8. [18], January 26, 1950.
9. [50], January 26, 1951.
10. [10, p. 122].

Communist viewpoint in that it made necessary imports more expensive in terms of domestic currency, thus adding to the inflationary pressures on prices. Depreciation may have increased foreign demand or have eased the exporters' profit margin, but the problem on the export side was essentially one of limited supply. Furthermore, continued depreciation would have led to a lack of confidence in the Chinese Communist currency at the very time they were attempting to establish the *Jen-min-pi* as the sole circulating medium of exchange. The history of continual depreciation under the Kuomintang also made further depreciation of the *Jen-min-pi* undesirable.

Table 4 also shows what happened to the exchange rate after the introduction of state foreign trading in March 1950.[15] The deflationary policies adopted in that month led to a 21 percent decline in the wholesale price index between March and September 1950 [49, p. 46]. Therefore, the parallel movement in domestic prices and the exchange rate continued immediately after March, the exchange rate falling by 26 percent between March and September. This parallel movement between domestic prices and the exchange rate was soon broken, when domestic wholesale prices resumed their upward movement in June. Between June 1950 and May 1951, the Chinese yuan was continually appreciated, the exchange rate falling by 41 percent. Wholesale prices, on the other hand, rose by 31 percent over the same period. Throughout 1951, wholesale prices continued to rise, but the exchange rate was not changed.

The severing of the relationship between the domestic price level and foreign price levels through the exchange rate was not the only factor favoring the adoption of state foreign trading companies. The purpose of the National Urban Supply Conference, held in February, was to discuss plans for the reallocation of supply and the adjustment of prices. The directive of the Government Administration Council that created the six foreign trade companies also instructed the Ministry of Trade to determine wholesale prices at "major" markets for commodities under the control of the state trading companies. This was the first systematic attempt made by the Chinese Communists to alter the domestic price structure and to give the government greater control over the allocation of resources, production, and distribution. The "containment" of the influence of foreign prices on the domestic price *level* could be achieved through a system of trade and

[15] Although restrictions had been placed on both who was permitted to trade and what goods were to be traded, Communist China's foreign trade was still carried on by private traders before March 1950. Private trade also continued to be important for a short period after March. For example, during the first six months of 1950, state foreign trading (including private trade on commission for state organs) was about 50 percent of the total foreign trade of Tientsin, Shanghai, Tsingtao, and other northern ports [22]. For the entire year, however, state foreign trading companies accounted for approximately 70 percent of Communist China's total foreign trade, and their share of the total had increased to 90 percent by 1952 [14].

exchange controls. It would also be possible, theoretically, to divorce the domestic price *structure* from the influence of foreign prices by means of such controls. The attempt to do so, however, would be administratively most difficult.

STATE TRADING AND THE MAINTENANCE OF
INDEPENDENT DOMESTIC PRICE LEVELS
AND STRUCTURES — A THEORETICAL ANALYSIS

The actual manner in which state trading isolates domestic prices from the influence of foreign prices and exchange rates is of great importance and merits more careful examination. The Ministry of Foreign Trade and the state trading companies are required to keep two sets of accounts, one in foreign currency (the external account) and the other in domestic currency (the internal account). The external account is important from the standpoint of receipt and expenditure of foreign exchange, while the internal balance shows whether the state trading companies are making profits or require subsidies. There is no requirement for both balances to be either in the same or in opposite directions.[16] An external deficit would require

---

[16] In international trade theory, under the assumption of free private trade and the absence of an offsetting policy by the monetary authorities, an export surplus (surplus in the external account) is associated with an increase in domestic expenditures (deficit in the internal account); it is associated with inflationary pressures. On the other hand, an import surplus (deficit in the external account) is associated with a decrease in domestic expenditures (surplus in the internal account); it is associated with deflationary pressures. With state trading companies, a deficit (or surplus) in the internal account indicates an excess (or deficit) in payments made by the state to domestic producers as against payments made to the state by domestic consumers. Therefore, the generalization concerning free private trade remains true even with the institution of state foreign trading companies, as long as the balance in the external account and that in the internal account are in opposite directions. In the case of free private trade, however — in theory at least — price adjustments and income adjustments (or, in the absence of the gold standard or fixed exchange rates, an adjustment in the exchange rate) tend to correct the external and internal balance. With state foreign trading, the relationship between these internal and external self-correcting tendencies is broken. Several non-Communist nations have also attempted to isolate the effect of external inflationary or deflationary pressures from their domestic price levels, but they have done so largely through monetary and fiscal measures and not by resorting to state trading. Furthermore, the importance of state trading lies not only in its ability to isolate the domestic price *level* from external pressures, but in its ability to free the domestic price *structure* from external pressures as well. It is also important to note that with state foreign trading having a complete monopoly of foreign trade, it is possible for both the domestic and the external balance to be in the same direction. Thus, there can be a deficit (or surplus) in the balance of trade associated with inflationary (or deflationary) pressures in the domestic economy. A deficit in the balance of trade with inflationary pressures domestically would signify that state trading companies were buying relatively expensive goods abroad and selling them relatively cheaply domestically and, at the same time, buying relatively expensive goods domestically and selling them cheaply abroad — at least to the extent where both the external and internal balances showed a deficit.

the spending of foreign exchange reserves or foreign borrowing, a decision that would be a matter of Chinese Communist policy. The internal balance (i.e., the profits or subsidies) would become a part of the state budget — also a matter of policy. Insofar as the effects of foreign trade are concerned, the Chinese Communists would be able to distort the domestic price level and structure as they desired.

While correct in principle, the above analysis ignores the effect of the exchange rate in determining the profits of the state trading companies. The effect of the exchange rate can best be seen in the equation for determining the total internal balance:

Profits on imports $= \Sigma P_m Q_m - E \Sigma (F_m Q_m)$, or Revenue — Cost,

Profits on exports $= E \Sigma (F_x Q_x) - \Sigma P_x Q_x$, or Revenue — Cost,

where

P_m = domestic price of imports,
P_x = domestic price of exports,
Q_m = quantity of imports,
Q_x = quantity of exports,
E = exchange rate in yuan/foreign currency,
F_x = foreign price of exports,
F_m = foreign price of imports.

Combining the profit on both imports and exports,

$$\text{Total internal balance} = \Sigma P_m Q_m - E \Sigma (F_m Q_m) - E \Sigma (F_x Q_x) - \Sigma P_x Q_x,$$
$$= (\Sigma P_m Q_m - \Sigma P_x Q_x) - E (\Sigma F_x Q_x - \Sigma F_m Q_m).$$

The total internal balance of the state trading companies is made up of two quantities. The first term in the final equation above may be called the real internal balance — i.e., the difference between the value of domestic sales and purchases of the state foreign trading companies. The second term in the equation represents the transactions between the state foreign trading companies and the Bank of China in buying and selling foreign exchange. Nonetheless, the second term is just as important in determining the net profit-and-loss position of the state foreign trading companies as the first. The reason for making a distinction between the two terms is that the first term is real in the sense that it determines the flow of funds between the state trading agencies and the domestic economy, while the second, which may be called the internal transfer balance, merely represents the transfer of funds from the Bank of China to the state budget, or from the state budget to the Bank of China.

For example, an export surplus in terms of foreign currencies, *at any exchange rate*, would mean that the state trading companies received more yuan from the Bank of China for the surrender of foreign exchange than they were paying to the Bank to acquire foreign currencies.[17] In this manner, the Bank of China would be transferring funds in domestic currency to the state trading corporations. On the other hand, an import surplus in terms of foreign currencies would mean that the state trading companies were, on balance, transferring funds to the Bank of China, and therefore reducing the total internal balance of the state trading companies that is to be passed on to the state budget. There is, of course, the problem of the origin and ultimate uses of these funds transferred between the Bank of China and the state budget; the internal transfer balance is important to the state trading companies inasmuch as it determines the extent of their profits or losses, and thus to the Ministry of Finance inasmuch as it determines the extent of the budget surplus or deficit. Nonetheless, the internal transfer balance is neither inflationary or deflationary *in itself* and can be described as the transfer of funds from one pocket of the state to another.

Since the individual export (import) transaction involves a domestic purchase (sale) at domestic prices, foreign sale (purchase) at foreign prices, and sale (purchase) of foreign currency to the Bank of China, the exchange rate does affect the profit or loss on individual exports. How important are these "profits" and "losses" in determining the commodity composition of the foreign trade of China? According to the Minister of Foreign Trade, there is generally a loss, in terms of domestic currency, on the export side, while profits are realized on imports [18] — an explicit admission that the official exchange rate overvalues the Chinese yuan. With state trading, however, imports are determined by the import requirements of domestic investment and production — i.e., the decisions of the state planners or the state enterprises — and are limited by the available foreign exchange. Furthermore, the Chinese Communists have continually stressed the desirability of replacing imports with domestic production to create an independent economy. On the export side, a balance is sought between the need for foreign exchange and the availability of export commodities, with continual emphasis being placed on the need for increased exports. In this sense, the Chinese Communists have attempted to limit what appears on paper to be a profitable business — i.e., imports. Of course, the "profit" and "loss" in individual transactions has little meaning, being largely determined by the exchange rate used.

[17] The internal transfer balance and the external balance are always of the same sign at any exchange rate.

[18] "In our country's trade with the capitalist countries, the prices of our import and export commodities are calculated on the basis of prices in the capitalist nations' international market. Since our country's domestic prices *are formulated by a different method*, after the external prices of our import and export commodities are converted into Jen-min-pi prices *according to the exchange rate* and compared with domestic prices, there is generally a decided difference — indicating a loss on exports and a gain on imports" [43, p. 714; emphasis added].

The manner in which the introduction of state trading has broken the interrelationship between domestic and foreign prices and has caused the exchange rate to lose its traditional significance can be summarized by looking at the three balances analyzed above. The external balance, the balance of merchandise trade in terms of foreign currencies, depends on foreign prices and the Chinese Communists' export and import schedules. Within the limits of the available foreign exchange, the Chinese Communists are able to maintain an import surplus without pressure on the exchange rate. The foreign exchange to pay for imports must come from reserves, foreign loans, and export earnings; but it does not come from purchase of foreign currencies with the yuan — i.e., the yuan is not an international currency.

The real internal balance, the balance of domestic purchases of exports and domestic sales of imports in terms of domestic currency, depends on domestic prices and the Chinese Communists' export and import schedules. The government accrues the gains from a positive balance and sustains the losses from a negative balance. *Ceteris paribus,* lower domestic prices for exports and higher domestic prices for imports increase the real internal balance; but there is nothing to prevent the Chinese Communists, if they so desired, from increasing the domestic price of export commodities and lowering the domestic price of import commodities, even to the point where a negative real balance resulted. If this were done, the government would be subsidizing foreign trade. The exchange rate, however, does not enter into the determination of the real internal balance.

The exchange rate does play a role in determining the total internal balance, through its effect on the internal transfer balance. The internal transfer balance is determined by the amount of exports and imports, the foreign prices, and the exchange rate; it is the external balance in terms of domestic currency (but not domestic prices). Only the size and not the sign of the internal transfer balance is determined by the exchange rate. Therefore, inasmuch as the internal transfer represents the transfer of funds from the Bank of China to the state budget (export surplus) or the transfer of funds from the state budget to the Bank of China (import surplus), the exchange rate becomes a matter of Chinese Communist policy. With state trading, the resulting isolation of the domestic price level and structure allows the government to set and maintain any exchange rate desired.

According to the Minister of Foreign Trade, the exchange rate does play a role in determining the domestic sales prices of certain imported commodities — i.e., those sold on commission.[19] Imports sold on commission

[19] "As to imported commodities, a portion are transferred to the organization which ordered them with a two or three percent fee added to the original import price in the manner of importation on commission and a portion are transferred to commercial organizations according to prices agreed to by the Ministry of Foreign Trade and the Ministry of Commerce" [43, p. 714].

include complete sets of equipment and a large portion of the imports of machinery, industrial raw materials, and scientific equipment, and are not produced domestically. In other words, in the absence of an existing domestic price, the foreign trade price is used to determine the domestic price. Insofar as these imports on commission are concerned, therefore, it is true that the exchange rate does have some significance in determining the real internal balance. Nonetheless, while in this instance the domestic price is determined by foreign prices and the exchange rate, the domestic price can be raised or lowered without changing the exchange rate, or the exchange rate could be changed without changing the domestic price.[20]

STATE TRADING AND BILATERAL TRADE AND PAYMENTS AGREEMENTS AS
OBSTACLES TO THE RATIONAL ALLOCATION OF RESOURCES ACCORDING
TO THE INTERNATIONAL DIVISION OF LABOR

The institution of state foreign trading has allowed the Chinese Communist planners to alter the domestic price level and structure to change the pattern of resource allocation and product distribution;[21] has placed the foreign trade of China in the hands of government bureaucrats, subject to the directives of the planners; and has given the planners monopoly power over China's exports and monopsony power over China's imports.[22] The planners have paid a high price for these advantages, however.

Even given the preference of the planners who must decide what commodities to trade and with whom, it is almost impossible to determine the gains from trade. With an exchange rate that overvalues the domestic currency, imports appear to be profitable and exports unprofitable. Inasmuch as the imports involve the necessity of exports, however, only by associating the loss in exports with the profits on imports can the planners determine even the nominal gains from trade. A more realistic exchange rate would

[20] Edward Ames believes that the domestic prices of a very large portion of Soviet imports are based on or are porportional to their foreign prices; he therefore argues that changes in the exchange rate have an inflationary or deflationary effect on the domestic economy [3] [5, p. 212]. It is not possible to estimate the portion of Communist China's total imports that are imported on commission — i.e., those whose domestic price is determined by the foreign price and the exchange rate. If it were assumed that all machinery and equipment were imported on commission, foreign prices and the exchange rate would have been used to determine the domestic prices of between 20 and 40 percent of Communist China's imports in 1953–1960 (Table A-2, Appendix to this paper).

[21] The statement here is restricted to the existence of the planners' ability to alter the domestic price level and structure free from the effect of foreign prices and the exchange rate. For an excellent study of the extent to which the planners have used changes in the price level and structure to change resource allocation and production distribution, see [39].

[22] Full utilization of this monopoly (monopsony) power in the non-Communist world depends on the lack of alternative suppliers (buyers), which is generally not the case.

allow a more realistic estimate of the nominal gains from trade, but a fundamental problem remains in the domestic price structure. If relative domestic
prices do not reflect opportunity or real costs, it becomes difficult for the
planners to determine what goods to import and export in a rational manner.
Relative changes in the domestic prices of export and import goods (i.e.,
through changes in prices for purposes of allocation, stimulation of production, tax revenue, and the like) which cause the relative nominal rates of
profit or loss to change need not be associated with changes in real costs.[23]

The above problem is a result of state trading and the isolation of the
domestic price level and structure, but Communist China's bilateral trade
agreements with the Communist bloc have added two more complicating
factors. The actual prices of the commodities traded are agreed upon in the
individual trade contracts, but the bilateral negotiations in connection with
the annual agreements establish the basis upon which the prices are to be
determined. The determination of these prices is a most important and difficult aspect of Sino–Communist bloc trade. It stems from the attempt to create
a "separate and independent" intra-bloc market, while at the same time
maintaining separate and independent price structures within each country.
Since 1950, all of the prices in intra-bloc trade have been expressed in trade
rubles, which do not represent equal purchasing power over resources and
commodities in each of the Communist countries, and its use in intra-bloc
trade is mainly as a unit of account.

In China's trade agreements with the Communist countries, the trade
ruble prices were based on world market prices at a particular time, with
conversion to rubles at the official exchange rate. The practice of pricing the
commodities in intra-bloc trade in nominal ruble equivalents of world prices
further distorts comparisons of real costs between partner countries, *even
if* real costs were accurately reflected in each country's domestic prices. Although, to be sure, the use of world prices hardly leads to a situation where
the traditional commodities traded are not those that would result from
considerations of comparative advantage, world prices are a poor guide in
determining the relative costs of new commodities between China and the
countries of the Communist bloc, what country should specialize in producing them, and at what rates they should be exchanged.

The payments mechanism adopted in Communist China's bilateral trade
and payments agreements with countries of the Communist bloc adds still
another complication to the determination of the gains from trade. There
is continued emphasis in these agreements on the desire to achieve bilaterally

[23] The Chinese Communists are well aware of the problem described in the above
paragraph. See [27, p. 28]. The European bloc countries are also aware that their
maintenance of autonomous domestic price structures is "an obstacle in the formation
of a rational, international division of labor in the system of socialist countries" [44,
p. 65].

balanced trade. Inasmuch as the actual balance depends on individually negotiated transactions, however, with no direct relationship between those contracts for exports and those for imports, China's bilateral trade with the individual countries of the Communist bloc has never resulted in an annual equality between exports and imports. Therefore, the bilateral trade and payments agreements have created a method of financing the individual trade transactions and provide a means for settling the annual balance.

As is the practice in all intra-bloc trade, China's trade agreements with the Communist countries provide for the creation of a ruble account in the People's Bank of China and in the state bank of the partner country.[24] A Chinese export leads to a Chinese credit in both state banks, while a Chinese import leads to a partner-country credit in both state banks. Thus, the account in both state banks should show the same balance; and with all prices and clearing accounts expressed in trade rubles, the exchange rate between the Chinese yuan and the ruble would not be involved.

The attempt to achieve an annual bilateral balance trade is, in principle, enforced through the method of settlement. The credits and debts in these bilateral ruble accounts are to be in balance at the end of a fixed period — usually a year but frequently six months. Provisions are included, however, that provide for any imbalance that may, and usually does, result. In general, the resulting imbalance is to be settled through trade in the next period — i.e., transferred to the next period's bilateral trade account. Despite the emphasis on the introduction of a multilateral clearing mechanism in intra-bloc trade in 1957, throughout the 1950s China's trade agreements with the countries of the Communist bloc included a provision for the transfer of accumulated balances in the bilateral trade ruble accounts to a third country. The prior approval of all three countries involved is required. The latter limitation appears to be the obstacle to the widespread use of this multilateral clearing system within the bloc — i.e., it is not automatic. Furthermore, if the prior approval of all three partners is acquired, there would be no need to include this clause in the payments agreements.[25]

[24] In general, three types of ruble accounts were created in the central banks of the partner countries: one to handle payments for imports and exports; one to handle payments in connection with credits and loans; and one to handle payments on non-commercial transactions. For a detailed study of the technicalities in the use of these accounts and the method of intra-bloc settlements, see [8, pp. 56–59, 64].

[25] Little is known of actual intra-bloc multilateral clearings, but the continued emphasis in the deliberations of the Council for Economic Mutual Assistance on the need to utilize a multilateral system of clearings in order to promote the socialist international division of labor, and the admission that the different price structures within the individual member countries of the bloc constitute one of the main obstacles to such a system, indicate that, while it exists on paper, little use has been made of this system. Frederic L. Pryor disagrees with this interpretation and argues that East European multilateral trade is not much less than Common Market multilateral trade (10 percent vs. 12 percent of total trade). His equation for determining the percent of

By limiting intra-bloc trade along bilateral lines, with prices and settlements in bilateral rubles rather than in multilateral rubles, even comparison of the prices of identical imports from or exports to alternative trading partners is made very difficult. If China receives 1,000 rubles for export commodity A from trading partner X and 1,050 rubles for the same export from trading partner Y, to which country should China export commodity A? The answer would depend on the ruble prices and types of commodities exported by countries X and Y to China, as China must use rubles earned from country X to buy commodities from country X, and the same is true in regard to trade with country Y. For example, if the general ruble price index of imports from country X was 98 and that for country Y was 104, then, under normal circumstances, it would be equally "preferable" to export commodity A to either country. Even leaving out of account the difficulty of comparing alternative trading partners on the basis of the availability of different imports, it would be necessary to draw up an index of import prices for each bloc trading partner, and each index would involve the difficult problems of comparability, weighting, and the like.[26] Hence, bilateral trade and payments agreements limit even further the integration of intra-bloc trade and the most efficient allocation of Communist bloc resources. A growing body of empirical and theoretical articles had appeared in the Communist bloc by the end of the 1950s on the problem of rational allocation of resources in both the domestic economy and foreign trade. The major obstacles to a solution of these problems, according to these articles, are the independent domestic price structures, the meaningless exchange rates, bilateral trade and payments agreements, and the goals of autarkic economic development. It is not surprising that these policies have made a rational allocation of resources within the Communist bloc most difficult; they are at cross-purposes with the international division of labor and the gains from trade.

multilateral trade, however, *assumes* that all trade not balanced bilaterally is settled multilaterally. This assumption contradicts the explicit provision in almost all of the intra-bloc bilateral payments agreements for transferring the bilateral trade balances to the next bilateral trading period. See [41, pp. 190–192]. Even so, the role of multilateral trade has a different importance in a situation where a country engages in total multilateral trade and in a situation where a country engages in bilateral trade, settling the remaining imbalances multilaterally. I am grateful to Professor Alan Brown for pointing out this additional qualification of Pryor's results.

[26] In trade with non-Communist, non-trade-agreement partners, the state trading companies would attempt to sell exports in their highest price market and to purchase imports in their lowest price market. This general rule would be altered, however, if the currencies involved were not freely convertible, if the quality and quantity of commodities were not similar, if the method of payments and interest rates differed, or if there were widely differing political relations between China and the partner countries. All of these qualifications have been important in China's trade with the non-Communist countries.

II

RATIONALE OF CHANGES IN THE LEVEL, DIRECTION, AND COMMODITY COMPOSITION OF COMMUNIST CHINA'S FOREIGN TRADE

Thus, our conclusions for Communist China are the same as those reached in similar studies of other Communist countries. The institutional reorganization of Communist China's foreign trade after 1949 enabled the planners to maintain an independent domestic price structure and meaningless exchange rate, but, at the same time, made it most difficult for the planners to estimate the gains from trade in individual foreign trade transactions. In this second section of the paper, I turn to an investigation of the actual foreign trade of Communist China and attempt to answer the question, upon what basis do the Chinese Communist planners determine the level, direction, and commodity composition of trade? What follows is not a definitive answer to this question, but a summary of preliminary findings, presented here for the purpose of stimulating further discussion and research.[27]

OVERALL RATIONALE OF COMMUNIST CHINA'S FOREIGN TRADE

Planning essentially involves the setting of targets for domestic industrial and agricultural production. In a closed economy, these targets must be made consistent with the domestic input-output relationships. With the possibility of foreign trade, certain of the required inputs — largely machinery and equipment and raw materials for industry — may be imported in exchange for certain of the non-required or available outputs. Furthermore, imports above these currently paid for by exports may be obtained on the basis of foreign exchange reserves and foreign loans. In other words, as far as foreign trade is concerned, import requirements of the plan must be consistent with the available foreign exchange, whether the foreign exchange comes from reserves, current exports, or foreign loans.

In 1950 through 1952, China's total trade grew rapidly, largely because of the increasing level of imports required for the rehabilitation effort during this period, although imports of some machinery and equipment for new additions to industrial capacity were also important. These imports were made possible by the rapidly increasing exports supplemented by foreign loans from the Soviet Union. Communist China's ability to borrow from the Soviet bloc, at least in the short run, was facilitated by the payments mechanism provided in China's payments agreements with these countries. China's ability to obtain both credit and required imports from the Soviet

---

[27] My estimates for the level, direction, and commodity composition of Communist China's trade are presented in the Appendix to this paper.

bloc and her inability to obtain them from the non-Communist countries were important factors in determining the direction of trade.[28]

Even with the introduction of planning — or at least centralized direction of the allocation of resources and distribution of production on a large scale — in 1953, the situation remained much the same from 1953 through 1955. Planned increases in industrial production determined the level of imports necessary to obtain these increases.[29] Some of the increases in industrial production and the necessary imports were grafted onto the plan in the form of complete sets of equipment or industrial plants supplied to Communist China under specific Soviet loans for this purpose.[30] After consideration of the available foreign loans, the necessary exports could be determined. With centralized control of the economy and state trading companies after 1952, it was possible, if desired, to assure this necessary level of exports, even if production levels projected were not achieved merely by reducing those commodities allocated for other purposes — i.e., by reducing the domestic per capita ration in the case of agricultural exports.

The turning point in 1955 marks the change in emphasis from imports to exports. With the large decline in foreign loan receipts and the beginning of a net capital outflow, imports were indirectly limited by Communist China's export capacity and, hence, domestic agricultural and textile production.[31] The change in emphasis from imports to exports, however, did not alter the importance of planning. In the new situation — i.e., during the repayment of foreign loans — exports were determined on the basis of planned increases in output or changes in the distribution of output.

The change in the direction of capital flows in 1955–1956 and the limits imposed by China's export capacity upon the level of imports led to a decline in the level of imports, between 1955 and 1957, of almost 25 percent. These declines led in turn to a decline in the level of investment in 1957, and thus to a significant reduction in the rate of growth. A major factor leading to the "great leap forward," I believe, is this causal relationship between the change in direction of capital flows in China's foreign trade, the need to reduce imports to current export earnings minus foreign loan re-

[28] Sino–Communist bloc trade was 44.9 percent of China's total trade in 1950 and 80.1 percent of the total by 1954. See Table A-3, Appendix.

[29] The increases in industrial production would be planned, of course, with the import requirements in mind; thus, the selection of import requirements and the planned increases in domestic production are part of the same decision. For example, imports of machinery and equipment accounted for 44.0 percent of total investment in machinery and equipment in 1953, 40.0 percent in 1954, 41.5 percent in 1955, 38.0 percent in 1956, and 42.0 percent in 1957 [14].

[30] Imports of complete sets of machinery and equipment reached a peak level in 1959, when they accounted for 30 percent of China's imports [14].

[31] Raw and processed agricultural products (including textiles) accounted for approximately 70 percent of Communist China's total exports throughout the period 1950–1964. See Table A-2, Appendix.

payments, and the decline in the rate of growth. Three important developments involved in the "great leap forward" — the decentralization of industry, the emphasis on native technology, and the large-scale mobilization of rural "disguised unemployment" (the commune movement) — were all related to an attempt to decrease expenditures by the central government on large imports of machinery and equipment from abroad.[32]

Initially, the "great leap forward" appeared to be a success. China's exports increased rapidly in 1958 and were almost 50 percent above their 1957 level in 1959. The Chinese Communists took advantage of these increased exports to nearly double their imports of machinery and equipment over the same period. By the end of 1959, however, it became evident that China was in the midst of an agricultural crisis. Because of the commodity composition of China's exports, *even during the agricultural crisis* the volume of those exports indicates probable developments in domestic agricultural output, with a one-year lag: the export levels were 64 in 1960 (1959 = 100), 68 in 1961, 69 in 1962, 67 in 1963, and 72 in 1964 [14]. Imports of foodstuffs replaced machinery and equipment as China's leading import after 1960, and the level of imports declined to less than two-thirds their level in 1959. Following the agricultural crisis in 1959, however, it is doubtful that planning of foreign trade was of operational importance; according to the Chinese Communists, effective planning of domestic economic activity was not to have been restored until 1966.

DETERMINANTS OF THE COMMODITY COMPOSITION OF EXPORTS

"As an agricultural country China's natural exports are mostly agricultural produce" [9, p. 3]. The year 1928 saw the peak of China's pre-1949 foreign trade, and her foreign trade in 1959 represents the peak year during the Communist period. In both years, exports of raw and processed agricultural products accounted for three-fourths of China's total exports.[33] Thus, while the Chinese Communists were able to increase the relative shares of non-foodstuffs and processed agricultural products in total agricultural-products exports between 1950 and 1961, exports of agricultural products as a whole remained the mainstay of China's export trade under the Communists.

With a relatively low rate of growth of agricultural production, exports represented a demand for relatively scarce resources. Furthermore, over the period as a whole, the gap between demand and supply widened con-

---

[32] The argument presented above does not mean that the forced reduction in imports in 1956 and 1957 was the only reason for the "great leap forward." There were, of course, several other important economic, political, and social reasons for this major change in development policy.

[33] For the commodity composition of China's export trade in 1953–1964, see Table A-2, Appendix.

siderably. Nonetheless, the need to export in order to finance necessary imports for industrialization gave priority to export demand. The fundamental question was, which agricultural exports?

A study of individual raw and processed agricultural products and mineral and metal exports in 1955–1960 indicates that the classification of export commodities in Table 5 is reconcilable with what is known concerning the domestic availability, domestic requirements, and world markets of these commodities.[34]

Foodstuffs, of all the agricultural products, were subject to the greatest pressure of a widening gap between supply and demand during the 1950s. During the First Five-Year Plan period, the average annual increase in food grain production was only 3.3 percent, while population growth was approximately 2 percent, and the average annual increase in the industrial use of food grains as inputs was 12.2 percent [25, pp. 7–8]. Therefore, per capita availability of food grains for consumption declined during the First Five-Year Plan period, and nationwide rationing of food grains was introduced by the end of 1955. The bumper harvest of 1958 relieved pressure on domestic consumption of food grains, and the daily per capita consumption of food grains is estimated to have increased to a peak of 2,133 calories per day in 1958–1959. The agricultural crisis in 1959, however, reduced the daily per capita calories consumed to less than 2,000; the level was maintained at slightly over 1,900 calories per day in 1960–1961 and 1961–1962 only by resorting to large-scale food-grain imports.[35]

Thus, exports of most foodstuffs accounted for a relatively small proportion of domestic production and displayed either a stable or a declining trend in the level of their export between 1955 and 1960. Included in this

[34] It may be objected that the simple relationship between planning and foreign trade depicted here — i.e., the reliance upon material balances and planned availability and requirements — is a gross oversimplification of actual practice. Specifically, it does not allow for changes in foreign prices to affect the commodity composition of China's foreign trade. For example, China's Commercial Councilor in Paris recently claimed that the import of wheat at $70 to $80 a ton, and the export of rice and soybeans at $120 a ton, was a deliberate economic policy. The problem is, of course, that China did not make a decision to export rice for imports of wheat. Throughout the 1950s, China exported about 1 or 2 percent of the domestic output of rice and about 10 percent of the domestic output of soybeans, and there are no indications that these percentages increased after 1960. The decision to import wheat was not made until after the domestic agricultural crisis and the resulting food crises, especially in the wheat-consuming northern urban areas. Finally, in 1961–1964, China's exports of cereals and oilseeds were less than 30 percent of her imports of cereals [14]. I would suggest that the Commercial Councilor's remarks were meant to counter Western press reports concerning continued Chinese exports of cereals even though food shortages existed in the domestic market. The Chinese Communists were, of course, influenced by the relatively low price on wheat in the world market and the availability of short-term credit when they made the decision to import wheat on a large scale at the end of 1960.

[35] Estimates of daily calories consumed per capita from food grains from [1, pp. 13, 16–17].

TABLE 5

CHANGES IN THE COMMODITY COMPOSITION (INDIVIDUAL
COMMODITIES) OF COMMUNIST CHINA'S EXPORT TRADE,
1955–1960
(Absolute values)

1. Exports that declined:

    Medium share of domestic production (about 10 percent): foodstuffs, oil-seeds (groundnuts and soybeans).

2. Exports that remained stable or declined:

    Small share of domestic production (5 percent or less): foodstuffs, meat and fish, and cereals; raw textile fibers (silk).

    Medium share of domestic production (about 10 percent): animal and vegetable materials, tobacco, and animal and vegetable oils and fats (edible vegetable oils).

    Large share of domestic production (20 percent or above): raw textile fibers (wool).

    Share of domestic production unknown: foodstuffs, dairy products and beverages; animal and vegetable materials, hides and skins, and wood, cork, and pulp; all minerals and metals.

3. Exports that remained stable or increased:

    Large share of domestic production (20 percent or above): foodstuffs, fruits and vegetables (oranges and tangerines, apples, and bananas), and tea.

4. Exports that increased greatly:

    Small share of domestic production (5 percent or less): raw textile fibers (cotton).

    Medium share of domestic production (about 10 percent): textile yarns and fabrics (cotton textiles).

NOTE: This table is a summary of the statistics, estimates, and sources for determining changes in the commodity composition of China's export trade presented in [14, pp. 154–156 and pp. 493–501]. Over 50 commodities were included in that study, representing over two-thirds of China's export trade.

category would be exports of meat and fish, cereal, and most probably dairy products. Other foodstuffs such as oilseeds, fruits, and tea, which were among China's traditional exports, accounted for a much larger proportion of domestic production. It was possible for the Chinese Communists to maintain these relatively high ratios to domestic production — especially of fruit and tea — and to allow a slight upward trend to their level of export, because their domestic production increased at a rapid rate and they did not represent an essential item in the pattern of domestic food consumption. Exports of oilseeds displayed a slight downward trend in the level of export because of the difficulty encountered in increasing domestic production. The divergent rate of growth of domestic production is only one possible explanation for the slight increase in the export of fruit and tea and the decline in the export of oilseeds. According to one Chinese source, taking the export earnings of one *mou* of soybeans as 100, the export earnings of one *mou* of tea is 350; apples, 750; and oranges, 1,650 [54]. The net effect of the various changes in the level of exports of individual categories of food-stuffs resulted in a rather stable level of total foodstuffs exports throughout the 1950s, accounting for approximately one-half of total exports in 1953 and about one-fourth of the total in 1960.

Two major opportunity costs worked against the export of animal and vegetable materials, oils and fats, and minerals and metals — categories of exports which failed to increase significantly between 1955 and 1960. First, there was the demand for food-grain production, which limited the available land and labor for the production of industrial crops. Second, there was the demand for industrial crops as inputs in the rapidly increasing Chinese domestic industrial production. Because of the relatively low rate of growth of agricultural industrial crops, many light industrial plants were "not able to operate at full capacity for lack of enough raw materials" during the First Five-Year Plan period [37, p. 23].

The rapid increase in domestic investment and industrial production also limited increases in the export of minerals and metals. According to one Communist Chinese source, the production of minerals and metals was unable to keep pace with domestic demand during the First Five-Year Plan period. For example, the production of both steel materials and cement increased at an average annual rate of 34 percent and 24 percent, respectively, but the domestic consumption of both commodities increased at an average annual rate of 42 percent over the same period [37, p. 5]. Therefore, while "approximately 15 percent of our total exports consist of mine products . . . under the circumstances, any large increase in exports is dependent upon a great expansion of industrial and agricultural production" [37, p. 7].

The increases in China's total exports during the latter part of the 1950s were due almost entirely to the large increases in her exports of textile products — more specifically, exports of cotton yarns and fabrics. Several factors were undoubtedly important in the selection of textile yarns and fabrics as China's leading export commodity. First, China's textile industry was the most developed of all industries in the pre-Communist period.[36] Furthermore, capacity in the textile industry could be expanded by utilizing domestically produced machinery, thus greatly reducing the problem of providing employment for the swelling numbers of urban workers; the ratio of investment per worker was lower in the textile industry than the aver-

[38] In 1947, the textile industry accounted for 44 percent of the employees in industry and 40 percent of the motive power used in industry; one out of every four factories was producing textile products [55, p. 37].

age for industry as a whole, and the difference between these two ratios was widening during the First Five-Year Plan period [32]. In addition, the profits of the textile industry, as an industry that produced consumer's goods, were a major source of indirect consumer taxes used to finance investment in heavy industry. Second, even though textile products were also rationed and failed to meet the First Five-Year Plan target, the production and per capita consumption of textiles, according to one Chinese source, increased faster than that of foodstuffs.[37] Third, inasmuch as the Soviet Union was by far the major trading partner of China during the 1950s and China had incurred a bilateral trade debt to that country in 1950–1955, the commodity composition of China's exports depended not only upon what commodities China would and could supply, but also upon what commodities the Soviet Union would accept as repayment of the earlier trade debt. The very large increase in the export of textile yarns and fabrics in 1959 was directly related to the Soviet agreement in that year to increase purchases of Chinese textiles to permit China to meet her export obligations to the Soviet Union. Finally, the Chinese Communists displayed every intent of increasing the proportion of processed agricultural products and, if possible, manufactured products in total exports. Finished textiles are included in the trade statistics as processed agricultural products. Nonetheless, the great increase in the export of textiles does represent a decline in the role of raw agricultural products and an increase in manufactured products in China's export trade.

Despite domestic shortages and rationing of cotton cloth because of the failure of both raw cotton and cotton cloth production to fulfill the First Five-Year Plan targets, and even though the domestic production of cotton textiles declined in both 1955 and 1957 following the poor agricultural years in 1954 and 1956, exports of textiles increased over fifteen-fold between 1953 and 1960. The emergence of textiles as China's leading export commodity is the dominant theme of the various changes in Communist China's export trade, 1950–1960.

In the light of these considerations, one could argue that the Chinese Communists planners so selected commodities for export that the resulting allocation of agricultural raw and processed and mining products would satisfy the minimum domestic requirements for consumption in industry and the minimum requirements for total export earnings. In the allocation of foodstuffs and textiles, inputs in industry and export requirements were of a higher priority than domestic consumption. Yet the Chinese Communist planners did attempt to maintain a minimum level of domestic per capita consumption following the agricultural crisis in 1959, when the minimum

[37] Between 1952 and 1957, according to a Chinese Communist source, food-grain production increased by 19.8 percent and per capita food-grain consumption increased by 13.2 percent; over the same period, cotton cloth production increased by 31 percent and per capita cotton cloth consumption increased by 28.5 percent [37, pp. 27–28].

requirements of domestic per capita consumption of food grains had to be met by imports and all categories of exports were greatly reduced.

It is important to note that the impact of planning upon the commodity composition of Communist China's export trade has been determined by examining the actual commodity composition of trade and hypothesizing a set of planners' decisions that would produce these results. No attempt has been made to determine the explicit value criterion used by the planners or the manner in which their decisions are made. Yet, our hypothesis is certainly consistent with their general discussion of the problem of export commodities. For example, according to Ch'en Yun, then Vice-Chairman of the Party, Vice-Premier of the State Council, and Chairman of the State Capital Construction Commission: "If we cannot save on the domestic consumption of such products (i.e., agricultural export commodities), we have no other staple exports and cannot import machinery and equipment for industrialization . . . Cutting down of domestic consumption and giving priorities to exports is a measure demanded not only by present needs but by those of the next ten or a dozen years. It will remain necessary until the imports of industrial equipment can be reduced, till our industry is on a firm footing" [9, p. 4].

III

CONCLUSION

In the first section of this paper, I have attempted to show that the Chinese Communists have adopted institutions (bilateral trade and payments agreements) and followed policies (autarkic economic development) that have made it difficult for even the planners themselves to determine the gains from trade as these gains are traditionally measured. In the second section, I have attempted to show that Communist China's foreign trade during the 1950s was compatible with an allocation of resources based on planned material balances, or the exchange of commodities available beyond the minimum needs of the domestic economy (for both production and consumption) for imports of producers' goods required for realization of the plan. The conclusions of both sections of this paper are identical with those of similar studies of the foreign trade of other Communist countries.[38]

These developments have made it almost impossible to determine the

[38] For one example: "In the practice of Soviet trade, there is a virtually complete divorce between internal and external prices. This is due partly to the nature of the internal price system, partly to a completely artificial exchange rate, and partly to the trade procedures adopted. . . . If Soviet prices were related to those of the West at any conceivable rate of exchange, and if decisions about imports were then based on profitability and comparative cost, the result would be a drastic revision of the import plan . . . which would be quite inconsistent with the Soviet planning system. . . . An artificial exchange rate makes such comparisons peculiarly difficult"

gains from trade as they are traditionally measured; the gains from trade to the Chinese Communists are inseparable from their own objectives. The economic goal with the highest priority during the period of China's transition to socialism was the maximization of growth rate, subject to a declining ratio of agricultural production to heavy industrial production in gross national product (i.e., to industrialization). The contribution of foreign trade to the attainment of their goals is viewed by the Chinese Communists in a similar manner:

Exports from our country are made to provide the means for the import of whole sets of equipment and materials needed for national construction, particularly heavy industrial development . . . If exports are too low, the need for imports will not be guaranteed, (and) the progress of industrialization will be slowed down [53].

By means of a simple model of the relationship between imports and domestic investment and output in the First Five-Year Plan period, 1953–1957, I have estimated that without the ability to exchange raw and processed agricultural products for producers' goods — both machinery and equipment for heavy industry and inputs in production in agriculture and light and heavy industry — from abroad, the *official* annual rate of growth of 10.9 percent would have been reduced to between 7.5 and 8.4 percent [14]. Despite the rather crude assumptions made concerning fixed proportions and the weaknesses of the basic data, these estimates indicate the relatively large impact of foreign trade on China's rate of growth. Using a similar model, Professor Alexander Eckstein estimates that without the

[38, p. 23]. And, "the plan must include the importation of a number of commodities, the need for which cannot be met from within the U.S.S.R. . . . The central authorities doubtless receive more applications for imported goods than can be paid for and the actual plan must be based on estimated export earnings. These, in turn, depend on the goods that can be made available for export. . . . In many cases there are competing demands for exportable goods at home . . . Gosplan must decide in such cases who is to go short. . . . The process appears to be totally unconnected with any consideration of relative prices," and "one searches Soviet textbooks in vain for a serious analysis of the very concept of comparative advantage" [38, pp. 21–23]. According to Ames, Soviet foreign trade seems to have been conducted along the following lines: Soviet imports provide mainly goods which are needed in the investment program and cannot be produced readily domestically, and Soviet exports consist of goods least needed in the investment program [5, p. 217]. This does not deny the argument made by Berliner and Holzman concerning the parallel shift in the structure of exports and the "overall" comparative advantage in the Soviet economy — i.e., from agricultural products to industrial products [7, Chap. 7] [21, pp. 310–311]. Put in the context of the argument presented in this paper, the "surplus" available for export in industrial output increased, and that available in agricultural output declined, over the course of Soviet industrialization; this change in the relative "surplus" was reflected in the structure of exports and in domestic prices. To show that considerations of comparative advantage were utilized in resource allocation in the foreign trade sector, it would be necessary to analyze the role of real prices (opportunity costs) in determining individual export and import commodities.

actual imports of machinery and equipment in 1953–1957, the *estimated* annual rate of growth of 6.5 percent would have been reduced to between 3 and 5 percent [16, p. 124].

Thus, the Chinese Communists have utilized institutions, policies, and foreign trade itself to secure the relatively high rate of growth actually achieved. Following the agricultural crisis in 1959, the dominant use of foreign trade has been to obtain foodstuffs and agricultural inputs (chemical fertilizers) to alleviate domestic shortages. Nonetheless, there is every indication that the present policies are short-run expediencies. We can expect a return in the near future to the goal of a relatively high rate of growth and planning and to the use of foreign trade as a means of obtaining necessary machinery and equipment in exchange for available exports of agricultural raw and processed products (including textiles).[39]

[39] This conclusion implicitly assumes, of course, that the present leadership and their long-run goals survive the current crises on the mainland. Even if the present leadership is overthrown, however, it is likely that the institutions and long-run goals of the present leadership will remain.

APPENDIX

The Level, Direction, and Commodity Composition of Communist China's Foreign Trade, 1949–1964

TABLE A-1

THE VOLUME AND BALANCE OF COMMUNIST CHINA'S
MERCHANDISE TRADE, 1949–1964
(Million U.S. dollars)

Item	1949	1950	1951	1952	1953	1954	1955
China's exports	390	660	760	790	1010	1150	1370
China's imports	350	680	1040	1050	1250	1330	1690
Total trade	740	1340	1800	1840	2260	2480	3060
Annual balance	+40	−20	−280	−260	−240	−180	−320
Cumulative balance	+40	+20	−260	−520	−760	−940	−1260

1956	1957	1958	1959	1960	1961	1962	1963	1964
1620	1600	1930	2160	1940	1480	1490	1510	1680
1460	1390	1840	2000	1910	1350	1060	1110	1290
3080	2990	3770	4160	3850	2830	2550	2620	2970
+160	+210	+90	+160	+30	+130	+430	+400	+390
−1100	−890	−800	−640	−610	−480	−50	+350	+740

NOTE: These statistics are based on data found in both Chinese Communist and non-Chinese Communist sources. For the purposes of complete coverage, they include estimates of Communist China's trade with the Asian satellites in all years, 1954–1964; for several of the European satellites in 1963–1964; and for Albania in 1954 and Rumania in 1954–1957. To value all of China's exports on an f.o.b. basis, an adjustment was made in the c.i.f. values for China's exports reported in the trade returns of China's non-Communist trading partners. All estimates in this table are presented to the nearest 10 million U.S. dollars.

SOURCE: Robert F. Dernberger, "Communist China's Foreign Trade and Capital Movements," Appendix A (unpublished manuscript).

TABLE A-2

THE COMMODITY COMPOSITION OF COMMUNIST CHINA'S FOREIGN TRADE, 1953–1964
(Percentages)

Commodity Type	1953	1954	1955	1956
Exports:				
I. Raw, semi-processed, & processed foodstuffs	50.0	49.6	45.5	40.4
II. Animal & vegetable materials, oils & fats	9.8	8.7	14.1	13.6
III. Textile fibers, yarns, & fabrics	13.6	14.0	16.6	18.3
X-1, (I, II, & III) raw & processed agricultural products	73.4	72.3	76.2	72
IV. Minerals, mineral fuels, metals, ores, & mineral & metal manufactures	12.5	12.9	17.1	16.2
V. Chemicals	3.5	3.1	2.1	3.2
VI. Machinery & equipment	...	...	1.1	0.8
VII. Manufactured goods	1.8	1.4	2.0	2.9
X-2 (IV, V, VI, & VII) mining & industrial products	17.8	17.4	22.3	23
X-3 (VIII) not specified	8.9	10.3	1.5	4
Imports:				
I. Raw, semi-processed, & processed foodstuffs	0.1	0.1	0.1	0.5
VII. Manufactured goods	3.2	1.6	3.3	4.7
M-1. Consumer goods and end products	3.3	1.7	3.4	5
II. Animal & vegetable materials, oils & fats	6.2	5.4	3.9	4.6
including: rubber	(n.a.)	(n.a.)	(3.0)	(4.2)
III. Textile fibers, yarn, & fabrics	3.8	3.9	7.0	5.8
IV. Minerals, mineral fuels, metals, ores, & mineral manufactures	16.7	16.9	14.6	18.6
V. Chemicals	8.9	11.2	9.4	9.2
Including: manufactured fertilizer	(n.a.)	(n.a.)	(4.0)	(5.2)
M-2 (II, III, IV, & V) producers' goods — raw materials	35.6	37.4	34.9	38
M-3 (VI) prod. goods — mach. & equip.	19.7	21.4	23.7	3C
M-4 (VIII) not specified	41.6	39.6	38.0	26

NOTE: The percentages for the commodity composition of Communist China's foreign trade are based on the incomplete detailed commodity trade returns of China's trading partners. Detailed commodity trade statistics were available for between 73.3 percent (1963) and 85.9 percent (1953) of China's total exports; the weighted average of available commodity trade statistics for China's exports for the entire period, 1953–1964, was 77.7 percent. On the import side, detailed commodity trade statistics were available for between 71.2 percent (1958) and 80.5 percent (1954), and the weighted average for the entire period, 1953–1964, was 73.3 percent. The following commodities are included in the eight major commodity classifications listed in Table A-2.

In raw, semi-processed, and processed foodstuffs: meat and fish; dairy products; cereals; fruit and vegetables; sugar, coffee, cocoa, chocolate, tea, and spices; beverages; oilseeds; foodstuffs and food preparations.

In animal and vegetable materials, oils and fats: tobacco; hides, skins, furs; rubber; wood, cork, and pulp; animal and vegetable materials, not specified; animal and vegetable oils and fats.

In textile fibers, yarns, and fabrics: raw textile fibers and products; textile yarns and fabrics.

In minerals, mineral fuels, metals, ores, and mineral and metal manufactures:

THE COMMODITY COMPOSITION OF COMMUNIST CHINA'S FOREIGN TRADE, 1953–1964
(Percentages)

1957	1958	1959	1960	1961	1962	1963	1964
33.7	37.5	30.2	29.3	15.5	22.7	27.2	32.6
15.0	12.2	10.0	8.8	5.7	5.6	7.1	7.4
22.5	24.0	33.8	38.2	44.1	41.3	39.1	29.8
71.2	73.7	74.0	76.3	65.3	69.6	73.4	69.8
17.5	14.5	11.8	13.3	19.9	17.7	12.9	13.4
2.6	2.9	1.7	1.7	1.9	2.3	2.9	3.2
0.6	0.5	0.9	0.1	0.3	0.3	0.8	0.8
3.7	7.3	6.2	5.8	6.9	8.1	8.1	6.4
22.4	25.2	20.6	20.9	29.0	28.4	24.7	23.8
4.5	1.2	5.4	2.8	5.7	1.9	2.0	6.5
1.6	1.1	0.2	0.1	34.1	41.1	39.1	42.3
4.4	4.2	1.9	2.1	1.9	3.4	3.0	4.3
6.0	5.3	2.1	2.2	36.0	44.5	42.1	46.6
8.7	6.5	7.8	5.7	7.6	9.4	5.1	4.8
(8.0)	(5.8)	(7.3)	(4.8)	(5.6)	(6.9)	(3.0)	(2.2)
10.0	7.8	6.4	9.1	7.7	8.4	11.9	9.4
18.4	33.1	25.0	29.0	21.2	18.4	15.8	13.0
10.7	9.6	7.7	5.7	6.6	7.8	13.4	11.6
(5.5)	(5.0)	(2.7)	(2.1)	(3.4)	(3.5)	(6.5)	(2.6)
47.8	57.0	46.9	49.5	43.1	44.0	46.2	38.8
31.9	27.7	39.8	38.7	13.1	4.6	7.3	11.9
14.2	10.0	11.2	9.7	7.9	7.0	4.5	2.7

minerals; mineral fuels; ores; metals; mineral manufactures; metal manufactures; glass, pottery, silver, and gems.

In chemicals: dyes and coloring materials, pharmaceutical products; essential oils and soaps, manufactured fertilizers; chemicals, chemical materials and products, not specified.

In machinery and equipment: power machinery; tractors and agricultural machinery and equipment; metal working machinery; electrical machinery; transportation machinery and equipment; oil drilling equipment; complete plants; mining and industrial equipment and machinery, not specified.

In manufactured goods: leather and furs; rubber; wood, cork, and paper manufactures, buildings, building fixtures, and furniture; handbags, clothes, and footwear; instruments, photo goods, watches, clocks, and musical instruments; manufactured goods, not specified.

In not specified: not specified, non-Communist countries; not specified, Soviet Union.

Detailed statistics for each of these 45 subcategories in the commodity composition of Communist China's foreign trade in 1955–1964 can be found in the source cited below.

SOURCE: Robert F. Dernberger, "Communist China's Foreign Trade and Capital Movements," Appendix B (unpublished manuscript).

TABLE A-3

THE DIRECTION OF COMMUNIST CHINA'S FOREIGN TRADE, 1950–1964[a]

(Percentages)

Item	1950	1951	1952	1953	1954	1955	1956	1957	1958	1959	1960	1961	1962	1963	1964
A. Communist countries[b]															
Chinese exports	33.7	46.5	65.5	65.9	75.9	72.7	70.4	70.5	70.2	75.7	70.5	67.3	64.4	57.3	47.4
Chinese imports	53.5	58.6	75.8	80.6	73.6	82.2	77.0	69.8	66.1	73.9	72.4	59.6	52.2	43.8	38.2
Total trade	44.9	53.0	71.0	73.7	80.1	77.2	73.4	70.1	68.5	74.8	71.4	63.8	59.6	51.9	43.7
B. Non-Communist countries[c]															
Chinese exports	66.4	53.5	34.4	34.2	24.1	27.3	29.9	29.5	29.5	24.3	29.5	32.7	35.6	42.7	52.6
Chinese imports	46.5	41.5	24.2	19.0	16.3	17.8	22.8	30.2	33.9	26.1	27.6	40.4	47.8	56.2	61.8
Total trade	55.2	47.2	29.2	26.4	20.0	22.5	26.6	29.8	31.5	25.2	28.6	36.2	40.4	48.1	56.3
Percentages of Communist China's total trade															
1. Soviet Union	44.2	53.0	63.9	61.0	57.1	54.6	52.3	46.7	44.0	53.2	46.9	36.1	32.5	25.9	17.7
2. European bloc	0.6	n.a.	7.1	12.7	19.2	18.9	17.8	19.6	20.4	17.7	18.5	12.9	9.8	9.2	9.4
3. Asian bloc	n.a.	n.a.	n.a.	n.a.	3.8	3.7	3.5	3.9	4.1	4.0	4.8	7.3	9.0	9.7	9.8
4. Europe	8.7	10.5	5.1	8.4	5.8	6.8	8.9	10.1	13.4	11.8	12.9	10.7	10.4	11.1	12.6
5. North America	12.2	12.2	1.4	0.4	0.1	0.1	0.2	0.2	0.3	0.1	0.3	3.5	4.4	3.1	3.8
6. Southeast Asia	7.2	9.8	9.8	5.9	5.1	5.1	6.1	6.4	6.4	6.3	6.5	7.1	8.0	9.7	8.6
7. Other Asia	25.6	23.5	12.0	10.7	7.8	8.6	9.2	10.0	8.6	5.0	6.1	11.6	13.2	19.2	23.8
8. Near East	0.5	0.2	0.5	0.5	0.6	0.9	1.2	2.3	1.6	1.3	1.7	1.8	2.2	2.9	2.9
9. Africa	0.7	0.7	0.3	0.3	0.5	0.7	0.7	0.6	0.9	0.6	1.0	1.4	1.2	1.9	2.0
10. South America	0.5	0.2	0.1	0.1	0.2	0.2	0.2	0.2	0.3	0.1	1.4	7.6	9.3	7.3	10.1

[a] Percentages for Sino-Communist country trade in 1950–1953 and for Sino–non-Communist country trade in 1962–1964 are based on incomplete data. Complete coverage is obtained in all other years, but does not include some estimates for China's trade with individual Communist countries.

[b] Includes Cuba in 1960–1963.

[c] Excludes Cuba in 1960–1963.

SOURCE: Robert F. Dernberger, "Communist China's Foreign Trade and Capital Movements," Appendix C (unpublished manuscript).

DISCUSSION
Richard Y. C. Yin

Inasmuch as Professor Dernberger has taken into account, in the present version of his paper, most of the points that I made in detailed comments on an earlier draft, I will limit my remarks to the following general issues: (1) the economic efficiency of foreign trade in China, and (2) the experience of China as a case study of foreign trade in a centrally planned economy.

The problem of economic efficiency is obviously Professor Dernberger's chief concern in this paper. This is evidenced by the title of the paper, as well as by other specific references in his analysis. The other two items listed in the title — prices and the exchange rate — turn out to have only a passive or even negative role. For as the author argues, an artificial price structure created by state trading and isolated from foreign prices through an arbitrary exchange rate would hinder efficient resource allocation. This, in a nutshell, appears to be the plot of the whole story.

One can heartily concur in the choice of this difficult subject for emphasis, both because it merits more attention in the discussion of China's foreign trade, and because efficiency is, after all, an important criterion for judging the comparative performance of different economic systems. It would seem useful, however, to bear in mind the two related questions that are simultaneously involved in this concept: (a) Does trade benefit China? and (b) Does trade benefit China as much as it should? The first question concerns the effect of trade on the economy, in terms of some such pre-established objective as rate of growth, as compared with the case where trade is absent. The second question has to do with deviations from the optimum, or the possibility of increasing the benefit from trade. It seems obvious that Dernberger's Part I deals essentially with the second question and his Parts II and III with the first. It is worth noting that, while Part I emphasizes the adverse or negative aspects of the institutional arrangements which make efficient handling of trade well-nigh impossible, the author has pushed on in Part II to an investigation into the basis upon which the Chinese Communist planners determine the level, direction, and commodity composition of trade, which he has found to be compatible with an allocation of resources based on the planned objectives. And later in Part III, the author makes specific reference to two estimates — one by himself in an earlier study and one by Professor Alexander Eckstein — which show that the annual rate of growth during 1953–1957, based either on official figures or on independent estimates, would have suffered if there had been no import of certain commodities essential to industrial growth. Only when all these parts are viewed together will we have a more balanced assessment of the problem of economic efficiency.

A related point may be raised concerning the possibility, or rather impossibility, of determining the "gains from trade" with an artificial exchange rate and an artificial domestic price structure. One has no particular objection on theoretical grounds to the author's contention that the price structure that does not reflect relative scarcities hinders efficient trade. The question is, how much of this is logical, *a priori* reasoning and how much is fact? What evidence do we have on the distorted price structure in China? Do we know enough about China's price policy, not to mention the actual determination and formulation of prices? Is there direct evidence of trade being inefficiently handled? Clearly the author cannot be expected to examine thoroughly these and other related problems, and one shares the author's view that much work on these aspects remains to be done.

As to the value of the Chinese experience as a possible case study of foreign trade in a centrally planned economy, the author has properly cautioned in his introductory pages against accepting without verification the hypothesis that similar institutions in each of the Communist countries will lead to the same results. In view of this caveat, and of the gaps of our knowledge about China's actuality — of which the absence of any reference to China's actual price structure is but one example — one may perhaps justly wonder whether the author's final acceptance (Part III) of the applicability of conclusions of similar studies of other Communist countries should not be somewhat qualified.

The author's detailed account of the evolution of some of the foreign trade institutions and his theoretical analysis of their possible consequences are of course useful materials for students interested in a generalized model of the foreign trade of a centrally planned economy. One is impressed by the difficulty of trying to identify the necessary features of foreign trade in such an economy. Whether bilateralism, for example, should be treated as an inherent feature of a centrally planned economy would seem to depend, according to Dernberger's analysis of pre-1940 Soviet Russia and post-1950 China, not only on central planning in the country in question but also on the existence of central planning in the economies of its trading partners. The explanation of the introduction of state trading in China also raises the question of whether it is a necessary feature of a centrally planned economy. As the author has pointed out, there are apparently other possible measures that could be used to combat inflation, to sever domestic from foreign prices, and to change the domestic price structure; and state trading itself permits varying degrees of monopoly and controls.

To conclude, there is no question that Professor Dernberger's "preliminary investigation" is a most impressive contribution. His diligence of research, his originality of analysis, and his depth of understanding are plainly evident. One should also stress the difficult nature of the task the author is undertaking. The attempt to unravel the workings of an economic system — the role of one sector of it — is a task that has been too long neglected and too frequently slighted. Over the years, the importance of such analyses has certainly not diminished.

REFERENCES

1. "Agricultural Study Forecasts Another Hungry Spring for Communist China," *Current Scene*, I:23 (January 22, 1962), pp. 1–21.
2. Allen, Robert Loring. *Soviet Economic Warfare* (Washington, D.C.: Public Affairs Press, 1960).
3. Ames, Edward. "The Exchange Rate in Soviet Type Economies," *Review of Economics and Statistics*, XXXV:4 (November 1953), pp. 337–342.
4. ———. "Soviet Bloc Currency Conversions," *American Economic Review*, XLIV:3 (June 1954), pp. 339–353.
5. ———. *Soviet Economic Processes* (Homewood, Ill.: Irwin, 1965).
6. Baykov, Alexander. *Soviet Foreign Trade* (Princeton: Princeton University Press, 1946).
7. Berliner, Joseph. *Soviet Economic Aid* (New York: Praeger, 1958).
8. Bystrov, F. "The Organization of International Settlements among the Socialist Countries," *Voprosy Ekonomiki*, No. 2 (1960); English translation in *Problems of Economics*, III:2 (June 1960), pp. 56–59, 64.
9. Ch'en Yun. "Bridging the Gap Between Supply and Demand," *People's China*, No. 22, November 16, 1954.
10. Cheng Chu-yuan. *Monetary Affairs of Communist China*, Communist China Research Series, Third Edition (Hong Kong: The Union Research Institute, 1959).
11. *Chung-hua Jen-min Kung-ho-kuo T'iao-yueh Chi* (Collection of Treaties of the Chinese People's Republic), thirteen volumes through 1964 (Peking: Legal Press and World Knowledge Press; Vol. I published in 1957, Vol. XIII published in 1965).
12. "Decision Concerning the Implementation of Cash Control in State Organs," *Hsin-hua Yueh-pao* (New China Monthly), II:1 (May 1950), p. 128.
13. "Decision on the Procedures Governing the Unification of State Trading throughout the Country," *Chung-yang Ts'ai-ching cheng-ts'e Fa-ling Hui-pien* (Concordance of Fiscal and Economic Policies and Ordinances of the Central People's Government) Vol. II, 1950, pp. 403–407.
14. Dernberger, Robert F. "Foreign Trade and Capital Movements of Communist China, 1949–1962" (Unpublished doctoral dissertation, Harvard University, 1965; references in this paper are to a revised version covering the years 1949–1965, mimeographed.)
15. Domke, Martin, and John Hazard. "State Trading and the Most-Favored-Nation Clause," *American Journal of International Law*, LII:1 (January 1958), pp. 55–68.
16. Eckstein, Alexander. *Communist China's Economic Growth and Foreign Trade* (New York: McGraw Hill, 1966).
17. "Economic Conditions in China in the Past Year," *New Construction*, I:10 (January 1950), p. 13.
18. *Far Eastern Economic Review*.

19. Gordon, Margaret S. *Barriers to World Trade* (New York: Macmillan, 1941).
20. Hazard, John. "State Trading in History and Theory," *Law and Contemporary Problems*, XXIV:2 (Spring 1959), pp. 243–255.
21. Holzman, Franklyn. "Foreign Trade," in Abram Bergson and Simon Kuznets (eds.), *Economic Trends in the Soviet Union* (Cambridge: Harvard University Press, 1963), pp. 283–332.
22. *Jen-min Jih-pao*, September 4, 1950.
23. *Jen-min Shou-Ts'e* (People's Handbook), 1952.
24. Johnson, Harry G. "The Theory of Tariff Structure, with Special Reference to World Trade and Development," in *Trade and Development* (Études et Travaux de L'Institute Universitaire de Hautes Études Internationales, No. 4, Génève, 1965).
25. Lee, T. C. "The Food Problem," *Contemporary China*, IV (Hong Kong: Hong Kong University Press, 1961), pp. 1–26.
26. Levine, Herbert S. "The Centralized Planning of Supply in Soviet Industry," U.S. Congress, Joint Economic Committee, *Comparisons of the United States and Soviet Economies* (Washington, D.C.: 1959), Part I, pp. 151–176.
27. Li Yung-sheng. "Unification of Import Commodity Exchange and Price Setting Methods," *Chi-hua Ching-chi* (Planned Economy), No. 4 (1958).
28. Mah Feng-hwa. *Communist China's Foreign Trade: Price Structure and Behavior, 1955–1959* (Santa Monica: The RAND Corporation, October 1963), RAND Memorandum RM-3825-RC.
29. ————. "First Five Year Plan and Its International Aspects," in C. F. Remer (ed.), *Three Essays on the International Economics of Communist China* (Ann Arbor: University of Michigan Press, 1959).
30. ————. "The Terms of Sino-Soviet Trade," in Li Choh-ming (ed.), *Industrial Development in Communist China* (New York: Praeger, 1964), pp. 174–191.
31. Maklakov, A. "From History of Socialist Planning in the Economy of the Chinese People's Republic," *Voprosy economiki* (October 1958); English translation in *Problems of Economics*, I:10 (February 1959), pp. 78–84.
32. Ma Yin-chu. "A New Theory of Population," *Hsin-hua Pan-yueh-k'an* (New China Semi-monthly), No. 15 (1957).
33. Meade, J. G. *The Theory of International Economic Policy*, Vol. I, *The Balance of Payments* (New York: Oxford University Press, 1951).
34. Mendershausen, Horst. "The Terms of Soviet-Satellite Trade: A Broadened Analysis," *Review of Economics and Statistics*, XLII:2 (May 1960), pp. 152–163.
35. ————. "Terms of Trade between the Soviet Union and Smaller Communist Countries," *Review of Economics and Statistics*, XLI:2 (May 1959), pp. 106–118.
36. Mikesell, Raymond F., and Jack N. Behrman. *Financing Free World Trade with the Sino-Soviet Bloc*, Princeton Studies in International Finance, No. 8 (Princeton: Princeton University Press, 1958).
37. Niu Chung-huang. *Relation between Production and Consumption During the First Five Year Plan in China* (Peking: 1959); English translation in CIA, Foreign Documents Division, *Translation*, No. 735.
38. Nove, Alec, and Desmond Donnelly. *Trade with Communist Countries* (London: Hutchinson of London, 1960).

39. Perkins, Dwight H. *Market Control and Planning in Communist China* (Cambridge: Harvard University Press, 1966).
40. "Price Fluctuations and the Basic Methods of Overcoming Them," *Hsin-hua Yueh-pao* (New China Monthly), I:3 (January 1950), p. 667.
41. Pryor, Frederic L. *The Communist Foreign Trade System* (Cambridge: Massachusetts Institute of Technology Press, 1963).
42. Remer, Charles F. *The Trade Agreements of Communist China* (Santa Monica: The RAND Corporation, February 1961), Paper P-2208.
43. "Report of Yeh Chi-chuang, Minister of Foreign Trade," *The Fourth Session of the First National People's Congress of the People's Republic of China* (Peking: People's Press, 1957).
44. Rolow, Aleksander. "Foreign Trade Prices and Effectiveness of Foreign Exchange in Production," *Gospodarka Planowa*, XV:4 (April 1960); English translation in JPRS, No. 7195 (November 30, 1960).
45. Röpke, Wilhelm. *International Economic Disintegration* (New York: Macmillan, 1942).
46. Schwartz, Harry. *Russia's Soviet Economy*, Second Edition (Englewood Cliffs: Prentice-Hall, 1958).
47. Smirnov, A. M. *International Currency and Credit Relations of the U.S.S.R.* (Moscow: 1960); English translation in JPRS, No. 7155 (November 29, 1960).
48. Spulber, Nicolas. "The Soviet Bloc Foreign Trade System," *Law and Contemporary Problems*, XXIV:3 (Summer 1959), pp. 420–434.
49. State Statistical Bureau. *Report of Fulfillment of the National Economic Plan of the People's Republic of China in 1955* (Peking: Foreign Languages Press, 1956).
50. *Ta Kung Pao*, Tientsin, January 26, 1951.
51. United Nations. *Economic Survey of Europe* (Geneva: Economic Commission for Europe, various years).
52. Yeh Chi-chuang. "Our Country's Foreign Trade in the Last Ten Years," *Hsin-hua Pan-yueh-k'an* (New China), No. 19, 1959.
53. ———. "The Promotion of Foreign Trade," *People's Daily*, September 28, 1956.
54. Wang Ti. "Make Proper Arrangements for Export Trade, Actively Organize the Supplies," *Ta Kung Pao*, Tientsin, October 13, 1957.
55. Wu Yuan-li. *An Economic Survey of Communist China* (New York: Bookman Association, 1956).

Foreign Trade of China:
A Summary Appraisal

ALEXANDER ECKSTEIN

In this brief comment I would like to make a few observations (a) on the contribution of the international economic sector to saving in Communist China, (b) the contribution of the same sector to investment, (c) the relationship between foreign trade and domestic economic planning, and (d) the effect of lagging agricultural development on foreign trade and on domestic economic growth during the Communist period as a whole, and during the "great leap forward" and the crisis following it in particular. Finally I would like to comment on some specific issues raised in the two papers by Professors Dernberger and Perkins.

GENERAL COMMENTS

In considering the contribution of the international sector to saving, we must differentiate between the situation in the 1950s and the 1960s. During the early 1950s — i.e., between 1950 and 1955 — China was a net importer of capital, primarily because of the substantial Soviet credits drawn upon at that time. Such credits amounted to about $1.4 billion.[1] The credits actually received in 1956 and 1957 were so small that repayments of the Soviet debt in these years greatly exceeded the last credit installments drawn. As a result, there was a significant shift in China's balance-of-payments position after 1955. Beginning in 1956 she became a net capital exporter, in part because of her repayment obligations and in part because of the fact that China started to extend foreign aid to other countries.

[1] The figure of $1.4 billion actually applies to the 1950–1957 period. However, credits extended in 1956 and 1957 were quite small, so that the greater part of these were drawn upon prior to 1956. For the sources of these estimates, see [1, pp. 154–159 and pp. 297–298]; see also [2, Table 5, pp. 22–23].

The net capital inflow for the 1950–1957 period may be estimated as about $430 million [2, Table 5]. This amount would constitute no more than about 0.3 to 0.4 percent of estimated gross national product for the 1950–1957 period as a whole.[2] On the basis of these calculations, net capital imports during the recovery and first five-year plan periods would have added no more than 1 percent to total savings.

As already indicated, beginning in 1956 and continuing to the present day Communist China has been a net exporter of capital. For the 1958–1964 period it is estimated that the net capital outflow may have amounted to as much as about $1.7 billion [2, Table 5, p. 22]. This may have constituted about 0.5 percent of the gross national product and possibly about 3 percent of the total saving for this period. In effect, then, total capital inflow through 1957 added about 1 percent to total resources available for financing investments. However, from 1958 on, capital outflow diminished the resources available for investment purposes by about 3 percent. If one takes the Chinese Communist period as a whole, the mainland still turns out to be a net exporter of capital, a most unusual condition for an underdeveloped country and a condition that — however marginally — imposes additional constraints on the possibilities of financing domestic investment.

It would, however, be misleading to confine an analysis of the role of the international sector to a consideration of net capital flows and their effect on total resources available for financing investments. An equally and perhaps even more important consideration is the role of the international sector, and most particularly of the foreign trade sector, as a highway for the transmittal of new technology, new goods, and new methods of production. Viewed in these terms, foreign trade played an extremely strategic role in Communist China's economic growth, particularly during the first ten years — i.e., during the period which the Chinese Communists characterized as the "ten great years," 1949–1959. Abstracting from the early recovery period, the import component of investment may be estimated to have been 20 to 40 percent, depending on what exchange rates are used for converting imports of complete plant equipment and machinery from the Soviet Union and East European countries to China [1, Chap. 4, pp. 117–130; pp. 321–322 n. 19]. Not only was the import component of capital formation quite large, but the particular type of industrialization that took place in the 1950s almost certainly would not have been possible without the ability to import machinery and other kinds of capital goods for expansion of investment goods capacity on the mainland.

Imports played an entirely different role in the 1960s. With the onset of the agricultural crisis, the character of the import bill was altered drastically.

[2] Based on the Liu-Yeh product estimates converted into dollars at the official rate of exchange. See [3].

Capital goods imports were compressed very sharply while food imports were increased markedly. Prior to 1961 the latter averaged around 2 to 2.5 percent a year; however, since 1961 they have constituted 30 to 40 percent of total imports. This necessarily meant that the import component of capital formation was much lower; in fact, it seems to be quite small in the 1960s. The principal contribution of imports in the 1960s has been the maintenance of economic and political stability. As Professor Perkins points out in his paper, these food imports can be regarded in a sense as an investment in the improvement of agricultural incentives. That is, these imports relieve the pressure on the countryside and increase the reliance of urban areas on imported foodstuffs. At the same time, by easing the urban pressures on food supply they make a very significant contribution to containing inflationary forces. They also have helped the regime to contain unrest at the depths of the food crisis. One may perhaps speculate that the pattern of the 1950s is not likely to be repeated. It is improbable that imports will again constitute such a large component of capital formation. In part because of the very experience of the 1950s, Mainland China's capacity to produce capital goods and plant equipment has been significantly augmented, and therefore her need to rely on imported components has been somewhat lessened. More importantly perhaps, to the extent that a post-Mao leadership will have learned some lessons from the "great leap forward" disaster, one may reasonably expect a different investment mix in the future, with less exclusive emphasis on the expansion of heavy industry, which in itself might lessen import dependence in capital formation.

Of course, all of the foregoing serves to illustrate the fundamental fact that these interrelationships among foreign trade, the international sector as a whole, and domestic goals and stability in China hinge on the trends and annual fluctuations in agricultural output. Given China's economic backwardness and the weight of agriculture in the national product — and, even more, in the labor force — agriculture acts as a most effective constraint on growth in all sectors of the economy including the international sector. Moreover, it acts as an effective constraint on investment levels, investment rates, the size and composition of the export bill, and the size and composition of imports. In these terms, the "great leap forward" may be viewed as a supreme effort initiated by the Chinese Communist leadership in an attempt to overcome this constraint by raising agricultural production, and thus correcting the growing disproportionalities, bottlenecks, and lack of complementarities which were apparent by the end of the first five-year plan period.

Dernberger is right in stressing the increased pressures on the agricultural sector and the growing constraints imposed by it in 1956 and 1957 because of the cessation of Soviet aid and the shift in China's position from a capital importer to a net capital exporter. However, it is misleading to suggest that this is the primary or the fundamental cause that drove the regime into the "great leap forward." It was only an aggravating and contributing factor. After all, as Perkins points out, had the Chinese followed a different investment and resource-allocation policy, the force of the agricultural constraints would not have been as great in the first place. On the other hand, it is perfectly true that if foreign aid were a free good and if the Chinese could have relied on the Soviets to advance credits and grants without limit, the agricultural constraints would never have operated.

It is similarly misleading to suggest that "the change in the direction of capital flows in 1955–1956 and the limits imposed by China's export capacity upon the level of imports led to a decline in the level of imports, between 1955 and 1957, of almost 25 percent." Actually imports increased from about $1.32–1.35 billion (the precise figure depending on what adjustments one makes for re-exports) in 1955 to $1.39–1.41 billion in 1957 [1, Table 4-1, p. 95]. This represents a 5 percent increase in import levels. It is, of course, true that there was a decline in imports between 1956 and 1957, but this was again primarily attributable to the particular investment policy and economic policy pursued in 1956. That year, investment was dramatically raised by 60 percent. This forced a significant increase in capital goods imports in 1956 and at the same time produced very acute bottlenecks, raw materials shortages, and inflationary pressures in consumer goods markets, so that the regime was forced to cut back investments in 1957. When the investment cutback in 1957 led in turn to a decline in investment goods demand, this was reflected in a decrease in total imports between 1956 and 1957. However, the 1957 imports were still above the 1955 levels. Of course, it is quite true that the bottlenecks and shortages of 1956 were aggravated by the sharp increase in exports, which were necessitated by the cessation of Soviet aid and the obligation to start repayment of these credits.

Dernberger and Perkins both touch upon the relationship between foreign trade and domestic economic planning. However, neither comes to grips with the problem explicitly and directly. To be more specific, we do not yet have a clear picture or real understanding of how the foreign trade sector is integrated into the domestic economic plan. We do not really know how the planners determine the level, direction, and commodity composition of foreign trade. Dernberger is quite right in stressing that, up to 1955, import plans were a function of domestic industrial production plans. Exports followed imports, and if the need arose, personal consumption at home was squeezed somewhat to insure the necessary level and composition of exports. This situation changed after 1955, when China became a net exporter of capital. To maintain an export surplus, exports had to be maximized and imports minimized. As a result, after 1955 imports followed exports — i.e., imports were planned as a function of export capacity.

It is unclear, however, just what is meant by the postulate that exports follow imports, or vice versa. Let us take the situation up to 1955. Presumably import requirements were derived from the material balances — i.e., from a summation of input requirements needed to obtain certain output targets for the final bill of goods. Presumably those inputs that could not be produced at home, because of a lack of either capacity or technical know-how, or that could be produced at home only at a very high cost, would be imported. Was this in fact how the Chinese Communists went about the task? Suppose they did, and then upon summing up import requirements found that these requirements exceeded export availabilities? How was plan consistency achieved in such a case?

One could think of several different alternatives. Was such consistency attained by planning for short-term balance-of-payments deficits — i.e. for short-term loans — which would then enable China to import over and above its export capacity? Alternatively, were imports adjusted downward without altering industrial production targets or other final targets; and, if so, was this done by tightening the input-output norms or by resorting to various means of import substitution with attendant consequences either in terms of lower quality or higher costs of production? Was consistency in some cases achieved by reducing output targets, thus lowering import requirements and in this way restoring import-export balance? Finally, was the adjustment made by raising exports at the expense of domestic consumption? Similarly, after 1955 when exports presumably led imports, how were these adjustments made? Suppose that, given certain export availabilities, import levels which could be financed were inadequate to meet production targets. Was consistency then restored by increasing exports at the expense of domestic consumption, or by reducing norms, or by reducing production targets?

This is a range of problems which needs very careful and thoroughgoing study. Admittedly, the materials available are extremely scarce, since the Chinese Communists have been particularly secretive about their planning practices in the international trade field. However, it is conceivable that a carefully designed interviewing project aimed at selected refugees in Hong Kong as well as businessmen and government trade officials from China's trading partner countries, supplemented by whatever material can be obtained from documentary sources both on the Chinese side and on the trading partner's side, could yield significant results.

SPECIFIC COMMENTS

Professor Dernberger, in his interesting paper, states that "while bilateral trade and payments agreements are neither necessary nor beneficial to a planned economy, the need for bilateral agreements for trade between

planned economies with state monopolies of foreign trade has made the annual negotiations of these agreements an integral part of the planning process." One can genuinely doubt whether multilateralism is compatible with a
system of foreign and internal trade monopolies based on internal prices
divorced from external prices and more or less divorced from true factor
costs. The experience of the East European countries with the Council for
Economic Mutual Assistance would bear this out. When internal prices are
divorced from scarcity relations and exchange rates do not approximate
purchasing power ratios, it is very difficult to see how multilateralism can
operate. This factor is reinforced by planning factors: namely, if import
components are essential for meeting certain high-priority targets, contracts must be concluded beforehand. Uncertainty, both on the import and
the export side, can be reduced if these can be placed in a bilateral barter
relationship, where one can be certain that the exports delivered in payment
for the imports will actually be bought by the trading partner. In such a case,
gains from trade and cost considerations are subordinated to the need to
meet high-priority targets.

Dernberger also maintains that state trade was introduced in China as
a means of inflationary control. As long as private traders were operating in
the international sector, exchange rates had to be more or less meaningful.
Is this really the case? The experience of many countries during the great
depression of the 1930s and again in the immediate post-war period, suggests that one can have foreign trade carried on by private business enterprises and yet have artificial exchange rates buttressed with exchange
controls, import quotas, export licensing, and other methods.

I would also like to enter a caveat in connection with the statement made
by Professor Perkins that "in a fundamental sense China's low level of
foreign economic assistance, which probably resulted in a reduction of the
size of her trade, has been a consequence of a deliberate desire to go it alone
in international politics." This probably overstates China's determination
at self-isolation and does not take into sufficient account the international
environment in which Communist China found herself after 1949. One can
genuinely question whether China entered the Korean War voluntarily or
whether circumstances forced her into it. If the latter, then the embargo and
trade controls imposed by the United States and its allies can hardly be
attributed to Chinese measures at self-isolation. I would only say that this
has been an interacting relationship, where other countries have attempted
to isolate China and China has reinforced the pattern through her own
foreign policy behavior.

The papers by Professors Dernberger and Perkins make an important
contribution to our understanding of the organization of Communist China's
foreign trade and its behavioral characteristics. Also they illuminate how

domestic policy decisions have affected the foreign trade sector, how domestic goals have constrained foreign trade, and how, by a feedback effect, these constraints have influenced domestic developments in turn. As I have attempted to point out, perhaps the most significant gap in our current state of knowledge concerning Chinese planning techniques and approaches falls in the area of foreign trade planning.

REFERENCES

1. Eckstein, Alexander. *Communist China's Economic Growth and Foreign Trade* (New York: McGraw-Hill, 1966).
2. Intelligence Report, Central Intelligence Agency. *Communist China's Balance of Payments 1950–1965* (Washington, D.C.: 1966).
3. Liu, T. C., and K. C. Yeh. *The Economy of the Chinese Mainland: National Income and Economic Development, 1933–1959* (Princeton: Princeton University Press, 1965).

Foreign Trade
of the U.S.S.R.

The Effects of Foreign Trade on Soviet Planning Practices*

HERBERT S. LEVINE

INTRODUCTION

Two possible approaches to the question of the effects of foreign trade on Soviet planning suggest themselves. One approach would be to investigate the effects of foreign trade on the decisions taken by Soviet planners — in other words, the effects of trade on the strategies of resource use in Soviet planning. The other approach would be to pursue the effects of trade on the ways in which planning decisions are reached — that is, on the methods and practices of Soviet centralized planning.

THE ROLE OF TRADE IN SOVIET PLANNING STRATEGY

The first approach has already been examined in depth in the literature on the Soviet economy.[1] Its dominant feature is the quantitatively insignificant role that foreign trade has played in the Soviet economy. Professor Holzman, for example, has shown that Soviet exports reached a plan-era peak of 3.5 percent of national income in 1930, fell to a low of 0.5 percent in 1937, and rose in the post-war period to a level of 2.3–2.6 percent by the end of the 'fifties.[2] In 1964, Soviet exports were still under 3 percent of national income.[3] This is not to say, however, that foreign trade has been

---

* I wish to acknowledge my indebtedness to Antonio Costa, John Hardt, and Erich Klinkmüller for the advice they gave me. Responsibility for what follows is unfortunately solely my own.

[1] See, for example, [11] and [14].

[2] [14, p. 290]. Exports and imports are of approximately the same order of magnitude for the years cited here.

[3] Holzman's 1959 figure extended by data in [30, p. 660] and [6, p. 105].

of no significance in Soviet growth. During the period of the First Five-Year Plan, with its concentration on industrial capital formation, imports of machinery and equipment assumed a position of great importance. By 1932, they rose to a level of 55 percent of total imports [14, p. 296]; and imports of certain types of machines (turbines, generators, boilers, machine tools, and metal-cutting machines) accounted for between 50 and 90 percent of the growth in the stock of these machines during the First Five-Year Plan period [14, p. 299]. Furthermore, imports of certain basic industrial materials (lead, tin, nickel, zinc, aluminum, and rubber) accounted for 90 to 100 percent of these materials consumed in the Soviet economy during much of this period [14, p. 299]. This dependence on imports for individual key items decreased after the early 'thirties — for some items, abruptly [4] — so that by 1937 imports of only copper, lead, tin, and nickel accounted for more than 20 percent of the total internal consumption of these materials; by the end of the 'fifties, no imports (on which Holzman presents data) accounted for more than 20 percent of internal use of the product, and in fact only one import (wool) accounted for more than 5 percent of internal use [14, p. 299]. Thus, during the period of the First Five-Year Plan, imports played a significant role in Soviet growth. Holzman argues that if there had been no trade at all, Soviet industrialization would have been "seriously retarded, if not almost completely stopped for a number of years. Soviet efforts to import in this period despite great handicaps [adverse terms of trade, insufficient and expensive credits] attest to the importance they attributed to imports." [5]

After the period of the First Five-Year Plan, however, foreign trade played a much less strategic role in Soviet growth as, with the construction of import-competing production capacity, the Soviet economy became more and more self-sufficient. This strategy of producing import substitutes at home rather than trading for them may be said to have lead to a misallocation of resources in the static sense, reducing real income in a given year below what it otherwise could have been. But in the dynamic sense the case may be the reverse. Holzman contends that the Soviet choice of across-the-board industrial development with little trade resulted in higher dynamic growth than would have been experienced under a strategy emphasizing agriculture development and more trade [14, pp. 322–325].

[4] The import of tractors, for example, dropped from almost 60 percent of the growth in tractor stock in 1931 to zero percent in 1932 [14, p. 299].

[5] [14, p. 318]. Holzman also argues, "On the other hand, the really crucial imports, those which conferred the greatest 'importer surpluses' — prototype machines, nonferrous and ferrous metals, and rubber — probably amounted to less than one-fifth of total imports. A sharp reduction in trade which left the Russians still importing these categories would have retarded growth, but certainly would not have precluded a fairly creditable pace of industrialization."

THE APPROACH TAKEN AND ITS DIFFICULTIES

In the present paper, these questions might have been pursued further. Some quarrel could be raised, for example, with Holzman's conclusions. He probably underestimates the potential gains from technological changes in agriculture. And there are other alternatives to industrialization–*cum*–self-sufficiency besides concentration on agricultural development. Some of these alternatives would have involved industrialization, but with a larger role for trade. However, Holzman's piece is very thorough both in scope of coverage and depth of analysis, and I doubt whether much could be added to what he and others have said.

I have chosen, therefore, to concentrate on the second approach to the topic: the effects of foreign trade on the methodology of Soviet planning. This approach, however, has proved to have its difficulties. First, since foreign trade has played such a small role in Soviet economic activity, its impact on Soviet planning practices has been correspondingly slight. A discussion concentrating on some of the discoverable effects may therefore make these effects appear to have been more important than they really were. In actuality, some of the "effects" to be discussed assumed rather the nature of tendencies-to-have-an-effect. Second, mainly because of the relative unimportance of foreign trade in Soviet general economic planning and the little influence it has had on Soviet planning practices, information on this question is meager. The literature that I have seen is rather uncommunicative on the methods used in foreign trade planning and the ways in which foreign trade planning fits in with general planning. The major sources on general planning have not been very helpful, even the otherwise fairly fruitful literature on materials supply planning.[6] And the specific literature on the organization, planning, and operation of foreign trade has little to say about planning. It is instead concerned almost exclusively with organization and technical matters of operation, especially in regard to dealing with foreign firms and markets. What follows, therefore, is to perhaps a larger extent than desirable based on deductions from small bits of information coupled frequently with creative extrapolations.

AUTARKY AND CENTRAL PLANNING

Before proceeding to the main issue, let us consider one more matter of a preliminary nature. To what extent were the quantitative insignificance of Soviet foreign trade and its consequent limited effect on Soviet planning

[6] For example, the chapter on the construction of material balances for such an important export product as petroleum, in [13, pp. 97–129], has practically nothing to say about exports. According to Holzman [14, p. 295], exports of petroleum in 1958 accounted for 8 to 22 percent of the total output of petroleum, depending on the type of petroleum product.

practices due to the presence of centralized planning itself? It is sometimes argued that Soviet leaders, especially in the 'thirties, pursued a policy of eliminating foreign trade (autarky) because central planners do not *like* foreign trade. Central planners, it is said, want complete control over all the economic variables relevant to achieving the economic objectives established for them. This creates in the planners an antipathy toward foreign trade, for trade would remove from their direct control a subset of relevant variables, and would (perhaps) involve added uncertainties (note that these are two separate issues.) [7]

It is probably true that the planners' desire for a wide span of control played a part in the drive to limit foreign trade. Furthermore, the extreme pressure for growth, exerted by the political leaders, may have intensified this drive in a manner somewhat similar to the way in which the pressure for rapid growth stimulated ministerial empire-building ("sectoral autarky") within the economy. It is not, however, the only factor that led to the low level of trade. First of all, given the large, diverse resource base of a continent-size country, the Soviet Union might be expected to experience a low and decreasing level of foreign trade as it industrialized. In the United States, the ratio of exports to national income fell from 7.5 percent in 1913 to 4 percent in 1958, despite attempts of the government, during much of this time, to increase the role of trade [18, p. 156]. Second, the shock of the sharp reversal of international terms of trade against the U.S.S.R. in the period of the early 'thirties when it did attempt to trade, and the inability of the Soviet Union to acquire sufficient international credits, also led to the decrease in trade.

Primarily, however, the policy of autarky reflected political considerations, the same considerations in fact which lay behind the policy of forced, rapid industrialization itself and which were instrumental in the adoption of highly centralized means of planning and control. These were the desire to catch up economically with the advanced capitalist nations of the West and to achieve military parity with them, in this way protecting and increasing the national sovereignty and power of the Soviet Union. [8] Soviet industrialization in the 'thirties was imbued with the spirit of gaining economic independence and strengthening the defense capabilities of the nation. These objectives were, in fact, stated in the U.S.S.R. Constitution as being among the aims of economic policy, and were cited by one Soviet foreign trade authority as

---

[7] Given the uncertainties of the Soviet internal supply system, it is not necessarily true that supply from abroad, especially from developed capitalist nations, would involve the Soviets in greater uncertainties. The case might well be the reverse. There would, though, be the added uncertainties of changes in foreign and international prices (again, especially with capitalist nations). However, whatever the actual balance as regards uncertainties, it is still true that foreign trade limits the exercise of direct control by central planners.

[8] See [10, pp. 17–18] and papers by J. Berliner and H. Levine in [24].

the basis for Soviet foreign trade planning [5, p. 62]. Another Soviet trade specialist, in writing of the period of the First Five-Year Plan, referred to the goal enunciated by Stalin in a famous speech in 1931: "The task before us was to liquidate in 10 years, those 50–100 years in which old Russia lagged behind other countries. . . ." [9] That these political factors were dominant in the *policy* of autarky (as differentiated from the *actuality* of growing self-sufficiency) can also be seen in the fact that the movement toward autarky began in the 1920s before the actual introduction of central planning, that it was altered after World War II vis-à-vis the nations within the Soviet bloc because of the "friendly" atmosphere prevailing among them, and that in more recent times it has lessened with regard to the developed capitalist world as a result of the Soviet's achievement of virtual military parity with the West and the reduction of hostility in this area.[10]

Furthermore, if the Soviet policy of trade aversion was primarily a result of the political considerations just mentioned, then it is not clear that "autarky" is the appropriate term to use to describe it. For the pursuit of economic independence does not require the total elimination of foreign trade. All it requires is that a country not be dependent on another country for any goods crucial to its economic existence.[11] Soviet economists today in fact argue that the Soviet Union is not now, and was not even in the 'thirties, interested in autarky: "While seeking economic independence from capitalist countries, the Soviet Union has never tried to achieve autarky . . ." [25, p. 3].

In sum, we are not just dealing with the tight circle whereby foreign trade had little effect on Soviet planning practices because foreign trade was insignificant relative to total Soviet economic activity, and foreign trade was relatively insignificant because Soviet central planners did not want it to affect their central planning practices. There were other and more important reasons for the reduced role of foreign trade in the Soviet economy.

DESCRIPTION OF FOREIGN TRADE ORGANIZATION AND PLANNING

ORGANIZATION

With foreign trade as insignificant in the Soviet economy as it was, one might think that it would have been possible for regular economic organizations to handle foreign trade activities. The planning and operation of exports and imports, and of transportation and money flows, could have been han-

[9] [22, p. 91] as cited in [14, p. 302].

[10] With regard to the most recent period, see the speech by Kosygin at the 23rd Party Congress, in [7, p. 20].

[11] For further discussion of this question, see the Introduction to this volume and [4].

dled through the regular channels of Gosplan and its various subdepartments, through the industrial ministries and their administrations for planning, supply, and sales (with perhaps the addition of foreign trade specialists), and through the ministries of transportation and finance. And the entire subset of trade planning considerations could have been coordinated by a subdepartment of Gosplan for foreign trade. However, foreign trade — insignificant though it was in the total picture — did possess enough peculiarities and did present sufficient problems in planning and operation (especially in dealing with foreign organizations) to have required, the Soviets decided, a separate structure of organizations.

The literature on the organization of Soviet foreign trade is fairly substantial,[12] while the literature on the planning of foreign trade is not. But since both of these issues are of importance to us here, let me sketch briefly the organizations involved in foreign trade and their functions, and outline, if perhaps in "idealized" form, the way in which the annual foreign trade plan is constructed.[13] There is no attempt, in what follows, to be complete. A number of organizations involved in foreign trade and details of plan construction have been omitted. The aim is to present only the highlights in order to provide a basis for our discussion of effects in the following section.

At the top of the Soviet foreign trade organization stands the *Ministry of Foreign Trade*. The Ministry is purely an administrative and regulatory body; it does not engage directly in operational work on foreign trade transactions. Its functions, in addition to the supervision of those bodies that do have operational responsibilities, involve the construction of foreign trade plans, the working out of tariff policies, and generally the development of measures to improve the conduct of Soviet foreign trade. Its staff includes a few administrations for export and import (constructed along consolidated branch lines), a number of administrations organized by groups of countries, and several functional administrations (for economic planning, finance, foreign exchange, legal matters, transportation, inspection of quality of export goods, and others).

To carry out its task of supervising the conduct of foreign trade, within the borders of the Soviet Union, the Ministry has a net of resident *commissioners* (*upol'nomochennye*) located primarily in areas where there are major producers of exports and in important port cities and shipping centers. The commissioners supervise the fulfillment of orders for the preparation and delivery of export goods, according to the proper specifications and schedules, with special attention to questions of the quality of machines and equipment produced for export. In especially important cases, the commis-

[12] See, especially, [2], [5], [28, pp. 3–17], [31], and [35, pp. 48–52]; for the prewar period, see [1].

[13] The descriptions of the organization and planning of foreign trade which follow are based primarily on the sources in the preceding footnote.

sioners report regularly on the progress of export orders to the Ministry and the relevant foreign trade associations (see below). The latter, in turn, keep the commissioners informed about export orders issued to industrial enterprises in their localities and about changes in these orders. In general, the commissioners are the "eyes" of the Ministry in their given localities.

In supervising the conduct of Soviet foreign trade outside the borders of the Soviet Union, the Ministry has *trade delegations* attached to the official Soviet diplomatic representation in foreign countries. The trade delegation represents the foreign trade interests of the Soviet Union in the country in which it is located, studies economic conditions and trade possibilities within that country, and advises the Ministry on how to improve trade and the conduct of trade with that country. It supervises the operational activities, within the host country, of Soviet organizations having the right to conduct foreign trade and often acts as the representative of these organizations in operational matters.

The direct operational conduct of Soviet foreign trade is performed by the *all-union foreign trade associations (ob'edineniia)*, which are *khozraschet* organizations having monopoly rights over the export and import of a defined group of products (of one or several branches of the economy).[14] Currently, they number more than forty, over half of them concerned with machinery, equipment, and instrument products.[15] The foreign trade association is empowered to enter into foreign trade transactions, and into banking, credit, and foreign exchange transactions with organizations both within the Soviet Union and abroad. In general, it acts as an intermediary between Soviet and foreign enterprises, carries out the administrative work involved, and assures the fulfillment of foreign trade contracts.[16] It is also responsible for working out the annual and long-term trade plans for the products within its competence, for developing means of improving the conduct of Soviet trade, and for studying foreign markets and firms with the aim of making better use of fluctuations of economic conditions abroad in buying and selling goods. To perform these functions, it has a number of operating (line) departments, and functional departments covering economic-planning, technology, market conditions (*kon'iunkturnyi otdel*), advertising, transport, foreign exchange and finance, accounting, and personnel. It also frequently maintains authorized agents within Soviet trade delegations abroad and keeps permanent offices at major Soviet port cities. Being *khozraschet* organizations, the foreign trade associations are expected to maintain a profitable

[14] For a list of the foreign trade associations and the products covered by each in 1958, see [5, pp. 41–43].

[15] For a complete list of foreign trade associations as of August 1966, see [33, p. 50].

[16] Foreign trade associations concerned with the importation of machinery and equipment have, in recent years, been responsible not only for supervising contract fulfillment, but also for seeing that the imported machinery is put into use in accordance with the economic plan [28, p. 12].

financial relationship between the income they earn from their commissions on foreign trade transactions and their expenditures.

In addition to these main foreign trade organizations, there are some others worth mentioning. In the late 1950s, the *State Committee for Foreign Economic Relations* was established to strengthen Soviet economic coopera- tion with the underdeveloped countries and also with the socialist bloc. It is mainly concerned with constructing and equipping industrial plants in for- eign countries in connection with the Soviet program of foreign aid and technical assistance. It has subordinate to it (rather than to the Ministry of Foreign Trade) several foreign trade associations organized to supply equip- ment and materials for these plants.

During the period of the regional form of economic administration (1957– 1965), *departments of foreign relations* were formed in many republics and economic regions, especially those near international borders, to help in the administration of foreign trade. There were also *commissions to aid export* established in each republic with such functions as uncovering new sources of export and checking the quality of exported commodities. Even though the Soviets in 1965 returned to the branch line (ministerial) form of economic administration, both these sets of organizations may still be in existence, for many republican organizations have been retained in an effort to maintain some territorial influence in administration. Whether they still exist, and, if so, what functions they now perform, is not clear (from the literature I have seen).

PLANNING

Proceeding now to a brief and idealized description of the construction of the foreign trade plan, let it first be noted that the foreign trade plan is a constituent part of the overall economic plan, both the annual and the per- spective plan. It would have been better to say foreign trade *plans*, for the foreign trade plan is really a series of interconnected plans: an import plan, an export plan, plans for the actual deliveries of these commodities, a trans- port plan, and a plan of income and expenditures.

The actual construction of the annual foreign trade plan begins, as does the construction of the overall annual economic plan,[17] with preliminary targets for the forthcoming plan ("control figures") worked out by Gosplan on the basis of, among other things, specific communications (from the Polit- buro, Council of Ministers) about the preferences and policies of political leaders, statistical knowledge of the current economic situation, technological information, and in the case of the foreign trade plan the long-term trade agreements then in existence.[18] In constructing the control figures, Gosplan

---

[17] For a description of the construction of the overall annual economic plan, see, among others, my [20, pp. 151–176] and [21, Chaps. V and VI].

[18] Long-term trade agreements are bilateral agreements, usually signed for five years, in which minimum trade flows of key products are indicated. These agreements have

puts together a set of rough, highly aggregative material balances (which it can compare with the set of empirical material balances reflecting the previous year's actual experience, to test for reasonableness). With these preliminary material balances, Gosplan is able to develop a set of preliminary import and export targets, which it sends to the Ministry of Foreign Trade. The planning administration of the Ministry checks these preliminary targets and transmits them to the relevant foreign trade associations. The latter do the basic work of constructing the plan. Operating within the guidelines set for them, they work up detailed import and export plans by type of product (within their established range), by country, and by method of international payment.

With regard to imports, the foreign trade associations have to disaggregate the control figures to the level of "funded" (centrally allocated in the annual state plan) commodities, in line with their estimates of the specific import needs of Soviet economic organizations; further, they have to check on the availability of these products abroad with respect to price, to means of international payment, and, if the product is not a standard variety of raw material, to many quality specifications. With exports, the problems are, *mutatis mutandis*, much the same, with the often more difficult problem of estimating the possibilities of selling planned exports in foreign markets, and the prices that might be received. The associations maintain a close connection, through the import and export administrations (of the Ministry of Foreign Trade), with the Ministry's administrations organized by countries, with the administrations of foreign exchange and finance, "and when necessary with the relevant departments of Gosplan" [5, p. 64].

When the foreign trade associations complete their plan drafts and submit them to the economic planning administration of the Ministry, there are bound, of course, to be inconsistencies in the consolidated foreign trade plan. Given the various overall physical and monetary targets and constraints, and the constraints of necessary bilateral payment balances with most individual countries, inconsistencies at this first consolidation would appear to be unavoidable. It is then the job of the planning administration of the Ministry to work out, with the foreign trade associations, changes in their drafts that will bring about a consolidated draft of the foreign trade plan, which the Ministry then submits to Gosplan.

Gosplan takes data from different parts of the Foreign Trade Ministry's draft and incorporates them into various balances: material balances (quantitative data on exports and imports of "funded" commodities), financial balances, transportation balances, and labor balances. And it proceeds, with the data it receives from other economic organizations, to work out a con-

not been treated as binding; they are more in the nature of orienting documents and are revised annually.

sistent draft of the national economic plan, altering in the process the Foreign Trade Ministry's draft of the foreign trade plan.

After the draft of the annual economic plan, and with it the foreign trade plan, has been confirmed by the Council of Ministers, the foreign trade associations are given allotments (*fondy*) for acquisition of the funded commodities they are to export.[19] On the basis of these, they send detailed orders for the delivery of export goods to the sales administrations of the producing ministries, who assign them in turn to individual producing enterprises.[20] It is then the task of the foreign trade associations to negotiate the sales of the export goods abroad, and, as described earlier, to supervise (with other organs of the Ministry of Foreign Trade and of the producing ministry) the precise and on-time fulfillment of the export orders during the course of the plan year. In this regard, the powers of the foreign trade associations apparently include changing the export production orders given to an enterprise — "the cancellation of an order, the changing of the schedule of deliveries, the changing of the quantity and assortment of a commodity, etc." [5, p. 38].

With regard to imports, the procedure is for the economic organization, which is allotted *fondy* in the annual economic plan for the acquisition of imported goods, to send a detailed order for specific goods within its allotment to the appropriate foreign trade association. In the case of machinery and equipment, this order is to be sent by the supply administration of the using-ministry, is to name the purchasing unit (enterprise, factory, or other organization), is to include very detailed information about the specifications of the machine or piece of equipment ordered, and is to indicate the estimated purchase price and the suggested foreign firm from which the purchase should be made. If the imported commodity is a raw material, food product, or other such standard item, it is apparently ordered from the foreign trade association by the sales administration of the ministry producing that product in the Soviet Union, and is distributed by it to the ultimate users.[21] The foreign trade associations check the import orders received,

[19] For the acquisition of non-funded commodities, the Ministry of Foreign Trade works out agreements with the producing ministries. See [5, pp. 197–198].

[20] In a recent article, a Soviet economist stated that with the change from the territorial principle back to the branch principle in the administration of Soviet industry, it is now easier to decide many of the operational questions connected with foreign trade. "Thus, the well founded choice of enterprises who will produce a given export commodity can now be accomplished by the organization most competent in this area — the all-union or union-republic branch ministry and its production associations. It will be able to work out the necessary technical measures and to control the actual progress of the delivery in close cooperation with the foreign trade organization" [26, p. 116].

[21] See [1, p. 35]. I have not, as yet, been able to discover what the role of the new State Committee for Material-Technical Supply is in the process of transmitting actual orders for exports and imports. Since this Committee is an outgrowth of the All-Union Sovnarkhoz and its main administrations of interrepublican deliveries, which were in-

make recommendations for revisions where appropriate, and proceed to negotiate the purchase of import goods from foreign suppliers.

THE EFFECTS OF FOREIGN TRADE ON SOVIET PLANNING PRACTICES

THE SEPARATE ORGANIZATION OF FOREIGN TRADE AND PROBLEMS OF COORDINATION

The first effect of the presence of foreign trade on Soviet planning practices, to be noted, results from its separate organizational structure. Let it be clear from the outset: I am not arguing that the Soviets should not have set up a separate organizational structure for foreign trade. Indeed, I think it was probably necessary for them to do so. What I am arguing is that in the total absence of foreign trade, there would, of course, have been no foreign trade organization. It was the presence of trade that led them to set up a separate organization, and this separate organization has had certain effects on Soviet planning practices. These effects are in the nature of problems of coordination.

The difficulties resulting from a lack of sufficient coordination among different planning and control organizations are quite common in the Soviet Union, and have been well described in the literature on the Soviet economy. Enterprises get output targets they cannot fulfill because they are not given enough financial funds. In the middle of a year, the output plan of an enterprise is changed but not its input supplies, and so forth. The separateness of the foreign trade organization adds to these problems.

Difficulties of coordination would arise, it is true, even if foreign trade were not conducted by separate organizational units, but by, say, subdepartments of Gosplan and of other organizations. However, the relationships between Organization A and Organization B are different from the relationships between subdepartment A and subdepartment B of one organization, because of the separate identities of the former and the single organizational identity of the latter. An example of this is the experience the Soviets have had with combining short-term and long-term planning in one planning organization and then separating the two functions into two separate organizations. When they are separate, there are frequent complaints of a lack of coordination between the two types of plans. When they are together, coordination between the two planning groups tends to be better and there seems to be less complaint about a lack of coordination between short- and long-term plans. (On the other hand, there are complaints that work on the long-

volved in the transmission process, it may now also play an active role. The system I have described is based primarily on Cherviakov (1958), which mainly concerns the pre-1957 situation and should therefore be rather relevant to the current situation.

term plan is often sacrificed to the more pressing needs of short-term planning.)

The foreign trade organizations have to deal, in export and import matters, with the industrial ministries; in transportation matters, with the Ministry of Transportation; and in balance-of-payments matters, with the Ministry of Finance and the State Banking System. To avoid inconsistencies, a change by any one of these organizations should go through the bureaucracies of the others. If it does not, inconsistencies will occur. As we have observed above, the foreign trade association has the right during the operation of the plan to change an export production order given to a producing enterprise, but it does not have the power to change other parts of the enterprise's plan to compensate for the change, and it appears unlikely that the other bureaucracies will make the required changes. This adds to the inconsistencies among plan indicators.

Furthermore, experience with Soviet matters teaches us that organizational differences can be manifested in unusual ways. For example, Soviet industrial ministries have used, and undoubtedly still use, different systems of materials classification.[22] Soviet foreign trade specialists speak of their "unified commodity nomenclature," but they do not say that it is the same nomenclature used by other economic organizations, thus adding to the confusion [5, pp. 70–72]. Another manifestation — perhaps not of great importance but particularly telling in this paper — is that separate organization tends to produce a separate literature. Thus, the separate literature on foreign trade planning is not coordinated with the literature on general economic planning.

While it is true that complaints are not over-frequently heard in the Soviet economic literature about coordination problems with respect to foreign trade organizations, this is because of the insignificant role that foreign trade plays in the Soviet economy. Foreign trade contributes its share to the general coordination malady in Soviet planning practice — but it is a small share. The satellite literature is, to be sure, quite different [23, Chap. II].

CEMA AND ECONOMIC COOPERATION IN THE BLOC

If the Council for Economic Mutual Assistance had been endowed with supranational planning powers over the countries of the Soviet bloc, then national economic planning within the Soviet Union would indeed have been affected. The locus of dominant preferences, the difficulty (and perhaps also the methodology) of working out the internal consistency of the plan, the degree of flexibility in planning calculations and decisions, and other aspects of Soviet planning practices would have been changed. But from the beginning it was made clear that CEMA was not to have such powers [17, p. 26].

[22] See the discussion in [16].

Its aim was to coordinate the economic activity of sovereign, independent nations. This emphasis on individual national sovereignty has been maintained throughout its existence, and is still stressed by the Soviets today (perhaps even more so than previously).[23]

Even without supranational teeth, however, CEMA may affect Soviet planning, depending on how it pursues the coordination of economic activity within the bloc. At first, apparently, this was attempted through long-term bilateral trade agreements. But it was soon discovered that it was not possible to use trade agreements to force the coordination of economic plans. The divergences existing in the latter led the trade flows to deviate (as a result of annual revisions of the trade agreements) from the long-term agreements. The approach then taken was to try to coordinate long-term plans more directly. This too, though, was not very successful. One Soviet author has stated that about all that was really attempted was the avoidance of duplication in the construction of new production facilities, in order to allow new plants to be built which were large enough to take advantage of economies of scale [15, p. 26]. In explaining why the coordination of long-term plans was not more successful, another Soviet author has said that the CEMA discussions occurred at too late a stage. They tried to coordinate the long-term plans of individual bloc nations after the directives (preliminary plan summaries) of the plans had already been confirmed by the respective countries [29, pp. 99–100].

At present, intra-bloc coordination is being attempted during the drawing up of the drafts for the long-term plans. In working on the coordination of long-term plans for the period 1966–1970, bilateral discussions were held among CEMA countries, as a result of which, preliminary agreements concerning mutual deliveries were reached. Also, rough trade balances were worked up for the most important types of products in the fuel and power, machine-building, metallurgical, and chemical sectors, which were combined by the staff of CEMA into summary (rough) trade balances. "And in turn the countries used these balances in the further work on the drafts of their national plans" [29, p. 100].

What it boils down to is that the coordination work of CEMA has had only a slight impact on Soviet planning practices (again, as differentiated from actual planning decisions taken). It has increased the flow and probably the quality of information about import and export possibilities, and has provided an arena in which trade negotiations and planning discussions

[23] "Therefore, international economic relations between socialist countries take the form of relations between sovereign owners of the means of production, and not as relations, built on the base of unified, international property . . . this is one of the basic differences between CEMA and imperialist economic organizations like the 'common market' which aspire to take for themselves functions of supra-national institutions" [19, p. 82].

could take place. The bilateral long-term trade agreements between bloc countries were apparently considered in the construction of the most recent five-year plan. And while these agreements have not been binding and have been revised from year to year, they were not completely ignored in the construction of the operational annual plan. As we shall see in the next section, this played a useful part in plan construction. But it also played a dysfunctional part, in that it added an element of inflexibility to the planning process and encouraged bureaucratic inertia in the year-to-year seeking of new, more effective structures of trade.[24]

TIME AND SEQUENCE PROBLEMS IN PLANNING

Two prominent problems in Soviet planning practices concern the time it takes to construct the annual plan, and the sequential nature of plan construction. As regards the first, the time it takes is excessive; the plan is often not completed until after the beginning of the plan year. As regards the second, the sequence of plan construction begins with a set of preliminary output targets sent down the planning hierarchy by Gosplan. On the basis of these targets, enterprises estimate input requirements and send them up the planning hierarchy to Gosplan, where a balanced plan is worked out. Output targets and input allocations are then sent down the hierarchy to the enterprises, which construct detailed lists of specific inputs required. These go back up the hierarchy, and ultimately the enterprise is assigned its operationally detailed output and input plans. Thus, original output targets lead to calculation of input needs; the calculated input needs lead to changes (and more detail) in output targets; these changes in output targets lead to changes (and more detail) in input requirements; and these changes and increased detail lead in turn to the enterprise plan (which involves further changes for the individual enterprise). The problem is that the enterprise is always one step behind. The information it last provided on its input needs pertained to the previous set of output targets, and therefore the inputs it is allocated in its official plan are not appropriate to the output targets it is actually assigned. A few more rounds would help, but as we have said, the plan is late as it is.

The question facing us here is whether the presence of foreign trade intensifies or reduces these difficulties. The answer depends very much on the magnitude of foreign trade. The literature on the East European economies stresses the intensification of these problems (especially the lateness of

[24] "One of the important tasks set by the 23rd Congress of CPSU . . . was the raising of the effectiveness of foreign trade . . . The fulfillment of the established aim is complicated by the fact that the five year trade agreements, concluded by the Soviet Union with the CEMA countries, have already pre-determined the volume and structure of Soviet foreign trade, and in particular Soviet deliveries of fuel and raw materials necessary for the normal development of the economies of fraternal countries" [8, p. 84].

plans) by the relatively significant foreign trade sectors found in these econ-omies [23, Chaps. II and III]. But the situation in the Soviet economy is not as clear.

To begin, the process of construction of the foreign trade plan, which is part of the construction of the official Soviet annual economic plan, does not include the process of negotiating the actual purchase and sale of imports and exports.[25] (The consequences of this will be discussed below.) Second, the strength of the time and sequence problems is to a great extent related to the discontinuous nature of Soviet planning. Each calendar year the entire plan is constructed "from scratch." The long-term trade agreements could be of help here, but their lack of firmness limits their effectiveness.

Turning now first to the problem of lateness, there is no indication, in the scant literature on Soviet foreign trade planning (that I have seen), that the Ministry of Foreign Trade's plan draft reaches Gosplan any later than do the drafts from the industrial and other ministries. Nor does there appear to be much reason, given the relatively small magnitude of Soviet trade, to expect it to do so. The presence of foreign trade, however, may tend to make Gosplan's balancing job more time-consuming. Since the foreign trade associations, which make estimates of imports and exports, and the produc-tion enterprises, which make estimates of import needs and export pro-duction, come from separate organizations, there is a good chance that their estimates will be far apart, thus adding to Gosplan's burden (this may be so even though both of their organizations began, presumably, with the same control figures).[26] Furthermore, though it may be handy to be able to close a material balance by increasing an import (see next section), it may well take considerable time to find a matching export to increase. This is especially true if the import is involved in bilateral trade with a socialist bloc country (as about 70 percent of Soviet imports currently are) [30, p. 660]. For then Gosplan might have to consult with the Ministry of Foreign Trade and its relevant country administration to find an appropriate poten-tial export for that particular country. Such interorganizational consultations, one might imagine, could take time.

As far as the sequencing problem is concerned, the separate organizational structures for foreign trade and production may again add to the problem. For the initial differences in import and export estimates, mentioned above, may mean (though not necessarily) that the sequencing divergence between output targets and input allocations in the final enterprise plan may end up being greater than would otherwise be the case. In other respects, foreign

[25] See "Planning," above; see also [5, p. 68].

[26] See [23, pp. 84–85] where Pryor shows that in East Germany, the subdepartments of machine-building and of foreign trade in the State Planning Commission used differ-ent control figures. This is a case of "subdepartmental barriers"; it runs counter to the argument made above in discussing the separate organization of foreign trade.

trade does not appear to add to the problem. For as the Soviets have organized their process of plan construction, the Ministry of Foreign Trade's plan draft and the drafts from the production ministries are constructed at the same time, and therefore no extra levels are added to the planning sequence.

After the official plan is constructed, however, and the actual purchases and sales are negotiated, sequencing-type problems do arise because of changes introduced during negotiations with trading partners. This is somewhat different from what occurs in domestic planning, where little change (in planned outputs and inputs) is introduced at the contracting stage. The situation is similar, though, to what occurs in the national economic plan throughout the year in which the plan is in operation, where changes are made in *ad hoc* fashion as a result of repeated divergences between the plan and reality. The sequencing-type problems that arise at this stage are more noxious than those discussed previously, which are part of the plan construction process, since, because they are treated on the spot, as it were, there is little chance and little attempt to make a balanced set of changes. In the example cited earlier, when a foreign trade association changes an export production order given to an enterprise, it will not — and indeed cannot — change the input and other plan allocations that the enterprise has been given. If it is a very important enterprise, Gosplan or some other superior body (including the Communist Party) may try to make the other required changes. But the impression derived from Soviet literature is that plan imbalances created by repeated changes during the course of the plan's operation are a serious source of difficulty.

The extent of the problems caused by changes at the stage of purchase and sale negotiations is related to the mechanism used to effect the purchase or sale. If the traded commodity is of a homogeneous, raw-material type, then it might be traded on a commodity exchange or at an auction. In such a case, the only source of change would be a divergence between the planned price and the actual price paid or received.[27] This might then lead to a change in the quantity of the commodity imported or exported, or changes in other imports or exports necessitated by the balance-of-payments effects of the price divergence. If, on the other hand, the commodity traded is a manufactured good, especially machinery or equipment, it is traded through direct negotiations with sellers and buyers. In such cases — and more forcibly in the case of Soviet exports than of Soviet imports — changes in the quantity and composition of traded goods are not infrequent. Thus, if the Soviets pursue the policy, as they say they want to do, of increasing the share of manufactured goods in their exports, then the impact on planning practices of changes at the stage of contract negotiations should be expected to increase.

[27] This could be handled, however, through operations in futures markets.

METHODOLOGY OF PHYSICAL PLANNING [28]

In this section, I should like to investigate the impact of foreign trade on Soviet balancing methodology, and to explore the ways in which certain aspects of foreign trade planning might appear to central planners accustomed to working with physical balances.

When the draft plans come into Gosplan from the Ministry of Foreign Trade, from the industrial ministries, and from other economic organizations, Gosplan, as we have pointed out, distributes the plan data to the individual material balances of the products covered by the state plan. Gosplan then has the task of working out the internal consistency of the total set of material balances. Difficulties arise in the Soviet methodology of closing balances (besides the difficulty of running into constraints on productive capacity) from the fact that any change in a planned output (or decrease in a planned supply) has a series of secondary effects in the direction of requiring more inputs (or in leading to a decrease in the planned output levels of those products that use the commodity, whose supply was decreased, as an input). If, however, Gosplan were to try to eradicate a shortfall in a particular material balance by raising (or introducing) imports of that deficit product, this would not lead to direct input secondary effects on the rest of the set of material balances, since the product would be produced abroad using foreign inputs. It might, therefore, be thought that increasing imports is an easy way of closing a material balance. However, an increase in imports would have secondary effects along other lines. The increase would cause the balance of foreign exchange to go into deficit, requiring corrective action. Such action would primarily involve changes in the planned production level of exports, thus leading to the secondary effects on other inputs and outputs in domestic production.

At this point, let me digress for a moment. Generally speaking, in any planning of domestic output levels, what is of concern is the importance of products, final or intermediate. Final products are valued in relation to their private and social utility (as determined by the society), and intermediate goods are valued in relation to their technical capabilities in the production of other goods.[29] Import planning involves both these aspects, but export planing involves only the latter.

In Soviet export planning, an export good is always an intermediate or producers' good, even if in physical form it is a consumers' good, for exports are planned to earn the foreign exchange necessary to acquire the desired imports (which are desired because of either the direct utility they give or

[28] For a discussion of similar issues, see Professor Brown's paper in this volume and [4]; see also [23, pp. 55–63].

[29] Let us ignore, here, the question of the psychic enjoyment Stalin may have derived from reading steel production figures.

their use in production). An export good is a producers' good, but it does not have a physical, engineering, input relationship with the goods it "produces." [30] Furthermore, a given export good does not "produce" any given import good, but is involved in the "production" of the aggregate of imports. This is true even under bilateral trade balancing, for bilateral trade is normally not — product for product — barter. Nevertheless, it may be of some value to think in terms of a relationship between a given export good and a given import good, a concept similar to the input norms of Soviet physical planning or the input coefficients of input-output analysis. In the latter, the coefficient a_{ij} indicates the amount of the ith product needed in the production of one unit of the jth product in a production process where every (non-zero) input in the amount a_{ij} ($i = 1 \ldots n$) is necessary to produce one unit of the jth product. An analogous "production" coefficient for exports and imports can be defined as v_{ij}, which indicates the amount of export of the ith good needed to "produce" a unit of import of the jth good, in a "production" process where the indicated amount of the export good will by itself "produce" a unit of the import good.

One of the important differences between the set of a's and the set of v's is that the a's vary as technology changes (also, if dealing with aggregate a's, as the composition of the aggregate changes), whereas the v's fluctuate as a direct result of changes in foreign trade prices — since, of course, they are nothing more than the commodity terms of trade, the ratio of the world market price of the import good to the world market price of the export good. This makes them a much more unstable set of coefficients. [31] And if the balance of foreign exchange is viewed as a constraint, the fluctuation of world prices contributes to the uncertainty of the internal consistency of annual economic plans.

Returning, now, to Gosplan's balancing problems, an increase in planned imports of the kth product would, all other things remaining constant, require either an increase in the export of any single ith product in the amount $v_{ik} \cdot \Delta M_k$ (where ΔM_k is the increase in imports of the kth product) or some changes in other balance-of-payments items. [32] Ignoring the latter, if planned exports were to be increased, this would cause the series of secondary effects through the system of material balances referred to above (unless Gosplan was lucky enough to find an exportable good with a surplus in its balance). [33] These effects could be avoided, however, by methods

---

[30] Exports could also be viewed as "producing" foreign exchange. But pursuing the thinking of Soviet physical planners, we shall not take this approach.

[31] See the relevant discussion in the article in [12, p. 79].

[32] Or a number of different exports could be increased, each in the amount $v_{ik} m_{ik}$, where m_{ik} = the units of the kth import good "produced" by the ith export good; $i = 1 \ldots n$, and $\Sigma m_{ik} = M_k$.

[33] If, as is likely given the structure of Soviet exports, it is the production of a raw material or a lowly fabricated export good which is to be increased, the secondary

analogous to norm-tightening in standard Soviet balancing methodology.[34] An increase in a planned import of the kth good could be balanced by an appropriate decrease in v_{ik} without any increase in the planned amount of export of the ith good. A decrease in v_{ik} would be brought about, not through a forced improvement in the efficiency of production, but through an increase in the estimate of the expected price at which the exports of the ith good will be sold, or a decrease in the expected purchase price of the kth good. Gosplan officials might even feel that the expected prices were falsely estimated in the first place (operation of the "safety factor" in Soviet planning practice) and, therefore, that a change might not cause any difficulties.

Norm-tightening in regard to the v's could work in two directions (as it does with the a's). That is, a deficit balance could be closed through an increase in planned imports and a decrease of a suitable v or set of v's, thus maintaining a planned balance of foreign exchange; or, if the deficit was in the material balance of an export good, the balance could be closed by decreasing the planned exports of the good and decreasing its v's.

There are obvious dangers in this balancing methodology. Closing a balance through increased imports, even with an increase in planned exports, has certain risks, for the exports still have to be sold, and if foreign markets are not receptive the relevant v's will rise, leading to strains in the domestic economy.[35] I have some doubts that forcing estimates of foreign market prices is a much-used method of achieving plan balances. Given the Soviet problems with balance of payments, the dangers of creating adverse balance-of-payments movements make the risks quite high, especially when the possibility of tightening the domestic input production norms frequently offers another way out. If, however, an increase of planned imports is the only way of closing a vital balance, I am sure it will be done, and ways of counteracting the increased drain on foreign exchange will be sought, including at times the tightening of the v coefficients. But I do not think that this step is taken lightly.

Pursuing this approach further, when the Soviets plan for the production

effects on other products might not be great. However, capacity constraints in the production of such goods might well be reached, which would mean that exports could be increased only at the expense of domestic uses of this good, which could lead in turn to secondary effects.

On the question of capacity limitations in bloc production of raw materials and some intriguing suggestions for its solution, see [8]. But see also [26, pp. 112–113].

Furthermore, the predominance of bilateral trade restricts the choice of export goods that can be used to cover an increase in imports.

[34] See [20] and [21].

[35] Professor Brown has kindly called to my attention the fact that the v's should be marginal coefficients rather than average coefficients if they are to be used for incremental adjustments. This is also true, in theory, of Leontief input-output coefficients, if they are to be used, in the inverted Leontief matrix, to calculate the effects of changes in final demand.

of a certain level of output of, say, the kth product, the set of input norms a_{ik} ($i = 1 \ldots n$) that they have constructed will determine how many units of *each* input material will be necessary to produce the desired amount of the kth product. However, when the Soviets plan an import of a certain amount of the kth product, the set of v_{ik}'s will not determine *which* export good will "produce" the desired import; it will only tell how much of any one of them would be necessary to "produce" the imports. Soviet production planning employs sets of fixed (i.e., invariant in the short run to price or scale changes, but subject to tightening) input coefficients, calculated primarily on the basis of engineering considerations rather than economic considerations (by which is meant the investigation of relative input productivities and conditions of input availabilities).[36] This leads to economic inefficiency, yet the limited selection of alternative production techniques and the availability of advanced foreign technologies reduce its cost. The "production" of imports by exports, however, vastly increases the scope of alternatives, the v's indicating only the terms on which any export can "produce" an import. The problem of choice, the choice of an advantageous set of exports, grows in significance. Soviet methods of physical planning, based as they are on engineering relationships with the primary aim of just achieving a balanced, feasible plan, are insufficient for foreign trade planning. As a Soviet article recently stated: "Both theory and practice demonstrate the error of the mechanical transfer of the forms and methods of economic behavior, which were developed within the individual socialist countries, to their foreign economic relations" [19, p. 82]. Thus, the presence of foreign trade, by greatly increasing the scope of economic choice, emphasizes the need for the development of rational decisionmaking procedures.

THE ECONOMIC REFORM

The pressure from the foreign trade sector for rationality in economic decisionmaking did not in the past have an overwhelming effect on Soviet planning practices. As Western economists have on occasion observed, rational, optimal planning has not been one of the Soviets' strong points. But now with the need for reform in economic planning and control methods generally accepted, this pressure from the foreign trade sector might be of some importance.[37] The growing literature on the calculation of the effectiveness of foreign trade is a case in point. In the past, foreign trade "theory" was very simple. Imports were used primarily to fill temporary gaps in the capital stock, and temporary and not-so-temporary gaps in the supply of inputs required in the domestic economy. Traditional exports and goods in

[36] For a discussion of Soviet norm construction, see [21, Ch. VIII].

[37] But see [19, p. 82], where the authors argue that reform is moving from the domestic economy to the foreign trade sector.

temporary surplus supply were then exported in amounts "necessary to pay for the imported goods, to form foreign exchange reserves, and to meet obligations for mutual deliveries and deliveries on credit" [5, p. 66]. But current discussions on the effectiveness of trade are becoming more sophisticated. And one of the central issues, as in domestic reform, is the development of a meaningful system of prices in the Soviet economy. The early articles, which only compared the ruble costs of producing exports with the ruble costs of producing import-competing goods, are giving way to articles that analyze the weaknesses of Soviet prices in making foreign trade decisions and that make suggestions for changes, including the inclusion of capital charges, more meaningful profit rates, economic rent, and the reflection of "the possible results of the good's utilization in the national economy." [38] Even the doctrine of comparative advantage, maligned in the past as a wicked tool of the capitalist world used to maintain the economic subjugation of underdeveloped agrarian nations, is now within the pale. In a recent article, a Soviet economist explained its principles, though without mention of its past history, Ricardo, or even wine and cloth [27, pp. 89–99].

Another important question is the effect that the foreign trade sector might have on the movement toward decentralization in Soviet planning practices. Because foreign trade depends, among other things, on prices and on supply and demand conditions in foreign markets, and because these conditions change regularly and rapidly, there is great need for decentralization in foreign trade decisionmaking. There have been some observable movements to make decisionmaking more responsive to the needs of trade. At the 23rd Party Congress, Kosygin stated: "Workers in industry must study the conditions for sale of their products both within the country and abroad, and the Ministry of Foreign Trade is obliged to give them the necessary information." [39] In a recent interview, the Deputy Chief of the Main Administration (of the Ministry of Foreign Trade) for the Export of

[38] [3, pp. 75–76]. See also other articles on the effectiveness of foreign trade in this journal volume. For discussions of the East European literature, see other issues of the journal.

[39] [7, p. 20]. It is clear that Kosygin is not happy with the progress of Soviet foreign trade and the performance of foreign trade organs:

"We are not yet making adequate use of the possibilities offered us by the development of foreign economic relations.

"The time has come to evaluate the role of foreign trade in a somewhat different way. Workers in the foreign trade organizations frequently shut themselves up in their own sphere, failing to give sufficient consideration to the fact that their entire activity should be subordinated to the task of raising the effectiveness of the national economy as a whole. It goes without saying that a long-range plan for foreign trade cannot foresee all the possibilities and changes that may arise in the international market, but for this very reason it is most important that workers in foreign trade have a thorough knowledge of the requirements of our economy and display initiative in posing questions of the most advantageous purchases and sales. On the other hand,

Machinery and Equipment to Capitalist Countries called for an increase in the direct participation of producers in trade negotiations. To aid in this, he announced that the large foreign trade association for machinery exports (*Mashinoeksport*) had been broken up into two smaller, less unwieldy, more specialized associations.[40]

But because of the need to maintain a balance-of-payments equilibrium, foreign trade can also strengthen centralization. The importance of the balance of payments and the supply of foreign exchange makes it unlikely that the regime will go too far in relaxing central control over foreign trade.[41]

Another way in which the foreign trade sector might affect current economic thinking in the Soviet Union is related to Soviet dealings with capitalist economies. Foreign trade specialists, first of all, intensively study capitalist business conditions and the ways in which capitalist economies actually operate. They are in a position to interpret for Russian economists and managers the ways in which real markets (rather than theoretical ones of the left or right) can, should, and should not operate. Second, in being forced to sell in markets that are not sellers' markets (as most have been in the Soviet Union), Soviet foreign trade officials are exposed to the requirement of meeting the needs of purchasers in terms of quality and timeliness of deliveries; they learn the importance of high-quality production and of such matters as providing service and spare parts on machines sold.[42]

Finally, trade itself will affect Soviet planning practices in the coming period. The importation of technically advanced machinery and equipment in the past has helped counteract the weaknesses of Soviet planning practices with respect to the pace and quality of technological change, and it is clear that the Soviet leaders intend to maintain and increase such imports. But, in addition, as Soviet trade relations with the West increase, men of Soviet industry will be more often exposed to Western products, to Western business methods and ways of industrial administration, and to Western businessmen — the way they act, the way they think, and the way they live. This breadth of contact may, indeed, turn out to be the single most important effect of foreign trade on Soviet planning practices.

workers in industry often regard foreign trade as something secondary. This totally incorrect view must be changed, and businesslike contacts between industry and foreign trade must be strengthened" [7, p. 19].

[40] [34, p. 11]. This is not necessarily an unmixed improvement. For, as argued above, the proliferation of separate organizations can lead to problems of coordination and communication.

[41] In the Instructions on the transition to the new economic system, published in [9], it was indicated that among the direct targets still to be sent from the center to enterprises was the output of export goods, in physical units.

[42] For example, they were able to get special premiums introduced, in December 1964, for the high-quality and timely delivery of exports (see [32, p. 46]). But also see a recent complaint that premiums are not high enough to be effective [26, p. 116].

DISCUSSION
Evsey D. Domar

Not being an institutional economist, I have little to say about Professor Levine's description of Soviet planning procedures as they relate to foreign trade. My general feeling is that actual Soviet planning is much less precise than he has implied. Many things happen, many goods are produced and distributed outside of any plan, while plans given to an enterprise frequently involve nothing more than an increment of a few percentage points over last year's output. The Liberman debates bear ample proof of this, and so do many discussions in the *Ekonomicheskaia Gazeta* and many references in Soviet fiction, not to mention my favorite *Krokodil*. Even the recent reforms, important and useful as they are, have not remedied these defects as yet.

In regard to Soviet foreign trade in particular, I have often wondered how good the Soviet trade officials are in carrying on their business — or, more broadly, how good *any* governmental officials (of nationalized industries in non-Communist countries) are in this game. So long as Soviet exports consisted of bulky staples like grain, lumber, petroleum, and even furs, perhaps no great business acumen was required. But the ability to sell a great variety of manufactured products certainly calls for that particular type of skill called "business sense." Do Soviet officials have it? Can they snatch profitable opportunities before their competitors discover them? How good are their forecasts of prices and of demand (or supply on the import side)? If they deal with corrupt government officials of underdeveloped countries (and not only of underdeveloped ones) do they offer bribes, rake-offs, and similar deals, like good capitalists? How honest are the Soviet officials themselves? Much information on this subject should be available among capitalist businessmen dealing with the Soviets. A skillful interviewer could produce a very interesting study.

My own acquaintance with Soviet exports pertains to Russian books. Here I can testify that they do not know the market, that they set prices, at least on books in economics and on statistical compendia, too low and provide too few copies. (Soviet economic journals are also rather cheap.) Do they simply add a certain markup to the ruble prices without considering the demand elasticity for different kinds of books? Since the ruble prices usually appear on the back cover, this is a testable hypothesis.

My next comment is about autarky. I agree with Levine that the Soviets are not against foreign trade as such. They merely do not want to be dependent on imports for essential economic inputs. For brevity, let the word "machines" stand for all such inputs, and let "toys" indicate all nonessential imports. For a country aiming at autarky, the ideal imports would consist of toys only. But this is true only in a final state of equilibrium which is not likely to arise. Since machines (in the above sense) are needed to make other machines, imports will for some time be heavily weighted with machines. In any given line, self-sufficiency will eventually be achieved, but by that time technological progress will require imports of other machines, and so on. Hence, such a country may keep on importing machinery (of different kinds, of course) and may never reach its ideal of importing toys only. On the other hand, a country not interested in self-sufficiency may happily keep on importing toys. Thus, a detailed study of imports over time is required to judge whether or not a given country is trying to achieve autarky. Superficial comparisons can be quite misleading.

Finally, a word about Levine's attempt to use input-output paraphernalia in discussing substitutions among Soviet imports and exports. The whole essence of the input-output method lies in rigid interrelationships between the outputs and the required inputs. Since this is clearly not the case between an increase in some imports and the required increment in some exports not in any way related to the specific imports, I do not feel that his use of coefficients clarifies the problem. Besides, reserves of foreign exchange blur any relationship that might otherwise have existed.

REFERENCES

1. Baykov, Alexander. *Soviet Foreign Trade* (Princeton: Princeton University Press, 1946).
2. Berman, Harold. "The Legal Framework of Trade between Planned and Market Economies: The Soviet-American Example," *Law and Contemporary Problems*, XXIV:3 (Summer 1959), pp. 482–528.
3. Borisenko, A. "On the Problems of Effectiveness of Socialist Foreign Trade," *American Review of Soviet and Eastern European Foreign Trade*, I:2 (March–April 1965), pp. 67–80.
4. Brown, Alan. "The Economics of Centrally Planned Foreign Trade: The Hungarian Experience" (Unpublished doctoral dissertation, Harvard University, 1966), Chap. VII.
5. Cherviakov, P. *Organizatsiia i tekhnika vneshnei torgovli SSSR* (Moscow: 1958).
6. Cohn, Stanley H. "Soviet Growth Retardation: Trends in Resource Availability and Efficiency," U.S. Congress, Joint Economic Committee, *New Directions in the Soviet Economy* (Washington, D.C.: 1966), Part II-A, pp. 99–132.
7. *Current Digest of the Soviet Press*, XVIII:14 (April 27, 1966), pp. 1–47.
8. Dudinskii, I. *Voprosy ekonomiki*, No. 4 (1966); translation in *American Review of Soviet and Eastern European Foreign Trade*, II:5 (September–October 1966), pp. 19–39.
9. *Ekonomicheskaia gazeta*, No. 50, December 1966.
10. Gerschenkron, Alexander. *Economic Backwardness in Historical Perspective* (Cambridge: Harvard University Press, 1962).
11. ———. *Economic Relations with the USSR* (New York: The Committee

on International Economic Policy in cooperation with the Carnegie Endowment for International Peace, 1945).

12. Glikman, P. *Voprosy ekonomiki*, No. 11 (1964).
13. Grebtsov, G., and L. Karpov. *Material'nye balansy v narodnokhoziaistvennom plane* (Moscow: 1960).
14. Holzman, Franklyn. "Foreign Trade," in Abram Bergson and Simon Kuznets (eds.), *Economic Trends in the Soviet Union* (Cambridge: Harvard University Press, 1963), pp. 283–332.
15. Ivanov, P. "Division of Labor and Coordination of Economic Plans," *American Review of Soviet and Eastern European Foreign Trade*, I:3 (May–June 1965), pp. 21–35.
16. Judy, Richard. "Information, Control, and Soviet Economic Management," in John P. Hardt *et al.* (eds.), *Mathematics and Computers in Soviet Economic Planning* (New Haven: Yale University Press, 1967).
17. Kaser, Michael. *Comecon* (London: Oxford University Press, 1965).
18. Kindleberger, Charles. *Foreign Trade and the National Economy* (New Haven: Yale University Press, 1962).
19. Ladygin, V., and Iu. Shiriaev. *Voprosy ekonomiki*, No. 5 (1966).
20. Levine, Herbert. "The Centralized Planning of Supply in Soviet Industry," U.S. Congress, Joint Economic Committee, *Comparisons of the United States and Soviet Economies* (Washington, D.C.: 1959), Part I, pp. 151–176.
21. ———. "A Study in Economic Planning" (Unpublished doctoral dissertation, Harvard University, 1961).
22. Mishustin, D. (ed.), *Vneshniaia torgovlia Sovetskogo Soiuza* (Moscow: 1938).
23. Pryor, Frederic L. *The Communist Foreign Trade System* (Cambridge: Massachusetts Institute of Technology Press, 1963).
24. Rosovsky, Henry (ed.), *Industrialization in Two Systems: Essays in Honor of Alexander Gerschenkron* (New York: Wiley, 1966).
25. Rubinshtein, G. *Vneshniaia torgovlia*, No. 5 (1960); translation in *Problems of Economics*, III:4 (August 1960), pp. 3–10.
26. ———. *Voprosy ekonomiki*, No. 9 (1966).
27. Shagalov, G. *Voprosy ekonomiki*, No. 6 (1965).
28. Shereshevskii, M. "Osnovnye cherty i zadachi organizatsii vneshnei torgovli SSSR posle vtoroi mirovoi voiny," *Voprosy vneshnei torgovli*, Inst. mezh. otnosh. (Moscow: 1960).
29. Sokolov, A. *Voprosy ekonomiki*, No. 1 (1967).
30. Tsentral'noe Statisticheskoe Upravlenie SSSR. *Narodnoe khoziaistvo SSSR v 1964g* (Moscow: 1965).
31. Vagnov, B. *Organizatsiia i tekhnika vneshnei torgovli SSSR i drugikh sotsialisticheskikh stran* (Moscow: 1963).
32. *Vneshniaia torgovlia*, No. 4 (1965).
33. *Vneshniaia torgovlia*, No. 8 (1966).
34. *Vneshniaia torgovlia*, No. 9 (1966).
35. Voronov, K. *Vneshniaia torgovlia*, No. 8 (1966).

Soviet Central Planning
and Its Impact on Foreign Trade
Behavior and Adjustment Mechanisms*

FRANKLYN D. HOLZMAN

This discussion of the impact of central planning on Soviet foreign trade is divided into two major sections. In the first section, some ideas that have appeared elsewhere [1] on autarky, state trading, and inconvertibility and bilateralism are summarized briefly. They are presented here for the "sake of completeness" at the suggestion of the editors of this volume. In the second, an attempt is made to indicate the ways in which some of the traditional market adjustment mechanisms operate (or fail to operate) in the economic relations between the Soviet Union and other nations. Much of the analysis contained in the second section, particularly that on "Income-Multiplier Effects," will appear obvious to readers familiar with the operation of Soviet-type economies. Nevertheless, there is a need to spell out precisely and formally the ways in which central planning practices affect the operation of automatic foreign trade adjustment mechanisms, and the consequences of this fact — and this is the major task of the present paper.

Before proceeding, a brief background sketch of the salient features of Soviet foreign trade history is in order.[2]

Russia of the late nineteenth and early twentieth centuries was a large trading nation. In addition to leading the world in exports of petroleum, she played an important role in the markets for grain, lumber, manganese,

* I am indebted to Charles Kindleberger for comments on an early draft, to the National Science Foundation for financial assistance, and to Frank Mandel for his warm support and encouragement.
[1] For example, in [3], [8], [9], [10], and [22].
[2] Taken primarily from [9].

flax, and many other products. She was, moreover, the world's largest importer of foreign capital. In 1913, just before the outbreak of World War I, trade (exports) is estimated to have amounted to slightly more than 10 percent of gross national product, a large figure for a nation of such size and diversity of resources. The 1917 Revolution and its aftermath (including Soviet expropriation of foreign properties, repudiation of all foreign debts, and the Western blockade) almost eliminated foreign trade completely for several years. While recovering gradually, trade remained at very low levels for at least a decade.

A moderately sharp increase occurred over the First Five-Year Plan period as a result of the decision to industrialize rapidly and on the basis of large imports of foreign machinery and equipment.[3] These imports were to be financed by an increase in exports, primarily of grains,[4] lumber, and consumers' goods. Total exports rose to a post-Revolution peak (never since equalled) of 3.5 percent of gross national product in 1930, and imports exceeded 4 percent of consumption in the same year. The use of foreign trade for industrialization purposes is highlighted by the fact that, over the First Plan period, consumers' goods amounted to only 7–8 percent of total imports, the rest consisting of producers' goods. As a result of the great depression, the Soviet strategy turned out to be much more costly than anticipated. While the Soviets were able to purchase machinery and equipment much more cheaply than expected in the declining world market, the prices of their exports fell even more drastically. Taking 1929 as 100, commodity terms of trade declined to a low of 71.5 in 1932 and 1933. Further, the Soviets incurred large deficits and were forced to borrow heavily at very high interest rates. Given these adverse terms and the fact that the most urgent import requirements of machinery and equipment had been satisfied, the Soviets beat a hasty retreat from world markets. By 1934, imports had declined to less than one-third their 1931 level; after 1937, and until World War II, trade (exports or imports) was consistently less than one-half of one percent of gross national product. In this period, the Soviets certainly approached what might be called a policy of almost complete autarky. They were trading at only a fraction of the optimum level, importing only the most essential raw materials (nonferrous metals and rubber) and machinery, and exporting just enough to balance their accounts.

The volume of Soviet trade increased rapidly in the post-war period, and exports (imports), which had risen to about 2.5 percent of gross national product in 1960, may by now have reached almost 3 percent. The rebirth was due, of course, to the fact that the Soviet Union was no longer isolated politically but had a large bloc of Communist nations with which she could

[3] For an elaboration of this point, see Herbert Levine's paper in this volume.
[4] A major factor in the decision to collectivize agriculture abruptly.

trade with less fear of compromising her economic and military independence. These nations do not constitute a "natural" trading bloc, as evidenced by the fact that most of them scarcely traded with each other before World War II. Trade with the bloc constituted only 15 and 5 percent, respectively, of total Soviet commerce in 1928 and 1938. Now, intra-bloc trade comprises from two-thirds to three-fourths of each bloc nation's trade, most of which obviously must represent "trade diversion" rather than "trade creation." The lack of natural complementarity among the bloc nations and the smallness of the group certainly militate against the achievement by them (exclusive of the U.S.S.R.) of gains from trade approaching those possible under pre-war circumstances. The profitability of intra-bloc trade is further hampered by problems of inconvertibility and bilateralism, to be discussed directly below.

A word should be said about Soviet entrance into the field of foreign assistance. Since 1954, the Soviets have extended over $5 billion in foreign aid to underdeveloped nations (by 1965), of which slightly less than half has resulted in deliveries. These nations also received, by 1965, about $4 billion in military aid.[5] Aid has also been extended to other bloc nations, the case of China in the 1950s being the one most publicized. While most of these loans, particularly those to the underdeveloped nations, have had an economic dimension — the Soviets stood to be repaid in commodities they needed and desired — the primary motivation for extending aid has obviously been political. This inference is inescapable when one considers the extension of 10- to 12-year, 2- to 2.5-percent loans in the context of the capital shortage and full employment of resources which have characterized the Soviet economy.

FOREIGN TRADE BEHAVIOR

The Soviet planning model with which we are concerned is the "old look" model, the one that approximated reality until the early 1960s in the Soviet Union, as well as in most of the Eastern European nations. The implications for foreign trade of the actual and proposed reforms in pricing, planning, and enterprise management are not considered here. What, then, are the major relevant features of the "old look"? First, planning in the Soviet Union is accomplished to a very great extent by centrally administered direct controls, with very little authority regarding level of output, product mix, or price; and with choice of customer or supplier being delegated to enterprises. Supply and demand for literally thousands of intermediate products are laboriously balanced by central planning organs utilizing the well-known method of balances. Enterprises are told when and where to ship their products, and

[5] Cf. [20, pp. 949 ff.].

where to purchase their supplies of all the commodities for which balances are drawn up. Under these circumstances it is understandable that the major target for enterprises is an output target rather than profit or some other success indicator.

Second, with the possible exception of wages, almost all costs and prices in the U.S.S.R. deviate from scarcity prices. This is due to extensive use of differential subsidies and turnover taxes, to failure to account properly for rent, interest, and profit, and to insensitivity of prices to market forces. This situation, which exists in all of the centrally planned economies, is now recognized as a problem by writers in Eastern Europe as well as by Western economists. It should also be mentioned that exchange rates among bloc nations were far from "equilibrium" rates before the changes of 1961, and probably still are. However, some, like the ruble, may now roughly equate internal and foreign trade prices for goods that the planners allow to be traded.

Finally, central planning has been, in effect, both over-full employment planning and rapid-growth planning. The strain created by these related planning objectives tends to have adverse effects on the balance of payments — the former by leading to sellers' markets (internally) and a general lack of concern for quality and buyers' needs, including those of foreign importers, and the latter by generating needs for imports.

Some consequences of these characteristics of central planning follow.

AUTARKY

It is a commonplace among economists working on the Eastern European economies that these nations trade a smaller percentage of their gross national products than market economies of comparable size, per capita income, and distribution of resources. This fact has been documented by many scholars.[6] It is probably not accurate to call this tendency autarky, for the nations of Eastern Europe do not try to do completely without trade. Rather, for reasons rational or irrational, to be noted below, they find themselves constrained to avoid many more trade opportunities that appear profitable than would a market economy. First, because of the centrally administered direct allocation system of implementing planning, a failure in almost any part of the intermediate product supply system will have repercussions in other parts of the system *which have to be adjusted by the planners*. The last clause of the preceding sentence is the crucial one.

[6] See, for example, [7, p. 312], [9, p. 290], [19, pp. 27 ff.], [23, pp. 279–280], and Pryor's "Discussion" in this volume.

It is important to note that foreign trade has been expanding more rapidly than GNP in most of the centrally planned economies in recent years; hence, the trade/GNP ratio has also been rising. As a result, some economists have questioned whether all of the centrally planned economies are, in fact, *still* trading at exceptionally low levels.

Adjustments to disruptions in supply have to be made in market economies as well, but they are made anonymously and probably more flexibly — by the invisible hand. In a centrally planned economy, the same few administrators are responsible for all disruptions; in a capitalist economy, the responsibilities are spread around. Under these circumstances, it is not unnatural for the planners to try to insulate themselves from disruption originating in the foreign trade sector, since that sector is outside their direct control. Second, all nations trade below the free trade optimum for reasons of military security — to reduce the potential risks of being subjected to economic warfare. This factor weighs more heavily on the political outgroup nations, which in this case happen to be the centrally planned economies, than the others, since the areas in which they can trade without such fears are more limited. Third, the chaotic character of internal prices makes it more difficult for the planners to determine where their comparative advantages and disadvantages lie. This added uncertainty undoubtedly reduces the volume of trade, while at the same time leading to uneconomic trade. Finally, relative to private enterprise economies, a bias against trade exists as a result of nationalization of industry. Among private enterprise economies, trade takes place wherever profitable opportunities are visible, unless the government takes explicit measures to stop it. Where industry is nationalized and the state directs economic activity, trade will not take place without explicit governmental decisions.

STATE TRADING: FOREIGN TRADE MONOPOLY

Professor Alexander Gerschenkron was certainly right when he said that ". . . economic planning of the type practiced in Russia is not feasible without the use of a foreign trade monopoly" [8, p. 18]. Given the problems of dovetailing intermediate products imported from abroad into the plan as described above, it appears inevitable that a high degree of centralization of foreign trade activity would be in order and that the bulk of trade would be planned in advance and implemented by trade agreements. This has been and is the situation in the Soviet Union, of course. If internal trade is decentralized, the situation may well change, as it has to some extent already in some of the Eastern European nations.

The existence of a foreign trade monopoly has at least three consequences for foreign trade behavior. First, foreign trade is conducted to obtain essential imports, with exports viewed as a necessary evil — to pay for the imports [8, p. 47]. The concern of capitalist nations is more equally divided between exports and imports, if they are not more concerned with the former for its employment effects. The second and related point is that the foreign trade monopoly often views exports and imports as interdependent in a barter sense. Profitability may then be assessed by the terms of trade rather than by evaluating the profitability of individual exports and imports taken separately. This approach makes possible (is necessitated by) trade under conditions of disequilibrium (overvalued) exchange rates and irrational internal prices. Third, given a state monopoly of foreign trade, tariffs are not necessary and, where they do exist, are largely redundant.

INCONVERTIBILITY AND BILATERALISM

The currencies of the centrally planned economies are as inconvertible as any in modern history, and intra-bloc trade is conducted along lines of almost complete bilateral balance. Factors responsible for the balance-of-payments problems that lead to inconvertibility and bilateralism among Western nations operate here also: rapid growth, over-full employment planning, repressed inflation, etc. Two other factors, of even greater importance — since they explain some unique features of the inconvertibility of bloc currencies — must be noted. First, it is difficult for planners to engage in "unplanned" trade originated by foreigners, since this, by definition, disrupts the plan with undesirable consequences, as noted above. Second, even if the plan were not in danger of disruption, foreigners would not be allowed to come in and shop around, purchasing goods at internal prices, because of the "irrationality" of these prices. Where internal prices are below cost, either in terms of actual outlays or in terms of opportunity cost in the eyes of the planners, export would involve losses to the economy.

These two factors are responsible for what has come to be known as commodity inconvertibility.[7] Commodity inconvertibility means not allowing foreigners who hold your currency to spend it on imports (from you). Thus, it is, in effect, a restriction on unplanned, unrequited (in goods) exports. This behavior is the direct antithesis of that of Western nations in balance-of-payments difficulties: unrequited exports are their goal. Western nations meet their balance-of-payments difficulties by placing limits on convertibility by residents into foreign currencies;[8] they leave non-residents free to convert at least current earnings. From the non-resident's point of view, bloc currencies are undesirable because of the substantial uncertainties regarding (1) what might be purchased with them in view of commodity inconvertibility and (2) prices. Non-residents do not have to worry, of course, since they are legally restricted from holding bloc currencies in the first place. A major consequence of inconvertibility of the sort described is that it is much more difficult to eliminate than inconvertibility, Western style. Since it results from certain peculiar characteristics of central planning, it cannot be eliminated without a change in planning techniques and institutions.[9]

[7] Cf. [3, pp. 430–431].
[8] That is, they restrict imports.
[9] For a discussion, see [10, pp. 257–263].

Inconvertibility always leads to bilateralism, and intra-bloc trade is no exception. Since no bloc nation is willing or is allowed to hold another's currency, trade must be bilaterally balanced.[10] Nevertheless, it would obviously be desirable for the bloc nations as a group to take advantage of those multilateral trading opportunities that must exist among them. It was primarily for this very purpose that the International Bank for Economic Cooperation was established in 1964. Presumably, each bloc nation is no longer to strive for bilateral balance with every other bloc nation, but is, within an "overall balance" constraint, to let imbalances fall where they may in the process of bilateral negotiations. Subsequent to the bilateral negotiations, a meeting of all nations is to be held in which surpluses and deficits are to be offset against each other wherever possible and additional trade is to be negotiated to remove the remaining imbalances.

Under the circumstances, the goal in view is very difficult to achieve, and it was entirely predictable that very little multilateralization would result. The achievement of overall intra-bloc balance is relatively easy via a series of bilateral balances with each partner, because the necessity of bilateral balance provides the negotiating nations with a relatively clearly defined limit regarding the extent of trade. That is to say, trade in each case is limited to the amount that the potential surplus country is willing to buy from the potential deficit country. Under the proposed system, the eight member nations have no guideline whatsoever regarding how much to trade with each of its seven partners. Each nation knows only that its seven bilateral imbalances must eventually add up to zero. While there exists an almost infinite variety of possible solutions to the problem for each nation, there is no strong economic basis for picking any particular solution over the others. Further, since the same problem confronts each of the eight nations, the solution to any of the twenty-eight intra-bloc imbalance problems affects the possible values in all or most of the other imbalances; and the strategy of any nation is likely to be in conflict with that of any other.

Despite the great and obvious difficulties that the bloc nations face in trying to achieve some bilateral imbalance in a framework of overall balance, one might expect to find some multilateralization if at least two further conditions prevailed: (1) the various bloc currencies were equally undesirable and (2) rewards and penalties accrued, respectively, to the overall surplus and deficit countries. It seems highly unlikely that the first condition prevails,[11] and the result is, of course, that the harder currency nations will not be will-

---

[10] This tendency is reinforced by the general unavailability of large reserves of hard currencies in the treasuries of most bloc nations. Furthermore, even if they have hard currencies, they prefer to conserve them for use in importing high-priority commodities from the West rather than to spend them within the bloc. Cf. [10, pp. 257–263].

[11] This does provide some, but not much, determinateness in the bilateral negotiation process.

ing to run surpluses with, or to accept offsets in the currencies of, the softer currency nations. Absence of the second condition means that the deficit countries have no incentive to eliminate their deficit on terms favorable to the creditor — in fact, their strong bargaining position (as recipients of unplanned credits from unwilling creditors) implies the reverse.[12] To sum up: given inconvertibility, multilateralization cannot be expected to work on any scale without either effective economic adjustment mechanisms or the establishment of a supranational authority with power to establish and enforce rules and penalties. Even then, final adjustment may require the acceptance of "uneconomic" trade by some trading partners.

SOME TRADITIONAL AUTOMATIC ADJUSTMENT MECHANISMS

In a classical system with fixed exchange rates, autonomous disturbances to the foreign trade sector affect the domestic economy through changes in income, money supply, prices, reserves, capital flows, and other channels. These changes in the domestic economy subsequently have an impact on the foreign trade sector of the nation in question and on its trading partners' economies; under most circumstances the result is to reduce the disequilibrium engendered by the initial disturbance. This sequence of changes and repercussions is usually referred to as the foreign trade adjustment mechanisms. To the extent that these "natural" adjustments occur, there is a tendency for an economy to move in the direction of balance in the balance of payments without the use of controls.

In a neo-Keynesian model, the adjustment mechanisms do not or are not allowed to function freely. The less the work performed by the adjustment mechanisms, the greater the need for recourse to methods that force a balance. Balance in this case reflects controlled disequilibrium rather than market equilibrium. A neo-Keynesian state has at least two major goals that lead it to interfere with the natural adjustment mechanisms, *viz.*, the maintenance of full or near-full employment and the maintenance of relatively stable price levels.[13] These goals are usually implemented by fiscal and monetary policies, although on difficult occasions direct controls may also be employed. Aside from government policy, international adjustment is frus-

[12] Recall that the European Payments Union, even with substantial financial assistance from the United States and even using economic incentive mechanisms, was not able to solve the problem of persistent debtors and creditors.

[13] There are, of course, national economic objectives with a higher priority than equilibrium or balance in trade. In the United Kingdom after World War II, for example, maintenance of the standard of living and further equalization of incomes were very high-priority objectives. In the early post-war periods, almost all European nations were unwilling to accept the "real wage" consequence of policies that would have resulted in immediate international balance.

trated in a neo-Keynesian model by the assumptions, which fit the facts for most capitalist nations, that wages and prices are relatively rigid downward.

There are at least five Soviet (centrally planned economy) goals that affect the operation of international adjustment mechanisms.[14] First, the state strives to achieve and maintain internal micro-balance, as viewed through the system of physical balances mentioned above. Once the annual plan, which includes commodity trade, is established, the Soviets are strongly motivated to avoid disturbances to the balances through unforeseen changes in foreign trade. Conversely, they try to make *ad hoc* changes in foreign trade plans to offset unforeseen disturbances of domestic origin to the physical balances.

Second, and this is a corollary of the first, the Soviets strive for full employment of resources — i.e., for macro-balance.

Third, they strongly prefer to use direct controls rather than indirect controls or free market responses for controlling interenterprise transactions and the foreign trade sector. This fact alone means that little reliance is placed on market adjustment mechanisms. In effect, the Soviet choice of direct controls to manage these large sectors of the economy so influences the possible adjustments to foreign trade disturbances that in some respects it makes redundant any consideration of the first two goals mentioned above, since pursuit of these goals prevents adjustment in roughly the same way.

Fourth, in the area of foreign trade, the Soviets pursue a goal (have a constraint) of overall short-run balance in payments and of bilateral balance in trade with other socialist nations, for reasons mentioned in the previous section. These goals are not independent of those mentioned, but stem in part, as we have shown, from the first and third.[15]

Finally, because relatively free markets are used to distribute consumers' goods and labor and because financial incentives do play a role, however limited, in interenterprise transactions, including those involving the foreign trade enterprises, the Soviets pursue financial policies designed to avoid repressed inflation and rationing. This objective appears to have relatively low priority in the Soviet scheme; nevertheless, it does explain some Soviet measures in the foreign trade sphere.

We turn now to the operation of adjustment mechanisms in the trade of the Soviet Union and other centrally planned economies. For lack of space, we will concentrate on income, price, and exchange rate adjustments. The assumption is made that a sudden change in trade takes place — for example,

[14] Before listing these goals, it must be noted that, in contrast with the neo-Keynesian case, government objectives do not necessarily lead to frustration of natural adjustment mechanisms. Rather, in some instances, the need to achieve these objectives leads the state, in the foreign-trade sphere, to simulate and stimulate market mechanisms, where they would otherwise be suppressed.

[15] That is, inconvertibility and bilateralism are the result in the U.S.S.R. of detailed central planning implemented by direct controls.

the loss of a large export market — which initially affects the balance of payments adversely. The subsequent adjustments are then noted. To provide benchmarks against which to evaluate the adjustments in a centrally planned economy, we first sketch briefly those that are likely to take place in the classical (i.e., laissez-faire) and neo-Keynesian models.

INCOME-MULTIPLIER EFFECTS

A decline in exports, in the classical model, leads to a decline in income, the extent of which depends on the value of the multiplier. The decline in income induces a decline in imports (as well as in consumption and investment from domestic resources, and in savings), which tends to reduce the balance-of-payments deficit caused by the drop in exports. The decline in income takes the form of unemployment if the economy was initially below full employment; if it was initially at full employment or over-full employment, there are fewer unemployment or real income effects and more declining price and money income effects. In the latter case, the extent of the decline in income and the resulting drops in expenditures on imports, consumption, and investment will depend on the extent to which the population is real-income conscious or subject to money illusion: if the former, expenditures will drop proportionately with prices and incomes; if the latter, expenditures will decline less rapidly and the adjustment to imbalance in the balance of payments will be less complete.

Repercussionary effects on, and from, other countries can make the adjustment more or less difficult, depending on the circumstances. In the case under consideration, the induced decline in imports in country A implies a decline in exports in country B (rest of the world), which leads to a decline in income in B and in imports from A. This leads to a renewal of the sequence described in the previous paragraph.[16] On the other hand, if country A had developed a deficit as the result of a rise in income and therefore imports, exports of B would rise, increasing B's income and imports from A, thereby improving A's position. The improvement would be offset, in part, however, by the subsequent rise in A's income and, again, imports.

Abstracting from repercussion multiplier effects, the processes described can be presented as follows. Let

(1) $$Y = C + I + X - M$$

where Y refers to income, C to consumption, I to investment, X to exports, and M to imports. Let

---

[16] If the original reduction of exports in A were the result of an autonomous reduction in imports in B (change of tastes), then B's income would rise, increasing imports and offsetting, in part, the original reduction in A's exports.

(2) $$C = a + cY$$
(3) $$I = b + iY$$
(4) $$M = e + mY$$

where c, i, and m are marginal propensities to consume, invest, and import, respectively; and a, b, and e are constants.

The relationship between the change in exports (ΔX) and the change in income (ΔY) is described by the following equation:

$$\Delta Y = \frac{-\Delta X}{1 - c - i + m} = \frac{-\Delta X}{s + m}$$

where s is the marginal propensity to save.

Dynamically, given $-\Delta X$,

$$-\Delta X \to -\Delta Y \to \begin{cases} -\Delta C \\ -\Delta I \\ -\Delta M \end{cases}$$

The usual end result of the above adjustments is that unemployment develops in the domestic economy (or inflation is reduced) and that the balance-of-payments deficit is reduced as a result of the decline in imports. The extent of the reduction in the deficit depends on the importance of m as a "leakage" in the circular flow. If m is the only leakage — that is, if the marginal propensity to save is zero — then and only then will the deficit caused by the drop in X be completely eliminated. Otherwise the income adjustment process works itself out, leaving the foreign trade sector with a deficit (assuming balance to begin with). At this point, balance must be achieved by price and other adjustment mechanisms, or by controls.[17]

The processes described above would occur to a reduced degree in the neo-Keynesian model. Income effects, particularly negative ones, would not be allowed to work themselves out completely, since any substantial amount of unemployment would not be acceptable. Monetary and fiscal policies would be used to offset the impact of a decline in exports by directly increasing government expenditures, by indirectly increasing expenditures on C and I by a reduction in tax rates, or by following a monetary policy that reduced interest rates. Where the deficit is serious, balance may be forced by the use of quotas and exchange controls. Such measures further reduce the income-adjusting effects of the initial disequilibrium.

There are few direct income effects and still fewer multiplier effects in a relatively pure planned economy such as that of the Soviet Union. There are several reasons for this, related to the overall objectives of the Soviets

[17] The exceptional case should be mentioned in which the inducement to invest (disinvest) is so large that the inducement to save is negative. In this event, the decline in M would exceed the decline in X.

mentioned above. First and fundamentally, the production and distribution of the real national product of the Soviet economy are determined, within certain broad limits, by the government by means of direct controls; they are not subject to the dictates of "free propensities" as is the case in the classical or neo-Keynesian models. Thus, while the accounting identity (1) is correct for capitalist and planned economies alike, the behavioral equations (2)–(4) apply only to the former. One might appropriately substitute for the behavioral equations an equation that views income as supply-determined, such as:

$$(5) \qquad\qquad Y = f\,(L,K)$$

where L is the quantity of labor and K the quantity of capital. In effect, then, gross national product is determined by Eq. (5), although it is affected by exogenous forces, of course, and allocated and distributed within broad limits via government decisions by Eq. (1).

Assume a sudden autonomous decline in exports. The Soviet government would react to implement its policies as follows. First, it would act to restore balance by (1) reducing imports [18] or (2) increasing (other) exports, including gold.[19] Since gold is mined on a large scale for export, it can be viewed here as just another commodity. To the extent that gold and other exports replace the lost exports, there should be, in theory, no income effects. Actually, since the Soviets may hold large stocks of gold and since gold output may be fairly insensitive to current changes in the quantity of gold exports, there may arise, in fact, a negative income effect, as unemployment in export industries is not automatically offset by increased employment in gold mining and processing.[20]

To the extent that balance is achieved instead by a reduction in imports, there will be, in theory, a negative income effect associated with the reduction in balanced trade (akin to the balanced-budget multiplier effect). This effect is apt to be in the neighborhood of unity and therefore of much less impact than that of the multiplier connected with a unilateral change in either exports or imports [14].

Second, even the balanced trade multiplier effect will not take effect, because of Soviet policies of maintaining full employment of resources. Should exports decline, not only would the Soviets reduce imports, they would also act relatively quickly to reemploy unemployed resources and to shift some

[18] The reduction in imports would be geared, of course, to minimizing the disturbance to the physical balances. We abstract here from the possibility of capital flows in order to concentrate on income effects.

[19] Hoeffding's paper in this volume presents empirical evidence for the parallel case of an increase in imports.

[20] For a modification of the traditional multiplier approach to account for this fact, see [14].

of these resources into the production of goods formerly imported. The (equal) reduction in X and M is offset by an equal increase in $C + I$, which replace, in part at least, the lost imports. The implementation of this policy in the Soviet Union may be presumed to be much quicker and more direct than the capitalist counterpart of compensating fiscal and monetary policies. By the same token, the extent to which internal income would adjust to a foreign trade disturbance in the Soviet economy would be even less than the adjustment in a typical capitalist economy, not to mention that of the free market model.

These income effects might properly be called employment effects — for it is not income that the Soviets maintain in their reaction to a trade deficit, but employment. In fact, the Soviets, in making the adjustments they do, would suffer a loss of real income as a result of lower productivity.[21] Such a decline in real income in the classical and Keynesian models would induce a decline in imports via the operation of the multiplier and the marginal propensity to import. This automatic reaction would not occur in the Soviet economy, for reasons already noted. There would undoubtedly be a reaction, but its precise nature would depend on specific circumstances, and planners' reactions to the circumstances, rather than on general rules.

So far we have shown why the income adjustment mechanism does not operate under conditions of central planning. One final point is that even if it did operate, it would not assist significantly in the balancing of payments in intra-bloc trade, which comprises the bulk of the trade of the Eastern European nations. This is because of bilateralism. Suppose that Soviet exports to one bloc nation were suddenly cut by 50 percent. If income effects were allowed to work themselves out, there would be an induced drop in Soviet imports. Since this drop would be spread over the total of Soviet trade, it would not move the Soviet balance of payments very far toward balance[22] — which requires, under conditions of bilateral trade, that the entire drop in imports be concentrated in the one country. Income effects are too undifferentiated geographically to have a significant equilibrating effect in bilateral trade.

To sum up: the income mechanism assists the foreign trade sector to adjust to "disturbances." It works most effectively in the classical model, less effectively in the neo-Keynesian model, and almost not at all in the central planning model. It is not allowed to work effectively in the latter two cases because of internal goals of higher priority than "market equilibrium in foreign trade."[23] To the extent that income adjustment does not

---

[21] This implies a change in the functional relationships, f, in Eq. (5), above.

[22] In fact, surpluses would develop with all other nations as a result of the deficit with the one.

[23] The internal and external goals are not always in conflict. For example, given inflation and a deficit caused by loss of exports, the resulting decline in income would lead in the direction of internal and external balance.

operate, the burden of adjustment to the disturbance falls primarily on other adjustment mechanisms (prices, exchange rates) and secondarily on the foreign trade sector itself, as reflected in a greater degree of controlled disequilibrium.

RELATIVE COMMODITY PRICE EFFECTS [24]

Assume a decline in demand for an export or group of exports in a classical free market economy. Export prices fall; unemployment develops in the export industries, leading to a fall in prices of factors (inputs) and of commodity prices generally. These effects are accentuated via the income multiplier. This has the following results: (1) the quantity of exports does not decline as much as if prices had remained stable; (2) to the extent that export prices decline more than other prices, and to the extent that the domestic population consumes exportables, more exportables will be purchased internally; and (3) since internal prices declined relative to external prices, import substitutes will be consumed at the expense of imports. Results (1) and (3) move the balance of payments back toward (but probably not to) balance. Results (2) and (3) move the economy back toward full employment. In fact, under the classical assumption of flexible internal commodity and factor prices, full employment will again be achieved. The return to full employment may worsen the payments deficit by inducing an increase in imports. However, imports will be at a lower level than before because (1) full-employment real income is lower with poorer terms of trade and (2) internal prices are lower (relative to external) than before. The end result is a return to full employment and an improvement, but not necessarily balance, in the balance of payments.

Price effects are considerably less powerful in restoring balance in the balance of payments in the neo-Keynesian model, largely because the model assumes a downward rigidity in prices (especially of industrial products) and wages characteristic of modern Western capitalist nations. The result is that, in the face of declining demand, prices do not decline or do not decline very much, and therefore do not moderate the impact on exports of the drop in demand. Furthermore, although more resources in export industries are unemployed as a result of price rigidities, these very rigidities prevent the reabsorption of these resources into import-competing and other industries. If the unemployment generated by price inflexibility were allowed to develop, a drop in imports would be induced. This effect is severely limited, however, by adherence to the full-employment goal.

Prices and wages *are* flexible upward in the neo-Keynesian model, particularly as the economy approaches full employment. The consequence is that

[24] In what follows we assume, unless stated otherwise, fixed exchange rates and supply-and-demand elasticities sufficiently large for price changes to move trade balances in the direction of equilibrium.

an increase in demand for exports *will* lead to a rise in the price of exports, to a withdrawal of resources from import-competing industries and a subsequent increase in imports, and so forth, thereby facilitating the adjustment process. A limit is also set to this process, however, by the stable price goal.

The net result of price effects and their repercussions in the neo-Keynesian model is that they contribute little to the elimination of balance-of-payments disequilibria except, perhaps, where a nation experiences an increase in demand for its exports under full-employment conditions.

We turn now to the Soviet foreign trade pricing mechanisms. Perhaps the major difference between the foreign trade pricing mechanisms of the Soviet Union and other centrally planned economies and those of capitalist nations is the complete divorce of foreign trade prices from internal prices. The implications of this fact are explored a little later. The centrally planned economies rely on world prices, as a first approximation, in trade among themselves as well as in trade with the West. These prices have no consistent or clearly defined relationship to their own internal prices. Reliance on world prices is necessary because: the internal prices of the bloc nations are not what might be called scarcity prices; further, they do not deviate from scarcity prices in any consistent fashion; and finally, internal price levels are not even approximately equated by bloc exchange rates. World prices constitute, as a first approximation, the only available consistent system of relative values for use in international trade.

Let us examine, first, Soviet trade with the West, then intra-bloc trade. The evidence suggests that Soviet foreign trade prices have reacted quite flexibly to changes in market conditions in trade with the West. (In fact, since Soviet trade is a small fraction of world trade in most markets, Soviet prices must follow world prices or trade ceases.) To pick a dramatic example, in the early 1930s when world prices collapsed as a result of the great depression, the Soviets lowered the prices of their agricultural exports, particularly grain, to less than 40 percent of the 1929 level in an effort to maintain receipts.[25] Such an adjustment to a decline in demand for a nation's exports is undoubtedly much greater than one would expect to find even in a classical world.[26]

Why did the Soviets allow prices to fall so low; or, more relevantly, why did they continue to export agricultural products when prices had fallen so low? Their behavior is easily understood in terms of the national goals described earlier. Primarily, they were motivated by the desire to safeguard

[25] Cf. [9].

[26] The world of the early 'thirties was, of course, decidedly unclassical, and world trading prices declined by almost as much as those at which the Soviets exported. One major difference between Soviet trade behavior and that of the capitalist nations in this period was that Western traders immediately contracted their exports, whereas for the first few years of the depression Soviet exports increased and did not fall below the 1929 volume until 1934. Cf. [9, p. 289].

the integrity of the Five-Year Plan, which was dependent on large imports of machinery and equipment from the West. Had they not been so motivated, exports would have been allowed to decline and imports would have been cut back to match the new level of exports. In effect, one might describe Soviet import behavior as having been consistent with an import-demand function that was perfectly inelastic with respect to price. Had the world prices of Soviet exports and imports fallen by equal amounts, then the Soviets would have been able to finance the target basket of imports with the same volume of exports. Under these circumstances, Soviet behavior would be consistent with having an export supply function that was also perfectly inelastic with respect to price.

The behavior described above would be impossible in the absence of a foreign trade monopoly which viewed exports and imports, not independently, but in barter terms. Thus, exports can be sold at a loss if the gain on imports bought with the foreign exchange earned is more than offsetting. In effect, the relevant prices to the planners are not the prices of imports *or* exports, but rather the terms of trade. From this point of view, an equal decline in export and import prices constitutes no change in price at all — hence, one would not expect a change in the quantities traded.

The next question is, what would happen if the terms of trade should change? In fact, in the early 'thirties, prices of Soviet exports fell by more than those of imports and the terms of trade declined from 100 in 1929 to 71.6 in 1932.[27] In the face of such an abrupt deterioration in the terms of trade, one might be inclined to infer that the Soviets experienced a loss on the transaction — certainly if pre-depression price relationships are viewed as normal. In fact, however, the Soviets view exports and imports not in "average cost" terms, but in terms of short-run marginal costs and opportunity costs. In particular, the loss to them of the machinery and equipment imports would have had considerable negative repercussions on their First Five-Year Plan, causing losses to the economy (as viewed by the planners) of a much greater value than the higher cost of the machinery. Whatever the nominal losses on sales of agricultural products, they were obviously less — in the eyes of the planners, though certainly not in the eyes of the hungry population — than the potential losses of having the flow of machinery and equipment into the country interrupted. The result was that the volume of trade expanded rapidly despite the steadily declining terms of trade [9].

If the terms of trade turn against the Soviets, then it is necessary to export a greater quantity in order to finance the same level of imports. These exports are usually taken from non-priority sectors of the economy. The interesting implication of this situation is that the supply curve of exports is not just

[27] Cf. [9, p. 305].

price-inelastic, but backward-sloping, approaching the shape of a rectangular hyperbola — that is, negative unit elasticity.

We are assuming that world prices are set by supply-and-demand forces, of which Soviet imports and exports make up a very small part; the latter, therefore, do not appreciably influence world prices. In the above case, for example, it is assumed that external forces push down the price at which the Soviets can export — but at the new price the Soviets can sell all they want. This is generally true, although it was not true in the greatly contracting 1929–1934 period.[28] What this means, in effect, is that the world demand for Soviet exports is very elastic, and so also is the world supply of goods the Soviets wish to import.[29] These high elasticities play a very important role in facilitating Soviet foreign trade adjustments.

Finally, it is important to note that, while we have stressed the inelasticity of Soviet import-demand, it is not, of course, completely inelastic. The same is true of exports. Cases can be cited of refusals to buy or sell because of unfavorable prices. This is particularly true over the medium or long run, when it is possible to make the necessary adjustments and thereby avoid, without undue loss, a relatively unfavorable exchange.

We turn now to intra-bloc trade. The external price flexibility that appears to characterize Soviet behavior in Western markets is largely missing in intra-bloc trade. In fact, almost every Soviet book on foreign trade boasts that an important superiority of intra-bloc over intra-Western trade is stability of prices. As noted above, intra-bloc trade takes world prices as a starting point for negotiation. However, prices in intra-bloc trade are not allowed to fluctuate concurrently with world prices; rather, prices of a single year are adhered to for several years. Thus, 1957 world prices were used at least until 1961;[30] more recently *some* 1961 prices have been substituted for those of 1957. Now it is true that world prices are reported to be only a "starting point" for negotiations between bloc nations. Subsequently, prices must be adjusted for a number of factors such as short-run fluctuations, the fact that the relative values of some commodities may be quite different within and without the bloc, and so forth. There also appears to be a certain amount of price-juggling at the time bilateral trade agreements are drawn up. This is almost inevitable, since bilateral balance is a function of quantities and prices and it may not always be practicable to achieve balance easily by just manipulating quantities. To the extent that there is an all-bloc unity of

[28] We ignore here the fact that most Western nations prefer to do business with other Western nations, and often force the Soviets to sell at a lower price and buy at a higher price if they want to trade. Cf. [11] and sources cited there.

[29] We are obviously ignoring here the special post-war circumstance of Western strategic controls.

[30] Cf. [16, Chap. 9]. Sándor Ausch [6] refers to prices on the socialist world market being set "for seven to eight years." An excellent article on pricing in bloc trade is [6, pp. 800–808], translated into English in [21].

prices adhered to at any given time (not to mention maintaining these prices over a period of time), the bilateral balancing is rendered much more difficult.[31] Use of price adjustments is probably particularly easy in the case of heterogeneous products such as machinery and equipment, where it is difficult, if not impossible, to establish a unified price.[32]

Despite many small deviations from the principle of a long-run, unified, stable, intra-bloc price based on world prices of some specific year, it appears that the principle is adhered to on a fairly large scale and particularly for the more homogeneous commodities.[33] Thus, for example, despite the decline in the world terms of trade of agricultural versus industrial commodities from 1957 on, and despite the fact that adherence to 1957 prices favored Bulgaria against East Germany and Czechoslovakia, a commensurate change was not made in intra-bloc prices as late as 1963, even though East Germany and Czechoslovakia both argued strongly for such a change.[34]

Fixed prices are probably maintained over long periods in international trade for the same reason that prices remain relatively fixed for long periods in internal trade: to simplify the task of the planners, narrowly conceived.[35] On the other hand, however, price stability in the face of changing economic conditions cannot but impede the development of healthy trade relationships. As Ausch points out [6, p. 5], these prices eventually reflect "neither the average costs of the CEMA countries nor the world-market price ratios, nor the conditions of supply and demand among the socialist countries." Current world prices do, as noted above, provide a consistent set of values for use in intra-bloc trade, something which so far cannot be generated out of the intra-bloc economic relationships per se.[36] They are acceptable to the members of the bloc, albeit with some modifications, because they are in fact real "opportunity cost" prices to the bloc nations at which (approximately) they can buy or sell if necessary. Old world prices — prices of more than

[31] A Czechoslovakian source, Slavomir Jiranek, suggests that there is not, in fact, unity of prices within the bloc: "The prices arrived at between pairs of socialist countries have varied, and have not created a single socialist market price." See [15, p. 57], translated from [17, No. 5 (1965)].

[32] Pryor contains the best discussion of the price-setting process in bilateral bargaining, based on the testimony of some East European economists. See [19, Chap. V].

[33] See also the statement by Slavomir Jiranek quoted in footnote 31.

[34] Taking 1959 as 100, the following trends are recorded:

	1957	1962	1963
Food and raw materials	107	97	100
Manufactures	102	103	103

SOURCE: [16, p. 157] (taken from United Nations sources).

[35] That is to say, it simplifies the problems of achieving "balance" but not of achieving "efficiency."

[36] "I should like to state that from the very beginning of the development of economic relations within the camp of socialism, world prices have been and still are used, for no one has been able to find a better objective measure of value equivalents" [18, p. 45]. (Original in [17, No. 5 (1965)].)

four or five years back — no longer have this justification. Buying or selling at "frozen world prices" involves, on some commodities, a substantial loss to some nations and a substantial gain to other nations, relative to trade at current world prices.[37] The result has been a partial breakdown from pure bilateralism on a country-country basis in which the only constraint is that exports to and imports from each partner be equal — a breakdown to a situation in which it is necessary, in addition, to achieve bilateral balance for various subcategories of goods with each partner. Thus, within overall bilateral balance, nations trade raw materials for raw materials, machinery for machinery, goods which can earn convertible currency in the West for like goods, and so forth.[38] In other words, with frozen world prices, there is a degeneration from "bilateralism" to a level of "barter," because the set of relative prices implied is no longer acceptable. The frozen world prices are used in the limited way in which they are still acceptable: as a measure of the value of (like) goods whose relative prices have not changed since the base period.

There are at least two major differences between the effects of price flexibility noted here in both East-West and intra-bloc trade and those in a free market economy. First, in the market economy, price flexibility — to the extent that it exists — moves both the external and internal markets toward balance and equilibrium. In the centrally planned economy, a major goal of foreign trade price flexibility is the achievement or preservation of physical balance in internal planning. Foreign trade price changes are also used to contribute to the achievement of balance in foreign trade. In both cases, of course, price flexibility is no more than a handmaiden to physical controls. As a result the balances achieved may be more "forced" — further from the free market optimum or equilibrium — than before. This can be illustrated by reference, again, to the situation in the early 'thirties. To assure imports of machinery, important to the plan, grain was exported at very low prices — certainly below cost by any reasonable method of calculation — despite famine conditions at home. Trade was almost balanced and internal physical balances and plans were preserved to a much greater extent than if trade had been cut back. But the external balance was certainly more "forced" than before, as suggested by the very disadvantageous terms of trade which resulted (were suffered).[39] Similarly, balance in the non-priority

---

[37] It is true that trading at current world prices may involve gains or losses to various bloc nations relative to trade at prices more appropriate to the intra-bloc market. However, with occasional adjustments, current world prices are nevertheless acceptable, because they provide the only consistent set of relative values available to the bloc which reflect "real opportunity cost."

[38] Cf. [6, p. 5]; also [16, p. 139].

[39] On the other hand, as noted above, Soviet refusal in the mid-'thirties to continue imports on a large scale at very adverse terms of trade suggests a price sensitivity that

sectors of the internal economy was more "forced," and, despite this, was not even achieved in all sectors — as evidenced by the rapid development in this period of industrial bottlenecks, and of repressed inflation and rationing in consumers' goods markets.

The second major difference (related to the first and perhaps the more basic) between price flexibility in Soviet trade and in free market trade is as follows. In trade under free market conditions, changes in the prices of exports and imports have an impact on the allocation of resources. If the price of an export rises and large profits result, production and exports will be increased either at the expense of other commodities or by the use of unemployed resources. Similar reasoning can be applied to a drop in the price of exports and to price changes in connection with imports. Price changes in Soviet trade feed back little, if at all, to the allocation of resources,[40] except perhaps with a very long lag. This happens for at least two major reasons.

First, the commodities (and their amounts) which are to be traded are largely established in advance in the Plan. The Ministry of Foreign Trade and the foreign trade associations which actually handle the buying and selling are not as interested (if at all) in making large profits as they are in just fulfilling their plans in quantitative terms. So, if commodities are allocated for sale abroad, an attempt is made to sell them even if prices decline. By the same token, a rise in prices will also have little or no effect on allocation, because it will usually be difficult or impossible for the foreign trade associations to obtain additional commodities (resources) for export. On the import side, the foreign trade associations will continue to buy despite a rise in prices, because to do otherwise would disrupt the operations of enterprises dependent upon imports. From another point of view, to fail to import would put the foreign trade associations in a position of not being able to fulfill their delivery quotas. A decline in import prices will also have little short-run impact, because the plans do not envisage the use of additional imports.

Second, the actual export-producing and import-using enterprises (or persons) are quite far removed from the locus of foreign trade.[41] The export-producing enterprises, in particular, have no incentive whatsoever to alter their plans to take account of changes in foreign trade prices. Their accounts are kept exclusively in internal prices, and it is irrelevant to them whether they sell to the foreign trade export associations or to domestic users. The prices they charge and their quantity targets make no distinction between

was conducive toward equilibrium in the foreign balance. This was possible because, over the long run, the physical balances (internal) were adjusted commensurately.

[40] Cf. [6].

[41] No longer true in all bloc nations.

the two;[42] or if there is a distinction, it is not related to prices on the world market. Furthermore, until very recently quantity targets have been much more important than profit and cost targets, thereby reducing still further the relevance of price factors. Domestic enterprises that consume imports, similarly, have nothing to gain or lose from changes in import prices. The price they pay is set without regard to the world price paid by the import association. Any gains or losses due to changes in world prices are absorbed initially by the foreign trade associations and subsequently by the state budget. Thus, there is no mechanism with regard to either export-producer or import-user which would lead either to take account of foreign trade prices in the course of its economic activities.

To sum up: In trade with the West, Soviet foreign trade prices are adjusted to changes in world prices so that the foreign trade plans may be fulfilled, thereby maintaining the integrity of the overall plan, of which the foreign trade plan is a part. This implies highly inelastic import-demand and export-supply functions. However, the interpretation of import-demand and export-supply elasticity is complicated by the fact that the foreign trade monopoly looks upon exports as payments for imports — that is, looks at terms of trade as the relevant price.[43] Under these circumstances, a simultaneous rise or decline in export and import prices constitutes, in fact, no change in price at all to the foreign trade monopoly, and one would therefore expect no changes in quantities demanded and supplied. Nevertheless, even where real terms of trade have declined, as in the early 'thirties, imports have been price-inelastic, at least in the short run, to preserve the plan, and the supply of exports has been backward-bending, to preserve the foreign trade balance. The ultimate burden of these adjustments is borne by the non-priority sectors of the economy — in this case, the final consumer. An essential facet of the ability of the Soviet economy to adjust to world trade, as described above, is the fact that it plays the role of a small competitor. Its export-supply and import-demand functions are inelastic; on the other hand, the world's import-demand and export-supply functions are very elastic. Hence, at any world price, the Soviets may, if they choose, export or import additional large quantities without affecting price.[44]

Intra-bloc trade differs in two respects from East-West trade. First, prices are relatively fixed for long periods of time. Second, partner supplies and

---

[42] Actually, a producer of consumers' goods may well sell without turnover tax to the foreign trade association but include turnover tax to domestic wholesalers. Since the turnover tax on sales to domestic users does not remain in his hands very long, he has no incentive to choose among buyers on this count. He might want to avoid selling to the foreign trade association, however, if his gross output performance increased by inclusion of turnover tax.

[43] In fact, in analyzing Soviet foreign trade behavior, one might well consider the elasticity of the offer curve to be the appropriate concept.

[44] See the discussion of capillarity in Neuberger's paper.

demands are inelastic (fixed by plan). These facts plus bilateralism and inconvertibility leave almost no mechanism (at least in the short run) for adjustment to changing requirements, either in terms of internal plans or in terms of balance in the balance of payments. The eventual irrelevance of frozen world prices as an acceptable standard of value causes further difficulty in trade.

In both intra-bloc and East-West trade, the significance of prices for "adjustment" is reduced by the lack of feedback to the domestic economy — the failure of the domestic economy to respond to signals from the foreign trade sector.

THE EXCHANGE RATES: GENERAL PRICE EFFECTS [45]

Occasional changes in the exchange rate, or freely floating rates, provide a very important and effective means of adjustment to payments difficulties. These mechanisms, when allowed to operate, assume most of the burden of adjustment. In the absence of inflationary pressures, and given favorable price elasticities that apparently are almost always present, a devaluation will reduce a payments deficit by reducing the price of exports to foreigners and increasing the price of imports to residents.[46] Freely floating rates, under the same favorable conditions, presumably prevent imbalances from developing, and, of course, a change in the exchange rate feeds back to the domestic economy and encourages an equilibrating reallocation of resources similar to that described in the previous discussion.

The Soviet and other centrally planned economies have followed a policy of maintaining the nominal exchange rate of their currencies fixed for long periods of time, and then making large changes. Since before the Revolution, only three significant changes in the nominal value of the foreign exchange ruble have been made: in 1936, 1950, and 1961. These changes, while each of substantial magnitude,[47] had absolutely no impact on Soviet foreign trade, as can be seen by comparing the pre- and post-revaluation quantities and internal prices of exports and imports. In Soviet foreign trade, the only function of the exchange rate is as a unit of account for converting foreign currency prices into local currency terms for the purpose of setting forth a balance of payments. This has to be the case under the Soviet conditions of pricing and planning, as described above.

[45] This discussion differs from the preceding one in being concerned primarily with changes in aggregate price levels and their implications.

[46] Under some conditions, strong reversal effects (e.g., rising income and therefore imports due to the improved trade balance) may make it difficult to eliminate the deficit. Cf. [2, pp. 22–42].

[47] The devaluation of 1936 left the ruble at 23 percent of its previous value; that of 1961 reduced its value from $0.25 to $0.111, but a simultaneous ten-fold internal price reduction raised the value to $1.11; while the revaluation of 1950 raised the value of the ruble by 32 percent.

The situation, then, is one in which (1) the nominal exchange rate has no economic significance for trade; (2) internal prices of tradables (or of any other commodities) do not react to external economic forces; (3) changes in internal prices do not affect the prices at which foreign trade takes place; and (4) foreign trade prices, on the other hand, do change in reaction to external forces — in fact, follow world prices in East-West trade. Given these conditions, let us consider the implications of regarding the price ratio between internal and external price levels, particularly of tradables, as representing the *de facto* exchange rate.[48] This may be considered reasonable in light of the fact that the official rate has no significance for foreign trade. In the Soviet case, and particularly in Soviet-West trade, the ratio changes whenever either the Soviet internal price level changes or the world price level of commodities traded by the Russians changes. It is not unreasonable to interpret this situation as constituting an implicit *de facto* freely floating exchange rate. Consider a situation in which either internal prices rise or external prices fall. Under free market conditions with a fixed exchange rate, exports would decline and imports would increase, leading to a foreign trade deficit. An immediate devaluation or the use of a freely floating exchange rate would restore trade precisely to its original position. In Soviet-West trade, the rise in internal prices would leave foreign trade prices — hence, quantities — unchanged; and a decline in world prices would be followed by a corresponding decline in Soviet export and import prices, again leaving the composition of trade unchanged.[49] In other words, the implicit exchange rate changes[50] with changes in internal or external prices, and the commodity structure of trade is preserved — just as if a truly freely floating exchange rate were in operation under conditions where the price levels of nations are inflating at different rates.

The situation in intra-bloc trade is similar for changes in internal price levels but slightly different for changes in foreign trade prices. Since the internal price levels of these countries do not affect foreign trade prices, our so-called implicit exchange rates are in effect freely flexible in intra-bloc trade with regard to differential changes in internal price levels. The difference in connection with foreign trade prices exists because the general external price level is, as pointed out above, more or less frozen, and aggregative changes are made infrequently. When such changes are made, the situation is more akin to one of pegged exchange rates in which all nations revalue

[48] More accurately, an exchange rate should reflect all forces affecting the supply of and demand for a nation's currency, including forces connected with capital flows. Criticisms of the "purchasing power parity" approach, used here as an approximation, are too well-known to need repeating.

[49] Recall that from the point of view of the foreign trade monopoly, the terms of trade are unchanged.

[50] In this case, declines in value.

simultaneously.[51] The fact that there is, in effect, a sort of adjustable-peg exchange rate system in intra-bloc trade and a freely floating rate system in world trade leads to inconsistency between the implicit rates in East-West and intra-bloc trade. This provides the conditions for arbitrage. In general, declining world prices strain the limitations under which intra-bloc trade operates, as there is a tendency for bloc nations to want to shift purchases of imports from East to West;[52] rising world prices provide a similar incentive to exporters.

The implicit exchange rate(s) of each bloc nation will also usually differ from its official nominal rate. Since all foreign trade transactions are converted internally at the official nominal rate, financial adjustments have to be made, as indicated earlier. Where the official rate overvalues (undervalues) the currency, nominal losses (profits) on exports will be matched by nominal profits (losses) on imports, the real terms of trade remaining unchanged.[53]

We have stressed the similarity between a freely floating exchange rate system and the ways in which the trade of centrally planned economies adjusts to aggregative changes in internal and external prices. This parallel may appear somewhat strained, and, in fact, the point should be emphasized that it is valid, as developed here, only for relationships between general levels of internal and external prices, not for changes in specific or relative prices. For example, assume a truly flexible exchange rate in a market economy. Assume that the internal prices of two exportables change, one up and one down, just offsetting each other — so that the export price index does not change. Under market conditions, the foreign trade prices of the commodities change in a manner corresponding to the change in internal prices. Under Soviet conditions, there would be no change in the foreign trade prices of the two commodities.

Another way to look at the same point: When a payments disequilibrium results from a non-parallel change in the general levels of internal and ex-

[51] Since world prices will usually not have changed proportionally, the change will favor those nations whose exports rise relatively in price or whose imports fall relatively in price. In terms of the discussion of this section, some nations will have devalued or revalued implicitly more than others. If world prices change proportionally, of course, the degree of revaluation is the same for all nations.

There is no particular reason to believe that changes in external prices move the implicit exchange rates in a direction that is more or (alternatively) less appropriate to intra-bloc trade. Because bloc nations do consider current world prices to be a true opportunity cost, the use of frozen prices does cause difficulties, as noted earlier, regardless of their appropriateness within the bloc.

[52] These tendencies exist in any case, because many very profitable opportunities for trade with the West are forgone, usually reluctantly, as a result of political commitments to favor intra-bloc trade.

[53] For minor "real" side effects of the difference between rates, see my review of [1] in [4 (June 1960), pp. 481–483]; also my forthcoming paper [13].

ternal prices — that is, from pure inflation or deflation — a return to market equilibrium through a change in the exchange rate leaves foreign trade exactly as it was under previous equilibrium conditions, with the commodity structure of trade unchanged and, consequently, no change in domestic resource allocation. In effect, it is a situation of this nature in Soviet trade which leads us to posit the idea of the implicit flexible exchange rate of the ruble. Assume now that there are differential shifts in demand or supply and prices, as well as overall inflation or deflation. Under these conditions, in the West, the quantities and types of goods traded tend to change, and changes in resource allocation are stimulated, even though balance-of-payments equilibrium has been reachieved by a change in exchange rate. Soviet trade, on the other hand, is much less sensitive to differential foreign trade price changes, in two respects. First, unless there are very large differential price changes, quantities traded will not be affected. Second, even if the quantities traded do change because of the development of large profits or losses, there is still very little, if any, feedback to the domestic economy in the form of reallocation of resources. Of course, to the extent that there are any changes in quantities traded and any feedback to the domestic economy, the similarity between our so-called implicit freely floating exchange rate and a freely floating exchange rate, Western style, is increased.[54]

CONCLUDING REMARKS

The purpose of this section was to examine the short-run adjustment made by the Soviet economy to external shocks originating in the foreign trade sector. The goals of the planners are such (preservation of internal micro- and macro-balance, preference for direct controls, necessity of bilateral trade balance) that most of the burden of adjustment must be borne by the foreign trade sector itself. That is to say, the internal economy, particularly the priority sectors, is protected insofar as possible from the consequences of a shock to the foreign trade sector, leaving the latter in a higher degree of controlled disequilibrium than before.

Income effects are prohibited by dedication to full employment and deliberate insulation of the economy from the effects of "propensities."

In trade with the West, changes in Soviet foreign trade prices are used very flexibly to achieve trade *balance*, though the result is often further from external *equilibrium* than before. The high-priority goal of internal micro-balance puts the Soviets in the position, in the short run, of having a demand for imports which is, in effect, completely price-inelastic. The supply sched-

[54] It is possible that changes in relative domestic Soviet prices (costs) might also influence trade decisions, although we have assumed so far that this is not the case. The evidence that I have seen suggests that domestic cost or price changes have no influence at all on Soviet foreign trade decisions, particularly in the short run.

ule of exports, being geared to the financing of a fixed basket of imports, tends to be inelastic or backward-sloping. Where an increase in exports is required because of an adverse shift in terms of trade, it tends to be met at the expense of non-priority sectors of the economy. Equal changes in Soviet export and import prices leave trade unchanged, as do changes in Soviet internal prices — an effect analogous to having a freely floating exchange rate. The foreign trade price changes, just noted, have no short-run impact at all, and very little long-run impact on the allocation of resources. In this sense, changes in prices serve a function similar to those on a consumers' goods market in which there is consumer choice but no consumer sovereignty. To pursue the analogy further, price changes will be greater where there is consumer choice but not sovereignty. This is because, under choice, the total burden of adjustment must be borne by price changes; whereas, under sovereignty, changes in quantity also occur. Similarly, in Soviet-West trade, quantities remain relatively rigid and prices must therefore fluctuate more than usual.

The price and quantity adjustments that assure balance, though not equilibrium, in Soviet trade with the West are facilitated by the fact that they (the Soviets) can trade multilaterally on Western markets and that their trade generally constitutes a small part of a large market (that is, foreign export-supply and import-demand functions tend to be highly elastic vis-à-vis Soviet trade). All of the qualities that facilitate balance in Soviet-West trade are largely missing from intra-bloc trade. Prices tend to remain fixed for long periods of time. Requirements of internal micro-balance put all bloc nations in the position of not being able to provide elastic import-demand or export-supply functions to facilitate each others' adjustments. Inconvertibility and bilateralism further reduce the possibilities of adjustment.

Other adjustment mechanisms than those studied above exist, but lack of space prohibits their analysis here.[55] The flow of foreign exchange reserves and gold play an important role in East-West trade, though not in intra-bloc trade. Long-term capital flows have similarities to and differences from those used in the West to facilitate "adjustment." Foreign trade shocks have minor monetary and financial effects on the internal economies of the Eastern nations, but these are not allowed to feed back to the trade sector.[56] Finally, the "bottleneck" effect from a sudden cutting off of intermediate products, which disturbs the high-priority internal micro-balance, is a subject that requires special study and provides an interesting case of differences in reaction between planned and unplanned economies.[57]

[55] These are developed in my forthcoming paper [13].

[56] These have been considered in [5, Chap. 13], [12], and [19, Appendix F].

[57] Alexander's "absorption" approach [2] provides another way of looking at the effectiveness of price and income adjustments in eliminating a "disequilibrium" in trade, but it would not be essentially different from the analysis presented above.

DISCUSSION

Joseph S. Berliner

Professor Holzman's paper studies the impact of central planning on foreign trade behavior by examining the operation of adjustment mechanisms in the Soviet economy. His method is to review the three chief adjustment mechanisms that operate in market economies — the income, price, and exchange-rate adjustment mechanisms — and then to examine the role of each in the Soviet economy.

A standard analytical approach in our field is to select a set of keys made to fit the locks of a market economy, and to use them to try to pick the locks of the Soviet economy. Very often they cannot, and that I judge to be Holzman's experience in this inquiry. With a single major exception, little is learned by searching for Soviet mechanisms equivalent to the income and price adjustment mechanisms in a market economy. The exception is an interesting argument by Holzman regarding an implicit exchange-rate adjustment mechanism in the Soviet economy, on which I shall comment below.

It is not an unexpected result that the notion of adjustment mechanisms does not prove to be very fruitful in interpreting Soviet foreign trade behavior. The reason is that the idea of a mechanism presupposes a set of autonomous parts that respond to various signals, such as parametric prices or profits; hence, it is an appropriate analogue for a decentralized system like a market. The centrally planned economy, however, is in this respect rather like a single accounting unit — a firm or a household. A decline in exports is registered directly in the accounts as a reduction in the stock of foreign exchange reserves. The response is a matter of deliberate policy, and not the result of a series of signals transmitted through a mechanism. By analogy, if an aircraft were operating on an automatic pilot system, it would be reasonable to study the aircraft's behavior by studying the adjustment mechanisms. But if it is operated by a live pilot, we would not normally look for mechanisms in explaining his behavior. Behavior in that case is the result of conscious policy, a decision process in which the left hand usually knows what the right hand is doing.

In fact, in the Soviet case, we know that the planning process operates with something less than perfect efficiency; the two "hands" of export and import do not articulate with perfect balance. Hence, it would appear to be useful to examine foreign trade behavior in terms of the complexities of the central planning process. But the guiding idea would then consist in centralized decisionmaking and administration rather than in a set of automatic mechanisms. The model would represent an ideal central planning and administrative system, and one would ask how closely the decisions of the actual Soviet planning system come to those of the ideal. One would study, for example, whether the commodities chosen for import and export are such as to maximize the gains from trade. Such an approach is likely to yield more useful results, in a study of the influence of central planning upon foreign trade behavior, than an approach based on a search for mechanisms.

Thus we find that there is no equivalent in the Soviet case for the income adjustment mechanism that operates in market economies, whether of the neoclassical or of the Keynesian variety. As Holzman puts it, there are no behavioral equations in the system's model; output is simply determined by the production function. Hence, a fall in the exports of some goods leads directly to measures to keep the flow of international payments in balance, by a reduction in imports or by the substitution of other goods for export, such as gold.

Holzman summarizes the analysis by writing that the income mechanism "is not allowed to work effectively" because of higher priority goals than market equilibrium in foreign trade. I do not quarrel with the meaning, but the formulation is such as to suggest that a centrally planned economy might conceivably allow it to work. Since the Soviet planners have the power to reduce imports directly, it hardly makes sense for them first to let incomes fall in order to motivate themselves to reduce imports. It is not merely that the income mechanism is not allowed to work, but that it simply makes no sense in the planned economy.

Analysis of the price adjustment mechanism is somewhat more complicated because of the existence in the Soviet economy of two sets of prices, domestic ruble prices and foreign trade prices, which are in fact world prices. In the market economy, there is a single set of prices; it is the changes in those prices that cause the allocation of resources to shift in such a manner as to offset the deficit caused by a fall in exports. But again, in the Soviet case the planners need no price signals to provide motivation for taking the measures needed to restore balance in international payments. They react directly, by cutting imports or allocating substitute goods for export, without changes in domestic prices. Hence, it would be appropriate to conclude that a price adjustment mechanism neither is used nor makes any sense in a centrally planned economy. Holzman does make this point when he examines differences in the concept of price flexibility as it applies in the Soviet economy and in the market economy. But most of his discussion deals with the evidence of Soviet flexibility in foreign trade prices, and it is presented as if this were also evidence of the operation of something like the price adjustment mechanism in market economies. If the question were put in these terms, I believe Holzman would agree that flexibility in foreign trade pricing is *not* equivalent to the price adjustment mechanism of market economies, because it does not affect the allocation of resources. The reallocation of resources in response to a fall in exports is done directly by the

Soviet planners, without the mediation of either an income or a price adjustment mechanism.

Thus, the adjustment mechanisms of a market are of no use in explaining
Soviet responses to changes in supply-and-demand conditions in foreign trade.
But it is somewhat different when we turn to adjustments to changes in price
levels. In the market economy, balance-of-payments difficulties arising
because of a general price inflation are met by changes in the exchange rate.
Ideally, a general increase in domestic prices, if accompanied by a simultaneous devaluation of the appropriate magnitude, would leave foreign trade
unchanged. It might seem that, since the Soviets keep the official exchange
rate constant for long periods of time, the exchange-rate mechanism is not
available for carrying out the adjustment process in this case. But Holzman
argues that this would be a superficial view, since the official exchange rate
is of no relevance in actual foreign trade behavior. Since the central planners
treat exports and imports in a single account, a doubling of the domestic
prices of both would leave the pattern of exports and imports unchanged.
This is identical with the effect of a price inflation in a market economy with
a freely floating exchange rate. To formalize the argument, he proposes that
we consider the real, or "implicit," ruble exchange rate to be the ratio of
domestic to world prices. Then a doubling of Soviet domestic prices would
lead, by definition, to a 50 percent reduction in the implicit exchange rate,
leaving the pattern of trade unchanged, exactly as in a market economy.
With this rather clever twist, Holzman's analytic method has yielded an
interesting fruit. The exchange-rate adjustment mechanism of the market
economy does operate implicitly in the Soviet case, and in much the same
form as in the market economy.

Let me turn now from these general comments to a few more specific ones.
First, the paper deals with the positive aspects of foreign trade behavior, and
not with the normative. I would like to suggest that the ability of the centrally planned economy to dispense with the income adjustment mechanism
is a source of efficiency. By any reasonable welfare standard, an economy that
has to rely on a fall in income and employment to activate foreign trade
adjustment mechanisms is paying a considerable cost. The Soviet foreign
trade monopoly, by its ability to react directly, can forgo this cost. This, of
course, is not the whole story. The centrally planned economy has other
sources of inefficiency: the well-known irrationality of Soviet prices, and
problems of economic administration, may lead to a non-optimal selection
of imports to be cut and substitute exports to be promoted. These problems,
however, are generic to central planning and not specific to the Soviet foreign
trade adjustment methods.

Second, Holzman points out that even if the income adjustment mechanism did operate, it would not have a significant effect in balancing intra-

bloc trade, because of bilateralism. That is, a drop in Soviet exports to one country would induce a drop in imports that would be spread over all countries, and thus would fail to balance trade with the country that originally reduced its purchases of Soviet exports. One might note a similar consequence of the Soviet foreign aid program to underdeveloped countries. Most of the aid agreements provide for soft-currency loans and are repaid in the form of Soviet imports of the main export commodities of the borrowing countries. Now if Soviet exports fall, these imports cannot be reduced to offset the loss of foreign exchange, for they are not paid for in foreign exchange. Hence, the burden of adjustment falls entirely on those commodities currently being imported from hard-currency countries, commodities that are likely to be of higher priority. Thus the soft-loan aid program has reduced the flexibility with which the Soviets can adjust to balance-of-payments deficits.

Third, Holzman argues that the flexibility of Soviet foreign trade prices leads to a more "forced" balance in international payments than would be attained under a market adjustment mechanism. His illustration is the Soviet export of grain and timber in the early 1930s at very low prices to maintain planned imports of machinery products. I would like to suggest that this interpretation confuses economic policy with economic organization. That is, the forcing of balance in international payments by heavy grain exports was a deliberate policy decision, and not at all a special property of the Soviet foreign trade balancing method. A different policy would have led to a less forced result, with no change in foreign trade methods. Hence, the effects of price flexibility in the Soviet and in the market economies would not differ in degree of "forcedness," except to the extent that Soviet policy dictated this result.

Finally, one might note that certain of the difficulties faced by the Soviet economy in adjusting to changes in world trading conditions spring from a practice of Soviet planning that also characterizes domestic economic policy. I refer to what has been called "tautness," one feature of which is a policy of low inventories of stocks. It is often pointed out that many problems of balancing the internal economy would be eased with larger inventories. The same is true of the external economy. The problems caused by bilateralism, and by inconvertibility of both currencies and commodities, would be greatly eased if the Soviets built up a stock of convertible foreign exchange and thereafter conducted all their trade in convertible currencies. Holzman has indeed proposed this in a paper published earlier this year. There are doubtless reasons why the Soviets might find the proposal uncongenial. The process of building up a stock of convertible foreign exchange by running a balance-of-payments surplus for several years would constitute, in effect, the granting of a long-term loan to the United States and Britain, although the Soviets

would earn interest on their holdings of dollars and sterling. Nor would they
enjoy the political role of dependence on convertible currencies for the conduct of their foreign trade, and presumably that of Eastern Europe too. But
one cannot reflect on the present difficulties in conducting foreign trade, as
they emerge from Holzman's review of adjustment mechanisms, without
being impressed by the advantages of using not only Western prices, which
they do, but also Western currencies.

REFERENCES

1. Aizenberg, I. *Voprosy valiutnogo kursa rublia* (Moscow: 1958).
2. Alexander, Sidney. "Effects of a Devaluation: A Simplified Synthesis of
   Elasticities and Absorption Approaches," *American Economic Review*,
   XLIX:1 (March 1959), pp. 22–42.
3. Altman, Oscar. "Russian Gold and the Ruble," *Staff Papers*, International
   Monetary Fund, VII:3 (April 1960).
4. *American Economic Review*, L:2 (June 1960), pp. 481–482.
5. Ames, Edward. *Soviet Economic Processes* (Homewood, Ill.: Irwin, 1965).
6. Ausch, Sándor. "Nemzetközi munkamegosztás és gazdasági mechanizmus"
   ("International Division of Labor and Economic Mechanism"), *Közgazdasági Szemle*, XII:7–8 (July–August 1965), pp. 800–808.
7. Dell, Sydney. *Trade Blocs and Common Markets* (New York: Knopf, 1963).
8. Gerschenkron, Alexander. *Economic Relations with the USSR.* (New
   York: The Committee on International Economic Policy in cooperation
   with the Carnegie Endowment for International Peace, 1945).
9. Holzman, Franklyn. "Foreign Trade," in Abram Bergson and Simon Kuznets
   (eds.), *Economic Trends in the Soviet Union* (Cambridge: Harvard University Press, 1963), pp. 283–332.
10. ———. "Foreign Trade Behavior of Centrally Planned Economies," in
    Henry Rosovsky (ed.), *Industrialization in Two Systems: Essays in Honor
    of Alexander Gerschenkron* (New York: Wiley, 1966), pp. 237–265.
11. ———. "More on Soviet Bloc Trade Discrimination," *Soviet Studies*, XVII:1
    (July 1965), pp. 44–65.
12. ———. "Some Financial Aspects of Soviet Foreign Trade," U.S. Congress,
    Joint Economic Committee, *Comparisons of the United States and Soviet
    Economies* (Washington D.C.: 1959), Part II, pp. 427–443.
13. ———. "Some Traditional Adjustment Mechanisms in the Foreign Trade
    of Centrally Planned Economies," to appear in the *Cahiers de L'ISEA*.
14. ———, and Arnold Zellner. "The Foreign Trade and Balanced Budget
    Multipliers," *American Economic Review*, XLVIII:1 (March 1958),
    pp. 73–91.
15. Jiranek, Slavomir. "The Position of the Czechoslovak Crown in International
    Relations," *American Review of Soviet and Eastern European Foreign
    Trade*, I:6 (November–December 1965), pp. 56–63.
16. Kaser, Michael. *Comecon* (London: Oxford University Press, 1965).
17. *Planovane hospodarstvi*, No. 5 (1965).
18. Pleva, Jan. "Foreign Trade and the New System of Managements," *Ameri-
    can Review of Soviet and Eastern European Foreign Trade*, I:6 (Novem-
    ber–December 1965), pp. 39–55.

19. Pryor, Frederic L. *The Communist Foreign Trade System* (Cambridge: Massachusetts Institute of Technology Press, 1963).
20. Tansky, Leo. "Soviet Foreign Aid to the Less Developed Countries," U.S. Congress, Joint Economic Committee, *New Directions in the Soviet Economy* (Washington, D.C.: 1966), Part IV, pp. 947–974.
21. Translations on East European Trade, No. 247, JPRS:34,547 (October 27, 1965).
22. Wyczalkowski, Marcin. "Communist Economics and Currency Convertibility," *Staff Papers*, International Monetary Fund, XIII:2 (July 1966).
23. Zauberman, Alfred. *Industrial Progress in Poland, Czechoslovakia and East Germany, 1937–1962* (London: Oxford University Press, 1964).

Recent Structural Changes and Balance-of-Payments Adjustments in Soviet Foreign Trade*

OLEG HOEFFDING

As every student of Soviet foreign trade and other international transactions knows, Soviet literature is exceedingly uncommunicative on the subject of the Soviet Union's balance of payments, in terms of both statistics and prose. Textbooks confine themselves to brief and arid descriptions of accounting principles. There is no academic or popular literature on balance-of-payments experience, theory, or policy. Public allusions to problems and difficulties that arise over international transactions and payments are extremely rare and commonly couched in terms of denouncing imperialist or monopolist discriminatory machinations.

Against this general background of silence, it is all the more gratifying, and somewhat surprising, that since 1955 the U.S.S.R. has chosen to publish very detailed and reasonably complete statistics of merchandise trade, by far the most important component of its international transactions.

The present paper uses this particular corpus of data in an attempt to find at least some partial answers to the question: How did the planners and directors of Soviet international transactions manipulate merchandise trade in order to help overcome the acute difficulties that the U.S.S.R. experienced in 1963–1965 in balancing its accounts with the non-Communist world?

We are only incidentally — and not quantitatively — concerned with other Soviet countermeasures against this recent balance-of-payments problem which have been more or less fully visible in the West and have attracted

* Any views expressed in this paper are those of the author. They should not be interpreted as reflecting the views of The RAND Corporation or the official opinion or policy of any of its governmental or private research sponsors.

considerable attention: notably the sharp increase in Soviet gold sales, and the intensified quest for Western long-term credits to finance purchases of producer durables.

In our scrutiny of Soviet foreign trade statistics we focus primarily on hard-currency trade, a term presently to be defined in a way that excludes Soviet trade not only with the Communist countries but also, largely, with underdeveloped countries. However, as will be seen, Soviet responses to the hard-currency deficit problem significantly affected the latter two categories of trade, and we cannot leave them entirely out of consideration.[1]

THE BACKGROUND OF THE PROBLEM

According to what is by now a well-established and excusable oversimplification, the Soviet balance-of-payments problem of 1963–1965 was brought on by the U.S.S.R.'s need to resort to large-scale grain imports from (mainly) the Americas and Australia, after a very poor crop in 1963 and exhaustion of Soviet grain reserves. Other factors undoubtedly contributed. For instance, on the import side, there were sharply rising purchases of machinery and equipment in Western Europe and Japan (not all of them credit-financed). On the export side, fixed commitments to Communist countries under long-term trade agreements, and to other countries receiving Soviet aid, may have impeded diversion of exports to hard-currency markets and also required additional hard-currency imports. There was also the more general problem posed by the Soviet Union's very slow progress in diversifying its exports to the industrial West by raising the share of manufactured goods.

It is excusable, however, to cast the grain imports of 1963–1965 as the villain of the piece, as they were clearly the dominant element in the sharp and sudden deterioration of the Soviet hard-currency balance of trade. But it is important to realize that they were only the climax of a significant shift in the commodity structure of Soviet foreign trade which, even during the 1950s, had turned the U.S.S.R. into a net importer of food. Between 1950 and 1960, the share of crude and processed foodstuffs in total Soviet exports had fallen from 20.6 to 13.1 percent. The decline of their share in exports to capitalist countries was from 37.3 to 11.9 percent. The share of foodstuffs in total imports, 17.5 percent in 1950, also declined but more moderately, to 14.8 percent in 1958, and 12.8 percent in 1960, when food imports from China started collapsing. The advent of large-scale wheat im-

---

[1] All statistical data on Soviet foreign trade in this paper (unless otherwise indicated) are cited or calculated from official Soviet statistics. The principal sources used are [7] and [8]. Some data omitted from these sources have been obtained from the annual volumes for 1960 through 1964 in the same series. All values are in current prices and in foreign trade rubles, at the official exchange rate established January 1, 1961: $1.00 = 0.90 ruble.

ports in 1963–1964 had a truly striking impact on the structure of Soviet trade, raising the share of food in total imports to 20.1 percent (36.2 percent of imports from capitalist countries), and leading to a drop of the food share in total exports to 7.7 percent [9, No. 11, pp. 7ff.]. Soviet summary data on the values of total food exports and imports (published for selected years only) are shown in Table 1.

TABLE 1

SOVIET TRADE IN CRUDE AND PROCESSED FOODSTUFFS
(Million rubles)

Item	1950	1955	1958	1960	1964
Imports	229.3	556.4	580.5	605.7	1,394.3
Exports	332.7	370.1	476.3	663.6	535.3
Balance	103.4	−186.3	−104.2	57.9	−859.0

SOURCE: *Vneshniaia torgovlia* 1965, No. 11, pp. 7 ff. 1950, 1955, and 1960 figures are calculated by applying percentage data given in the source to total export and import values. No precise definition of "crude and processed foodstuffs" is given by the source. Probably the figures represent the sums of the values of Group 7 (Raw materials for the production of foodstuffs) and 8 (Foodstuffs) in the Soviet foreign trade commodity classification.

A salient aspect of this transition process was the fact that in the 1950s, and even until 1962, it was contained within the Communist countries. Underdeveloped countries contributed modestly to the expansion of food imports from the late 'fifties on. By contrast, until 1962, the U.S.S.R. kept imports of foodstuffs from the industrial West at a very low level, and in most years was able to realize modest net earnings of hard currencies in its food trade with this group of countries.

THE DIMENSIONS OF THE PROBLEM

Any account of the magnitude of the hard-currency balance-of-payments problem encountered by the U.S.S.R. should be prefaced by a warning that the Soviet difficulty, measured in absolute terms, was but a turbulence in a teapot by the standards we associate with payments crises afflicting large Western economies. The figures denoting the Soviet case fall far short of the heroic dimensions of Britain's sterling crises or United States gold drains. In 1964, the worst year, the Soviet hard-currency trade deficit was of the order of only about half a billion dollars. The modest absolute values, of course, reflect the fact that Soviet trade with the West is still quite small if compared with that of major market economies intensively tied into world trade.

However, it will presently be seen that the Soviet deficits were quite large relative to this modest scale of its total hard-currency trade. If current official U.S. estimates of Soviet gold reserves — some $2 billion in early 1964 — are anywhere near the truth, the U.S.S.R. experienced these deficits when its reserve position was uncomfortably tight. Also, again according to official U.S. estimates, Soviet gold sales in 1963–1964 were running at about $500 million a year, or more than double its annual gold production.[2] Finally, as Professor Holzman notes in his contribution to this volume, the U.S.S.R. economy has no built-in automatic "adjustment mechanisms" to counteract international disequilibria. Nor, it should be noted, has it access to the resources of the International Monetary Fund, or other sources of international liquidity (except limited trade credits) available to Western economies in balance-of-payments trouble.

In short, however undramatic the absolute figures, one may assume that the U.S.S.R. had good reasons to take its 1963–1965 problem quite seriously. In addition, the scope and vigor of Soviet adjustments to the problem, discussed below, indicate that it did take it quite seriously.

Before we proceed to outline the dimensions of the problem, the term "hard-currency trade," as we use it here, must be defined. It is a definition that does *not* aim at precise numerical measurement of Soviet hard-currency trade, which is not the object of the paper. The purpose of the definition is to approximately isolate that segment of Soviet foreign trade in which exports and imports are quite preponderantly transacted in convertible currencies, or against credits extended in such currencies, and which is free of special trading arrangements such as clearing agreements, barter transactions, deliveries under economic aid credits or shipments in repayment of such credits, and the like.

This definition excludes Soviet trade with all Communist countries in Europe (including Yugoslavia), Asia, and the Caribbean. It also excludes trade with Finland, conducted largely under a ruble clearing agreement. The latter does provide for small Soviet payments (40 million rubles a year) in convertible currency, a complication which we ignore [4, pp. 489–490].

It also excludes Soviet trade with all underdeveloped countries, except for trade in two commodities presently to be mentioned. The countries excluded are those constituting the category designated "capitalist developing countries" (hereinafter CDC) in Soviet foreign trade statistics. This covers all of Asia except Japan (and including Turkey), Africa except the Union of South Africa (with whom the U.S.S.R. has acknowledged no trade since

---

[2] According to the U.S. Bureau of Mines [5, pp. 515 ff.], Soviet gold sales in 1964 were about $500 million, "nearly as much as in 1963." Soviet gold production, according to the same source, averaged $126 million in 1955–1959, and then moved as follows ($ million):

1960	1961	1962	1963	1964
144	154	168	179	196

TABLE 2

SOVIET HARD-CURRENCY TRADE, 1959–1965
(Million rubles)

Type of Trade	1959	1960	1961	1962	1963	1964	1965
Exports to HC area	649.3	752.3	829.0	873.3	934.8	982.0	1,149.0
Imports from HC area	562.2	840.1	854.9	996.1	1,084.0	1,435.9	1,250.6
Balance with HC area	87.1	−87.8	−25.9	−122.8	−149.2	−453.9	−102.0
Imports of rubber and copper[a]	149.9	132.7	178.7	168.4	136.5	59.2	95.7
Total HC imports	712.1	972.8	1,033.6	1,164.5	1,220.5	1,495.1	1,346.3
Balance	−62.8	−220.5	−204.6	−291.2	−285.7	−513.1	−197.3

[a] From countries identified in text.

1960), and all of Latin America (except Cuba). The summary exclusion of this large group of countries is quite arbitrary. Undoubtedly it includes quite a few countries in which the Soviet Union spends and earns convertible currencies. On the whole, however, Soviet trade and aid are so closely intermingled in this group, and so much trade is conducted under ruble or local-currency clearing agreements or by barter that even a major research effort (which we have not attempted) probably would not succeed in sorting out hard-currency from other trade.

To make partial amends for summarily excluding the entire CDC group, we include in our definition of hard-currency trade Soviet imports of rubber from Malaya and Thailand and of copper from Zambia, Uganda, Mexico, and Peru — all countries with whom the U.S.S.R. has no special trading arrangements. This inclusion is not insignificant: rubber imports from Malaya and Thailand alone accounted for one-third of total Soviet imports from the CDC in 1960.

The hard-currency *area* covered by our definition, then, consists of all of non-Communist Europe (except Finland), Japan, the United States, Canada, Australia, and New Zealand. Soviet hard-currency *trade*, as we define it, consists of trade with this area, plus the rubber and copper imports just mentioned.[3]

[3] In the tables that follow, the abbreviation HC stands for hard currency.

In Table 2 we summarize the overall changes in Soviet hard-currency trade in 1959–1965. It will be seen that this trade resulted in deficits in all these years. In 1962–1965, the years which will concern us most, the 1963 deficit was slightly smaller than in 1962. The 1964 deficit is conspicuously large, but that of 1965 is actually smaller than any recorded since 1959. These phenomena — not, perhaps, on the surface consistent with what we have characterized above as an acute balance-of-payments problem extend-

TABLE 3

GEOGRAPHIC DISTRIBUTION OF SOVIET TRADE
WITH HARD-CURRENCY AREA, 1959–1965
(Million rubles)

Type of Trade, by Area	1959	1960	1961	1962	1963	1964	1965
Europe							
Exports	592.4	656.5	700.6	753.2	796.8	809.2	938.1
Imports	501.5	690.2	674.3	803.6	697.8	698.4	707.3
Balance	90.9	−33.7	26.3	−50.4	99.0	110.8	230.8
Japan							
Exports	30.0	68.5	101.7	101.7	111.5	148.2	166.4
Imports	21.1	55.4	59.9	131.2	148.9	173.9	159.6
Balance	8.9	13.1	41.8	−29.5	−37.4	−25.7	6.8
Other Non-Europe[a]							
Exports	26.9	27.3	26.7	18.4	26.5	24.6	44.5
Imports	39.6	94.5	120.7	61.3	237.3	563.6	383.7
Balance	−12.7	−67.2	−94.0	−42.9	−210.8	−539.0	−339.2

[a] Canada, United States, Australia, New Zealand.

ing over three years, 1963–1965 — require explanation in terms of (a) the geographic distribution of Soviet hard-currency trade, and (b) Soviet counter-measures against the disequilibrating forces it faced in 1963–1965.

As shown in Table 3, the deterioration of the Soviet trade balance with the hard-currency area in 1963–1965 was entirely confined to non-European countries other than Japan or, in other words, the countries which figured as the principal suppliers of wheat to the U.S.S.R. in these years: Canada, the United States, and Australia. In trade with these countries, the U.S.S.R. had incurred import surpluses prior to 1963, but these remained modest in size until the onset of the massive wheat imports in 1963. Soviet exports to these countries had been almost negligibly small and they remained so in 1963–1965, although some gain was made in the latter year.

On the other hand, Soviet trade balances with Western Europe and Japan improved very substantially in 1963–1965, from a combined deficit of 80 million rubles in 1962 to a surplus of 238 million rubles in 1965. As shown in Table 2, substantial hard-currency savings were also realized by reducing imports of rubber and copper, from an average of 157 million rubles a year in 1959–1962 to one of 97 million rubles in 1963–1965.

Thus — and this brings us to our first observation on Soviet strategy in countering its problem — the U.S.S.R., in the absence of opportunities for bilaterally balancing its deficit with the wheat suppliers, evidently undertook a very determined effort to finance this deficit not only by increased gold sales, but also by generating trade surpluses — or reducing deficits — with its other hard-currency trade partners. This triangular balancing operation — accomplished by a combination of import restriction and export expansion to be examined in greater detail below — contributed substantially to the striking reduction of the overall hard-currency trade deficit from 1964 to 1965, by 316 million rubles. About one-half of this reduction, however, was due to a decline of grain purchases in 1965, by 156 million rubles.

TRADE IN FOOD, 1959–1965

In Table 4 we summarize Soviet data on trade in food in 1959–1965 with the hard-currency area and with Communist countries. The term "food" here covers crude and processed foodstuffs (including coarse grains), beverages, tobacco, and tobacco manufactures.

As regards hard-currency trade, the table shows that apart from the large imports from non-European countries in 1963–1965, which are almost entirely accounted for by grain and flour, the U.S.S.R. also sharply increased food imports from Europe, tripling them by 1965 over 1962. This increase may be substantially understated by Soviet foreign trade statistics, which do not report any food imports from West Germany in 1963 and 1964, although this country is elsewhere reported to have exported 402,000 tons of wheat and flour to the U.S.S.R. in fiscal 1963–1964 [10, p. 3]. The increases of food imports from Europe reported by Soviet statistics in 1963 and 1964 were made up largely of meat and dairy products. The increase in 1965, however, is entirely due to wheat imports from France; other food imports from Europe showed a slight decline.

On the other hand, the U.S.S.R. sharply curtailed its food exports to hard-currency countries (mainly in Europe), but not until 1964. This was achieved largely by a near-total suspension of grain exports to these countries. The recovery of food exports in 1965, in turn, largely represents the reappearance of some exports of barley and other coarse grains, but not of wheat.

Turning to food trade with Communist countries, it appears that the U.S.S.R. was quite successful in sharing its problem with the European members of this group, both by contracting exports and expanding imports. Here again, the most prominent Soviet reaction on the export side was a severe curtailment of grain exports. Wheat exports to Bulgaria, Czechoslovakia, East Germany, Hungary, and Poland declined moderately in 1963, to 2.6 million tons from 2.8 million in 1962, and then precipitously to 1.3 million tons in 1964 and 1.1 million tons in 1965. In the latter year, only East Germany and Czechoslovakia received Soviet wheat, at roughly half the scale of 1962–1963 exports. Rumania was a special case: In 1963, it *exported*

TABLE 4

SOVIET TRADE IN FOOD, 1959–1965
(Million rubles)

Type of Trade, by Area	1959	1960	1961	1962	1963	1964	1965
HC Area:							
Exports	78.4	76.5	123.3	91.0	110.2	49.1	84.1
Imports:							
Europe	30.1	34.0	26.5	28.2	36.3	61.7	94.7
Non-Europe	10.5	....ᵃ	27.7	2.4	168.7	490.2	290.9
Total	40.7	34.0	54.2	30.6	205.0	551.9	385.6
Balance	37.8	42.5	69.0	60.4	−94.8	−502.8	−301.5
Communist Countries:							
Europe							
Exports	537.4	426.0	399.9	505.1	466.6	306.0	309.3
Imports	178.4	197.7	275.1	244.5	299.0	342.0	405.5
Balance	359.0	228.4	124.8	260.5	167.6	−35.9	−96.2
Asia							
Exports	15.1	13.2	45.3	33.0	12.8	10.3	18.7
Imports	285.5	177.5	52.2	76.3	56.2	83.4	120.4
Balance	−270.4	−164.3	−6.9	−43.3	−43.4	−73.1	−101.7
Cuba							
Exports	....ᵃ	10.9	33.2	73.3	86.4	70.4	81.5
Imports	6.7	93.4	270.4	183.9	126.5	229.2	278.8
Balance	−6.7	−82.5	−237.2	−110.6	−40.1	−158.8	−197.3
Total							
Exports	552.5	450.1	478.4	611.4	565.8	386.7	409.5
Imports	470.6	468.6	597.7	504.7	481.7	654.6	757.4
Balance	81.9	−18.5	−119.3	106.7	84.1	−267.9	−395.2
Finland							
Exports	37.2	27.6	20.5	30.6	28.9	20.0	7.5
Imports	0.9	1.3	0.9	1.2	2.1	9.3	18.1
Balance	36.3	26.3	19.6	29.4	26.8	10.7	−10.6

ᵃ None reported or negligible.

395,000 tons of wheat to the U.S.S.R., and another 5,000 tons in 1964; but in 1964 it also *imported* 400,000 tons from the U.S.S.R., which suggests that this was a loan transaction providing for Soviet repayment in kind. In 1965, Rumania re-emerged as a wheat exporter to the U.S.S.R., supplying 172,000 tons. This, however, represented only 9 million rubles of the large total 1965 increase in food imports from this region, by 64 million rubles. All countries except East Germany shared in this increase, with Bulgaria and Poland contributing the largest portions.

On the whole, in 1963–1965 the U.S.S.R. succeeded in reducing its food exports to European Communist countries by 196 million rubles below the 1962 level or by 39 percent, and in raising its imports by 161 million, or 66 percent. By doing so, it reversed the traditional large export surplus in its food trade with this area, 261 million rubles in 1962, into a sizable import surplus of 96 million rubles in 1965. Curtailment of grain exports to Eastern Europe must have contributed directly and significantly to containing the Soviet hard-currency trade deficit in these years. The import expansion, to some extent, should have had a similar effect. Thus, there was an increase of Soviet imports from Eastern Europe of meat and dairy products — which it was also importing from hard-currency countries — from 16 million rubles in 1963 to 69 million rubles in 1965. One should note, however, that a major portion of the import increase consisted of relatively "non-essential" products — such as fruit, wine, and cigarettes — of which Soviet hard-currency imports are negligibly small. Thus — evidently in the absence of serious balance-of-payments constraints in trade with this region — the U.S.S.R. was able to draw on imports from Eastern Europe to supplement and vary the solid and liquid diet of Soviet consumers, and did not have to impose an austerity regime on this segment of its imports.

Table 4 indicates that the 1962–1965 changes in Soviet food trade with Asian Communist countries were very similar to those observed in Eastern Europe. Soviet food exports, never large, were sharply cut — again, mainly at the expense of wheat and other cereals — and imports were sharply increased. A revival of meat imports from China accounted for much of this increase. However, the U.S.S.R. also obtained modest amounts of wheat from Mongolia and, in 1965, of rice from North Korea. The upshot was a restoration of the Soviet food import surplus from this group, which had been nearly wiped out by 1961 by the elimination of food imports from China, to 102 million rubles in 1965.

Cuba was an exceptional case among the Soviet Union's Communist trade partners. Soviet exports (or re-exports) of wheat and other grains were well maintained, as were exports of meat and other foodstuffs. This, presumably, was in recognition of the fact that Cuba's large sugar exports to the U.S.S.R.

provide not only a welcome addition to Soviet carbohydrate supply but also a re-exportable commodity of some importance in financing trade with underdeveloped countries and Finland.

It is of interest that the pattern of change in Soviet food trade with Communist countries in Europe and Asia was precisely replicated, on a small scale, in its trade with Finland (see Table 4). Here, Soviet exports of wheat and rye were severely cut in 1963 and 1964, and virtually stopped in 1965 (when, however, some barley and corn was substituted). As a result, food exports by 1965 dropped to one-quarter of their 1962 value. By contrast, Soviet food imports from Finland, quite small until 1963, increased steeply in 1964–1965.

On the whole, then, it is clear that in 1963–1965 the U.S.S.R. took very vigorous action to readjust its food trade with Communist countries (and Finland) so as to economize on hard-currency outlays on food — mainly by severely restricting grain exports to Eastern European recipients — while at the same time it sharply stepped up food imports from these soft-currency markets.

One may note, from Table 4, that the sum of the deterioration in its food trade balance with hard-currency countries from 1962 to 1965, 362 million rubles, was less than that of the technical deterioration (or improvement, in terms of Soviet objectives) of its food trade balance with Communist countries and Finland, 542 million rubles. This comparison, however, has to be qualified by the caution that the equivalence of the foreign trade ruble in the two market areas should not be taken for granted.

We have not systematically examined whether similar readjustments occurred in food trade with non-Communist underdeveloped countries — the CDC group. It seems clear, however, that here too the U.S.S.R. used what limited opportunities it had for increasing grain imports from, and cutting exports to, this group. Total grain imports from CDC rose from 12 million rubles in 1962 and 18 million rubles in 1963 to 40 million in 1964 and 61 million in 1965, as a result of wheat imports from Argentina, and increased rice imports from Southeast Asia and Egypt. Since the U.S.S.R. had all along been very sparing in exporting grain to the CDC (with Brazil the only major recipient in 1960–1963), there was little scope for withholding of grain from these markets, but they were not neglected. Exports of wheat and flour to this group, 30 million rubles in 1962 and 18 million in 1963, dwindled to less than one million rubles in 1964 and two million in 1965.

Other Soviet food imports from CDC — notably coffee, cocoa, tea, and fruit — increased substantially in 1962–1965, again suggesting that the U.S.S.R. was under no compulsion to practice austerity in its soft-currency food trade.

HARD-CURRENCY NONFOOD TRADE

In Table 5 we summarize data on Soviet hard-currency trade other than in food, obtained by deducting the values of hard-currency food trade in Table 4 from the total values in Table 2.

It will be seen that in nonfood trade with the hard-currency area the U.S.S.R. in 1960–1962 incurred substantial deficits, which were further augmented by the large imports of rubber and copper from what we presume to be hard-currency sources in the CDC group. Both the hard-currency area

TABLE 5

SOVIET NONFOOD HARD-CURRENCY TRADE, 1959–1965
(Million rubles)

Type of Trade	1959	1960	1961	1962	1963	1964	1965
1. Nonfood trade with HC area:							
Exports	570.9	675.8	705.7	782.3	824.6	932.9	1,064.9
Imports	521.5	806.1	800.7	965.5	879.0	884.0	865.0
Balance	49.4	−130.3	−95.0	−183.2	−54.4	48.9	199.9
2. Imports of rubber and copper [a]	149.9	132.7	178.7	168.4	136.5	59.2	95.7
3. Total HC balance	−100.5	−263.0	−273.7	−351.6	−190.9	−10.3	104.2

[a] From countries identified in text.
SOURCE: Tables 2 and 4, above.

deficit and the total hard-currency trade deficit (which, as defined above, includes rubber and copper imports) reached a peak in 1962, which marked a distinct turning point; the hard-currency area deficit was sharply reduced in 1963, and turned into a surplus in 1964–1965, for a total gain by 1965 over 1962 of 383 million rubles. The total deficit in hard-currency trade moved similarly, but was not reversed until 1965. The improvement by 1965 over 1962 amounted to 456 million rubles.

One may infer from these changes that the Soviet Union, when forced to resort to heavy grain purchases from the West and to restrict food exports, embarked on a very determined effort to improve its hard-currency balance of nonfood trade.

This effort took the form of import restriction as well as export expansion. Initially, as one might expect, the adjustment was mainly restrictive. As shown in Table 6, import cuts accounted for 118 million rubles of the balance-of-trade improvement in 1963 by 161 million rubles. In 1964, however, export gains contributed more than import cuts, and in 1965 the entire improvement was on account of export expansion, with a slight increase in imports. For the 1963–1965 period as a whole, 62 percent of the balance-of-trade gains was achieved by export expansion.

We now examine how Soviet export expansion and import restriction were distributed by commodity groups during the readjustment phase of 1963–1965. In this we are assisted by a Soviet source that permits a labor-saving if not fully precise approach to the problem. The annual *Vneshniaia torgovlia SSSR* volumes do not publish a breakdown of trade by country

TABLE 6

CHANGES IN TOTAL NONFOOD HARD-CURRENCY BALANCE,
1962–1965
(Million rubles)

Item	1962–1963	1963–1964	1964–1965	1962–1965
Improvement in Balance	160.7	180.6	114.5	455.8
Export gains	42.3	108.3	132.0	282.6
Import cuts	118.4	72.3	−17.5 [a]	173.2

[a] Import increase.
SOURCE: Table 5.

groupings and by commodity groups. However, such a breakdown, for the years of concern to us, has appeared in a supplement to the journal *Vneshniaia torgovlia* [6]. It tabulates exports and imports of "principal commodities" to and from "socialist countries" and "capitalist countries," subdividing the latter into two groups, "industrially developed" and "developing" countries. The "industrially developed" group almost exactly corresponds to our "hard-currency area." The only difference is that it includes Finland, which is excluded by our definition.[4] Thus, by subtracting trade with Finland in each of the commodity groups listed from the figures shown for trade with "industrially developed countries," one should obtain the value of trade with our "hard-currency area" for each commodity group. Unfortunately, the Soviet tabulation is flawed by reporting trade in some commodities in physical units only, rather than in rubles. Since it reports trade on foodstuffs mostly in physical units, we could not use it for our calculations on Soviet food trade. Fortunately, however, nonfood commodity trade is reported mostly in rubles, with only one important exception, crude oil

[4] No explicit definition of the country groupings used for "capitalist countries" in Soviet statistics has, to our knowledge, ever been published. However, their coverage can be reconstructed from data appearing in a Foreign Trade Ministry publication [2, pp. 52–53, 65–66].

and petroleum products. With this exception, the commodity group values for exports and imports in our Tables 7 and 9, below, have been compiled from this source, by deducting trade with Finland in each case from the value of trade with "industrially developed capitalist countries." In Table 7, hard-currency exports of crude oil and petroleum products have been calculated from Soviet country-by-commodity statistics.

The coverage of the Soviet summary data is not comprehensive, but the resulting commodity breakdown covers 82 to 89 percent of total hard-currency nonfood exports and 78 to 82 percent of imports during the years in question, enough to permit some interesting insights into shifts in the commodity composition of this segment of Soviet trade in this turbulent period.

Table 7 shows the commodity structure of nonfood hard-currency exports in 1962–1965. A first general impression is that the rapid export expansion achieved in these years was quite preponderantly sustained by raw materials and semi-manufactures. Exports of the three groups that can be identified as clearly representing manufactured goods — machinery and equipment,

TABLE 7

NONFOOD EXPORTS TO HARD-CURRENCY AREA
BY COMMODITY GROUP, 1962–1965[a]
(Million rubles)

	Commodity Group[b]	1962	1963	1964	1965
1	Machinery and equipment	10.1	9.6	14.1	24.8
20	Solid fuels	58.9	78.2	81.8	75.1
21, 22	Crude oil, petroleum products	191.0	220.1	214.7	214.4
24	Metallic ores and concentrates	22.9	23.4	25.8	34.3
26	Iron and steel	57.7	58.1	81.5	92.6
27	Nonferrous metals	28.1	28.0	65.4	70.9
30	Chemicals	13.4	15.7	15.2	18.3
50	Wood, pulp, paper	180.6	184.2	235.1	243.7
51	Textile raw materials and semi-manufactures	39.3	36.4	34.4	60.6
52	Furs	40.6	59.0	49.5	48.1
96	Drugs, cosmetics, etc.	1.4	1.6	2.3	1.8
970	Consumer durables	1.2	2.0	3.2	5.3
	Total itemized	645.2	716.3	823.0	889.9
	Unspecified[c]	137.1	108.3	109.9	175.0
Total nonfood exports to HC area[d]		782.3	824.6	932.9	1,064.9

[a] See text for sources.
[b] Numbers represent classification in Soviet foreign trade commodity code.
[c] Difference between itemized total and total nonfood exports to hard-currency area (Table 5, first row).
[d] Table 5, first row.

consumer durables, and drugs and cosmetics — increased sharply in relative terms, between them from 13 million rubles in 1962 to 32 million in 1965. However, by 1965 they still accounted for only 3 percent of total nonfood hard-currency exports, and they contributed only 19 million rubles to a total expansion of such exports by 283 million.

However, even if traditional Soviet export commodities loomed large in the export expansion, a remarkably large share of it was accounted for by products that are relative newcomers to the Soviet export trade. Somewhat arbitrarily, one may classify the commodity groups in Table 7 in three categories:

A. "Traditional" raw materials and semi-manufactures: solid fuels, petroleum, ores and concentrates, wood, etc., textile materials, furs.

B. "New" raw materials and semi-manufactures: iron and steel, nonferrous metals, chemicals.[5]

C. Manufactures: machinery, drugs, etc., consumer durables.

One finds that the percentage share of each group in 1962 and 1965, and its contribution to the total increase in nonfood hard-currency exports during these years, was as follows:

| | *Percent of Total Exports* | | *Increase, 1962 to 1965* | |
Commodity Group	1962	1965	Million Rubles	Percent of Total Increase
A	68.2	63.5	142.9	50.5
B	12.7	17.0	82.6	29.2
C	1.6	3.0	19.2	6.8
Unspecified	17.6	16.4	37.9	13.4

Thus, Group A, which accounted for more than two-thirds of total exports in 1962, contributed only one-half of the 1962–1965 export expansion; Groups B and C, with a 1962 share of 14 percent, accounted for 36 percent of the increase.

From this, one may possibly infer that the U.S.S.R. found it easier to expand exports in this period by diversifying its commodity offerings, through introduction or expansion of "new" product exports, rather than by further pressing sales of "traditional" goods, although it clearly did not neglect pressing them. However, our examination of the changes in commodity composition is not detailed enough to positively establish this proposition.

[5] The assignment of iron and steel to "new" products is dubious, but may be warranted by the lesser share of pig iron (a "traditional" product) and the increased share of rolled steel and ferro-alloys in Soviet exports of ferrous metals since World War II.

Two commodity groups may be mentioned where expansion definitely reflected introduction of new products: nonferrous metals and, in a peculiar way, unspecified commodities. Exports of nonferrous metals to the west — mainly of lead, zinc, and aluminum — did not assume significant proportions until the late 1950s, and were subject to considerable fluctuations. As shown in Table 7, they increased very rapidly in 1964–1965, from 28 million rubles in 1962 and 1963 to 71 million in 1965, or by 43 million rubles. Two metals accounted for 36 million rubles of this increase: aluminum exports rose from 12 million rubles in 1962 to 24 million in 1965, and in 1965 Soviet foreign trade statistics for the first time reported exports of nickel, 12.5 million rubles' worth to the United Kingdom. The increase in aluminum, presumably, signified a systematic effort to step up sales of a metal that had figured in Soviet exports for some years. The appearance of nickel, however, was quite a novel phenomenon, suggesting that Soviet imports of nickel concentrate from Cuba — together, possibly, with expanded domestic production (on which the U.S.S.R. does not publish statistics) — have turned it from a net importer into a net exporter of this metal. Soviet imports of nickel from the "free world" (as reported by the U.S. Department of Commerce) started dwindling soon after the Cuban revolution, while imports from Cuba of what is identified only as "metallic ores and concentrates" first appeared in Soviet statistics in 1963.[6]

	1959	1960	1961	1962	1963	1964	1965
U.S.S.R. imports of nickel from "free world" ($ million)	7.69	10.34	15.25	5.45	5.29	0.06	0.01
U.S.S.R. imports of "ores and concentrates" from Cuba (million rubles)	....	....	....	....	20.0	26.4	25.8

An alternative possibility is that the U.S.S.R. drew on its nickel stockpile to supplement its hard-currency earnings. There are indications, presently to be reviewed, that this occurred in the case of other commodities, which brings us, first, to the unspecified nonfood exports shown in Table 7, above.

Exports in this category dropped in 1963–1964 but then rose sharply in 1965, from 110 to 175 million rubles, an increase nearly equal in ruble terms to that in total itemized exports in Table 7.

A very detailed scrutiny of Soviet country-by-commodity statistics, which

---

[6] The U.S.S.R. has not published data on its total imports of nickel. The only imports it has reported are those from France. These ran steadily at close to 5 million rubles a year in 1959–1963; none are reported for 1964–1965.

we have not attempted, might provide some explanations for this behavior, but there is reason to believe that it would not, at least as far as the increase in 1965 is concerned. The U.S. Department of Commerce compilations on East-West trade show that in 1965 there was a marked increase in "free world" imports from the U.S.S.R. of certain commodities that have never been explicitly reported in published Soviet statistics, although they are included in the Soviet foreign trade commodity classification. The items involved are, mainly, precious metals other than gold and diamonds. "Free

TABLE 8

"FREE WORLD" IMPORTS OF PRECIOUS METALS
AND STONES, 1959–1965
(Million dollars)

Item	1959	1960	1961	1962	1963	1964	1965
Silver, un-worked and partly worked	0.61	0.62	0.31	.....	1.09	.....	13.60
Platinum and similar metals	16.52	22.48	23.89	27.16	35.39	33.86	73.91
Other and un-specified silver, platinum, gems, and jewelry	0.03	3.29	.....	.....	.....	.....	.....
Diamonds, ex-cept industrial	.....	.....	.....	.....	.....	.....	25.92
	17.16	26.39	24.20	27.16	36.48	33.86	113.43

SOURCE: U.S. Department of Commerce, Summaries of Country-by-Commodity series, Free-World Countries Imports, for 1959 through 1965.

world" imports of these items from the U.S.S.R. in 1959–1965 are shown in Table 8.

It will be seen that the total of these imports, after rising moderately in 1962–1964, more than trebled in 1965, increasing by $80 million to $113 million. By coincidence or otherwise, the ruble equivalent of the increase, 72 million, is fairly close to that of unspecified Soviet exports in Table 7, 65 million rubles.

We have not attempted to track down the distribution of these imports by recipient countries. However, the United Kingdom was a principal recipient in 1965, importing $46 million's worth, as compared with only $3 million in 1964.[7] British 1965 imports accounted for most of the "free world's" total imports from the U.S.S.R. of silver ($12.2 million out of $13.6 million) and diamonds ($24.5 million out of $25.9 million). Soviet statistics of ex-

[7] According to the U.S. Department of Commerce data.

ports to the United Kingdom contain an indication that the value of trade
in the above items (as well as, undoubtedly, other commodities) is included
in the export totals, although not identified in the commodity breakdown.
In recent years, there has been a widening gap between reported Soviet total
exports to the United Kingdom and the total itemized by commodity:

	1963	1964	1965
Total U.S.S.R. exports to U.K., million rubles	193.5	214.7	259.8
Itemized exports, million rubles	178.2	190.6	209.7
Unspecified exports, million rubles	15.3	24.1	50.1
Unspecified exports, percent of total	7.9	12.3	19.3

Our surmise that exports of silver, platinum, and diamonds may be included in the unspecified residual calls for one qualification: Soviet statistics
of exports to the United Kingdom do mention exports of "precious stones"
(not specified as diamonds) in the years 1963, 1964, and 1965, in rising
but minute amounts: respectively, 15, 328, and 981 *thousand* rubles.

If, nevertheless, our surmise is correct, and if Soviet statistics follow the
same practice for countries other than Britain, then exports in this special
class of commodities might well be included in the unspecified residual in
Table 7, and would help to account for its behavior in 1964–1965.

But even if we are wrong, the Department of Commerce data on Western
imports in this class are of considerable interest in themselves, particularly
as regards the increase in 1965. Its magnitude — and the first appearance of
major silver and diamond exports — strongly suggests sales from stocks in
excess of current production.

If this was the case, such exports should be regarded as "balancing items"
functionally akin to gold sales rather than as current transactions on merchandise account. If they are included in the unspecified residual of hard-
currency nonfood merchandise exports (Table 7), Soviet statistics considerably overstate the actual improvement in the hard-currency balance on
merchandise account in 1965. As we have seen, the increase in the residual
amounted to nearly half the total increase in this category of Soviet exports.

One may also wonder whether the sharp increase of silver, platinum, and
diamond exports in 1965 indicated by the Department of Commerce data,
and their magnitude, might not signify increased Soviet concern over the
rate of their "gold drain" and a decision to draw down reserves of commodities as readily convertible into foreign exchange as gold.

IMPORTS

If the expansion of Soviet hard-currency nonfood exports in 1962–1965 was
rather widely and unevenly spread over a variety of commodity groups, the
record of Soviet imports in the same category presents quite a different pic-

TABLE 9

SOVIET HARD-CURRENCY NONFOOD IMPORTS, 1962–1965 [a]
(Million rubles)

Commodity Group [b]	1962	1963	1964	1965
A. *HC Area Imports*				
1 Machinery and equipment	414.9	412.2	499.4	368.3
26 Iron and steel	218.0	126.7	57.6	95.0
27 Nonferrous metals	48.1	46.7	9.7	11.1
30 Chemicals	39.6	59.0	68.1	102.3
50 Wood, pulp, paper	9.8	10.1	12.3	16.2
51 Textile fibers and semi-manufactures	72.4	81.6	71.2	82.9
.. Unspecified [c]	162.7	142.7	165.7	189.2
Total [d]	965.5	879.0	884.0	865.0
B. *HC Imports from CDC* [e]				
Crude rubber	150.0	122.1	56.8	95.7
Copper	18.4	14.4	2.4	...
Total	168.4	136.5	59.2	95.7
C. *Total HC Nonfood Imports*				
(A + B)	1,133.9	1,015.5	943.2	960.7

[a] See text for sources.
[b] Numbers represent classification in Soviet foreign trade commodity code.
[c] Difference between itemized total and total hard-currency nonfood imports (Table 5, second row).
[d] Table 5, second row.
[e] Table 5, item 2.

ture. As shown in Table 9, the net reduction in 1962–1965 — by 173 million rubles or 15 percent — was heavily concentrated in relatively few commodity groups. Imports in all other groups, as well as unspecified imports, increased from 1962 to 1965.

This contrast between the changes in exports and imports presumably reflects the simple fact that a foreign trade monopoly, geared into a central planning system, will enjoy much greater freedom in manipulating imports from private-enterprise economies than exports to them. Decisions on what to buy and what not to buy can be taken unilaterally by the planners according to their preferences and priorities (although, in practice, probably after much internal bargaining and compromising of conflicting departmental claims). Export transactions, on the other hand, can only be consummated with the consent of foreign buyers not subject to the planners' command.

We shall see, however, that the freedom of the Soviet authorities to restrict imports was subject to at least two external constraints: They had to go on taking delivery of long-lead-time items presumably ordered before the onset of the restrictionist phase; and some of the hard-currency savings

TABLE 10

COMMODITY COMPOSITION OF HARD-CURRENCY
NONFOOD IMPORTS
(Percent of total)

Commodity Group	1962	1963	1964	1965
A. Machinery and equipment	36.5	40.6	52.9	38.3
B. Metals and rubber	38.3	30.5	13.4	21.0
C. Other and unspecified	25.1	28.9	33.6	40.6

SOURCE: Table 9.

realized by cutting imports of certain commodities apparently were offset
by obligations to maintain exports of these commodities to Communist countries. We shall also see that during this period one particular import restriction was imposed on the U.S.S.R. by an outside party, to wit, NATO.

Restrictions on nonfood imports from the hard-currency area in 1963–
1964 fell quite preponderantly on iron and steel and nonferrous metals. There
was also a drastic reduction of rubber and copper imports from hard-currency
sources in the CDC area. Concurrently, imports of machinery and equipment, by far the largest commodity group, increased sharply in 1964, while
imports of all other commodity groups were at or above the 1962 level. In
1965, as imports of all other commodity groups except nonferrous metals
increased, there was a conspicuous drop in imports of machinery and equipment.

These divergent movements produced some remarkable shifts in the commodity mix of this segment of Soviet imports, if one groups them, as we do
in Table 10, into:

A. Machinery and equipment
B. Metals and rubber
C. Other

The annual changes in the import values for the same three commodity
groups in 1963–1965 were as follows, in million of rubles:

	1963 / 1962	1964 / 1963	1965 / 1964
A	−2.7	+87.2	−131.1
B	−124.6	−183.4	+75.3
C	+8.9	+23.9	+73.3
Total	−118.4	−72.3	+17.5

The behavior of *machinery and equipment* imports probably reflects the
overlapping operation of two factors:

a. Some considerable portion of imports in this group was purchased against credits, and there was less immediate pressure to curtail such purchases. Since credit transactions were involved, it should be noted that trade statistics do not truly reflect the impact of imports in this group on the Soviet hard-currency balance on current account. Imports of equipment purchased under credits will be recorded at full value in the year of delivery, whereas the major part of the payment due will be deferred for some years.

TABLE 11

SOVIET HARD-CURRENCY IMPORTS OF MACHINERY
AND EQUIPMENT BY TYPE
(Million rubles)

Type of Machinery and Equipment[a]	1962	1963	1964	1965
100 Metal-cutting machine tools	13.0	21.8	24.3	18.5
140 Food industry equipment	53.5	29.5	5.1	12.3
144 Light industry equipment	19.1	14.7	17.0	18.9
150 Chemical industry equipment	78.6	111.2	102.2	99.1
151 Woodworking, pulp, and paper industry equipment	56.5	62.2	54.9	12.5
192 Ships and ship equipment	29.4	57.0	192.7	88.1
... Other machinery and equipment[b]	164.8	115.8	103.2	118.9

[a] Numbers represent classification in Soviet foreign trade commodity code.
[b] Difference between itemized total and total hard-currency imports of machinery and equipment, Table 9.

To this extent, unfortunately unknown to us, our data understate the actual hard-currency savings realized by the U.S.S.R. through import restrictions during the years under review.

b. A substantial part of machinery and equipment imports consists of items subject to long production lead times after the placing of purchase orders. This, obviously, imposes some rigidity on imports of this kind in a generally restrictionist import policy phase: Short of reneging on contracts, items on order will have to be accepted and, unless credit-financed, paid for.

The fact that Soviet machinery and equipment imports rose to a peak in 1964 and then dropped sharply in 1965 suggests that this time-lag was operative in our case; the decline in 1965, conversely, probably represents the delayed effect of Soviet decisions to curtail purchases made, perhaps, in 1963.

We have not studied in detail the changes in imports within the machinery and equipment group. However, a partial breakdown by major component categories, computed from country-by-commodity data and presented in Table 11, indicates that both the import expansion in 1962–1964 and the decline in 1965 were very largely accounted for by a distinctly long-lead-time item, namely, ships.

Imports of ships from hard-currency countries in 1964 exceeded those in 1962 by 163 million rubles, compared with an increase in total machinery and equipment imports from these countries by 85 million rubles. In 1965, imports of ships declined by 105 million rubles, while the total decline was 131 million rubles.

Since, presumably, one objective of the rapid expansion of the Soviet merchant fleet, of which the ship imports are a reflection, is to reduce hard-currency outlays for shipping services, it appears that the Soviet authorities decided to subordinate this long-run goal to the exigencies of their present balance-of-payments situation. That foreign exchange savings rather than other reasons were the motive for the heavy cutback in ship imports is suggested by the fact that Soviet imports of ships from Communist European countries increased steadily in 1962–1965, from 195 to 262 million rubles.

The sharp reduction in *iron and steel* imports in 1963–1964 cannot be entirely attributed to restrictive Soviet policy. A fairly large proportion of it is traceable to the effects of the embargo imposed by NATO in November 1962 on the export of large-diameter pipe to the U.S.S.R. The impact of this measure may not be fully reflected in Soviet statistics, as they identify only two NATO countries, Germany and Italy, as having engaged in this trade. However, they make it clear that these countries were the principal NATO suppliers. For 1962, Soviet statistics put total imports of large-diameter pipe at 88 million rubles, of which 60 million rubles were from Germany and Italy. Another 25 million rubles were accounted for by Czechoslovakia, East Germany, and Poland. The following figures indicate approximately the effect of the NATO embargo on Soviet hard-currency iron and steel imports (in millions of rubles):

	1960	1961	1962	1963	1964	1965
Total HC iron and steel imports	227.2	173.8	218.0	126.7	57.6	95.0
Large-diameter pipe imports from Germany and Italy	33.5	22.9	60.2	9.2	....	....
Sweden [a]	(5.1)	(2.8)	(2.7)	9.5	8.5	7.2
Other iron and steel imports	193.7	150.9	157.8	108.0	49.1	87.8

[a] The figures in parentheses are total imports of pipe; we have assumed they were not of large-diameter pipe, for which no figures are given for 1960–1962.

It will be seen that most of the increase in total iron and steel imports in 1962 was accounted for by large-diameter pipe, 37 out of 44 million rubles. The latter also accounted for 51 million rubles of a 91 million ruble decline in total iron and steel imports in 1963. No imports of large-diameter pipe from Germany and Italy are reported for 1964 and 1965, but Sweden evidently stepped into the trade. Considering that the total decline in hard-currency nonfood imports in 1963 amounted to 119 million rubles, the contribution of the pipe embargo to the initial reduction of such exports was clearly quite substantial.

However, we also find that Soviet imports of other iron and steel declined sharply in 1963–1964, presumably because of restrictions imposed on balance-of-payments grounds. However irksome the NATO embargo may have been to pipeline builders in the U.S.S.R., its balance-of-payments planners may have regarded it as a useful windfall.

The striking decline in *rubber and copper* imports in 1963–1964 was undoubtedly another Soviet response to the mounting hard-currency deficit. It affected not only the copper imports from CDC shown in Table 9, but also accounted for the drop in imports of nonferrous metals from the hard-currency area (in millions of rubles):

	1962	1963	1964	1965
Nonferrous metal imports from HC area:	48.1	46.7	9.7	11.1
Of which, copper	40.9	34.5	3.7	...
Other metals	7.2	12.2	6.0	11.1

In the case of both rubber and copper, the Soviet hard-currency savings achieved by import restrictions were probably cut into by continued Soviet exports to Communist countries, as shown in Table 12, presumably because of firm obligations under trade agreements with these countries.[8] In the case of rubber, these encroachments were relatively small, less than Soviet rubber imports from what we take to be soft-currency sources. Copper exports, however, were close to imports in 1962–1963, and in 1964–1965 the U.S.S.R. was in the unusual position of being a net exporter of copper, to the tune of some 50 million rubles a year.

Admittedly, our surmise that these exports reduced Soviet hard-currency savings is speculative: the possibility that the recipients paid for them in convertible exchange cannot be ruled out, and it is also possible that the deliveries to Communist countries were intended for incorporation into products to be exported to the U.S.S.R.

In the absence of Soviet statistics on domestic production and consumption of both copper and synthetic rubber, it is also impossible to rule out the possibility that the U.S.S.R. approached, and in the case of copper

[8] As indicated in Table 12, there were also small copper exports to unspecified other countries. The reported total exports, except in 1963, exceed the total of exports itemized by country in Soviet statistics.

achieved, self-sufficiency during this period. However, the abruptness of
the import reductions, their coincidence with many other symptoms of
balance-of-payments stress, and the revival of crude rubber imports in
1965 make this most unlikely.

In fact, it seems much more likely that the U.S.S.R. drew on stockpiles of
these commodities to achieve the large hard-currency savings realized on
their account. In the case of copper it had an added incentive for doing so

TABLE 12

SOVIET IMPORTS AND EXPORTS OF RUBBER AND COPPER, 1962–1965
(Million rubles)

Item	1962	1963	1964	1965
Rubber				
Imports from HC sources	150.0	122.1	56.8	95.7
Other imports	35.3	24.8	26.7	27.7
Total imports	185.3	146.9	83.5	123.4
Exports to Communist countries	12.8	8.8	10.8	10.7
Copper [a]				
Imports from HC area	40.9	34.5	3.7	....
Other HC imports	18.4	14.4	2.4	....
Total HC imports	59.3	48.9	6.1	....
Exports to Communist countries	40.4	40.9	44.5	53.3
Total exports	41.0	40.9	51.2	54.2

[a] Copper imports (from Western Europe and other countries, defined in the text as
hard-currency area) listed here as "Imports from HC area" were included as "Nonferrous metals" in Table 9.

because of the sharp rise of world market copper prices in 1963–1965. This,
however, was not true for rubber, where Soviet import prices (judged by
unit values of imports from Malaya) were fairly stable during this period.

Few useful observations can be offered without further research on the
reasons that induced the Soviet authorities to maintain or increase certain
categories of imports during this period of general retrenchment. We have
seen above (Table 9 and text) that they did one or the other in the case of
chemicals, pulp and paper, and (after an initial cutback in 1963) unspecified
commodities, for a total increase by 106 million rubles by 1965 over 1962.
Nearly two-thirds of this was accounted for by chemicals, probably mainly
destined for Soviet heavy industry. However, imports of textile fibers (mainly
wool and synthetic fiber) increased moderately, from a fairly high starting
point in 1962. This and, more important, the fact that producer durables

and materials used mainly for producer goods bore the brunt of import restrictions, suggests that the Soviet authorities did not attempt to shift the burden of the hard-currency deficit to the consumer. This is not a surprising finding, for two reasons. First, the share of consumer goods and consumer-oriented materials in hard-currency imports was so small that it could not have yielded significant foreign exchange savings. Second, the whole balance-of-payments gap of 1963–1965 would not have opened if the Soviet author-ities had been disposed to balance the grain deficit by consumer austerity instead of imports.

On the other hand, our limited attempt to study the incidence of changes within the machinery and equipment group suggests that traditional Soviet industrial priorities may have been at work in shaping import policy. Al-though the heaviest cutback in 1965 fell on ships, food industry equipment became an early casualty, light industry equipment imports remained at a low level, and group 151 — mainly cellulose and papermaking equipment — was sharply cut back in 1965. By contrast, imports of chemical industry equipment remained well above the 1962 level, and those of machine tools increased.

CONCLUSION

The main general conclusion emerging from our study seems to be that Soviet responses to their balance-of-payments problem were speedy, vigor-ous, and comprehensive. Assuming that the decision to import grain was made about mid-1963, the scope of reactions, mainly of the restrictive kind, recorded in the trade statistics even for that year is impressive. By 1964, a full-scale redeployment of trade to deal with the new situation — and to contain the gold drain — must have been in full swing. As we have seen, the counter-measures were by no means confined to hard-currency trade. Food trade with Communist countries was profoundly affected, both by restricting Soviet exports and generating additional imports. Even the limited opportunities for doing likewise in trade with non-Communist underdeveloped countries were not neglected.

In its hard-currency trade, in spite of a marked deterioration of its trade balance in food even with Western Europe, the U.S.S.R. carried out a highly successful maneuver in 1962–1965 to produce substantial net earn-ings with Europe and Japan, to be applied to its deficits with the overseas grain suppliers. In our survey of nonfood trade we found that more than half of the improvement in the Soviet trade balance was achieved by export expansion. This is an interesting finding, in the light of the old saying that when your balance of payments is limping, it is always easier to shorten the long import leg than vice versa. Undoubtedly, the very healthy economic con-dition of the Soviet Union's capitalist trade partners greatly assisted their export drive. We have also noted that, especially in 1965, export expansion included some rather unusual sales — of platinum, silver, and diamonds — whose status as current-account transactions is dubious.

However, we also found that the U.S.S.R. did not stop short of drastic import restrictions, and that possibly — in the case of machinery and equipment — it was initially compelled by contractual obligations to maintain imports at a higher level than it might have preferred.

Rubber and copper were conspicuous among the restricted imports. Here again — and in conjunction with the fact that exports of these commodities to Communist countries were maintained — we mentioned the possibility of the drawing down of Soviet stockpiles.

This raises the broader question of whether the U.S.S.R. may not rather widely and systematically rely on management of reserves other than gold and foreign exchange in balancing its external accounts. In a sense, the progressive depletion of Soviet grain reserves prior to 1963 was a measure that kept the balance-of-payments problem latent until then. When it became acute, Soviet authorities very possibly drew on other commodity stockpiles to ease the gold outflow and help maintain other imports.

Needless to say, the concept of commodity inventories performing an international equilibrating function is not new in Western balance-of-payments theory. Thus, Professor Haberler considers "accumulation and decumulation of inventories of internationally traded commodities" as a possible "subtle" form of "accommodating transactions," without endorsing the notion. He adds: "Some writers, perhaps like Sir Roy Harrod, regard them [i.e., inventories] as part of a country's international reserve, a close substitute for gold movements and short-term capital flows" [1, p. 16].

However, the equilibrating function of commodity inventory changes in a market economy probably could only be exercised in what Soviet writers would call an "elemental" fashion (*stikhi'no*). In a centrally directed economy, equipped with a monopoly of foreign trade and a highly institutionalized and long-established system of "state reserves," there should be much greater opportunities for systematic and deliberate management of commodity reserves in an equilibrating role.

At least a hint that this is the case in the U.S.S.R. was provided by what Mr. V. F. Garbuzov, Soviet Minister of Finance, said to the March 1965 plenary session of the Central Committee: "In order to support the economic development of the country we have been compelled to resort to the utilization of previously accumulated material and foreign exchange (*valiutnykh*) reserves . . ." [3, p. 127].

Garbuzov's language is somewhat obscure, but the mention of *valuta* (which would include gold) and "material" reserves in one breath is intriguing, and one may speculate that the "material" reserves he had in mind were not confined to grain.

To conclude, our findings indicate that the opportunities available to Moscow planners for handling balance-of-payments crises by manipulating foreign trade are great enough to arouse the envy of their counterparts in Western capitals besieged by similar problems. But the Western planners may console themselves by the thought that they can fall back on various cooperative cushions of international liquidity, whereas Moscow remains, in this respect, out in the cold.

DISCUSSION

Aurelius Morgner

Dr. Hoeffding's paper is very illuminating in its explanation of how a centrally planned economy such as the U.S.S.R. meets a balance-of-payments problem. Western economies use up monetary reserves, meanwhile resorting to corrective measures such as the adjustment of relative wage-price structure, income levels, and interest rates. Dissatisfied by the process of adjustment such steps are likely to involve, they may jump to devaluation, or more likely to exchange control. Centrally planned economies, on the other hand, manipulate their merchandise trade directly.

That the U.S.S.R. should not attempt to summarize in some form its economic relations with the rest of the world seems amazing. Even less-developed countries these days devise foreign exchange budgets as part of the planning process *ex ante*, and provide the International Monetary Fund with balance-of-payments statements *ex post* for publication. Doubtless, somewhere in the Soviet planning mechanism likely foreign exchange earnings and needs are estimated, and policies for commodity trade are formulated, in attempts to fill the gap. In less-developed countries, foreign exchange budgets are usually not divulged except to international agencies and foreign governments from whom balance-of-payments aid may be sought. The Soviet Union, of course, has no one to convince of its exchange needs nor any obligation to supply any information *ex post* to the International Monetary Fund, since it is not a member.

Dr. Hoeffding, therefore, is to be congratulated for organizing Soviet trade statistics in such a form as to show how the Soviet Union was able to generate surpluses (or cut deficits) with its major hard-currency trade partners (Western Europe and Japan) in order to pay the Americas and Australia for expanded wheat imports, which were a "dominant element" in the sharp deterioration in Soviet hard-currency balance of trade in the 1963–1965 period. It would be interesting to know if the Soviets have bothered to analyze their own trade statistics *ex post* in the fashion that Hoeffding has done. How ironic, if Hoeffding's account should actually furnish Soviet economists with an explanation of how the U.S.S.R., in fact, met its balance-of-payments problems in the 1963–1965 grain crisis period!

It is to be hoped that Hoeffding will continue these analyses of Russian trade statistics and try to devise at least some skeleton outlines of a Balance-of-Payments Statement for the U.S.S.R. Certainly, some information must be available somewhere relative to the amount and nature of Soviet credits, on the basis of which something could be done with the capital accounts section, which can hardly be treated as nonexistent.

For the Soviet Union must make some marginal adjustments through changes in its foreign exchange holdings. While, as pointed out by Hoeffding, alterations in the size of stocks of commodities should not be overlooked as part of an adjustment mechanism, Soviet planning is generally supposed to operate under marked tautness with respect to inventories, in contrast with the capitalist West. That the Soviet Union should maintain such large stocks of copper and rubber in the face of general inventory scarceness suggests that these two items are stockpiled for military reasons. The United States, too, has used the release of part of its metal stockpiles to alleviate balance-of-payments problems, although this was incidental to international metal price control problems. The concept of accumulation and decumulation of inventories of internationally traded commodities as a means of adjusting reserves may be as significant for the United States, with its large military stockpiles of metals and large holdings of agricultural commodity surpluses, as for the Soviet Union.

What is most interesting about the U.S.S.R. balance-of-payments experience in 1963–1965 is that the Soviet Union should have been willing to make such relatively substantial adjustments in its foreign trade in order to furnish the Soviet economy with possibly 500 to 800 million rubles more food imports than food exports to offset the decline in domestic food production. The amount, expressed in per capita terms, is not great — two or three dollars per year per person, concentrated in one commodity, bread.

In past periods it has been charged that, even in the face of famines, the Soviet Union maintained food exports to pay for equipment imports. That the Soviet Union in the present era should substantially alter the composition of its trade, run down gold holdings and materials stockpiles, so that consumers would not be inconvenienced, shows a remarkable solicitude for the consumer. Perhaps the planners were so attached to their own figures for "planned" wheat consumption, based upon the past, that they felt impelled to maintain these figures for the economy by filling the gap through imports, at the expense of sizable concentrated trade adjustments. Could not the economy of the U.S.S.R. possibly have been sustained with less wheat consumption and a major adjustment of food consumption patterns, combined with what would appear to be, at most, a modest reduction of a few percentage points in the level of food consumption?

In an economy guided wholly by competitive markets, altered conditions in one market will affect other markets through an elaborate system of trade-offs, and the effect of the change, while extensive, will be moderate. At the other extreme, one can envision a centrally planned economy where adjustments for any deficit in the plan may be concentrated on a few items, in the belief that this will minimize disturbances to the plan.

Were the U.S.S.R. a competitive market economy employing a flexible exchange rate, the response to the wheat shortage would have been a rise in the domestic price of wheat, reduced consumption of wheat, and increased output and consumption of rice, potatoes, and other quickly grown foods. Also, increased import of wheat and the other staples would have caused a depreciation of the exchange rate, dampening all imports and expanding exports. While much change would have occurred, the adjustments would presumably have been small in comparison with the major adjustments in trade made by the planners.

Hoeffding speaks of Moscow planners — probably facetiously — as having powers in balance-of-payment crises "great enough to arouse the envy of their counterparts in Western capitals besieged by similar problems." But in Western capitals emergency tariffs, quota restrictions, and finally exchange controls permit some of the trade-off capability that is so important to diffuse the impact of restriction and to minimize its costs. Western planners merely try to balance trade in conditions that do not permit its automatic balancing; it is not their function to determine the actual composition of trade. They have no cause to envy their Moscow colleagues unless they are also willing to assume the burdens of central planning.

REFERENCES

1. Haberler, Gottfried. *Money in the International Economy* (Cambridge: Harvard University Press, 1965).
2. Kadyshev, V. P. *SSSR na vneshnikh rynkakh* (Moscow: 1964).
3. *Plenum Tsentral'nogo Komiteta Kommunisticheskoi Partii Sovetskogo Soiuza 24–26 marta 1965 g. Stenograficheskii otchet* (Moscow: 1965).
4. *Sbornik torgovykh dogovorov i soglashenii SSSR s inostrannymi gosudarstvami* (Moscow: 1961).
5. U.S. Bureau of Mines. *Minerals Yearbook 1964* (Washington, D.C.: 1965), Vol. I.
6. *Vneshniaia torgovlia Sovetskogo Soiuza za 1960–1965 gg. (Statisticheskie dannye ob ob'eme vneshnei torgovli SSSR, eksporte i importe vazhneishikh tovarov)*, supplement to *Vneshniaia torgovlia*, No. 8 (1966).
7. *Vneshniaia torgovlia SSSR za 1965 god* (Moscow: 1965).
8. *Vneshniaia torgovlia SSSR za 1959–1963 gody* (Moscow: 1965).
9. *Vneshniaia torgovlia*, No. 11 (1965).
10. Volin, L., and H. Walters. "Soviet Grain Imports," *Foreign Agriculture Economics*, U.S. Department of Agriculture (Washington, D.C.: September 1965).

Foreign Trade of the U.S.S.R.:
A Summary Appraisal

GREGORY GROSSMAN

One could not very well say that either Soviet foreign trade or the Soviet economic system (including the system of central planning, of course) has been neglected by Western observers over the decades during which both have been in existence. It is therefore the more remarkable that so little attention has been paid to the mutual relations and mutual impact of the two, either in the West or — for that matter — among Soviet economists as well. And insofar as the problem has received attention in the Western literature, it is the state operation of Soviet foreign trade that has enjoyed predominant attention. Thus, at various times, Western writers have preoccupied themselves with such questions as the possibility and proclivity of state-operated trade to engage in dumping, to be used as an instrument of the government's foreign policy, to disrupt world markets and to be conducted with varying degrees of disregard of profitability in the usual sense. Much less attention has been paid to the impact of foreign trade on the organizational structure of the Soviet economy or on the methods and conduct of planning, and vice versa.

True, this observation pertains primarily to the U.S.S.R. itself, not to the other countries that espoused the Soviet economic system after World War II. With the conspicuous exception of China, these countries have been — and, particularly as a result of forced-draft industrialization under Communist regimes, have become — so very much more dependent on foreign trade than the Soviet Union that the question of the connection between their foreign trade (including their difficulties in earning foreign exchange) and their domestic economic institutions has perforce attracted a good deal of attention both in the West and in the East European countries themselves. Much of the discussion of the proposed and, to date, partly realized economic reforms in the East European countries has indeed revolved around the problem that is the theme of the present Conference. And to a significant extent *all* of the recent economic reforms or proposed reforms in Eastern Europe — though not in the Soviet Union — have as a main purpose making the given socialist economy more effective as an earner of foreign exchange and as a gainer from the international division of labor. Thus, the present Conference at once serves to correct a long-standing neglect in our comprehension of the working of the Soviet-type economic system and to investigate a problem of the highest topical interest in most Communist countries.

My own comments are, however, confined almost entirely to the Soviet economy, being inspired specifically by the two interesting papers of Professors Holzman and Levine. These two papers look at the relationship between international trade and central planning from, so to say, opposite standpoints. Professor Levine asks, what effects has foreign trade had on the practice of Soviet Planning? *Per contra*, Professor Holzman investigates the effect of the Soviet institutional setup in general, and of Soviet planning in particular, on the conduct of Soviet foreign trade, with special reference to the mechanism of adjustment in international accounts. Although their probings are careful and deep, both authors, interestingly, find relatively little to report — in part, because of serious lacunae in our knowledge of the relevant facts, but in part also (I daresay) because little *systematic* information may remain to be discovered on these two subjects.

Let me address myself to Professor Levine's paper first. If I understand the author correctly, his conclusion is that foreign trade has left hardly a mark on the institutional structure of the Soviet economy and on its planning practice (with the obvious exception of that sector of the economy which is directly engaged in the conduct or planning of foreign economic relations). I agree. This is not to say that foreign trade and other facets of international economic relations have been unimportant in Soviet history. Though small in relation to gross national product and other aggregate measures, foreign economic relations have been of great significance to Soviet industrialization, to the military and space efforts, and (since the mid-'fifties) to consumer morale.[1] Nevertheless, it is difficult to point to any aspect of the institutional

---

[1] Among other things, foreign economic relations perform the important function of raising technological standards in the Soviet economy (1) by channeling technologically advanced articles and technological information into the country, and (2) by forcing the Soviets to compete with technologically sophisticated producers in foreign markets. Moreover, foreign economic relations may also add force to certain domestic decisions regarding long-term use of resources. For instance, the recent agreement with Fiat to build a large automobile plant in the U.S.S.R., and similar agreements with other Western concerns, lend the force of international commitment to the decision to "motorize" the country, thereby to some degree binding future Soviet governments that may have different preferences.

setup which can be said to have been significantly shaped by the influence of foreign economic relations. Or, to put it otherwise, it is difficult to point to any Soviet institution that, most probably, would now be significantly different in the event that Soviet foreign trade had been only a small fraction of what it actually was during the past four decades.

A major qualification to this blanket assertion comes to mind. (It is entirely conjectural, and shall be mentioned below.) Otherwise, the exceptions are all very minor and as such tend to "prove the rule." For example, although great pressure is put on enterprises to fill export orders, I know of only one case where an enterprise's success indicator is expressed in foreign trade rubles. This is in maritime transport, where — since 1960 — a ship's plan is measured in terms of revenue in foreign trade rubles, and premiums to personnel afloat are based on this indicator (as well as some others).[2] The rationale is clear. The U.S.S.R. has been extensively chartering foreign vessels to carry its maritime traffic; a consequence of greater activity by its own fleet is to reduce the need to charter foreign vessels. Hence, foreign exchange is a logical unit of measure of the performance of Soviet ships. But surely there must be other places where better performance by a Soviet enterprise could have a clear and favorable effect on the balance of payments. Why, then, are there no other cases — known to me, at least — of an enterprise's success indicator being expressed in foreign trade rubles? (I believe, many cases could be found in the East European countries — a possibility notable not only for itself but also because it is undoubtedly known to Soviet authorities.) Is it because, in regulating maritime transport, the relevant ministry may be concerned both with economizing on foreign exchange allotted to it for chartering foreign vessels and with setting success indicators for individual enterprises (ships) — hence, may be administratively in a position to act rationally, to attune the success indicator to the need for *valuta*? In all, or nearly all, other cases the two functions are administratively separate. Thus, although petroleum and its products are major foreign exchange earners, the oil extracting and refining enterprises are not (to our knowledge) instructed to value these commodities at the prices in foreign markets for the purpose of measuring plan fulfillment and rewarding personnel. The relevant ministry probably derives no direct benefit from greater export of petroleum and petroleum products — the direct benefits are appropriated by the administratively distinct foreign trading enterprises — and therefore may have no interest in shaping success indicators accordingly.

Surely, if foreign trade played a quantitatively greater role in the Soviet economy, its influence on economic institutions and planning procedures would be more observable, and even such administrative impediments as have been suggested would not always stand in the way. The experience of

---

[2] See [1, pp. 699 ff.].

the East European countries indicates it. But in addition to the (small) quantitative importance of foreign trade in the Soviet economy, its geographical distribution and commodity structure may also be relevant here. In the post-war era some 70 percent of Soviet trade has been with other Communist countries, most of it conducted on the basis of trade agreements and with countries that are in no position to be choosy about specifications and quality. Thus, the need to reform domestic institutions and planning procedures in order to cater to these markets has not been very pressing. On the other hand, Soviet exports to the non-Communist world are largely composed of staple raw materials and semi-manufactures. Here, too, the dictates of the foreign market place relatively little pressure on the domestic economic system. (Of course, one could say that the composition of Soviet exports to the non-Communist world is what it is because of rigidities of the domestic economic system.) It may be, therefore, that Soviet institutions and planning procedures suffer their severest test when the U.S.S.R. exports fairly sophisticated equipment to the non-Communist underdeveloped countries. Such successes as the construction of the Bhilai steel mill in India may well have been a *tour de force*, one that might not have been possible if such cases were more numerous.

I now return to the major qualification mentioned earlier. The imperatives of foreign trade may not have had a significant influence on the Soviet economic system, as Levine argues (and I concur), *after* the system was established. But might not the prospective need to earn large amounts of foreign exchange in the course of rapid industrialization have shaped the system importantly *at the time* of its formation? Let us assume for a moment that, in 1929, there was no reason to plan for very large grain exports to earn the foreign exchange requirements dictated by the First Five-Year Plan. (Let us imagine that gold production could have been increased relatively cheaply and in sufficient amounts to cover all foreseeable foreign exchange needs.) To be sure, the anticipated rise in the urban population and the planned-for improvement in its diet would still have called for rapidly growing government procurements of grain, a difficult task in view of the "marketing crisis" of the later 'twenties. But would Stalin have ordered a collectivization drive of the same extent and severity, and persisted with it in the face of catastrophic consequences, had he not also intended to immediately begin large exports of grain? (Such exports rose from a mere 260 thousand metric tons in 1929, to 4,841 thousand tons in 1930, and to 5,178 thousand tons in 1931, then declined to 1,808 thousand tons in 1932 and 1,760 thousand tons in 1933. But Stalin may well have been aiming at something like the 10 million tons that had been exported annually by Russia just before World War I.) Needless to say, Soviet history would have been quite different with a different collectivization experience, and perhaps even Soviet planning procedures and the institutional structure outside agriculture would not have been quite the same either. But as with all grand conjectures, the details are better left to the reader's imagination.

As already noted, the Soviet economic reform of 1965, unlike the concurrent economic reforms in the East European countries, does not seem to have been in any large measure motivated by foreign trade considerations. Yet I would agree with Levine in his cautious view (in the last section of the paper) that the notions of rationality which are beginning to emerge in the U.S.S.R. with regard to the foreign trade sector (quite a few years after they emerged in Eastern Europe) may extend into the rest of the economy. (One reason that, in the experience of Communist countries except the U.S.S.R., notions of rationality tend to emerge relatively early in the foreign trade sector is that this sector is blessed with a rather simple, almost unidimensional objective, the earning of foreign exchange. It is easy to incorporate this objective into formal optimizing rules. The objective for the rest of the economy is much harder to define, as the surfeit of Soviet literature on and around this subject since 1956 amply shows.) Yet there is the simultaneous danger that shortage of foreign exchange will also cause the retention of certain central controls, thus seriously holding back the impetus toward decentralization brought about by the reformist measures. Witness what Professor Neuberger says in his paper in the present volume regarding Yugoslavia: "In the Yugoslav case, the foreign exchange system appears to have become one of the last bastions of strength for those elements who oppose decentralization."

Turning now to Professor Holzman's interesting paper, I feel that its value lies largely in demonstrating the limits — in this case, the very severe limits — to the application of conventional "Western" analytical apparatus to conditions where the basic assumptions of that apparatus are not fully satisfied. True, the Soviets *must* do something to "adjust" to balance-of-payments imperatives; they cannot spend more foreign exchange than they get. There are also propensities and elasticities in the Soviet economy with respect to foreign trade, though these are occasioned by planners' policies and routines as well as by the more familiar behavioral reactions of consumers and producers. What there may not be is an "adjustment mechanism" in the cybernetic sense — i.e., in the sense of a more or less automatic tendency to equilibrium (or equilibria) brought about by predictable reactions of economic agents to certain signals and a reciprocal feedback effect on these signals. To put it differently, the Western analytical apparatus presupposes a market economy; this presupposition is lacking in the Soviet economy.

Holzman's notion of an implicit flexible exchange rate in the Soviet case is an intriguing one, and may be helpful in visualizing the adjustment process. I am not sure, however, that it contributes much to an understanding of the way the Soviet balance of payments is "balanced." The fact remains that this balancing is performed administratively, by rationing out such amounts of foreign exchange as are available and by invoking other administrative means to possibly augment the supply of foreign exchange.

It does not necessarily follow that the Soviet foreign exchange rationing authorities go about their business entirely arbitrarily. No doubt they follow certain principles in allocating the scarce supply of *valuta* to competing claimants and in trying to enhance foreign exchange. For instance, they no doubt refer to a certain fairly definite hierarchy of priorities. And it may be that those who stand much closer to this process than do Western observers could even predict the planners' response in a given conjuncture of foreign exchange demand and supply. Moreover, one can discover the nature of their reactions subsequently in the form of actual exports, imports, and credit transactions. Dr. Hoeffding's paper in the present volume attempts to do just this in the wake of the extraordinary purchases of grain in 1963–1964. Yet, can one properly speak of an "adjustment mechanism"? But since I agree entirely with Professor Berliner's extensive comments on this point, there is no need to dwell on this point further, save for one relatively minor aspect to which I now turn.

Holzman makes the generally valid point that there should be no income effects (domestically), as the Soviets make up for a shortfall in some exports by substituting other exports. He also adds the valid qualification that if the new exports are drawn from a pre-existing gold stock, then there would be a negative income effect, no income being created domestically in the given period. (Indeed, this would be true if the new exports came from *any* pre-existing inventory.) Another consideration might be mentioned here, one that is prompted by the well-known divorce between the Soviet domestic price structure and the world price structure. That is, the domestic income generated by a million dollars' worth (at world prices) of one domestically produced commodity may be quite different from that generated by a million dollars' worth of another. Thus, a million dollars' worth of exported coal generates much more household income in the Soviet economy than does a million dollars' worth of exported crude oil, the former being relatively expensive to mine and the latter relatively cheap to extract. Thus, substitution of new exports for a shortfall in other exports may in fact have significant income effects at home. (This is, of course, not a uniquely Soviet phenomenon but holds true wherever there is an important divorce between domestic and world prices — and, one might add, wherever the share of "government" within the price (e.g., indirect taxes, state-collected profits or rents) varies considerably among commodities. For instance, it would be true for exports of price-supported agricultural products from the United States, ignoring exports from the pre-existing inventory.)

A word, finally, on an old conundrum: Why do Communist countries trade among themselves at (more or less) world prices? Holzman gives first a number of reasons for the irrationality of internal prices and exchange rates; then he points out that world prices, after all, represent the real alternatives for any Communist country's trade. It seems to me that this reason alone is quite sufficient to explain the phenomenon (assuming, of course, that each Communist country tries to obtain the best prices for its exports and pay the least for its imports). World prices are, so to say, parametric from the standpoint of any Communist country, since, as a rule, it can do little or nothing to affect them. The principle of foreign exchange maximization therefore requires that the Communist countries trade at world market prices among themselves as well, quite regardless of the degree of rationality of internal price structures and exchange rates. In other words, granted the maximization postulate, it is the deviations from world market prices in Communist intra-bloc trade that have to be explained, not the trading at such prices.

REFERENCE

1. Popov-Cherkasov, I. N. (ed.), *Organizatsiia platy rabochikh SSSR; sbornik normativnykh aktov* (Moscow: 1965).

Conclusion
and Future Prospects

Central Planning and Its Legacies: Implications for Foreign Trade*

EGON NEUBERGER

In the voluminous literature on the relative merits of the Soviet-type system of central planning,[1] one key aspect has been relatively neglected — the legacies this system bequeathes to the system or systems that follow it. Marx, Schumpeter, and others have discussed the transition problem from capitalism to socialism and the legacies that socialism inherits from capitalism. I suggest that now is the time to begin a similar discussion of the transition from Soviet-type socialism to a new system, and of the desirable and undesirable legacies that this system will inherit. This paper is an exploratory attempt to initiate a discussion of the "legacy problem," with special attention to its implications for foreign trade.[2]

* I wish to thank the American Philosophical Society for making it possible for me to visit Yugoslavia; this paper would not have been written without that visit. I am grateful to the many Yugoslav colleagues who informed, encouraged, and argued with me. Comments by participants in a RAND seminar forced me to recast and expand the paper; I wish to thank particularly Abraham Becker, Edmund Dews, Evsey Domar, Oleg Hoeffding, Nancy Nimitz, and George Rosen. Professor Alan Brown, who has discussed the paper with me at every stage and has offered valuable criticism, deserves special thanks.

[1] The following studies provide a good survey of writings on this topic. They have been extremely helpful to me in defining key elements of the Soviet-type system of central planning and their consequences: [2, pp. 355–403], [6], [11], [17, pp. 38–44], [28, pp. 57–80], [35, pp. 29–38], [40, pp. 38–44], and [49].

To provide the reader of this volume with a short description of the Soviet-type system of central planning (CPE), including its advantages and disadvantages during its own lifetime, Professor Alan Brown and myself have prepared the Appendix, "Basic Features of a Centrally Planned Economy." This appendix lays the groundwork for the discussion in this paper of the legacies of CPEs and provides a useful introduction to all the papers in this volume.

[2] A more comprehensive discussion of the legacy problem may be found in [31]. The present paper represents a revised and considerably condensed version of the referenced paper.

A study of the possible legacies of a system of central planning of the Soviet type (CPE) may serve three functions: (1) to explore the possible problems of transition that the U.S.S.R. and the countries of Eastern Europe currently face in groping for a new system to replace the model built by Stalin in his heyday and imitated in Eastern Europe, (2) to assist leaders in underdeveloped countries searching for ways to develop their economies, in order to gain a more complete picture of the possible gains and losses from selection of either the full Soviet-type model of economic development or some of its key elements, and possibly (3) to provide insights for students of centralized bureaucratic systems in general.

My belief that the time has come to study the legacy problem in connection with Soviet-type systems rests on empirical observation and not on a strict stage theory of economic history. Until recently, it appeared that the Soviet-type system, or one very similar to it, could remain in effect indefinitely, with Yugoslavia the only country to declare it obsolete. Students of CPEs have dealt primarily with the Soviet economy, and despite Khrushchev's bluster and tinkering, his heirs inherited an economic system that did not differ in essentials from the one Khrushchev himself inherited. However, beginning with 1965, even the Soviet Union began following the lead of the smaller Eastern European countries and initiated a policy of economic reform which is thought by some observers to represent a Trojan horse that will lead to more radical transformations. Thus, while it was quite natural to ignore the legacy problem in the past, the logic of recent developments makes it highly desirable to make a start at filling this gap.

Yugoslavia was one of the first countries to follow the Soviet Union in adopting the Soviet-type model in 1947, and was also the first country to abandon it. Only five years later, in 1952, it began moving toward a system of market socialism based on worker management. Fifteen years later, in 1967, Yugoslavia has moved very far from its original system of economic management, but the transition has been relatively slow, difficult, and painful — and even now Yugoslavia is still struggling with some of the legacies of the Stalinist system. It is significant that, despite its relatively short reign, this system was able to sink its roots deeply enough into minds and institutions to leave behind important legacies.[3]

[3] On the other hand, the short duration of the system in Yugoslavia did not permit Yugoslav leaders to modify the system during its lifetime to eliminate some of the more deleterious aspects of Stalinism. Since virtually all of the present-day CPEs are engaging in such modifications, this will make some aspects of the legacy problem somewhat less serious. In addition, some specific features of the Yugoslav situation force us to be careful in simply applying the Yugoslav case to forecasting the nature and significance of the legacy problem in the CPEs. The leaders of CPEs, as well as their economic consultants, are studying the Yugoslav experience very carefully and have the opportunity to learn from Yugoslav achievements and mistakes. The existence of very great regional differences in economic development and the connection of this with

The present Yugoslav system is, of course, not the only possible alternative to the CPE. As I have argued in a previous paper [33], two basic reform alternatives are open to a Communist country: (1) a strengthening and improvement of the central planning mechanism by using the new tools of information technology, the cybernetic solution, and (2) adoption of a system in which the central authorities exercise control over the economic development strategy, but use a relatively decentralized market system to implement this strategy — the "visible hand." I would argue that the probable Yugoslav system of the future will be one of a visible-hand type, with the important specific feature that workers will take over the role of stockholders in the enterprises.[4]

For the purposes of this paper, I shall not deal with the first reform alternative; this decision is based on a lack of empirical data and on my judgment that an extreme cybernetic solution, not based on decentralization and the use of markets, is not possible in the near future. If I should be proved wrong, then a companionpiece dealing with this problem would be very fruitful.

KEY ELEMENTS OF A CPE

Although there is no accepted list of key elements of the Soviet-type system, let me suggest the following:

1. Social ownership of the means of production — *"social ownership."*

2. A high-pressure economy with a high rate of forced saving at the macro-level and with taut planning of outputs, inputs, and inventories at the micro-level — *"pressure economy."*

3. A centralized, bureaucratic management of the economy, with detailed physical planning and supply — *"command economy."*

4. Planning based on priorities, with complete dominance of political, ideological, and social criteria of economic policy over economic criteria. For example, primacy of industry over agriculture, producers' goods over consumers' goods, material goods over services (except for high priority of education, especially technical education of the labor force) — *"priority economy."*

5. Output-oriented planning, with stress on ever-increasing quantities of output, achieved with massive infusions of inputs of labor and capital — *"extensive development."* [5]

the nationality problem in Yugoslavia, as well as the bold experiment with worker self-management, have certainly affected the Yugoslav experience and must be taken into account in applying this experience to the CPEs.

[4] This does not exhaust the possibilities by any means. For the most complete treatment of the alternatives, see [49, Chaps. 1 and 4].

[5] This term has gained wide acceptance in Eastern Europe as a shorthand description of the policies followed under the Stalinist system; I am adapting it to describe the specific feature described above. See [14].

6. Primacy of domestic economic considerations over foreign trade, for-eign trade plans being merely addenda to domestic plans — "*closed economy.*"

These key elements lead to desirable and undesirable consequences dur-ing the lifetime of the Soviet-type system, as described in the Appendix to this volume. The key elements also cause certain positive and negative legacies, which form the heart of this paper.[6]

REASONS FOR THE PROBABLE DEMISE OF THE CPE

For the purpose of justifying the importance of studying the transition prob-lems facing the U.S.S.R. and Eastern European countries, it is sufficient to show that they are entering, or are about to enter, a transition period. As in-dicated earlier, this is in fact happening. However, in order to argue that a full evaluation of the relative merits of a CPE as a model for economic de-velopment requires a careful consideration of the legacy problem, it is neces-sary to show that such a system is not likely to last forever, or for such a long period as to make the legacies of little importance at any reasonable rate of time discount. The analogy of the purchase of a new car may be useful. The probable resale value is not the major factor in choosing a car. It has virtually no importance if one expects to keep the car for many years. However, if one believes that it will be necessary or desirable to trade the car in relatively soon, then a neglect of resale value does not lead to a rational choice. I am not suggesting that leaders of underdeveloped countries go around shopping for an economic system. I do believe, however, that a thor-ough study of the legacy problem, one of the heretofore neglected areas, is important to enable them to get a more nearly complete picture of the rela-tive merit of any given system, Soviet-type or other.

I shall try to indicate briefly that there are reasons to believe that the CPE is not a "model for all seasons."[7] Just as Marx has argued that the capi-talist system digs its own grave — both by its successes, which make it less

[6] My classification of consequences as desirable and undesirable, and of legacies as positive and negative, rests, of course, on the preference function of the system's directors of any given country. To make my discussion applicable to as broad a range of circumstances as possible, I have assumed a preference function in which economic growth and unification of the country are dominant parameters. In addition, I have assumed that, at any given time, maximization of consumer welfare and reduction of income inequality are subsidiary parameters. If the reader wishes to delete any of these or to add other parameters, such as central control for its own sake, he is free to alter my evaluation of the desirability of any given consequence or legacy.

[7] An extremely stimulating and enlightening discussion of this topic, by some of the leading experts in the field, may be found in [43]. Among the innumerable other studies dealing with this subject, let me mention three that argue that a new system is neces-sary. These are by Soviet, Eastern European, and Western authors: [12, p. 2], [41, pp. 3–6], and [34, pp. 185–195].

necessary, and by its failures, which make it less desirable — I shall argue that the Soviet-type system does likewise.

This is likely to be true in a large, well-endowed economy, where domestic factors play the major role, such as the U.S.S.R.; the probable life of the system will be shorter in a small, less potentially self-sufficient country, where foreign economic relations play a much more crucial role, such as Yugoslavia or Hungary.

DOMESTIC FACTORS

As an economy develops, the problems faced by the system's directors [8] change greatly. There is a shift from radical, discrete transformations of the economy which are useful in the "take-off," to smaller marginal changes which characterize a more mature economy. The greater sophistication of government leaders and technicians makes them more impatient with the crudeness of the Stalinist model, and the larger supply of trained and politically reliable (or at least neutral) managers and staff personnel make decentralization seem more feasible. The increases in income and sophistication of the population lead to a demand for better quality and a greater variety of consumer goods, including a highly embarrassing accumulation of unsalable stocks. The efficiency of appeals to ideological fervor and promises of future pies in the sky diminishes, and the use of totalitarian techniques and extreme pressure tactics in the economic sphere becomes counterproductive.

Hirschman's analogy of the Berlitz model is quite useful in this connection [16, pp. 47–49]. The Stalinist model is like a teacher of French who, counting on the enthusiasm of the student and his own power of coercion, imposes on the student a rate of learning much greater than the student would voluntarily undertake on his own. This is likely to result in a relatively rapid rate of learning at the beginning; but as the student begins to feel increasingly unhappy at the amount of practice required of him and as he progresses toward the stage of having to learn the fine points of the language, he becomes more and more restive and his rate of learning per hour of practice diminishes. This presents a dilemma to the teacher. If he persists in coercing the student, he may face either an open revolt in which the student refuses to study French, or, even more likely, a situation where the student goes through the motions of studying but does not learn very much. On the other hand, if the teacher reduces the load on the student, the student may react to it by demanding an even lower load. Once the teacher *begins* by using the coercive method, he becomes a threatening figure to the student and will have great difficulty in gaining the student's willing co-

---

[8] I am using Professor Abram Bergson's excellent shorthand term for describing decisionmakers in an economic system.

operation at a later stage. This analogy would seem to describe quite well the situation in post-war Eastern Europe, especially the 1956 Polish and Hungarian "events," and the difficulty Gomulka and Kadar are still having in gaining whole-hearted cooperation from their peoples [29, p. 454].

Significant changes of an objective type take place during the process of development under the CPE which combine to make it less and less desirable. The rate of growth of national income, for example, may tend to fall. There are many possible reasons for a slowdown. A rise in capital/output ratios will require an increased rate of investment to maintain a given rate of growth in output. The pressing demands of the population for more and better goods and services will create strong demands for a reduction in the rate of investment and a shift in the allocation of investment resources toward the former "buffer sectors" (agriculture, housing, consumer goods industries, and services). The increased complexity of planning raises the necessary inputs into information while it reduces the qualitative and quantitative outputs from information [33]. The possibility of living off borrowed technology is reduced, and research and development becomes essential on a much broader front than earlier. There are increased difficulties, even in applying foreign technology, as the economy moves from the relatively simpler technology of steel and steel fabricating to the more complex technology of electronic computers and automatic control mechanisms. The benefits of extensive development by massive infusions of unskilled labor decline sharply. The problems of labor incentives and efficient organization of productive units become more important. The continued lag of agriculture and the difficulties experienced in attempting to plan this sector contribute to the need to find other solutions.[9]

All of these, as well as other factors not mentioned, make the extensive development, command economy, pressure economy, priority economy, and other elements of the CPE less and less useful as time passes and the economy develops.

INTERNATIONAL ECONOMIC FACTORS

It is probably not too farfetched to argue that, no matter how serious the domestic arguments for abandonment of the CPE, in a small country [10] the problems faced in the field of foreign trade are the crucial ones in forcing changes in the system. This is a major theme of Professor Brown's discussion of the dynamic changes in the foreign trade performance of a CPE, in

[9] [4] makes the interesting point that the difficulties faced by central planners in the agricultural and the foreign trade sectors have many similarities.

[10] We may merely define as small, for our purposes, any country where a very high degree of self-sufficiency would be extremely costly, because of small population, low per capita income, or poor endowment with natural resources.

this volume. Excruciating dilemmas face the system's directors in their attempts to handle the two major, interrelated problems in the field of foreign trade: the balance-of-payments problems (total and regional) and the problem of relatively low gains from trade (primarily poor single-factoral terms of trade, in some cases poor income terms of trade, and, as pointed out by Brown, also poor commodity terms of trade). Because of the importance and complexity of this problem, I shall not attempt to provide a superficial summary of his argument, but shall merely refer the reader to his paper in this volume and to his dissertation [3].

A leading Hungarian foreign trade expert writing in a Yugoslav journal states the case forcibly for participation in an international division of labor:

International division of labor is called upon to create a basis upon which modern technology can affirm its tremendous, today barely discernible possibilities for the speeding up of economic development. We would go even further: we consider it beyond argument that in the rapid tempo of economic development in the period 1950–60, the wider international division of labor played a role which is hard to exaggerate and that the development of the majority of countries obtained the major impulses from the arena of the international division of labor on the world market [47, p. 597].

Once the system's directors, in a small country, begin to doubt the value of the CPE and begin to consider the possibility of replacing it with a more decentralized system and one that abandons the closed economy feature, the very considerable advantages of a closer integration into the world market, or at least a larger regional market, become even more evident.[11] As a matter of fact, these advantages become one of the factors militating in favor of replacing the Stalinist model with a new one. Joining an international division of labor brings with it the advantages of specialization according to existing comparative advantage, or more important, the development of new, potential areas of comparative advantage. It makes it possible to capitalize on economies of scale which the small domestic market did not permit. By acting as a countervailing power, foreign trade reduces the ability of monopolistic or oligopolistic giants to exercise their market power. Thereby, it reduces the need to give up the benefits of decentralization to maintain some control over these firms. In addition, the competition from firms in more advanced countries is likely to provide a stronger stimulus toward a more rapid rate of technological and product innovation, toward higher quality production, toward more cost consciousness, and the like, over a wide range of economic activities, than the basically administrative methods of the command economy have provided under the Soviet-type system.

[11] The dangers inherent in depending on world markets, such as the possibility of long-term falling commodity terms of trade, demand-induced fluctuations in export earnings, and dangers of economic or political blackmail, have been so widely dealt with in the literature that little would be gained in discussing them here.

LEGACIES OF THE CPE

According to the time period during which a legacy exerts its influence, there are two types of legacies and two types of "quasi-legacies."

I would consider as "quasi-legacies":

1. The forces in the CPE that create ideological and psychological barriers and statistical deficiencies which prevent the system's directors from recognizing the fact that abandoning the system would serve their own ends better than maintaining it — the "recognition lag."

2. Irreversible alterations in institutions or mores which narrow the meaningful options of successor systems open to the system's directors.

The true "legacies" are:

1. Forces that create obstacles to the implementation of a decision by the system's directors to replace the system — delaying the change, making the transition period more painful, and possibly even deflecting the path followed during the transition, thereby leading to a result different from that decided upon by the system's directors.

2. The consequences of the CPE that outlast both this system and the transition period, and that constitute the inheritance of the new system.

The "quasi-legacies" can, by definition, be only negative. The first true legacy is also bound to be negative, unless one assumes that the system's directors have made a mistake in deciding to abandon the old system and have chosen an unsuitable successor system. The second legacy can, of course, be both positive and negative. The distinction among these four categories is very hard to draw, because we cannot demarcate the time periods sufficiently exactly. It is useful primarily to clarify our thinking about the legacy problem. For purposes of exposition, I shall divide the legacies into three categories: (1) ideological, political, psychological, and sociological; (2) institutional; and (3) economic — although the boundaries are not completely distinct and there is some overlapping.

POSITIVE LEGACIES

In order to divide the legacies into positive and negative ones, it is necessary to define the criteria by which the division is made. I am using the hypothetical preference function, discussed earlier, for this purpose.

Unless the pressure on the population is so severe as to bring about complete disillusionment and revulsion, the growth-orientation and the psychology of high investment rates are likely to continue into the transition period. This may be considered to be a major positive legacy; however, it may also have some undesirable aspects. If the country had a relatively developed economy when it adopted the CPE — as did, for example, Czechoslovakia — then an excessively strong growth-orientation may prove counterproductive. Even in a country which had been underdeveloped, the legacy of growth-orientation could have undesirable effects. If capital/output ratios are rising and rates of growth of output are falling, an attempt to maintain high growth rates requires increases in the rate of investment at the cost of consumption and exports. In addition, the transition period may be a time for consolidation and not rapid growth.

The new system is likely to inherit a larger capital stock from the CPE than from a system in which the priority economy element played a smaller role. If, as is quite likely, the new capital embodies significant amounts of new technology, the overall productivity of the economy may also be higher. In addition to being a positive legacy in its own right, this could exert a positive influence both on the balance of payments and on the gains from trade, by increasing export possibilities or reducing import requirements.

In addition, the likelihood of a large number of unfinished projects may make the transition period smoother by permitting large increases in output from relatively small incremental investments. However, the unfinished projects may also make the transition more difficult. Their completion may not necessarily be rational on the basis of cost-benefit analyses; but it may be very difficult psychologically and politically to abandon them. In such cases, they will either take resources away from other, more useful projects, or will force a higher rate of investment than may be desirable.

The relatively smaller degree of income inequality, brought about mainly by the absence of private ownership of the means of production, is likely to continue even after the CPE has been abandoned, since it is not probable that the successor system would be one of complete private ownership of all means of production. Private ownership in agriculture, services, and small-scale industry is quite likely to be reintroduced, but not in large-scale industry or social overhead sectors.

The successor system will inherit an economy that has been transformed from an agricultural to a primarily industrial economy, or has, at least, been started on this road. This is, of course, not necessarily an unmitigated blessing, but it would probably be regarded as such by both the leaders of countries now having a CPE and those of present-day underdeveloped countries.

If the policy of unifying the country and working toward greater equalization of regional differences in development is successful, the successor system will find its own job much easier. Its political problems will be reduced and it will be able to concentrate more closely on economic and other policies. However, recent Yugoslav experience leads to some possible questioning of this optimistic evaluation.

The great emphasis on education, skill training, and transformation of the peasantry into industrial laborers may provide the successor system with the most beneficial legacies of all.

The increased educational and skill level of the population is likely to raise labor productivity and make possible the operation of technologically advanced branches of production. This is likely to yield favorable legacies in the field of foreign trade as well as in the domestic economy. It should be noted that it may also create some political problems if the system's directors desire to retain all political power in their own hands.

NEGATIVE LEGACIES

IDEOLOGICAL, POLITICAL, PSYCHOLOGICAL, AND SOCIOLOGICAL LEGACIES

Every major economic system either is established by ideologists or develops an ideology during its lifetime. The ruling ideology exercises some influence over the thoughts and actions of the system's directors. It tends to delay their acceptance of the fact that conditions have changed in such a way as to make the system backed by this ideology obsolete. It also forecloses certain reform options, makes the transition to a new system more difficult, and is likely to exert some influence on the new system, so long as this system is introduced from above by the old system's directors.

Every economic system that has been in operation for any length of time is difficult to abandon, owing to the force of inertia and uncertainty. The existing conditions, no matter how bad, are at least familiar — while the alternatives are always uncertain and therefore likely to be frightening.

Closely connected with this is the fact that the system builds up a set of vested interests. In the case of the CPE, the vested interests consist of party functionaries, government planners and bureaucrats (who find much of their raison d'etre, and much of their power, in meddling in economic affairs),[12] scholars (who obtained their academic credentials by writing panegyrics to the system and may honestly believe in the glory of the system and the correctness of their own theories of it), and enterprise managers (who have learned the ropes and developed ways to beat the system). These individuals have little to gain and much to lose from the abandonment of a system that has enabled them to rise to leading roles in their respective bureaucracies. There is one other vested interest not generally included in such a list — the workers, who may or may not particularly like the system

---

[12] A leading Hungarian economist, in writing about the difficulties of introducing a new economic model in Hungary, states that: "The greatest difficulty, whose weight it is difficult to overrate, lies in the fact that, on the one hand, the leaders — in the broader sense of the word, not only a few dozen, but several thousand of them — have to implement those changes, while on the other, the majority of those leaders have become too used to current methods, and it is difficult for them to change. We have to reckon with this, all the more so as there will be among the modifications some which require methods of leadership different from the previous one, and some of them will require a change of leaders" [13, p. 17].

but who tend to feel the possible threat of a new system very strongly. They fear the possible loss of their jobs, the danger that they will have to work harder to earn the same real wage, and the price adjustments likely to accompany the transition, which may result in a lowering of their real wages. Since any reform is likely to be imposed from above and the workers have good reason to mistrust government actions, they are quite likely to join the other vested interests in opposing changes, even though the ultimate results of the changes may be to bring about significant improvements in their circumstances.[13] It may not be inappropriate to talk about the CPE as creating a "confidence gap" (euphemistically called "reserved trust") between the leaders and the population, thereby bequeathing a significant negative legacy to the successor system.

The CPE turns the individual into an object of manipulation and changes initiative, good cheer, and enthusiasm into apathy and indifference. I would follow Professor Holesovsky in arguing that one of the most significant, although seldom-mentioned, legacies of a CPE is the destruction of *élan vital*, a production input for which there is no close substitute.[14]

The extensive development element and the other elements that lead to lower productivity not only make export expansion more difficult, but also create great pressures against import liberalization on the part of the workers and managers in enterprises threatened by competition from imports. This has already happened in Yugoslavia.

The CPE breeds an interventionist psychology and an opposition to, and misunderstanding of, the operation of a market system.[15] This legacy acts to delay the introduction of a decentralized system and makes the transition much longer and more difficult. It results in the introduction of half-measures, which are bound to bring more difficulties than solutions, and thereby strengthen the hand of all those opposed to giving up the key elements of the Soviet-type system.[16]

This interventionist legacy is likely to be particularly strong in the crucial fields of foreign trade and foreign exchange, where, because of the other legacies and various exogenous factors, the balance-of-payments situation presents a serious problem. Balance-of-payments difficulties provide a powerful force for the retention of state intervention in this area.

[13] This is not merely a hypothetical argument; it appears to be a significant factor in the Czech reform attempts.

[14] [18]. The reference to "reserved trust" is to [19, p. 3], while the reference to the killing of initiative, good cheer, and enthusiasm is to [45, p. 26].

[15] For example, a Yugoslav economist stressed the point that the city fathers of Zagreb cannot comprehend the fact that the citizens of their city would not starve if they did not assure a sufficient supply of food, either by direct administrative action or by setting up a controlled monopoly enterprise.

[16] The early decentralization experiments in Poland and Czechoslovakia may be viewed in precisely this light.

In addition to fostering an interventionist psychology, the CPE also breeds an engineering, perfectionist bias. The adherents of a centralized, command economy believe that it is, at least potentially, a perfect system. They oppose a system whose actual performance might surpass that of the actual centralized system, but which can make no claim to ultimate perfection. (The analogy of believers in perfect competition may not be inappropriate in this connection.)

It might be noted that the more extreme and radical any economic system is, the stronger these ideological, psychological, and sociological legacies tend to be.

When and if a successor system is established, it will inherit from the CPE "entrepreneurs" who are not trained to be independent, cost-conscious, new-product-oriented, or particularly concerned with financial liquidity or solvency. Neither are they likely to be experienced in those skills essential to selling in a competitive world market or a competitive buyers' market at home.[17] They are likely, instead, to be oriented toward short-run goals and to be unconcerned with the more difficult problem of operating with a long time horizon.

The physical planning and taut planning aspects of the CPE lead to a sellers' market and a system of incentives for production and not sale. This results in a situation where enterprises pay relatively little attention to quality, to timely deliveries, or to after-sale servicing or warranties on their products. In addition, monetary fines are not very effective instruments for countering this attitude, since the payment of fines does not affect the incomes of managers significantly. This makes contracts much less effective than they are in market economies. The situation does not change very quickly, even after physical planning and taut planning are no longer in existence [48]. This legacy is particularly harmful in the field of exports and constitutes one of the major reasons a country like Yugoslavia finds it difficult to promote the exports of its industrial products on highly competitive, convertible currency markets.[18]

As indicated earlier, the priority economy, pressure economy, and com-

[17] The London *Economist* presents a very interesting example of this problem. The technical manager of the Bucharest Machine Tool Factory has argued that his plant uses predominantly modern West German and Swiss equipment, gets the most qualified workers by paying them high wages, and produces a product of high quality. However, the cumbersome centralized planning system and the lack of an advertising and sales department have prevented his firm from successful competition in world markets [8, p. 1022].

[18] A high official in the sales department of a major Yugoslav industrial firm explains the inability of his firm to export to the U.S. market in large part by the fact that it is not able to meet the strict delivery terms required by most U.S. importers. In a discussion, he told me that although part of the problem lies in possible bottlenecks in the production process of his own firm, the major blame must be placed on late

mand economy elements combine to yield a legacy of investment projects that have not proved to be economically sound. When this legacy is combined with an unwillingness to admit mistakes, especially big mistakes, the successor system inherits "white elephants" that are continually nurtured at the expense of the rest of the economy. The need to devote investment resources to these white elephants, and the retention by them of scarce managerial and technical talent, make it more difficult to develop those sectors of the economy which could participate effectively in export activity. The Yugoslav experience is quite instructive in this connection; to the best of my knowledge, no large industrial firm has yet been liquidated, although there appears to be no shortage of candidates. Considerable opposition exists to the substitution of open unemployment for the disguised unemployment created by the extensive development under the CPE, adding further weight to the opposition against closing down large enterprises.[19]

INSTITUTIONAL LEGACIES

One of the major legacies of the CPE is a price system divorced from both domestic and foreign scarcity relationships. This "irrationality" is troublesome during the life of the system, but it becomes worse when attempts are made to decentralize the system and introduce market elements. The gingerly way in which Liberman and other Soviet economists have handled the price problem is symptomatic of this. As will be shown in the section on Yugoslavia, reforming a price system to make it reflect scarcities is one of the truly difficult tasks faced by those attempting to replace a CPE with a new system. Radical changes in the relative prices of inputs and outputs affect the income distribution among regions, among branches of the economy, among firms within a given branch, among workers in a given enterprise, and among different classes of consumers. Even the fiscal agencies at the national and local levels are hit by changes in indirect taxes, necessitated by price changes, and by changes in the prices of goods and services they purchase. Of course, the further out of line the prices are, the more difficult is the process of realignment.

deliveries by its suppliers. In the case of inputs from domestic sources, contracts were often not met; in the case of imports, the fault generally lay, not with the foreign exporters, but with the difficulties in obtaining the necessary foreign exchange on time.

[19] In a public opinion poll conducted in Yugoslavia after introduction of the 1965 reforms, workers were asked what they believed should be done with enterprises that operated for a long time with losses, and whether they would advocate firing excess workers. To the first question, 36 percent said that such enterprises should be liquidated, 35 percent that they should be merged with successful enterprises, and 16 percent that they should be helped to continue. To the second question, 48 percent answered that excess workers should be fired, 45 percent opposed firing anyone, and 74 percent of all workers said they were willing to give up part of their income to prevent the need for firing anyone [5, pp. 131–132].

The effect of irrational prices on the conduct of centrally planned foreign trade is examined in Professor Brown's paper in this volume. Continuation of such prices after the transformation of the economy toward a decentralized market system has begun results in the chronic need for various fiscal or other government instruments to prevent the prices from leading to a misallocation of resources in export or import activity.

A much less difficult, but not insignificant, problem is presented by the need to alter unrealistic exchange rates. A change in exchange rates without a thoroughgoing reform of domestic prices solves none of the important problems. Yugoslav devaluations in 1952 and 1961 managed to get the average dinar/dollar rate temporarily closer to the average purchasing power parity of the two currencies, but the dinar/dollar rates for individual products were still very much further out of line than in most market economies without a legacy of an "irrational" price system.

Closely connected with the existence of unrealistic, generally overvalued exchange rates is a highly centralized foreign exchange system. The dismantling of such a system is one of the more difficult tasks of the transition period. Despite the reforms of 1952, 1961, and 1965, strong elements of central control over foreign exchange still exist in Yugoslavia. There appear to be two main explanations for this: (1) The difficulties of expanding exports sufficiently to assure balance-of-payments equilibrium make foreign exchange very scarce. This requires strong controls, unless the leaders are willing to adopt a system of flexible exchange rates. (2) In the Yugoslav case, the foreign exchange system appears to have become one of the last bastions of strength for those elements who oppose decentralization.

An admittedly secondary cause of continued balance-of-payments problems is the difficulty of adapting the organizational network in foreign trade to the needs of a decentralized economic system. It is not possible overnight to alter a bureaucratic system of foreign trade monopoly into an appropriate network of foreign trade organizations. It is easier to decree the organizational changes than it is to retrain the personnel and create a flexible and efficient network at home and abroad. Connected with this is the difficulty in shifting from a pattern of trade dependent on bilateral clearing arrangements to one of flexible, unplanned market relationships. Furthermore, since continuation of the bilateral arrangements has advantages to a country that has depended heavily on them, they are likely to be continued. This necessitates some types of controls to assure the fulfillment of the quotas agreed upon in the trade agreements, and prevents the abandonment of exchange and trade controls over enterprises.

A more important institutional change, perhaps, if a decentralized market system is to operate effectively, is the creation of a satisfactory mechanism for transferring investment resources from those who do the saving to those who do the investing — i.e., some type of capital market. Unless some satisfactory mechanism is developed to replace the centralized system of investment allocation, no truly decentralized economic system is viable. The creation of a capital market, or the reëstablishment of one that has been dismantled, is a very difficult, time-consuming process under any circumstances. The legacy of the CPE is that this process will begin much later and under much less favorable conditions.[20]

According to Yugoslav economists with whom I have spoken, the irrational price system, the centralized foreign exchange system, and the lack of a capital market are among the most damaging legacies in Yugoslavia.

ECONOMIC LEGACIES

The closed economy principle of the CPE leaves extremely significant legacies to the successor system. In a CPE, domestic factors are emphasized and foreign trade is relegated to an ancillary position, with imports consisting of commodities necessary for fulfillment of domestic production plans and exports consisting primarily of commodities in which a temporary surplus exists. This means that no special effort is made to develop important export sectors, and that the human and material capital stock is not likely to be suitable for rapid inclusion into an international division of labor. A Yugoslav economist, writing in 1966, stated that:

> The planning system itself is relatively responsible for the still present elements of autarchic, closed economy. The starting point of our planning used to be, predominantly, internal balance sheets, which inevitably created, or at least, tended to create, a closed, "balanced," self-sufficient economic structure. Exchange with foreign countries was mostly reduced to the exports of surpluses and imports of deficits (from the viewpoint of the internal material balance sheets). No systematic and resolute orientation towards fitting our economy into the international division of labour existed, even in those instances where either present or future comparative advantages could have been estimated. The result is well known: the insufficient exports, and consequently imports potential of the Yugoslav economy and a persistent deficit in the balance of current account, slowing down the rate of economic growth.[21]

The absence of effective export sectors is one of the factors that explain the generally low levels of foreign exchange reserves, an inconvertible currency, and either a balance-of-payments deficit or a balance in international accounts purchased at the cost of a low export/income ratio and a less

---

[20] For a somewhat more comprehensive discussion of this important issue, see [31].

[21] [25, pp. 2–3]. Another Yugoslav economist makes a similar point, arguing that it was only in 1957 that the first significant step was taken to include the criterion of foreign exchange results as a major factor in investment policy, and that even as late as the middle 1960s emphasis was still being placed on short-run balance-of-payments effects instead of on long-run development of those sectors of the economy where present or probable future comparative advantage exists [27, pp. 476 and 480].

than optimal geographic pattern of trade. As shown by Professor Brown, the dynamic changes during the operation of the CPE are likely to yield a legacy of a highly inelastic offer curve, because of a low price elasticity of demand for imports (as imports tend to contain an ever greater proportion of higher priority products) and a low price elasticity of supply of exports (because of the aversion of planners to alter plans in order to change the amount of goods available for export, and the fact that as the priority of products entering exports rises, there is an even greater unwillingness to respond to possible increases in export prices by increasing export quantities). The income elasticity of demand for imports is likely to be high because of the operation of the trade expansion multiplier. In order to maintain a balance in international accounts, this causes a high income elasticity of demand for foreign exchange, which forces an expansion of exports. This is true even though planners will not willingly release goods for export, since their cost, in terms of planners' preferences, will rise as more high-priority products must be exported.

The probability of suffering from regional balance-of-payments problems in the transition period and the early stages of the successor regime can be evaluated in terms of Hirschman's concept of "exportability" [16, pp. 169–171]. The relatively low degree of exportability of the rapidly growing sector under the CPE — i.e., primarily the investment goods sector — explains the difficulties experienced in trying to export to convertible markets. The country does not find it easy to supply, at competitive prices, goods comparable to those already sold in convertible markets; it does not have many goods that are new and superior. The rapidly growing sectors in CPEs correspond to the slowly growing sectors in most underdeveloped countries, but to the rapidly growing sectors in advanced industrial countries.

The pattern of development under the CPE works against the country's becoming overly dependent on a monocultural export industry, and this may be considered to be one advantage of this approach. However, while considerable effort has been given in the literature to an analysis of the dangers of excessive specialization, little attention has been paid to the danger of a completely home-market-oriented development with excessive diversification of exports, which may be one of the legacies of the CPE. In this system, despite an aversion to foreign trade, imports are likely to be very important as providers of new technology and scarce raw materials, and a safety valve in case of failures in the domestic planning system. Exports, aside from some traditional agricultural exports (whose importance gradually declines), are likely to be commodities that are produced for the home market and happen to be in temporary excess supply. In the absence of sectors specialized for exports, the need to pay for imports forces the government to use a battery of administrative or indirect instruments to stimulate the export of all types of goods, regardless of their suitability for export. This leads to great diversification of exports, as more and more different types of goods are pushed into export markets.[22]

The legacies of this approach are : (1) inferior single-factoral terms of trade, as no effort is made to benefit from specialization or economies of scale; (2) no assurance of dependable sources of foreign exchange earnings in the long run, which forces the successor system to try to develop such sources; (3) the absence of important export products, which makes it impossible for the country to gain significant benefits in tariff bargaining or in negotiations leading to entry into a regional economic union; (4) the concentration of firms on the domestic market, which makes lesser demands in terms of quality, new products, packaging, and finishing, and which makes it difficult to stimulate producing firms to abandon the domestic market or the less exacting clearing area markets for the much more demanding convertible area markets; (5) the absence of a compulsion to develop expertise in export marketing, which results in a lack of trained personnel and tested policies; and (6) the absence of a constituency in favor of exports, since few firms specialize in this field.

Closely connected with the issue of commodity diversification is the concept of capillarity.[23] Dr. Pertot describes this concept as follows:

Our surpluses available for export, singly and in toto, turn out to be so small on the world scale, that in given cases they are often able, as if by the principle of capillarity, to find access and exit on world markets through the tiny pores of the world economic fabric, and that in doing so, in many cases not only do not threaten anyone's economic interests, but our foreign trade partners are not even conscious of such additional exports from our country [36, p. 382].

Thus, capillarity means, in effect, that the country finds itself in a position similar to that of a pure competitor facing a perfectly elastic demand curve.

While commodity diversification has important advantages and costs, the advantages of capillarity clearly outweigh its disadvantages. The advantages are that the country is less subject to political blackmail or to economic changes in one particular trading partner, that it faces a more elastic foreign offer curve, which permits an expansion of exports without deterioration in the commodity terms of trade, and that it has no need to invest in market surveys, trade networks in foreign countries, advertising, and so forth. The

[22] A study of concentration in international trade showed that Yugoslav exports were highly diversified. Yugoslavia ranked 38th out of 44 countries, and the countries with lower coefficients of concentration were industrially developed countries of Western Europe and the United States. The study did not include data on Soviet-type economies [26, p. 12].

[23] An excellent discussion of diversification and capillarity in Yugoslavia may be found in [36] and [10].

Egon Neuberger

negative legacies from a policy based on capillarity include a lack of expertise in specific markets, resulting in an inability to take advantage of favorable market conditions in a foreign market when these arise, and higher administrative and transportation costs for shipping many different items to many different markets.

The priority principle of the CPE results in two important legacies: the need to compensate for the highly unbalanced investment structure, and the likely danger of the eruption of open inflation. The concentration of investment resources and of the best trained and most effective human resources in the priority sectors in the CPE imposes the burden of having to make major investments in material and human resources for the former buffer sectors, such as agriculture, housing, and consumers' goods industries. Since even the producers' goods industries may have an unbalanced structure, investments might be necessary to develop those which were relatively neglected earlier — e.g., chemicals. Thus, the success achieved by operation of the priority principle is, at least partly, negated by the need to compensate for deficiencies in the capital stock structure. The CPE tends to operate under a condition of repressed inflation. When attempts are made to relax the controls of the command economy, open inflation threatens and there is a strong temptation to impose stringent price controls.[24] The imposition of such controls will delay the introduction of a new market system or emasculate it. The danger of initiating open inflation is heightened by the need to realign relative prices, since it is usually easier to raise input and output prices than to lower them, and this is especially true of wages. This tendency is likely to be enforced by the need to raise food prices to provide incentives to the peasants. Unless the exchange rate is realigned before the command economy is dismantled, the devaluation itself is likely to put pressure on the price level. Any inflationary pressure will, of course, place additional strain on the balance of payments.

THE YUGOSLAV EXPERIENCE

A significant proportion of Yugoslav economists believe that the legacy problem has been an important contributory cause for the adverse, and possibly also for the important positive, developments in the Yugoslav economy since 1952.[25] However, neither these economists nor I would argue that the legacies are a sufficient or necessary condition for explaining all the developments in the Yugoslav economy from 1952 to 1967.

[24] As indicated in the next section, this is precisely what happened in Yugoslavia.

[25] The whole brunt of the so-called "White Paper" written in 1962 was that the problems faced by Yugoslavia during the 1961–1962 economic difficulties were due primarily to incomplete removal of the vestiges of the old system [23, pp. 147–299].

THREE YUGOSLAV STATEMENTS ON THE LEGACY PROBLEM

Dr. Vladimir Bakaric, the leader of the League of Communists of Croatia, and a prominent liberal statesman, presents the essence of the dilemma faced by the system's directors in a country that adopts the CPE and then attempts to replace it with a new, more suitable system. For this reason, I shall present a lengthy extract from his statement.

Here exist two issues. The first is the obvious fact that disproportions keep accumulating, and that the longer the old relations are kept, the more disproportions will arise and it will become ever more difficult to control them. The giving of "freedom by the spoonful" does not present the possibility of a solution for the simple reason that there have been established such relationships that partial attempts, measures which retain as dominant the existing, in essence administrative methods of running [the economy] can no longer provide a solution. Such a method actually means only the postponement of a solution. On the other hand, if suddenly we were to leave everything to an automatism, if suddenly we were to permit such a conflict of forces which would lead to the elimination from our economy of all which according to its present capabilities could not exist, it is most likely that the depth of disproportions which have been created up to this time would show up so forcefully that the question would arise whether we could stand by and let the process take its full course. . . . It is most likely that, in the very fact that it is relatively easy to see the whole difficulty of getting out of the situation, is hidden the cause of the inclination toward interventions which in fact mean the solidifying of the old system. Such an approach, in any case, does not provide the basis for a solution of the problem. Difficulties which are in their essence the product of the old system cannot be overcome with methods which are suitable for that system. Meanwhile, the periodic aggravation of one of the basic disproportions — the deficit in the balance of payments — shows that it is no longer possible to depend on measures which do not lead to a more rapid solution of the structural problems of our economy. Moreover, the ever shorter intervals between balance of payments difficulties, show that it is becoming dangerous to postpone deeper and bolder actions, with the adoption of classical measures, and especially with the help of foreign credits; these methods and these resources should be utilized to make such changes in the economic system and in exchange with foreign countries that will initiate the process of the liquidation of disproportions on the basis of a greater productivity of labor. This means that we must move toward freer economic relationships, and in these newly created conditions intervene to prevent the disproportions from having too brutal consequences. More precisely: change over to a system of freer action of economic laws with the possibility of regulation.[26]

A statement by two Yugoslav economists, published in 1965, emphasizes the continued existence of significant legacies, even at that late date:

Our whole economic system is unfinished, so that one should regard it more as a transitional category which contains in itself elements of the old and the new (we suppose future). Under the new form there often hides the old content, so

[26] Dr. Vladimir Bakaric, in an interview in [9, October 10, 1964], quoted in [7].

that, objectively regarded, *that which is old in the present system is more than dominant.*[27]

Yugoslavia's chief ideologist and President of the National Assembly, Edvard Kardelj, argued in an interview published shortly after the introduction of the 1965 reform that the current troubles

lie in the fact that the whole of our system is still burdened with excessive state intervention. . . . In the sphere of extended reproduction, the financing of international trade, i.e. in the foreign exchange system, in the credit system, etc. the old system still exerts its influence, i.e. there exists excessive state intervention ([21] as reported in [38]).

STATISTICAL SURVEY

A brief statistical survey of Yugoslav economic developments serves to place the problem in its proper perspective. Looking at the rate of growth in national income and industrial output, it appears either that no legacy problem exists or that the positive legacies outweigh the negative ones by a considerable margin. When the balance of trade and balance of payments are considered, the opposite impression is gained.

Yugoslav national income grew from 11.5 billion new dinars (in 1960 constant prices) in 1947 to 14.8 billion new dinars in 1951, fell to 12.8 billion new dinars in 1952, rose to 15.1 billion new dinars in 1953, and reached 38.5 billion new dinars in 1965. The average annual rates of growth were 6.5 percent between 1947 and 1951, 2.1 percent between 1947 and 1952 (1952 was an extremely poor harvest year), and 7.9 percent between 1953 and 1965 (1952 is eliminated, since it would show a more rapid rate of growth than is warranted).[28]

An even more dynamic picture is presented by the industrial component of national income, which had an average annual growth rate of 11.9 percent from 1952 to 1965 [20, p. 78] [44, p. 105]. A slightly different set of data presenting the indexes of physical volume of industrial output shows a growth rate of 12.4 percent for that period [20, p. 77] [44, p. 105]. However, during the earlier period, in good part because of the wrenching effect on the economy of the break with Stalin, the industrial output grew very rapidly

[27] [15] as quoted in [7, p. 58] (emphasis is mine).

[28] The rates of growth were calculated in the usual manner of obtaining the compound rate of yearly growth between the beginning and the terminal year, since no more sophisticated measure seems necessary for our purposes. Yugoslav statisticians have some qualms about the quality of these statistics, especially about the price deflators used to obtain the series in constant prices, but I do not believe that even the most sophisticated recalculations would change the results sufficiently to prevent the Yugoslav economy from appearing as a very dynamic one. The use of 1960 prices as the base, rather than 1947 or 1952 prices, eliminates one of the major sources of upward bias in an economy that is being rapidly transformed. The rates of growth were calculated from data in [20, p. 77] and [44, p. 105].

from 1947 to 1949, but then stagnated until 1952, giving a rate of growth of 6.5 percent a year for the entire period during which the CPE may be considered as having held full sway in Yugoslavia [20].

Agricultural output fluctuated very widely throughout the period, and showed no long-term trends during the Stalinist period. After decollectivization, the agricultural component of national income grew at the rate of 4.3 percent a year from the average of 1952–1954 to the average of 1963–1965.[29]

The performance of the Yugoslav economy presented here is impressive, but the picture is not complete. The rapid growth of output was based, in large part, on the use of extensive development — i.e., very high rates of gross investment and large-scale additions to the industrial labor force. For the period 1952–1963, Rockwell has calculated the exponential growth rates of value added in the total social sector of the Yugoslav economy at 9.9 percent a year, with capital inputs growing at 6.2 percent and labor inputs at 7.2 percent a year [39, Table II]. In the industry and mining sector during that same period, value added grew at 11.3 percent, capital inputs at 8.2 percent, and labor inputs at 7.1 percent [39, Table III].

More important, the favorable picture of Yugoslav growth does not take into account the very great contribution of foreign economic aid and the inflow of foreign government loan capital, which permitted Yugoslavia to run a large import surplus during the post-Stalinist period.

Table 1 presents the balance of trade available for the whole post-war period. It is clear from this table that the picture of Yugoslavia as seen through its foreign trade is quite different from the picture presented by the data on national income and industrial output. It is thus not surprising that foreign trade has been one of the sectors most troublesome to Yugoslav leaders, although by no means the only one. The picture is considerably better when the balance on current account, including invisibles such as tourism, transport, and emigrants' remittances, is considered, rather than merely the merchandise balance. In every year, Yugoslavia had a positive balance in these items, and part of the import surplus was financed by these invisibles. In 1962 and 1963 invisibles covered 58 percent of the import surplus; in 1964 they covered 46 percent; and in 1965 they actually covered in excess of 100 percent — and thus for the first time since 1949 Yugoslavia had a surplus on current account [44, p. 115]. A stimulating Yugoslav economist, Professor Rudolf Bićanić, has suggested that foreign trade is like criminal law. Each is the most sensitive sector in its own area. A study of the foreign trade system of a country will give a good insight into the whole economic

---

[29] By taking three-year averages, it is possible to reduce somewhat the effect of particularly good and particularly disastrous harvests. Calculated from [20, p. 78] and [44, p. 105].

TABLE 1

BALANCE OF TRADE OF YUGOSLAVIA, 1947–1966
(Millions of new dinars, at the exchange rate of 12.5 new dinars = $1)

Year	Exports	Imports	Balance of Trade	Export-Import Ratio (%)
1947	2,046.1	2,075.9	− 29.8	98.6
1948	3,711.8	3,831.0	− 119.2	96.9
1949	2,483.7	3,685.2	−1,201.5	67.4
1950	1,929.4	2,883.4	− 954.0	66.9
1951	2,234.0	4,796.4	−2,562.4	46.6
1952	3,081.5	4,663.4	−1,581.9	66.1
1953	2,324.7	4,941.2	−2,616.5	47.0
1954	3,004.7	4,242.4	−1,237.7	70.8
1955	3,207.3	5,511.9	−2,304.6	58.2
1956	4,042.1	5,926.7	−1,884.6	68.2
1957	4,938.8	8,266.3	−3,327.5	59.7
1958	5,517.4	8,562.5	−3,045.1	64.4
1959	5,958.0	8,589.7	−2,631.7	69.4
1960	7,076.9	10,329.7	−3,252.8	68.5
1961	7,111.1	11,378.4	−4,267.3	62.5
1962	8,631.0	11,096.5	−2,465.5	77.8
1963	9,879.3	13,207.8	−3,328.5	74.8
1964	11,164.4	16,539.7	−5,375.3	67.5
1965	13,643.8	16,099.4	−2,455.5	84.7
1966	15,251.0	19,692.9	−4,441.9	77.4

NOTE: Imports are c.i.f., exports f.o.b. Yugoslav border. From 1951 on, imports include goods financed by foreign economic aid and U.S. agricultural surpluses; these unrequited imports ranged between 0.7 and 1.7 billion new dinars, thus covering a significant proportion of the deficit in the merchandise account; or, putting it differently, making possible an excess of imports over exports. *Statisticki Godisnjak 1966*, p. 213.

SOURCE: *Statisticki Godisnjak SFRJ 1967* (Belgrade: Federal Statistical Administration, 1967), p. 204.

system, just as the study of criminal law will give a good picture of the whole legal system of a country.[30]

CONTROLS OVER PRICES

Many possible legacies in Yugoslavia are worthy of attention, such as the difficulties encountered in trying to decentralize the banking system and make it act on market principles,[31] the efforts to change the structure of investments, the struggle against inflation and the realignment of relative prices, and the efforts to dismantle the administrative system of foreign exchange controls.[32]

[30] Discussion with Prof. Rudolf Bićanić, Zagreb, September 17, 1966.

[31] For example, President Tito stated at the beginning of 1967 that "the banking system is still not good. I do not know of a single bank that has completely adapted itself to the intentions of the Economic Reform [of 1965]." Statement made on television series "Current Topics," and reported in [50, No. 18 (January 17, 1967)].

[32] Let me mention a significant caveat at this point. I do not, of course, claim that,

TABLE 2

VALUE OF OUTPUT SUBJECT TO PRICE CONTROL
(Percentages)

Branch	1958	1961	1962
Total industry	31.2	28.6	67.0
Electric energy	100.0	100.0	100.0
Coal	97.0	97.0	76.2
Oil	42.3	54.5	96.0
Ferrous metallurgy	100.0	100.0	100.0
Nonferrous metallurgy	41.2	27.4	93.0
Nonmetals	0.0	0.0	70.6
Metal fabricating	0.0	0.0	51.6
Shipbuilding [a]	0.0	0.0	0.0
Electrical industry	0.0	0.0	84.8
Chemical industry	31.2	30.3	81.4
Construction materials	0.0	0.0	65.0
Wood industry	23.8	22.7	79.0
Paper industry	0.0	10.8	96.1
Textile industry	0.0	0.0	55.0
Leather and footwear	0.0	0.0	82.1
Rubber industry	0.0	0.0	72.5
Food processing	41.1	34.5	66.6
Tobacco	100.0	100.0	100.0
Miscellaneous industry	0.0	0.0	4.6

[a] The absence of controls over prices in the shipbuilding industry is misleading; the reason is that shipbuilding is predominantly oriented toward export markets, so there is less need for control over prices.

SOURCE: [7, p. 71]. Since the authors do not indicate exactly what types of price controls are included, and one can only infer that they are talking about wholesale prices, it is necessary to view the data in this table with some caution. However, the ubiquity and importance of some type of administrative control over prices, whether price ceilings or requirements that firms must announce their intention to raise prices in advance, is evident.

However, in the brief space available, I shall deal with only two legacies, both of which have great significance for foreign trade: the problem of the irrational price system and the problem of the foreign trade and exchange system.

A vivid illustration of the difficulties encountered in Yugoslavia in attempting to shift from central planning to a system of market socialism is the persistence, nay the increase, in the proportion of the output subject to controls over prices. As Table 2 indicates, there was an apparent rise in the proportion of goods subject to price control from 1958 to 1962, with a slight decrease in 1961. Furthermore, in connection with the 1965 reform of the

if some feature of Yugoslav economic history since 1952 fits into my general discussion of the legacy problem, it is necessarily a legacy from the Stalinist period in Yugoslavia. All I am arguing is that such features illustrate some possible aspects of the legacy problem and lend some support to my claim that this problem is worthy of study.

economic system, the Yugoslav regime imposed a broad price freeze, thus providing a comprehensive and direct control over prices.

Despite controls over prices, the cost of living index still more than doubled between 1952 and 1964, even according to official statistics [20, p. 235].

The CPE's command economy and closed economy elements cause significant divergences between domestic prices and prices on world markets. I have argued earlier that it is difficult to eliminate these divergences, and the Yugoslav case lends strong support to this claim. As long as domestic prices differ widely from those in foreign markets, instruments must be developed which bring these two sets of prices sufficiently into line to permit trade to take place. In the CPE this problem is skirted by the expedient of not permitting prices to determine export and import decisions and of subsidizing foreign trade firms that take losses and taxing those that make profits because of the price divergences. Once this primacy of centralized, direct, physical planning is abandoned, either domestic prices must be changed to correspond to world prices or administrative and financial instruments must be developed to compensate for the divergences. The use of such instruments is not a satisfactory substitute for a price reform that enables the market to operate freely, since they can never be as flexible as the market mechanism and they always contain the danger of bureaucratic meddling in the detailed affairs of the economy. As late as 1965, the Yugoslav price structure was still far from satisfying the need for a reliable yardstick of value for purposes of decisions on the allocation of resources within the economy or in foreign trade. The Yugoslav Minister of Finance, Kiro Gligorov, in a speech to the Federal Assembly on June 9, 1965, argued strongly in favor of the considerable shifts in prices which were part of the 1965 reform. He argued that the low prices for energy, raw materials and semi-manufactured products, and transport — all of which are relatively scarce in Yugoslavia — should be raised relative to the prices of manufactured products. In addition, imports were subsidized by a low effective exchange rate of 800 to 900 dinars to the dollar, while exports of manufactured products were subsidized by a much higher rate, averaging 1,055 dinars to the dollar. He further stressed that this condition will place a burden on the economy for the next fifteen or twenty years, as some large investment projects were being started on the basis of faulty calculations. The benefit of liberalizing trade lies in the fact that the veil is removed and true relations are revealed when trade is based on world market prices. [33, 34]

[33] Kiro Gligorov speech of June 9, 1965 to the Federal Assembly, in [37, pp. 13–14].
[34] A Yugoslav economist told me that he believed Yugoslav prices to have been far out of line. He said that, if prices were changed to represent those on world markets, it was quite possible that some of the Slovenian factories, which are now held up as models of efficiency, would prove unprofitable. He argued that these enterprises had paid very low prices for raw materials and food, both from other regions of Yugoslavia

The need for a significant realignment of prices by administrative means, and the raising of the general price level in the process, as part of the 1965 reform, exemplifies some of the legacy problems discussed earlier. The plan was to raise the general price level by 24 percent over the 1964 level, with prices in industry and mining rising by 14 percent, in agriculture by 32 percent, in transport by 26 percent, in construction by 22 percent, and in other activities by 45 percent [7, p. 132]. Within industry, prices of processing branches were to rise by only 8 percent, and raw material prices by three times as much. The range of individual price changes was, of course, much greater. For example, the price rise for iron ore was set in the range of 41 to 59 percent, for aluminum at 45 percent, and for crude steel at 63 percent; while prices of medicines were to fall by 9 percent, of cotton fab-rics by 6 percent, and of rubber footwear by 10 percent [7, pp. 133–137] Since a major aim of this reform was to enable Yugoslavia to enter more fully into an international division of labor, these price changes reflect, in part, the disparities that had existed between domestic and world prices prior to the reform and that were to be removed.

FOREIGN TRADE AND FOREIGN EXCHANGE SYSTEM

In line with the gradual transformation of the Yugoslav economic system from a CPE to a "visible hand" system, the Yugoslav government has worked to modify the centralized foreign trade and foreign exchange system. How-ever, just as with the banking system,[35] Yugoslav leaders were ambivalent about the desirability of introducing market elements into the foreign trade and exchange systems. While the need to provide greater independence for enterprises dictated decentralization in the field of foreign trade, the bal-ance-of-payments problem, the need to meet obligations under bilateral clearing agreements, and the desire to keep some of the crucial levers of control at the central level all militated against complete abandonment of the command economy and priority economy elements in foreign trade and foreign exchange. Thus, despite valiant attempts in 1952 and again in 1961 toward a more liberal, market-oriented trade and exchange system, the progress has been halting. Even the important 1965 reform, while providing some of the necessary conditions (a policy of deflation, devaluation, and price adjustments), did not result in an immediate transition toward a free foreign trade and exchange system.[36]

and from abroad, and were assured high, protected prices for their products in the domestic markets. With increases in the prices of raw materials and food (and therefore payments to workers), and with competition from imports, the situation of these manufacturing enterprises would change radically. If this rather extreme forecast approximates reality, it provides very interesting evidence on the legacy problem.

[35] See my paper, [32].

[36] Thus, a Yugoslav economist wrote in 1966 that the reforms in the foreign sector of the Yugoslav economy lagged behind those in the domestic sector [30].

In a decision published in August 1966 [42, No. 32, August 10, 1966, pp. 655–656], the principle of compulsory cession of foreign exchange earnings to the National Bank was confirmed, but the amount of foreign exchange which exporters could keep and use freely (retention quota) was raised for most products over that provided in March 1966 [42, No. 10, March 9, 1966, pp. 203–204]. In addition, the mere promise that exporting enterprises could purchase given amounts of foreign exchange from the bank was changed to actual retention of the appropriate percentage of foreign exchange earnings, and to a provision that enterprises exporting 51 percent or more of their output might use all the foreign exchange in their bank account to buy raw materials or intermediate products [42, No. 32, August 10, 1966, pp. 654–655]. This piecemeal approach to increasing the freedom of enterprises to use the foreign exchange they earned was opposed in a joint proposal of the Economic Chambers of Belgrade, Zagreb, and Sarajevo, in which they suggested the introduction of a completely decentralized foreign exchange system.[37] While this proposal was not adopted and there are serious doubts as to whether the particular plan recommended would have proved feasible, it provides evidence that, although forces exist in Yugoslavia which wish to eliminate central control over foreign exchange, the system's directors are not yet ready to eliminate this important lever of control.[38]

Just as steps were taken in 1966 to modify incrementally the foreign exchange system, a decree by the Federal Executive Council in September of that year provided for a considerable liberalization of foreign trade in 1967 [22, pp. 1 and 7]. Despite this liberalization, however, about 44 percent of raw materials and semi-manufactured goods, 77 percent of consumer goods, and 50 percent of capital goods imports were left under central control [51, p. 8].

The continuation of significant central controls over foreign trade and foreign exchange, some fifteen years after the first attempts to move toward a "visible hand" regime with worker self-management, is a function of the objective balance-of-payments situation and the views of the system's directors. I do not wish to argue that the persistence of central controls may

[37] This proposal provided that enterprises keep the major share of foreign exchange receipts and cede to the central government only enough to cover the foreign exchange needs of the government. Enterprises that do not earn foreign exchange could no longer obtain it from the government, but would have to make arrangements to obtain it from those that do, either directly or through banks. The proposal aimed at eliminating the redistribution of foreign exchange through central organs, while still avoiding an open market for foreign exchange, since this would, under Yugoslav conditions, result in a fluctuating market exchange rate above the official one. Radio Zagreb broadcast, August 1, 1966.

[38] An interesting aspect of the Yugoslav system is that banks have taken over the basic functions of foreign exchange control. For example, by control over foreign exchange and credit they assure the fulfillment by enterprises of obligations undertaken by the government in its bilateral clearing agreements with socialist countries.

be explained simply as a legacy of the CPE. I would suggest, however, that the difficulties experienced in expanding exports — especially to convertible currency markets — are due, in part, to some of the legacies discussed here. Similarly, the leaders' beliefs are also influenced by their experiences during the centrally planned period and the difficulties faced in the period of transition.[39]

CONCLUDING REMARKS

Since there is no shortage of analyses of the operation of the centrally planned economy, I have chosen to focus on the less crucial, but relatively neglected, issue of the system's probable legacies. To repeat the automobile analogy, let us assume that safety, frequency of repair, comfort, roadability, and other characteristics have been fully studied, but that resale value has for some reason been neglected. In that case the marginal benefit from studying relative resale values and informing potential buyers that there are considerable differences between various cars in this respect might well exceed the marginal benefit from duplicating the studies of the cars' operational characteristics.

Focusing on legacies is useful in helping us understand somewhat better the actions and decisions of Communist countries that are considering significant alterations in their economic systems or that have already begun the process of substituting a successor regime for the CPE. In addition, whatever our judgment may be of the merit of the CPE as an engine of economic development, inclusion of the legacy problem appears to change the equation in such a way as to make the system look less desirable. While positive legacies are very important, the negative legacies seem to outweigh them (when the evaluation is based on reasonable assumptions regarding the preference functions of countries potentially interested in the system). For a full comparative analysis, it would be necessary, of course, to study the merits of other potential economic systems in terms of their success during their lifetime and of their legacies.

Evaluating the legacies of the full-fledged Stalinist-type CPE may remind one of probating the will of a straw man, since it is not likely that leaders of many present-day underdeveloped countries wish or are able to establish such a system. A useful line of investigation for future work in this field would surely be a more profound analysis of the relationship between individual key elements of the CPE and their consequences during the life of the system, and between the key elements and the legacies they will leave. This analysis might focus on a search for modifications of the CPE that

---

[39] The unfortunate results of the 1961 reform, in which an attempt was made to abandon the closed economy element, have made Yugoslav leaders more cautious about the speed of implementing changes in the foreign sector.

would keep the major desirable consequences and legacies, but eliminate or reduce the undesirable ones. Modifications may be possible which allow one to have one's cake and eat it too. Probably more important is the possibility of discovering trade-offs in which one gives up some small part of the positive results in order to reduce considerably some of the negative results. Let me suggest briefly some of the questions that should be considered in such an analysis: (1) Is a less extreme version of the social ownership element possible, one in which only the "commanding heights" are socialized, without giving up the major benefits of the CPE? (2) Could the macro-level element of the pressure economy (i.e., the high rate of forced saving) and the key features of the priority economy be achieved without invoking the extreme Stalinist version of the command economy, pressure economy, and priority economy? This may be one of the key questions, since many of the undesirable features of the CPE and its legacies result from the command economy and from the extremes to which the pressure economy and priority economy are pushed in the pure model.[40] (3) Should extensive development be practiced, or should one start with a more balanced approach, paying more attention to the questions of productivity, costs, and quality even at the early stages of development? (4) Would it not be better to adopt a modified version of the closed economy element, in which an attempt was made from the very beginning to prepare the economy for eventual inclusion in an international division of labor?

The aim of this analysis of modified Soviet-type models would be to discover whether such systems would be feasible, and if feasible, whether they would be appropriate for the initial stages of development as well as (with minor modifications) for the more mature stages, thus eliminating or alleviating the legacy problem. If it were found that, by giving up some of the extreme features of the Stalinist model, the rate of development would be reduced in the early stages (and this is not a foregone conclusion, by any means), it would still be necessary to compare this loss with the possible gains from eliminating or reducing some of the most undesirable legacies of the extreme model.

If my claim is accepted that legacies represent an important additional

---

[40] The significance of establishing a system that permits rational choice, especially at the early stages of development, is stressed in Peter Wiles's pungent comment: "It is a mere fallacy, however often it is repeated by however high authority, that poverty and underdevelopment gives us more excuse for arbitrary choices, while rationality becomes important only when a certain prosperity has already been achieved. Obviously the exact opposite is the case. For arbitrary choices are wasteful choices, and a poor man can afford waste less than a rich. True, a rich man or country faces many more choices, and the subject acquires greater intellectual interest, what with fuel policy, higher education policy, choice between techniques, choice between road and rail, etc., etc. But the dull choice between bread and potatoes is more important than these in terms of human welfare" [49, p. 95].

dimension in the study of comparative economic systems, then one of the major results of this approach is to open up large and unmapped new areas of economic research.

DISCUSSION

Benjamin N. Ward

Professor Neuberger's notion of legacies is a very interesting one, well worth further study. This note attempts to make the notion of legacy a little more explicit, considers some problems in applying the notion in practice, and opts for a less sophisticated approach to the discussion of possible future paths for the Soviet bloc countries.

The legacy problem faced by Neuberger's underdeveloped country in making a choice among alternative economic systems can be sketched as follows. Suppose there are two economies, identical with each other in all respects, including their history. One suddenly becomes a Soviet-type economy. Both then run along through time for some years, experiencing identical environments, *mutatis mutandis*. Then the Soviet-type economy changes into a decentralized socialist economy, making extensive use of markets. The two economies continue to run for a few more years. All differences between the two economies after this second shift are legacies.

Legacies are thus not difficult to identify in principle, emerging as they do from a study of the comparative dynamics of the relevant model. However, the empirical isolation of legacies is a very difficult matter, and there is a serious risk that empirical analysis will produce false legacies. There are three principal reasons for this. First, both economies being compared are steadily changing, so each is different from itself at a different point of time. Hence, if the appropriate starting time for the market economy is not chosen, apparent legacies may well represent differences that would disappear if one of the economies were run forward or backward for a few periods. Not only would the false legacies disappear as the comparison moved toward a more appropriate starting time, but probably some true legacies that did not show up in the previous comparison would begin to appear. Second, legacies may vary widely, depending on the initial conditions and the nature of such exogenous factors as the size of the country and its level of development, the nature of its resources, and its level of economic and political security. Legacies correctly identified for one set of conditions may be false for another. Finally, there is the dearth of empirical evidence. Only one country so far fits the requirement of having first adopted a Soviet type of economic organization and then having discarded it for a kind of market socialism. So empirical comparisons must be limited to Yugoslavia or some other country whose initial conditions and environment closely parallel those of Yugoslavia.

Neuberger has not attempted such a comparison. His comparison appears to be between actual practice in a Soviet-type economy — and Yugoslavia — and an efficient ideal whose organization is not specified clearly. This can be misleading for the choice-situation which concerns him, since it tends to create false negative legacies of the Soviet type of system. Ignoring the many difficulties, let me offer a few casual, empirical comments on legacies. I select Greece as the economy for comparison with Yugoslavia. Greece is a capitalist market economy with initial conditions in the late 'forties somewhat similar to those in Yugoslavia just after World War II. A decade or so ago Greece was approximately the world's median country with respect to both GNP and per capita GNP, Yugoslavia having somewhat more of the former and less of the latter. Both have had successful growth experiences in the past dozen years, and both owe some considerable portion of their success to substantial foreign aid. The two countries can pass at least a very weak test of similarity and appropriateness for the intended comparison.[41]

The "positive legacies" listed by Neuberger are unchanged by shifting to a Greek-Yugoslav comparison. With respect to growth-orientation, high investment rate, higher capital stock, lesser income inequality, more rapid development of industry, and education, Yugoslavia appears to be on the predicted side of Greece.[42] It should be noted that this is true even though Greece has had an unusually high growth rate for a developing capitalist economy. A number of the "negative legacies" remain unchanged too, so attention will be limited to one or two cases where Neuberger's legacies do not seem to emerge.

First, the entrepreneurial deficiencies attributed to the Soviet-type system are largely shared by the Greeks. The underdeveloped markets of an underdeveloped economy are apparently not a very satisfactory training ground for "cost-conscious, new-product-oriented" businessmen, "experienced in those skills essential to selling in a competitive world market or a competitive buyers' market at home." Like their counterparts, they "are likely . . . to be oriented toward short-run goals." These are easily observable features of the Greek economic scene. The legacies in this area which survive are the lack of concern with financial liquidity and perhaps some aspects of "independence" [1].

[41] Unfortunately, these and the succeeding comparative statements cannot be defended in a short comment. Further effort at comparison can be found in my "Capitalism vs. Socialism: A Small Country Version" (mimeographed).

[42] Because the Greek population is ethnically homogeneous, regional comparisons with Yugoslavia are not very revealing with respect to systemic legacies; so we ignore Neuberger's point concerning the equalization of regional differences, under "Positive Legacies."

The asserted negative legacies in foreign trade are another area in which an empirical comparison changes the picture. Greece has shown no great ability to promote the exports of its industrial or agricultural products effectively on highly competitive, convertible currency markets. Also its system of trade protection permits an undesirable domestic price structure to persist. And Greece too seems to suffer from "the absence of a compulsion to develop expertise in export marketing," and to have no "constituency . . . in favor of exports, since few firms specialize in this field" [45, Chaps. 2, 5, and 6] [24, Chaps. 5, 7, and 8].

Further extension of this comparison would produce further qualifications to Neuberger's list of legacies, though I doubt that these would change the picture decisively. The important thing to note is simply that the market economy changes too, is also subject to the pressures and inertias of vested interests and to the inefficiencies of an operating economy. Perhaps most important of all, it too is an underdeveloped economy; it is all too easy, in comparisons with an ideal, to identify falsely the legacies of underdevelopment with systemic legacies.

The choice-of-system problem faced by an underdeveloped country is not the only application of the legacy theory proposed by Neuberger. He also suggests using it in discussing the prospects of Soviet bloc countries now in various early stages of decentralizing their economic administration. For this legacy problem, by our earlier sketch, the second country also becomes a Soviet-type economy, but one that continues in that state for some time after the first state has decentralized. The relevant legacies are then those differences between the two economies which exist after the second economy also decentralizes.

This comparison must be purely speculative at the moment, since there are no empirical candidates for comparison with Yugoslavia. It also serves to point up a rigidity in the legacy approach. What one would like to do is to identify the specific aspects of persisting Soviet-type organization which produce specific legacies. Neuberger has asserted a number of such connections, but they are extremely difficult to isolate empirically from other causal connections in a dynamic environment. A model might be used to generate such results by varying limited aspects of the organization, as Neuberger suggests, but this has not yet been done.

The legacy approach does not prove to be very useful for this part of Neuberger's problem. A better technique, perhaps, is simply to compare the similarities and differences between Yugoslavia on the eve of its decentralization and the East European Communist states on the apparent eve of theirs, without bothering too much about the dynamic causal chains. This is especially appropriate when strong emphasis is placed on the role of attitudes as the inertial force preserving negative aspects of the Soviet type of economy, as is done by Neuberger. Let me suggest two or three ways in which the situations differ.

First, the external environment faced by the Eastern bloc countries today is very different from that of Yugoslavia fifteen years ago. Instead of hostility there is relative harmony within the socialist camp in Europe, with the autonomy of individual states growing in the absence of any serious threat to security. Instead of a Cominform embargo, there is an effort to develop more extensive trade and more flexible methods of trading. And the coincidence in the timing of serious discussions of change within the Eastern bloc countries suggests that band-wagon effects may play a role in decentralization decisions.

Second, their status as followers offers the prospective decentralizers some opportunity to profit from Yugoslavia's experience. There may be an element of this, for example, in the intention of the Eastern bloc countries to preserve a strong set of price controls under their new regimes. Perhaps more related to ideology than to experience is the firm avoidance of any commitment to worker management in the latter-day reforms; however, the rather steady "opening" of Yugoslav society to various intellectual and political currents is a reminder of the connection between market flows and information flows. By the standard measures, Yugoslavia's performance since decentralization has been very good; nevertheless, a rickety patchwork surrounds the Yugoslav system of economic control which must give Eastern planners pause and add force to the inertias described by Neuberger.

Third, the technical skill of a large and increasing number of economists in the Eastern bloc countries is today much greater than that of the Yugoslav economists of fifteen years ago. This applies most particularly to the understanding of the role of prices in economic decisionmaking and to properties of planning schemes. Let me add that this comment does not apply to the Yugoslavia of today, which possesses a number of very competent economists. Nor need the Yugoslavia of fifteen years ago have given anything to today's Eastern bloc in terms of the enthusiasm with which it eulogized the "laws of supply and demand" as regulators of economic activity.

Finally, the Eastern bloc economies are in a generally healthier state than was Yugoslavia in 1950. Most of them, perhaps even Czechoslovakia, can expect further growth at respectable rates to accompany a no-more-than-marginal reform. Thus the major ideological and political pressures that were at work in Yugoslavia are either muted or absent in most Eastern bloc countries today. This is by no means to suggest that substantial, irreversible reforms will not occur. What it does suggest is that there will be an eager search for halfway houses, a greater reluctance to let the market settle policy issues than was true of the Yugoslav leaders.

Neuberger has listed a number of legacies that survive at least a casual inspection. In addition, the notion of legacy itself, with its apparent ability to provide causal connections between relatively abrupt organizational change and longer-run economic outcomes, may with further development turn out to be a very useful tool of comparative analysis. I share his hope that others will follow him into this new area of research.

REFERENCES

1. Alexander, A. *Greek Industrialists* (Athens: Center for Economic Research, 1964).
2. Baran, Paul A. "National Economic Planning," in Bernard F. Haley (ed.), *A Survey of Contemporary Economics* (Homewood, Ill.: Irwin, 1952), II, pp. 355–403.
3. Brown, Alan A. "The Economics of Centrally Planned Foreign Trade: The Hungarian Experience" (Unpublished doctoral dissertation, Harvard University, 1966), Chap. VII.
4. ———, and Y. C. Yin. "Communist Economics: Reform vs. Orthodoxy," *Communist Affairs*, III:1 (January–February 1965), pp. 3–9.
5. Damjanovic, Mijat, and others. *Jugoslavensko Javno Mnenje o Privrednoj Reformi 1965 Godine*, in *Godisnjak 1965* (Belgrade: Institut Drustvenih Nauka, 1966).
6. Dobb, Maurice. *Soviet Economic Development Since 1917*, Fifth Edition (London: Routledge and Paul, 1960).
7. Dzeba, K., and M. Beslac. *Privredna Reforma: Sto i Zasto se Mijenja* (Zagreb: Stvarnost, 1965).
8. *The Economist*. December 3–9, 1966.
9. *Ekonomska Politika*, October 10, 1964.
10. "Elementi za utvrdjivanje nekih specificnih osobenosti u nasem izvozu," V. Pertot, *Ekonomist*, No. 4 (1960), pp. 617–661. Cf. [36], below.
11. Erlich, Alexander. "Development Strategy and Planning: The Soviet Experience," Conference on Economic Planning, sponsored by Universities–NBER, Princeton, November, 1964.
12. Fedorenko, N. "Vazhnaia ekonomicheskaia problema," *Pravda*, January 17, 1965.
13. Friss, I. "The Party and Some Important Topical Tasks of Economic Science," *Társadalmi Szemle* (August–September 1965); as translated in Radio Free Europe, Hungarian Press Survey, No. 1635 (September 3, 1966).
14. Goldman, Josef. "Systems of Planning and Management," JPRS, Translations on Economic Organization and Management in Eastern Europe 28988, No. 455 (March 3, 1965).
15. Gorupic, Drago, and Ivo Perisin. "Prosirena reprodukcija i njeno financiranje," *Ekonomski Pregled*, Nos. 2–3 (1965).
16. Hirschman, Albert O. *The Strategy of Economic Development* (New Haven: Yale University Press, 1958).

17. Hoeffding, Oleg. "State Planning and Forced Industrialization," *Problems of Communism*, VIII:6 (November–December 1959), pp. 38–44.
18. Holesovsky, Vaclav. "Planning Reforms in Czechoslovakia," paper presented to the Second Annual Convention of the American Association for the Advancement of Slavic Studies, Washington, D.C., March 30, 1967.
19. *Hospodarske noviny*, Nos. 51–52 (1966).
20. *Jugoslavija, 1945–1964, Statisticki Pregled* (Belgrade: Federal Statistical Administration, 1965).
21. Kardelj, Edvard, *Borba*, November 27, 1965.
22. Korosec, Joze. "More Than Half of Imports Liberalized," *Yugoslav Export*, November 1, 1966.
23. "Materijali sa Savjetovanja Naucne Sekcije Saveza Drustava Ekonomista Jugoslavije" (Zagreb, 18–20 januara 1963), *Ekonomski Pregled*, Nos. 3–5 (1963), pp. 147–299.
24. McCorkle, Chester O. *Fruit and Vegetable Marketing in the Economic Development of Greece* (Athens: Center for Economic Research, 1962).
25. Mesaric, Milan. *Notes on the Yugoslav Planning System* (Zagreb: Ekonomski Institut, 1966).
26. Michaely, Michael. *Concentration in International Trade* (Amsterdam: North-Holland Publishing Company, 1962).
27. Miskovic, Dobrivoje. "Investicije i Platni Bilans," *Ekonomika Preduzeca*, XIII:7 (1965).
28. Montias, John M. "The Soviet Model and the Underdeveloped Areas," in Nicolas Spulber (ed.), *Study of the Soviet Economy* (Bloomington: University of Indiana, 1961).
29. "Mr. Kadar's Albatross," *The Economist*, October 29, 1966.
30. Mrkusic, Z. "Razvoj jugoslavenskog sistema spoljne trgovine," Trece Medunarodno Savetovanje Privrednika i Pravnika, Zagreb, 15–17 September, 1966.
31. Neuberger, Egon. *Central Planning and Its Legacies*, (Santa Monica: The RAND Corporation, December 1966), Paper P-3492.
32. ———. "Centralization versus Decentralization: The Case of Yugoslav Banking," *American Slavic and East European Review*, XVIII:3 (October 1959), pp. 361–373.
33. ———. "Libermanism, Computopia, and Visible Hand: The Question of Informational Efficiency," *American Economic Review*, LVI:2 (May 1966), pp. 131–144.
34. Nove, Alec. "The Changing Role of Soviet Prices," *Economics of Planning* (December 1963), pp. 185–195.
35. ———. "The Soviet Model and Underdeveloped Countries," *International Affairs*, XXXVII:1 (January 1961), pp. 29–38.
36. Pertot, Vladimir. "Neke osobenosti u strukturi i geografskoj usmerenosti naseg isvoza," *Ekonomist*, No. 3 (1960), pp. 380–426. See also [10], above.
37. *Privredne Reforme*, Belgrade, 1965.
38. Radio Free Europe, Yugoslav Internal Affairs (November 30, 1965).
39. Rockwell, Charles S. "Product Growth and Factor Inputs in Yugoslavia: Some Cross-Sectional Results," paper prepared for the American-Yugoslav Seminar, Belgrade, 4–9 July 1966.
40. Seton, Francis. "Planning and Economic Growth: Asia, Africa, and the Soviet Model," *Soviet Survey*, No. 31 (January–March 1960), pp. 38–44.

41. Sik, O. "Improvement of System of Planned Management," *Rude Pravo* (November 22, 1963); in JPRS, Translations on Economic Organization and Management in Eastern Europe 26256, No. 369 (September 3, 1964), pp. 1–20.
42. *Sluzbeni List SFRJ*, XXII.
43. "Soviet Economic Performance and Reform: Some Problems of Analysis and Prognosis — A Round-Table Discussion," *Slavic Review*, XXXV:2 (June 1966), pp. 222–246.
44. *Statisticki Godisnjak SFRJ 1967* (Belgrade: Federal Statistical Administration, 1967).
45. Tomasek, Ladislav. "Vztah filosofie a ekonomie a nove zasady rizeni," *Planovane hospodarstvi*, XVIII:2 (1965).
46. Triantis, S. G. *Common Market and Economic Development: The E.E.C. and Greece* (Athens: Center for Economic Research, 1965).
47. Vajda, Imre. "Privredni Razvoj i Medjunarodna Podela Rada," *Ekonomist*, No. 4 (1965).
48. Vukovic, D. "Dueli Koncar-Natronka," *Borba*, September 26, 1966, p. 5.
49. Wiles, P. J. D. *The Political Economy of Communism* (Cambridge: Harvard University Press, 1962).
50. *Yugoslav Facts and Views*, No. 18, January 17, 1967.
51. *Yugoslav News Bulletin*, V:392, January 10, 1967.

On Prospects for
Communist Foreign Trade

ABRAM BERGSON

As a final discussant on our program, I have been given a broad mandate. Rather than try to comment at all systematically on the many issues that might merit attention, perhaps it will be fitting if I turn to the future. In the light of the interesting essays that have been presented, I propose to inquire very briefly into the possible impact on foreign trade of an outstanding feature of the current Communist scene: the trend toward economic rationality in planning. This trend is relatively new, and its future course is still uncertain; but assuming that the trend continues, how will Communist foreign trade be affected?

The question might be raised regarding Communist trade generally, but of particular interest is the trade of the U.S.S.R. and Eastern Europe, where the trend toward economic rationality seems most manifest. A logically prior issue concerns the degree to which Communist foreign trade is now affected by economic irrationality. If I may turn first to this matter, economic rationality in respect of foreign trade is usually taken to mean conformity with the principles of contemporary Western trade theory — that is to say, conformity with free trade norms corresponding to comparative advantage, these norms being construed with due regard to the country's "preferences." The identity of economic rationality and such norms, however, may not be complete; and for familiar reasons a divergence may obtain for the Communist countries in question. For the moment, however, I shall pass by this complexity. Provisionally, therefore, I take the free trade norms corresponding to comparative advantage as the standard of economic rationality.

In speculating about the future impact of the trend toward economic rationality, we are interested in the volume, structure, and direction of trade.

We also wish to know, therefore, how each facet may be affected now by a divergence from free trade norms.

To begin with volume, the question at issue here, of course, is in effect whether and to what extent Communist participation in foreign trade has been restricted below the level called for by free trade norms. And this is much the same thing as the question that Professor Haberler has posed: Does the trade of a Communist country tend to be smaller relative to its gross national product than that of a "comparable" capitalist country — that is, one of similar size, resource endowment, and the like?

The two questions are much but not entirely the same, for the foreign trade of capitalist countries, too, diverges from free trade norms. Also, the structure of final demand, particularly the choice between investment and consumption, tends to be different under the two systems. For this reason, as is rarely considered, trade participation might differ even if free trade norms ruled in both cases.

Still, if the volume of trade of capitalist countries diverges from the free trade level, it is usually in the downward direction. Moreover, one surmises, though this is less certain, that the inordinate stress on investment under Communism would tend rather to increase participation there, at least in early stages, and perhaps even at later stages in smaller countries. Especially in these circumstances investment should outrun domestic machinery production. While the extent of the excess of the former should depend on the country's aptitude for machinery production, the emphasis on investment should tend to stimulate net imports of machinery and foreign trade generally. This was, of course, the experience of the U.S.S.R. under the First Five-Year Plan, and Professor Montias' essay suggests that it has also been the experience in Eastern Europe for more extended periods.

By implication, if trade participation by Communist countries should indeed tend to be below that in capitalist countries, this would in itself indicate a corresponding tendency under Communism for trade to be below the free trade level. Yet, while Professor Haberler poses the question concerning comparative trade participation under the two systems, he properly answers it only hypothetically, for it must be acknowledged that this complex theme still awaits a sufficiently comprehensive and systematic inquiry.

The hypothesis, however, is that Communist trade participation tends to be relatively low, and the evidence for this surely is weighty in the case of the chief of the countries in question, the U.S.S.R. Here in 1964, for example, foreign trade (exports plus imports) amounted to but 5.3 percent of the gross national product. With all due allowance for the continental dimensions of the U.S.S.R., this must be an inordinately low level of trade participation for that country.[1]

[1] In the United States, foreign trade during 1954–1963 averaged 7.9 percent of the

As for the Communist countries of Eastern Europe, here especially I think more research is in order; but perhaps I do not misread the readily available, though somewhat conflicting, evidence in thinking that at least in a number of cases trade participation is probably relatively low.[2]

But in trying to judge whether and to what extent trade volume may be below the free trade level, we are able to refer not only to trade participation rates but to a variety of other evidence concerning the policies pursued, and this too is illuminating. Thus, in directing the development of their economies the "system's directors" in Communist countries (if I may use a convenient expression that I have employed elsewhere) have sought expressly to expand industry, especially basic branches, on a broad front, and so to limit dependence on foreign trade. By all accounts, the system's directors have done so partly for ideological, military, and political reasons; but apparently their policy of autarky also reflects an inordinate antipathy, under centralized planning, for the uncertainties of world trade, and often a lack of understanding of the economic costs that the policy entails. The concern has been especially to limit trade with the capitalist West, but trade with other Communist countries seems sometimes viewed with misgivings also.

Under policies such as these, it would be surprising indeed if Communist trade participation were not often below the free trade level. The force of this tendency, however, must have been somewhat weakened insofar as some industries that were developed may have proved not so costly as "adults" as they did as "infants," and hence not so much in conflict with comparative advantage as they were initially. Also, in developing new industries the system's directors apparently have not always anticipated fully the requirements these have generated for supporting imports of materials. Especially in the smaller countries, this probably has tended to cancel some steps towards autarky.[3]

I conclude that Communist participation in foreign trade probably is often, though not necessarily always, below the free trade level. It may be hoped that further research will soon permit us to be more definite on this important matter.

If the volume of foreign trade is uneconomically low, the structure too (to come to this aspect) must diverge from that called for by comparative advantage, for the reduced volume presumably in itself distorts structure

GNP. At least in current prices, the corresponding ratio was still larger at an earlier stage when per capita GNP in the United States was nearer the current Soviet level. On Soviet and U.S. trade participation rates, see [4, p. 108], [5, p. 281], [9, p. 290], [11, pp. 312–314], and [13, p. 660].

[2] See especially [2], [7, pp. 898 ff.], [10, pp. 111 ff.], and [12, pp. 23 ff.].

[3] On Communist trade policies, see especially [2], [9], [10], and [12]; also the Conference papers of Spulber, Brown, and Holzman.

relative to what it would be if volume were not reduced. But the structure of Communist foreign trade must be distorted beyond this. Thus, with due allowance again for the possibility that some costly "infants" have become less costly "adults," there can hardly be a doubt that numerous branches have been developed to an uneconomic degree, with the result that even within limits of the reduced overall volume the assortment of both imports and exports diverges from that called for by comparative advantage. Among different branches, probably it is most often those in basic industry that have been developed unduly, but an inordinate stress on the production of one or another branch could easily have occurred elsewhere as well.

There is room for more research on the determinants of the structure, as well as the volume, of Communist foreign trade; but I believe that there is evidence enough for these generalizations. For one thing, there are the facts on Communist economic policies already referred to. Imaginably, domestic production could have been fostered and imports limited in such a way that different industries would have been affected in a more or less uniform way, and with little effect on the structure of trade. But the system's directors in Communist countries have sought rather to favor some industries over others, and apparently often with little regard to costs. For another, even where costs have been a concern, the system's directors in undertaking any meaningful appraisal have been handicapped again and again by their imperfect understanding of costs and by distortions in their own prices. The imperfect Communist understanding of costs and the distortions in Communist prices are proverbial features of the Communist scene, and there is no need to labor them here. Finally, Western studies of Communist foreign trade, such as those of Professor Pryor and Professor Brown, supply an abundance of examples which fairly clearly illustrate the distortions that are in question [12, pp. 28ff.].

I have said that the Communist trade structure has tended to diverge from free trade norms. As I read the evidence, the divergence must often have been of a very gross sort.

To refer finally to the direction of Communist trade, I can be brief on this. The economic policies that have been described, while limiting trade generally, obviously have tended to restrict it especially with the non-Communist countries, particularly the capitalist West, and this fact is readily confirmed. Thus, of Russia's total foreign trade (imports plus exports) in 1964, 59.6 percent was conducted with Communist countries in Eastern Europe, and 69.7 percent with Communist countries generally. Industrial countries in the West accounted for only 20.0 percent of total trade, and less-developed non-Communist countries for the remaining 10.3 percent. Of the trade of Eastern European Communist countries in 1964, 15.4 percent was conducted with each other, 46.7 percent with the U.S.S.R., and 67.2 percent with Communist countries generally. Trade with the industrial West accounted for only 24.0 percent of the total, and that with the less-developed non-Communist countries for 8.8 percent.[4]

One need not probe much beyond these facts to become aware of the degree to which the share of the capitalist West in the trade of the U.S.S.R. and Communist Eastern Europe must be below the free trade level. One or two further figures may be of interest: of the total trade of non-Communist countries in 1964, that with the U.S.S.R. and all of Eastern Europe accounted for only 3.6 percent, or less than the share of the trade of non-Communist countries with a single one of their number, the Netherlands [14].

I have been identifying economic rationality in foreign trade with free trade norms corresponding to comparative advantage. As the primers teach, this identification is permissible for a country that trades only in competitive markets. Should a country enjoy any monopoly power abroad, however, economic rationality would dictate that the country sometimes diverge from free trade norms. In doing so it might be able to benefit materially. To what extent have the Communist countries enjoyed and exploited monopoly power in respect of their foreign trade?

The question is familiar and also still somewhat controversial. But perhaps I shall not be doing violence to the known facts if I hold that, in view of limitations the Communist countries have found it expedient to observe in their trade with the non-Communist world, these countries must often enjoy monopoly power in their trade with one another; that this must be true especially of the U.S.S.R. in its trade with its Communist neighbors; and that nevertheless, under the established practice of taking "world prices" as a point of departure for fixing intra–Communist bloc trade terms, such monopoly power, at least in very recent years, probably has not often been exploited very fully. So far as Communist trade fails to conform to free trade norms, monopoly power must be a factor; but it probably is not among the weightier ones with which we have to deal.[5]

So far I have also tacitly ignored Western trade controls. As Professor Spulber explains, such controls are of rather diverse sorts, but they might all be viewed as affecting adversely the terms on which Communist countries can trade with the West. So far as economic rationality is understood to represent an appropriate adaptation to available terms, therefore, the controls — strictly speaking — cannot be considered to be a cause of irrationality on the Communist side. But if Communist trade with the West is relatively limited, such controls are a factor, along with Communist poli-

[4] For the trade of Eastern European countries, shipments of one of these countries to another are counted only once. See [3] and [8, p. 922].

[5] On the determination of prices in intra–Communist bloc trade, see especially [10, Chap. IX] and [12, Chap. V].

cies; and what has been said thus far about the level and direction of Communist trade must be read accordingly.

If the foregoing is correct, we have some basis to answer the question posed at the outset concerning the impact on Communist trade of a continuing trend toward economic rationality. Thus, should this trend persist in the Communist countries, there should be a tendency for the volume of foreign trade to rise not only absolutely but relative to national income. There should also be consequential changes in resource allocation among branches, probably often at the expense of some branches in basic industry. Such changes would tend to be accompanied by changes in the structure of exports and imports. Finally, trade flows too should tend to be redirected, and often in favor of trade with the capitalist West.[6]

Will the trend toward economic rationality persist, and if so with what force? How rapidly might it affect trade? To refer first to the second question, the shift toward conformity with free trade norms presumably could not be very rapid, at best. Even if planning should become completely rational today, it surely would take time for such norms to be fully observed; for reallocations are required not only of labor but of capital, and often there would have to be further adaptations in labor training as well.

Moreover, as implied, I have been referring throughout to comparative costs in the long run, where capital as well as labor is indeed allocable. The shift toward rationality, however, would tend initially to give expression especially to comparative advantage in the short run, where capital reallocations are limited. Even so, trade no doubt would have to change, but the change might be of a rather different character from that called for, as the imperatives of long-run comparative advantage are felt. In the U.S.S.R., for example, it is often suggested that from the standpoint of comparative costs the government should now be buying more agricultural products abroad, payment being made through exports of machinery. This I am sure is true in terms of short-run comparative costs, but very likely there has been underinvestment of capital in agriculture. Should this underinvestment be repaired, one wonders whether the comparative disadvantage of agriculture would continue, or if so to what extent.

As to whether and to what extent the trend toward economic rationality will persist, this is properly the subject of another inquiry; but this theme has been discussed here by Professor Neuberger, and perhaps I should make a few observations on it. While I do not think I differ much from him, the prospects for economic rationality do not seem quite so bright to

---

[6] Of course, a trend toward economic rationality might imaginably bring a tendency toward fuller exploitation of monopoly power; but any resulting additional divergencies from free trade norms should be limited, insofar as the increase in economic rationality generally would also tend to weaken monopoly power.

me as some other writers have assumed. Thus, while the system's directors are by all accounts more understanding of and concerned with economic rationality than they used to be, their understanding and concern both still leave something to be desired. It would be surprising if this should not continue to be so in the visible future.

Also, even if the system's directors should be fully understanding of and devoutly concerned with economic rationality, it does not follow that the corresponding precepts could be quickly followed in actual practice. On the contrary, difficulties can be anticipated at many points. This was already evident from the celebrated theoretic exchanges on socialist economic rationality of the inter-war period; and subsequent writings, including Professor Haberler's contribution to this Conference, provide no basis to challenge this conclusion.[7]

The trend toward economic rationality is often manifesting itself in a shift from the traditional Soviet type of planning, where decisionmaking is notably centralized, to an alternative kind stressing decentralization and market-like institutions. In judging the possible consequences of this shift, it is rather sobering to learn that in Yugoslavia, fifteen years after a substantial reform of this sort was initiated, a prominent figure in that country should inform us, as quoted by Professor Neuberger,[8] that disproportions are still so great that

. . . if suddenly we were to permit such a conflict of forces which would lead to the elimination from our economy of all which according to its present capabilities could not exist, it is most likely that the depth of the disproportions which have been created up to this time would show up so forcefully that the question would arise whether we could stand by and let the process take its full course.

Perhaps other countries will learn from the Yugoslav experience, but we know that consequential maladjustments are pervasive, and curiously these are circumstances with which market institutions have special difficulty in grappling. I refer particularly to the familiar limitations of the market in assuring an appropriate resource allocation where indivisibilities are present. The gross reallocations now called for necessarily will often entail indivisible adjustments.

If economic rationality is not likely to be quite the potent force some imagine, I do not wish by any means to discount it altogether. Forces making for economic irrationality probably are especially deep-seated in the area of foreign trade, at least with respect to the aversion to trade with capitalist countries; but even this should not be beyond the reach of change. Time forbids me to explore here recent trends in Communist foreign trade, but evidence abounds that lately divergencies from comparative advantage

[7] See [1, Chap. 9]; and Abram Bergson, "Market Socialism Revisited" (forthcoming).
[8] See also [6, December 3, 1966, p. 21].

generally may already have been somewhat ameliorated because of increasing economic rationality. This must be affecting Communist trade now, therefore, and I for one would be surprised if it did not continue to do so.

Such trade, of course, will also be affected by other factors. In any complete account one would have to consider that, along with the trend toward economic rationality, there are many indications of changing ends, including an increasing concern for consumption (so that the system's directors are often less prone than they were formerly to increase, at the expense of consumption, the share of output going to investment), and an increasing concern for consumers' evaluations of different consumers' goods. Also, as Professor Spulber has explained, Western trade controls have evolved in the course of time, and are not what they used to be, but they will presumably continue to evolve in the future. Then, too, changes are in progress in Western trade policies generally, including most importantly the development of the Common Market. Last but not least, all the Communist countries are in the process of industrialization, and will continue to be in the future.

While these factors, too, must leave their imprint on Communist foreign trade, just what this will be must be left to separate inquiry. The trend toward economic rationality, however, should not be the least of the forces in motion. It has also seemed to merit special attention because of its relative novelty.

REFERENCES

1. Bergson, Abram. *Essays in Normative Economics* (Cambridge: Harvard University Press, 1966).
2. Brown, Alan. "The Economics of Centrally Planned Foreign Trade: The Hungarian Experience" (Unpublished doctoral dissertation, Harvard University, 1966).
3. Central Intelligence Agency. "Foreign Trade of the European Satellites in 1965" (Washington, D.C.: 1966).
4. Cohn, Stanley H. "Soviet Growth Retardation," U.S. Congress, Joint Economic Committee, *New Directions in the Soviet Economy* (Washington, D.C.: 1966), Part II-A, pp. 99–132.
5. Deutsch, K. W., and A. Eckstein. "National Industrialization and the Declining Share of the International Economic Sector, 1890–1959," *World Politics*, Volume XIII:2 (January 1961), pp. 267–299.
6. *The Economist*, December 3, 1966, p. 21.
7. Ernst, Maurice. "Postwar Economic Growth in Eastern Europe," U.S. Congress, Joint Economic Committee, *New Directions in the Soviet Economy* (Washington, D.C.: 1966), Part IV, pp. 875–916.
8. Heiss, Herta W. "The Soviet Union in the World Market," U.S. Congress, Joint Economic Committee, *New Directions in the Soviet Economy* (Washington, D.C.: 1966), Part IV, pp. 917–933.
9. Holzman, Franklyn. "Foreign Trade" in Abram Bergson and Simon Kuznets

(eds.), *Economic Trends in the Soviet Union* (Cambridge: Harvard University Press, 1963), pp. 283–332.
10. Kaser, Michael. *Comecon* (London: Oxford University Press, 1965).
11. Kuznets, Simon. *Modern Economic Growth* (New Haven: Yale University Press, 1966).
12. Pryor, Frederic L. *The Communist Foreign Trade System* (Cambridge: Massachusetts Institute of Technology Press, 1963).
13. Tsentral'noe Statisticheskoe Upravlenie SSSR. *Narodnoe khoziaistvo SSSR v 1964g* (Moscow: 1965).
14. United States Department of State. *The Battle Act Report, 1965* (Washington, D.C.: February 1966).

Notes on Some Theoretical Problems Posed by the Foreign Trade of Centrally Planned Economies

HARRY G. JOHNSON

INTRODUCTION

I attended the Conference on International Trade and Central Planning in my capacity as an international trade theorist, and claim no qualifications on the subject other than amateur interest in the centrally planned economies and in their foreign trade. In the course of reading the papers and participating in the discussions, I came to the conclusion — which I expressed in my concluding comments on the Conference — that the predominant approach to the trade problems of the centrally planned economies was distorted by excessive emphasis on the characteristics of these economies as planned economies in contrast to market economies, and that participants were neither exploiting the available tools and concepts of international trade theory nor asking the sort of questions that an international trade theorist would naturally be inclined to ask. Since those concluding comments were intended primarily to stimulate the authors of the major papers presented at the Conference to revise their papers extensively before publication, it would be an anachronism to include them *in extenso* in the volume of the Conference proceedings. In their place, I offer some notes on theoretical approaches to the problems which occurred to me in the course of the Conference. I have not read the revised papers, and as mentioned I do not claim any expertise on the centrally planned economies and their foreign trade; I should therefore wish these notes to be regarded as extremely tentative, and intended to suggest hypotheses and research projects to the specialists in the field.

TOWARD A GENERAL THEORY OF
FOREIGN TRADE POLICY

For a variety of reasons unnecessary to elaborate on here, economic research on the Communist countries has been dominated by interest in the consequences and problems of central planning, which distinguishes these countries' economic systems from the market or "mixed" economies of the countries of the West, and especially the "free enterprise" United States. The domination of research by this distinguishing characteristic has, in my judgment, distorted the conception and analysis of the trade problems and policies of these countries by diverting attention from other and more relevant characteristics in which the centrally planned economies resemble non-centrally planned or at least non-Communist countries. In the first place, the economic situation of the centrally planned economies, and their policy objectives, are very similar to those of the less-developed countries of the world — due allowance being made for the fact that countries cannot be divided neatly into three homogeneous categories of developed, less-developed, and centrally planned according to the doctrines of the United Nations Conference on Trade and Development, but form a spectrum along the two dimensions of degree of development and degree of centralization of economic decisionmaking. Consequently, many of the phenomena of economic policy observed in centrally planned economies are better understood as phenomena associated with the attempt to promote rapid economic growth of a backward country by concentrating economic policies on that objective, than as phenomena associated with central planning as such. This is especially true of the costs incurred and the mistakes made in the pursuit of rapid industrial growth.

In the second place, the ideology of Communism to the contrary, the centrally planned economies are nation-states, and their economic policies are nationalistic in character. In this respect they resemble not only the less-developed countries, but also the developed countries of the world, though this resemblance may be difficult for the Western scholar to appreciate, for two major reasons. One is that the European scholar is accustomed to respect the nationalism of his own country's policies as part of the natural order of things, and to defend nationalistic policies in terms of the more flattering logic of the social good and the assumption that the trained intelligence is easily capable of improving on the working of market forces; the American scholar, on the other hand, has developed a mythology of the self-seeking cupidity of the Congressional system to explain away nationalistic policies as mere aberrations from a liberal international ideal that is assumed to govern American economic policy. The other is that nationalistic economic policies in market economies are implemented through two major means that preserve the appearance of free private competition — tariff, tax, and subsidy policies, which operate impersonally to set the cost-price framework within which private competition operates, and government expenditure policy, whereby it is accepted as legitimate for government to discriminate against foreigners and in favor of nationals.

If one considers the foreign trade and related international economic policies actually pursued by the various countries of the world, without the prior assumption that there must be a significant difference of kind between the centrally planned and the market economies because of their contrasting economic systems, or between the developed and the less-developed countries because of their differing stages of development, one is forcibly impressed by two common general characteristics. First, all countries to a greater or lesser degree pursue restrictive foreign trade policies that prevent them from gaining the full efficiency of resource utilization indicated as possible by the theory of comparative advantage. Moreover, while these policies are frequently defended on the grounds that inefficiency in the short run will be amply recompensed by superior efficiency in the long run — the well-known infant industry or infant-economy argument for protection — there is no evidence to support this on-the-face-of-the-matter paradoxical assumption. Second, these restrictive trade policies are almost universally devoted to maintaining and expanding industrial production in the economy, a characteristic clearly associated with an ideology of nationalism in which industry is crucial to national power and economic growth.

Faced with these phenomena, economists have generally followed one of two alternative courses. One has been to refine the theoretical arguments for protection as a policy superior to free trade, and to rely on a selective interpretation of economic history to substitute for empirical testing of hypotheses against hard evidence. The other has been to accept the comparative-advantage argument for free trade as a point of reference, and to use departures from a free trade policy, or the difference between the results of actual policy and what would be likely under a free trade or "rational socialist price-system" policy, to measure the avoidable inefficiency of a protectionist or centrally planned economic system.

The latter approach is a useful and illuminating one when properly applied, as will be discussed in the next section. But it does leave its practitioners with a serious unanswered question: why, if free trade or its equivalent in terms of rational central planning of trade is the most efficient economic policy, do countries persistently restrict their trade by protecting their industry by tariffs or by planning policy? The only answer that can be given, in terms of traditional trade theory, is that for some reason or other countries or their governments are perversely irrational. This is not a scientifically satisfactory answer; essentially it explains nothing.

Dissatisfaction with these two alternatives — of believing that the market system operates so consistently perversely that almost any interference with it will lead to improved economic performance in the long run, or of believing that governments are consistently economically irrational — has led me in my recent work, building on some insights from Albert Breton into the nature of economic nationalism [1] [6], to attempt to develop a theory of protectionism that would incorporate this policy within the framework of maximization-subject-to-constraints which constitutes formal economic theory, and thus permit rational explanation of a variety of forms of behavior in the field of commercial policy, as well as generating testable hypotheses [4]. The theory postulates that government is a rational process in which politicians achieve and retain office by promising and implementing policies desired by the public; that the presence of industrial production in a country is a collective consumption good, from which the public derives satisfaction additional to the private satisfaction provided by the products of that industry, and for which it is prepared to sacrifice private consumption via the inefficiency entailed by protection; and that a rational government will push protection to the point where the marginal cost of protecting industrial production is equal to the marginal social utility derived from collective consumption of it. The extent to which protectionism is carried will therefore be determined jointly by the strength of the "preference for industrial production" and the excesses over world costs entailed in establishing industries in which the protecting country lacks comparative advantage. A country might have a strong preference for industrial production, yet remain largely dependent on imported supplies because the cost of import-substitution was extremely high; or it might, on the contrary, have a relatively weak preference for industrial production, yet possess a large protected industrial sector because its comparative disadvantage in industry was relatively small.

In view of Professor Wiles' rather snide strictures on Dr. Breton's work on nationalism, it seems necessary to point out here that this kind of application of the public-goods concept to economic policies is not "intellectual imperialism." The theory does not attempt to explain why people are nationalistic, or why nationalism focuses on the production of industrial goods, any more than traditional economic theory attempts to explain why people prefer some goods for private consumption to others. Its purpose is to bring policies that involve an economic cost (by the economist's usual criteria) within the economist's framework of choice among alternatives. Nor does it merely "give a piece of politics an economic name"; its purpose is to explain phenomena that otherwise would have to be assigned to irrational causes, and to provide predictions of how commercial policy will react to exogenous changes. In my perhaps biased judgment, the theory does prove useful in its original context of commercial policy behavior: it explains such otherwise puzzling phenomena as the principle of reciprocity in tariff nego- tiations, the incentive to form discriminatory customs unions and free trade areas, and the tendency of such discriminatory arrangements to be confined to countries at a comparable stage of development.[1]

In the context of the foreign trade problems and policies of the centrally planned economies, the "preference for industrial production" model also provides some guidelines, insights, and predictions. To begin with, it sug- gests that it is hopelessly naive and futile to attempt to appraise the foreign trade policies of these economies in terms of "autarky" as an objective.[2] A more sophisticated approach would envisage these countries as seeking certain industrial objectives, possibly according to a set of weights attached to the various industries reflecting their assumed social importance, subject to limitations of cost determined by the initial structure of the national econ- omy. A rational policy of this kind might well involve less contraction of international trade than the notion of autarky would suggest, for several reasons. First, some types of goods might not be considered desirable to produce, or to produce in larger quantities as a deliberate policy, either be- cause they were non-industrial or because they were considered industrially "inferior." Second, since industrial products enter the industrial complex as both inputs and outputs, the high-cost production of industrial inputs might so seriously damage the efficiency of the user industries that it would be preferable to import the inputs; this is a major reason why countries gen- erally give less protection to their capital goods industries than to their con- sumer goods industries. For the same reason, it might be more efficient from the point of view of long-run promotion of industrialization to attempt to force the expansion of traditional non-industrial exports in order to be able to pay for imports of capital equipment — the policy adopted by China in recent years. Third, a country might well be in, or arrive at, the position in

[1] In the broader context of nationalistic economic policies, the public-goods approach to a theory of nationalism provides predictions, for example, of what industries will tend to be nationalized.

[2] An objection should in any case be raised against the crude technique of attempting to investigate "autarkic" policies by means of the statistics of trade-to-income ratios. Though such ratios have been widely used in the exploration of all sorts of comprehen- sive hypotheses — e.g., that countries become more self-sufficient as they develop, or that world growth is biased against the exports of the less-developed countries — they pose an insoluble identification problem, since they reflect the general equilibrium out- come of both economic factors (demand and supply) and economic policies designed to alter the influence of the economic factors, in all the countries involved in the inter- national economic system. Thus, for example, it would seem an impossible task to determine, without a large-scale econometric exercise, how far any tendencies toward increased self-sufficiency in Eastern Europe could be attributed to autarkic policies there, as distinct from the discrimination against trade with the Communist countries that has been part of the strategy of the cold war.

which it was more economical to export industrial goods of the type it was capable of producing, even at a cost significantly above the world level at current exchange rates, than to attempt further high-cost import substitution. This problem has begun to afflict the less-developed countries of the non-Communist world, and is responsible for their current demands for preferences for their industrial products in the markets of the developed countries. Finally, the process of forced industrialization must eventually encounter a resource constraint in the form of inadequate domestic supplies of foodstuffs, which must be made good by imports paid for by exports of industrial goods. As Professor Wiles pointed out during the Conference, it is now the industrial exporters among the Eastern European countries that have the weaker positions in the Communist world, and those with surplus foodstuffs that have the bargaining power.

The analytical approach to the commercial policies of the centrally planned economies outlined above suggests a rather different set of questions for research than have heretofore been posed. Specifically, one would like to know how much, in terms of real resources, the trade policies of these countries have cost them, by comparison with a free trade policy; how much of this cost has been a necessary cost of the kind of development and industrialization policy they have adopted as a means to the implementation of national objectives, and how much has been unnecessary waste, the result of inconsistencies and inefficiencies of the central control system; and, of course, how far, if at all, this apparent waste (by the standards of Western economies) can be justified empirically by a quantifiable payoff in terms of learning-by-doing, externalities, and the other arguments adduced by economic theory in support of protectionist policies as a means of promoting economic development.

TRADE POLICY AND THE EFFICIENCY
OF RESOURCE ALLOCATION

The assumption that tariffs and other forms of protection involve important wastes of real resources is deeply ingrained in the orthodox tradition of international trade theory. Consequently Western students of the trade policies of the centrally planned economies have tended to find, in the limited amount of their trade, the apparently arbitrary basis on which decisions about the items and quantities to trade are made, and the dominance of bilateral trading agreements, a serious source of inefficiency and economic waste. This waste in turn appears difficult to reconcile with the high recorded rates of economic growth that many of these countries have achieved.

The apparent paradox is not a real one, however, since static inefficiency of resource *allocation* is not inconsistent with a high rate of resource *accu-*

mulation. An economy may use its resources very inefficiently, yet be augmenting them rapidly (though still using them inefficiently), by dint of massive saving and investment out of its current income. In such a case, the
removal of the static inefficiency of resource allocation could increase the
economy's growth rate transitionally, by superimposing a once-over gain
in output from given resources on the growth of output due to the accumulation of resources, and thereafter could be used either to achieve an increase
in the growth rate, by permitting an increase in saving consistently with no
reduction in consumption, or to increase consumption without sacrificing
growth.[3]

The real question concerns the magnitude of the real income losses from
inefficient trade and specialization policies, which (as mentioned) are usually
assumed to be substantial. There are, however, reasons for believing that
such static losses from resource misallocation, while significant enough to
merit attention and measurement, are not in general likely to loom very
large either in the explanation of international differences in productivity
and real income per head, or as an offset to the achievement of high rates of
economic growth.

Before presenting these reasons, it is worth recording that the papers and
discussions of the Conference cast serious doubt on the traditional assumption that bilateral trading is necessarily a serious source of inefficiency. The
reason is an interesting one, since it illustrates the danger of theorizing on
the basis of identification of words with assumed facts. The usual analysis
of the inefficiency of bilateralism, as compared with multilateralism, assumes
that, like barter, bilateralism involves the exchange of goods that each recipient intends to use himself; hence the presumption that the requirement of
balance in the exchange involves a less satisfactory arrangement than could
be obtained by the exchange of goods against money and money against
goods in a multilateral market. But the argument loses much of its force,
for both bilateralism and barter, if the parties are not assumed to have to consume the goods received in exchange, but may barter them away again in trade
with third parties. This is, in fact, what some of the Eastern European countries have been doing. In that case, bilateral trading appears as a means of
avoiding the explicit use of money, but not as a partitioning of the market
into segregated sectors with widely different exchange ratios; and the economic waste involved may be only the rather trivial cost of shipping goods
to their final users by more indirect routes and through the hands of more
transactors than would be the case in a market employing money.

---

[3] It is theoretically possible that part or all of the output gain will be swallowed up
by increased inefficiency of resource allocation, if the growth of the economy is biased
toward the expansion of inefficient industries at the expense of efficient industries. On
this point, see [5].

The main argument concerns the probable magnitude of the cost of protection, and contends that this cost is likely in most cases to be a relatively small fraction of national income.[4] The contention rests on two considerations: the proper formula for calculating the cost of protection as a proportion of national income, and the likelihood that governments and their public will be aware that protection imposes an economic cost and will not be willing to forgo too much real income in pursuit of the objectives to be implemented by protection.

Technically, the cost of protection can be decomposed into three parts: the consumption cost or loss of consumers' surplus resulting from obliging consumers to pay prices for importable goods which are higher than the alternative opportunity cost in world markets; the production cost resulting from the production of goods domestically at a resource cost above the cost of producing the goods indirectly by producing exports and using the proceeds to import the goods; and (a negative cost) the gain obtained via higher prices for exports, or lower prices of imports, resulting from the restriction of trade.

For most countries, the terms-of-trade gain can probably be taken as negligible. Contrary to the usual assumption, it is probably true that the large developed countries rather than the small less-developed countries stand to reap this potential gain from protectionism. For the centrally planned economies, however, it may well be the case — given the general view that demands for their exports are probably not very elastic — that the terms-of-trade gain from trade restriction is substantial, perhaps enough to outweigh the consumption and production costs.

Ignoring the possibility of gain on the terms of trade, which necessarily reduces the cost of protection, the magnitudes of the production and consumption costs depend on the rate of protection, the elasticities of demand and supply, and the ratios of consumption and production of the protected goods to national income. Approximately, the cost of protection as a proportion of national income may be formulated as

$$k = \tfrac{1}{2} \sum_i \left(\frac{t_i}{1 + t_i} \right)^2 (c_i \eta_i + p_i \epsilon_i),$$

where t_i is the rate of protection of the ith industry, η_i and ϵ_i are the elasticities of consumption demand and domestic supply, and c_i and p_i are the ratios of consumption expenditure and value of domestic production to national income. The essential characteristic of this formula is that all the factors except η_i and ϵ_i are fractions, and that the elasticities are, according to the

[4] For a fuller development of the argument, see [2]; for computations of the cost of self-sufficiency and its dependence on the economic structure of the economy, which confirms the general proposition advanced here, see [3].

bulk of the empirical evidence, unlikely to be very large numbers. Consequently, since the formula involves multiplying together elements that are mostly fractions, the result is likely to be a still smaller fraction. In fact, the available empirical estimates (which unfortunately have generally been derived by much cruder methods) point to costs of protection running well under 10 percent of national income (6 percent for Australia, 4 percent for Canada, under 1 percent for the United States).

Figures of this magnitude cannot be dismissed as insignificant reductions of the potential standard of living. But, on the other hand, they do not go far toward explaining the large differences that exist between national levels of productivity; and they amount at most to one or two years' normal growth of the economy.

The formula above supports the argument that normally protective policies do not involve a major loss of efficiency; but it also suggests the circumstances in which the loss might be much more substantial. Specifically, a substantial loss of efficiency could be sustained by an economy whose economic structure was such that under free trade conditions it would be highly specialized on production for the world market, and that attempts to reduce its dependence on trade and increase its self-sufficiency would encounter rapidly rising costs of import-substitution.

It would be an interesting research project to calculate the cost of protection in one or more of the centrally planned economies (including any terms-of-trade effects) to determine how great a waste of potential output was involved. The exercise might usefully be undertaken for several years, and thus possibly throw some light on the dynamic effects, if any, of forcing industrialization by protectionist policies. It would, of course, miss some effects of the trade policies of these countries which are additional to the static misallocation effects analysed by trade theory but extremely difficult to quantify. One such is the cost of uncertainty and interruption of imported goods. Another is the possible effect of protectionism in forcing the choice of domestic technologies and capital goods inferior in productivity to what could be obtained through trade.

REFERENCES

1. Breton, Albert. "The Economics of Nationalism," *Journal of Political Economy*, LXXII:4 (August 1964), pp. 376–386.
2. Johnson, Harry. "The Cost of Protection and the Scientific Tariff," *Journal of Political Economy*, LXVIII:4 (August 1960), pp. 327–345.
3. ———. "The Costs of Protection and of Self-sufficiency," *Quarterly Journal of Economics*, LXXIX:3 (August 1965), pp. 356–372.
4. ———. "An Economic Theory of Protectionism, Tariff Bargaining, and the

Formation of Customs Unions," *Journal of Political Economy*, LXXIII:3 (June 1965), pp. 256–283.

5. Johnson, Harry. "The Possibility of Income Losses from Increased Efficiency on Factor Accumulation in the Presence of Tariffs," *Economic Journal*, LXXVII:305 (March 1967), pp. 151–154.

6. ———. "A Theoretical Model of Economic Nationalism in New and Developing States," *Political Science Quarterly*, LXXX:2 (June 1965), pp. 169–185.

Appendix

Basic Features of a
Centrally Planned Economy

ALAN A. BROWN
and
EGON NEUBERGER

Since most of the papers in this book assume some acquaintance with Soviet-type centrally planned economies (CPEs),[1] readers who are not specialists in this field may find this brief, self-contained analytical summary of such economic systems useful. This Appendix may also be of interest to economists who are familiar with the existing literature on CPEs, since this exposition — with its emphasis on a logical sequence of analytical steps — differs from the usual descriptions of CPEs. As a joint effort of the editors, it attempts to blend analyses of CPEs taken from their respective Conference papers.

We may identify the basic features of a CPE in terms of its objectives and *modi operandi*. Let us consider these in sequence under five major headings: objectives and key elements, planning mechanisms, desired effects, undesired consequences, and adjustment mechanisms.[2]

[1] As a cautionary note, we may add that this conceptual model attempts to illuminate only the traditional CPE; it does not deal with recent changes resulting from economic reforms.

[2] The sketch of the closed CPE which follows was inspired by Professor David Granick's imaginative organizational model of Soviet planning [7, pp. 109–130]. An increasing number of Western economists have also constructed models of CPEs, and only a few of these can be listed here. Professor Bergson, in one of his recent works, presents an analytical framework of the Soviet economy within which he interprets Soviet behavior patterns and assesses economic efficiency [2]. Professor Montias, in his appraisal of the Polish experience, provides a thorough introduction to the theory of central planning [15]. Professors Balassa and Kornai both use theoretical models of central planning to analyze economic planning in Hungary [1] [13]. A very comprehensive treatment of different models of CPEs and of some alternative Communist economic systems appears in a book by Professor Wiles [20]. The fruits of a collective undertaking on various aspects of planning in the Soviet Union and in East Europe have been published in a volume edited by Professor Grossman; the editor's Introduction contains not only a summary of the other contributions but also a succinct model of CPEs [9]. Also, an earlier article by Professor Grossman serves as a useful

OBJECTIVES AND KEY ELEMENTS

OBJECTIVES [3]

Rapid Growth and Industrialization.[4] Planners in traditional CPEs aim at a very high rate of economic growth, as a rule much higher than the rate maintained in market-type economies (MTEs). Not all economic sectors, however, are promoted equally; the result is unbalanced growth. Expansion of industrial sectors is stressed — more specifically, producers' goods and particularly certain heavy industries, such as mining, metallurgy, and machinery production. Attempts to satisfy an ever-increasing demand for industrial inputs lead to a chronic neglect of agriculture, a trend enhanced by the planners' ideological orientation (i.e., their mistrust and fear of the peasantry). Unbalanced industrial growth is generally pursued without regard for the relative resource endowment of individual CPEs.

Centralization. This term is a shorthand expression that includes both *centralized planning and centralized control* of economic activities. Thus, centralization means, on the one hand, that important planning decisions are reserved to the system's directors (to use Professor Bergson's expression), and, on the other, that decisions are communicated to operational units by direct commands or directives. This implies a set of institutional mechanisms whose function is to assure the fulfillment of commands.[5] Centralization, it may be added, is at once an important policy objective and a *modus operandi* of the system (via certain mechanisms to be discussed below). The planners have a revealed preference for centralization per se, pursuing it even at the expense of growth.

KEY ELEMENTS

The basic goals of rapid growth and centralization give direction and shape to the system. The following six key elements represent a relatively complete shorthand description of the CPE.

Socialist Economy (or *Social Ownership*) — According to Western economic terminology, public ownership of the means of production. (While this is one of the independent goals, it is also a means of achieving the goal of centralization, and to some extent the goal of rapid growth.)

Command Economy — Centralized bureaucratic management of the economy, with detailed physical planning and supply.

Pressure Economy — Emphasis on a high rate of forced savings at the macro-level; and on taut planning of outputs, inputs, and inventories at the micro-level.

Priority Economy — Planning based on priorities, reflecting the dominance of political and ideological criteria over economic considerations in the overall

theoretical frame of reference for Soviet-type systems [8]. In a *Festschrift* honoring Professor Gerschenkron, there are several models of Soviet planning [18]. Attention will be called, as we proceed, to other contributions relating to specific features of CPEs.

[3] Although preference functions are obviously multidimensional, we attempt to call attention here only to those goals that have been explicitly and strongly stressed by the planners.

[4] For a recent discussion of the genesis of the Soviet system's directors' preoccupation with growth, see Professor Berliner's article, "The Economics of Overtaking and Surpassing," in [18, pp. 159–185].

[5] E.g., as described by Professor Grossman in [8].

formulation of economic policy; e.g., primacy of industry over agriculture, of producers' goods over consumers' goods, and of material goods over services — except for high priority of education, especially technical education of the labor force.

Extensive Development [6] — Output-oriented planning, with stress on ever-increasing quantities of output, achieved with massive infusions of labor and capital inputs.

Closed Economy — Primacy of domestic economic considerations over the exigencies of foreign trade, foreign trade plans being merely addenda to domestic plans. (This is again an independent goal, as well as a means of achieving the goal of centralization.)

PLANNING MECHANISMS

Every economic system requires certain mechanisms, or institutional devices, to achieve its basic goals. In a CPE the planning mechanisms are designed to foster rapid economic growth (particularly in the high-priority sectors) and to safeguard centralization. We may identify three primary mechanisms (vertical coordination and control, system of material balances, and taut planning) and three secondary mechanisms (discontinuous planning, discontinuous incentives, and multiple criteria).

PRIMARY PLANNING MECHANISMS

Vertical Coordination and Control [7] means a predominant reliance on vertical channels of coordination and control as a basic method of centralization. This emphasis on the "vertical connections" in economy (i.e., direct orders from above) reflects an effort by the planners to reduce their dependence on the "horizontal connections" (i.e., spontaneous, immediate contacts among operational units).[8] This mechanism manifests itself in a three-fold separation of economic activities: (i) among different sectors of the economy (*intersectoral separation*), (ii) among the enterprises in given sectors (*interfirm separation*), and (iii) among departments within given administrative or producing units, as within a ministry or firm (*interdepartmental separation*).

System of Material Balances is a technique to achieve consistency among the various plans.[9] It has two important aspects: (i) *physical planning*, the balancing of equations in physical units to assure a flow of supplies mainly to high-priority sectors, and (ii) *sequential planning*, the use of successive approximations rather than simultaneous equations to facilitate the planning process.

[6] This term has gained wide acceptance in Eastern Europe as a descriptive reference to the policies followed under the Stalinist system; we are adapting it to describe the specific feature described below. See [6].

[7] János Kornai in his "Model of Economic Mechanisms" distinguishes between vertical connections ("a matter of authority and subordination") and horizontal connections (which "involve contacts [of an enterprise] with other enterprises . . . [all] having equal legal rights and standing") [13, pp. 191 ff.].

[8] Kornai says, ". . . these vertical connexions are the dominant ones . . . The influences which result from direct contacts between enterprises are dwarfed by those which reach them from the centre" [13, p. 194].

[9] For a detailed description of this method of coordination, see [14] and [16].

Taut Planning aims at the swiftest possible central mobilization of all available resources — by means of continual sellers' markets — to facilitate rapid growth. It also serves as a technique to motivate operational units.[10] We may distinguish three aspects of taut planning: (i) *output (target) maximization*, (ii) *input (or input coefficient) minimization*, and (iii) *inventory minimization*.

SECONDARY PLANNING MECHANISMS

Discontinuous Planning may be viewed as an elongation of the Robertsonian "planning day" (or Hicksian "week"), i.e., the period during which plans are supposed to remain unchanged.[11] This is also a device to facilitate central planning, since the planners attempt to keep relatively long "planning days" (they sanction interrelated plan revisions only infrequently or discontinuously) so as to minimize the burden of planning.

Discontinuous Incentives imply a sharp line of demarcation in the incentive system between success and failure. The purpose is to encourage fulfillment of a centrally specified output pattern. To achieve this purpose, the incentive system is designed to offer rewards if the plans are fulfilled 100 percent (particularly, the physical output plan); failure is defined as falling short of the established quotas. Consequently, little attention is paid to differences of degree.[12]

Multiple Criteria mean the absence of a single common standard of value, whether in the planning process (e.g., prices) or in the control mechanism (e.g., profits).[13] The tendency to postulate output targets and inputs norms in non-additive, heterogeneous units is functionally related to the system of material balances (i.e., to physical planning). Multiple criteria are also used in assessing the fulfillment of plans, i.e., in measuring the performance of operational units. Thus, multiple criteria and the corresponding proliferation of instructions are means of safeguarding central control, although they often do not accomplish this purpose satisfactorily.[14]

DESIRED EFFECTS[15]

The CPE is able, at least theoretically, to produce certain effects that, given the preferences of the system's directors, are considered desirable. It should

[10] The operational characteristics of taut planning are analyzed by Professor Hunter [12]. Recently, Professor Levine has evaluated this method in his essay, "Pressure and Planning in the Soviet Economy" [18, pp. 266–285].

[11] J. R. Hicks says, "I shall define a week as that period of time during which variations in prices can be neglected. For theoretical purposes this means that prices will be supposed to change, not continuously, but at short intervals" [10, pp. 122–123].

[12] Castigating the practice of "turning '100 percent' into a fetish," Kornai says, "premiums are not paid until the degree of fulfillment of the relevant plan index reaches 100 percent" [13, p. 128].

[13] According to Levine, "the system of instructions lacks an all-embracing criterion, which, at least in theory, is provided by profits in a market economy" [14, pp. 170–171].

[14] Kornai writes that "excessive centralization inevitably leads to an undue proliferation of instructions" [13, p. 204]. "The more instructions are given, the greater the tendency of ministries and other highly placed authorities to 'dictate' and to rely on ordering people about" [13, p. 203].

[15] The most comprehensive treatment may be found in [20, pp. 253–263], where many of the points listed below are discussed at length.

be noted that, in practice, some of these effects are attenuated or altogether negated for reasons to be discussed as we proceed.

SOCIO-ECONOMIC REORGANIZATION

Formation of a New Elite. The system is able to orient the whole country toward the goal of economic development, replacing those uninterested in or hostile to rapid growth and centralization with a new elite of greater reliability. The new cadres are fully committed to the fundamental objectives of the system. This is accomplished by substituting a new ruling ideology for the old, and shifting power to adherents of the new ideology. The change is aided by the key elements cited above, especially social ownership, the pressure economy, and the command economy.

Income Distribution. Social ownership makes economic development possible without resort to a highly unequal income distribution, a precondition usually considered necessary to attain a sufficiently high level of investment from private voluntary saving. In practice, however, the wage differentials needed for incentive purposes and the lack of progressive taxes combine to widen the dispersion of disposable incomes in CPEs.

Population Policy. The CPE, by focusing on economic development and giving power to a new elite imbued with a development ideology, should be in a strong position to deal with one of the most crucial issues facing underdeveloped countries — the problem of population growth. But none of the key elements of the system deals directly with this question, and none of the countries that have adopted such a system has developed a consistent long-term population policy.[16]

MOBILIZATION OF INPUTS

Capital Formation. The elements of social ownership, the pressure economy, and the command economy are used to impose very high rates of forced saving and investment, with the corollary effect of greater capital formation than under alternative economic systems.

Labor Recruitment. Extensive development, the priority economy, and the socialist economy facilitate the utilization of relatively abundant agricultural labor and unemployed urban labor, as well as the recruitment of women into the labor force.

Labor Training. Another desirable effect is the improvement of the educational levels and vocational skills of the population, a goal promoted by both the priority economy and social ownership (since education becomes a more important avenue of social mobility).

ACCELERATION AND CHANNELING OF ECONOMIC DEVELOPMENT

Growth of GNP. The pressure economy, the priority economy, and extensive development are jointly utilized to achieve a rapid increase of the gross national product, although not necessarily of the standard of living.

Direction of Development. An important function of the priority economy, the command economy, and social ownership is the ability to concentrate on high-priority objectives (e.g., giving the lion's share of investment funds to industry,

[16] An excellent discussion of the ramifications of this omission may be found in [11].

especially to its favored branches) and to bring about a rapid structural transformation of the economy.

Regional Development. Attempts to bring the less-developed regions of the country to the more-developed level — together with a corollary tendency toward greater socio-political cohesiveness — are also promoted by the priority economy, the command economy, and social ownership.

ALLEVIATION OF MARKET IMPERFECTIONS

Externalities. The ability to internalize external economies and diseconomies, while clearly a theoretical effect of the CPE — particularly of the command economy, the priority economy, and social ownership — is not easily realized in practice, since central planning organs are not monolithic units and do not have the necessary data and tools to assess externalities accurately.

Restrictive Influences. Social ownership, the pressure economy, and the command economy can be used, with at least partial success, to reduce monopolistic misallocation of resources and organizational slacks by tightly controlling managerial power and severely limiting trade-union interference.

Technological Progress. Control over management and labor and the absence of artificial monopolies based on patents foster a more rapid diffusion of existing technological knowledge. This desirable effect is related to social ownership and certain features of the command economy. Other elements of the system, however — such as the pressure economy, the closed economy, and extensive development — tend to work in the opposite direction.

PROMOTION OF ECONOMIC STABILITY

Price-Wage Stabilization. Elements of the CPE (the command economy and the closed economy) enable the system's directors to control undesirable price and wage fluctuations. If severe inflationary pressures do build up periodically, as has happened in the past, they can be prevented from affecting resource allocation in part by controlling the wage-price spiral.

Insulation from International Business Cycles. CPEs also have more power than MTEs to prevent, at least for a time, external cyclical pressures and disturbances in the balance of payments from dominating domestic economic policies; this is a primary effect not only of the closed economy but also of the command economy. The system's directors do not feel the need to engage in a stop-go policy of investment and growth, nor have the banks the authority to insist on it.

UNDESIRED CONSEQUENCES

We turn now to various undesired consequences of CPEs, rooted in the objectives, key elements, and specific features of the planning system.[17] Although these undesired consequences are interrelated, we may separate them for analytical

[17] Operationally, it would be difficult to determine whether the emphasis on growth or that on centralization were fundamentally more responsible for the undesired consequences. Although in practice they are joint products, Professor Levine has recently tried to separate the causes analytically, assigning most of the blame to pressure in the system [18, especially pp. 269 ff.].

purposes into four major categories: administrative inefficiencies, unreliable valuation criteria, microeconomic inefficiencies, and macroeconomic problems.

ADMINISTRATIVE INEFFICIENCIES

Formal Organization. In its traditional form, the CPE is hypercentralized (i.e., its centralization interferes with economic efficiency) [18] and rigidly organized. Its features, which are embedded in the bureaucratic framework of the command economy, lead to various macroeconomic maladjustments. The absence of flexibility pervades all sectors of the economy, from the Central Planning Board to every subordinate level. It presents serious problems, periodically, in the supply system (where cumulative shortages can arise because of the unavailability of crucial inputs through legal channels, regardless of prices that firms may be willing to pay) and particularly in foreign trade (where potential gains depend on flexible responses to ephemeral changes). First among the specific problems is an overemphasis on vertical coordination and control channels (and a corresponding neglect of horizontal links among the enterprises), which increases the need for more information in the formulation and implementation of plans.[19] This, along with discontinuities in planning, leads to (i) lags in administrative response, (ii) the neglect of special requirements or atypical conditions, and (iii) cumulative shortages, which are rendered particularly acute by taut planning (e.g., efforts to keep reserves as low as possible). Thus, the planning mechanisms not only create initial bottlenecks but also generate further repercussions.

Informal Bargaining. On close inspection, it appears that the CPE, in spite of its highly centralized formal organization, is not a system of rational decision-making by an omniscient and monolithic unit. Although vertical command channels are overemphasized officially, the formulation and implementation of plans are pervaded at all levels by bargaining. Results more often reflect the power of individuals than the intrinsic strength of their case, and our attempts to explain or predict the behavior of CPEs may be better served at times by tools of game theory than by traditional economic theories of rational resource allocation.

UNRELIABLE VALUATION CRITERIA

Domestic Prices. There are nonsystematic aberrations of domestic prices both from prevailing scarcity ratios and from planners' preferences,[20] primarily because several features of the system tend to immobilize the market mechanism.[21]

[18] This problem has frequently been discussed in Western economic literature. For example, Professor Levine in his analysis of the Soviet supply system gives many examples of macroeconomic maladjustment in the Soviet economy [14, especially pp. 167–170]. Also, most of Kornai's book is devoted to these problems [13].

[19] Evaluating the informational efficiency of the Soviet system, Egon Neuberger argues: "The increasing information intensiveness of the Soviet economy partly explains the search for new economic methods in the U.S.S.R." [17, p. 133].

[20] The irrationality of Soviet prices was discussed by Professor Wiles and others in a series of articles during the 1950s. (See [19] and replies in *Soviet Studies*.) For a thorough discussion of the Soviet price system, see [4].

[21] Other fundamental problems include ideological mistrust and a lack of intellectual appreciation of the market mechanism, but the desire for centralization and the use of centralized devices of the system are probably the most important reasons for the irrationality of the prices. As Professor Grossman has expressed it: "But most important, to be workable, a market mechanism would require a dispersion of power

Without a trial-and-error method, it would be difficult to establish a set of economically meaningful prices for even a handful of basic commodities (e.g., to derive synthetic or shadow prices by means of mathematical programming); and, in any case, the problem of the lack of price flexibility would remain. In a centralized economic system, interrelated price adjustments or general price reforms are too costly and can be undertaken only at infrequent intervals. Several key elements of the system — the command economy, the priority economy, and the closed economy — militate against rational pricing in a CPE. The inability of the planners to formulate economically meaningful and sufficiently flexible prices may also be directly attributed to certain specific planning mechanisms. First, the emphasis on vertical channels and the corresponding neglect of horizontal connections among operational units slows the transmission and reduces the reliability of information. Second, material balancing, with its stress on quota fulfillment in physical terms, delegates financial accounting to a subsidiary role in the planning process. Third, taut planning and its corollary, periodic supply shortages, inhibit equilibrium pricing.

Exchange Rates. Closely connected with irrational domestic prices is the system of generally arbitrary exchange rates. Both the command economy and the priority economy are to blame, although the closed-economy element is chiefly responsible. While foreign trade decisions are not made primarily on the basis of official exchange rates, the lack of reliable and explicit comparisons between external prices and internal costs tends to interfere with planning as well as with control. Arbitrary exchange rates, like irrational domestic prices, are a contributory cause of macro- and microeconomic inefficiencies.

MICROECONOMIC INEFFICIENCIES

Incentive System.[22] Within the pressure economy and the command economy, multiple criteria and discontinuous incentives give rise to a series of problems at the microeconomic level. Both of these aspects of the planning system tend to make incentives dysfunctional: (i) multiple criteria lead to uncertainties, or *ambiguous motivation*; and (ii) discontinuous incentives lead to an exaggerated schism between success and failure, or *dichotomous motivation*. The final consequence is an all-or-nothing philosophy. First, up to a point, there are strong incentives for *simulation* (a familiar manifestation of this is the "assortment problem," the willful misclassification of commodities to show favorable results) and *storming* (regular seasonal spurts in production to fulfill the quota). Second, when simulation is not likely to help, the performance of enterprises tends to suffer more than necessary because of temporary lethargy and (especially) illicit *hoarding*, which occurs to facilitate plan fulfillment in subsequent periods.

Productivity. Extensive development, the pressure economy, the closed economy, and the command economy are jointly responsible for various microeconomic inefficiencies: slow rate of technological and product innovation, poor quality of output, and low productivity of labor and capital (long gestation period, inefficient choice of investment or its location, low-capacity utilization because of

and a degree of slack in the economy that the regime may be unwilling to grant" [9, pp. 9–10].

[22] The Soviet incentive system is analyzed in detail by Professor Berliner [3]. He explains and documents various microeconomic problems that are here only briefly mentioned.

supply bottlenecks, and inadequate charges for capital use). At the same time, excessive inventories of unneeded inputs and unsold outputs accumulate.

Firm Size and Specialization. Elements of the command economy, the pressure economy, the priority economy, and the closed economy lead to a pattern of interfirm relationships with: (i) a bias toward giant plants with high transport costs and unused capacity, as well as an absence of smaller enterprises needed to provide forward and backward linkages; and (ii) the presence of nonspecialized enterprises, aiming at narrow self-sufficiency, producing many commodities in small series, and engaging in subcontracting as little as possible.

MACROECONOMIC PROBLEMS

Consumer Satisfaction. The priority economy, the command economy, and social ownership tend to keep consumer satisfactions at relatively low levels because of the high rates of forced saving, the low priority of agriculture and consumer goods industries, and the neglect of service industries (which in turn lead to such corollary problems as the wrong assortment of products in terms of type, size, and style, and the unavailability of products in certain localities).

Agriculture. The past collectivization of agriculture and the low priority assigned to it subsequently (keeping agricultural incomes low and making life miserable for peasants) — the consequences of social ownership and the priority economy — have caused an exodus of the best workers from agriculture. While this neglect of agriculture makes extensive development possible and allows increases in industrial output, it nonetheless debilitates long-term agricultural performance, increases social problems in overcrowded cities, reduces — as mentioned above — the level of consumer satisfaction, and contributes to balance-of-payments problems.

International Specialization. The closed economy, the command economy, and the priority economy are responsible for the relative neglect of traditional export industries and the failure to develop new specialized export industries based on present or prospective comparative advantage. As a result, CPEs become dependent on the exportation of commodities that happen to be in temporary excess of domestic needs. Similarly, the lack of an optimal long-term import policy leads to the importation of commodities in temporary short supply, rather than those in which the country has a comparative disadvantage.

ADJUSTMENT MECHANISMS

CPEs employ certain adjustment mechanisms in an attempt to deal with the undesirable consequences discussed above. These mechanisms may be divided into external and internal safety valves. The *external safety valves*, or *ad hoc* imports, which are often used to alleviate planning errors or unforeseen disturbances, are discussed in some detail in one of the papers above.[23] By *domestic safety valves* is meant the semilegal mechanisms whose function is to introduce a measure of flexibility — by means of informal decentralization — into the rigidly centralized system. Two allied devices, selective violation of instructions and priority planning, are also used to cope with some of the undesired consequences.

[23] See Alan Brown, "Towards a Theory of Centrally Planned Foreign Trade," in [5].

414 *Alan A. Brown and Egon Neuberger*

Selective Violation of Instructions. Informally, planning authorities are inclined to overlook a case of the neglect of certain instructions by enterprises so long as the more important instructions are observed (chiefly, the fulfillment of physical output plans). There is, as it were, a hierarchy among instructions, the more important ones being safeguarded at the expense of the less important.[24]

Priority Planning. There is a similar hierarchy among various branches of production, i.e., among products of different industries. Thus, priority planning is a means of assuring fulfillments, or overfulfillments, of high-priority output targets — ranking high in the preferences of the system's directors. This occurs at the expense of low-priority goods — commodities that the directors consider to be more expendable, at least in the short run (traditionally, agricultural products and consumer goods).[25]

REFERENCES

1. Balassa, Bela A. *The Hungarian Experience in Economic Planning* (New Haven: Yale University Press, 1959).
2. Bergson, Abram. *The Economics of Soviet Planning* (New Haven: Yale University Press, 1964).
3. Berliner, Joseph S. *Factory and Manager in the U.S.S.R.* (Cambridge: Harvard University Press, 1963).
4. Bornstein, Morris. "The Soviet Price System," *American Economic Review*, LII:1 (March 1962), pp. 64–103.
5. Brown, Alan A., and Egon Neuberger (eds.). *International Trade and Central Planning* (Berkeley: University of California Press, 1968).
6. Goldman, Josef. "System of Planning and Management," JPRS, Translations on Economic Organization and Management in Eastern Europe 28988, No. 455 (March 3, 1965).
7. Granick, David. "An Organizational Model of Soviet Industrial Planning," *Journal of Political Economy*, LXVII:2 (April 1959), pp. 109–130.
8. Grossman, Gregory. "Notes for a Theory of the Command Economy," *Soviet Studies*, XV:2 (October 1963), pp. 101–123.
9. ———— (ed.). *Value and Plan: Economic Calculation and Organization in Eastern Europe* (Berkeley: University of California Press, 1960).
10. Hicks, John R. *Value and Capital*, 2nd edition (Oxford: Clarendon Press, 1946).
11. Hoeffding, Oleg. "State Planning and Forced Industrialization," *Problems of Communism*, VIII:6 (November–December 1959).
12. Hunter, Holland. "Optimal Tautness in Developmental Planning," *Economic Development and Cultural Change*, IX:4 (July 1961), pp. 561-572.
13. Kornai, Janos. *Overcentralization in Economic Administration: A Critical*

[24] Let us once again cite Kornai: "According to what their consequences are, some instructions have much 'authority' and 'weight,' and are very effective, while others are of more or less formal importance only, having their existence only on paper. Thus, a definite order of the importance of the tasks which arise in the course of the economic process is formed" [13, p. 122].

[25] This process in Soviet planning is described by Professor Levine as follows: "Another method is the substitution of nondeficit materials for the deficit. . . . Throughout the balancing process, the priority principle is at work" [14, p. 164].

Analysis Based on Experience in Hungarian Light Industry, translated by John Knapp (London: Oxford University Press, 1959).

14. Levine, Herbert S. "The Centralized Planning of Supply in Soviet Industry," in U.S. Congress, Joint Economic Committee, *Comparisons of the United States and Soviet Economies* (1959), pp. 151–176.

15. Montias, John Michael. *Central Planning in Poland* (New Haven: Yale University Press, 1962).

16. ———. "Planning with Material Balances," *American Economic Review*, XLIX:5 (December 1959).

17. Neuberger, Egon. "Libermanism, Computopia, and Visible Hand: The Question of Informational Efficiency," *American Economic Review*, LVI:2 (May 1966), pp. 131–144.

18. Rosovsky, Henry (ed.). *Industrialization in Two Systems: Essays in Honor of Alexander Gerschenkron* (New York: John Wiley, 1966).

19. Wiles, P. J. D. "Are Adjusted Rubles Rational?," *Soviet Studies*, VII:2 (October 1955), pp. 143–160.

20. ———. *The Political Economy of Communism* (Cambridge: Harvard University Press, 1962).

Selected Bibliography

OFFICIAL AND OTHER COMMUNIST SOURCES

BOOKS, DOCUMENTS AND PAMPHLETS

Adatok és adalékok [Facts and Figures] (Budapest: Központi Statisztikai Hivatal, 1957).

Aizenberg, I. *Voprosy valiutnogo kursa rublia [Problems of the Ruble Exchange Rate]* (Moscow: 1958).

Anuarul statistic al Republicii Socialiste România [Annual Statistics of the Socialist Republic of Rumania] (Bucharest: various years).

Cherviakov, P. *Organizatsiia i tekhnika vneshnei torgovli SSSR [Organization and Technique of the Foreign Trade of the U.S.S.R.]* (Moscow: 1958).

Chung-hua Jen-min Kung-ho-kuo T'iao-yüeh Chi [Collection of Treaties of the Chinese People's Republic]. Thirteen volumes through 1964 (Peking: Legal Press and World Knowledge Press; Vol. I published in 1957, Vol. XIII published in 1965).

Dezvoltarea agriculturii R.P.R.: Culegere de date statistice [Development of the Agriculture of the P.R.R.: Collection of Statistical Data] (Bucharest: 1965).

Džeba, K., and M. Beslac. *Privredna reforma: što i zašto se mijenja [Economic Reform: What and Why the Change]* (Zagreb: Stvarnost, 1965).

First Five-Year Plan for Development of the National Economy of the People's Republic of China in 1953–1957 (Peking: Foreign Languages Press, 1956).

Grebtsov, G., and L. Karpov. *Material'nye balansy v narodnokhoziaistvennom plane [Material Balances in the National Economic Plan]* (Moscow: 1960).

Ikonomichesko i sotsialno razvitie na NRB [Economic and Social Development of the P.R.B.] (Sofia: Bŭlgarska akademiya na naukite, 1964).

Jen-min Shou-ts'e [People's Handbook] (Peking: various years).

Jugoslavija, 1945–1964, statistički pregled [Yugoslavia, 1945–1964, Statistical Survey] (Belgrade: Federal Statistical Administration, 1965).

Kadyshev, V. P. *SSSR na vneshnikh rynkakh [U.S.S.R. in Foreign Markets]* (Moscow: 1964).

Kornai, János. *Overcentralization in Economic Administration: A Critical Analysis Based on Experience in Hungarian Light Industry*, translated by John Knapp (London: Oxford University Press, 1959).

Külkereskedelmi Kislexikon [Small Encyclopedia of Foreign Trade] (Budapest: Közgazdasági és Jogi Könyvkiadó, 1960).

Levente, M., E. Barat, and M. Bulgaru. *Analiza statistico-economica a agriculturii* [*Statistical-Economic Analysis of Agriculture*] (Bucharest: 1961).

Mesarić, Milan. *Notes on the Yugoslav Planning System* (Zagreb: Ekonomski Institut, 1966).

Mishustin, D. (ed.). *Vneshniaia torgovlia Sovetskogo Soiuza* [*Foreign Trade of the Soviet Union*] (Moscow: 1938).

Nagy, Imre. *On Communism* (New York: Praeger, 1957).

Niu Chung-huang. *Relation Between Production and Consumption During the First Five-Year Plan in China* (Peking: 1959); English translation in CIA, Foreign Documents Division, *Translation*, No. 735.

Plenum Tsentral'nogo Komiteta Kommunisticheskoi Partii Sovetskogo Soiuza 24–26 marta 1965 g. Stenograficheskii otchet [*Plenum of the Central Committee of the Communist Party of the Soviet Union, March 24–26, 1965, Stenographic Record*] (Moscow: 1965).

Polska w liczbach 1944–1958 [*Poland in Figures, 1944–1958*] (Warsaw: 1959).

Popisakov, G. *Vŭnshna tŭrgovia na N.R. Bŭlgaria* [*Foreign Trade of the P.R. of Bulgaria*] (Sofia: 1959).

Popov-Cherkasov, I. N. (ed.). *Organizatsiia platy rabochikh SSSR; sbornik normativnykh aktov* [*Organization of Workers' Wages in the U.S.S.R.; Collection of Basic Regulations*] (Moscow: 1965).

Razvitie narodnogo khoziaistva Narodnoi Respubliki Bolgarii (statisticheskie pokazateli) [*Development of the National Economy of the People's Republic of Bulgaria (Statistical Indexes)*] (Moscow: 1958).

Rocznik statistyczny [*Statistical Yearbook*] (Warsaw: Polskie Wydawnictwa Gospodarcze, various years).

Sbornik torgovykh dogovorov i soglashenii SSSR s inostrannymi gosudarstvami [*Collection of Trade Treaties and Agreements of the U.S.S.R. with Foreign States*] (Moscow: 1961).

Smirnov, A. M. *International Currency and Credit Relations of the U.S.S.R.* (Moscow: 1960); English translation in JPRS, No. 7155 (November 29, 1960).

Stalin, Joseph. *Economic Problems of Socialism in the USSR* (New York: International Publishers, 1952).

State Statistical Bureau. *Report of Fulfillment of the National Economic Plan of the People's Republic of China in 1955* (Peking: Foreign Languages Press, 1956).

————. *Ten Great Years* (Peking: Foreign Languages Press, 1960).

Statisticheski godishniak na N.R. Bŭlgaria [*Statistical Yearbook of the P.R. of Bulgaria*] (Sofia: various years).

Statistički Godišnjak SFRJ [*Statistical Yearbook of the SFRY*] (Belgrade: Federal Statistical Administration, various years).

Statisztikai Évkönyv [*Statistical Yearbook*] (Budapest: Központi Statisztikai Hivatal, various years).

Tsenral'no Statistchesko Upravlenia [Central Statistical Administration]. *Vŭnshna tŭrgovia na N. R. Bŭlgaria: Statisticheski sbornik* [*Foreign Trade of the P.R. of Bulgaria: Statistical Handbook*] (Sofia: various years).

Tsentral'noe Statisticheskoe Upravlenie SSSR [Central Statistical Administration of the U.S.S.R.]. *Narodnoe khoziaistvo SSSR* [*National Economy of the U.S.S.R.*] (Moscow: various years).

Vagnov, B. *Organizatsiia i tekhnika vneshnei torgovli SSSR i drugikh sotsialisticheskikh stran* [*Organization and Technique of Foreign Trade of the U.S.S.R. and Other Socialist Countries*] (Moscow: 1963).

Vajda, Imre. *Szocialista Külkereskedelem* [*Socialist Foreign Trade*] (Budapest: Közgazdasági és Jogi Könyvkiadó, 1963).

Vneshniaia torgovlia SSSR za 1959–1963 gody [*Foreign Trade of the U.S.S.R. in 1959–1963*] (Moscow: 1965; also various years).

Vneshniaia torgovlia Sovetskogo Soiuza za 1960–1965 gg. (*Statisticheskie dannye ob ob'eme vneshnei torgovli SSSR, eksporte i importe vazhneishikh tovarov*) [*Foreign Trade of the Soviet Union in 1960–1965* (*Statistical Data on the Volume of Foreign Trade of the U.S.S.R., Exports and Imports of Major Commodities*)], supplement to *Vneshniaia torgovlia*, No. 8 (1966).

Wacker, V., and B. Malý (eds.). *Mezinárodní socialistická dělba práce* [*International Socialist Division of Labor*] (Prague: 1964).

Yen Chung-p'ing. *Chung-kuo Chin-tai Ching-chi Shih T'ung-chi Tzu-liao Hsüanchi* [*Compendium of Selected Statistics on the Economic History of Contemporary China*] (Peking: Science Press, 1955).

Zala, J. (ed.). *Gazdaságstatisztika* [*Economic Statistics*] (Budapest: Közgazdasági és Jogi Könyvkiadó, 1959).

ARTICLES AND PAPERS

Akar, László. "A külkereskedelmi tervezés fejlesztéséről" ["On the Development of Foreign Trade Planning"], *Külkereskedelem*, II:6 (June 1958), pp. 1–2.

Ausch, Sándor. "Nemzetközi munkamegosztás és gazdasági mechanizmus" ["International Division of Labor and Economic Mechanism"], *Közgazdasági Szemle*, XII:7–8 (July-August 1965), pp. 800–808.

Bakos, György. "A termelés anyagi ösztönzése a külkereskedelmi célkitüzések elérésére" ["Material Incentives in Production to Achieve Foreign Trade Programmes"], *Külkereskedelem*, V:5 (May 1961), pp. 10–13.

Balázsy, Sándor. "A külkereskedelem gazdaságosságához" ["On the Economic Efficiency of Foreign Trade"], *Közgazdasági Szemle*, IV:3 (March 1957), pp. 303–320.

Borisenko, A. "On the Problems of Effectiveness of Socialist Foreign Trade," *American Review of Soviet and Eastern European Foreign Trade*, I:2 (March-April 1965), pp. 67–80.

Bystrov, F. "The Organization of International Settlements among the Socialist Countries," *Voprosy ekonomiki*, No. 2 (1960); English translation in *Problems of Economics*, III:2 (June 1960), pp. 56–59, 64.

Ch'en Yun. "Bridging the Gap between Supply and Demand," *People's China*, No. 22, November 16, 1954.

Damjanović, Mijat, *et al.* "Jugoslavensko javno mnenje o privrednoj reformi 1965 godine" ["Yugoslav Public Opinion on the Economic Reform of 1965"], in *Godišnjak 1965* [*Yearbook 1965*] (Belgrade: Institut Društvenih Nauka, 1966).

"Decision Concerning the Implementation of Cash Control in State Organs," *Hsin-hua Yüeh-pao*, II:1 (May 1950), p. 128.

"Decision on the Procedures Governing the Unification of State Trading throughout the Country," *Chung-yang Ts'ai-ching Cheng-ts'e Fa-ling Hui-pien* [*Concordance of Fiscal and Economic Policies and Ordinances of the Central People's Government*], Vol. II (1950), pp. 403–407.

Déri, Gusztáv. "Utazói tapasztalatok Közép-Amerikában" ["Experiences of Commercial Travelers in Central America"], *Külkereskedelem*, III:7 (July 1959), pp. 20–21.

Dudinskii, I. "The Problem of Fuels and Raw Materials in the Comecon Countries and the Ways to Solve It," *Voprosy ekonomiki*, No. 4 (1966); translation in *American Review of Soviet and Eastern European Foreign Trade*, II:5 (September-October 1966), pp. 19–39.

"Economic Conditions in China in the Past Year," *Hsin Chien-she*, I:10 (January 1950).

Facsády, Kálmán, and László Várkonyi. "Prémiumrendszer a külkereskedelemben" ["Premium System in Foreign Trade"], *Külkereskedelem*, II:6 (June 1958), pp. 9–12.

Fedorenko, N. "Vazhnaia ekonomicheskaia problema" ["An Important Economic Problem"], *Pravda*, January 17, 1965.

Fiszel, H. *Gospodarka planowa*, Nos. 7–8 (1957), pp. 27–30; cited in *Közgazdasági Szemle*, V:6 (June 1958), pp. 614–625.

Friss, I. "The Party and Some Important Topical Tasks of Economic Science," *Társadalmi Szemle* (August–September 1965); as translated in Radio Free Europe, Hungarian Press Survey, No. 1635 (September 3, 1966).

Goldman, Josef. "Systems of Planning and Management," *Rudé právo* (January 29, 1965); in JPRS, Translations on Economic Organization and Management in Eastern Europe 28988, No. 445 (March 3, 1965).

Gorupić, Drago, and Ivo Perišin. "Proširena reprodukcija i njeno financiranje" ["Expanded Reproduction and its Financing"], *Ekonomski pregled*, Nos. 2–3 (1965).

Hamburger, László. "Az exportforgalmi jutalék és az árkiegyenlítési prémiumrendszer néhány hiányossága" ["Some Shortcomings of the Export Turnover Bonus and of the Price-Equalization Premium Systems"], *Külkereskedelem*, III:1 (January 1959), pp. 19–20.

Hantos, Miklós. "A külkereskedelem vállalati prémiumrendszeréről" ["On the Premium System of the FTEs"], *Külkereskedelem*, IV:3 (March 1960), pp. 7–9.

———, and László Várkonyi. "A külkereskedelmi prémiumrendszer módosításáról" ["On the Modification of the Foreign Trade Prémium System"], *Külkereskedelem*, III:5 (May 1959), pp. 12–15.

Illyés, Éva. "A külkereskedelem szerepe és tervezésének jelenlegi feladatai" ["The Role of Foreign Trade and the Current Tasks of its Planning"], *Társadalmi Szemle*, IX:5 (May 1954).

Ivanov, P. "Division of Labor and Coordination of Economic Plans," *American Review of Soviet and Eastern European Foreign Trade*, I:3 (May–June 1965), pp. 21–35.

Jiranek, Slavomir. "The Position of the Czechoslovak Crown in International Relations," *American Review of Soviet and Eastern European Foreign Trade*, I:6 (November–December 1965), pp. 56–63.

Kálmán, Dezsö. "Az importmunka felelössége" ["Responsibility of the Import Work"], *Külkereskedelem*, III:8 (August 1959), pp. 10–11.

Karádi, Gyula. "Új vonások külkereskedelmünkben" ["New Trends in Our Foreign Trade"], *Közgadasági Szemle*, VI:11 (November 1959), pp. 1141–1158.

Katus, László. "Termelöi árrendezés, import ármegállapitás" ["Producer Price Reform, Import Price Determination"], *Külkereskedelem*, II:3 (March 1958), pp. 13–14.

Korošec, Joze. "More Than Half of Imports Liberalized," *Yugoslav Export*, November 1, 1966.

Lakos, Gyula. "A helyi és kisipari export néhány problémájáról" ["On Some Problems of Local and Small-Scale Industrial Exports"], *Külkereskedelem*, I:2 (November 1957), pp. 7–8.

Li Fu-ch'un. "Report on the Draft 1960 National Economic Plan" (March 30, 1960), *Second Session of the Second National People's Congress of the People's Republic of China (Documents)* (Peking: Foreign Languages Press, 1960), pp. 1–48.

Li Yung-sheng. "Unification of Import Commodity Exchange and Price Setting Methods," *Chi-hua Ching-chi*, No. 4 (1958).

Liska, Tibor, and Antal Máriás. "A gazdaságosság és a nemzetközi munkamegosztás" ["Economic Efficiency and International Division of Labor"], *Közgazdasági Szemle*, I:1 (October 1954), pp. 75–94.

Maklakov, A. "From History of Socialist Planning in the Economy of the Chinese People's Republic," *Voprosy ekonomiki* (October 1958); English translation in *Problems of Economics*, I:10 (February 1959), pp. 78–84.

"Materijali sa savjetovanja naučne sekcije saveza društava ekonomista Jugoslavije" ["Material from the Conference of the Scientific Section of the Association of the Societies of the Economists of Yugoslavia"] (Zagreb, January 18–20, 1963), *Ekonomski pregled*, Nos. 3–5 (1963), pp. 147–199.

Ma Yin-chu. "A New Theory of Population," *Hsin-hua Pan-yüeh-k'an*, No. 15 (1957).

Mišković, Dobrivoje. "Investicije i platni bilans" ["Investment and Financial Balance"], *Ekonomika preduzeca*, XIII:7 (1965).

Mrkušić, Z. "Razvoj jugoslavenskog sistema spoljne trgovine" ["The Development of Yugoslav System of Foreign Trade"], Treće medjunarodno savetovanje privrednika i pravnika [Third International Symposium of Economists and Lawyers], Zagreb, September 15–17, 1966.

"Napirenden: A külkereskedelem harmadik ötéves terve" ["Agenda: The Third Five Year Plan of Foreign Trade"], *Külkereskedelem*, X:7 (July 1966), pp. 193–194.

Pajestka, J. "An Interpretation of the First Stage of Poland's Economic Development" in *Studies on the Theory of Reproduction and Prices* (Warsaw: 1964).

Pertot, Vladimir. "Elementi za utvrdjivanje nekih specifičnih osobenosti u našem izvozu" ["Elements in Ascertaining Some Specific Characteristics of Our Exports"], *Ekonomist*, No. 4 (1960), pp. 617–661.

———. "Neke osobenosti u strukturi i geografskoj usmerenosti našeg izvoza" ["Some Characteristics in the Structure and Geographical Direction of Our Exports"], *Ekonomist*, No. 3 (1960), pp. 380–426.

Pleva, Jan. "Foreign Trade and the New System of Managements," *American Review of Soviet and Eastern Foreign Trade*, I:6 (November-December 1965), pp. 39–55.

Po I-po. "Report on the Results of the 1956 Plan and the Draft 1957 Plan," *Chung-hua Jen-min Kung-ho-kuo Fa-kuei Hui-pien* [*Compendium of Laws and Regulations of the People's Republic of China*] (Peking), No. 6, pp. 145–178.

"Price Fluctuations and the Basic Methods of Overcoming Them," *Hsin-hua Yüeh-pao*, I:3 (January 1950), p. 667.

"Report of Yeh Chi-chuang, Minister of Foreign Trade," *The Fourth Session of the First National People's Congress of the People's Republic of China* (Peking: People's Press, 1957).

Rolow, Aleksander. "Foreign Trade Prices and Effectiveness of Foreign Exchange in Production," *Gospodarka planowa*, XV:4 (April 1960); English translation in JPRS, No. 7195 (November 30, 1960).

Rubinshtein, G. "The Development of Soviet Imports," *Vneshniaia torgovlia*, No. 5 (1960); translation in *Problems of Economics*, III:4 (August 1960), pp. 3–10.

Sattler, Tamás. "Gazdaságos aluminiumkohászati segédanyag import" ["Economical Importation of Auxiliary Materials for Aluminum Metallurgy"], *Külkereskedelem*, III:12 (December 1959), pp. 8–11.

Savov, M., and N. Velichkov. "Spetsializatsiata na proizvodstvoto i tsenite v tŭrgoviita mezhdu sotsialisticheskite strani" ["Specialization in Production and Pricing in the Trade among Socialist Countries"], *Planovo stopanstvo i statistika*, No. 7 (1966).

Sebestyén, Tibor. "A Chemolimpex és az ipar együttmüködése az importban" ["Cooperation of Chemolimpex and Industry in Importing"], *Külkereskedelem*, III:2 (February 1959), pp. 24–25.

Shereshevskii, M. "Osnovnye cherty i zadachi organizatsii vneshnei torgovli SSSR posle vtoroi mirovoi voiny" ["Basic Characteristics and Tasks of the Organization of Foreign Trade of the U.S.S.R. after the Second World War"], *Voprosy vneshnei torgovli* [*Problems of Foreign Trade*] (Moscow: Inst. mezh. otnosh., 1960).

Šik, O. "Improvement of System of Planned Management," *Rudé právo* (November 22, 1963); in JPRS, Translations on Economic Organization and Management in Eastern Europe 26256, No. 369 (September 3, 1964), pp. 1–20.

Szabó, Tibor, and Tamás Sugár. "A külkereskedelem ipari kapcsolatai és ösztönzési rendszerek a szocialista országokban" ["Relations between Foreign Trade and Industry and the Incentive Systems in Socialist Countries"], *Külkereskedelem*, IV:2 (February 1960), pp. 4–9.

Szányi, Jenő. "Moszkvai tapasztalatok . . . " ["Experiences from Moscow . . ."], *Külkereskedelem*, I:3 (December 1957), pp. 15–16.

Tallós, György. "Az 1958 évi külkereskedelmi tervről" ["On the 1958 Foreign Trade Plan"], *Külkereskedelem*, II:3 (March 1958), pp. 1–3.

———. "Az 1959 évi külkereskedelmi tervől" ["On the 1959 Foreign Trade Plan"], *Külkereskedelem*, III:1 (January 1959), pp. 1–3.

Tomasek, Ladislav. "Vztah filosofie a ekonomie a nove zasady rizeni" ["The Relation of Philosophy and Economy to the New Economic Model"], *Plánované hospodářství*, XVIII:2 (1965).

Vajda, Imre. "Privredni razvoj i medjunarodna podela rada" ["Economic Development and International Division of Labor"], *Ekonomist*, No. 4 (1965).

Vuković, D. "Dueli Končar-Natronka" ["Duel Between *Končar* and *Natronka*"] *Borba*, September 26, 1966, p. 5.

Wang Ti. "Make Proper Arrangements for Export Trade, Actively Organize the Supplies," *Ta Kung Pao*, Tientsin, October 13, 1957.

Yeh Chi-chuang. "A Discussion of Foreign Trade," *Jen-min Shou-ts'e, 1958* [*People's Handbook, 1958*], pp. 557–559.

——. "Our Country's Foreign Trade in the Last Ten Years," *Hsin-hua Pan-yüeh-k'an*, No. 19 (1959).

——. "The Promotion of Foreign Trade," *Jen-min Jih-pao*, September 28, 1956.

"Zur Aussenhandelskonferenz" ["On the Foreign Trade Conference"], *Aussenhandel*, No. 3 (1958).

SELECTED PERIODICALS

Der Aussenhandel [*Foreign Trade*] (East Berlin: semimonthly).

Borba [*Struggle*] (Belgrade and Zagreb: Organ of the Socialist Alliance of the Working People of Yugoslavia, daily).

Chi-hua Ching-chi [*Planned Economy*] (Peking: monthly).

Ekonomicheskaia gazeta [*Economic Gazette*] (Moscow: weekly).

Ekonomika preduzeća [*Economic Enterprises*] (Belgrade: monthly).

Ekonomist [*Economist*] (Belgrade: quarterly).

Ekonomista [*Economist*] (Warsaw: bimonthly).

Ekonomska politika [*Political Economy*] (Belgrade: weekly).

Ekonomski pregled [*Economic Review*] (Zagreb: monthly).

Figyelö [*Observer*] (Budapest: biweekly).

Gospodarka planowa [*Planned Economy*] (Warsaw: monthly).

Handel zagraniczny [*Foreign Trade*] (Warsaw: monthly).

Hospodářské noviny [*New Economy*] (Prague: weekly).

Hsin Chien-she [*New Construction*] (Peking: monthly).

Hsin-hua Pan-yüeh-k'an [*New China Semimonthly*] (Peking: semimonthly).

Hsin-hua Yüeh-pao [*New China Monthly*] (Peking: monthly).

Jen-min Jih-pao [*People's Daily*] (Peking: Organ of the Communist Party of China, daily).

Közgazdasági Szemle [*Economic Review*] (Budapest: monthly).

Külkereskedelem [*Foreign Trade*] (Budapest: monthly).

Népszabadsag [*People's Freedom*] (Budapest: Organ of the Hungarian Socialist Workers' Party, daily).

Neues Deutschland [*New Germany*] (East Berlin: Organ of the Central Committee of SED, daily).

People's China (Peking: semimonthly).

Plánované hospodářství [*Planned Economy*] (Prague: 10 times yearly).

Planovo stopanstvo i statistika [*Planned Economy and Statistics*] (Sofia: 10 times yearly).

Planovoe khoziaistvo [*Planned Economy*] (Moscow: monthly).

Pravda [*Truth*] (Moscow: Organ of the Central Committee of the CPSU, daily).

Probleme economice [*Problems of Economics*] (Bucharest: monthly).

Rabotnichesko delo [*Workers' Task*] (Sofia: Organ of the Central Committee of the Communist Party of Bulgaria, daily).

Rudé právo [*Red Right*] (Prague: Organ of the Communist Party of Czechoslovakia, daily).

Scîntea [*Spark*] (Bucharest: Organ of the Rumanian Communist Party, daily).

Statisztikai Havi Közlemények [*Statistical Monthly Bulletins*] (Budapest: monthly).

Statisztikai Szemle [*Statistical Review*] (Budapest: monthly).

Ta Kung Pao [*Impartial Daily*] (Tientsin and Peking: daily).

Társadalmi Szemle [*Social Review*] (Budapest: monthly).

Trybuna ludu [*People's Tribune*] (Warsaw: Organ of the Central Committee of the Polish United Workers' Party, daily).

Vneshniaia torgovlia [*Foreign Trade*] (Moscow: monthly).

Voprosy ekonomiki [*Economic Problems*] (Moscow: monthly).

Vŭnshna tŭrgovia [*Foreign Trade*] (Sofia: monthly).

Yugoslav Export (Belgrade: bimonthly).

Yugoslav Facts and Views (New York: Yugoslav Information Center, irregular).

Zahraniční obchod [*Foreign Trade*] (Prague: monthly).

NOTE: In addition, the reader is referred to such standard collections of translations from Communist countries as those of the Joint Publications Research Service (JPRS); the IASP (International Arts and Sciences Press) journals such as *Chinese Economic Studies, Eastern European Economics, Mathematical Studies in Economics and Statistics in the USSR and Eastern Europe, Problems of Economics, Soviet and Eastern European Foreign Trade* (formerly *The American Review of Soviet and Eastern European Foreign Trade*); the Press Surveys of Radio Free Europe; and *The Current Digest of the Soviet Press*.

WESTERN SOURCES

BOOKS, DOCUMENTS AND UNPUBLISHED DISSERTATIONS

Alexander, A. *Greek Industrialists* (Athens: Center for Economic Research, 1964).

Allen, Robert Loring. *Soviet Economic Warfare* (Washington, D.C.: Public Affairs Press, 1960).

Ames, Edward. *Soviet Economic Processes* (Homewood, Ill.: Irwin, 1965).

Balassa, Bela A. *The Hungarian Experience in Economic Planning* (New Haven: Yale University Press, 1959).

Baumol, William J. *Economic Dynamics* (New York: Macmillan, 1951).

Baykov, Alexander. *Soviet Foreign Trade* (Princeton: Princeton University Press, 1946).

Bergson, Abram. *The Economics of Soviet Planning* (New Haven: Yale University Press, 1964).

————. *Essays in Normative Economics* (Cambridge: Harvard University Press, 1966).

Bergson, Abram, and Simon Kuznets (eds.). *Economic Trends in the Soviet Union* (Cambridge: Harvard University Press, 1963).

Berliner, Joseph S. *Factory and Manager in the USSR* (Cambridge: Harvard University Press, 1957).

————. *Soviet Economic Aid* (New York: Praeger, 1958).

Brown, Alan A. "The Economics of Centrally Planned Foreign Trade: The Hungarian Experience" (Unpublished doctoral dissertation, Harvard University, 1966).

Central Intelligence Agency. *Foreign Trade of the European Satellites in 1965* (Washington, D.C.: 1966).

Chenery, Hollis B., and P. G. Clark. *Interindustry Economics* (New York: Wiley, 1959).

Cheng, Chu-yuan. *Monetary Affairs of Communist China*, Third Edition, Communist China Problem Research Series (Hong Kong: The Union Research Institute, 1959).

Clark, Colin. *The Conditions of Economic Progress*, Third Edition (London: Macmillan, 1957).

Dell, Sydney. *Trade Blocs and Common Markets* (New York: Knopf, 1963).

Dernberger, Robert F. "Foreign Trade and Capital Movements of Communist China, 1949–1962" (Unpublished doctoral dissertation, Harvard University, 1965).

Dickinson, H. D. *Economics of Socialism* (London: 1937).

Dobb, Maurice. *Economic Theory and Socialism* (New York: International Publishers, 1955).

————. *Soviet Economic Development Since 1917*, Fifth Edition (London: Routledge and Paul, 1960).

East-West Trade: A Compilation of Views of Businessmen, Bankers and Academic Experts. U.S. Congress, Senate Committee on Foreign Relations (Washington, D.C.: 1964).

Eckstein, Alexander. *Communist China's Economic Growth and Foreign Trade* (New York: McGraw-Hill, 1966).

Gerschenkron, Alexander. *Economic Backwardness in Historical Perspective* (Cambridge: Harvard University Press, 1962).

————. *Economic Relations with the USSR* (New York: The Committee on International Economic Policy in Cooperation with the Carnegie Endowment for International Peace, 1945).

Gordon, Margaret S. *Barriers to World Trade* (New York: Macmillan, 1941).

Gordon, Wendell C. *International Trade: Goods, People, and Ideas* (New York: Alfred Knopf, 1962).

Grossman, Gregory (ed.). *Value and Plan: Economic Calculation and Organization in Eastern Europe* (Berkeley and Los Angeles: University of California Press, 1960).

Haberler, Gottfried. *Money in the International Economy* (Cambridge: Harvard University Press, 1965).

————. *A Survey of International Trade Theory*, Revised and Enlarged Edition, Special Papers in International Economics, No. 1, July 1961 (Princeton: International Finance Section, Princeton University, 1961).

————. *The Theory of International Trade*, English translation (London: William Hodge, 1936).

Herman, Leon M. *A Background Study on East-West Trade.* U.S. Congress, Senate Committee on Foreign Relations (Washington, D.C.: 1965).

Hicks, John R. *Value and Capital,* Second Edition (Oxford: Clarendon Press, 1946).

Hirschman, Albert O. *The Strategy of Economic Development* (New Haven: Yale University Press, 1958).

India, 1960 (Delhi: Government of India, 1960).

Iversen, Carl. *Aspects of the Theory of International Capital Movements* (Copenhagen: Levin and Munksgaard, 1936).

Kaser, Michael. *Comecon* (London: Oxford University Press, 1965).

Kindleberger, Charles. *Foreign Trade and the National Economy* (New Haven: Yale University Press, 1962).

Kuznets, Simon. *Modern Economic Growth* (New Haven: Yale University Press, 1966).

————. *Six Lectures on Economic Growth* (Glencoe: Free Press, 1959).

League of Nations. *Statistical Yearbook, 1933/4* (Geneva: 1934).

Lerner, Abba P. *The Economics of Control* (New York: Macmillan, 1944).

Levine, Herbert S. "A Study in Economic Planning" (Unpublished doctoral dissertation, Harvard University, 1961).

Liu, T. C., and K. C. Yeh. *The Economy of the Chinese Mainland: National Income and Economic Development, 1933–1959* (Princeton: Princeton University Press, 1965).

Machlup, Fritz. *The Production and Distribution of Knowledge in the United States* (Princeton: Princeton University Press, 1962).

Mah, Feng-hwa. *Communist China's Foreign Trade: Price Structure and Behavior, 1955–1959* (Santa Monica: The RAND Corporation, October 1963), RAND Memorandum RM-3825-RC.

Marshall, Alfred. *Money, Credit and Commerce* (London: Macmillan, 1923).

McCorkle, Chester O. *Fruit and Vegetable Marketing in the Economic Development of Greece* (Athens: Center for Economic Research, 1962).

McKitterick, Nathaniel. *East-West Trade: The Background of U.S. Policy* (New York: The Twentieth Century Fund, 1966).

Meade, J. E. *The Theory of International Economic Policy;* Vol. I, *The Balance of Payments;* Vol. II, *Trade and Welfare* (London: Oxford University Press, 1951 and 1955).

Michaely, Michael. *Concentration in International Trade* (Amsterdam: North-Holland Publishing Company, 1962).

Mikesell, Raymond F., and Jack N. Behrman. *Financing Free World Trade with the Sino-Soviet Bloc,* Princeton Studies in International Finance, No. 8 (Princeton: Princeton University Press, 1958).

Montias, John Michael. *Central Planning in Poland* (New Haven: Yale University Press, 1962).

————. *Economic Development in Communist Rumania* (Cambridge: Massachusetts Institute of Technology Press, 1967).

Neuberger, Egon. *Central Planning and Its Legacies* (Santa Monica: The RAND Corporation, December 1966), Paper P-3492.

Nove, Alec. *The Soviet Economy: An Introduction,* Revised Edition (New York: Praeger, 1965).

Nove, Alec, and Desmond Donnelly. *Trade with Communist Countries* (London: Hutchinson of London, 1960).

Perkins, Dwight H. *Market Control and Planning in Communist China* (Cambridge: Harvard University Press, 1966).

Pryor, Frederic L. *The Communist Foreign Trade System* (Cambridge: Massachusetts Institute of Technology Press, 1963).

Remer, Charles F. *The Trade Agreements of Communist China* (Santa Monica: The RAND Corporation, February 1961), P-2208.

The Report to the President of the Special Committee on U.S. Trade Relations with East European Countries and the Soviet Union (Washington, D.C.: April 29, 1965).

Research Analysis Corporation. *The 1959 Soviet Intersectoral Flow Table* (Washington, D.C.: November 1964), Vols. I and II.

Röpke, Wilhelm. *International Economic Disintegration* (New York: Macmillan, 1942).

Rosovsky, Henry. *Capital Formation in Japan* (Glencoe: Free Press, 1961).

——— (ed.). *Industrialization in Two Systems: Essays in Honor of Alexander Gerschenkron* (New York: Wiley, 1966).

Schelling, Thomas C. *International Economics* (Boston: Allyn and Bacon, 1958).

Schenk, Fritz. *Die Magie der Planwirtschaft* [*The Magic of Planned Economy*] (Cologne: Kiepenheuer und Witsch, 1960).

Schumpeter, Joseph A. *Socialism, Capitalism and Democracy* (New York: Harper, 1947).

Schwartz, Harry. *Russia's Soviet Economy*, Second Edition (Englewood Cliffs: Prentice-Hall, 1958).

Solow, Robert. *Capital Theory and the Rate of Return* (Amsterdam: North-Holland Publication, 1963).

Spulber, Nicolas. *The Economics of Communist Eastern Europe* (Cambridge and New York: The Technology Press of Massachusetts Institute of Technology and Wiley, 1957).

Triantis, S. G. *Common Market and Economic Development: The E.E.C. and Greece* (Athens: Center for Economic Research, 1965).

United Nations. *Demographic Yearbook* (New York: various years).

———. *Economic Bulletin for Europe* (Geneva: various issues; three times a year).

———. *Economic Survey of Europe* (Geneva: Economic Commission for Europe, various years).

———. *Statistical Yearbook* (New York: various years).

———. *Yearbook of International Trade Statistics* (New York: various years).

U. S. Bureau of Mines. *Minerals Yearbook 1964* (Washington, D.C.: 1965), Vol. I.

U. S. Department of Commerce. *Summaries of Country-by-Commodity Series* (Washington, D.C.: various years).

U. S. Department of State. *The Battle Act Report, 1965* (Washington, D.C.: February 1966).

U. S. Directorate of Intelligence. *Communist China's Balance of Payments 1950–1965* (Washington, D.C.: 1966).

United States-Japan Trade Council. *United States Exports to Japan by Customs District of Shipment, 1965* (Washington, D.C.: 1966).

Wiles, P. J. D. *Communist International Economics* (forthcoming).

———. *The Political Economy of Communism* (Cambridge: Harvard University Press, 1962).

Wu, Yuan-li. *An Economic Survey of Communist China* (New York: Bookman Association, 1956).

Yntema, Theodore O. *A Mathematical Reformulation of the General Theory of International Trade* (Chicago: University of Chicago Press, 1932).

Zauberman, Alfred. *Industrial Progress in Poland, Czechoslovakia and East Germany, 1937–1962* (London: Oxford University Press, 1964).

ARTICLES AND PAPERS

"Agricultural Study Forecasts Another Hungry Spring for Communist China," *Current Scene*, I:23 (January 22, 1962), p. 1–21.

Alexander, Sidney. "Effects of a Devaluation: A Simplified Synthesis of Elasticities and Absorption Approaches," *American Economic Review*, XLIX:1 (March 1959), pp. 22–42.

Altman, Oscar. "Russian Gold and the Ruble," *Staff Papers*, International Monetary Fund, VII:3 (April 1960).

Ames, Edward. "The Exchange Rate in Soviet Type Economies," *Review of Economics and Statistics*, XXXV:4 (November 1953), pp. 337–342.

———. "Soviet Bloc Currency Conversions," *American Economic Review*, XLIV:3 (June 1954), pp. 339–353.

Balassa, Bela. "Planning in an Open Economy," *Kyklos*, XIX:3 (1966), pp. 385–403.

Baran, Paul A. "National Economic Planning," in Bernard F. Haley (ed.), *A Survey of Contemporary Economics* (Homewood, Ill.: Irwin, 1952), II, pp. 355–403.

Berman, Harold. "The Legal Framework of Trade between Planned and Market Economies: The Soviet-American Example," *Law and Contemporary Problems*, XXIV:3 (Summer 1959), pp. 482–528.

Bornstein, Morris. "A Comparison of Soviet and United States National Product," U.S. Congress, Joint Economic Committee, *Comparisons of the United States and Soviet Economies* (Washington, D.C.: 1959), Part II, pp. 377–395.

———. "The Soviet Price System," *American Economic Review*, LII:1 (March 1962), pp. 64–103.

Breton, Albert. "The Economics of Nationalism," *Journal of Political Economy*, LXXII:4 (August 1964), pp. 376–386.

Brown, Alan A. "Centrally-Planned Foreign Trade and Economic Efficiency," *American Economist*, V:2 (November 1961), pp. 11–28.

———, and Richard Yin. "Communist Economics: Reforms vs. Orthodoxy," *Communist Affairs*, III:1 (January-February, 1965), pp. 3–9.

Campbell, Robert. "On the Theory of Economic Administration," in Henry Rosovsky (ed.), *Industrialization in Two Systems: Essays in Honor of Alexander Gerschenkron* (New York: Wiley, 1966), pp. 186–203.

"China in World Trade," *Current Scene*, IV:3 (February 1, 1966), Part I, pp. 1–8; and IV:4 (February 15, 1966), Part II, pp. 1–11.

Cohn, Stanley H. "Soviet Growth Retardation: Trends in Resource Availability and Efficiency," U.S. Congress, Joint Economic Committee, *New Directions in the Soviet Economy* (Washington, D.C.: 1966), Part II-A, pp. 99–132.

"Decision for an Upsurge," *Current Scene*, III:17 (April 15, 1965), pp. 1–10.

Dernberger, Robert F. "First Five Year Plan and Its International Aspects," in C. F. Remer (ed.), *Three Essays on the International Economics of Communist China* (Ann Arbor: University of Michigan Press, 1959).

Deutsch, K. W., and A. Eckstein. "National Industrialization and the Declining Share of the International Economic Sector, 1890–1959," *World Politics*, Volume XIII:2 (January 1961), pp. 267–299.

Domke, Martin, and John Hazard. "State Trading and the Most-Favored-Nation Clause," *American Journal of International Law*, LII:1 (January 1958), pp. 55–68.

Erlich, Alexander. "Development Strategy and Planning: The Soviet Experience," Conference on Economic Planning, Sponsored by Universities–NBER, Princeton, November 1964.

Ernst, Maurice. "Postwar Economic Growth in Eastern Europe," U.S. Congress, Joint Economic Committee, *New Directions in the Soviet Economy* (Washington, D.C.: 1966), Part IV, pp. 875–916.

Granick, David. "An Organizational Model of Soviet Industrial Planning," *Journal of Political Economy*, LXVII:2 (April 1959), pp. 109–130.

Grossman, Gregory. "Innovation and Information in the Soviet Economy," *American Economic Review*, LVI:2 (May 1966), pp. 118–158.

———. "Notes for a Theory of the Command Economy," *Soviet Studies*, XV:2 (October 1963), pp. 101–123.

Haberler, Gottfried. "An Assessment of the Current Relevance of the Theory of Comparative Advantage to Agricultural Production and Trade," *International Journal of Agrarian Affairs*, IV:3 (May 1964), pp. 130–149.

———. "Economic Consequences of a Divided World," *The Review of Politics*, XVIII:1 (January 1956), pp. 3–22.

Hazard, John. "State Trading in History and Theory," *Law and Contemporary Problems*, XXIV:2 (Spring 1959), pp. 243–255.

Heiss, Herta W. "The Soviet Union in the World Market," U.S. Congress, Joint Economic Committee, *New Directions in the Soviet Economy* (Washington, D.C.: 1966), Part IV, pp. 917–933.

Hoeffding, Oleg. "State Planning and Forced Industrialization," *Problems of Communism*, VIII:6 (November-December, 1959), pp. 38–44.

Holesovsky, Vaclav. "Planning Reforms in Czechoslovakia," paper presented to the Second Annual Convention of the American Association for the Advancement of Slavic Studies, Washington, D.C., March 30, 1967.

Holzman, Franklyn D. "Foreign Trade," in Abram Bergson and Simon Kuznets (eds.), *Economic Trends in the Soviet Union* (Cambridge: Harvard University Press, 1963), pp. 283–332.

———. "Foreign Trade Behavior of Centrally-Planned Economies," in Henry Rosovsky (ed.), *Industrialization in Two Systems: Essays in Honor of Alexander Gerschenkron* (New York: Wiley, 1966), pp. 237–265.

———. "More on Soviet Bloc Trade Discrimination," *Soviet Studies*, XVII:1 (July 1965), pp. 44–65.

———. "Some Financial Aspects of Soviet Foreign Trade," U.S. Congress, Joint

Economic Committee, *Comparisons of the United States and Soviet Economies* (Washington, D.C.: 1959), Part II, pp. 427–443.

Holzman, Franklyn D. "Some Traditional Adjustment Mechanisms in the Foreign Trade of Centrally Planned Economies," to appear in the *Cahiers de L'ISEA*.

———. "Soviet Foreign Trade and the United States Market," U.S. Congress, Joint Economic Committee, *New Directions in the Soviet Economy* (Washington, D.C.: 1966), Part IV, pp. 935–946.

———, and Arnold Zellner. "The Foreign Trade and Balanced Budget Multipliers," *American Economic Review*, XLVIII:1 (March 1958), pp. 73–91.

Hoselitz, Bert F. "Socialism, Communism and International Trade," *Journal of Political Economy*, LVII:3 (June 1949), pp. 227–241.

———. "Socialist Planning and International Economic Relations," *American Economic Review*, XXXIII:4 (December 1943), pp. 839–851.

"How Switch Trading Works," *The Economist*, January 14, 1966.

Hunter, Holland. "Optimal Tautness in Developmental Planning," *Economic Development and Cultural Change*, IX:4 (July 1961), pp. 561–572.

———. "Transport in Soviet and Chinese Development," *Economic Development and Cultural Change*, XIV:1 (October 1965), pp. 71–84.

Ishikawa, S. "Strategy of Foreign Trade Under Planned Economic Development — with Special Reference to China's Experience," *Hitotsubashi Journal of Economics* (January 1965).

Johnson, D. Gale. "The Environment for Technological Change in Soviet Agriculture," *American Economic Review*, LVI:2 (May 1966), pp. 145–153.

Johnson, Harry G. "The Cost of Protection and the Scientific Tariff," *Journal of Political Economy*, LXVIII:4 (August 1960), pp. 327–345.

———. "The Costs of Protection and of Self-sufficiency," *Quarterly Journal of Economics*, LXXIX:3 (August 1965), pp. 356–372.

———. "An Economic Theory of Protectionism, Tariff Bargaining, and the Formation of Customs Unions," *Journal of Political Economy*, LXXIII:3 (June 1965), pp. 256–283.

———. "The Possibility of Income Losses from Increased Efficiency on Factor Accumulation in the Presence of Tariffs," *Economic Journal*, LXXVII:305 (March 1967), pp. 151–154.

———. "A Theoretical Model of Nationalism in New and Developing States," *Political Science Quarterly*, LXXX:2 (June 1965), pp. 169–185.

———. "The Theory of Tariff Structure with Special Reference to World Trade and Development," in *Trade and Development* (Etudes et Travaux de L'Institute Universitaire de Hautes Etudes Internationales, No. 4, Geneve, 1965).

Judy, Richard. "Information, Control, and Soviet Economic Management," in John P. Hardt, *et al.* (eds.), *Mathematics and Computers in Soviet Economic Planning* (New Haven: Yale University Press, 1967).

Kalecki, M. "The Principle of Increasing Risk," *Economica*, N.S., IV:4 (November 1937), pp. 440–447.

Lange, Oscar. "On the Economic Theory of Socialism," in Benjamin E. Lippincott (ed.), *On the Economic Theory of Socialism* (Minneapolis: University of Minnesota Press, 1938), pp. 55–143.

Lee, T. C. "The Food Problem," *Contemporary China*, IV (Hong Kong: Hong Kong University Press, 1961), pp. 1–26.

Lerner, Abba P. "Economic Liberalism in the Postwar World," in Seymour

Harris (ed.), *Postwar Economic Problems* (New York: McGraw-Hill, 1943), pp. 127–139.

Levine, Herbert S. "The Centralized Planning of Supply in Soviet Industry," U.S. Congress, Joint Economic Committee, *Comparisons of the United States and Soviet Economies* (Washington, D.C.: 1959), Part I, pp. 151–176.

MacDougall, Colina. "Eight Plants for Peking," *Far Eastern Economic Review*, XLIII:4 (January 23, 1964), pp. 156–158.

MacDougall, G. D. A. "British and American Exports: A Study Suggested by the Theory of Comparative Costs"; Part I, *Economic Journal*, LXI (December 1951), pp. 697–724; Part II, *Economic Journal*, LXII (September 1952), pp. 487–521.

Machlup, Fritz. "The Supply of Inventors and Inventions," *Weltwirtschaftliches Archiv*, LXXXV:2 (1960), p. 210–254.

Mah, Feng-hwa. "The Terms of Sino-Soviet Trade," in Choh-ming Li (ed.), *Industrial Development in Communist China* (New York: Praeger, 1964), pp. 174–191.

Mendershausen, Horst. "The Terms of Soviet-Satellite Trade: A Broadened Analysis," *Review of Economics and Statistics*, XLII:2 (May 1960), pp. 152–163.

———. "Terms of Trade between the Soviet Union and Smaller Communist Countries," *Review of Economics and Statistics*, XLI:2 (May 1959), pp. 106–118.

Metzger, Stanley D. "Federal Regulation and Prohibition of Trade with Iron Curtain Countries," *Law and Contemporary Problems*, XXIX:4 (Autumn 1964), pp. 1000–1018.

Montias, John Michael. "Economic Nationalism in Eastern Europe: Forty Years of Continuity and Change," *Journal of International Affairs*, XX:1 (1966), pp. 51–61.

———. "Planning with Material Balances," *American Economic Review*, XLIV:5 (December 1959), pp. 963–985.

———. "The Soviet Model and the Underdeveloped Areas," in Nicolas Spulber (ed.), *Study of the Soviet Economy* (Bloomington: University of Indiana, 1961).

"Mr. Kadar's Albatross," *The Economist*, October 29, 1966.

Neuberger, Egon. "Centralization versus Decentralization: The Case of Yugoslav Banking," *American Slavic and East European Review*, XVIII:3 (October 1959), pp. 361–373.

———. "Libermanism, Computopia, and Visible Hand: The Question of Informational Efficiency," *American Economic Review*, LVI:2 (May 1966), pp. 131–144.

"Note on Post-war Developments in East European Trade," United Nations, *Economic Bulletin for Europe*, XVI:2 (Geneva: 1964).

Nove, Alec. "The Changing Role of Soviet Prices," *Economics of Planning* (December 1963), pp. 185–195.

———. "The Soviet Model and Underdeveloped Countries," *International Affairs*, XXXVII:1 (January 1961), pp. 29–38.

Pryor, Frederic L. "Trade Barriers of Capitalist and Communist Nations Against Foodstuffs Exported by Tropical Underdeveloped Nations," *Review of Economics and Statistics*, XLIII:4 (November 1966), pp. 406–412.

Pryor, Frederic L., and George Staller. "The Dollar Values of the Gross National Products in Eastern Europe 1955," *Economics of Planning*, VI:1 (1966), pp. 1–26.

Rockwell, Charles S. "Product Growth and Factor Inputs in Yugoslavia: Some Cross-Sectional Results," paper prepared for the American-Yugoslav Seminar, Belgrade, 4–9 July 1966.

Seton, Francis. "Planning and Economic Growth: Asia, Africa, and the Soviet Model," *Soviet Survey*, No. 31 (January-March, 1960), pp. 38–44.

"Soviet Economic Performance and Reform: Some Problems of Analysis and Prognosis — A Round-Table Discussion," *Slavic Review*, XXXV:2 (June 1966), pp. 222–246.

Spulber, Nicolas. "Effects of the Embargo on Soviet Trade," *Harvard Business Review*, XXX:6 (November-December, 1952), pp. 122–128.

———. "National Income and Product," in Stephen Fischer-Galati (ed.), *Romania* (New York: Praeger, 1957).

———. "The Soviet Bloc Foreign Trade System," *Law and Contemporary Problems*, XXIV:3 (Summer 1959), pp. 420–434.

Staller, George J. "Fluctuations in Economic Activity: Planned and Free Market Economies, 1950–1960," *American Economic Review*, LIV:4 (June 1964), Part I, pp. 385–395.

———. "Patterns of Stability in Foreign Trade, OECD and Comecon," *American Economic Review*, XLVII:4 (September 1967), pp. 879–888.

Svendsen, Knud Erik. "Notes on the Economic Relations between the East European Countries," *Economy and Economics of the East European Countries, Development and Applicability*, Ost Okonomi, Special Number (Oslo: Norwegian Institute of International Affairs, 1961).

Tansky, Leo. "Soviet Foreign Aid to the Less Developed Countries," U.S. Congress, Joint Economic Committee, *New Directions in the Soviet Economy* (Washington, D.C.: 1966), Part IV, pp. 947–974.

"Trade Expansion and Regional Groupings," in *Proceedings of the United Nations Conference on Trade and Development, Geneva, 23 March–16 June 1964*, VI, Part I (New York: United Nations, 1964).

Viner, Jacob. "International Relations between State-Controlled National Economies," *American Economic Review*, XXXIV, Supplement (March 1944), pp. 315–329; reprinted in Howard S. Ellis and Lloyd A. Metzler (eds.), *Readings in the Theory of International Trade* (Philadelphia: The Blakiston Company, 1950), pp. 437–456.

Volin, L., and H. Walters. "Soviet Grain Imports," *Foreign Agriculture Economics*, U.S. Department of Agriculture (Washington, D.C.: September 1965).

Wilczynski, J. "The Theory of Comparative Costs and Centrally Planned Economies," *Economic Journal*, LXXV:297 (March 1965), pp. 63–80.

Wiles, P. J. D. "Are Adjusted Rubles Rational?," *Soviet Studies*, VII:2 (October 1955), pp. 143–160.

Wyczalkowski, Marcin. "Communist Economics and Currency Convertibility," *Staff Papers*, International Monetary Fund, XIII:2 (July 1966).

Index of Names Cited

The letter "n" following a page number identifies a footnote; the letter "r," a reference in the text; "R," a name in a reference list; "t," a table. Names appearing in the bibliography are not included in the index.

Aizenberg, I. P., 303nr, 310R.
Akar, László, 67nr, 68nr, 99R.
Alexander, Alec P., 378r, 381R.
Alexander, Sidney S., 301nr, 305nr, 310R.
Allen, Robert L., 119n, 120n, 211nr, 243R.
Altman, Oscar, 280nr, 285nr, 310R.
Ames, Edward, 203nr, 223n, 234–235n, 243R, 305nr, 310R.
Apel, Erich, 171.
Ausch, Sándor, 296n, 297, 298nr, 299nr, 310R.

Bakaric, Vladimir, 367.
Bakos, György, 70nr, 79nr, 80nr, 99R.
Balassa, Bela A., 42nr, 53R, 57n, 99R, 405n, 414R.
Balázsy, Sándor, 66–67nr, 99R.
Baldwin, Robert E., 5, 19, 46.
Baran, Paul A., 64, 99R, 349nr, 381R.
Barat, E., 157t.
Bauer, Otto, 30.
Baumol, William J., 78n, 99R.
Baykov, Alexander, 17r, 28R, 243R, 260nr, 264nr, 278R.
Behrman, Jack N., 204r, 205nr, 211nr, 213n, 244R.
Bergson, Abram, 6, 8, 23, 24, 27, 32r, 53R, 57n, 99R, 100R, 178nr, 200R, 244R, 279R, 310R, 353n, 384, 390n, 391R, 405n, 406, 414R.
Berliner, Joseph S., 21, 99R, 234–235n, 243R, 258n, 306, 345, 406n, 412, 414R.
Berman, Harold, 260nr, 278R.
Beslac, M., 271tr, 373r, 381R.
Bicanic, Rudolf, 369–370.
Bogomolov, O. O., 172n.

Borisenko, A., 275nr, 278R.
Bornstein, Morris, 22, 23, 99R, 100R, 126, 411nr, 414R.
Breton, Albert, 167–168, 173R, 396, 401R.
Brown, Alan A., 3, 7, 8, 12, 18, 19, 22, 35n, 42, 44, 46, 49, 51, 53R, 57, 58nr, 59nr, 60nr, 61, 63nr, 66nr, 66–67nr, 76nr, 77nr, 86nr, 87r, 88r, 90nr, 91nr, 92nr, 94–99, 100R, 166, 167, 169, 226n, 259nr, 271n, 273n, 278R, 349n, 354–355, 362, 364, 381R, 386n, 386nr, 387, 391R, 405, 413n, 414R.
Bukharin, Nikolai I., 215.
Bulgaru, M., 157t.
Bystrov, F., 225nr, 243R.

Campbell, Robert W., 7, 11, 19, 57–58, 91n, 94, 100R.
Castro, Fidel, 202.
Chamberlin, Edward H., 38, 50.
Chao, Kang, 178n.
Ch'en Yun, 229r, 234, 243R.
Chenery, Hollis B., 180tr, 189nr, 191nr, 197, 200R.
Cheng Chu-yuan, 217tr, 243R.
Cherviakov, P., 259r, 260nr, 261nr, 263r, 264r, 264nr, 264–265n, 266r, 269nr, 275r, 278R.
Clark, Colin, 163nr, 164R.
Clark, John B., 34n.
Clark, Paul G., 180tr, 189nr, 191nr, 197, 200R.
Cohn, Stanley H., 255nr, 278R, 385–386nr, 391R.

Damjanović, Mijat, 361nr, 381R.
Dell, Sidney, 283nr, 310R.
Déri, Gusztáv, 84nr, 100R.

Dernberger, Robert F., 7, 12, 16–18, 180tr, 181tr, 184tr, 185r, 189r, 195tr, 200R, 202, 218nr, 228nr, 229r, 230nr, 231tr, 235r, 237t, 239t, 240t, 241–243, 243R, 246–252.
Deutsch, Karl W., 385–386nr, 391R.
Dickinson, Henry D., 30–31, 31n, 34–36, 53R.
Dobb, Maurice, 64, 100R, 349nr, 381R.
Domar, Evsey D., 9, 10, 19, 277.
Domke, Martin, 213tr, 243R.
Donnelly, Desmond, 234–235nr, 244R.
Dudinskii, I., 118n, 129R, 268nr, 272–273nr, 278R.
Dzeba, K., 371tr, 373r, 381R.

Eckstein, Alexander, 13, 16, 17, 19, 178n, 180t, 180tr, 182r, 182nr, 189r, 200R, 235–236, 241, 243R, 246, 246nr, 247r, 249r, 252R, 385–386nr, 391R.
Ellis, Howard S., 102R.
Engels, Friedrich, 29.
Erlich, Alexander, 349nr, 381R.
Ernst, Maurice, 386nr, 391R.

Facsády, Kálmán, 79nr, 100R.
Fedorenko, N., 352nr, 381R.
Fischer-Galati, Stephen, 165R.
Fiszel, H., 66n, 100R.
Friss, István, 358nr, 381R.

Galbraith, John K., 38, 51.
Garbuzov, Vasilii F., 336.
Gay, László, 83n.
Gerschenkron, Alexander, 35nr, 53R, 58n, 255nr, 258nr, 278R, 280nr, 284, 310R, 405–406n.
Gligorov, Kiro, 372.
Glickman, P., 272nr, 279R.
Goldman, Josef, 351nr, 381R, 407nr, 414R.
Gomulka, Wladislaw, 354.
Gordon, Margaret S., 205r, 244R.
Gordon, Wendell C., 73nr, 100R.
Gorupić, Drago, 25r, 28R, 367–368n, 381R.
Granick, David, 57n, 100R, 405n, 414R.
Grebtsov, G., 257nr, 279R.
Grossman, Gregory, 4, 19, 40nr, 53R, 57–58n, 100R, 340, 405n, 406n, 411–412n, 414R.

Haberler, Gottfried, 3, 6, 18, 19, 24, 27, 29, 35nr, 38nr, 46–52, 53R, 59n, 75n, 76nr, 100R, 194n, 336, 339R, 385, 390.
Haley, Bernard F., 99R, 381R.

Hamburger, László, 70nr, 97nr, 100R.
Hantos, Miklós, 79nr, 88nr, 100R.
Hardt, John, 279R.
Harris, Seymour E., 53R.
Harrod, Sir Roy, 336.
Hayek, Friedrich A., 38.
Hazard, John, 213tr, 215r, 243R, 244R.
Heiss, Herta W., 388nr, 391R.
Herman, Leon M., 107r, 110r, 125r, 129R.
Hicks, John R., 68n, 83n, 100R, 408n, 414R.
Hilferding, Rudolf, 30.
Hirschman, Albert O., 353, 364, 381R.
Hoeffding, Oleg, 4, 13, 20–21, 291n, 312, 337–339, 345, 349nr, 382R, 404nr, 414R.
Holesovsky, Vaclav, 359, 382R.
Holzman, Franklyn D., 7, 16, 17–18, 21, 46, 59n, 65n, 75n, 83n, 100–101R, 170–171, 178nr, 200R, 204, 234–235n, 244R, 255–257, 257n, 259nr, 279R, 280, 280nr, 283nr, 285nr, 286nr, 291r, 291nr, 294nr, 295r, 295nr, 296nr, 303nr, 305nr, 306–310, 310R, 315, 341, 344–346, 385–386nr, 386n, 391R.
Hoselitz, Bert F., 30nr, 53R.
Hunter, Holland, 64n, 101R, 190nr, 200R, 408n, 414R.

Illyés, Éva, 60nr, 101R.
Ishikawa, Shigeru, 189nr, 200R.
Ivanov, P., 267r, 279R.
Iverson, Carl, 73nr, 101R.

Jiranek, Slavomir, 297n, 310R.
Johnson, D. Gale, 40nr, 53R.
Johnson, Harry G., 5, 6, 18, 25–27, 166, 167, 173R, 203n, 244R, 393, 396r, 399nr, 400nr, 401–402R.
Judy, Richard, 266nr, 279R.

Kadar, János, 354.
Kadyshev, V. P., 323nr, 339R.
Kalecki, Michal, 62n, 101R.
Kálmán, Dezsö, 69nr, 70nr, 101R.
Karádi, Gyula, 67nr, 101R.
Kardelj, Edvard, 368, 368r, 382R.
Karpov, L., 257nr, 279R.
Kaser, Michael, 266r, 279R, 296nr, 297nr, 298nr, 310R, 386nr, 388nr, 392R.
Katus, László, 72nr, 101R.
Kautsky, Benedict, 30.
Khrushchev, Nikita, 167, 350.

Kindleberger, Charles P., 258r, 279R.
Kornai, János, 57n, 101R, 405n, 407n, 408n, 411n, 414n, 414R.
Korosec, Joze, 374r, 382R.
Kosygin, Alexei N., 275.
Kuznets, Simon, 100R, 179nr, 200R, 244R, 279R, 310R, 385–386nr, 391R, 392R.

Ladygin, V., 267nr, 274r, 274nr, 279R.
Lakos, Gyula, 78nr, 101R.
Lange, Oskar, 30, 34–36, 52, 53R.
Lee, T. C., 230r, 244R.
Lenin, Valdimir I., 17, 215.
Lerner, Abba P., 31, 31n, 34, 52, 53R.
Levente, M., 157t.
Levine, Herbert S., 7, 16, 18, 19, 64nr, 75n, 101R, 205r, 244R, 255, 258n, 262nr, 273nr, 274nr, 277–278, 279R, 341–344, 407nr, 408n, 410n, 411n, 414n, 414R.
Li Choh-ming, 244R.
Li Fu-ch'un, 184tr, 200R.
Li Yung-sheng, 224nr, 244R.
Liberman, Yevsey G., 277, 361.
Lippencott, Benjamin, 53R.
Liska, Tibor, 12r, 28R, 58nr, 59n, 67n, 91r, 101R.
List, Friedrich, 30.
Liu, Ta-chung, 16, 180tr, 183nr, 184tr, 186n, 199, 200R, 247nr, 252R.

Ma, Y., 233r, 244R.
MacDougall, Colina, 192nr, 200R.
MacDougall, *Sir* Donald, 32n, 53R.
MacDougall, George Donald Alastair *see* MacDougall, *Sir* Donald
Machlup, Fritz, 40n, 53R.
Mah, Feng-hwa, 188nr, 200R, 203nr, 244R.
Maklakov, A., 209nr, 244R.
Malenkov, Georgii M., 167.
Maly, B., 133t, 135–137nr, 165R.
Mao Tse-tung, 179.
Marias, Antal, 12r, 28R, 58nr, 59n, 67n, 91r, 101R.
Marshall, Alfred, 45, 73n, 75n, 101R.
Marx, Karl, 3, 15, 29, 30, 167, 171, 349, 352.
McCorkle, Chester O., 379r, 382R.
McKitterick, Nathaniel, 106nr, 129R.
Meade, James E., 244R.
Mendershausen, Horst, 171, 203nr, 244R.
Mesarić, Milan, 363nr, 382R.
Metzger, Stanley D., 106nr, 109–110nr, 129R.

Metzler, Lloyd A., 102R.
Michaely, Michael, 365nr, 382R.
Mikesell, Raymond F., 204r, 205nr, 211nr, 213n, 244R.
Miller, Marcus, 106n, 125.
Mishustin, D., 259nr, 279R.
Mišković, Dobrivoje, 363nr, 382R.
Montias, John Michael, 7, 13, 14, 57n, 79nr, 101R, 130, 130nr, 132t, 138t, 139nr, 157t, 158nr, 159–164, 164R, 166, 170, 349nr, 382R, 385, 405n, 407nr, 415R.
Morgner, Aurelius, 20, 337.
Mrkušić, Z., 373nr, 382R.
Myrdal, Gunnar, 41, 171.

Nagy, Imre, 88r, 90r, 91, 101R, 167.
Neuberger, Egon, 3, 19, 23, 24, 28r, 40nr, 51, 52, 53R, 92, 92n, 102R, 300n, 344, 349, 349nr, 351r, 354r, 363nr, 373nr, 377–381, 382R, 389–390, 405, 411n, 414R, 415R.
Niu Chung-huang, 232r, 233nr, 244R.
Nove, Alec, 102R, 234–235nr, 244R, 349nr, 352nr, 382R.

Pajestka, J., 67nr, 102R.
Pareto, Vilfredo, 52, 168.
Perkins, Dwight H., 7, 9, 10, 12, 13, 15, 16, 20, 177, 184tr, 185nr, 199–200, 201R, 223nr, 245R, 246–252.
Perisin, Ivo, 25r, 28R, 367–368r, 381R.
Pertot, Vladimir, 365nr, 382R.
Pleva, Jan, 297nr, 310R.
Po I-po, 195r, 201R.
Popisakov, G., 132t, 133t, 138t, 142r, 165R.
Popov-Cherkasov, I. N., 342nr, 346R.
Prebisch, Raul, 41, 171.
Pryor, Frederic L., 8, 14, 59n, 65nr, 67nr 80nr, 102R, 123nr, 124nr, 128r, 129R, 159, 163nr, 165R, 203nr, 209r, 225–226n, 245R, 266r, 269r, 269nr, 271nr, 279R, 283nr, 297n, 305nr, 311R, 386nr, 387, 392R.

Remer, Charles F., 244R, 245R.
Ricardo, David, 275.
Robinson, Joan, 50.
Rockwell, Charles S., 369, 382R.
Rolow, Aleksander, 224nr, 245R.
Röpke, Wilhelm, 245R.
Rosenstein-Rodan, Paul N., 38n, 50.
Rosovsky, Henry, 57–58nr, 100R, 101R, 102R, 173R, 190r, 201R, 279R, 310R, 405–406nr, 415R.

Rubinshtein, G., 259r, 264nr, 272–273nr, 276nr, 279R.

Sattler, Tamás, 78nr, 102R.
Savov, M., 133nr, 165R.
Schelling, Thomas C., 59n, 62nr, 102R.
Schenk, Fritz, 160nr, 165R.
Schumpeter, Joseph A., 37, 38, 51, 53R, 349.
Schwartz, Harry, 205n, 245R.
Scitovsky, Tibor, 38n, 50.
Sebestyén, Tibor, 78nr, 102R.
Seton, Francis, 349nr, 382R.
Shagalov, G., 275r, 279R.
Shereshevskii, M., 260nr, 261nr, 279R.
Shiriaev, I., 267nr, 274r, 274nr, 279R.
Šik, Ota, 352nr, 383R.
Simunek, D., 123n.
Singer, Hans W., 41.
Smirnov, A., 245R.
Smith, Adam, 41, 177.
Sokolov, A., 267r, 279R.
Solow, Robert, 34n, 53R.
Sombart, Werner, 73n.
Spulber, Nicolas, 7, 13, 22–23, 83nr, 102R, 104, 120nr, 126–129, 129R, 139nr, 165R, 166, 170, 245R, 382R, 386n, 388, 391.
Stalin, Joseph, 4, 15, 19, 63, 102R, 168, 170, 171, 259, 271n, 343, 350, 368.
Staller, George J., 14, 78nr, 162r, 163nr, 164, 165R.
Sugár, Tamás, 65nr, 79nr, 80nr, 102R.
Svendsen, Knud Erik, 123nr, 129R.
Szabó, Tibor, 65nr, 79nr, 80nr, 102R.
Szányi, Jenö, 70nr, 79nr, 80nr, 102R.

Tallós, György, 67nr, 68nr, 83nr, 102R.
Tansky, Leo, 282nr, 311R.

Ti Chao-pi, 216n.
Tito, Josip Broz, 370n.
Tomasek, Ladislav, 359nr, 379r, 383R.
Triantis, Stephen G., 383R.

Vagnov, B., 260nr, 279R.
Vajda, Imre, 88–89n, 102R, 355r, 383R.
Várkonyi, László, 79nr, 100R.
Velichkov, N., 133nr, 165R.
Viner, Jacob, 31n, 54R, 63, 102R.
Volin, Lazar, 318r, 339R.
Voronov, K., 260nr, 279R.
Vuković, D., 360r, 383R.

Wacker, V., 133t, 135–137nr, 165R.
Walters, Harry, 318r, 339R.
Wang, Ti, 232r, 245R.
Ward, Benjamin, 24, 377.
Wilczynski, J., 32n, 54R, 58nr, 102R.
Wiles, Peter J. D., 9, 13, 15, 23, 25, 57n, 102–103R, 166, 170r, 171nr, 173R, 349nr, 351nr, 376n, 383R, 396, 398, 405n, 408nr, 411n, 415R.
Wu, Yuan-li, 232nr, 245R.
Wyczalkowski, Marcin, 280nr, 311R.

Yeh Chi-chuang, 195, 201R, 209n, 235r, 245R.
Yeh, Kung-chiu, 180tr, 183nr, 184tr, 200R, 247nr, 252R.
Yen Chung-p'ing, 180tr, 181tr, 201R.
Yin, Richard Y. C., 17, 76nr, 92nr, 100R, 241, 354nr, 381R.
Yntema, Theodore O., 73nr, 103R.

Zala, Julia, 66nr, 103R.
Zauberman, Alfred, 283nr, 311R.
Zellner, Arnold, 291r, 291nr, 310R.

Subject Index

The letter "n" following a page number identifies a footnote; "t," a table. Footnotes are indexed only when they include material not immediately relevant to the text on the particular page where they occur.

The classifications in this index are made principally on the basis of economic concepts or terms. Information on specific countries and geographic areas (see Table of Contents) should be sought under the appropriate economic terms. Because connectives and relational phrases (e.g., "influence on") are omitted in subentries, relationships between levels of entries are frequently implicit rather than explicit, and the reader may find it useful to check cross-references and cross-listings.

Absorption approach, 305n
Adjustment mechanisms, trade, 20–23, 78–79, 85, 211–213, 224–225, 227, 280–310, 315, 338, 344, 345, 390, 405, 413–414
  See also Balance of payments; Trade: adjustment
Administration, CPEs, 284, 410–411
Administrative inefficiencies, 411
Agreements. *See* Bilateral: agreements; Trade: agreements
Agriculture:
  balance of payments, 20, 413
  development, 198, 246
  importance, 16, 183, 193, 199, 406–407
  output, 148–150
    China, 16, 192, 194–195, 199, 229, 248
    Poland, 141t
    Yugoslavia, 369
  problems
    CPEs, 27, 71
    China, 183, 185–186, 193, 194–195, 229–230, 233–234, 236, 247–249, 406
  procurements, 154–155, 157, 158
  See also Collectivization; Exports: agricultural; Imports: agricultural; Trade: agricultural

Albania, 122, 131, 209n
"Anarchy of the market," 63
Arbitrage, 303
Autarky:
  concept, 9–10, 58–59, 62n, 85, 283–284
  countries
    CPEs, 7, 9, 26, 32–33, 58–59, 162, 164, 169, 226, 257–259, 283–284, 386, 397–398
    China, 10, 167, 177–178, 189–191, 199, 234
    Czechoslovakia, 167
    East Europe, 116, 162–164, 167
    U.S.S.R., 32–33, 167, 258–259, 277, 281
    West Europe, 162–164
  ex ante, 9–10
  existence, 59
  ex post, 9, 10
  fluctuations, 162–164
  machine building, 170
  Marxism, 169
  measurement, 163–164
  model, 162, 164
  Stalin, 167
  trade aversion, 62
  trade level, 7
  See also Self-sufficiency

Balance:
"overall," 286
physical, 288, 291, 298
U.S.S.R., 271–274, 282–283, 288, 414n
See also Bilateral: balance
Balance of payments:
adjustment, 4, 8, 20–21, 27, 59, 160, 276, 287–293, 335, 344–345, 362
classical system, 287, 289, 293
factors influencing, 342, 357, 359, 366, 410
foreign exchange policy, 309–310
planning, 283
problems
CPEs, 4–5, 18, 27, 47, 74, 84, 89, 96, 171, 337, 355, 362–366, 413
China, 250
Hungary, 85, 88, 90–92
LDCs, 47–49, 337
MTEs, 18, 74, 285, 289, 294, 308, 315
U.S.S.R., 20, 273, 312–339
U.S.A., 338
Yugoslavia, 363, 367, 373
situation
CPEs, 4, 73, 246, 374
U.S.S.R., 20, 276, 288, 302, 312–339
theory, 336
trade, 77, 83n, 272, 288–289, 290–292, 359, 368
Balance of trade, 197, 271, 273, 297n, 298n, 306, 309, 369
Bulgaria, 137, 141
CPEs, 12, 83, 144, 285–287, 298
neo-Keynesian system, 290
Poland, 137, 140
Rumania, 137–139, 158
simulation model, 144
U.S.S.R., 313, 318, 323
Yugoslavia, 368–369
Balances, material. *See* Material balances
Bargaining:
CPEs, 79n, 411
East Europe, 20, 320–321
U.S.S.R., 20, 320–321
Barter, 45, 251, 272, 315, 316
See also Bilateral: trade; Trade
Benefit denial, 62, 65–70, 78, 82, 94, 96
incentives, 70
macroeconomic efficiency, 66
material balances, 67
planning, 68
subjective, 65
valuation standards, 65
vertical coordination and control, 66

Bilateral:
agreements
payments, 84, 205, 209, 225n, 227, 263
trade and payments, 44, 83, 123, 204–226, 250–251, 285–287
See also Trade: agreements
arrangements, 362
balance
CPEs, 83, 286, 288
payments, 12
prices, 296–297
trade, 12, 285–287, 298
bargaining price, 297n
barter relationship, 251
negotiations, 286
ruble accounts, 225–226
trade, 18, 44, 84, 225n, 226n, 304, 399
balance, 225–226
CPEs, 44, 206
China, 211–213, 223–226, 233
effects, 292
U.S.S.R., 206, 272
See also Exports; Imports; Trade
Bilateralism, 8, 16–18, 86, 89, 212t, 213, 285–287
CEMA, 128
countries
CPEs, 205, 206–207, 209, 242, 292, 298, 301, 305, 308–309
China, 209–213
East Europe, 44n, 206–207, 209
MTEs, 205, 207n, 285
U.S.S.R., 288n
degree, 18, 45
problems, 17, 18, 286, 309
re-exports, 12, 18, 44n, 45, 81, 86, 87, 399
See also Multilateralism
Bottlenecks. *See* Supply: problems
Bulgaria, 105n, 134, 137, 138t, 171, 320
Bureaucrats, 223, 358
Buyers' market, 95–96

Cadres, foreign trade, 65, 66, 69, 95, 276
Canada, 108, 203, 316, 317
Capillarity, 365–366
Capital:
accounts, 338
allocations, 389
borrowing, 158–159
flows, 228–229, 247, 249, 287, 302n, 305
formation, 247–248, 409
goods
CPEs, 27, 401

Capital (cont'd):
China, 248
development, 158–159
imports, 158–159, 247–248
Rumania, 158–159
inputs
CPEs, 158–159, 407
Rumania, 158
Yugoslavia, 369
intensity, 167
market
MTEs, 362–363
Yugoslavia, 363
output ratio, 148n, 161n, 172, 354, 357
productivity, 148–150, 158
savings, 197
shortage, 282
simulation model, 148–154, 160, 161n
stock
CPEs, 357, 363, 366
Greece, 378
Rumania, 158
Yugoslavia, 378
Capitalist economy. *See* Market-Type Economies
CEMA. *See* Council for Economic Mutual Assistance
Centrally Planned Economies (CPEs):
abandonment, 350, 354
analyses, 7, 57, 71, 205, 306, 340, 351, 354, 359, 376, 378, 405n–406n
autarky, 7, 9, 26, 58–59, 162, 257–259, 283–284, 397–398
balance of payments, 20–21, 74, 91
comparative advantage, 284, 355, 390
See also Comparative costs
consequences, 352, 356, 375–376, 405, 408–413
institutional mechanism, 16–23
See also Adjustment mechanisms; Centrally Planned Economies: key features
institutions, 242, 341–344
key features, 11, 16–17, 23, 37, 57–59, 62, 78, 204, 205, 206, 351–352, 355, 375, 394, 405–414
legacies. *See* Legacies
objectives, 405–406, 410–411
output, 268–269, 283, 408
perfectionist bias, 360
policies, 58–59, 396–398
rationality, 4, 23–25, 384–391
specialization, 413
U.S.S.R., 57–58, 110–116, 205–206, 337–339, 350

(CPEs) (cont'd):
workers, 358–359
See also Command economy
Central control:
CPEs, 65, 90, 351, 406, 408
China, 228
Yugoslavia, 374–375
Centralization:
CPEs, 63, 69, 78–79, 81, 406–410
trade, 78–79, 80–81, 169, 196, 276, 284, 373
U.S.S.R., 284
See also Decentralization
Central Planners. *See* Planners
Ceylon, 182, 210–211, 213
CG. *See* Consultative Group
China:
aid, 179, 227–228
budget deficit, 216
capital exports, 246–247
capital imports, 249
commune movement, 229
currency, 216–219
domestic production, 183, 185–186, 199
"great leap forward," 193, 196, 228–229, 246, 248–249
industry, 191, 192–193, 197
institutional model, 215
investment, 197–198
isolation, 251
key commodities, 190
Marx, 167
National Urban Supply Conference, 216, 218
relations
Japan, 182–183
North Korea, 206–207, 251
North Vietnam, 206–207
trading partners, 181, 196, 202, 206–207
U.S.S.R., 172, 179, 183, 186, 193, 196–197, 206–207, 233, 249
U.S.A., 186
resources, 247
"ten great years," 247
Classical system, 289–293
Clearing system, 211–213, 225–226, 315–316
Closed economy, 373
CPEs, 352, 355, 363, 372, 376, 407, 410, 412–413
Collectivization:
CPEs, 413
Rumania, 157n

Collectivization (cont'd):
U.S.S.R., 19, 343–344
Yugoslavia, 369
COMECON. *See* Council for Economic Mutual Assistance
Command economy, 351, 354, 355, 360–361, 372, 376, 406, 409, 413
See also Centrally Planned Economies
Commodity:
assortment, 71
classification, 266, 327
diversification, 365
exchange, 270
funded, 263–264
imbalances, 198
inconvertibility, 285
inventories, 336, 338
reserves, 20–21, 328, 336
Common Market. *See* European Economic Community
Communist China. *See* China
Comparative advantage, 24, 49, 224, 225, 226, 355, 386–387, 395, 396
countries
CPEs, 284, 390
China, 178, 189, 194
LDCs, 177
U.S.S.R., 235, 274–275, 389
Yugoslavia, 363
rationality, 384, 389–391
Comparative costs, 32, 33, 38n, 49, 58, 66, 389, 396, 398, 400–401
Comparative statics, 62
Competition, 31–38, 45, 50–52, 341n, 394–395
Conference on International Trade and Central Planning, 5–6, 9, 23, 25–26, 27, 33
Consultative Group (CG), 108–110
China Committee (CHINCOM), 109–110
Coordinating Committee (COCOM), 109–110, 121n
See also Embargo
Consumer:
goods
Bulgaria, 141–142
CPEs, 170, 351, 391, 406–407
China, 194, 198, 233
Rumania, 139
U.S.S.R., 281, 298–299, 320, 324–325, 335
satisfaction, 413
Consumption:
classical system, 289–293

Consumption (cont'd):
countries
CPEs, 391
China, 185, 195–196, 198, 230–231, 233–234
Rumania, 154–158
U.S.S.R., 20–21, 233, 238t–239t, 281
growth, 399
simulation model, 150, 154, 160, 161n
Control:
figures
East Germany, 269n
U.S.S.R., 262–263, 269
mechanism, 290–291, 296n, 298, 373–374, 408
organizations, 265
Convertibility, 285–287, 333
See also Inconvertibility
Coordination, 66–67, 72, 123–124, 267–268, 407
Cost:
average, 297
considerations, 169, 251
differentials, 190, 198
factor, 251
implicit, 62–65, 94–95
marginal, 295
prices, 224, 283
real, 82, 223–224
relative, 224
sensitivity, 62–65, 68, 78, 82, 94–95
trade, 66, 295, 304n, 396, 398, 400–401
understanding, 387
See also Comparative costs
Cost-of-living index, 372
Council for Economic Mutual Assistance (CEMA), 116–119, 251, 266–268
countries
Bulgaria, 118
Czechoslovakia, 105n, 106n, 116, 171–173
East Germany, 116, 171–173
Hungary, 118
Poland, 118, 167
Rumania, 105n, 117, 167, 171–172
U.S.S.R., 105n, 118n, 122–126, 167, 171–173, 266–268
Yugoslavia, 172
Marxism, 166–167
CPEs. *See* Centrally Planned Economies
Credits:
CPEs, 84, 88, 124
China, 179n, 195, 225, 249
CEMA, 127

Credits (cont'd):
  East Europe, 127–128, 137, 367
  Hungary, 88–92
  MTEs, 119, 122, 124, 128, 312–313
  U.S.S.R., 89n, 137, 246, 256, 274–275, 281, 315, 331, 338
Crisisphilia, 79–81, 89
Cuba, 127n, 173, 202, 207n, 320–321, 326
Currencies:
  CPEs, 285–287, 298
  China, 216–218, 223–224
  East Europe, 285, 309–310
  U.S.S.R., 309–310, 315–316
  See also Hard-currency
Current account transactions, 328, 336
Customs unions, 396–397
Cybernetic solution, 351
Czechoslovakia:
  CEMA, 105n, 106n, 116, 171–173
  Marx, 167

Decentralization:
  benefits, 43–45, 355
  countries
    CPEs, 43–45, 353, 361–363, 379
    China, 229
    East Europe, 259, 284, 379–380
    Yugoslavia, 167, 344, 361–363
  cybernetics, 351
  Marx, 167
  trade, 275–276, 373–375
  See also Centralization
Decentralized socialism, Lange-Lerner, 52
Decentralized system, CPEs, 34–35, 306, 355, 359
Deflation, CPEs, 35–36, 219n, 304, 373
Demand, 77–78, 130, 273n, 304, 308, 385
  curve, 36, 38, 45
  final, 273n
Depressions, 34–37, 44, 51, 205, 281
Devaluation, 301–302, 308, 337, 362, 366, 373
Development:
  countries
    CPEs, 47–52, 158–159, 350, 352, 364, 409–410
    China, 177–178, 181, 188–193, 229n
    CEMA, 128
    LDCs, 47–52
    Rumania, 158–159
  strategy
    CPEs, 158–159, 351
    China, 196–198

Development (cont'd):
  See also Extensive development; Growth
DF (*Deviza forint*). *See* Foreign exchange: forint
Direct controls, 287–288, 291
Directors, system's:
  CPEs, 4, 355, 356, 358, 386–387, 408, 410, 414
  problems, 353, 355, 367, 391
  rationality, 390
  U.S.S.R., 312, 406n
  Yugoslavia, 374
  See also Planners
Discontinuous incentives, 69, 407, 408, 412
Discontinuous planning. *See* Planning: discontinuous
Disequilibrium, 45, 59, 74, 75, 97, 287, 290, 303–304, 305n, 315, 317
Dumping, 340
Dynamics. *See* Fluctuations; Trade: pattern
Dysfunctional incentives, 69, 70, 78, 275–276, 412

East. *See* Centrally Planned Economies
East Europe:
  CEMA, 251
  economy, 162, 205
  GNP, 163
East Germany, 15, 105n, 118, 121n, 169, 170–171, 173, 320
Economic:
  activity, 35, 257, 259, 267
  administration, 308
  aid
    China, 179, 211, 246, 251
    investment policy, 249
    LDCs, 309
    U.S.S.R., 179, 227, 249, 262, 282, 309, 313
    Yugoslavia, 369
    See also Loans
  dependence, 120
  efficiency
    centralization, 411
    information, 275–276, 411
    LDCs, 39
    MTEs, 39n
    trade, 66, 241, 274, 297n, 308, 399
    U.S.S.R., 405n
    See also Profitability, trade
  fluctuations. *See* Fluctuations
  growth, 37, 399
    CPEs, 71, 394, 398, 406, 407

Economic (cont'd):
  China, 16, 178, 199, 247
  MTEs, 406
  U.S.S.R., 406
  Yugoslavia, 363
  history, 370n–371n, 395
  integration, 31–33, 117
  literature
    balance of payments, 312
    CPEs, 3, 226, 268–269, 349, 405
    East Europe, 65, 79n, 85
    trade, 16, 18, 29, 44, 203n, 225, 257, 260, 266, 269, 270, 274, 275n, 340
  objectives, 290–291, 344
  "offensive," 211
  organization, 205, 263, 266
  policies
    CPEs, 249, 387, 394, 395, 397, 406–407, 410
    nationalism, 394–395, 396, 397n
    protection, 36
    U.S.S.R., 259
  problems
    CPEs, 340–341, 397–399
    China, 194–196
  rationality, 4, 19, 23, 24, 344, 384–391
  reforms
    CPEs, 17, 23, 76n, 351, 366, 405
    Czechoslovakia, 359n
    East Europe, 4, 340–341, 344, 350, 359, 380
    Hungary, 79, 91–92
    U.S.S.R., 4, 274–276, 277, 341, 344, 350
    Yugoslavia, 361n, 362, 368, 370n, 372–373, 390
    See also Transition problem
  relations
    CPEs, 107–110, 113, 122–126, 266–268
    East Europe, 119, 127, 205n–206n
    U.S.S.R., 110, 113, 120, 124, 127, 280–281, 337, 341–342
  rent, 275
  system, 340, 352, 358, 373, 376n, 395, 405n
  theory, 30–31, 32, 33–38, 276, 394–398, 411
  warfare, 284
Economies of scale, 267
Economists:
  CPEs, 67, 80n, 106
  East Europe, 4, 33, 44, 57, 58, 67, 283, 297n, 380
  Hungary, 59, 60, 67, 68, 72, 78n, 80n, 89

Economists (cont'd):
  MTEs, 4–5, 25, 30, 32, 35, 57, 58, 73n, 166, 167, 169, 177, 194, 274, 283, 396, 405n
  Marxist, 3
  U.S.S.R., 32, 45, 259, 264n, 275, 276, 340, 361
  Yugoslavia, 24–25, 359n, 363, 366–368, 369, 372n, 373n, 380
Efficiency. *See* Economic: efficiency; Trade: efficiency index
Elasticity:
  expectations, 83n
  income, import demand, 186, 364
  substitution, 81
  supply and demand, 96, 97, 300–301, 400
  trade, 21, 22, 70, 73, 75, 78n, 79, 82, 86n–87n, 96, 295–296, 300–301, 344, 364
  See also Exports: demand; Exports: supply; Imports: demand
Embargo, 7, 15, 22–23, 104–129, 170, 171, 181, 182–183, 190, 196, 251, 332, 333, 380
  effects, 22, 127, 128, 129, 170, 332
  Far East, 109n, 110, 127, 181, 182–183, 190, 196, 209, 251
  list, 108, 109, 110
  NATO, 127, 332, 333
  U.S.A., 109n, 110, 127, 181, 182–183, 190, 251
  See also Consultative Group (CG)
Employment:
  neo-Keynesian system, 287
  Rumania, 155, 157, 158
  U.S.S.R., 292
Entrepreneurs, 19, 24, 26, 37–38, 39–42, 43–45, 52, 360, 378
Equilibrium:
  CPEs, 78, 85, 344
  objectives, 287
  regions, 82, 88
  theories, 35, 38n
  trade, 62, 77, 84, 88, 96, 98, 283, 292, 304
  See also Adjustment mechanisms; Balance of payments: adjustment; Fluctuations
European Economic Community (EEC; Common Market), 44, 124n, 126, 391
European Payments Union, 287n
Exchange control, 17, 203n, 218–219, 251, 290, 337, 339, 362

Exchange rate:
adjustments, 219n, 288, 301, 306
countries
  CPEs, 13, 17, 21–22, 44, 65, 70, 220,
    226, 283, 301–304, 308, 346, 362,
    366, 412
  China, 169, 178n, 202, 203n, 216–
    218, 220–224, 227, 241, 242, 251
  EEC, 44–45
  U.S.S.R., 13, 169, 234n, 285, 294,
    301–304, 308, 313n, 412
  Yugoslavia, 362, 372, 374n
depreciation, 339
floating, 301, 302, 303, 304
market, 21–22, 44, 287, 302, 303, 304,
  308, 339
mechanism, 308
nominal, 17, 21, 234n, 242, 251, 302,
  303, 304, 308, 344
official, 13, 21, 178n, 221, 224–226,
  247n, 302, 303, 308, 313n, 374
PEP-index, 66n
prices, 21, 227, 251, 301–304, 346,
  362, 412
purchasing power parity, 21–22
trade policy, 154, 399
See also Foreign exchange
Exchange ratios, 154, 399
Exports:
agricultural
  Canada, 203
  CPEs, 27
  China, 180–186, 191, 194–196, 228,
    229, 230–232, 236–237, 248
  Cuba, 320–321
  East Europe, 117
  Rumania, 142, 154, 155–158, 319–
    320
  simulation model, 145–146, 153
  U.S.S.R., 313, 318–321, 338, 343
  U.S.A., 181–182
  West Germany, 318
arrangements, triangular, 124
commodities
  China, 179
  U.S.S.R., 264, 325
commodity composition
  China, 183, 194, 195, 223, 229–234,
    237t–239t
  determinants, 229–234
  U.S.S.R., 277, 324–335, 343
consumer goods
  Bulgaria, 141–142
  China, 194
  simulation model, 161n
controls, 13, 22, 107–110, 126–129

Exports (cont'd):
countries
  CPEs, 70, 75, 76, 127, 223–226, 251,
    284, 295–296, 306, 329, 346, 364,
    389, 400, 413
  China, 12, 41n, 172, 178–186, 187,
    193, 194–196, 198, 199–200, 203,
    220–222, 223, 225, 227–234, 235–
    237, 248–250
  East Europe, 113, 117, 121
  East Germany, 113
  Hungary, 86–87, 93, 124
  LDCs, 47, 397n
  MTEs, 113, 117, 119, 128
  Poland, 117, 124n, 141t
  Rumania, 117, 139n, 145–146, 154–
    158, 159n, 170, 319–320
  U.S.S.R., 113, 116, 117, 121, 124,
    127, 255, 263, 264n, 269–274,
    278, 291–292, 294n, 295–296, 300,
    302, 305, 313, 317–321, 322–324,
    324–328, 329–330, 333, 335–336,
    338, 343, 345
  U.S.A., 35n, 107–108, 113, 182
  Yugoslavia, 360, 365n, 372
demand, 75–76, 230, 293, 296, 400
diversification, 365
earnings, China, 180–181, 185, 186,
  192, 193, 222, 229, 232, 233–234
effect on planning, 272–273
expansion, 87, 181–182, 187, 188n, 193,
  199, 227, 249, 318, 325, 359, 364,
  365, 397
  LDCs, 47
  U.S.S.R., 323–328, 335–336
  Yugoslavia, 375
import-intensive, 11, 12, 77, 86
income effects, 289, 292
industries, 299, 413
level
  CPEs, 49, 75, 95
  China, 49, 179, 181, 183, 191, 193,
    194, 228, 229
  East Europe, 179n
  U.S.S.R., 294n, 295
machinery
  CPEs, 11–12, 27
  Hungary, 86
  Poland, 166
  U.S.S.R., 324–325
manufactured goods
  LDCs, 398
  Poland, 131
  Rumania, 131, 145–146
  U.S.S.R., 313, 324–325

Exports (cont'd):
potential, China, 178–186, 199, 228–229, 249, 250
price effects, 294
price index, 303
priority, 75, 77
problems
CPEs, 69, 70, 75, 413
China, 183, 186, 194–195, 221–222
U.S.S.R., 263, 270
ratio-to-income
CPEs, 46–47
Hungary, 60n, 89
LDCs, 47
U.S.S.R., 255, 281, 282
See also Trade: ratio-to-income
raw material
China, 172, 194, 232
Rumania, 121, 127, 145, 154, 170
U.S.S.R., 117, 127, 170, 172, 324, 325n, 326, 328, 333n, 336, 345
restrictions. *See* Exports: controls
supply, 21, 73, 79, 82, 295, 300, 304–305, 364
surplus
China, 15–16, 88, 159, 219n, 220–221, 222, 249, 320
Poland, 118n
textiles, 194, 195–196, 199, 232–233
See also Re-exports; Trade
Expropriation, 281
Extensive development:
CPEs, 351, 354, 361, 376, 407, 409, 410, 412–413
definition, 407
effect on trade, 359
Yugoslavia, 359, 369
External economies. *See* Externalities
Externalities, 31, 34–38, 51, 398, 410

Feedback effects, 67
Financial:
accounting, 412
balances, 263
incentives, 288
policies, 288
Fiscal policy:
MTEs, 292
neo-Keynesian, 287, 290
Flexibility:
CPEs, 78–79, 83, 89, 126, 411
dilemma, 18–19, 73, 78–81, 86, 89, 96, 98
MTEs, 126
Fluctuations, 10, 35, 64, 194–195
autarky, 162–164

Fluctuations (cont'd):
CPEs, 70, 89–92, 155n, 410
export earnings, 177
transmission, 63
Forced saving, 409
Foreign debts. *See* Credits
Foreign exchange:
balance of payments, 271, 359, 362
countries
CPEs, 14, 66, 68, 70, 80, 183, 185, 341, 362, 365
China, 15, 188, 191, 192, 193–195, 219–222, 227
Hungary, 67, 78n, 91
LDCs, 337
Poland, 67, 140
Rumania, 158–159
U.S.S.R., 263, 271, 272n, 309–310, 328, 332, 335, 336, 337, 338, 341–345
Yugoslavia, 344, 362–363, 368, 370, 373–375
earnings
CPEs, 4, 14, 70, 80, 365
China, 15, 191, 193–195
Hungary, 67
Poland, 67
U.S.S.R., 337
Yugoslavia, 374
forint (DF), 13, 74n–75n, 88
industrialization, 145, 159
New Course, 137, 140
reserves, 20, 64, 68, 219–221, 274–275, 278, 305, 306, 336, 363
rubles, 13, 206, 225–226, 342
See also Convertibility; Exchange rate
Foreign trade. *See* Trade
Foreign trade associations. *See* Foreign Trade Enterprises
Foreign trade cadres, 65, 66, 69, 95
Foreign Trade Enterprises (FTEs):
countries
CPEs, 66–70, 81, 86
East Europe, 17, 66–67
U.S.S.R., 261–262, 263, 264, 269, 270, 274, 284, 299, 300, 342
crisisphilia, 79–80
incentives, 68
plans, 68
prices, 70
See also State trading; Producing enterprises
Foreign trade monopolies, 16–17, 41, 206, 207, 251, 284, 285, 295, 300, 302n, 308, 329, 336, 362
Free-enterprise economy, 38, 52

Free market, 33n, 288, 298
Free trade, 29–30, 32, 170, 207, 219n, 384–385, 387, 388–389, 395, 397, 401
FTEs. *See* Foreign Trade Enterprises
Full employment, 288, 293–294, 304
Funded commodities, 263–264

Gains from trade, 67, 82, 226, 251, 355
  bilateralism, 81
  countries
    CPEs, 24, 26, 65, 68, 81–83, 282
    China, 17, 202–203, 204, 223–224, 234–235, 242
    Hungary, 65
    MTEs, 65
    U.S.S.R., 307
  technology, 357
  See also Trade: benefits
General Agreement on Tariffs and Trade (GATT), 105–106
Goals:
  CPEs, 292, 406
  neo-Keynesian model, 292–293, 294
  U.S.S.R., 288, 294–295, 304
Gold:
  flow, 305, 314, 328, 335, 336
  production, 291, 315, 343
  reserves, 20–21, 291, 315, 338
  sales, 312–313, 315, 318
  standard, 219n
Great Britain. *See* United Kingdom
"Great leap forward," 193, 196, 228–229, 246, 248–249
Greece, 378–379
Gresham's law, 44n
Gross National Product (GNP):
  countries
    CPEs, 13, 96–97, 291, 409
    China, 178n, 179, 189, 235, 247
    Greece, 378
    Japan, 189
    U.S.S.R., 291, 385n–386n
    U.S.A., 385n–386n
    Yugoslavia, 378
  simulation model, 148, 150, 162
  See also Income
Growth:
  competition, 38
  countries
    CPEs, 39, 47, 71, 74, 357, 406, 408–409, 410n
    China, 186–193, 194, 196–198, 235–236, 246, 248
    Czechoslovakia, 380
    LDCs, 47

Growth (cont'd):
    Rumania, 154–155
    U.S.S.R., 255–256, 258
  long-run, 35
  orientation, 356, 378
  rate
    CPEs, 357, 380
    China, 229, 235–236
    Greece, 378
  resource allocation, 398–399
  short-run effects, 161
  See also Development; Extensive development

Hard-currency:
  area, 316, 322–323, 328, 337
  saving, 317–318, 329–330, 333–334
  trade, 314–335
"Hicksian week," 408
High priority:
  commodities, 76, 77, 96–97
  sectors, 40, 77–78, 79, 90, 96, 406–407
  trade, 73–77, 79, 82
  See also Low priority; Priority
Hoarding, 412
Hong King, 41n, 250
Horizontal connections, 407
Hungary:
  Central Statistical Office, 65, 90, 91
  documents, 70, 76n, 87, 88, 91, 94
  revolution, 354

"Ideological goods," 25, 168
Ideology, 358, 394
  See also Marxism
Imperialism, 15, 63, 172–173
Import Certificate Delivery Verification (ICDV), 108
Imports:
  ad hoc, 74, 81–82, 90–91
  agricultural
    China, 185–186, 229–230, 248, 313
    Hungary, 90
    Rumania, 142
    U.S.S.R., 313–314
  capital goods, 158–159, 397
    China, 187n, 188, 189, 196, 234, 235, 246, 247–249
    Rumania, 158
    simulation model, 150, 153, 161n
  consumption goods, 281
  controls, 37
  countries
    Bulgaria, 14
    CPEs, 10, 81–82, 84, 170, 413
    China, 186, 193, 196, 204–205, 209,

Imports (cont'd):
   220–221, 222–223, 225, 229n, 246–250
   East Europe, 113, 117, 122
   Hungary, 74n–75n, 78n, 85–88, 90–91
   MTEs, 104, 113, 327
   Rumania, 14, 117
   U.S.S.R., 113, 117–118, 121, 256, 271–272, 291n, 296, 314, 320, 332, 336–338
demand
   CPEs, 12, 71, 74
elasticity, 73, 75, 295, 296, 300, 305, 364
discontinuous incentives, 69
external safety valve, 413
financing, 281, 295, 331
funded commodities, 263
growth, 11, 89, 186–193
hard-currency, 313, 320, 324, 328–329, 330, 331–333, 335
high-priority, 74, 75, 79, 82, 374
induced demand, 77–78, 93, 289–290
intensity, 11, 12, 77
level
   China, 229, 249
   classical system, 293
   U.S.S.R., 281, 295, 314
low-priority, 74
machinery, 9, 14, 142, 281
   Bulgaria, 131–134, 137, 141, 142
   CPEs, 385
   China, 223, 227, 228n, 229, 235
   Poland, 131–132, 133–134, 137–139, 142
   Rumania, 131–132, 134–135, 136, 137–139, 154, 158
   U.S.S.R., 113, 117, 256, 264, 276, 281, 295, 298, 309, 313, 330–332, 336
   See also Exports: machinery; Trade: machinery
metals, 326, 333
nonessential, 74, 75
plans, 234n, 249
policies
   CPEs, 108, 187, 331, 334–335
   China, 193, 221–222, 397
   U.S.S.R., 318, 322, 323, 329–331, 333–336
prices, 169, 300, 302, 346
ratio-to-income, 47, 60, 89, 93, 136n
   See also Trade: ratio-to-income
raw materials, 145n, 154–155, 189, 256, 316–318, 322, 330, 332–334
requirements

Imports (cont'd):
   China, 193, 250
   U.S.S.R., 118, 263, 269
restrictions. *See* Imports: controls
self-sufficiency, 190–191
subsidies, 169
substitution, 15, 26, 47, 96, 120n, 121, 131, 152, 250, 278, 396, 398, 401
surpluses, 118n, 213, 215–216, 220–221, 222, 317
technology, 364
trade agreements, 223–226
See also Re-imports
Incentives, 70, 78, 79, 408, 412
   See also Discontinuous incentives; Dysfunctional incentives
Income:
adjustment-mechanism, 21, 219n, 287–293, 305n, 306–310, 337
distribution, 361, 409
effects on trade, 289–292, 304, 345
inequality, 357, 378
redistribution, 168–169
U.S.S.R., 256, 292, 345
U.K., 287n
See also Gross National Product; Trade: ratio-to-income
Inconvertibility:
bilateralism, 8, 16, 17, 285–287
problems, 18, 285, 288n, 309, 363
See also Convertibility
India, 173, 182, 194, 209–210
Indirect controls, 288
Industrial:
development, 22, 66, 71, 191, 257, 298–299, 378, 397, 406
goods, 248, 396–398
growth
   Rumania, 154–155, 158
   Yugoslavia, 368, 369
Industrialization:
CEMA, 122–123, 127
countries
   CPEs, 5, 23, 49, 51, 52, 71, 74, 82, 391, 406–407
   China, 15–16, 193, 196, 228, 230, 232, 235, 247
   Hungary, 85
   LDCs, 25, 47
   U.S.S.R., 48, 235, 256, 258–259, 264n, 281, 341
forced, 398
foreign exchange, 159, 343
policies, 48–49, 401
postwar, 113, 134, 137
socialist, 130, 159

Inflation:
 CPEs, 35–36, 219n, 242, 366, 410
 China, 17, 215–219, 249, 251
 LDCs, 39n
 trade, 290, 292, 304, 366
 U.S.S.R., 288, 298–299, 301
 Yugoslavia, 370
Innovation, 37–39
Input-output:
 allocations, 268–269
 coefficients, 64, 145–146, 148, 152, 197,
  272–274, 278, 408
Interdepartmental separation, 67, 407
Interest rates, 290, 337
Interfirm separation, 66–67, 407
Internal transfer balance, 220–222
International Bank for Economic Cooper-
  ation, 286
International Bank for Reconstruction and
  Development (IBRD), 40–41
International Development Association
  (IDA), 41
International division of labor, 32–33,
  42n, 43, 59, 60, 202–204, 223,
  224n, 225n, 226, 341, 355, 363,
  373
International Monetary Fund (IMF), 206,
  315, 337
International trade. *See* Trade
Intersectoral separation, 66, 275–276, 407
Investment:
 allocation, 32, 38n, 39, 354
 countries
  CPEs, 357, 364, 385, 391, 409
  China, 14, 15–16, 178, 187, 188, 191,
   197–198, 233, 248, 249
  Rumania, 134–135, 159, 162
  U.S.S.R., 24, 389
  West Europe, 162
  Yugoslavia, 363n, 369–372
 cycles, 160, 162
 foreign, 48
 growth, 170
 maximization, 143, 144
 program
  China, 186–190, 192–193, 216
  U.S.S.R., 113, 235n
 simulation model, 147–148, 150, 153,
  154, 160–162
Invisible hand, 31, 284

Japan, 109, 126n, 182–183, 189, 197, 316–
  317, 337
Jen-min-pi. *See* Exchange rate: China
Joint-stock companies, 120, 139n, 205n–
  206n

Korean War, 113, 134, 179, 181, 182–183,
  196, 251
 See also North Korea

Labor:
 balances, 263
 CPEs, 354, 369, 407, 409
 cost, 32n, 155–157
 output ratio, 160n
 productivity, 154, 155, 157, 158, 358
 theory of value, 32, 169
Law of value, 63
LDCs. *See* Less Developed Countries
Legacies:
 categories, 356, 359, 377, 379, 381
 CPEs, 27, 350–351, 352–353, 375–377
 economic, 363–366, 375
 education, 357
 empirical, 377–378
 export, 360
 false, 377–378
 identification, 377
 ideological, 358–361
 inflation, 366
 institutional, 361–363
 interventionist, 359–360
 investment, 360–361, 366
 negative, 352, 356, 358–366, 375, 376,
  378, 379
 political, 358–361
 positive, 352, 356–358, 375–376, 378
 price, 361–362, 370–373
 psychological, 358–361
 qualifications, 379
 quasi-, 356
 sociological, 358–361
 Stalin, 350n, 375, 377n
 trade, 24–25, 27, 92, 349–381
Lerner's Rule, 31
Less-Developed Countries (LDCs), 5, 40–
  41, 46–50, 143, 170–171, 177, 180–
  181, 211, 277, 282, 337, 394–395,
  398
Liquidity, international, 337
Loans, 92, 142–143, 147, 222, 227–229,
  250, 282, 309, 319–320, 369
 See also Credits; Economic: aid
Low priority:
 commodities, 73–76, 77, 96–97
 industries, 75–78, 97
 sectors, 90, 96
 See also High priority; Priority

Machinery:
 countries
  Bulgaria, 132t, 133t, 135n, 141–142

Machinery (cont'd):
    CPEs, 13–15, 22, 27, 77, 131, 170,
       171
    China, 172, 188, 197, 233
    Czechoslovakia, 172
    East Europe, 169–170, 172
    Poland, 132t, 133t, 135n, 140
    Rumania, 162, 171
    U.S.S.R., 132t, 133t, 134–135, 172
    trade, *See* Exports: machinery; Imports:
       machinery; Trade: machinery
Macro-balance, 288–292
Macroeconomic problems, 66, 409–413
Managers:
    enterprise
       CPEs, 31, 41, 42n, 276, 358–359
       MTEs, 39–41
    See also Cadres, foreign trade
Marginalism, 34n
Marginal propensities, 289–293
    See also Trade: ratio-to-income
Maritime transport, 342
Market:
    adjustment mechanisms, 280
    buyers', 95–96
    free, 288, 298
    forces, 31–32
    imperfections, 410
    mechanisms, 33n, 51, 288n, 411
    multilateral, 286, 399
    sellers', 69
    socialism, 350, 371
    system, 351
    See also Free-enterprise economy
Marketing problem, 193, 343
Market-Type Economies (MTEs), 3, 82,
    173, 276, 362–363, 398
Marshall Plan, 206
Marxism:
    autarky, 169
    ideology, 29, 30–33, 45, 63
    imperialism, 172–173
    interpretation in CPEs, 166–167
    trade theory, 29–30
Material balances:
    countries
       CPEs, 19, 66, 204–205, 408, 412
       China, 197–198, 200, 209n, 234, 250
       East Germany, 67n
       Poland, 67
       U.S.S.R., 263, 269, 271–272, 282–
         283, 288, 414n
    method, 67, 271–274, 407
    trade, 66–67, 194, 272
MFN. *See* Most-Favored-Nation clause
Micro-balance, 288, 301–304, 305

Microeconomic inefficiencies, 412–413
Military aid, 282
Miller Report, 106n, 125
Monetary policies:
    MTEs, 292
    neo-Keynesian, 287–290
Monopoly:
    embargo, 120–122
    exploitation, 24, 388, 389n
    import restriction, 37
    innovation, 38
    restrictions, 410
    See also Foreign trade monopolies
**Moscow International Economic Confer-
    ence,** 209
Most-Favored-Nation clause (MFN),
    105–106, 124, 126, 128, 213n
MTEs, *See* Market-Type Economies
Multilateralism, 44n, 45, 123, 128, 251,
    286–287, 399
Multiplier:
    Keynesian, 289–292
    trade expansion. *See* Trade: expansion
       multiplier

National income. *See* Gross National
    Product
Nationalism, 5, 31, 32, 46–47, 63, 167–
    169, 394–397
National Monetary Conference, China,
    216
Neo-Keynesian model, 289–293
New Course, 119, 135n, 137–142, 160n
NFE-index (Net foreign exchange earn-
    ing index), 66n, 69–70
"Nondeficit commodities," 75
North Atlantic Treaty Organization
    (NATO), 109, 126–128, 332
North Korea, 206–207, 209n, 320
    See also Korean War
North Vietnam, 206–207

Offer curve, 73, 75, 82, 86, 96, 300, 364,
    365
Oligopoly, 31, 50–51
Opportunity costs, 118n, 192, 223–224,
    232, 235, 295, 298n
**Organization for Economic Cooperation
    and Development** (OECD), 113,
    124

Pareto optimality, 52, 168
PEP-index (Price equalization index), 66n,
    69–70
Planners:
    autarky, 190

Planners (cont'd):
  balance of payments, 27, 333, 337
  countries
    CPEs, 31–32, 283, 308, 358, 380,
      406–407, 412
    China, 178–179, 194–198, 203–204,
      209, 221, 223–224, 227–228, 233–
      234, 249, 250
    MTEs, 32, 337, 339
    U.S.S.R., 21, 258, 271–272, 292, 295,
      304, 307–308, 312, 329, 338, 339
    trade, 194–198, 204, 221, 223–224, 227,
      258, 271–272, 285, 292, 297, 304,
      307, 312, 329, 364
  See also Directors, system's
Planning:
  autarky, 257–259, 281, 283–284
  countries
    CPEs, 26, 31–32, 34, 48–52, 63–65,
      66–68, 79, 97, 204–205, 206, 267,
      283, 292–294, 298, 349–351, 354,
      363, 394, 406–408, 410–411
    China, 178, 186–198, 203–204, 206–
      209, 213, 215–218, 250–252
    East Europe, 4, 57–58, 106, 282
    Hungary, 57n, 61, 84–85, 90–92, 405n
    LDCs, 47–49
    U.S.S.R., 57–58, 205–206, 242, 255–
      310, 338–339, 340–344, 405n, 414n
    Yugoslavia, 363, 371–375
  discontinuous, 66, 68, 269, 407–408, 411
  domestic, 15–17, 19, 64, 83, 229, 249,
    251–252, 270, 271, 364
  growth, 38n, 283
  flexibility, 78–80, 89
  mechanisms, 26, 46–47, 52, 337, 351,
    405, 407–408, 411–412
  physical, 16–17, 271–274, 351, 360,
    372, 406–408
  problems, 49, 52, 308, 339, 394
  rationality, 390
  Robertsonian "planning day," 408
  Sequential, 268–270, 407
  targets, 116, 227
  trade, 64–67, 78–80, 178–179, 242,
    284–285, 308, 329
    CPEs, 6–7, 16, 18–19, 22–23, 26, 66–
      67, 116–117, 122–124, 128–129,
      203, 262–265, 395
    China, 194–198, 203–204, 207–209,
      229, 234, 241–242, 246, 252
    Hungary, 61, 67n, 85–92
    U.S.S.R., 19–21, 89, 255–310, 338–
      339, 340–341
    Yugoslavia, 373, 375

Planning (cont'd):
  See also Material balances; Priority
    planning; Taut planning
Plans:
  annual, 195, 262–265, 268–269, 272,
    288
  balance, 271–274
  CPEs, 67, 78–84, 288, 407–408, 414
  construction, 268–270
  drafts, 269–271
  Five-year, 16, 75n, 92n, 195, 230–233,
    235, 247, 256, 259, 281, 295, 343,
    385
  fulfillment, 69–70, 80, 290, 299, 408
  trade
    CPEs, 67–68, 78–79, 352, 407
    China, 195, 198, 209n, 230–233, 235
    East Germany, 67n, 80n
    Hungary, 68n
    U.S.S.R., 256–259, 260, 262–265,
      269–270, 277, 288, 299
Poland, 66n, 118, 126, 134, 135n, 137,
  140, 142, 167, 172, 320, 354
Population, 191n, 230, 309, 409
Preference functions, 27, 65, 215, 223,
  356, 375, 396–397, 406n, 411
Pressure economy, 351, 354, 360–361,
  376, 406, 409, 410, 412–413
Price:
  adjustment, 22, 36, 288, 290, 305, 306–
    308, 373, 412
  controls, 338, 366, 370–373, 380
  determination, 16–17, 242, 297n, 388
  effects on trade, 21, 293–304
  equalization, 65, 66, 69, 70, 169
  equalization index (PEP-index), 66n,
    69–70
  flexibility, 70, 79, 293–304, 305, 307,
    309, 371–372, 408n, 410, 412
  level
    CPEs, 223–224, 302
    China, 216–223
    MTEs, 219n
    neo-Keynesian, 287
    U.S.S.R., 294
  mechanism, 32, 34–38, 43, 168
  reform, 91, 372, 412
  structure
    CPEs, 17, 65, 118, 215, 223–226,
      242, 346, 372, 379, 387
    China, 17, 218–224, 227, 242
    MTEs, 307
    trade, 17, 204, 296–297
    U.S.S.R., 345
  system, 49, 65, 361, 363, 395, 411n
  theory, 33–34

Prices:
allocation of resources, 49–50, 283, 294, 307–308, 362–363
bilateral balance, 296–297
export, 64, 186, 221n, 281, 294, 296, 299, 302, 364, 400
external, 22, 75, 78n, 222–223, 230, 234n, 241, 251, 273, 293, 299, 302–305
frozen, 301, 302, 303n
import, 64, 75, 79, 169, 194, 221n, 226, 295, 300, 302, 346, 400
internal
classical system, 293
countries
CPEs, 13, 21, 47–48, 65, 70, 76, 222–226, 283–284, 294, 303–304, 362, 366, 372, 408, 411
China, 188n, 204, 215–219, 221n, 222–224
MTEs, 303, 308
U.S.S.R., 13, 234n, 235, 275, 285, 302, 305, 307–308, 411n, 412
Yugoslavia, 362–363, 368, 372–373
factor cost, 251
world market, 64, 163, 234n, 298n, 308, 345
intra-CEMA, 122, 124, 226, 296, 297n, 298n, 305
market, 43–44
parametric function, 36–38, 380
relative, 50, 61, 298, 361, 370
ruble, 224, 225, 226
scarcity, 24, 76, 251, 283, 361
shadow, 34, 45, 412
trade, 13, 17, 79, 80n, 83, 95, 118, 120, 121, 122, 123, 137, 140, 141, 144, 270, 272, 275, 283, 287, 293–304, 307–310, 364
world, 19, 21, 48, 64, 70, 188n, 202, 224, 258, 272, 294–298, 300, 302, 303n, 346, 372, 388
See also Exchange rate
Pricing, 31, 45, 92, 412
Priority:
concept, 96–97, 366
dichotomous, 75–77, 90
dilemma, 12, 73–74, 78–81, 82, 85, 96–99
economy, 351, 354, 360–361, 373, 376, 406–407, 409–410, 412, 413
planning, 13, 75–76, 345, 413–414
See also High-priority: Low priority
Producers' goods, 139, 271–272, 281, 351, 406–407

Producing enterprises:
East Europe, 17
Hungary, 72n
Poland, 66n
U.S.S.R., 264, 266
See also Foreign Trade Enterprises
Productivity, 76n, 292, 412–413
Profitability, trade, 284–285, 340
See also Economic: efficiency, trade
Profits:
MTEs, 408n
U.S.S.R., 275, 306
Propensity-to-trade. *See* Trade: ratio-to-income
Protectionism, 5, 29, 30, 170, 395–401
Public goods, 25, 167–169, 396–398
See also "Ideological goods"
Purchasing power parity, 21–22, 251, 302n, 362

Quantitative controls list, 108, 109
Quantity adjustments, 305
Quotas, 69–70, 79–80, 160n, 251, 290, 299, 362, 408, 412

Rationality, economic. *See* Economic: rationality
Rationing, 288, 298–299, 345
Ratios:
investment, 162
procurement, 152, 153, 154n, 159
trade. *See* Trade: ratio-to-income
Raw materials, 113, 117–118, 120, 142n, 158, 160, 170, 172, 177, 187, 194
See also Exports: raw material; Imports: raw material
Real wages:
Europe, 287n
Rumania, 154–155, 158
simulation model, 148–150, 152–153, 160
Reciprocal demand. *See* Offer curve
Recognition lag, 356
Re-exports, 12, 18, 44n, 45, 81, 86, 87, 399
Reforms. *See* Economic: reforms
Re-imports, 12, 86, 87
Reparations, 120, 139n, 205–206
Reserves:
commodity, 20–21, 328, 336, 338
emergency, 72
foreign exchange, 20, 64, 68, 219–221, 274–275, 278, 305, 306, 336, 363
gold, 20–21, 291, 315, 338
trade, 70–71, 74, 91, 222, 287, 336–337

Resources:
allocation
countries
CPEs, 17, 32–34, 40, 72, 226, 389, 410
China, 203–204, 218–219, 222–226, 228, 234, 241, 247, 249
MTEs, 34–37, 304
U.S.S.R., 124, 256, 299, 305, 307
Yugoslavia, 372
efficiency, 398–401
growth, 398–399
limitations, 390
rationality, 389
theories, 45, 411
trade, 299, 304–305, 307, 325, 362
endowment, 71, 406
full employment, 282, 291
structure, 46
unemployed, 299
Restrictions. *See* Exports: controls; Imports: controls; Trade: controls
Revisionists, 202
Risks, 37, 38, 41–43, 62, 83
Rubles. *See* Foreign exchange: rubles
Rumania:
CEMA, 105n, 117, 167, 171–172
input coefficients, 145–146
policies, 124, 134n, 139

Safety valves, 71–72, 74, 79,· 81, 90, 413
Saving:
CPEs, 351, 376, 406
China, 246–247
classical system, 289
neo-Keynesian model, 290n
"Sectoral autarky," 258
Self-sufficiency:
autarky, 10–11, 58–59, 62n
CPEs, 9–11
East Europe, 85, 94, 397n
trade restriction, 62, 401
U.S.S.R., 10, 256, 259, 278, 333–334
Sellers' market, 69, 72, 95–96
Sequential planning, 268–270, 407
Service sector, 406–407
Simulation model, 143–164
agriculture, 147, 152, 153–154, 160
balance of payments, 146
balance of trade, 147
capital goods, 147, 150–153, 161n
coefficients, 145–146, 147–148, 160, 163–164
consumption, 147, 150, 154, 160, 161n
cyclical behavior, 162

Socialist economy:
centralization, 52, 377, 406
definition, 406
growth, 406
planning, 30–31
See also Centrally Planned Economies
Social ownership, 351, 376, 406, 409–410, 413
Sombart's Law, 73n
Soviet-type economy. *See* Centrally Planned Economies
Soviet Union. *See* Union of Soviet Socialist Republics
Specialization, 131, 171, 364, 399
Stalinist model, 350, 353, 355, 376
State trading:
agencies, 203, 205, 219–221, 228, 284–285
China, 215–226, 228, 241, 242
East Europe, 215
U.S.S.R., 205
See also Foreign Trade Enterprises
Steel, 71n, 117, 118, 142, 188, 189, 192, 194, 324t, 332
"Storming," 70, 80, 412
Strategic embargo. *See* Embargo
Subsidies, 169–170, 283
Successor systems, 356, 357, 361
Supply problems, 71, 80, 87, 89–91, 283–284, 297, 299, 304–305, 411
Surveillance list, 108, 109
Swing credits, 83, 213, 214nt–215nt
Switch-deals, 44n
System's directors. *See* Directors, system's

Tariffs:
CPEs, 105–106, 124, 215, 260, 285
MTEs, 31, 49, 105–106, 203n, 339, 395–398
Taut planning:
CPEs, 64, 66, 68, 72, 86, 97, 360, 406, 411
benefit denial, 68
cost sensitivity, 68
definition, 64, 408
domestic sectors, 35, 64, 407, 408n, 412
trade, 64, 68, 72, 74
U.S.S.R., 309
Technology, 64, 357, 401
CPEs, 22, 39–40, 351, 354, 355, 410
China, 197, 229
trade, 15, 170, 172–173, 272, 355, 357, 364
U.S.S.R., 40, 341n
Terms of trade:
Bogomolov, 172

Terms of trade (cont'd):
  classical system, 293
  countries
    CPEs, 21, 68, 75n, 76, 84, 96, 170,
      302n, 303, 355, 388, 400
    Czechoslovakia, 171
    East Germany, 171
    Hungary, 85, 86, 88, 90, 91, 92
    Rumania, 157n
    U.S.S.R., 171, 256, 258, 272, 281,
      285, 295, 297, 298, 300, 305
  deterioration, 76, 80, 84–86, 89–92, 98,
    295
  exploitation, 171
  factoral, 73, 76, 97, 355
  legacies, 365
Textile industry, 232–234
Tied agreements, 66n–67n
Trade:
  adjustment
    CPEs, 288–289, 293, 308–309
    classical system, 289, 292
    neo-Keynesian model, 289, 292–293
    U.S.S.R., 288, 312–339
    See also Adjustment mechanisms,
      trade
  agreements
    Albania, 206, 209n
    Bulgaria, 206
    CPEs, 78, 80–81, 83, 123, 124, 171,
      183n, 204–226, 250–251, 262,
      268n, 269, 285–287, 308t, 313, 333,
      341n, 343
    China, 204–226, 234, 308t
    Cuba, 207n
    Czechoslovakia, 206
    East Germany, 171, 206
    Europe, 205
    Hungary, 206
    Japan, 209
    MTEs, 83, 124, 204, 209–213, 341n
    North Korea, 206–207, 209n
    North Vietnam, 206–207
    Outer Mongolia, 207
    Poland, 206
    Rumania, 206
    U.S.S.R., 171, 183, 205–206, 262,
      268–269, 313, 316, 333, 341n, 343
    West Germany, 210
    Yugoslavia, 207n
    See also Bilateral agreements: trade
      and payments
  agricultural, 27, 117, 160, 180, 229–
    232, 246, 314–315, 318–321, 319t
  allocation of resources, 32, 299
  ambivalence, 62, 72–84

Trade (cont'd):
  aversion, 11, 26, 42, 43, 62–70, 72–
    73, 79, 85, 86, 96, 390
  balance. *See* Balance of payments; Bal-
    ance of trade
  benefits
    CPEs, 66, 96, 120n
    China, 241
  bilateral. *See* Bilateral: trade
  cadres. *See* Cadres, foreign trade
  centralization, 78–79, 80–81, 169, 196,
    276, 284, 373
  commodity composition
    CPEs, 26, 46, 64, 73, 81, 115t, 160n
    China, 13, 182, 196–197, 203, 221,
      227, 240, 249
    East Europe, 13, 60–61, 131, 132,
      159
    MTEs, 115t, 339
    simulation model, 162
    U.S.S.R., 13, 304, 313, 324, 338, 343
    See also Trade: structure
  controls, 65, 288, 388–389
    See also Trade: restrictions
  CEMA, 105, 110–129, 130–133, 143,
    144n, 160, 209
  countries
    Africa, 315–316
    Argentina, 321
    Australia, 317
    Bulgaria, 118–119, 319, 320
    Burma, 213
    Canada, 203, 317
    CPEs
      MTEs, 124, 386–387
      Other CPEs, 83–84, 91n, 118–119,
        137, 167, 204–226, 282, 296–
        297, 300, 386
    Ceylon, 210–211, 213
    China
      Burma, 213
      Canada, 203
      CPEs, 118–119, 206–207, 224–
        226
      Ceylon, 210–211, 213
      Cuba, 202
      Egypt, 213
      Hungary, 85–93
      India, 209–211
      Indonesia, 213
      Japan, 182–183
      MTEs, 108–109, 209–213, 221n,
        226n
      North Korea, 206–207
      North Vietnam, 206–207
      Outer Mongolia, 207

Trade: countries (cont'd):
  Pakistan, 211
  Sudan, 211
  U.S.S.R., 183, 206, 227–228, 233, 320
  West Germany, 210
Cuba, 110, 202, 316, 320–321
Czechoslovakia, 118, 170, 172, 319
East Europe, 116, 118n, 205, 320, 384, 387, 399
East Germany, 118–119, 319, 320
Egypt, 213, 321
Europe, 44, 164, 210, 337
Finland, 117, 315, 321
France, 118–119, 318
Hungary, 87–88, 118, 319
India, 209–211
Indonesia, 213
Italy, 117, 121n, 332–333
Japan, 182–183, 210, 313, 315, 317–318
Latin America, 315–316
LDCs, 186, 313, 315, 321, 335
MTEs
  Bulgaria, 118–119
  CPEs, 107–110, 113, 124, 386-388
  China, 108–109, 209–213, 221n, 226n
  Netherlands, 388
  Poland, 117
  Rumania, 118–119, 171
  U.S.S.R., 35n, 113–116, 117, 121, 125, 294, 314–317, 321, 324
Middle East, 118–119
Netherlands, 388
North Korea, 108, 206–207, 320
North Vietnam, 110, 206–207
Outer Mongolia, 207, 320
Pakistan, 211
Poland, 106n, 117, 118n, 320
Rumania, 117–119, 171, 319–320
Sudan, 211
Sweden, 117, 121n
Switzerland, 117
Turkey, 315
U.S.S.R.,
  Africa, 315–316
  Argentina, 321
  Australia, 317
  Bulgaria, 319, 320
  Canada, 317
  CPEs, 282, 313, 343, 387–388
  China, 183, 206, 227–228, 233, 320
  Cuba, 316, 320–321

Trade: countries (cont'd):
  Czechoslovakia, 319
  East Europe, 116, 118n, 320, 384, 387
  East Germany, 319, 320
  Egypt, 321
  France, 318
  Finland, 117, 315, 321
  Hungary, 319
  Italy, 117, 121n, 332–333
  Japan, 313, 315, 317–318
  LDCs, 313, 315, 321, 335, 387
  MTEs, 35n, 113–117, 121, 125, 294, 313–317, 324, 343, 387
  North Korea, 320
  Outer Mongolia, 207, 320
  Poland, 118n, 320
  Rumania, 319–320
  Sweden, 121n
  Turkey, 315
  United Kingdom, 117
  U.S.A., 35n, 317
  West Europe, 162–164, 313, 317–318
  West Germany, 318
  Yugoslavia, 315
U.S.A., 35n, 107–110, 113, 173, 179, 182, 316–317
West Europe, 313, 317–318
West Germany, 117, 210, 318
Yugoslavia, 315
delegations, 261, 266, 276
development, 196–197, 235, 255–256, 281, 391
dialectics model, 72
direction
  CPEs, 81–82, 84, 87–88, 127, 196, 282, 292, 387–388
  China, 196, 227–234, 240t, 249
  Hungary, 61, 87–88
  MTEs, 88, 384–385
  U.S.S.R., 316t, 317t, 322t, 335
  See also Trade: proportions; Trade: structure
dominance, 18, 110–113, 171
effects, 43, 65, 160n, 253–279, 288–289, 290, 291, 292, 341
  See also Trade: role
efficiency index, 92n
  NFE-index, 66n, 69–70
  PEP-index, 66n, 69–70
  See also Economic: efficiency
elasticity. See Elasticity: trade
enterprises. See Foreign Trade Enterprises
entrepreneurs, 39–40

Trade (cont'd):
expansion, 11, 26, 60, 73, 85, 86, 97, 119
expansion multiplier, 12, 21, 77–78, 86, 87, 90, 92–93, 364
financing, 183n, 209n, 211–213, 228, 315, 331, 368
flexibility, 78, 411
goals, 235, 241, 288
hard currency, 313–337
  agricultural, 318–321
  definition, 316
  exports, 324–328
  imports, 328–335
  non-agricultural, 322–335
implicit cost, 64, 65
income effects. *See* Income: effects of trade
investment, 162, 193
legacies, 24–25, 27, 92, 349–381
level, 7, 8–13, 49, 77, 80n, 96, 387
  CPEs, 7, 8–13, 14, 18, 26, 46, 62, 70, 72, 73, 81, 85–87, 95, 111t, 112t, 119, 122, 126, 130, 284, 384–391
  China, 11, 12, 179, 196, 209n, 227, 234, 235–241, 249
  East Europe, 12, 14, 59, 113–114, 159, 162–164
  free trade, 384–385, 386
  Hungary, 60, 61, 85–87
  MTEs, 111t
  Rumania, 154
  U.S.S.R., 12, 116, 130, 258, 269, 281, 295, 313–314, 385–386
  Yugoslavia, 396–370
machinery
  Bulgaria, 142
  CPEs, 13–15, 22, 77, 130, 131, 160, 166, 172
  China, 172, 197
  Czechoslovakia, 172
  East Europe, 131t, 132t, 156t–157t, 170
  Poland, 135n, 140, 166, 172
  Rumania, 135n, 156t–157t, 162, 171, 172
  simulation model, 153
  U.S.S.R., 19, 172, 331t
  Yugoslavia, 172
  See also Exports: machinery; Imports: machinery; Machinery
multilateral, 205, 225n, 226n, 305
opportunities, 116–120, 283
organization
  CPEs, 16, 128, 204, 242

Trade: organization (cont'd):
  China, 202–204, 227, 251
  East Germany, 269n
  U.S.S.R., 259–265, 269, 275n–276n, 340–342
pattern
  CPEs, 58–59, 73, 113, 114t, 131–143, 167, 354–355, 362
  MTEs, 73, 308
  U.S.S.R., 308, 321
  See also Trade: structure
policy, 25, 68, 78, 79, 80, 89, 168, 393–401
  CPEs, 43, 105–107, 199
  China, 16, 178
  East Europe, 10, 23, 125–126
  Hungary, 60–61
  LDCs, 47–48
  MTEs, 5, 32, 105–107, 124, 391
  U.S.S.R., 9–10, 125, 160, 337
  U.S.A., 127
price effects. *See* Price: effects on trade
prices. *See* Prices
problems
  CPEs, 4–5, 26, 29–30, 39, 46, 70, 82, 128, 282, 308, 349–352, 354–355, 369, 397–398
  China, 196, 197, 198
  LDCs, 46, 48
  U.S.S.R., 142, 290, 292, 302, 314, 349–352
proclivity, 11, 26, 42n, 43, 62, 71–74, 85, 96
propensity. *See* Trade: ratio–to–income
proportions
  CPEs, 121–122, 124, 125t, 207, 282, 387
  China, 207
  Czechoslovakia, 117
  East Europe, 110–117, 121–122, 387–388
  Hungary, 61
  U.S.S.R., 113–116, 282, 294, 313–314, 387–391
  U.S.A., 113
  See also Trade: direction
ratio–to–income
  CPEs, 8, 11, 12, 13, 14, 46–49, 60, 73, 397n
  China, 8–9, 11, 16, 178, 179, 186, 190, 197–199
  East Europe, 163, 164n, 283
  Hungary, 8, 60, 90
  LDCs, 48–49
  MTEs, 11, 45, 46
  simulation model, 153–154

Trade: ratio–to–income (cont'd):
U.S.S.R., 10, 11, 20, 259, 281, 341, 385
U.S.A., 385
West Europe, 8, 164n
See also Exports: ratio–to–income; Imports: ratio–to–income
raw materials. *See* Exports: raw materials; Imports: raw materials; Raw materials
relations, 18, 63, 96, 110–113, 171, 182–183, 196, 206–207, 213, 276
reorientation dilemma, 81–84
restrictions
autarky, 59, 62
CPEs, 59, 108–109, 388, 391, 400
China, 108–109, 210, 218–219, 251
MTEs, 107, 122, 126, 128, 388
U.S.S.R., 119, 160n, 332
U.S.A., 107–110, 119, 126–127
See also Embargo; Exports: controls; Imports: controls; Quotas; Tariffs; Trade: controls
role
China, 247
industrialization, 257
U.S.S.R., 255–257, 259, 266, 275n, 276, 342
U.S.A., 258
See also Trade: effects
rubles. *See* Foreign exchange: rubles
safety valve function, 71–72, 74, 79, 81, 90, 413
structure, 8, 13–16, 80, 163, 169, 268, 312–319, 384–387
See also Trade: commodity composition; Trade: direction; Trade: pattern
uncertainties, 25, 40–42, 68, 83–84, 251
See also Bilateralism; Exports; Imports
Transition problem, 349, 350, 352
Transportation:
China, 193
U.S.S.R., 263, 342
Turnover tax, 13, 283, 300n

Uncertainties:
forecasting, 71
innovation, 37–38
trade, 25, 40–42, 68, 83–84, 251
Undeveloped economies. *See* Less–Developed Countries

Undertrading, 42–45
See also Trade: aversion
Unemployment:
classical system, 289–293
disguised, 361
neo-Keynesian model, 290, 293–294
Union of Soviet Socialist Republics (U.S.S.R.):
CPEs, 57–58, 110–116, 205–206, 337–339, 350
China, 172, 179, 183, 193, 196–197, 206–207, 233, 246
competitive aspects, 17, 20–21, 113, 235, 255–256, 273, 300, 304, 309, 338–339, 405n
MTEs, 173, 276
United Kingdom, 63, 108, 109, 173, 287n, 314, 326, 327–328
United Nations, 40–41, 105, 126, 206, 210–211, 394
United States of America (U.S.A.):
legislative acts, 107–108, 109–110

Valuation standards, 65–66, 411–412
Vertical connections, 407, 411–412
Vested interests, 37, 358–359
Visible hand, 351, 373–375

Wages:
adjustment, 337
costs, 147, 150, 160, 161n
differentials, 409
MTEs, 288, 294
real, 148–155, 158, 160, 287n
scarcity prices, 283
See also Incentives; Labor
West. *See* Market-Type Economies
World markets, 127–128, 281, 309, 340, 355

Yugoslavia:
banking system, 370, 373
CPE, 350, 368–369, 380
China, 207n
CEMA, 105n, 172
dinar/dollar rate, 362
economy, 350–351, 366, 368–369, 373, 378–381
GATT, 106n
legacies, 350, 361, 366–375, 378, 379–380
Marx, 167
regional differences, 357